Britain's Glorious Aircraft Industry

Britain's Glorious Aircraft Industry

100 Years of Success, Setback and Change

J Paul Hodgson

AIR WORLD

First published in Great Britain in 2020 by
Pen & Sword Air World
An imprint of
Pen & Sword Books Ltd
Yorkshire – Philadelphia

ISBN 978 1 52677 466 8

A CIP catalogue record for this book is
available from the British Library.

Typeset by Mac Style
Printed and bound in the UK by TJ Books Ltd,
Padstow, Cornwall.

Pen & Sword Books Limited incorporates the imprints of Atlas,
Archaeology, Aviation, Discovery, Family History, Fiction, History,
Maritime, Military, Military Classics, Politics, Select, Transport,
True Crime, Air World, Frontline Publishing, Leo Cooper, Remember
When, Seaforth Publishing, The Praetorian Press, Wharncliffe Local
History, Wharncliffe Transport, Wharncliffe True Crime and
White Owl.

For a complete list of Pen & Sword titles please contact

PEN & SWORD BOOKS LIMITED
47 Church Street, Barnsley, South Yorkshire, S70 2AS, England
E-mail: enquiries@pen-and-sword.co.uk
Website: www.pen-and-sword.co.uk

Or

PEN AND SWORD BOOKS
1950 Lawrence Rd, Havertown, PA 19083, USA
E-mail: Uspen-and-sword@casematepublishers.com
Website: www.penandswordbooks.com

Contents

Foreword		vi
Acknowledgements		vii
List of Abbreviations		viii
Aeronautical Terminology		xi
Introduction: About this Book		xiv

Chapter 1   The Very Beginnings   1

Chapter 2   From 1908 to 1939   4

Chapter 3   The Second World War, 1939 to 1945   82

Chapter 4   About Aircraft Engines – The Changes To Come   104

Chapter 5   The Post-Second World War Years, 1946 to 1959   112

Chapter 6   Turbulent Years, 1960 to 1975   179

Chapter 7   International Collaboration, 1960 to 1975   227

Chapter 8   More Turbulence, 1976 to 2010   252

Chapter 9   Industry Technical Progress and Commercial-Political Issues   289

Chapter 10   Late Additions, Even More Turbulence, the Mistakes   307

Chapter 11   "Glory" and Conclusions   320

Post Scriptum   332
Index of Personalities   333
Bibliography   336

Appendix 1: The Thirty British Aircraft Industry Companies of 1946   343
Appendix 2: The British Aircraft Industry/Government Interaction Timeline
   (1940 Onwards)   349
Appendix 3: British Air Ministry Aircraft Specification Process   354
Appendix 4: Plowden Report on the British Aircraft Industry, 1965   356
Appendix 5: USA Offshore Procurement Contracts for Aircraft in Europe   359
Appendix 6: The Boeing-Airbus Dispute on Trade Subsidies to Aircraft
   Programmes   361
Appendix 7: British Military and Civil Aircraft 1900–1919   363
Appendix 8: British Military And Civil Aircraft 1920–1929   388
Appendix 9: British Military and Civil Aircraft 1930–1939   409
Appendix 10: British Military and Civil Aircraft 1940–1949   432
Appendix 11: British Military and Civil Aircraft 1950–1959   449
Appendix 12: British Military and Civil Aircraft 1960–1969   462
Appendix 13: British Military and Civil Aircraft 1970–2019   470
Appendix 14: British Experimental Aircraft 1919–2019   477

Foreword

How did this book come to be written?

Since I was about 8-years-old, I have been interested in aeroplanes and aviation matters, becoming an aero-modeller as a schoolboy. Still at school, at 16-years-old I had my personal first flight, in a de Havilland Dragon Rapide biplane, as part of a week's work experience at Brough, courtesy of Blackburn and General Aircraft. My career of choice inevitably became to be an aircraft designer. On starting a degree course in Aeronautical Engineering, I simply wrote to A.V. Roe & Co. (Avro), to enquire about "undergraduate vacation work experience". I was offered a six week period in the summer of 1963 and, by the end of that, I became a signed-up undergraduate apprentice. Seventeen years after retiring from my job as an aircraft Chief Designer with BAE Systems, I found myself starting to write the story of the British aircraft industry. Why/how did a book come about?

Not long after retiring, out of interest I compiled enough information to create a lecture on the subject. When I presented this, it was well-received. A question which arose was "when is the book coming out?" Initially dubious, I researched some more and began to write the whole story in greater detail. My aim was a book which told of one hundred years of the technical, industrial and political background to the formation and eventual fate of all 129 aircraft companies formed in Britain. Deciding what to include and what to exclude was not as simple as I had expected. Some historical and technical detail had to be explained in a limited space, imposing a degree of simplification. The achievements are illustrated by the stories of many individual aircraft projects. All aircraft types actually produced are listed, dated and quantified, in a series of appendices.

I found the whole experience interesting, illuminating and exhilarating. I have to admit that there were some occasional feelings of regretful reflection about "what might have been" for various companies which were thriving at the end of the Second World War, but did not survive, in any form, into the twenty-first century.

Here is the book. I hope you find it as interesting to read as I found in writing it.

J.Paul Hodgson, June 2020

Acknowledgements

I would like to express my gratitude to all those who have assisted me in creating this book. Especial thanks go to the readers of my early drafts, notably my dear wife Diana, brother Ian, long-time friends and colleagues Alan Fieldhouse and Martin Renshaw, and the chairman of the Manchester branch of the Royal Aeronautical Society, Thurai Rahulan. They all had the stamina to read every word, do a little preliminary proofreading and make helpful and honest comments and criticisms. I must particularly acknowledge the quiet patience of my wife over the three years it took to research the information, keeping herself quietly amused whilst I searched for out-of-print books and information on the internet, and pounded my laptop keyboard (with only two fingers!).

Lastly, I am grateful for the friendly advice and patience of my publishers and, particularly, my editor Ken Patterson, in helping me to convert the manuscript into a tighter and more consistent narrative.

List of Abbreviations

A&AEE	Aircraft and Armaments Experimental Establishment (UK)
ACM	Air Chief Marshal (RAF)
ADF	Automatic Direction Finding (radio navigation aid)
AEW	Airborne Early Warning
AM	Air Marshal (RAF)
AMDP	Air Member (of the Air Council) for Development and Production
AMRD	Air Member (of the Air Council) for Research and Development
AOC	Air Officer Commanding (RAF)
AOP	Air Observation Post (army)
ARA	Aircraft Research Association (UK industry, now independent aeronautical consultancy)
ARB	Air Registration Board (incorporated into CAA, 1972)
ARC	Aeronautical Research Committee (UK)
AST/ASR	Air Staff Target/Air Staff Requirement
ATC	Air Training Corps (RAF)
AVM	Air Vice-Marshal (RAF)
BA	British Airways (merged BOAC and BEA)
BAC	British Aircraft Corporation
BBMF	Battle of Britain Memorial Flight (RAF)
BEA	British European Airways
BOAC	British Overseas Airways Corporation
Brexit	British decision to exit European Union (referendum vote, June 2016)
BSAA	British South American Airways
BVR	Beyond Visual Range
CAA	Civil Aviation Authority (UK)... acts as UK agent of EASA
CAS	Chief of the Air Staff
CATBAR	Catapult-Assisted Take-off But Arrested Landing (aircraft carrier)
cc.	cubic centimetres (1,000 cc. = 1 litre)
CIA	Central Intelligence Agency (USA)
CNC	Computer Numerically Controlled (machining of material)
CRO	Civilian Repair Organisation
CTOL	Conventional Take-Off and Landing
DERA	Defence Evaluation and Research Agency (UK)
DSTL	Defence Science and Technology Laboratory
EASA	European Aviation Safety Agency (est. in European Union 2002)
ECM	Electronic Countermeasures
EFIS	Electronic Flight Instrument System
EICAS	Engine Indicating and Crew Alert System
ELINT	Electronic Intelligence
EROPS	Extended Range Operations (multi-engined civil airliners)
ESM	Electronic Surveillance Measures
EST	Eastern Standard Time (USA)
ETOPS	Extended (Range) Twin-Engined Operations (civil airliners)

EU	European Union (originally European Economic Community)
EW	Electronic Warfare (encompassing ECM and ESM)
FAA	(1) Fleet Air Arm (UK Royal Navy Air Arm)
	(2) Federal Aviation Administration (USA equivalent to European EASA)
FAI	Fédération Aéronautique Internationale
FARs	Federal Airworthiness Requirements (USA)
FASS	Fore and Aft Scanning System
FLIR	Forward-Looking Infrared (sensor)
GMT	Greenwich Mean Time
GPO	General Post Office (UK)
GRC	(John) Glenn Research Center (NASA, USA)
GVA	Gross Value Added (in-house value added by a country or company)
HE	High Explosive
HP	Horsepower (engine: 1 HP = 746 Watts)
HSA	Hawker Siddeley Aviation
HSD	Hawker Siddeley Dynamics
IR	Infrared (sensor)
JAA	Joint Airworthiness Authority (Europe)
JARs	Joint Airworthiness Requirements (Europe)
JATO	Jet-Assisted Take-Off (really RATO, Rocket-Assisted)
kg.	kilogram weight (1 kg = 2.205 lbs. 1,000 kg = 1 tonne (US metric ton))
km.	kilometre (1 km. = 0.6214 miles)
lb.	pound mass
lbf.	pound force
LAPG	London Aircraft Production Group (of factories)
m.	metre (1 m. = 3.28084 ft. = 39.37 inches)
MAP	Ministry of Aircraft Production (UK)
MI.6	Military Intelligence 6 (UK Secret Service, Foreign Desk)
MLW	Maximum Landing Weight
MoA	Ministry of Aviation (UK)
MoD	Ministry of Defence (UK)
MoD(PE)	Ministry of Defence Procurement Executive (UK)
MoS	Ministry of Supply (UK)
mph	Miles per hour (1 mph = 0.868 knots)
MTOW	Maximum Take-Off Weight
MWDA	Mutual Weapons Development Agency (NATO)
NAC	National Air Communications (UK)
NACA	National Advisory Committee for Aeronautics (USA: incorporated into NASA, 1958)
NASA	National Aeronautics and Space Administration (USA)
NATO	North Atlantic Treaty Organisation
NBMR	NATO Basic Military Requirement (document)
NGTE	National Gas Turbine Establishment (UK)
NPV	Net Present Value (A value representing all historic and future costs referred to a present-year value, 2019 in this document)
OEM	Original Equipment Manufacturer
ONERA	Office National d'Etudes et de Recherches Aérospatiales (French Aerospace Lab.)
OR	Operational Requirement (UK Armed services)
OSS	Office of Strategic Services (USA)
PV	Private Venture (not paid for by the government)
RAAF	Royal Australian Air Force

RAE	Royal Aircraft Establishment (renamed 1988, as Royal Aerospace Establishment)
RAF	Royal Air Force (UK)
RAFVR	Royal Air Force Volunteer Reserve
RAMC	Royal Army Medical Corps
RAN	Royal Australian Navy
RCAF	Royal Canadian Air Force
RFC	Royal Flying Corps (of the army, merged into the RAF, 1918)
RN	Royal Navy (UK)
RNAS	Royal Naval Air Service (of RN, merged into the RAF, 1918)
RNLI	Royal National Lifeboat Institution (UK)
RNVR	Royal Naval Volunteer Reserve (UK)
RNZAF	Royal New Zealand Air Force
RPAV	Remotely Piloted Air Vehicle
RSRE	Royal Signals and Radar Establishment (UK)
(R)SAAF	(Royal) South African Air Force
SAAF	South African Air Force
SBAC	Society of British Aerospace Constructors (until 1964, Society of British Aircraft Companies)
SHP	Shaft Horse Power
SIGINT	Signals Intelligence
SOE	Special Operations Executive (WW2 forerunner of UK MI.6)
SST	Supersonic Transport (airliner)
STOL	Short Take-Off and Landing
STOVL	Short Take-Off, Vertical Landing
TMR	Thrust Measuring Rig (Rolls-Royce)
UAV	Unmanned Air Vehicle
U-boat	U-boot, German shortened version of "Unterseeboot" (submarine)
UK	United Kingdom of Great Britain and Northern Ireland
USA	Unites States of America
USAF	United States Air Force
USAAF	United States Army Air Force
USMC	United States Marine Corps
USN	Unites States Navy
USSR	Union of Soviet Socialist Republics (Soviet Union)
VTOL	Vertical Take-Off and Landing
WIP	Work in Progress (production work, pre-delivery)
WW1	The First World War, 1914–1918
WW2	The Second World War, 1939–1945

Aeronautical Terminology

Actuator	mechanical force device (e.g. to operate powered flying control)
Aerofoil	cross-section of wing in flight direction (or other wing-shaped surface)
Aero-isoclinic (wing)	common wing incidence along span as air loads deflect structure
Aerostatic lift	lighter-than-air (balloon/dirigible) lift
Aileron	control surface on wing trailing edge used for roll control
Aircraft range	maximum possible safe flight distance, with diversion reserve
Aircraft service ceiling	maximum approved operating altitude above mean sea level
Alclad	high-strength light alloy, clad with thin coating of high-purity aluminium (corrosion resistant): developed in 1920s, obsolescent.
Anhedral	wing or tailplane spanwise downwards slope angle, relative to fuselage (opposite to more common dihedral, upwards)
Balloon	lighter-than-air flying machine, either tethered on a winch-controlled cable or is blown along by the wind, whatever the direction.
Block fuel	total fuel on board at engine start (including reserves for diversion)
Boundary layer	the air layer "from immediately adjacent to a surface in motion (where it is at rest, relative to the surface) to the point where it has the same velocity as the surface.... boundary layers grow thicker from the leading edge to the trailing edge, sometimes separating from the surface, causing vortices to form in separated airflow.
Cannon	in aircraft, an automatic weapon, usually explosive ammunition
C_D	drag coefficient (a non-dimensional measure of drag characteristics)
C_L	lift coefficient (a non-dimensional measure of lift characteristics)
Collective (helicopter rotor pitch)	control of rotor blade incidence, to create more or less lift
Creep	very slow permanent deformation, building up due to repeated applied loads (particularly metals, also influenced by temperature)

Cyclic (helicopter rotor pitch)	control of rotor blade incidence as rotor rotates, to control pitch/roll
Dihedral	wing or tailplane span-wise upwards slope angle, relative to fuselage
Dirigible	lighter-than-air flying machine with motive power, steerable
Dry thrust (jet turbine engine)	thrust level without reheat
Duraluminium (Dural)	trade name for an age-hardened high-strength copper-aluminium alloy- modern terminology defines as the 2000 series of alloys
Elevator	control surface on tailplane trailing edge used for pitch control
Empennage	tailplane and fin(s) of an aeroplane
Fail Safe	a structural design philosophy whereby any developing defect will become apparent (at inspection intervals) before the defect becomes critical
Fin	Vertical Stabiliser (for yaw stability)
Flak	anti-aircraft fire (derived from First World War German term 'Flugabwehrgeschütz' (Flag))
Float Plane	aircraft with floats which, at rest, keep the fuselage out of water
Flutter	aerodynamically-induced rapid and large-amplitude structural oscillation of wing or control surface
Flying Boat	aircraft which, at rest, has the fuselage floating in water
Foster Mounting	Machine gun (Lewis type) mounting on biplane top wing, firing over propeller, with slide to allow access for drum magazine change
'g'	1 'g' is the accelerating force due to gravity at the earth's surface (makes 1 lb. mass apply a force of 1 lb. weight on the scales)
Gallon (Imperial)	volume of 10 pounds of water (= 1.2 US gallons)
Geodesic (construction)	elements which follow lines on a three-dimensional curved surface
Glider	aircraft without motive power, usually launched by towing, once launched using rising air (thermals or hill-wave) to continue flying
Gull Wing	wing with "crank" mid-span: inboard dihedral and outboard anhedral
Knot	speed of one nautical mile per hour (1 knot = 1.152 mph)
Laminar Flow	airflow without "turbulence"
Lewis gun	Light machine gun with rotary drum magazine
Longeron	length-wise load bearing structural element, usually of fuselage
Machine gun	an automatic weapon, usually solid (non-explosive) ammunition
Mach Number	the fraction of the local speed of sound at which the flow of a gas (such as air) or liquid over an object (such as an aircraft) which is moving in that gas or liquid. (Mach 1 = 760 mph in air at sea level)

Maximum Landing Weight (MLW)	maximum permitted aircraft weight for landing
Maximum Take-Off Weight (MTOW)	maximum permitted aircraft weight at start of take-off run (weight is usually in pounds (lbs.) or tonnes, where 1 tonne = 1,000 kg = 2204.6 lb = 1 short ton (US))
Monocoque	shell structure, where the "skin" is a major load-bearing element
Nautical Mile	equivalent to 1 degree of latitude change (= 1.15 miles = 1.851 km.)
'Q' feel	Control column artificial feel forces felt by the pilot proportional to the dynamic pressure 'Q' (which is a function of the square of the airspeeed and the air density)
Reheat (jet turbine)	burn extra fuel in exhaust to produce additional thrust (afterburner)
Rib	structural element of wing, tailplane or fin (defines aerofoil shape)
Roll (angle)	left/right vertical rotation about line of flight
Rudder	control surface on fin trailing edge used for yaw control
Safe Life	a structural design philosophy whereby a calculated life (with a reserve factor) in expected flying hours is established, reaching which requires a structural replacement
Sailplane	a high-performance glider
Scarff Ring	a machine gun ring mounting used on aircraft, with bungee cord weight/balance relief, to facilitate air gunner/observer manual gun manoeuvring, when aiming at moving targets
Spar	main span-wise load-bearing structural element (of wing, tailplane)
Stringer	subsidiary load-bearing lengthwise element (of fuselage, wing)
Swarf	shards of metal cut off during machining of parts
Tonne	Metric ton (1 tonne = 1,000kg. = 2,205lb.)
Warren Truss	A girder or structure with the top and bottom elements braced by a series of alternating equilateral triangles of supporting braces
Wet thrust (jet turbine engine)	thrust level with reheat
Wing Aspect Ratio	ratio of wing span to average chord (a measure of slimness of the wing planform)
Wing Camber	the degree to which the chord-wise wing section is curved
Wing Chord	straight-line distance, wing leading edge to trailing edge
Wing Incidence	the angle between the wing cord line and the airspeed vector
Wing Section	shape of the aerofoil used for the wing or other aerodynamic surface
Wing Span	straight-line distance, wing tip to wing tip
Yaw (angle)	azimuth rotation about line of flight

Unless otherwise stated, the date in text and appendices for each aircraft type is the date of the first flight.

Introduction: About this Book

Many books have been published on the subject of the history of flight, aviation in general, individual aircraft, or aircraft companies. Some of these have served as a useful starting point for this book, which is intended to focus on the story of the British aircraft industry as a whole. This book charts the complete one hundred and twelve years of the industry between 1908 and 2020, its successes, setbacks and changes. All known attempts to start an aircraft design-and-make company in Britain are included. Aeronautical technology development is described against the backdrop of political, industrial and commercial influences and major world events. To help illustrate progress, the book contains the project stories of individual prominent aircraft types, or groups of types, which were actually produced and highlights dramatic technology leaps alongside their sometimes eye-watering cost.

After the initial experimenters, once the First World War started in 1914 the rate of new aircraft designs emerging every year accelerated, as the rapid developments forced by war caused a mushrooming of incremental improvement. The rate of new types created per year reduced during the 1920s but numbers increased again in the 1930s. After the Second World War, as aircraft became much more sophisticated, taking more time and money to design, develop, test and produce, numbers of new designs became a lot lower. The technology explosion peaks in the 1940s and 1950s, as the "heyday" of British aircraft design, presaged an overdue rational reduction in the number of different companies. Eventually, collaboration within Europe (and, latterly, with North America) created the opportunity for the British aircraft industry to share in larger markets, for fewer types of more sophisticated and expensive civil and military aircraft.

Occasionally, the story hovers briefly over the territory of aircraft engines, their development and production, because the availability of powerful and fuel-efficient engines is an integral enabling part of aircraft development.

The book title is "Britain's **Glorious** Aircraft Industry". The concluding analysis suggests which were the glory periods or projects in the last one hundred and twelve years, at least from an aircraft designer's perspective. The body of the main text is the evidence for the conclusion.

Appendices list heavier-than-air aircraft types designed-and-produced by a British company, including prototypes of aircraft sold later as an improved or different type. The dates of first flight, numbers made and a brief summary of characteristics are included. Club build aircraft and companies supplying self or home build-to-plan, kit-build and microlight aircraft, motor-gliders, man-powered or para-glider type aircraft and replica aircraft are not included. If any aircraft type outside these exclusions has been missed, the fault is that of the author. The book is definitely not intended as a comprehensive catalogue of all the physical and performance details of every single variant of all UK designed and manufactured aircraft, and all the individual factories and establishments involved. Ron Smith's twenty-first century five-volume catalogue is a comprehensive record of British aircraft manufacturing establishments, including subcontract and British companies which built aircraft not of British origin (see Bibliography).

A definition of "Britain's Glorious Aircraft Industry" as described in this book is, at its simplest:

> "*British industrial activity for commercial gain, in the design, development and manufacture of heavier-than-air aeroplanes*".

Participation in all three of the design, development and manufacture of aircraft processes is an essential ingredient to the definition of the companies which constitute the industry described herein. Build-to-Print sub-contract companies are generally not included, but wartime support from sub-contractors and shadow factories is recognised. Suppliers of aircraft engines, aircraft parts and equipment are not included, thus making the boundary more restricted than the "Aerospace" larger entity.

Chapter 1

The Very Beginnings

Mankind dreamed of winged flight "free as a bird" for centuries. Some 2,000 years before the Common Era (BCE, or 2,000 BC in old money) the kite was invented in China. Old records show that the Chinese were flying man-lifting kites in the mid-sixth century BCE. Over 400 years BCE, the Greek mythology story of Icarus and his disastrous flight is one of the earliest references to flying freely, without a connection to the ground. Leonardo da Vinci (b. 1452, d. 1519) had ideas on a number of designs for a flying machine. In the seventeenth, eighteenth and nineteenth centuries there were other theoretical and practical scientific aeronautical pioneers, in several countries.

The most successful experimenter, who also approached flying as a scientifically-based investigation, was the English baronet Sir George Cayley (b. 27 December 1773, d. 15 December 1857). His sixty-year aeronautical efforts, experiments with gliders of his own design, and his scientific aeronautical publications all earned him a posthumous worldwide reputation, as the "father of the aeroplane". Although important, this pre-twentieth century British aviation *pre-industry* history activity is not part of this book.

After the first manned true controlled powered flight of the "Flyer" of brothers Orville and Wilbur Wright, in the USA on 17 December 1903, many aeronautical enthusiasts took great heart. Several were keen to emulate the Wright brothers' success, keen to be the first to design, build and fly a machine of their own in their own country. Various short, low hops, often under poor control, were achieved by the earliest early twentieth century aircraft experimenters in Britain. The unavailability of a suitable lightweight engine was a limiting factor in many attempts – the Wright brothers had had to design their own engine.

With the aim of encouraging the development of aviation in Britain, Lord Northcliffe (proprietor of the *Daily Mail* British newspaper) offered several prizes for "firsts" in aviation. The first one announced was in 1906:- £10,000 for the first to fly from London to Manchester (won by Frenchman Louis Paulhan in 1910). Prize money started at £100 for the "best" successful model aeroplane (won by Alliott Verdon Roe in 1906, but only £75 actually awarded). Noting that £100 in 1906 would be equivalent to over £11,500 in 2019, the aviation pioneers responded. *Daily Mail* and other prizes for pioneering achievements continued to be announced, in the UK and the rest of the world. The Daily Mail prize of £1,000 for the first person to fly in a heavier-than-air aircraft across the English channel was won by Frenchman Louis Blériot on 25 July 1909, in a monoplane of his own design. The last *Daily Mail* aviation prize was won in 1930, when Amy Johnson won a prize of £10,000 for the first solo female flight from Britain to Australia.

In 1908–09, two credible competing claims emerged for the first powered true controlled flight of an aircraft designed and built in Britain. These claims were between two experimental aircraft, the British Army Aeroplane No.1 of USA-born Colonel Samuel Franklin Cody, and the Roe 1 Triplane of the English-born Alliott Verdon Roe. Colonel Cody had to wait to be allowed to transfer the 50 HP French Antoinette engine to his new aircraft, from the British Army's experimental lighter-than-air Dirigible No. 1, "Nilli Secundus" on which Cody had been previously working. The

Cody Army Aeroplane No. 1 is now recognised as the first aircraft designed and built in Britain which flew successfully, at Farnborough (Hampshire) on 16 October 1908. The aircraft empty weight was around 2,500lb (1,134kg) to which fuel and pilot weights would be added.

It is also recognised that the first flight of an all-British aircraft (i.e. aircraft and engine designed and made in Britain) was by the Roe 1 triplane, using a 9 HP JAP engine, at Walthamstow Marshes, London, on 10 June 1909. This signalled the imminent end of the purely experimental stage in the UK.

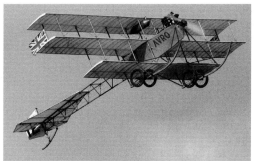

Avro Triplane (replica). (*TSRL – Own work, CC BY-SA 3.0*)

The aircraft industry story in Britain began with the Short Brothers partnership, formed in November 1908 by Horace Leonard, Albert Eustace and Hugh Oswald Short, as the first organisation in Britain to offer to produce a self-propelled aeroplane for sale, to their own design, or to the designs of others, should they so wish. The brothers had decided that the future of aviation was in heavier-than-air aeroplanes rather than the lighter-than-air balloon or dirigible craft. Unfortunately, their first in-house aeroplane never flew. This was Short Biplane No. 1, designed to an overall requirement of Frank McClean.[1] Powered by a 30 HP engine, in November 1909 it barely left the ground, stalling as it left the ground and crashing, becoming damaged beyond repair.

Shorts Biplane No.2 was specifically commissioned by John Moore-Brabazon,[2] in a bid to win a £1,000 *Daily Mail* prize for the first flight by a British pilot in an all-British aircraft around a closed circuit of one mile. In October 1909 the prize was duly won by Brabazon. At first, most successful Short Brothers aircraft sales were, however, licence-built Wright flyers (the improved Model A). Meanwhile, Shorts created and flew several different aircraft and, in September 1911, Frank McClean flew the world's first successful twin-engined aircraft,

Short S.39 Triple Twin. (*Flight magazine archive from FlightGlobal, CC BY-SA 4.0*)

Shorts model S.39 Triple Twin. This had two French Gnome 50 HP engines, with three propellers, one engine and pusher propeller behind the pilot and a tractor propeller on each wing, contra-rotating chain-driven by a second engine in front of the pilot. The S.39 was subsequently purchased by the British Admiralty.

The first British aeroplane manufacturing company to be registered based on public subscription (rather than private money) was the Handley Page Company, in Barking

---

1. Francis McClean had personal wealth and went on to commission and fly many aircraft from Shorts, often created to his personal order. He was commissioned in the Royal Naval Air Service on the outbreak of the First World War.
2. In May 1909, John Moore-Brabazon was the first person to make a flight in Britain and obtained the first British pilot's licence in March 1910.

(Essex), on 17 June 1909, registered by founder Frederick Handley Page. Starting with the Handley page Type A, the company built two unsuccessful monoplanes (the first crashed when the first attempt to turn the aircraft in flight was made) and a biplane to someone else's design which Handley page soon "disowned". The first Handley Page design to fly truly successfully was his Type D (later renamed as the HP.4) in 1910, but it took a few years for the fledgling company to create a useable and saleable flying machine.

After the 1909 success of his Roe 1 triplane, Alliott Verdon Roe and his elder brother Humphrey Verdon Roe started their then privately-funded company, on 1 January 1910 in Manchester (Lancashire). Humphrey provided financial support for the venture, using the resources of the webbing company which he had inherited. The second successful Roe design was a sturdier version of the first, with a more powerful engine. Two were constructed, one of which was sold. The longest recorded flight of the type was 600ft. (180m.). The 'Avro' acronym was soon adopted.

The 1908 founding of the Short Brothers aircraft company is the starting point for the remainder of this book, which attempts to describe what happened to the British aircraft industry in the one hundred and twelve years which followed. It tells the story of the changes which these years would bring. Alongside the technology explosion in the aeronautical world, the political, commercial and industrial events, policies and personalities form most of the answers to the "What?, Where?, When?, How?, Who? and Why?".

Chapter 2

From 1908 to 1939

2.1 The Founding of UK Aircraft Companies, to the End of the First World War

Enthusiasts starting the business of heavier-than-air aircraft design and manufacture before the First World War (WW1) were often told that "they were mad or foolish" and that "aircraft which were aeroplanes were inherently unsafe". Aeroplane pioneers were also advised, on the other hand, that lighter-than-air aircraft (balloons and dirigibles) were safe and useful, as observation or survey platforms (especially useful in wartime, tethered of course). In Britain, after an official investigation into the potential of military aeronautics, the War Office actually stopped all work investigating aeroplanes of any kind. In reply to a 1908 letter from Alliot Verdon Roe, the British War Office declared opinion was "… we do not consider that aeroplanes will be of any possible use for war purposes". However, even before the opening shots of the First World War were heard, there was rapid evolutionary progress in aeroplane capability which soon proved attractive for wartime use. Initially, this was seen by many as potential fast, long-range and uninhibited scouting capability. Progress in providing Britain with suitable aircraft was lamentably slow. One year before the First World War broke out, the British armed forces only had one hundred and twenty aircraft, out of which just fifty-three were fit to fly. Of these, only twenty-three were fully serviceable. Additionally, all British aircraft were inferior in performance to the best in French and German service.

Meanwhile, USA-born Samuel F. Cody had campaigned to build a self-propelled aeroplane at the Army Balloon Factory at Farnborough (originally established at Woolwich as the Army Balloon School in 1878). This finally resulted, in 1908, in the first aeroplane-style aircraft in Britain to make a complete self-propelled flight, the Cody-designed British Army Aeroplane No.1. The Farnborough facility was renamed as the "Royal Aircraft Factory" in 1912. The Admiralty established their Air Department in 1910. By that time, only two years after Short Brothers had started their aircraft business, seven independent aircraft partnerships or companies were designing and building aircraft "for gain" in the UK:- Short Brothers partnership (1908), Martin and Handasyde (1908), Handley Page Company (1909), Howard Theophilis Wright and brother Warwick Joseph Wright (1909, private partnership), A.V. Roe and Company (1910), the Blair Atholl Syndicate (building the designs of John William Dunne from 1910) and Bristol and Colonial Aeroplane founded in 1910 as a private company, by Sir George White and family, owners of Bristol Tramways and Carriage. Other pioneers quickly followed, such as Robert Blackburn who designed and flew his first aircraft in 1909 and his more successful second in 1911 at Filey, founding his aircraft company in Leeds in 1911.

John William Dunne commenced designing gliders whilst employed at the Army Balloon Factory. He had ideas about tailless inherently stable arrow-head winged aircraft ("arrow head wing planform" = swept back, but simply as a stability improver, not a transonic/supersonic feature!). He designed several different versions (eight in all) and had them built between 1907 and 1912 (three gliders before his first powered aircraft D.4 "hopped" in 1908). When the government curtailed all aeroplane development in 1909, he became independent. His designs were financed for construction by the Blair Atholl Syndicate in Scotland, which involved Charles Richard Fairey as managing director and the Duke of Atholl as chairman. Dunne's D.8 biplane flew in 1912 and went on to be built under licence, in France and in the USA. He retired from flying due to ill health before the First World War started and the syndicate was wound up.

After initial attempts by Bristol and Colonial to licence-build and fly examples of the Zodiac aircraft (designed by Frenchman Gabriel Voisin) had not been successful enough, Sir George was advised to seek a licence to produce French Henri Farman biplanes instead. However, that licence was being negotiated by George Holt Thomas (eventually to found the Aircraft Manufacturing Company in 1912, based in North London). George White's Chief Engineer was convinced he could design a copy of the Farman machine, partly based on the great detail published in the "*Flight*" magazine[1]. This revised design eventually became the Bristol Boxkite of 1910, which was to become the most-produced British aircraft before the beginning of the First World War (seventy-eight in total). The first production order came from the British government on 14 March 1911 and the first aircraft was delivered sixty-five days later. The original Bristol Boxkite unit sale price of around one thousand pounds equates to over one hundred thousand pounds in 2019.

More than one aspirational aircraft designer-constructor used land within the Brooklands motor racing circuit (opened in 1907, in Weybridge, Surrey) as a flight test facility. Aviator Thomas Octave Murdoch Sopwith, along with Frederic Sigrist and others, set up the Sopwith aircraft company at Brooklands in 1912. By 1914, with several flying schools alongside budding new aircraft designer-constructors, Brooklands airfield became the foremost aviation centre in Britain. Brooklands was used as a test site by A.V. Roe, Sopwith, the Aviation department of Vickers Limited and by Martin & Handasyde. Now a name "lost in history", in 1915 Martin & Handasyde became the limited company Martinsyde Ltd. and was the third-largest British aircraft manufacturer during the First World War.

After the opening of hostilities, the requirement for aircraft during the first year of the war vastly increased. Inventive new design thoughts and the burgeoning business situation caused more new aircraft companies to be formed. Of eventual significance, two companies in particular emerged <u>during</u> the war:

- Supermarine Aviation: Noel Pemberton-Billing had founded his own aircraft company in 1913 at Woolston, near Southampton, and soon focused his attention on the design and build of an anti-Zeppelin aircraft. He was a great proponent of the potential of aviation in Britain, despite the initial relative disinterest of many in the government and armed forces. His efforts at creating an aircraft company resulted in one aircraft which was under-powered and crashed during testing. He became detached from his company's day-to-day affairs and, when elected an MP in 1916, sold his shares to his factory manager Hubert Scott-Paine. The company was renamed "Supermarine Aviation", after the telegraph address of the company.
- Fairey Aviation: Short Brothers Chief Engineer was Charles Richard Fairey. With the help of another Shorts employee, Belgian First World War refugee Ernest Oscar Tips, Fairey established Fairey Aviation at Hayes, Middlesex, in 1915, using the airfield at Northolt for flight testing until 1929, later moving to the area that was to become part of London Heathrow airport.

---

1. The Farman biplane, itself a derivative and significant improvement of the earlier Voisin design, included an elevator control well ahead of the wing (similar to the origial Wright Flyer). The Voisin and Farman had an additional fixed tailplane. Henri Farman filed for patent infringement by Bristol, later dropped because of design improvements made by Bristol.

Some companies were initially and specifically established to build the designs of other companies, under licence. Other existing companies and new companies established themselves exclusively as pure production factories, building-to-print the designs of others. Not all those involved were engineering companies. The woodworking skills and factory equipment of large furniture makers, shopfitters etc. were often employed.

Table 2.1 below shows the twenty-four organisations in Britain which were designing and building aircraft for commercial gain at the end of the war. Some were originally founded by enthusiasts turning a hobby into a business and some were ex-employees of companies such as Avro, Shorts and Handley Page. Some were patriots (or opportunists, or both) such as Samuel Waring (of retailers Waring and Gillow) who founded Nieuport and General Aviation (initially to build French Nieuports under licence for the RFC) and British Aerial Transport, to build the designs of Dutchman Frederick Koolhoven. From 1915, Ruffy, Arnell and Baumann Aviation had produced adaptations of the French Caudron company for use in the Ruffy, Arnell and Baumann flying school. In 1918 the company was absorbed as the third aircraft company taken over by Samuel Waring, being renamed the Alliance Aeroplane Company. Another short-lived aircraft design and make activity was founded by Frederick Sage in 1916, as an extension to his shop-fitting business (being used to manufacture aircraft from the designs of others, in the early years of the war).

Table 2.1: UK Aircraft Companies & Partnerships Trading by the End of the First World War.

Company/Partnership/Sole Proprietor	Year Est.	First Location
Short Brothers	1908	Battersea, London
Martin & Handasyde (1915 Martinsyde)	1908	Woking
Handley Page	1909	Barking
Howard T. Wright	1909	London
A.V. Roe and Company	1910	Manchester
Bristol and Colonial Aeroplane Co.	1910	Bristol
Vickers Limited (Aviation Dept.)	1911	London and Kent
Grahame-White Aviation Co.	1911	Hendon, London
Blackburn Aeroplane	1911	Leeds
Aircraft Manufacturing Company (Airco)	1912	Hendon, London
Royal Aircraft Factory (ex-Army Balloon)	1912	Farnborough
Sopwith Aviation Company	1912	Brooklands (Weybridge)
Armstrong-Whitworth (Aerial Dept.)	1912	Newcastle-on-Tyne
Aircraft Manufacturing Co. Ltd. (Airco)	1912	Birmingham
London & Provincial Aviation	1913	Hendon, London
Parnall and Sons (from 1916, own design)	1914	Bristol
Pemberton-Billing (Supermarine 1916)	1913	Southampton
Fairey Aviation Company Limited	1915	Hayes
Frederick Sage (aircraft department)	1916	Holborn, London
Nieuport and General	1916	Cricklewood, London
Sunbeam (1912 motor engineers)	1916	Wolverhampton

Company/Partnership/Sole Proprietor	Year Est.	First Location
Mann-Egerton	1916	Norwich
British Aerial Transport	1917	Mayfair, London
Alliance Aeroplane	1918	London
Aircraft production-only companies that later designed their own aircraft		
Boulton-Paul (ironmongers in 1757)	1915	Norwich
Petters Ltd. (Aircraft Works)	1915	Yeovil
Austin Motors (Aircraft Dept.)	1917	Birmingham

In the list at the end of table 2.1 are three examples of "producers which never delivered their own designs of aircraft" <u>until after</u> the 1914–18 war. Two of them were Boulton-Paul's "aircraft division" and the Petters aircraft works. The later Westland name for the Petters works arose because Mrs Petter had used the term to describe the land on which was built a new Petters foundry in 1913 as "the west land". The new factory was offered by Petters board for war work. It became an aircraft factory in 1915. In 1935, Petters split off their post-war aircraft activity as a separate company, Westland Aircraft Ltd, of Yeovil, Somerset. The last name in the list is Austin Motors, which also designed six aircraft of their own during 1917–20, but these only reached the prototype stage, never entering series production. Aircraft activity at Austin Motors ceased in 1920 (later revived for the Second World War, as part of a government-inspired expansion of war production). John North was chief designer at Austin, previously working at the Grahame-White company. He moved to be chief designer for Boulton-Paul in Norwich, in 1917.

2.2 The Aircraft of the First World War and Advances in Aircraft Capability

As in the rest of the world, the first British aircraft design attempts were incredibly flimsy, accident-prone, and incapable of carrying a significant useful payload a significant distance. However, the 1909 French first crossing of the English Channel by the monoplane of Louis Blériot opened the eyes of many to the fact that aircraft development was starting to accelerate.

By 1912 the Royal Aircraft Factory had built and flown their Geoffrey de Havilland-designed B.E.2, capable of carrying a pilot and passenger some 150 miles, able to fulfil the army scout function mentioned earlier, but vulnerable when attacked by armed enemy scout aircraft. Eventually, a 224lb (100kg) bomb-carrying capability was added, for a single crew operation. Some 3,500 B.E.2 (in five distinct variants, "2a" to "2e") were produced and served in the First World War. Other aircraft from other organisations emerged quickly, responding to aircraft capability improvement

Royal Aircraft Factory
B.E.2c. (*Author's collection*)

requirements stimulated by actual war. Improvements to speed, ceiling altitude and range/endurance followed thick and fast, appearing as "incredible technical magic" to the uninformed observer.

Soon, air warfare became lethal, as opposing aircrews started to shoot hand-held pistols and rifles at each other. The more lethal airframe-mounted machine guns were soon added – the fighter aircraft was born. The world's first purpose-built fighter aircraft was the Vickers F.B.5 "Gunbus", introduced into British service on 5 February 1915. (F.B. stood for "Fighter Biplane".) The first purpose-designed bomber aircraft were designed just before the war, the 1913 Bristol T.B.8 being the first British example. Shortly after the start of the war, crews of scout aircraft started to drop hand-held grenades and small bombs on tactical ground targets. Purpose-built bombers became capable of comparatively long-range air raids, with a significant weapon load to attack targets such as supply depots or factories.

The Avro 504 was the most-produced First World War British aircraft, costing nearly £500 each (equivalent to £45,000 in 2019 terms). It was the first British aircraft to strafe troops on the ground, as well as being the first British aircraft to make a bombing raid over Germany. It was also the first Allied aeroplane to be downed by enemy anti-aircraft fire.

The list in Appendix 7 includes all the British types which were produced and flown in the years 1908–1919, including the many experimental types created prior to the outbreak of war. Table 2.2 below gives a few of the principle characteristics of the most well-known British wartime aircraft (all biplanes). Eighty-seven different aircraft types were produced as part of the war effort, used for communication, reconnaissance, pilot-training, aerial combat, and bombing.

Table 2.2: Some of the Most Well-Known UK-Designed Aircraft of the First World War (in-service 1914–18)

Company/ Factory	Aircraft Type	First Flight	Number built (total)	Number of		T-Off Engine HP (each)	Pwr./ Wt. (HP/lb)	Max Speed (mph)	Ceiling (ft.)
				Crew	Engine				
Royal A/craft Fac.	B.E.2c	1914	>3,000	2	1	90	0.0383	72	10,000
A.V.Roe	504	1913	8,896 (by end of WW1)	2	1	110 (504K)	0.0601 (504K)	90 (504K)	16,000 (504K)
Vickers	F.B.5	1914	224	2	1	100	0.0488	70	9,000
Sopwith	1½-Strutter	1916	5,939	2	1	130	0.0605	100	15,500
Sopwith	Pup	1916	1,770	1	1	80	0.0653	111	17,500
Airco	DH.4	1916	6,295	2	1	275* to 445	0.0792*	143	22,000
Royal A/craft Fac.	S.E.5	1916	5,205	1	1	200	0.1006	138	17,000
Sopwith	Camel	1916	5,490	1	1	130	0.0895	113	19,000
A'strg-Whitworth	F.K.8	1916	1,650	2	1	160	0.0569	95	13,000
Bristol	Fighter F.2B	1917	5,277	2	1	275	0.0848	123	18,000
Handley Page	HP O/400	1917	553	4-5	2	360	0.0539	98	8,500
Sopwith	Dragon	1918	200	1	1	360	0.1689	150	25,000
Vickers	Vimy	1918	~125 .	3	2	360	0.0662	104	7,000

Avro 504K. (*TSRL – Own work, CC BY-SA 3.0*)

In the two years between the 1914 B.E.2c (in itself, a significant redesign of the 1912 B.E.2a) and the 1916 Airco DH.4, installed engine power had more than tripled and power-to-weight ratio had more than doubled. Even though maximum take-off weights (MTOW) had increased, speed had doubled and ceiling height more than doubled. Endurance of the DH.4 was 15 per cent greater than the B.E.2c, all despite a 70 per cent increase in aircraft empty weight (therefore ruggedness). Detailed assessments which include fuel capacity and consumption, rate of climb, range and armament weight (including gun calibre and total ammunition weight, bomb or bullet) reveal more about the magically rapid aircraft performance improvements during the four years of the war.

Nearly 2,000 DH.4 were produced in Britain. Because the USA was unprepared for air warfare when they joined the allies in 1917, the USA standardised on the DH.4 and

Airco DH.4, with Rolls-Royce engine. (*BAE Systems*)

licence-produced 4,846 of them, using USA Liberty L-12 engines. These heavier but more powerful engines changed the performance of the DH.4, the first USA-built machines servIng in France in February 1918). The Bristol F.2B and the Royal Aircraft Factory SE.5A were also selected by the USA but production in America had hardly started by the end of the war and activity on these aircraft was soon wound up, with less than fifty F2.B and sixty SE.5A completed.

The 1917 Airco DH.9 single-engined bomber was a development of the DH.4, and large orders were placed for the RAF, in anticipation of higher performance. The

Airco DH.9. (*Author's collection*)

Armstrong Siddeley Puma engine of the DH.9 turned out to be unreliable and, to enter service, had to be de-rated from a nominal 360 HP to 230 HP. This severely compromised DH.9 performance. Over 4,000 DH.9 were built between 1917 and 1920 but many did not survive combat use.

Westland were contracted by Airco to design a revised aircraft, the DH.9A, with a larger wing span and the newly-available 400 HP American Liberty L-12 engine. This version of the aircraft entered RAF service in July 1918 and 1,997 were eventually completed, many after the war as the "standard" RAF aircraft. The RAF only retired their last DH.9A in 1931. Several hundred DH.9A were licence-produced in Spain and over 2,400 unlicenced copies were produced in Russia.

Aircraft capability improvement came either from intrinsic industrial ingenuity, increasing science-based understanding of aerodynamic and lightweight structural design principles, and the availability of more powerful and efficient lightweight engines and propellers. Some capability improvement was forced by the escalating requirements expressed by the armed forces. To illustrate progressive capability improvement, three more examples.

Airco DH9A. (*Author's collection*)

The Emergence of a Very Capable Fighter

From the data listed in Table 2.2 on the selected aircraft designs, the improving performance of aircraft during the First World War can be sensed from the increases in installed engine power (Horse Power, HP) and the aircraft power-to-weight ratio (HP per lb), and from the consequential increases in overall performance.

After twelve months war service, it became apparent that the 1914 B.E.2c was an outdated and vulnerable reconnaissance aircraft (see Table 2.2). This encouraged Chief Designer Frank Sowter Barnwell at the Bristol Company to propose the Bristol R.2 design, with a 150 HP Hispano-Suiza engine (Hispano-Suiza engines eventually powered over half the Allied aircraft of the First World War). The emergent higher power Falcon engine from Rolls-Royce allowed the proposal to be upgraded by Barnwell to the September 1916 F.2A, a reconnaissance aircraft with realisable air-to-air self-defence dog fighting capabilities.

Named the Bristol Fighter (eventual nickname Brisfit), it was found by aircrew to be the only reconnaissance aircraft rugged enough to carry out the fast and tight manoeuvres previously reserved to single-seat fighters (albeit the F.2A having fairly "heavy" aileron control), and with serious firepower of its own, having the forward firing fixed machine gun with the advantage of a rear gunner and his twin machine guns behind the pilot. Frank Barnwell had served as a pilot in the RFC for the first year of the war and was awarded a medal, the Air Force Cross. This experience influenced the design of the Brisfit to make it a practical, performing war machine. The definitive October

Bristol Fighter F.2B (*BAE Systems*)

1917 F.2B two-seater (with up-rated engines compared with the initial F.2A) offered the performance of a high-speed (123 mph maximum) well-armed manoeuvrable single-seat fighter aircraft. The F.2B Brisfit was well able to more than hold its own against an equal number of intercepting enemy single-seat fighters. Thirty-nine RAF squadrons were finally equipped with the Bristol Fighter and it remained in production after the end of the war, with some exported. A total of 5,277 Bristol F.2B were built by the end of 1927.

A Paralyser of an Aircraft

Warplane performance requirements were sometimes loosely expressed. At the time of the first German Zeppelin airship air raid on London, on 31 May 1915, the Admiralty was responsible for the defence of the city. The Royal Naval Air Service (RNAS) flying arm of the Admiralty had remained in the UK, unlike the army Royal Flying Corps (RFC). Winston Churchill, as First Lord of the Admiralty, was responsible for the defence of London. After the unopposed Zeppelin London raid, there was a forceful top-level Admiralty request for the industry to build "a bloody paralyser of an aeroplane" (sic), able to bomb Berlin! This resulted in three twin-engined aircraft types:- the 1916 Handley Page HP.O/100 and (later, in 1917) the improved version, the HP.O/400, and the Vickers Vimy.

The ultimate bloody paralyser British heavy bomber was the 1918 four-engined Handley Page V/1500 (engines in pusher-tractor paired configuration). This had the range to bomb Berlin from an airfield in Norfolk (500 miles away). Maximum range was 1,300 miles, maximum bombload was 7,500lbs. This was a remarkable advance on the single-engined B.E.2c (a redesigned B.E.2b, the B.E.2c entered RFC service at the start of the war in 1914 with

Handley Page V/1500 (c. 1920). (*Author's collection*)

224lbs bomb-carrying capability and a maximum range of 200 miles). Three of the first few V/1500 examples were readied for a raid on Berlin (to fly on to Prague, after the Austro-Hungarian forces had previously surrendered, on 3 November 1918). As they prepared to taxi out, they were stopped by an excited member of the ground crew, shouting that the armistice had been declared (effective at 5.00 am that day, 11 November 1918). V/1500 aircraft were not to see action. Parts for sixty-three aircraft sets were built, forty sets being completely assembled.

After initial concepts had been debated with the RFC, the Vickers twin-engined "paralyser" proposal offered better load-carrying and range capability than the HP.O/400 was eventually to offer. Vickers' detail design process for "a bloody paralyser" started on 16 August 1917 and a first flight was achieved only ninety-two days later, on 30 November 1917. Named the Vimy, one hundred and twelve were completed as a result of wartime contracts, with the Royal Aircraft Establishment (the new 1919 name of the Royal Aircraft Factory) completing some. The Vimy cost over £20,000 each in 1919 (around £1.5 million in 2019 terms).

Vickers Vimy. (*Author's collection*)

Vimy production ceased in 1920, with some 733 aircraft built. The type did enter service in 1918 but never saw First World War action. However, the Vimy replaced the Handley Page O/400 in post-war service. The Vimy also became famous as the aircraft in which John William Alcock and Arthur Whitten Brown made the first non-stop Atlantic crossing, from Newfoundland to Ireland, landing on the coast of Galway at 08.40 am on 15 June 1919. Total flight time was sixteen hours fifty-seven minutes, covering 1,880 miles at an average groundspeed of 111 mph (there was a following wind, although not always good weather).

The Vimy design endured in the adapted design of the "Vimy Commercial" passenger/freight carrier and as the air-ambulance/troop carrier which the RAF named the Vernon. It was the foundation of the uprated (re-engined) design of the Vickers Virginia heavy bomber, introduced into RAF service in 1924, and its transport sister aircraft the Vickers Victoria. Altogether, 997 aircraft of this Vickers family were eventually built. Unfortunately, the Virginia was accident-prone and eighty-one of the one hundred and twenty-four were damaged beyond repair by the time the type was withdrawn from service in 1941. The Virginia remained the most numerous bomber in RAF service until overtaken in the late 1930s by the last biplane bomber to enter RAF service, the 1933 Handley Page Heyford (which, in practical terms, was obsolescent before it flew!).

Seaplanes and the Birth of the Flat-top Aircraft Carrier

Early aeroplane experimenters considered the possible advantages of take-off and landing on water, thus requiring little advance survey and planning for an airfield facility and with an "unlimited" runway. Seaplane is the defining term, divided into the floatplane (the fuselage out of the water, usually on fuselage-mounted port and starboard floats) and flying boat, (whereby the fuselage is also a floating hull, most often stabilised on the water by floats mounted under each wing). The USA aircraft designer Glen Curtis built the first seaplane to be called a flying boat, in 1913, but there had been earlier floating-hull seaplanes designed in France. One of the first series of British seaplane experiments was conducted by Edward Wakefield and Oscar Gnosspelius on Lake Windermere in 1911–12 using a Curtis-style aircraft, built to order by A.V. Roe & Co. (Avro). Aircraft manufacturers Blackburn, Shorts, Supermarine, Vickers and Sopwith designed and built seaplanes during and after the First World War.

In general, the flying boat was at first thought to have the potential to be the largest aircraft (of any kind) because of the "unrestricted" airfield length needed, and thus likely to have the longest range and/or payload capability. The power required for seaplane take-off was not inconsiderable, even when reaching aquaplaning speed, and the weight of a rigid-surface waterproof hull and/or floats was a significant consideration. Spray ingestion considerations meant high mountings of the engines. With the growth of aircraft engine power, the size of large land-based bomber aircraft increased in the latter years of the First World War such that good payload/range was no longer the exclusive domain of the flying boat. Both the floatplane and flying boat continued development such that RAF and RN seaplanes continued to be used into the 1940s. There were also very large (for the time) flying boats in airline service in the 1930s.

An airborne observer at modest altitude enables army groups to see well over the natural horizon and to photograph enemy positions from above. Naval commanders at sea wished for the same. Out to sea, far from land, this hardly seemed possible. The Royal Navy was determined to develop "the impossible".

The British and German navies used airships as "reconnaissance scouts" but this was mostly restricted to the North Sea, with airships often operating from land bases. The Royal Navy had ambitions for a more self-contained capability, ideally extended to operating reconnaissance and torpedo bomber aircraft, and fighter aircraft to shoot down the scouting enemy airships, all from their own ship decks.

A means of operating an aeroplane from a large ship was required. On 14 November 1910, USA civilian aviator Eugene Ely had piloted the first aircraft take-off from an anchored ship's bow, using a temporary slightly downward sloping 80ft wooden deck (the aircraft touched the water before climbing away). On 18 January 1911, he landed on an anchored larger ship, USS *Pennsylvania*, with a 120ft aft upward-sloping temporary deck, with ropes across weighted with sandbags and hooks on the landing gear, to act as makeshift arrestor gear. The first take-off from a moving ship was by Royal Navy Commander Charles Samson, on the 9 May 1912, flying a Short S.27 biplane (airframe number S.38) from HMS *Hibernia* using a temporary ramp. Later he repeated this with streamlined inflated floats fitted, to land on the water. The deck landing process was not immediately developed further, partly because aircraft designs with higher take-off and landing speeds were emerging, plus unresolved concerns about operations under way at sea, with a heaving/pitching and rolling deck.

For the early years of the war, the Royal Navy and other navies developed the tedious procedure of stopping the ship (which might also heighten the risk of a submarine torpedo attack) and using a crane to place a seaplane on the (calm) sea surface, later used to recover the aircraft after landing. An elderly naval vessel was converted into a seaplane carrier (HMS *Hermes* in 1913, eventually sunk by enemy action in 1914). The Royal Navy had the design of a new commercial steamer changed during build, to become the first ship in history with the sole purpose of being an aircraft carrier, HMS *Ark Royal*. With the superstructure moved aft, an aircraft hangar in front and a flat deck in front of that, *Ark Royal* was commissioned in September 1914. The initial aircraft were four floatplanes and two standard landplanes (landplanes were carried to the operational area, off-loaded and transported to an appropriate nearby airfield). The flat deck was used for running-up engines of any aircraft. *Ark Royal* aircraft provided aerial reconnaissance during the Gallipoli campaign of 1915 but ship speed was too slow for operations with the Grand Fleet.

Following successful trials using existing floatplanes, the first RNAS aircraft specifically designed for take-off from ships was the 1917 Fairey Campania floatplane torpedo bomber, with wheeled bogies (attached to the floats) and using a 245ft flight deck constructed over the superstructure and between the modified split (forward) funnel of HMS *Campania* (an ocean liner converted to seaplane carrier). The bogies were jettisoned after take-off. At the end of a mission, the aircraft landed on the sea and was craned aboard.

Whilst under construction in 1916–17, the British battle cruiser HMS *Furious* was modified, replacing the forward guns with a flat wooden decking, from which a Sopwith Pup (fighter biplane with a wheeled undercarriage) might be launched (stalling air speed 31 mph, take-off/landing speed less than 40 mph).

HMS *Furious'* top speed would be over 30 mph (35 mph maximum reached in sea trials) and, by steaming into wind, would leave the aircraft trying to land (or take off) at relative speed of around 5–15 mph, due to the wind-over-the-deck speed of perhaps some 20–30 mph. To land, the aircraft could, in theory, be flown "alongside" the ship steaming into wind, from stern to forward of the central superstructure, then "side-slipped" by the pilot to place it in a position to land on the forward decking at a very low close-to-zero relative speed. An aircraft with a low stalling speed would be

First Landing on Moving Ship (Edward Dunning, Sopwith Pup). (*Author's collection*)

essential. Testing the theory would be hazardous, with no aircraft brakes or on-deck aircraft arrestor gear – but trials began. On 2 August 1917, Squadron Commander Edwin Harris Dunning of the RNAS made the first wheeled aircraft successful take-off and landing, from/to a moving ship, using a Sopwith Pup and HMS *Furious*. As the aircraft touched down, naval ratings had been ordered to rush after it as it slowed to less than walking pace and grab hold of straps specially attached for the purpose. Dunning lost his life a few days later, on his third landing, crashing and going over the side of HMS *Furious*. The ship took a while to turn and return to the floating wreckage, where Dunning was found to have been drowned in the cockpit.

In June 1918, HMS *Furious* was recommissioned with a second (landing) deck aft of the superstructure (aft guns removed). However, air turbulence around the superstructure and funnel was sufficient to make aircraft approaching to land on the afterdeck very difficult to control. On 17 July 1918, HMS *Furious* launched seven Sopwith Camels for a bombing raid on the Zeppelin sheds at Tøndern in Denmark. The raid destroyed two Zeppelins and a captive balloon. On return, it was intended that the aircraft were to ditch near *Furious*. Shortage of fuel caused three forced landings in Denmark and three ditchings, where two pilots were rescued and one was drowned. After the war, experience with HMS *Argus* (see below) eventually caused HMS *Furious* to be modified into a complete "flat top" aircraft carrier (recommissioned in 1925).

An incomplete ocean liner in build in a Scottish shipyard for an Italian company, the *Conte Rosso*, was converted into HMS *Argus*, an aircraft carrier with a retractable pilot house to make it a true flat-top (commissioned September 1918).

To accommodate a number of aircraft, *Argus* had forward and aft lifts to move aircraft between the flight deck and the hangar deck. *Argus* was the first full length flight deck equipped aircraft carrier in the world, with sixteen aircraft in her hangar (including two floatplanes), aircraft fuel and servicing facilities. With a long service life, the last take-off from the deck of HMS *Argus* was on 27 September 1944. HMS *Eagle* (commissioned 1924) was the first aircraft carrier with the now familiar starboard (right hand) side superstructure and complete full length flight deck. (Starboard side because pilots' aborted landings generally were found to include a port turn climb-away.)

With the true flat-top, the global power-projection capability of the modern aircraft carrier was born.

Systems Technology Development

Of course, industries and armed forces in other combatant countries made other advances in many areas. It was a "game of leap-frog" to some extent. Two more aviation systems technology examples:

- Early single-seat biplane fighter aircraft, for example, often had a fixed machine gun on top of the top wing, firing <u>over</u> the propeller arc from above the pilot's head. On 1 April 1915, the French airman Roland Garros had successfully shot down an enemy aircraft, firing through the propeller-fitted "bullet deflectors made of steel" on each of the blades. This had allowed the machine gun to be mounted lower, in the pilot's sight line (and just in front of the cockpit, easier to reload with a new magazine in flight). Later in the same month, Garros either had fuel feed trouble and/or was shot down, but he landed safely behind enemy lines. However, he failed to properly set fire to his aircraft. The Dutch aircraft designer Anton Fokker was shown Garros' captured aircraft and ordered to develop an equivalent for German fighter aircraft. Fokker's design team had already been thinking about an alternative (better) idea, to permit firing through the propeller arc. They quickly created a working example of a "firing synchroniser" operated by the propeller shaft. This synchronised the machine gun actual firing capability to the intervals each propeller blade was not in the line of fire. After a ground demonstration (and initial scepticism from the German High Command), the synchroniser gear was finally proven in action by making its first "kill" on 1 August 1915. This was a major improvement and a key contributor to the heavy allied aircraft losses during the year-long 1915–16 German Fokker Eindeker aircraft "Scourge" (as the British press called it). By the autumn of 1916, gun-engine synchroniser mechanisms became standard for all combatant single-engined tractor propeller-driven fighter aircraft (until guns started to be mounted remotely in the wings of the late-1930s monoplane fighters).

- One area of aviation technology improvement during the First World War was the altitude capability. Height was an important advantage to fighter aircraft: diving <u>down</u> on an enemy aircraft gave the attacking aircraft the upper hand. The RFC had encountered the problem of pilot altitude sickness from the days of the B.E.2, which had an altitude ceiling of 10,000 feet. The British S.E.5A of 1916 was capable of reaching 17,000 feet and, by the last year of the war, aircraft were capable of flying at more than 20,000 feet. Aircrew could not physically go that high without oxygen breathing equipment. In addition, the normal average air temperature of -9°C at 12,000 feet drops to –25°C at 20,000 feet.

An RFC squadron commanding officer recalled:

> "I found that pushing the [Foster mounted on top wing] Lewis gun back into the fixed position (while flying in the open cockpit of the single-seater SE5A) at high altitude called for an effort that was almost superhuman. We had no supply of oxygen in those days, and I found that my strength at height fell off considerably. It was difficult enough to change the double drum of ammunition on the Lewis gun without having to manhandle the gun into position for an attack and fly the aircraft at the same time. There were others who had the same experience, and more often than not we had to dive down to a lower altitude before we could reload."

One British fighter aircraft, the Sopwith Snipe, certainly carried oxygen equipment when it went out to France, shortly before the November 1918 Armistice. A former Snipe pilot recalled that, "though we had oxygen bottles and masks fitted in the Snipe (for patrols at over 20,000 feet), the cylinder was a very small one and you'd had it after a few gulps".

The Germans in the last year of the war possessed a fast two-seater reconnaissance aircraft with a service ceiling of 24,000 feet and an endurance of three and a half hours. With a high-compression engine with good power output at altitude, its crews were accustomed to making long flights deep into the rear of the Allied lines, unmolested by enemy fighters. For the sake of weight-saving, the aircraft had only the observer's machine gun and no forward-firing weapon. Liquid oxygen equipment was carried and the crews' flight suits were electrically heated (average air temperature at 24,000 ft. is –33°C).

For the British, the "Independent Air Force" was established, as independent from army or navy command (just before the army RFC and navy RNAS were changing, to become the new RAF service in April 1918). A squadron of the Independent Air Force possessed two special DH4 high-flying reconnaissance aircraft (fitted with larger DH.9A wings, giving a higher ceiling), to support their bombing campaign. No bombs were carried by the special DH.4, and machine gun ammunition was much reduced. An engine-driven generator heated the crew's flight clothing, camera and guns. Compressed oxygen was breathed above 15,000 feet (via a pressure-reducing regulator valve).

Table 2.3: Change in Power-to-Weight Ratio of Aircraft During the First World War.

Type	Aircraft	In Service	Installed HP	MTOW (lb)	HP/lb
Fighter	Airco DH.1	1915	80	2,044	0.0342
	Matinsyde Buzzard	1918	300	2,398	0.1251
Reconnaissance	Royal A'cft. Fty B.E.2c	1914	90	2,350	0.0383
	Bristol F.2B	1917	275	3,243	0.0803
Light Bomber	Royal A'cft. Fty.R.E.7	1915	150	3,450	0.0435
	Airco DH.9A	1918	400	4,645	0.0861
Heavy bomber	Handley Page O/100	1916	520	14,013	0.0371
	Handley Page V/1500	1918	1,500	30,000	0.0500

There were many, many other improvements in aircraft design and construction detail. The most telling were the engine developments and the payload/armament improvements. The power-to weight ratios for different classes of aircraft (fighter, reconnaissance, light bomber, heavy bomber) all improved. The examples in Table 2.3 above illustrate the improvement in power-to-weight ratio as the war progressed.

Maximising Aircraft Production Capacity in the First World War

All of Great Britain's aircraft designer-manufacturer companies did not always have sufficient orders of their own designs to completely fill all their individual factories at the same time. The required total British aircraft production war demand could not allow capacity to remain unused. The government sometimes placed direct orders for aircraft designed by one organisation on the factories of others, as an alternative to the original designer-manufacturer organising "make-to-print" licence-build subcontract arrangements. A direct government-controlled aircraft design example was the Royal Aircraft Factory S.E.5A aircraft extensive production contract (2,000 aircraft) with the Austin Motors factory in Birmingham.

In the first months of the war, the supply of aircraft of new (improved) design to service with the RFC was hampered by the mutual business competitive relationship between different aircraft manufacturers, despite government powers to dictate where production should be undertaken. On the 29 March 1915, a number of British aircraft manufacturers and industrialists met to try to establish a mutually acceptable way forward. Notable personalities attending were Herbert Austin (Austin Motors), Frederick Handley Page (Handley Page Aircraft), Humphrey Verdon Roe (Managing Director, A.V. Roe) and E.B. Parker (Short Brothers). The group agreed to share their design information among a number of other third parties to allow new designs to be produced quickly in quantity. The third party factories joined those being run by the government already accepted as manufacturing centres by the group.

As a direct consequence, the Society of British Aircraft Constructors (SBAC) was founded on 23 March 1916, when more than forty aircraft design companies and parts manufacturing and assembly companies were joined to this grouping. The aircraft engine design and manufacturing companies which were not also part of an aircraft design group were soon included. SBAC were soon influential outside the aircraft manufacturing industry, after the First World War approaching Lloyd's of London to start the inspection and insurance of aircraft (similar to Lloyd's commercial shipping insurance activities). This helped to promote commercial aviation activity in Britain. The SBAC organisation renamed itself as the Society of British Aerospace Companies in 1964, forming an industry voice for British companies manufacturing aircraft, aircraft equipment, aerospace vehicles and associated equipment of any kind. (In 2009, SBAC merged with two other trade associations to form the Aerospace, Defence and Security Group, known as the ADS Group).

A major aircraft production issue was the large number of different engines in service. By 1918, forty-four different engine types were in use in RFC/RNAS aircraft. This was partly due to the uncontrolled separated engine company frequent improvements and some new and, it has to be said, impressive developments. Lack of basic materials added to the problem and engine unreliability due to poor quality control was a source of frustration. In 1915, Armstrong Whitworth had 100 complete B.E.2, but without engines and, in 1918, no less than 400 S.E.5A were awaiting engines. The Bristol Fighter was flown with less powerful engines due to shortage of its Roll Royce Falcon engine and the Martinsyde F3 production rate was reduced for lack of the same engine. At one stage, 200 Sopwith Camel aircraft were in store awaiting engines.

In 1917, in order to help achieve required total rates of aircraft production, the Minister of Munitions (Winston Churchill, after returning from serving in the army for a period on the Western front) commissioned the opening of large-capacity National Aircraft Factories. This was done by "simple conversion", rather than taking the time to design and build purpose-built factories from scratch. The manufacture of any successful aircraft design could be allocated to these factories as required. Four factories were commissioned: Waddon (Croydon), managed by Holland, Hannard & Cubbitt (civil engineers) to build single-engined DH.9 light bombers; Heaton Chapel (Stockport), managed by Crossley Motors, also used to build DH.9 bombers; Aintree (Liverpool), managed by the Cunard Steamship Company to build Bristol F.2B fighter/reconnaissance aircraft and Ham (Surrey), leased by Sopwith Aircraft, to build Sopwith Snipe, Dolphin and Salamander fighter types.

Less than ten years after the formation of the first aircraft company, in July 1917 the Minster of Munitions reported to parliament that, "no fewer than 1,000 factories are engaged on some process or other connected with the construction and equipment of the flying machine".

The main "Allied" powers at the start of the First World War were the "Triple Entente" of Great Britain, France and Russia; joined by Serbia, with Italy joining in 1915. Their adversaries were the "Central Powers", Germany, Austria-Hungary and the Ottoman Empire, with Bulgaria joining in 1915. Only France, Britain and Germany (and, to a much lesser extent, Russia and Italy) had both a significant air force and a broadly-based aircraft industry. The total number of aircraft of all types produced and used by combatant countries was over 200,000. Over a half of this number were lost: 116,250 aircraft shot down, crashed, or damaged on the ground (some in ground/sea transportation). It was a sad fact that, for every member of allied aircrew killed in action, two were killed in accidents (many in training). Of the allied aircraft used in the war, the UK had produced some 40 per cent, a total of 58,144. Of these, 22,171 (less than 40 per cent) survived beyond the end of the war on 11 November 1918.

Controlling Experimental Aircraft during the First World War
The first aircraft designer-producers in Britain were a growing number of amateur and professional enthusiasts. All were really "experimenters", finding out about how to design an aircraft. During the First Word War there were many unsolicited aircraft proposals to the government and, eventually, regulations were passed, partly to prevent crackpot ideas consuming scarce materials and effort. On 30 March 1917, under wartime Defence Regulation powers, it became an offence to produce an experimental aircraft without authority (i.e. without a licence for each experimental type proposed). This was intended to avoid diverting effort and consumption of war materials unnecessarily.

For experimental aircraft, a requirement would be drawn up and approved, and competitive tenders invited. It was also recognised that an original idea might be created which could have a beneficial outcome but about which the government could be totally unaware. To cater for such eventualities, application for a Private Venture (PV) licence could be made and, after notional approval, suitable materials could be allocated (to such an extent as an engine, as well as specific materials). This would encourage those with possibly fruitful ideas but without significant resources, in order to pursue alternative offerings from the established designer-manufacturers, even for a type already in service which might be improved or replaced by incorporation of a novel idea.

The experimental aircraft would be registered as an 'X' category for each of the examples produced against the licence. The total number of 'X' registrations issued before the end of the war was twenty-five and twenty licences were created. However, only one of the 'X' categories was for a truly experimental research reason (the last one, X25), the Boulton Paul P.6. Table 2.4 below shows actually used 'X' registrations.

The 'X' system seems to have been used on a slightly haphazard basis. Records of some use continuing for a year or so after the war may exist (incomplete?). Early experimental designs which were built between 1908 and 1919 ('X' registered or not) are all listed in their respective categories in Appendix 7.

Table 2.4: UK Licenced Experimental Aircraft During the First World War.

'X' numbers	1st Flight	Allocated	Licence	Aircraft Category/Type	Purpose
X1		not used			
X2, X3, X4	1918	Sopwith	?	2FR.2 Bulldog fighter	
X7, X8	1917	Sopwith	L.14	2B.2 Rhino bomber	1st twin-engined spec.
X10, X11	1917	Sopwith	L.16	3F.2 Hippo fighter	to replace Bristol Fighter
X14	1917	S.E. Saunders	L.13	T.1 fighter/reconnais[nce.]	new proposal
X15, X16, X17	1918	Austin	L.17	A.F.T. Osprey fighter	to replace Sopwith Camel
X19, X20	1918	A-Whitworth	L.18	F.M.4 Armadillo	to Air Board A.1(a) spec.
X25	1919	Boulton-Paul	?	Boulton-Paul P.6	aerofoil research for P.9
X16, X17 Austin Ospreys abandoned incomplete. X5, X6, X9, X12-X13, X18, X21-X24 came to nothing.					

The 'X' system fell into disuse but the basic idea of special registration of experimental prototypes was re-invented in 1929 (amended in style but preserved in principle in 1948). For civil-registered flying of aircraft in Britain where the aircraft was/is a pre-Type Certificate of Airworthiness test aircraft, or the aircraft is not intended for a British-based end-operator, temporary registration would be applied (the CAA 'B class' test serials register) during development or production testing being carried out in Britain.

Ignoring prototypes of aircraft intended for series production, Appendix 14 lists British purely experimental aircraft from 1920 onwards, cross referencing where they are mentioned in the main text.

2.3 British Government Control of Aviation Matters, 1908 to 1939

Formation of the Air Ministry

In 1912 the Air Committee had been formed, as an intermediary between the (rival) flying armed services (the Army, controlled by the General Staff, and the Navy, controlled by the Admiralty). The Royal Flying Corps (RFC) was created in 1913 by an amalgamation of naval and army aviation. Just before the outbreak of war in 1914, the Royal Navy (RN) unilaterally reformed the naval wing of the RFC into the Royal Naval Air Service (RNAS), under the authority of the Admiralty. This left the army in charge of the remainder of the RFC, after the majority of the aircraft at that time had been allocated back to the RNAS.

The Air Committee did not hold executive authority and proved fairly ineffective. Due to serious problems with actual supply of aircraft and real equipment operational problems in the overall control of air warfare, the Joint War Air Committee replaced the Air Committee in 1916. This proved little more effective at forcing the Admiralty to co-operate and liaise effectively over aviation policy, equipment supply and air operations. The Joint War Air Committee was replaced by the Air Board on 15 May 1916, chaired by a cabinet minister. The Admiralty still did not co-operate fully and a second Air Board was established in January 1917, with a president specifically chosen by the Prime Minister David Lloyd George. There was some improvement in the Admiralty contribution but full integration was still not achieved. Lloyd George, rather sceptical of the idea of a separate air force, created a two-man committee of himself and a member of the War Cabinet, General Jan Christian Smuts, to consider means by which the management of British military aviation could be improved. On 17 August 1917, General Smuts reported to the War Council that a separate branch of the armed forces was needed, merging the RFC and the RNAS. After some reluctant "conversions", thus was created the Royal Air Force (RAF), on 1 April 1918, their aircraft equipment needs administered by a new government department, the Air Ministry. The Air Board was replaced by the Air Council, to be responsible for all matters in the control of the newly-formed RAF and its equipment. The Air Council was to be chaired by a new ministerial position, the Secretary of State for Air, with various very senior RAF officers as "Air Members", each with a specific area of responsibility within the RAF. In 1919, the Air Ministry also became responsible for civil aviation matters in Britain.

There had been media unrest about reported British air warfare inferiority, driven by the lack of development of radically more capable aircraft, to compete with the superior designs in service with the French air force ally and, particularly, with the enemy in France and Belgium during 1915–16. The obsolescent inadequacies of the B.E.2 aircraft were particularly highlighted in parliament by Noel Pemberton Billing MP. The net result was the Burbidge Committee enquiry, which concluded in March 1916 that, by 1915, an "unofficial" policy had emerged which imposed RFC service standardisation to use aircraft designed by the Royal Aircraft Factory (i.e. by the government). This was compared with the government 1908 reply to A.V. Roe "… we do not consider that aeroplanes will be of any possible use for war purposes". The Burbidge enquiry concluded that this standardisation should cease. The Air Board did not think that this went far enough, and further required that the Royal Aircraft Factory remit should not include actual service aircraft design and development, and should be restrained to aeronautical technology research and development. Forthwith, the RFC should be able to acquire suitable aircraft designed and produced by the burgeoning private industry. Ironically, the last Royal Aircraft Factory aircraft design to enter service was the 1916 S.E.5 which, after the initially chosen engine was changed from a 150HP version to a 200 HP unit in 1917, entered service as the S.E.5A. It became one of the most effective fighter aircraft on the Western Front – 5,205 S.E.5s were built, designed by Henry Folland, later of Nieuport, Gloster and Folland aircraft companies, and John Kenworthy, later of Austin, Westland and Redwing aircraft companies.

From 1918 to 1939, the new Air Ministry had the responsibility for most aviation matters in Britain and the specification, design standards, supply and operational regulation of aircraft for all government aircraft (essentially, the Army, RAF and RN). At the start of the Second World War in 1939, the actual supply of aircraft to the government became the responsibility of a newly-created Ministry of Supply (MoS). The Ministry of Aircraft Production (MAP) was established in 1940, as a wartime-only emergency measure, subsuming the aircraft part of MoS supply responsibilities (see section 3.2). After the Second World War, the government aeronautical research establishments were also brought under MoS control. The Air Ministry retained its other responsibilities until 1964, when it was merged with the War Office and the Admiralty to create the Ministry of Defence.

Civil aviation was formally not permitted to restart until 1 May 1919. The government regulated civil aviation aircraft registration and standards and, as the technology progressed, also regulated airports and air traffic control capability (which was pretty primitive until the later development of radio navigation equipment for aircraft use). From 1924, the Air Ministry issued the specifications for new airliners to be operated by the government-supported monopoly airline Imperial Airways.

The 1936 Air Navigation Act caused the responsibilities (of the government Civil Aviation Department) for certification and regulation of all aircraft types on the British civil register to be divested to a new Air Registration Board (ARB), becoming effective in 1937. This placed the setting of standards of design approval for British-operated civil aircraft (whether of British origin or from another country), testing and manufacturing approval, registration and the licensing of operation and maintenance of aircraft, all in the hands of an independent aviation body, staffed and led by aviation professionals. The British civil aircraft industry and airlines operated under the ARB rules and standards.

2.4 British Civil Aircraft, 1920 to 1929

By the end of the First Word War on 11 November 1918, over half of the aircraft produced by belligerents had been shot down, crashed, or damaged in some way. During the last 103 days of the war, the new RAF had lost 2,692 aircraft from all causes and had received 2,647 replacements (180 per week on average). By that time, Britain had the largest aircraft industry in the world and the largest air force in the world. For the whole war, nearly 60,000 aircraft in total had been produced in Britain, 62 per cent of which had been lost. That still left a large number of aircraft surplus to military requirements after peace was established.

The inevitable after-the-war dramatic and immediate downturn in new military aircraft demand was illustrated by the reduction of RAF total personnel, from 296,000 in March 1919 to 34,280 during 1920. There was not a civil aviation policy for the future, other than that declared in 1920 by War and Air Minister Winston Churchill, who said that if commercial air transport was to fly, "it must do it by itself" but added "the government must not get in the way" and "should smooth the way". Not subsidising civil air transport was not the attitude of other governments; in fiscal year 1921–1922, the French government subsidised commercial aircraft operations to the tune of £1.39 million (£73 million in 2019 terms), compared with a UK grant of £88,000. The British government view was that government direct subsidy of airline operations, with the attendant civil service controls, would "constrain and enfeeble" the growth in civil air transport which the government desired, although the provision of airports and other infrastructure services was to become a recognised and accepted government-sponsorship area as an important parallel "enabler". However, for British aircraft manufacturers, commercial air transport was not a well-placed proposition to replace more than a fraction of the wartime aircraft demand.

Within most of Britain, the very good rail network and relatively short distances between important centres mitigated urgent consideration of acquisition of new aircraft for domestic air services. The domestic commercial air operations market was unclear and adaptation of surplus wartime aircraft did not provide a durable, sensible profit-making environment for most of the aircraft manufacturers. Somehow, if the aircraft industry was to survive, at least a modest replacement for the wartime aeroplane market would have to be created.

Commercial Airliners

With an entrepreneurial eye towards life after the end of the war, in 1916 George Holt Thomas (owner of the Airco aircraft company) registered the first British airline, Air Transport and Travel. The initial fleet consisted of two single-engined Airco DH4 light bombers, modified by having a glazed but cramped two-passenger cabin behind the pilot, who remained in the existing position on top of the

Airco DH4 Airliner G-EAMU (winner of 1922 King's Cup). (*Author's collection*)

fuselage. After modifications were completed, an international service from London to Paris was inaugurated on 25 August 1919, eleven weeks before the end of the First World War. Scheduled services had to wait until the war was over. Following the 1920 sale of Airco to the BSA Company, the airline was re-established by BSA as Daimler Airway.

Handley Page similarly founded an airline, Handley Page Transport. They converted their O/400 bombers into passenger-carrying aircraft, in quantities which were relatively small. Only twenty-seven of 554 O/400 bombers built were converted into passenger-carrying/freight transports. Ship owner Instone also started a private London-Paris service in 1919. Adaptation of the wartime larger bomber designs, by changing the fuselage into an enclosed passenger cabin, was a quick way for manufacturers to create reasonably-sized passenger aircraft. The possibility of conversion of existing (surplus) aircraft (rather than completely new-build) also seemed a relatively simple task. The new Air Ministry controlled the features/capacity of all aircraft (military and civil) in the early days after the end of the war, including limits to capacity and the start of civil airworthiness regulation.

The largest aircraft seated ten to twelve passengers and were the Vickers "Vimy Commercial" and the Handley Page O/7, O/10 and O/11 (adaptations of the O/400 bomber design). The resulting aircraft had fairly primitive passenger accommodation. China ordered twelve O/7 and 100 Vimy Commercial (only forty-three completed). Fifty-five more Vimy Commercial were acquired by the RAF, renamed as the Vickers Vernon transport aircraft.

Vickers Vimy Commercial (1920 Prototype). (*Author's collection*)

Handley Page developed their first purpose-built passenger aircraft 'W' series (W8, W8b-W8f, W9 and W.10), starting with the foundation O/400 (O/7 etc.) and produced twenty-five, nearly half of which were assembled under licence in Belgium for a Belgian airline. The prototype W8 was exhibited at the 1919 Paris Air Show and was the world's first airliner to be fitted with a lavatory. The first to enter service in 1921 was the twelve-passenger W8b. Handley Page Air Transport and Imperial Airways used these 'W' types (later retrospectively allocated HP "type numbers").

Vimy Commercial Interior. (*Flight magazine archive from Flightglobal, CC BY-SA 4.0*)

The few airlines in Britain had to cease operations for a few weeks in the spring of 1921, due to lack of finance (revenue flying had virtually ceased in the preceding winter). Britain, with the world's largest air force, was relying on subsidised foreign airlines for any air travel! It was finally realised that British civil air transport business needed significant actual external support. This would assist a self-sufficient air transport industry to grow and flourish, alongside a concomitant commercial aircraft industry. Some supportive statements were made by several prominent persons, arguing that the British Empire needed good air transport links to "hold it together like sea transport has done for 150 years".

Despite a (relatively small) level of government subsidy introduced in 1921 for cross-channel routes to the continent, not one of the four British airlines was making a profit in 1923. Notably, these four airlines (plus the former Air Transport and Travel pre-cursor of Daimler Airway) had crashed (written off) nineteen other aircraft, in the four year period between the beginning of 1920 and the end of 1923.

There were four scheduled airlines operating in Britain by 1923: BSA-owned Daimler Airway (established in 1920, ex-Air Transport and Travel), Handley Page Travel (established 1919), Instone Air Line (established 1920) and British Marine Air Navigation (established 1923). In 1923, these were operating several different aircraft, varying in size and range capability:

Aircraft Type	No. of Aircraft	Max. Passengers (Crew)	Cruising Speed (mph)	Max. Range (miles)
de Havilland DH.4A	1	2 (1)	~100	470
de Havilland DH.18	1	8 (1)	100	400
de Havilland DH. 34	12	10 (2)	105	365
Handley Page Type W8b	4	12 (2)	90	500
Supermarine Sea Eagle	3	6 (2)	~80	230
Vickers Vimy Commercial	1	10 (1)	~75	450
Vickers Type 61 Vulcan	3	8 (1)	~95	430
Westland Limousine	2	4 (1)	90	520

Eventually, in 1924 the UK government agreed to promote the merger of the four airlines then operating into a single unit. Part of the reasoning was that continental European airlines of the time were heavily subsidised by their respective governments, the subsidy enabling those flying in/out of Britain being able to undercut British operators.

The new government-supported monopoly airline of 1924 was called "Imperial Airways". Exactly the same solution as was already in effect in the continental countries, to enable national commercial air transport systems to develop. However, the subsidy in Britain had to spread over a more ambitious objective – the task of connecting the worldwide British Empire with air travel. Sir Eric Campbell Geddes (Government ex-railway transportation and shell supply supremo, MP and First Lord of the Admiralty in 1917, all during the First World War, and a post-war director of Dunlop Rubber) was appointed Chairman. He had no previous background of any kind in aviation, but he was a recognised successful reorganiser and cost-cutter. In his appointment to Imperial airways, he was enjoined to "turn subsidy into profit" as soon as practicable.

Imperial Airways was to be supported financially from the public purse for the next ten years, on the "quid-pro-quo" of an expanding network of domestic and international air transport services. This was not a magic wand solution, but Britain was at last (hopefully) just about "up and running" in the commercial air transport business. Only domestically-produced aircraft were to be used by Imperial Airways, thus hoping to provide some stimulus for the aircraft industry. Production volumes of aircraft produced specifically to Imperial Airways requirements, however, generally turned out to be quite small. Various other charter-style airlines and air taxi style services were established later (into the 1930s), but none of these became large enough to acquire significant aircraft fleets, let alone new aircraft.

There were no radio navigation aids to aid safe flying in poor weather, or at night. Pilots used hand-held compass, maps, rivers, canals, roads and railway lines etc. to find their way. Forced landings, due to engine problems and/or weather were not uncommon. On one flight of a passenger conversion of an HP.O/400 from London to Paris there were seventeen unplanned (in a field) landings before the eighteenth in Paris. Pilots sometimes landed to clean engine spark plugs to correct engine misfiring, other minor repairs, or the weather/visibility deteriorating. Operations would have been unacceptably hazardous for flights in fog, or at night, except for clear-air evening sunset flights with a visible horizon, where pilots could follow a few special routes where lines of lights (or fires) on the ground marked the way. Until the invention of the gyroscopic horizon indicator by Elmer Amrose Sperry in 1929, the only instrument for indicating level flight was little better than an advanced version of a spirit level, subject to many external influences in flight other than just gravity. First use of a gyroscopic artificial horizon in an aircraft took place in 1929, in the USA.

The early 1920s aircraft passenger may have been adventurous and excited but was also likely to be cold and perhaps perceived to be at significant risk, relative to other means of transport. Early 1920s airliners had a less-than-comfortable cabin, in the early days maybe with lightweight wicker seats. The cabin

Armstrong Whitworth AW.154 Argosy. (*Author's collection*)

was unheated and very likely without toilet facilities or safety equipment. Passenger seat belts were not fitted as standard until the mid-1920s (and not in every aircraft, even then). Cabin attendants (if any) used megaphones to make announcements, in cabin ambient noise levels as high as 120 decibels. By 1926, Armstrong-Whitworth had developed and flown the purpose-built three-engined, 20-seater passenger airliner AW.154 Argosy (developed to an Imperial Airways requirement, only seven sold).

Pilots remained in exposed cockpits as late as in the AW.154 Argosy. Some pilots objected to fully enclosed cockpits, partly for vision reasons in periods of rain or mist. Some pilots carried hammers, to break the glass of an enclosed cockpit in the event of emergency exit needs.

On a "standard" 15°C day at sea level, any flight at 5,000ft altitude would be in an atmosphere with an

AW.154 Argosy Interior. (*Author's collection*)

ambient temperature of 5°C, dropping to 0°C at 8,000ft. On a winter's day, the air temperature could be down to –15°C or lower at 8,000ft. Above 10,000ft altitude, cabin pressurisation or oxygen-breathing equipment would have been essential to maintain pilot and passenger full consciousness (hence the modern practice of pressurised passenger cabins to maintain a cabin altitude of 8,000ft or less). The problem was recognised and, in 1921, the USA experimentally adapted an Airco DH.9A aircraft as the first aircraft to fly with a pressurised cockpit module. Airliner cabin pressurisation was not to arrive until 1938, in the USA Boeing 307 Stratoliner.

Safety regulation in civil aviation started in Britain as early as 1911, the first formal control being enabled by the Aerial Navigation Act 1911. Amendments to regulations concerning civil air operations continued even during the First World War, when very little such flying took place. On 1 May 1919, the position of Controller General of Civil Aviation was established in Britain. At first, civil air safety improvement focused most heavily on safety in the aircraft operations without too much attention on airspace control (initially, there were no airborne radio facilities to facilitate this). The aircraft as a machine required an approval of the design and a Certificate of Airworthiness. Aircraft in their own right had been improving from the beginning but errors in airmanship, navigation (especially in poor visibility), maintenance or servicing were the cause of many accidents. Over the period 1926 to 1933, of the 355 civil aircraft non-fatal and fatal accidents (forty-four per year!) to aircraft on the UK civil register, only 30 per cent were due to design or manufacturing inadequacies, or engine failure, aircraft structural or equipment failures, or inadequate maintenance of the aircraft itself.

By about 1922–23, a clearer and more proactive British government civil aviation policy started to be slowly developed. This was in the context of air transport initially focused mostly on the needs of communication and transport of key people between the various domains of the British Empire, both domestically and internationally.

Airships were thought to be the only likely option for really long-range high-capacity passenger flights. After the 1916-to-1920 Royal Navy R.31, R.32, R.33 and R.34 experimental military airships, the R.100 and R.101 airship contracts were part of government thinking. Much effort and money was to be expended on these two large "experimental" airships. The intent was to demonstrate long-range transport technology for routes to the corners of the Empire.

The R.100 was a government fixed price contract on a specially-created Vickers Armstrong company subsidiary, the Airship Guarantee Company. The R.101 was contracted to a Government-employed team, supported for all costs. Planning called for construction to start in 1925 but this did not happen until 1927.

The R.100 required a crew of thirty-seven, carried up to one hundred passengers, with a large dining room/lounge and downward-looking passenger observation facilities. The R.101 required a crew of forty-two and accommodated fifty passengers (in a closer to ocean-liner and more spacious style of accommodation and recreation areas than on the R.100). The R.100 set off on a demonstration flight to Canada on 29 July 1930. The crossing took seventy-eight hours. Following a short series of demonstrations, it was flown back to Britain, arriving on 15 August after a flight of a little under fifty-eight hours.

Unfortunately, on 5 October 1930, the R.101 demonstration flight to India crashed in transit in France, killing forty-eight people (including H.M. Secretary of State for Air, Lord Thomson). There were six survivors (two others who survived the crash died later in hospital). After a public enquiry and much public and political furore, further airship development was abandoned and the R.100 was scrapped in 1931. This signalled the end of British activity in passenger airships, so "bigger/better aeroplanes" eventually would be required.

The civil aircraft designers and producers might advise "what size and capability of aircraft might be made available" but were expected to respond to market requirements, which were very meagre to start with. Similar difficulties were experienced in other countries. Other than a German Zeppelin airship airline of 1909, Hungary saw the first airline in the world to use aeroplanes, established on 22 December 1910. By the end of 1919 there were seventeen airlines in the world, two of which were in Britain, eleven more were in the rest of Europe, two were in the United States and two were in Columbia. By the end of 1929, a total of eighty-seven airlines had been formed in the world but thirty-one of these had either ceased operations or had merged with other operators.

The world's first scheduled airmail service had started in Britain in 1911. Immediately after the First World War, the UK General Post Office (the GPO) again offered an air mail service. Airmail carriers were approved from the few fledgling British airlines and flying services companies, mostly operating within domestic borders, or government mail on RAF flights to Empire destinations. A premium price for GPO air mail was not allowed, so lack of finance restricted air mail development in Britain. The service slowly expanded over the next fifteen years to include most of the regions of the British Empire. Airmail services around the Mediterranean Sea and the Middle East were to be developed by the RAF. Most other countries were equally slow to develop non-government airmail services, although much of an aircraft's payload was often dominated by mail. The USA became a lively airmail environment in the early 1920s, postal services being established in the US constitution[2].

At the end of 1929, world airlines numbered sixty-four. Originally using converted surplus wartime aircraft, many airlines often started as little more than "air mail or air-taxi services". Higher capacity true passenger-carrying aircraft slowly started to appear but airlines only required small fleets, unlike the combatant large military fleets of the war.

In most of the further reaches of the British Empire, air transport needs supplied from Britain were entirely a Royal Air Force province until 1933. Local airlines were created in some parts of the empire. Qantas (Queensland and Northern Territory Air Service)

---

2. The United States Post Office Department started airmail public services in 1918. From May 1918 to January 1920, US Post Office Air Services earned US$22 million. A new federal law in 1926 forced airlines to be used as airmail carriers (rather than government aircraft). By 1931, airmail revenue of USA airlines was 85% of the total. Passengers "flying with the mail" helped to make air travel more widely appreciated in that country, stimulating growth.

was (and remains) an Australian airline founded in 1921. Qantas' first aircraft was an Avro 504K, able to carry just a pilot and two passengers, in open cockpits. Between 1926 and 1928, Qantas and other Australian airlines licence-built a total of sixteen of the 1923 single-engined enclosed cabin de Havilland four-passenger DH.50 biplane, with three more built in Brussels and seven in Prague. The DH.50 was a reworked and updated version of the DH.9 bomber design, the pilot remaining in an open cockpit positioned aft of the cabin. It was the first aircraft used by the Australian Royal Flying Doctor Service. Of the thirty-eight DH.50s produced, de Havilland themselves only built seventeen, mostly for Imperial Airways. For Britain, the commercial air transport market was very slow to develop, via the "Imperial Airways only" monopoly.

This highlights the question "Why did British airliners of the 1920s not sell well?" Was a market opportunity missed? Many countries were influenced by many factors which mitigated inclination to import foreign airliners. No British aircraft company sold many airliners between 1920 and 1929. Why?

Among the factors were:

- Governments "conditional support" based on using aircraft from a particular source e.g. Imperial Airways use of only British aircraft – a comparable practice used elsewhere (German government-run monopoly Deutsche Lufthansa had an all German-supplied fleet).
- Imperial Airways focused on minimising spend (to try to operate with a low subsidy), consequently ordering few aircraft compared with airlines in other European countries and inhibiting the used of new technology, in order to keep new aircraft acquisition cost low.
- British aircraft manufacturers having insufficient financial resources to finance a "PV" airliner.
- Airline started up by aircraft manufacturer (using own aircraft exclusively) e.g. French airline founded by Farman brothers using Farman aircraft exclusively, Handley Page Transport use of converted/redesigned O/400 bombers for passenger use.
- Start-up airline use of (cheap-to-buy) ex-military aircraft (converted) e.g. Swedish use of ex-RN AD flying boats, converted by Supermarine Aircraft into the Supermarine Channel, to carry three passengers (in open cockpits).
- British aircraft not suited to requirements of operators in parts of some countries, especially in demanding operations from "hot and high" (low air density) airfields.

The "emergent big market" would be in the USA, which, by the early 1930s, started to favour larger and longer-range aircraft, such as the 1933 Boeing 247 (range 745 miles) and the 1934 Douglas DC-2 (over 1,000 miles range). Within Britain, where large centres of population were less far apart and very well-connected by rail, there was not an equivalent emergent demand.

It would seem that many potential civil airliner designer-manufacturers in Britain either could not gain access to most overseas areas (except via the RAF transport fleet or Imperial airways), or could not (or did not) afford to try. This seriously limited the UK industry new airliner market opportunity.

Civil Utility, Sports and Trainer Aircraft

General utility aircraft (mostly two seaters) were one area where demand grew, for those wealthy enough. Sports aircraft (powered and gliders) would be sold in the 1920s and pilot-training aircraft (i.e. easy-to-fly) were developed. In both Britain and elsewhere, the "flying circus, or barnstorming" circuit for air displays and air experiences was extremely popular, stimulating demand for utility/sports aircraft. In the early 1930s,

Alan Cobham's Flying Circus became the most well-known in Britain, using up to fourteen aircraft. Publicity from high-profile prizes helped, such as those for the Lord Northcliffe (*Daily Mail*) round-Britain air race (£5,000), or the Australian government prize for the fastest flight from London to Australia (£10,000).

This London-Australia prize was won in 1928 by Australian Bert Hinkler in a single-seater Avro Avian biplane, taking a record fifteen and a half days. A prize of £10,000 in 1928 would have been the equivalent of almost £600,000 in 2019 and a new DH.60 Moth aircraft cost around £650 to buy in 1930. Designed to compete with the de Havilland DH.60, 405 Avians were built before production ended.

There were one or two other notable successful British civil utility aircraft successes in the 1920s. From 1925, the de Havilland developments of the utility two-seat biplane DH.60 "Moth Series" became the most popular light two-seat aircraft in the world.

The DH.60 original Cirrus engine was "half an air-cooled Renault 8G V8 engine" designed by Frank Bernard Halford[3], using Renault parts (ex-war RAF ADC engine stock) designed into a new crankcase by Halford. The DH.60 was an immediate success but the availability of Renault parts was insufficient to keep up with demand, so Frank Halford designed a new engine, the 100 HP DH Gypsy I engine, to replace the Cirrus. This ultimately helped to generate some 1,900 DH.60 Moth sales, between 1925 and the end of type production in 1935. It was sold widely in the world, and effectively started the de Havilland engines business in 1926.

DH.60 Cirrus Moth. (*BAE Systems*)

The DH.80 Puss Moth 2/3-seater high wing single-engined monoplane of 1929 also sold reasonably well (total 284 built by 1933 end of production). Puss Moths were used to break a number of aviation records. The most famous occasions were when Jim Mollinson completed the first solo east-west Atlantic crossing in August 1932, from Portmarnock Strand, near Dublin to New Brunswick, Canada, and the first east-west crossing of the South Atlantic (from England, three days to Brazil via Africa). In February 1933, Mollinson's wife Amy Johnson made record flights between England and Cape Town using a Puss Moth. In the 1934 MacRobertson Air Race from the UK to Australia, a Puss Moth finished overall seventh and second on handicap, in a time of ten days sixteen hours.

DH.80 Puss Moth. (*MilburneOne, CC BY-SA 2.5*)

The war-interrupted Schneider Trophy Seaplane races were run annually, in 1913 and 1914 and from 1920 to 1927, then biennially to allow more development time, until 1931. The competition was a very high-profile prestigious international speed trial, with the winner likely to be most interested in the prestige and publicity. Races were at least 150 miles long, over timed laps of a triangular

---

3. Frank Halford and Harry Ricardo founded the Cirrus Aero-Engine company in 1923, bought out in 1931 by Hermes to form Cirrus-Hermes, in turn acquired by Blackburn Aircraft in 1937. Halford established a consulting company and designed engines for various engine manufacturers, including Napier and de Havilland, until joining de Havilland in 1944 to run de Havilland's jet turbine engine business (see section 4.2).

course. The British Supermarine S.5 (1927), then S.6 (1929) won, and then the S.6B won the trophy for the third consecutive time in 1931 (and therefore the trophy outright), at a record average speed of 340mph. The 1931 win became a foregone conclusion, because the Italian and French contenders did not finish their preparations in time to compete. In the days immediately following the 1931 trophy race, and fitted with

Supermarine S6.B. (*BAE Systems*)

a specially-prepared 2,600HP engine using high-octane fuel, the S.6B broke the world straight-line air speed record. Flying 400 metres above sea level, the S6B was the first machine to fly at over 400mph, the record speed being set at 407.5mph. Just ten years previously, the record stood at 211.91mph. The RAF only had a service aircraft capable of such speeds in the latter part of the Second World War – the 1942 Spitfire Mk IX, with a 1,560HP Merlin 61 engine, achieved over 400mph at 27,000ft.

2.5 British Military Aircraft, 1920 to 1929

The government disposed of many of the military aircraft which had survived the First World War, by selling the entire stock of surplus aircraft, engines and the like. More than 10,000 aircraft and 35,000 engines were for sale. The Aircraft Disposal Company (ADC) was formed in 1920, with Handley Page awarded the contract to act as sole managing agents. The government were to receive £1,000,000 immediately (equivalent to £50 million in 2019 terms), plus 50 per cent of the profit from sales. Frederick Handley Page raised the £1,000,000 by issuing debenture shares in his aircraft company and acquired the managing agent contract. After one full financial year of operations, ADC had a profit of £1,000,000, able to remit £500,000 as the profit share to the government. After a change of name to ADC Aircraft in 1925, the disposal company still had enough material to be able to continue operations until wound up in 1930. Most of the sales went into civilian hands (mostly for adaptation and use in start-up transport enterprises, or simple salvage and reuse of materials).

Aviation matters needing continuous government attention in the first few years after the war involved the organisation of the newly-formed RAF (as the third armed and independent service in the UK), and the newly-created Air Ministry, responsible for military and civil aviation in Britain. The Air Ministry did not control the production of all civil aircraft but it was the organisation through which the civil airline operations were regulated and for which the Air Ministry became responsible.

Immediately the war ended, the Admiralty and the Army General staff began a campaign aimed at restoring the RNAS and RFC, seeking to dismember the RAF in the process. This campaign slowly became increasingly strident and vitriolic and lasted in full fury until 1923, with later short-lived re-enactions until well into the 1930s. The first RAF Chief of the Air Staff (CAS) was Major General Hugh Trenchard, who had led the RFC and the interim so-called "Independent" Air Force (independent from the army and navy) in the latter stages of the war. In 1919 the new Air Minister was Winston Churchill (who combined the role with that of War Minister). Churchill was air-minded, vigorously supported Trenchard and believed that the RAF should collaborate with the Navy and the Army but must actually be independently led, in order to directly prosecute aerial offence or defence activities according to any campaign objectives prioritised by the government. For other than specific "combined operations", or for planned tactical offence, there would often be little reason to involve naval and/or army resources in RAF activity. The main protagonist desirous of dismembering the RAF was Admiral of the Fleet, Lord David Beatty. Senior members of the cabinet were continually involved in diverting argument on the matter.

By happenstance, the RAF were handed a helpful "lifeline" in their fight for survival, when Hugh Trenchard took the chance to offer to suppress an armed revolt, in a sparsely inhabited, fairly bleak and troublesome part of Somaliland, at the Horn of Africa. Somaliland had been divided into British and Italian controlled areas since 1887. Armed revolt by the fanatical and religiously-inspired Mohammed Abdulla Hassan and his followers had been continual from the end of the nineteenth century, the latest insurrection recommencing in earnest in 1919. The RAF proposal would be at a cost which was far below that which the army said could be managed. Senior army officers had muttered "maybe two divisions (five or six brigades, some 30,000 or more personnel) with significant transport needed, with road and/or rail building". It was suggested that, to deploy two divisions into such an area would be an exercise costing millions of pounds, even before any real in-country action could be mounted. Trenchard advised that the RAF could solve the problem with a squadron of twelve DH.9 light bombers. This would be a counter-insurgency operation, in conjunction with a couple of brigades-worth of colonial troops already in-area, which included the Somali Camel Corps and other colonial African and Indian Army troops. Some bombs, machine-gun bullets and aviation fuel would be the only additional cost. Senior army staff fiercely expressed the view that they would only have to go in and rescue the situation from an RAF disaster, but the air-minded War Minister and the Prime Minister accepted the RAF plan. A total of 219 RAF personnel, with sixteen motor vehicles and tenting equipment, were eventually deployed to Somaliland. Operations would be from temporary unpaved air strips pre-prepared by local labour. Sites were surveyed in advance by the RAF commanding officer and a number of airfield construction personnel infiltrated into country disguised as a party of geologist oil prospectors. Stiff airborne bombing and machine-gun firing responses to the revolt of unmechanised and superstitious armed rebels, bandits, tribesmen and the like turned out to be enough. In a twenty-three day campaign and at a cost of £77,000 (less than £4 million in 2019 terms), the Dervish "Mad Mullah" of Somaliland was defeated – the cheapest war in history, as described by the Colonial Office at the time. The usefulness of RAF independent action was vindicated and continued to be used to "maintain the peace" in similar disturbances elsewhere, well into the 1930s. Of course, all such operations did not face an opposing air force, a fact conveniently ignored when celebrating the Somaliland success.

By 1924, the arguments over the permanence of the RAF establishment had just about subsided but it remained the case for a further decade that the RAF were significantly less-well financed than the other two armed services. Battleships, destroyers, heavy guns and armoured vehicles cost more than the wooden stick-and-string biplanes used by the RAF! The "war to end all wars" had not long ended, so sponsoring the acquisition of new, improved aircraft designs for the RAF was only given serious financial support (slowly-rising) in the mid-1930s. This was despite the indisputable fact that the aerial threat (bombers) had been shown to be an effective war tactic in the First World War and the European continent was only a short flight away. Total cost estimates (for both new equipment and operating expense) for the RAF were by far the lowest of the armed forces after 1918, only reaching levels comparable to the other services as the next world conflict loomed, see table 2.5 below.

Table 2.5: UK Armed Forces Annual Cost Allocation Estimates, 1920 to 1938.

Year	Actual service estimates (£)			At 2019 inflation levels (£ billion)		
	Navy	Army	RAF	Navy	Army	RAF
1920	90,872,300	125,000,000	22,992,230	3.937	5.416	0.996
1924	55,800,000	45,000,000	14,861,000	3.308	2.688	0.881
1929	55,865,000	40,545,000	16,960,000	3.464	2.514	1.052
1934	56,550,000	39,600,000	17,561,000	3.957	2.771	1.229
1938	96,117,500	85,357,000	73,501,000	6.320	5.612	4.833

Aircraft and pilots flying on behalf of the RN were assigned by the RAF to the Fleet Air Arm (FAA) of the RN, formed in 1924. The FAA became self-contained within the RN in May 1939, with the so-called "Inskip Award", named after the minister co-ordinating the pre-Second World War rearmament process.

Based on the growth seen in the post-1918 French Air Force, a potential but unlikely threat could be easily imagined. With a little complacency, the reality of an airborne threat from any armed nation within flying range of London was, however, deemed "remote" (and would therefore not receive major UK government resource allocation for a counter until the next decade). Given the RAF "article of faith" premise that, in a mass attack, "some bombers will always succeed in getting through", this inattention to air defence was not the most logical defence planning to guarantee national security. Most overseas countries were also slow to order new military aircraft in quantity, except for France and the USA. At first, the USA had been slow to build on the pioneering of the Wright brothers and was in "catch-up" mode after joining in the war in 1917. The Treaty of Versailles banned Germany from recreating an air force but allowed civil aircraft development – the 1930s were to see a change.

In the early 1920s, there were ongoing production contract completions of UK military aircraft wartime designs, sometimes with relatively minor improvement or adaptations. However, the inevitable abrupt halt to most military aircraft production soon after the Armistice was a serious industry (and government) problem. A heavy retrospective 80 per cent tax burden was placed on aircraft and other war material manufacturers, to reclaim "excess war profits". Production facilities were closed and workers laid off. Retained profits made during the war and the tailing off of some wartime contracts cushioned some manufacturers for a while, but when would significant new military aircraft orders emerge?

Some new military aircraft were procured from the mid-1920s onwards. Examples were:

- RAF specification 26/27 required a replacement of the 1917 DH.9A (see section 2.2), using DH.9A parts (of which the RAF still held a large stock of spares) but encouraging the use of an all-metal structure aircraft. Westland, designers of the DH.9-to-DH.9A changes on behalf of Airco, were successful with their 1927 Wapiti aircraft proposal, using metal for the fuselage (later extending to metal structure for the wings) and built 558 (twenty-seven more were licence-built in South Africa). As a PV, Westland later enhanced the Wapiti, with a more powerful engine and an enclosed cockpit, naming the new design as the Wallace. This first flew in 1931. RAF specification 19/32 was finally issued to obtain 104 new-build Wallace and sixty-eight conversions from Wapiti.
- In 1923, Avro improved the wartime standard Avro 504 pilot-training aircraft, producing the 504N. The RAF purchased 516 of these and overseas sales of fifty-

one more helped. These sales were over and above conversion of 147 existing Avro 504Ks to 504N standard.

- Further military adaptations of the Vickers Vimy were purchased by the RAF (124 Virginia bombers and ninety-seven Victoria transports) and 124 Blackburn Dart torpedo bombers were acquired by the RN.
- Armstrong Whitworth Siskin III fighter-bombers (the RAF's "first all-metal" aircraft) were built for the RAF (sixty-four of the 1922 Siskin III and 340 more of the 1926 Siskin IIIA) plus seventy-nine exported. There were few other significant RAF or RN fleet enhancements before the end of the 1920s, although the Bristol Bulldog started to replace the Siskin fleet in 1929.

2.6 Total British Civil and Military Aircraft Production, 1920 to 1929

By 1929, a grand total of eighty-four attempts to form aircraft design and manufacture organisations had been established in Britain since 1908 (however fleetingly). Apart from the aircraft exceptions noted above, however, both the civil and military aircraft markets of the 1920s were hardly buoyant. Several aircraft companies ceased trading by 1930. Twenty-one aircraft design-and-build organisations existed at the end of the First World War, fourteen of which survived into the 1930s. Ten new UK actual companies started up in the 1920s but only seven of these survived into the 1930s, as shown in table 2.6 below.

Including the "casualty" companies which were still in business in 1920 but did not survive into the 1930s, the total number of British aircraft new 1920s designs (of all types whose first flight was in the decade 1920 to 1929) are also shown in Table 2.6 below, together with the total production (beyond 1929, to the last one of each 1920s type).

Table 2.6: 1920s UK Aircraft Design and Manufacture Total Production (to end-of-line, beyond 1930).

Company Name	Founded (started aircraft work)	Survived beyond 1939?	Number of Aircraft (to end of production)	
			Types (to 1929)	Produced (grand total)
ABC Motors (Aircraft/Motor engines, motors only 1929-on)	1929	1929	1	1
Aircraft Manufacturing Company (Airco), pre-sale to BSA/DH	1912	1920	1	9 (by DH)
Air Navigation & Engineering	1919	1926	4	8
Alliance	1918	1920	0	0
Armstrong Whitworth	1912	yes	10	1,585
Austin Motor (motor engineering only, post-1924)	1917	"1924"	1	1
A.V. Roe (Avro)	1910	yes	14	1,084
Beardmore (ceased aircraft activity in 1930)	1886 (1913)	"1930"	3	3
Blackburn	1914	yes	15	341
Boulton & Paul (general engineers in 1900)	(1915)	yes	7	34
Bristol (including 1920 restructure from Bristol & Colonial)	1910	yes	23	500

Company Name	Founded (started aircraft work)	Survived beyond 1939?	Number of Aircraft (to end of production)	
			Types (to 1929)	Produced (grand total)
Cierva (ceased trading 1938, revived 1943)	1926	yes	5	>35
Civilian Aircraft	1928	1933	1	5
de Havilland (after Airco assets acquired from BSA)	1920	yes	19	2,295
English Electric (no aircraft design dept. 1927 to 1945)	(1922)	1926	2	8
Fairey	1915	yes	11	537
George Parnall (1935, Parnall Aircraft, after acquiring Hendy)	1916	yes	2	3
Grahame White Aviation	1911	1924	0	0
Handasyde	1920	1923	3	29
Handley Page	1909	yes	10	98
Hawker (1920-on, after Sopwith assets acquired)	1920	yes	12	1,249
Hendy Aircraft	1928	1935	2	2
Martin & Handasyde (1915, Martinsyde)	1908	1922	1	1
Nieuport & General (before 1920 close-down)	1916	1920	2	1
Pemberton-Billing (1916-on, Supermarine)	1913	yes	13	122
S.E. Saunders, then Saunders-Roe (Saro) in 1929	1920	yes	5	16
Simmonds (renamed Spartan 1930)	1928	1935	1	48
Shorts	1908	yes	9	21
Sopwith (voluntary liquidation 1920, became Hawker)	1913	1920	1	1
Vickers (Aircraft Division)	1911	yes	22	842
Westland (1915 Petters division, 1935 separate company)	1915	yes	11	632
		Totals	228	9,611

Appendix 8 lists all British military and civil types which were designed and first flown in the years 1920–1929, together with the total numbers of each type eventually produced. Almost half of the new types produced were unsuccessful prototypes, with a few purely experimental machines.

The grand overall total of combined military and civil British aircraft type designs of the 1920s was two hundred and thirty-five. Some 70 per cent of the total of these types would be delivered in the 1920s, leading to some 9,000 actual aircraft sales (deliveries) in those ten years, including types designed before 1920. Fewer than 200 of the 9,000 were classed as Civil or Military Transports. Comparing the yearly average total of 16,000 aircraft produced by British industry during the war, the total number of aircraft actually produced in the 1920s was disastrously low. For the whole decade, the rate of aircraft production per year was less than 6 per cent of the war total average annual production rate, and the ten-year total number was not much more than one half of one year's war production.

It is noteworthy that over half the war production total had been either Geoffrey de Havilland (DH) types (Royal Aircraft Factory or Airco) or Sopwith company design, and that this production dominance continued into the 1920s (from the de Havilland and Hawker companies).

Really long-range British commercial aviation hopes for the future had been pinned on large airships (at the time, high-lift, but flammable hydrogen-filled, rather than the rarer, more expensive non-flammable but not quite so light helium). After the airship demise, it was clear that long-range commercial passenger travel would have to await new and significant developments in winged aircraft. For all commercial aviation, improved navigation aids and development of air transport infrastructure would also be needed. Grass airfields were still very much the 'norm', needing fuel storage, aircraft maintenance and passenger-handling facilities, before fare-paying passenger air transport could offer regular and reliable domestic air travel, let alone comfortable international services.

2.7 British Civil and Military Aircraft Success, 1930 to 1939

Utility, Trainers, Transport and Sports Aircraft

Apart from the continuing 1930s Count Ferdinand von Zeppelin airship programme in Germany, for longer range commercial flights, it was clear that new and significant development in long-range large passenger/freight aeroplanes eventually would be required. Continuing extensive development of air transport infrastructure would also be needed before fare-paying passenger air transport could offer regular long-range travel, let alone intercontinental services. The establishing of a significant air services market would be a prerequisite for a self-supporting and expanding service network, a side-by-side enabler being the availability of suitable aircraft.

Quite a bit of chicken-and-egg! An ever-present feature of most manufactured-goods markets. Many utility civil aircraft of the period were also used as pilot training aircraft for both civil and military personnel and transport aircraft were used by both civil and military operators. In the UK and elsewhere, the 1930s was, therefore, a period of a part-combined civil/military UK market, alongside a much larger military market for fighters and light bombers, and a small market for true airliners.

From 1925, there had been glimmerings of one or two successes in the general civil aircraft marketplace, with production continuing through into 1930s business. There were some successful sales of good numbers of smaller aircraft in the 1930s, many to overseas customers. Avro was one company which had managed some modest success with the 1926 Avro Avian (a direct competitor with the more successful de Havilland DH.60 Moths, nevertheless having been useful "continuation business"). Avro and many other aircraft companies sometimes needed diversification support. For example, from time-to-time Avro was to make car body parts and billiard tables, among other things.

For de Havilland, by the mid-1930s the more advanced de Havilland DH.82 Tiger Moth of 1931 more than overtook the ubiquitous and successful DH.60 Moth series. Not to be confused with the 1927 monoplane DH.71 Tiger Moth racing aircraft, the DH.82 started out as a more powerful version of the DH.60 biplane (initially named the DH.60T). The DH.82 development included easier front cockpit access and better pilot vision. By the start of the Second World War, 1,424 Tiger Moths had been produced (much accelerated production in the Second World War would make the final total 8,868 by 1945, Morris Motors in Oxford producing 3,433 between 1941 and the end of the Second World War).

Hillman's Airways, operators of the three-to-four passenger 1932 DH.83 Fox Moth single-engined biplane requested that a larger capacity twin-

DH.82 Tiger Moth. (*BAE Systems*)

engined derivative be made available. The resulting twin-engined six-to-ten passenger 1932 aircraft DH.84 Dragon had modest success, 202 being built, eighty-seven of which were built in Australia. In response to a Britain-India-Malaya-Australia initiative to try to create an Empire air mail and passenger service, Australian airline Qantas ordered a then non-existent four-engined larger derivative of the DH.84 Dragon, for the Australia-Singapore legs of the service. This resulted in the 1934 DH.86 Dragon Express, (maximum range 760 miles), sixty-two of which were built. Designed

in a hurry, the DH.86 had design deficiencies mainly associated with lateral stability, which haunted the life of the type.

The numerically most successful 1930s British airliner was the 1934 twin-engined smaller derivative of the DH.86, the twin-engined DH.89 Dragon Rapide short haul airliner (six-to-eight passenger biplane, maximum range 573 miles).

Before the end of 1939, 205 DH.89 Dragon Rapides were produced, for commercial and private use. Total production was a final 727, over 500 of which were the RAF "Dominie"

DH.89 Dragon Rapide. (*Author's collection*)

variant, used in the Second World War for communications, training and air ambulance purposes. From the mid-1930s onwards, the Tiger Moth success, combined with the Dragon series of biplanes, caused de Havilland to have to use major subcontractors to support the total company workload. De Havilland had opened

overseas subsidiaries in Canada and Australia in 1927 and aircraft for these countries were assembled there (later, these subsidiaries designed and made improved versions of the DH.82 Tiger Moth).

A special de Havilland design was the DH.88 Comet Racer, developed specifically as a technology development activity, with high-profile prestige and publicity, to participate in the 1934 MacRobertson Air Race

DH.88 Comet Racer. (*BAE Systems*)

from the United Kingdom to Australia. The distance would be approximately 11,300 miles and the prize for the winner was £40,000. If orders were placed by 28 February 1934 by any prospective race entrant, de Havilland commited to deliver a DH.88 at a knock-down price of £5,000 each (£350,000 in 2019 terms), in time to start the race (take-off time dawn on 20 October 1934). Three aircraft were ordered.

A significant departure from conventional 1930s aircraft designs, the DH.88 was an advanced two-seat, twin-engined monoplane aircraft, with ash formers and spruce double-curvature skin. It had a fully-glazed cockpit and retractable undercarriage. Three examples were sold and the one purchased by Arthur Octavius (A.O.) Edwards (a hotel manager) and flown by Charles William Anderson Scott and Tom Campbell Black, won the race in a time of seventy-one hours and eighteen seconds. A total of five of this special aircraft were finally constructed.

In 1932, from within his newly-formed aircraft design company, Edgar Percival designed his first aircraft, the single-engined pilot-and-two passenger Percival Gull. The company did not have production facilities until it moved to Gravesend in 1934, so the prototype Gull was produced by the British Aircraft Company in Kent. The next twenty-four production aircraft were produced by Parnall Aircraft in Gloucestershire, until the new Gravesend Percival facility was opened. The Gull was heavily influenced by the 1929 Henderson Hendy 302 racer, which Percival had previously owned and raced. The Gull in its most powerful version was the D.3 Six model, with a 205HP de Havilland Gypsy Six engine, capable of a maximum speed of 178 mph. In 1936 Amy Johnson flew her Gull Six from London (Gravesend) to Cape Town in South Africa, recapturing the record in a time of seventy-eight hours and twenty-nine minutes, including refuelling stops and six hours sleep, and was eleven hours less than the previous record. In total, forty-eight Percival Gulls were built.

The Gull Six was developed as a specialist racing aircraft, the Mew Gull, which achieved a maximum speed of 265 mph. A modern commentator has retrospectively described the aircraft as "the Holy Grail of British air racing". Just six Mew Gulls were built. From its first appearance until the outbreak of the Second World War, Mew Gulls were dominant in British air racing and consistently recorded the fastest times. The basic Gull design led to ninety of the 1935 three-passenger Vega Gull, in turn leading to the Percival Proctor training aircraft, first flight October 1939 and used by the RAF (1,143 Proctors built).

Percival Mew Gull. (*Author's collection*)

British Commercial Airliners and their Use

Just as during the 1920s, countries with airlines and aircraft industries of their own tended to support their own industry, when new aircraft were being considered by airlines. In truth, at the beginning of the 1930s, the airliner-making part of the UK industry was smaller than in France, Germany and Italy. The level of government support to airlines differed, which influenced the domestic airliner market. In 1932, France had eight and a half times the number of airliners in service than numbers in Britain, Germany had five and a half times and Italy had two and a half times. Corresponding actual total airliner mileages flown were 2.8 times, 7.9 times and 1.6 times respectively, so only Germany had greater mileage per aircraft than Britain. For much of the 1930s, the British state-owned airline Imperial Airways operated a varied fleet of quite small numbers of different British aircraft. One or two were built to very specific and aeronautically unambitious Imperial Airways requirements, which did not sell to other operators in the UK, or overseas.

An example is the HP.42 and HP.45 large biplane airliner pair. First flight was in 1930, entering service in 1931 in two versions, externally almost identical. The HP.42(E) was used on the longer Empire routes and the HP.42(W) was used on European routes. The HP.42(W) was known as the HP.45 within Handley Page, with

Handley Page HP.42. (*Author's collection*)

supercharged engines, more passengers and less luggage space than the HP.42. Spacious, comfortable, reliable, safe, but slow, cruising at 100 mph, 500 miles maximum range. The only ones sold were the eight to Imperial Airways. Handley Page complained that they were not allowed to do better, by the Imperial Airways unambitious specification (in the interests of keeping aircraft acquisition cost low).

Really long distance air travel in the 1930s was not for the faint-hearted. The first all-the-way Australia-England service of 1935 included a ten hop Qantas airline service Brisbane-Singapore, taking three days with overnight stops. The Qantas aircraft was the four-engined ten-to-twelve passenger DH.86 Express biplane noted earlier, cruising at 140mph, with only sandwiches from the co-pilot for refreshment. Twenty-one further hops and nine days later, the combined Imperial/Trans-India/Qantas service from Brisbane arrived in London, at a total fare of £166 (£11,500 in 2019 terms). Due to political disputes on air transport routes, parts of this journey were by rail.

Imperial Airways decided that the Empire connections to South Africa and Australia required large, comfortable flying boats. As a floating body, flying boats were inconvenient and time-consuming for on-water passenger and baggage embarkation and disembarkation, refuelling and maintenance activities. However, the lack of adequate airfield facilities in parts of the British Empire meant that this type of aircraft suited routes involving (relatively) isolated places, such as on or near the coast of East Africa, and of Malaya. Difficult to staff and provision, it was still easier to set up coastal, river or lakeside waypoint destinations than land plane airfields, quite likely to be invaded by local herds of goats, cattle, antelope or other large wildlife – fishermen, crocodiles and semi-submerged dead tree trunks were possible water hazards! Shorts produced the S.23 and S.30 Empire Class flying boats for Imperial and Qantas Empire Airways. These had two decks, for just twenty-four first class passengers, with sufficient space to walk around. Aircraft range was 760 miles. Their average cost was over £40,000 each, equating to some £2.6 million in 2019 terms. The S.23 shared design features with the RAF Short S.25 Sunderland armed maritime patrol aircraft (749 built, particularly used in the Second World War Atlantic anti-submarine (U-boat) campaign and in the Far East theatre).

Shorts Quote: "We don't build aircraft that float, we build ships that fly."

The first Short Empire Flying Boat commenced operation in 1937. Jointly owned and operated by Qantas and Imperial Airways, in July 1938 Qantas Empire Airways started an Empire Class England-Australia (Southampton-Sydney) return service. Cruising at 165mph in an Empire Class flying boat, with overnight stop-overs it took nine and a half days. Operations were curtailed by the Japanese advances towards the Malay Peninsula and Australia in the Second World War.

Short Mayo Composite. (*Author's collection*)

An inventive suggestion of extending range to transatlantic, by Imperial Airways Technical Manager R.H. Mayo, was a composite "piggy back" flying boat combination. Shorts responded with the Shorts S.21 Maia, designed to hold the smaller S.20 Mercury on top of the fuselage, as a "composite pair". Mercury would be released to independent flight after take-off and initial climb. This would allow Mercury to carry more weight (fuel) at take-off than it would otherwise be possible with an unassisted launch. Just one set was built, first flying in 1937. Mercury (with 1,120lbs of newspapers and other media as payload, in the floats) and air-launched by Maia, completed the first commercial ever heavier-than-air East-West Atlantic aircraft crossing in July 1938, from Shannon in the west of Ireland to Boucherville near Montreal, Canada, in twenty hours twenty-one minutes. Taking off from Montreal after refuelling and going on to New York, the flight resulted in London newspapers on New York streets only one day after publication – a sensation at the time. After special range-enhancement modifications to Mercury, in October 1938 the composite pair achieved a 6,045 mile flight, air-launching a Mercury non-stop flight from Dundee (Scotland) to Alexander Bay (north-west of South Africa), a still-standing record for a seaplane.

At the end of 1938 the Imperial Airways fleet consisted of the following airliners:

Imperial Airways Airliners in 1938 # denotes Flying Boats	passenger capacity	range (miles)	cruise (mph)	engines per a'cft.	number of a'cft.
Avro 618 Ten	8	348	100	3	1
Armstrong Whitworth AW.15 Atalanta	17	640	118	4	3
Armstrong Whitworth AW.27 Ensign	40	1,370	180	4	1
		(total number of AW.27 on order 14)			
de Havilland DH.86 Express	12	760	142	4	9
de Havilland DH.91 Albatross	22	1,040	210	4	2
		(total number of DH.91 on order 7)			
Handley Page HP.42	24	500	100	4	4
Handley Page HP.45	38	500	100	4	4
Short S.8 Calcutta#	15	650	97	3	1
Short L.17 Scylla	39	500	~110	4	2
Short Mayo Composite#: S.20 Mercury & S.21 Maia	10 18	3,900 850	195 ~182	4 4	1 1
	(separated)	*S.20 range with composite air launch*			
Short S.23# Empire Class	20	760	164	4	23
Short S.30# Empire Class	24	760	164	4	1
		(total number of S.30 on order 9)			

The Mayo Composite was a technical achievement, in reality probably conceived as a long range air mail carrier rather than an economical soundly-based passenger air service machine. In retrospect, it was really "a bit of a stunt" and not a true commercial passenger airliner solution. Three larger versions of the Empire Class flying boat concept were built, the thirty-eight passenger Short S.26 (80 per cent increase in MTOW, 45 per cent bigger wing, more powerful engines, 3,200 miles range). Intended for transatlantic and the longest Empire routes, first flight was in July 1939. All three S.26 were commandeered before entering Imperial Airways fleet and were converted for wartime use, sometimes used as transatlantic aircraft operated on behalf of the government by Imperial Airways' successor, BOAC. They were mainly used for flying stores and equipment to Nigeria and other African destinations, as an urgent logistics support contribution to the trans-Africa supply route to the Near and Middle East (see also Boeing 341 Clipper, below). They were also used to fly important personnel between the west coast of Ireland and North America (see section 5.4).

Due to the start of the Second World War, the USA Pan American airline no longer needed the last three (of twelve) Boeing 341 Clipper flying boats being built, the first flight being in 1938. These large aircraft had capacity to carry up to seventy-four passengers (pre-1940, used by USA airline Pan American on Pacific and Atlantic routes, having nearly 3,700 miles normal maximum range or up to 4,900 miles at "overloaded" weight). After the Second World War started in Europe, the transatlantic route was no longer viable for Pan American and the last three Boeing 341 Clipper flying boats under construction were therefore sold to the UK in August 1940, for BOAC use. These were to be most often used on wartime "urgent" freight flying from Britain to Nigeria in West Africa, as part of the long (Mediterranean and Sahara-avoiding) trans-Africa air supply route to the Middle and Far East. The disadvantage was that the Clippers each required special servicing after only 120 hours' flying, with a very large number of special parts used. This made it uneconomic to service outside the USA... so the aircraft returned to the USA for each service.

The pre-1939 Imperial Airways highest capacity airliner was the four-engined Armstrong Whitworth Ensign, able to carry forty passengers, with a maximum range of 1,370 miles and a cruising speed of 180mph. Delivery of the first of the fourteen was expected in 1936 but Ensign production had to be moved to another Hawker Group factory at Hamble, due to the Armstrong Whitworth facilities in Coventry being fully occupied by Armstrong Whitworth Whitley bomber production. Imperial Airways were themselves responsible for some of the delays to Ensign production, by changing detailed requirements. The aircraft did not enter service until 1938.

Armstrong Whitworth AW.27 Ensign. (*Author's collection*)

The most modern-looking Imperial Airways airliner in 1938 was the de Havilland DH.91 Albatross (first flight 1937). Notably, the Albatross used the synthetic resin bonding of plywood first used in the DH.88 Comet Racer and the ply-balsa-ply moulded sandwich construction later used in

DH.91 Albatross. (*Author's collection*)

the wartime DH.98 Mosquito bomber. This construction technique was lightweight and aerodynamically smooth but could suffer from long-term deterioration, due to moisture ingress. Initially conceived as a mailplane, the Albatross cruised at 210mph, had a range of 1,040 miles and could carry twenty-two passengers. Only seven were built, the Second World War intervening before any more could be made.

In 1931, an initially private company airline Hillman Airways was formed, starting operation out of Romford (Essex) to Clacton, then to Continental destinations in France and Belgium. In 1933, British Spartan Aircraft Ltd. (after being taken over by Saunders Roe and moving to the Isle of Wight) founded Spartan Airlines, operating domestic flights. The railway companies obtained authority to operate airline services, the main result being Southern Railways' air service from London to the Isle of Wight, subcontracted on a cost-sharing basis to Spartan Airways. In 1935, a Spartan sister company, United Airways, operated out of Blackpool, offering flights to the Isle of Man. Also in 1935, British Continental Airways was established, operating services out of Croydon (Surrey) to Belgian, French and Netherlands destinations, later extended to Scandinavian cities.

There were a number of other small operators of commercial aircraft offering passenger, freight and air mail services within Great Britain between 1931 and 1933. Some sixteen new operators became airborne, with one to four aircraft each. Fleets did not include new aircraft, thus not supporting the aircraft manufacturers' order books. None of these operators lasted more than a year and the least-successful carried out just one week of flying operations.

On 30 September 1935, Allied British Airways was formed, merging the publicly quoted company Hillman Airways with the private companies of Spartan Airlines and United Airways. Highland Airways, which operated from a Scottish base, was quickly added. On 30 October 1935 the name of the combined airline was changed to British Airways Ltd, as a public limited company (not the same British Airways as formed in the 1970s from the merger of BOAC and BEA).

Encouraged by the government, in 1936 the new British Airways Ltd. absorbed British Continental Airways. After the merger, the combined British Airways Ltd. fleet consisted of thirty-seven aircraft, namely:-

Armstrong Whitworth 154 Argosy (20 passenger)	1
de Havilland DH.80 Puss Moth (1 or 2 passenger)	1
de Havilland DH.83 Fox Moth (3 passenger)	1
de Havilland DH.84 Dragon (6 to 10 passenger)	9
de Havilland DH.86 Express (10 to 12 passenger)	4
de Havilland DH.89 Dragon Rapide (8 passenger)	8
Saro A.19 Cloud flying boat (8 passenger)	1
Spartan Cruiser (8 passenger)	12

(1 Cruiser I, 7 Cruiser II, 4 Cruiser III)

Importantly, British Airways Ltd. was deliberately not constrained to using British aircraft. The company acquired six pre-owned Dutch sixteen-passenger Fokker F.XIIs, two fifteen-passenger Fokker F.VIIIs, three seventeen-passenger German Junkers 52s, at least seven USA ten-passenger Lockheed Electra Model 10 and one fourteen-passenger Super Electra Model 14. The Electra cruising speed was nearly twice that of the Imperial Airways HP.42, because the 100mph HP.42 had been deliberately specified by Imperial Airways at this speed to keep the design simple and cost down, as noted earlier. The British Airways Electra was the only sensible small-medium airliner option in Britain with the necessary range (840 miles maximum) for the three diplomatic visits of Prime Minister Neville Chamberlain to Munich in 1938. The final journey, returning with the

"Peace in our time" Munich Agreement (the infamous "paper signed by Herr Hitler" waved in front of the press by the British Prime Minister after returning on the final journey), was in the Electra Model 14.

A six-passenger Lockheed 12A Electra Junior was also flown under the British Airways "banner" on civilian private flights over Germany, with concealed cameras operated by remote control. Sidney Cotton was the flight arranger. Just before war broke out in 1939, Cotton engineered a joy ride observation flight over a number of German military airfields, accompanied by senior German Air Force officer General Albert Kesselring, Commander of a primary division (Luftflotte 1) of the German Air Force (Luftwaffe) based in Berlin. Cotton reached under his seat and operated the hidden remote cameras during the flight.

On 29 August 1939, four days before the outbreak of the Second World War on 1 September, the British government started to implement the Air Navigation (Restriction in Time of War) Order, 1939. The aircraft and the administrations of British Airways Ltd (BAL) and Imperial Airways were physically transferred to Bristol (Whitchurch) Airport, to be operated jointly by the Air Ministry National Air Communications (NAC). At the same time, the fleets of all other small private operators were dispersed (away from obvious air raid areas) and all civilian air transport was brought under the control of NAC. On the outbreak of the Second World War, non-essential civil air operations were suspended and many civil aircraft were requisitioned by the UK government, for allocation to the war effort.

On 1 April 1940, British Airways Ltd. and Imperial Airways Ltd. were officially combined into a new state-owned airline, British Overseas Airways Corporation (BOAC), a publically listed company but totally owned and directed by the government. BOAC was largely aimed at responding to essential international air transport requirements of members of the government, senior armed forces officers, government officials (and arms industry leaders/experts from time to time). BOAC also provided a long-range air logistics supply and communications service for the armed forces. At the beginning, they had a mixed fleet of eighty-two aircraft, many of which were flying boats. They operated 54,000 miles of air routes, to the Near and Middle East, Australia via India and Singapore, South Africa and North and South America. Total air miles per year approached nineteen million. Some routes were to be through enemy-held territory, such as BOAC civil-registered DH Mosquitos flying the shortest distance through the Nazi-controlled airspace between Norway and Denmark, en-route to/from Sweden, mostly ferrying Swedish ball bearings to Britain. Other civilian-operated aircraft operating entirely within the British Isles conducted operations under the National Air Communications mandate. In June 1940, this responsibility was transferred from the NAC to the Associated Airways Joint Committee. Nine different smaller airlines were involved, some of which helped to rescue civilian and service personnel when France and the Channel Islands were being overrun by German forces. This domestic air service maintained essential wartime air transport and communication with Scottish Islands, Northern Ireland and other internal routes in the rest of Britain.

Hints of the airliner future

There were significant civil sales successes of three particular USA airliners:

> The up to fourteen-passenger twin-engined Lockheed Electra monoplane (Models 10, 12 and 14) was first flown in 1934. The Electra was fast (cruising at 215mph) and sales total was an impressive 633 (and the aircraft went on to be the basis of the 2,941 Lockheed Hudson bomber/reconnaissance aircraft of the Second World War).

The 1934 14-passenger Douglas DC-2 twin-engined monoplane airliner had a cruising speed of 174mph and sold over 190 examples worldwide (sixty-three of them to the US military). A KLM DC-2 airliner came second in the October 1934 MacRobertson "race to Australia" (the race won outright by the DH.88 Comet racer), and a Boeing 247 close behind in third place. The DC-2 took ninety hours and thirteen minutes elapsed time, spending eighty-one hours ten minutes in the air.

In 1936, the DC-2 was followed up by its thirty-passenger developed version, the DC-3, which cruised at 207mph. By the time the USA entered the Second World War at the end of 1941, 607 DC-3s had been sold, to thirteen different USA airlines and eleven others worldwide (none in Britain). Cost of a DC-3 was US$79,500 in 1939, around US$1.4 million in 2019 terms (in 1939 the dollar/£ exchange rate was around 5 dollars to the pound, compared with 1.1 to 1.3 in 2019). The DC-3 was militarised during the Second World War for the USA Army Air Force (USAAF) and the RAF, into the ubiquitous C-47 Skytrain/ Dakota, 10,174 of which were eventually built.

All three of these new USA airliners were of all-metal construction and had retractable undercarriages.

There was also more than a hint about future airliner operations at high altitude. Until 1938, all transport aircraft (civil or military) were normally limited to maximum altitudes of around 8,000ft due to discomfort caused by lack of oxygen in the high atmosphere. For some people, altitude sickness can result at altitudes lower than 8,000ft, especially if the altitude is achieved relatively quickly and maintained. By 10,000ft altitude, pilot (and passenger) faculties start to be affected and by 12,000ft significant effects are likely to be experienced. As noted previously (section 2.2), high flying 1918 military reconnaissance operations up to 24,000ft were carried out by the German air force with oxygen-breathing equipment and heated flight suits, but this would clearly be inappropriate for passenger use in airliners.

An experimental pressurised Lockheed Electra 10 flew in 1937 (with a redesigned fuselage having the flight deck and part of the cabin pressurised and high power engines, becoming the one and only XC-35). This was sufficiently successful to become the executive transport of the USA Assistant Secretary of War. In 1938, Boeing produced the first commercial airliner with a pressurised cabin, the 307 Stratoliner thirty-three-passenger aircraft. The aircraft ceiling was over 23,000ft and the pressurisation provided an 8,000ft cabin pressure altitude while flying up to 15,000ft. Cruising speed was 215mph. The pressurisation system also warmed the cabin air from the -25°C of the atmosphere at 20,000ft. Part of the motive was to allow airlines to fly direct routes over the Rocky Mountains in the west of the USA. The 307 was based on the four-engined Boeing B-17 Fortress bomber with a new pressurised fuselage. It had a maximum still air range of 1,758 miles. The first one crashed on a demonstration test in March 1939, whilst recovering from a spin caused by an inherent aerodynamic problem inherited from the B-17, the recovery causing the wing structure to fail. The accident killed all aboard, including the Dutch airline KLM technical director, a representative of the Dutch air ministry, the Boeing Chief Aerodynamicist, the Boeing Chief Engineer and a representative of the USA airline TWA. The source of the problem was identified and corrected (and applied to the B-17) and nine more Stratoliner aircraft were built before the USA entered the Second World War, causing five of the ten aircraft to be reallocated to the USAAF.

In 1938, Britain also made a belated move to create more modern and competitive airliner products. In specifications 14/38 and 15/38, the Air Ministry in Britain requested proposals for new long-range (Imperial Airways Empire routes) and medium range (European routes, for use by British Airways Ltd) airliners, all with pressurised cabins. Shorts proposed their S.32 design for the 14/38 long-range type. Four other companies responded to the medium range requirements of 15/38, including the Fairey and General Aircraft companies. Shorts received a contract for three prototypes of their S.32 landplane proposal, range 3,420 miles and a cruising speed of 246mph. Three S.32 commenced build but the need to prioritise bomber production (the Short Stirling heavy bomber) meant none were complete when war intervened to halt airliner production.

In October 1938, Fairey received a contract for the development of two prototypes *and* twelve production models of their FC.1 airliner proposal response to 15/38, having a range of 1,700 miles and a cruising speed of 225mph. The founder of Fairey, Charles Fairey, is said to have spent over £1 million of his own money (equivalent to £65 million in 2019 terms) on the FC.1, but the whole project was cancelled on the outbreak of war. A revival attempt after the war, with newer engines, failed to gain traction over the output recommendations of the Brabazon Committee (see section 5.2).

General Aircraft had responded to 15/38 with their GAL.40 proposal, which included a research aircraft, the GAL.41. Although the GAL.40 was not selected for the contract, the GAL.41 aircraft (a modified GAL.ST-25 four-seat twin-engined "monospar" monoplane) was registered as T-0222 (UK government military register) and embarked on an experimental programme to test the pressurisation process and research the design principles of cabin pressurisation. The GAL.41 used an auxiliary (motor car) engine fitted with a supercharger fan to generate sufficient air pressure to fly up to 15,000ft whilst maintaining a sea level pressure altitude in a two-seat module, in a revised fuselage. If flight at higher altitudes could be achieved (ST-25 normal service ceiling limit was 16,000ft) this would cause the module pressure to decrease accordingly. In 1939 the GAL.41 became the first British aircraft to fly with a pressurised cabin. It was grounded in 1941.

The Road to Rearmament in the 1930s

In the 1920s, the UK domestic political scene had been most concerned with Irish Nationalism, economic stagnation, the unrest in domestic labour markets, women's suffrage and the perceived continuing threat of "revolutionary contagion" from Russia and elsewhere. With the emergence of a credible third force in politics (the Labour party) the old certainties and voting habits were more volatile, leading to four General Elections between the end of 1918 and the end of the 1920s. The Labour-minority government of 1929 only lasted two years. The economic woes continued into the 1930s.

The stock market crash of 1929 in the USA presaged what was to become a 1930s almost decade-long worldwide industrial depression. The period was known as the Great Depression or the Great Slump. Britain's economy was hardly booming in the 1920s and started to be more seriously stressed as the 1930s began. General economic relief from the depression in Britain mostly would be confined to the interwar subsidised suburban and slum-clearance house-building boom (e.g. London "Metroland") and specific government initiatives (which included the government-supported contracts for the new ocean-going liners RMS *Queen Mary*, in 1931, and RMS *Queen Elizabeth*, in 1936).

After the 1931 General Election, occasioned by a financial crisis, the British population overwhelmingly voted for a "National Government" (a pre-election coalition platform). Ramsay MacDonald was leader of the Labour party and Prime Minister in the outgoing Labour government. He reluctantly agreed to be leader of the National Government platform, which precipitated his expulsion from the Labour party. All this disaffected members of the Labour party and many Labour MPs, to the extent that, in the event, the multi-party National Government Cabinet led a parliament with 470 of the 554 seats occupied by Conservatives, but based on a National Government mandate.

MacDonald formed a government cabinet which included himself, Clement Attlee as the new leader of the Labour party and two other Labour members, two from the Liberal party and four from the Conservative party. One of them was Stanley Baldwin, who had been Conservative Prime Minister twice in the 1920s. Baldwin's position was Lord President of the Council, the senior cabinet position after the Prime Minister. This often required him to act as Prime Minister, due to MacDonald's poor health. MacDonald focused much personal attention on foreign affairs, intimately involving himself in the 1932–1934 Geneva disarmament conference. Baldwin was supportive of the idea of not provoking the German Chancellor Adolf Hitler (elected 1933). Baldwin's consequent prevarication on the idea of increasing the UK's military strength allowed time to pass, whilst it was slowly becoming obvious that war clouds were starting to gather. The prevarication caused the need for RAF aircraft fleet modernisation to become a protracted political argument, not helped by Baldwin's nomination of the Marquis of Londonderry, Charles Vane-Tempest-Stewart, as Secretary of State for Air in the new 1931 cabinet.

Londonderry tried to straddle the appeasement/rearmament divide, requesting new aircraft (bomber) authorisations and supporting planning for new fighters for the RAF but, at the same time, supporting the popular "appeasement profile". His refusal to cease from promoting the rearmament of the RAF made him an enemy of Clement Atlee, the Labour leader within the cabinet, the Labour party as a whole, and the Treasury. Coupled with an unimaginative, cautious and ultra-conservative RAF Chief of the Air Staff in Edward Ellington (later described by senior RAF officer Wilfrid Freeman as "the worst CAS we ever had"), the case for spending money on new RAF equipment initiatives languished. This prevented important activities from being seriously progressed, such as planning for best RAF use of emerging new technology, development of dispersed battle-damage repair depots and modernisation of the RAF aircraft fleet.

The ineffectiveness of Londonderry's influence on the government finally ended in 1935, when he was removed as Air Minister and moved to Lord Privy Seal (replacing Anthony Eden) and Leader of the House of Lords. He continued in his role as a member of the Anglo-German Fellowship, visiting Germany and hosting visits from German politicians and diplomats. This caused him to attract the nickname of "Londonderry Herr". During Londonderry's visit to Germany in October 1936, Hitler indiscreetly advised his embryo ambitions of extending German territory into parts of Czechoslovakia and Poland. Londonderry was not a supporter of any such move and immediately passed the information to the British government. "Appeasement" in the cause of peace remained as British policy, but, in reality, just bought time for the rearming of British forces.

Baldwin replaced MacDonald as Prime Minister, winning the General Election in June 1935 with a large Conservative majority. The new Air Minister was Philip Cunliffe-Lister (born Lloyd-Graeme but changed his name in 1924 on his wife inheriting the Cunliffe-Lister Masham estate) and newly ennobled as the Viscount Swinton. He was a most effective advocate for the RAF needs, as the new government collectively came to realise that "rearmament" had become an urgent issue. This was a bit of an about-face for many, including Anthony Eden, a former Undersecretary of State for Foreign Affairs in the national government. Like many who had served in and seen the horrors of the First World War, Eden had hoped for and believed in supporting a disarmament agenda, to appease Hitler's Nazi government. However, he and others eventually came to realise that this was a policy doomed to failure. Belatedly recognising the dangers from the rising belligerence of Germany after Adolf Hitler became Chancellor in 1933, a government major rearmament policy was finally publically declared in 1936. From then on, manufacturing industry in Britain started to seriously revive. The military aircraft industry clearly benefitted. For the RAF planners, rearmament did not start in earnest until 1935, quickly gathering momentum.

In the 1930s, Avro were to succeed in the military market with a new two-seater. The RAF wooden-framed Avro 504 was replaced by the 1929 metal-framed Avro 621 Tutor. The Tutor was later developed into the Avro 626 Prefect. Behind the Tutor's normal two cockpits the Prefect had a third, with a Scarff ring for mounting a machine gun. This aircraft was normally used for navigation, wireless and gunnery training. Including sales to foreign air forces, 606 Tutors and 198 Prefects were sold. Avro derived the Avro Cadet club/training/utility series from the Tutor, selling 133 of them.

A major boost to Avro fortunes was to come. In 1934 Imperial Airways bought two four-passenger Avro 652 airliners for operations in India. Meanwhile, the UK government was seeking a maritime patrol aircraft. Avro submitted the 652A, a modified version of the 652. This proposal and a version of the DH.89 Dragon Rapide were favoured and two of each were ordered, for a fly-off evaluation. The Avro aircraft was selected on 25 May 1935 and an initial order for 174 placed in July 1935, the aircraft type named as the Anson.

Avro 652A Anson. (*Oren Rozen, CC BY-SA 3.0*)

The Anson was built in large quantities and used in several different guises, fifty-six being built to a civil standard (up to nine-passenger) version known as the Avro XIX. The final grand total was 11,020 aircraft, remaining in production until 1952. The Anson was to become second only to the Vickers Wellington bomber, in terms of the number produced of British multi-engine aircraft types.

Anticipating inevitable conflict, in 1937 the RAF raised Operational Requirement OR.42 for a large number of multi-engined training aircraft, primarily aimed at producing crew for the planned medium and heavy bombers – pilots, flight engineers, navigators, bomb aimers, wireless operators and air gunners. Specification T.23/36 resulted in the Airspeed AS.10 Oxford, derived from the design of the AS.6 Envoy small airliner (two pilot seats and six passengers). First flight was on 19 June 1937. The Avro Anson was also considered. Deemed a little "too easy" to fly as a pilot training aircraft, the Anson did operate as a navigation and wireless operator trainer. Notably, the Oxford was found to have a significant flight vice. Recovery from a flat spin was found to be impossible and special measures to ensure aircrew could reach the door to parachute out were employed – a knotted rope to the door, to help pull themselves against the centripetal force of the spin!

Built by Airspeed, de Havilland, Percival and Standard Motors, a total of 8,751 Oxfords were produced eventually, mostly for RAF use. For the RAF, all initial multi-engined flight deck crew training, plus complete bomber aircrew initial flight training, were possible on the RAF Oxford. It was also used as a casualty evacuation and communications aircraft and in a maritime patrol mode.

Oxfords were also used by the RAAF, RCAF and the RSAAF. The USAAF in Britain used RAF Oxfords on loan. Several new aircraft were built after the war, as general purpose aircraft and airliners for overseas customers and 152 surplus Oxfords were converted to the post-war AS.65 Consul airliner.

Fighters and Bombers

From 1934 onwards, the Air Ministry devised a series of "Schemes" setting out successive views of the needs for new aircraft types, by number and operational role, and the associated expansion in the number of RAF airfields. Labelled alphabetically as shown in Table 2.7 below, these aimed to be realistic and based on reasoned argument concerning the current (at the time) assessment of the political situation. Requirements were dominated by bombers and fighters. The bomber had highest numbers, due to the RAF and government view that the best deterrent would be the threat of retaliatory bombing, on the basis "some bombers will always get through", which begged the question about priority for UK defending fighters.

Table 2.7: Air Ministry RAF/RN Aircraft Strength Planning Schemes.

	Cabinet Approval Date	Number of Aircraft (Home)			Addit^L A/C Overseas	Date to be complete		
		Fighters	Bombers	Other				
Scheme A	July 1934	336	500	124	292	1939	Eventual possible 1942 scheme 'M' outcome	
Scheme C	May 1935	420	816	276	292	1937		
Scheme F	February 1936	420	990	326	468	1939		
Scheme L	March 1938	608	1,360	413	389	1942	Fighter	Bomber
Scheme M	November 1938	640	1,352	389	nil	1942	800	1,360
Schemes B, D, E, G never reached formal issue, overtaken by events								
Schemes H, J, K were approved but were also overtaken by events								

The actual British military aircraft strength during the Second World War was to greatly exceed even the Scheme 'M' plan, just from UK sources. The wartime "Lend Lease" supply of aircraft from the USA would significantly augment the aircraft produced in Britain which would see British war service (see section 3.2).

The production of combat aircraft in 1930s decade started modestly, beginning with selection of the two-seater Hawker Hart light biplane bombers to satisfy the marginally out-of-date Specification 12/26. Over 1,000 of this type (all variants) were to be built between 1929 and 1936. This was not a strategic threat to Germany from Britain, to upset the political European disarmament negotiations, with only a 500lb per aircraft bomb load and the distance between Britain and Germany greater than the combat range of the Hart. Between 1931 and 1938 the Hart was also made in several variants: Audax (761); navalised version the Osprey (142); Hardy (47); Hector (179). The Demon two-seat fighter was also derived from the Hart and the RAF eventually had 305.

Hawker Hart. (*Author's collection*)

Avro built 287 Audax and subsequently designed and made twenty-four modernised versions (engine change) called the Avro type 674, for use in Egypt. Armstrong Whitworth, Gloster, Bristol and Westland also manufactured the Hart type and its variants. The Hart was eventually developed into the Hawker Hind, of which 527 were made between 1934 and 1938. This made a grand total of 3,067 aircraft of direct Hart origin over a nine-year period.

Alongside the Hart, 275 single-seat 1931 Hawker Fury biplane fighters derived from the Hart would also see RAF service. The grand total of all aircraft with "a bit of Hart in them" would finally reach well over 4,000 in service with the RAF, the RN and twenty overseas air forces.

In the 1930s, some senior RAF commanders were reluctant to move from the biplane fighter era, partly because of the excellent manoeuvrability of biplanes. There was also a history of mistrust of the structural integrity of monoplanes, stemming from the First World War RFC scrapping and banning all monoplanes. This had followed accidents caused by wing failure on two different monoplane aircraft during the early years of that conflict. In similar vein, fixed undercarriages were seen as more reliable than the complication (and weight) of retracting ones, and dope-impregnated fabric-covered structures much easier and quicker to repair from any damage (battle or otherwise) than all-metal frames and skins. The Air Ministry specification for the Fury replacement had been under discussion since 1930 (F.7/30) which, in 1932, had resulted in orders of prototypes for the eight compliant responses. Aircraft capable of being more heavily armed than those already in service and also capable of at least 250mph were part of this specification. The RAF-preferred engine was the Rolls-Royce 700HP steam circuit (evaporative cooling) Goshawk.

A biplane was not specifically requested but institutional senior RAF thinking remained biased in that direction. Using PV funds, Hawker built and proposed their PV.3, an enlarged Fury, re-engined with the Goshawk. This was rejected in favour of what became the 1934 Gloster Gladiator, an enclosed-cockpit fast biplane with a radial Bristol Mercury 830HP air-cooled engine, first flying in 1934 (253mph maximum speed, service ceiling 32,800ft altitude). This was to be the last biplane fighter to enter RAF service and saw action in the Second World War. For the Gloster Aircraft Company, the Gladiator was a success, with 747 built.

Gloster Gladiator, Shuttleworth Trust Collection restored aircraft. (*BAE Systems*)

In the early 1930s, Fairey Aviation were pursuing ideas about a new naval reconnaissance/torpedo bomber aircraft, partly as a PV, partly sponsored by a request from the Greek Navy and partly based on the emergent Air Ministry specifications M.1/30 and S.9/30 for a carrier-capable aircraft. After advising the Air Ministry and Admiralty of the work done for Greece, a revised UK specification S.15/33 resulted in Fairey's naval biplane Tactical Strike and Reconnaissance aircraft TSR.1, later to be named the Swordfish.

The design was constrained by the navy thinking that an observer was an absolute essential, and the fact (then) that the torpedoes to be used were too fragile to be air-launched into the sea at high speed.

Fairey Swordfish (restoration). (*Tony Higsett, CC BY-SA 2.0*)

With modest wind-over-deck speeds, the low speed performance allowed Swordfish operations without catapult-assisted launch or arrestor gear landing. The first prototype flew on 17 April 1934 and the type entered service with the Fleet Air Arm in February 1936. The Swordfish three-seater biplane (nominally pilot, observer and radio operator/rear gunner in a reconnaissance role) often flew with only two crew members, with a semi-permanent auxiliary fuel tank installed in the second (normally observer) cockpit. In total, 2,391 Swordfish were built (692 by Fairey and 1,699 by Blackburn). In pure aircraft terms, it was obsolescent by the start of the Second World War. It was nicknamed "the Stringbag", due to the large variety of stores carried. Nevertheless, the Swordfish was involved in many actions in the Second World War, three of which had important strategic consequences:

- After the fall of France in June 1940, on the third and fourth of July 1940, two squadrons of Swordfish launched from HMS *Ark Royal* were involved in the major naval attack on part (40 per cent by tonnage) of the French naval fleet docked in a French Algerian harbour, at Mers-el-Kébir. The controversial attack objective was to guarantee that the French warships could never be brought under the control of Germany.
- On 11 November 1940, Swordfish from HMS *Illustrious* launched a successful night torpedo attack on Italian warships, in harbour at Taranto on the "heel" of Italy. Illuminated by some aircraft dropping flares and others pressing home a torpedo attack, three Italian battleships were heavily damaged and a heavy cruiser and two destroyers were damaged.

  After the attack, the Japanese Naval Attaché to Berlin visited Tarantino and his report influenced the Japanese surprise attack on the American fleet in Pearl Harbour on 7 December 1941.
- The third prominent success was the crippling of the steering of the German battleship *Bismarck*, as she raced for the shelter of the harbour at Brest, on the north-western seaboard of France, to escape the large British fleet of capital ships giving chase in the Atlantic. A torpedo from a Swordfish flown off HMS *Ark Royal* did the damage. On 27 May 1941, Bismarck was caught and sunk by the fleet.

The Fairey Swordfish is cited as having been directly involved with the destruction of more tonnage of warships in the Second World War than any other single Allied aircraft type. Their use early in the Second World War more than confirmed the promise of the Tøndern air raid from HMS *Furious* in 1918 (see section 2.2).

The Hurricane and the Spitfire
In July 1934, a major expansion of the RAF was announced, with the number of Britain-based squadrons to be increased from fifty-two to seventy-five. The intention was to bring the total first-line strength to 128 squadrons within five years (a squadron could vary in size, from twelve or sixteen (typically), up to twenty plus aircraft).

Alongside the Fury biplane derivative for the F.7/30 specification, Hawker had simultaneously proposed the alternative of a monoplane derivative of the Fury. This was also rejected. In May 1934, RAF specification F.5/34 for a new 300mph fighter was issued, this time with an air-cooled engine preferred. Bristol, Gloster, Martin Baker and Vickers prototypes were authorised, only one of which was assessed as matching the speed requirement and none were ordered into production. The Managing Director of the Hawker Siddeley Group aviation business, Frank Spriggs, had authorised PV funding for Hawker Chief Designer Sydney Camm to pursue a major revision to his monoplane design. It seemed difficult, however, to match emerging new requirements in terms of top speed, because a suitable fully developed powerful enough engine was not readily available. Camm created a seriously revised high speed design by changing the engine to the (in-development) 1,000HP Rolls-Royce PV.12 (the early version of the liquid-cooled 27 litre 12-cylinder Merlin) and fitting a retracting undercarriage. After presentation of this revised private venture proposal, a one-tenth scale model was authorised, for wind tunnel tests in the National Physical Laboratories. The results were so promising that the Air Ministry go-ahead for a prototype was given before the end of 1934. Hawker formally submitted their design proposal to a new specification F.36/34, which was directly based on the new monoplane design.

In this way, the Hawker Hurricane monoplane fighter was born, later to be famed during the Battle of Britain. Adapting well-tried techniques developed by Hawker during the 1930s, the Hurricane had a Warren truss primary structure (braced using metal tubes) but much of the external shape was created with the traditional technique of dope-impregnated fabric over wooden formers, ribs and stringers. The prototype first flew on 6 November 1935. In May 1936, prior to formal production go-ahead, Hawker commited their own money to building 1,000 Hurricanes and hiring 280 more skilled production workers. Over 500 Hurricanes were in service by the outbreak of the Second World War, with a further 3,500 on order. A duraluminium monocoque wing design was introduced in 1939. With increased wing strength, the aircraft could utilise the increases in power from later Merlin engines. A total of 14,583 Hurricanes were to be produced.

During the whole period between 1930 and 1939, a combined total of over 4,000 Hawker-designed aircraft were delivered.

The other famous British Battle of Britain fighter aircraft had some of its origins in the Supermarine S.6 and S6.B seaplanes of Schneider trophy fame (see section 2.4). Supermarine had failed to impress the RAF (or anyone else!) with the type 224 fixed undercarriage gull-winged monoplane submission to meet the same F.7/30 specification as the winning Gloster Gladiator. Chief Designer Reginald J. Mitchell (designer of the Schneider Trophy winning aircraft) and his team had not fully understood all the intricacies of "more than just high speed", for a successful fighter. For the later F.5/34 requirement, at first Mitchell changed the wing of the Type 224 proposal for a new Type 300 design, with a retracting undercarriage, but (at first) still retained the 700HP Goshawk engine from the F.7/30 submission. However, with the agreement of Sir Robert McLean (Vickers/Supermarine chairman) and the chairman of Rolls-Royce (contributing £7,500 and the PV.12 new 1,000HP engine), Mitchell radically revised the final version of the Supermarine Type 300 proposal.

Responses from the Air Ministry to the initial suggestions were mixed (Supermarine seen as "designers of flying boats"). Air Vice-Marshal Freeman, appointed in 1936 as Air Member for Research and Development (AMRD) in the Air Council (later, Sir Wilfrid Freeman, Air Chief Marshal and Vice Chief of the Air Staff) eventually had to persuade some of his senior colleagues that they should not rely only on their new and exciting Hurricane monoplane.

One senior RAF person Freeman did not have to convince was Air Chief Marshal Hugh Dowding, appointed Commander-in-Chief Fighter Command in July 1936. Dowding had been AMRD prior to Freeman's appointment and the responsible authority for aircraft specification F.5/34 and the F.10/35 specification for more powerful fighter armament. He did not have complete faith in the First World War continuing government-accepted RAF (Hugh Trenchard) declared premise that "some bombers will always get through" and the consequential reliance on the complete deterrence effectiveness of the threat of retaliating with a large bomber fleet. Dowding pursued the enhancement of a system of actual defence in the air for Britain, which eventually was to consist of large numbers of fast fighters held on the ground (not on air patrol) until they could be launched (scrambled) and directed by radio to intercept the known track of incoming bombers. This was not a new concept but the British development of radar enabled enemy aircraft position and track to be more accurately determined early enough. By combining radar data and coastal ground observer information, all collated at RAF Bentley Priory (Fighter Command headquarters), this allowed a complete, topical and continuously updated "state-of-the-attack" to be graphically displayed. Interception flights of fast fighters would be scrambled from the most appropriate airfields in the optimum way, at RAF Bentley Priory telephone direct line instruction. With the development of 360° scanning radar, by 1941 the system became an even more effective "Ground Controlled Interception (GCI)" total defended airspace facility, rather than "Ground Controlled Predicted Interception".

As well as the change of engine[4], the new Supermarine fighter structure was a completely new design. The fuselage became a steel and duraluminium metal-framed semi-monocoque, with Alclad skinning forming an overall compound (3-dimensional curved) surface. The wings used flush-riveted light alloy structure and skinning. For aerodynamic and structural efficiency reasons Mitchell, advised by his Canadian-born aerodynamicist Beverley Shenstone, adopted a twin semi-elliptical planform for each wing, major axis slightly skewed forward at the tip to keep the centre of lift close to the main wing spar, with the spar at right angles to the fuselage. This minimised wing twist under air load. It also enabled more wing area and internal volume, compared with a straight taper wing of the same span and root chord with the same aerodynamic thin-ness (low thickness-chord ratio).

Recalled in Alfred Price's *"Spitfire: A Documentary History"*, Shenstone later said:

> "I remember once discussing the wing shape with him [Mitchell] and he commented: 'I don't give a b..... whether it's elliptical or not, so long as it covers the guns!'. The ellipse was simply the most efficient aerodynamic shape and also allowed us the thinnest possible wing with sufficient room inside to carry the necessary structure and things we wanted to cram in. And it looked nice."

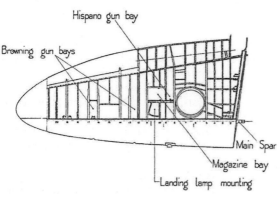

Spitfire (Mk.V) Wing Structure. (*Author's collection*)

As on the Hurricane, a retractable undercarriage was included. Due to the Spitfire thin wing internal space limitations in accommodating an undercarriage extend/retraction mechanism (and taking advantage of the strength and space at the deepest part of the wing), the undercarriage mount was close to the wing root and close to the main spar structural strength, with the wheels retracting outboard and slightly aftwards up into the wing behind the spar.

---

4. Later, in 1942, Freeman had to lobby hard for the Rolls-Royce engine (1940 Merlin XX, with two-speed supercharger) to be substituted for the original Allison engine in the North American Mustang P-51A (designed and produced in the USA under an order by Britain, but with unimpressive performance above 15,000ft). With the engine change and (later) with more fuel capacity, the P-51B version of the aircraft made it the only (very capable) fighter able to provide high altitude escort cover for Allied bombers, all the way to Berlin.

The undercarriage actuator was anchored within the fuselage profile. The design reduced wing spar bending loads when landing but also resulted in a narrow undercarriage track, making taxi and take-off/landing operations (steering control) more difficult than the wider-track Hurricane.

After a final bold private commitment in November 1934 by Supermarine, to commence design detailing, on 1 December 1934 an order was placed for the Supermarine Type 300, "a prototype fighter of R.J. Mitchell design", to specification F.7/30, amended by F.37/34 (formally signed off on 3 January 1935).

One of the remaining problems was the cooling of the powerful PV12 engine and its engine oil. At maximum power, some 400 kilowatts of heat needed dispersing. Officially, the revision described in F.37/34 still specified the same kind of steam circuit evaporative cooling system as F.7/30, coupled to the new PV.12 engine. This would be heavy, particularly vulnerable to battle damage and difficult to engineer the coolant condensate collection successfully for inverted (negative 'g') flight. Water-ethylene glycol engine coolant, which boiled at much higher temperatures than just water, was introduced with the Merlin engine. This still required coolant cooling. In 1935, F.W. Meredith at RAE developed the principles of the ducted radiator (now known as the Meredith effect), which actually generates exhaust thrust from the heat added to the air passing through the radiator. This compensates for a good proportion of radiator air drag. Using a ducted radiator method obviated the complication and much of the weight which would be associated with an evaporative cooling system. Both the Hurricane and Spitfire Merlin engines were cooled using a ducted radiator in a sealed liquid system (as were later aircraft, and versions of the German Me. Bf 109 - also modern Formula 1 racing cars). The method requires significant airspeed to be effective, the design thus limiting static ground-running time to "minutes in single figures".

Also in 1935 the government successfully negotiated a licence for BSA to produce USA Browning machine guns in Britain. These were reliably jam-free, able to be mounted on the nose or on strong wings, remote from the pilot. "Not less than six but eight are desirable" 0.303 inch calibre machine guns were added by Air Ministry specification F.10/35 for new production fighter aircraft. For a while, eight machine guns were to be the armament for all new fighters, thus including both the Spitfire and the Hurricane, to increase firepower at the latest higher flying speeds. The average time guns would actually be trained on target would only be about two seconds, eight guns totalling approximately 300 bullets fired in that time. First flight of the Spitfire prototype was in March 1936. The total cost of this prototype was £15,776, equivalent to over one million pounds in 2019 terms. Before the first test reports had been formally issued ("the aeroplane is simple to fly and has no vices and can be flown by the average fully trained service fighter pilot") in July 1936 the production specification F.16/36 for the first 300 aircraft was issued by the Air Ministry.

Thus the Spitfire was born. On 4 August 1938 the first Supermarine Spitfire production model entered service. Some 400 Spitfires were in service as the war began one year later, with 2,000 more on order. Eventually, a total of 20,351 were to be produced.

Hawker Hurricane and Supermarine Spitfire (*Richard Paver*)

The differences between the Hurricane and the Spitfire were more than external appearance. Initially comparable, the Spitfire would be developed to have a significantly higher top speed and service ceiling, enjoying more sophisticated thin-wing aerodynamics and structural design features and, for its time, was *extremely* manoeuvrable with excellent handling qualities.

The Spitfire had mostly metal internal structure and flush-riveted metal skinning. The whole was therefore more complicated to build than the Hurricane. Spitfires required 15,200 man hours to produce versus 10,300 hours for the Hurricane. The first 310 Spitfires cost an average of £6,033 each to build, compared with the early Hurricane cost of £4,000 each. It took nearly twice as much effort to build a Spitfire than its main opponent during the Second World War Battle of Britain (the German Messerschmitt Me.109) and it was often more difficult to repair than the Hurricane after battle damage. RAF battle commanders (and many of the pilots themselves) of these two fighter aircraft came to feel that they were a complementary pair, especially at altitudes above and below 15,000ft. Hurricanes often would be assigned to attack enemy bombers whilst Spitfires best tackled their fighter escorts at the higher altitudes, but this was not a rigid rule. Air battles got very confused!

The 1944 Better-than-Spitfire Fighter Aircraft That Never Served

In 1929, James Martin (like many other enthusiasts in that era) established himself as an aircraft designer. He started in some semi-derelict ex-army huts in Buckinghamshire, with some hand tools and two employees, to design and build a two-seat sports monoplane. At that time, most contemporaries (big and small) most often produced biplane designs. The first aircraft M.1 was a sound design but sales did not materialise, due to the great depression and a collapse in the sports aircraft market. In 1935 he was joined by Captain Valentine Baker (a competent ex-RFC pilot) who was also to act as company test pilot for the newly-established Martin Baker aircraft company. The company embarked on a new civil two-seater monoplane (the MB.1) which embodied many innovations. Almost before this was finished, the ambition leapt to the 1934 Air Ministry Specification F.5/34, to produce a 300+ mph fixed-undercarriage fighter. As described earlier, this was subsequently amended to be specified to create the first to be fitted with eight wing-mounted machine guns. The resulting Napier Dagger powered MB.2 monoplane design paid great attention to ease of servicing and repairs (the Dagger, also used in the Hereford bomber, proved not to be a reliable engine). The prototype first flew in 1938 and achieved a level flight speed of 320mph. It was sent to the Aircraft Experimental Unit at Martelsham Heath near Ipswich, in Suffolk (renamed the Aircraft and Armament Experimental Establishment [A&AEE], moved to Boscombe Down in Wiltshire in 1939). None of the four submissions for F.5/34 from industry went into production but the MB.2 compared fairly favourably with submissions from the established Vickers, Gloster and Bristol companies, especially in the ease of maintenance.

In a memorandum of 1939, the A&AEE chief technical officer remarked that the MB.2 had been a good response to F.5/34, but that the specification had been overtaken by later developments and, therefore, the MB.2 would have been obsolescent by the time it could have been introduced into service (the Hawker Hurricane went into service at the end of 1937). It was particularly noted that Martin Baker should be encouraged to tender for the new specification F.18/39, specified as a future replacement for the Spitfire and Hurricane. The A&AEE Wing Commander was sufficiently impressed to request that Captain Baker (as Martin Baker test pilot) be permitted to be allowed flights in the (still officially secret) Spitfire and Hurricane, to become personally familiar with flying properties of the most modern fighter aircraft. Uniquely, approval was given for civilian Valentine Baker to be granted such access, on the basis that the company would pay for the costs involved and insuring the aircraft. The costs incurred for the flight were £16.7s.6d (£16.38) per hour for the Hurricane, equivalent to £1,080 in 2019 (insured for £7,250, equivalent to over £480,000 in 2019) and £20.5s.0d (£20.25) per hour for the Spitfire, equivalent to £1,320 in 2019 (insured for £8,000, equivalent to over £530,000 in 2019). In 1939, new (never delivered) Spitfires for Estonia were priced at £12,500, complete with armament.

In the summer of 1939, Martin Baker were asked to produce three prototypes of a response to F.18/39, a remarkable achievement for such a small company which had yet to produce a single military aircraft. No other company was invited to tender. A completely new design was to be created, as the MB.3, powered by the Napier Sabre 2,000HP engine. After an encouraging first flight on 31 August 1943, when Valentine Baker had reported excellent flight characteristics, the MB.3 crashed during take-off on its second flight, due to engine failure, killing Baker in the process. The partly built second prototype was completed as the MB.5, this time with the ultimate development of the Rolls-Royce twelve-cylinder piston engines, the thirty-seven litre Griffon engine which powered the latest version of the Spitfire (first flight 1941, resulting in the 1942 Spitfire Mk.XII). The MB.5 used the Griffon Mk.83, (2,340HP with 130-octane fuel) and had a pair of constant-speed contra-rotating propellers, preventing the heavy ground swing during the take-off which was a feature of the Griffon-powered single-propeller Spitfire.

With a first flight in May 1944, the MB.5 top speed turned out to be 460mph at 20,000ft. This level of performance was only exceeded by the Spitfire development into the Supermarine Spiteful, first flown one month later in 1944 and only seventeen of which were built, including two prototypes. The MB.5 had twice as much range as the Spiteful. In October 1944 James Martin was informed that, excellent though the MB.5 was, it would not be going into production, due to the fact that the established Allied air superiority as the war was drawing to a close did not warrant a new "best piston-engined fighter aircraft" expenditure – the new jet age was clearly going to provide even faster/higher-flying aircraft. The fulsome A&AEE MB.5 assessment report was small consolation. Briefly, James Martin considered a jet version of the MB.5 but other activities were on his mind.

Martin Baker had already become involved in specialised equipment for military aircraft. In particular, James Martin had long had an interest in aircrew safety and aircraft escape systems. In 1944, his company was awarded a contract to make special studies for aircrew escape from the new "even faster" jet fighters which were emerging. This founded the Martin Baker aircrew ejection seat business, still in existence and (by 2020) having been responsible for the saving of over 7,600 aircrew lives, in many different air forces.

Britain Rearms With New Bomber Aircraft Designs
A significant number of new military aircraft were to be actually designed in the period from the early 1930s to 1939. Military aircraft in Britain were normally developed and procured using an "Air Ministry Aircraft Specification" as a starting document, stating performance, armament, payload and other requirements (see Appendix 3). This might be issued some time before a procurement decision, as many aircraft companies submitted proposals in response and prototypes of the most promising often would be authorised and flown, for competitive evaluation.

After 1935, as a "new technology hedging of bets", more than one type of each bomber and fighter requirement was sometimes to be authorised for production (as described previously for Hurricane and Spitfire). In all, there were at least 182 Air Ministry specifications for new aircraft or major upgrades in the years 1930 to

1939. Some sixty of these 182 specifications led to new aircraft production beyond prototype stage. From 1935 onwards, the whole UK military aircraft industry started to move back onto the front foot. Although significant discussions were between the RAF and/or the RN, the aircraft industry and government technical establishments (such as the RAE) were normal, not all RAF/RN specifications were "open enough" to allow unusual submissions to be properly evaluated. The development of the Hawker Hurricane and Supermarine Spitfire fighter aircraft were cases in point. These aircraft had been generated by industry chief designer persistence and their companies' PV backing, in the face of entrenched opposition from some senior persons in the RAF. The effort finally had led to over 900 new and very capable monoplane RAF fighter aircraft in service by the end of 1939, with a lot more to come before the air battles of 1940. The influential and vigorous support of the Air Council Air Member for Research and Development, Air Vice-Marshal Wilfrid Freeman, was key to opening this particular door.

The rearmament environment also led to activation of requirements for bomber types of military aircraft. New RAF specifications had been prepared in the early 1930s but the proposals in response by the aircraft companies needed "refinement", before satisfactory selections could be made. In particular, the rearmament decision provided impetus for the go-ahead on new RAF bombers, resulting in follow-up of bomber requirements, some of which originated in the early 1930s but needing reconsideration:

a. Twin-engined medium bomber to specification B.9/32 which became the Handley Page Hampden. (In 1936 an initial production order for 180 placed on Handley Page and 100 more on Shorts.)

b. Twin-engined medium bomber to specification B.9/32 – updated 1936 (for Vickers Wellington). (In 1936 a production order for 180 Wellingtons was placed on Vickers and in 1937 Gloster were given orders to produce 200 and Armstrong Whitworth were given an order for sixty-four.)

c. Twin-engined medium bomber to specification B.3/34 became Armstrong Whitworth Whitley. (In 1935 two orders totaling eighty aircraft placed on Armstrong Whitworth – unusually, before the prototype had flown.)

d. Light bomber adaptation of the twin-engined Bristol 142 eight-passenger airliner, which had had its first flight in April 1935. It was originally ordered for the RAF modified as a bomber, to a specially drawn up specification B.28/35 as the Type 142M, which became the Bolingbroke, soon renamed as the Blenheim by the Air Ministry. An initial contract for 135 aircraft was placed in September 1935. The type 142 became the type number for the Blenheim and the airliner became Bristol Type 143, the first 143 being the only one which was completed.

e. Four-engined heavy bomber, to specification B.12/36 with a maximum bomb load of 14,000lb became Supermarine 317, Short S.29 Stirling and, in 1939, the Handley Page HP.57 Halifax. In 1938 Shorts received two orders totalling 200 aircraft. *Immediately* after the 1938 "Munich Peace Agreement" (signed by Germany, Britain, France and Italy in the early hours of 30 September 1938), orders were increased to 1,500. Early in the same year, Handley Page received an order for 100 HP.57 Halifax, again before the prototype had flown.)

f. Twin-engined long-range medium-heavy bomber to specification P.13/36 with a maximum bomb load of 10,000lb (became Avro Type 679 Manchester). In 1937 Avro received an order for 200 aircraft, two years before the prototype flew, with the Handley Page HP.56 as a "back-up" design – at Air Ministry request, the HP.56 design was later amended into the four-engined HP.57 Halifax.

The biggest bombers would cost around £50,000 each, over £3.25 million in 2019 terms.

The idea of a bomber with a capability of delivering a 10,000lb load or greater, over a long-range, attracted the RAF and the Air Ministry, thinking of a strategic bombing campaign in the looming potential war. Bombers specified by the Air Ministry, up until 1935, had a maximum bomb load around 4,000lb. Lack of experience in Britain of the design of a large and complex four-engined heavy aircraft (by mid-1930s standards) was of concern. The authorisation process for production of the Stirling, Halifax and Manchester was not straightforward. Actual production authorisation was supported by an analysis of the relative cost effectiveness of the "the Heavy" and "the Medium" types, for a bombing offensive which could penetrate as far as the German interior, based on delivering 4,000 tons of bombs overall:

	Heavy Bomber	Medium Bomber
Average bomb load (lb.)	10,000	2,500 (at long-range)
Number of aircraft required	896	3,584
Cost (£ million)	47	79
Labour units needed	1,926	3,584
Number of engines needed	3,584	7,168
Aircrew numbers	6,720	22,400
Flying schools ratio	1	4
Maintenance personnel	14,000	42,000

This analysis was created in mid-1938 by Air Marshal Wilfrid Freeman, promoted as Air Member of the Air Council for Development and Production, and Air Vice-Marshal Arthur Tedder[5] (previously AOC Far East, reassigned to handle Research and Development within Wilfrid Freeman's function). The effectiveness of medium bombers for other than strategic long-range penetration missions was not questioned at the time, so the new Vickers Wellington medium bomber production would continue.

The technical, operational and economic evidence for the introduction of the heavy bomber seemed incontrovertible but the simple implementation of a policy to create such an offensive force would add some 55 per cent to the existing RAF budget. This would raise the RAF share of rearmament expense to 40 per cent overall, given that the need for more air defence fighters was not going to be compromised. During 1937–38, the Treasury resisted the heavy bomber proposition, a stance effectively endorsed by Prime Minister Neville Chamberlain's continued belief in the possibility of avoiding war by appeasement. Lord Londonderry's October 1936 revelation of Hitler's ambition to acquire German-speaking parts of Czechoslovakia and Poland (see section 2.3) had not overcome the Treasury position. The actual annexation of the German-speaking Sudetenland in Czechoslovakia, which began on 1 October 1938, probably caused a final government rethink and production of all these strategic bomber types was authorised "off the drawing board" by the end of that year.

The Vickers Wellington
In February 1933, Vickers tendered for the design of the twin-engined medium bomber, October 1932 specification B.9/32. Awarded a contract to design and build two

---

5. Later, as an Air Chief Marshal, Arthur Tedder became Deputy Supreme Allied Commander to Supreme Allied Commander USA General Dwight D. Eisenhower, for the Allied operations in the 1944 Normandy landings and subsequent successful Western European campaign against Germany and the other Axis countries.

Vickers Wellington (battle damaged).
(*Author's collection*)

Wellington Geodesic Structure.
(*Kroidkrensen, CC BY-SA 4.0*)

prototypes in February 1933, during three years of discussions, design proposals, actual design and starting prototype build, Vickers had influenced the Air Ministry and the RAF to accept a revised and more ambitious aircraft, with higher-powered engines and a new style of construction. The structure used the geodesic multiple redundant approach propounded by Vickers' structural engineer Barnes Wallis. This had previously been used in his work on airships and the Vickers Wellesley light bomber. A test specimen of this kind of construction at RAE demonstrated the capability of enduring nearly twice the maximum load required without any permanent damage. The geodesic style in light alloy, covered with doped fabric, was adopted for the fuselage, wings and empennage structure of what became the Wellington bomber.

This structure was resilient to extensive battle damage and returned home when other aircraft would have been destroyed with the same amount of damage. It was, however, more difficult and time-consuming to build or repair than the more conventional longeron-frame-stringer style of other aircraft.

First flight of the prototype was in June 1936, with service entry two years later, in October 1938. Capable of carrying a 4,500lb bomb load, the Wellington was assigned many roles other than bombing, as the heavy bombers (Lancaster and Halifax in particular) took over the bombing offensive in the later years of the war. Built in sixteen variants, Wellingtons remained in production from 1936 to the end of the war and became the most-produced multi-engined aircraft ever produced in Britain, with 11,461 completed.

The Handley Page Halifax, the Short Stirling and the Avro Manchester/Lancaster

The Air Ministry had prepared two bomber specifications, B.12/36 for a four-engined aircraft and P.13/36 for a two-engined aircraft. In the event, the Supermarine type 316, with four 1,300HP Bristol Hercules engines, a forecast high maximum speed of over 330mph and a bomb load maximum of 14,000lb, was viewed favourably as the B.12/36 aircraft. The Type 316 design was soon amended, to become the type 317 with a larger wing and twin-fin tail. The "heavy-medium" Handley Page HP.56 design, with twin 1,780HP Rolls-Royce Vulture engines and the similarly-powered Avro 679 Manchester, each with 10,000lb maximum bomb loads, were favoured as the P.13/36 aircraft.

Prototype development of all three was authorised early in 1937, with the Handley Page HP.56 aircraft placed as "back-up" to the Avro Manchester. The ill health and subsequent June 1937 death of Supermarine's Chief Designer R.J. Mitchell created doubt in the Air Ministry's mind about the Supermarine ability to deliver the type 317, so development of two prototypes of the "back-up" Shorts S.29 Stirling, with the same engines as the Supermarine 317 and a maximum bomb load of 14,000lb, was also authorised in 1937. An air raid on the Supermarine factory on the twenty-fourth day of the Second World War destroyed the two incomplete type 317 prototypes. Further effort on the Type 317 was not pursued.

By mid-1937, problems with the Vulture engine were starting to appear and the Air Ministry asked Handley Page to change their twin-engine heavy-medium bomber design to a four-engined design using Rolls-Royce Merlin engines. This created the HP.57 Halifax, basically in line with the B.12/36 specification. This was ordered for production in January 1938, well before its first flight, which happened fifty-two days after the 3 September 1939 outbreak of the Second World War. The main Halifax variant (HP.61) production was to use Bristol Hercules engines. Avro soldiered on with the Manchester, in the hope that the Vulture engine would ultimately "come good" (but soon quietly started design work on a stretched-wing version of the Manchester, with four Merlin engines). First flight of the Manchester was on 25 July 1939, just thirty-nine days before the outbreak of war, whilst the first flight of the Short Stirling was on 14 May 1939 (less than four months before the war). The Stirling became the first four-engined heavy bomber into RAF service, notably a few years after the USAAF Boeing B-17 Flying Fortress and about the same time as the USAAF Consolidated B-24 Liberator four-engined medium-heavy bombers (both 8,000lb maximum bomb load). For reasons of urgency, the Stirling design retained much in common with the Sunderland flying boat, with an adaptation of the wing and use of the upper part of the fuselage above the lower deck and boat hull, which were replaced by a new fuselage element with a large bomb bay. An RAF request for a cropped wing (reputedly for hangar door size limits) forced more changes, including more powerful engines. The result turned out to be relatively heavy, with an empty weight some 12,000lb. more than its eventual other RAF heavy bomber counterparts and with a maximum altitude capability several thousand feet lower.

The revised "four-engined Manchester" was officially authorised to go ahead as a prototype exercise by May 1940. Air Vice-Marshal Wilfrid Freeman, formerly Air Council Air Member for Research and Development (AMRD) but promoted to Air Marshal with increased responsibility for the overall research, development *and* production portfolio (AMDP), then made a judgement of the Avro Manchester/Vulture situation. This resulted in a request in a letter dated 29 July 1940 for Avro to replace the Manchester production line with a Handley Page HP.57 Halifax bomber line. The day after the letter was received Avro responded with a personal presentation to the Air Marshal. The presentation was made by Roy Dobson (Managing Director) and Roy Chadwick (Chief Designer). As a result, Freeman put on hold the change to the Halifax line, allowing the order for two prototype "four-engined Manchesters" to proceed (initially named as the Manchester III), clearly with a "hurry up" exhortation. The aircraft had its first flight just five months later (see section 3.1). The success of this Manchester development caused Freeman to energetically pursue full production authorisation. The development of the two-engined Manchester into the four-engined Lancaster had created an aircraft basically exceeding the operational requirements of B.12/36.... Roy Chadwick, Avro Chief Designer, later wrote to Freeman: "I am confident that the Lancaster will prove to be the outstanding aircraft of the war, and it is largely due to you that it has come into existence".[6]

---

6. Anthony Furse: "*Wilfrid Freeman – The Genius Behind Allied Survival and Air Supremacy 1939 to 1945*".

Airliner Becomes Successful Fighter Bomber

The Bristol Type 142 eight-seater airliner was created after a challenge to the British industry to produce the fastest civil aircraft in Europe. The challenge was made by the Chairman of the *Daily Mail* newspaper empire, Lord Rothsmere. Bristol Chief Designer Frank Barnwell and his Assistant Chief Leslie Frise[7] responded with a high-powered and stretched version of the unbuilt Bristol Type 135. Thus was the Bristol type 142 produced, first flying on 12 April 1935.

It was faster than any RAF aircraft then in service, with a demonstrated 307mph clearly attracting attention. It was ordered as a light bomber to a specially drawn up specification B.28/35, with a requirement to reposition the wing from low wing to mid wing, allowing a reasonable bomb bay underneath, as the Type 142M. The twin engines were changed from the 500HP Bristol Aquila to the 960HP Bristol Mercury. Named the Bolingbroke – it was renamed Blenheim by the Air Ministry – of which 4,442 were built.

Responding to the requirements of specifications M.15/35 and G.24/35 for a land-based maritime patrol aircraft with torpedo bombing capability, the design of the Blenheim light bomber was soon adapted to become the Bristol Type 152 Beaufort. The main changes were an increase in wing span, a change of engines from Bristol Mercury to Bristol Taurus (20 per cent more power), an increase in bomb bay size, a full time navigator alongside the pilot, with camera station, radio operator and bomb-aiming duties shared between two other crew members, thus adding an extra crew member.

The Beaufort was ordered into production off the drawing board (as an urgent need), at the same time as the Blackburn B.26 Botha was also similarly ordered (580 Bothas were built and operated by the RAF but they were not a great success, with a high accident rate). The Beaufort's first flight was on 15 October 1938. Due to roll stability issues requiring aerodynamic refinement, series production was not initiated until November 1939. A total of 1,121 Beauforts operated with UK maritime forces (RAF Coastal Command and the Fleet Air Arm) and 700 were built in Australia to operate with the RAAF.

Frank Barnwell was killed in 1938 in a crash in his privately designed and built light monplane. Leslie Frise took over his mantle at Bristol. In a PV study originally begun by Frank Barnwell prior to his death, the Beaufort was assessed as a potential foundation of a new long-range fighter-bomber, able to carry a significant bomb load and mount two cannon in the nose. Even eight wing-mounted machine guns in the Spitfires and Hurricanes could not deliver enough firepower to ensure a destructive hit on large aircraft, during the short intervals when a target could be held in the sights in air-to-air combat. The Westland Whirlwind four-cannon interceptor to specification F.7/35 was due to fulfil the requirement for an airborne cannon-firing aircraft but, as an interim measure, F.11/37 was issued for a version of the Beaufort adapted to become the Bristol Type 156, as a cannon-armed night fighter against enemy bombers. Nose mounting was considered essential, because a jammed wing-mounted cannon (not that uncommon in early installations) could cause the recoil of a single cannon on the opposite wing to be sufficient to critically affect the aircraft aim. The basic Bristol airframe design had the required underlying structural strength.

With a pair of Bristol Hercules engines 40 per cent more powerful than the Bristol Taurus engines of the Beaufort, and a larger propeller (requiring a longer undercarriage and mounting the engines centrally in the wing rather than the Beaufort underslung position, all to provide the necessary propeller tip ground clearance), the idea took

---

7. Leslie Frise had been at Bristol since 1915. Resigning in 1946 due to ill health, two years later he became Technical Director at Percival Aircraft, moving to Blackburn Aircraft in 1956 as Director of Special Projects.

root. The resulting aircraft was to be some 50mph faster than its antecedent Beaufort. Air Ministry specification F.11/37 was configured to suit and issued for the Bristol Type 156, named by the RAF as the Beaufighter in March 1939. In order to start flight testing as soon as possible and accelerate the introduction into service, much of the design remained identical to the Beaufort, enabling the same production tooling to be used in many areas. First flight was on 17 July 1939, only seven weeks before the outbreak of the Second World War.

The latest 1,600HP Bristol Hercules engine was in demand for other aircraft and the Beaufighter proposal changed, to substitute the 1,730HP Rolls-Royce Griffon engine instead. At the time, this was actually reserved for the Fairey Fulmar replacement, the two-crew Fairey Firefly carrier-born fighter/reconnaissance aircraft. Consequently, the Air Ministry opted for the less powerful (1,280HP) Rolls-Royce Merlin XX (in the same installation as used on Avro Lancasters) as an interim measure.

Bristol Beaufighter (note armament under wings). (*BAE Systems*)

This lasted until the Hercules-powered version of the aircraft appeared in 1942. By the time of introduction into service in 1940, the Beaufighter had acquired four nose-mounted cannon and an additional six machine guns mounted in the wings (two port, four starboard). This was fearsome armament.

As a nightfighter, Beaufighters would replace the 1937 Boulton-Paul Defiant, which was constrained by not having a forward-firing gun but used twin pairs of turret-mounted machine guns operated by an air gunner to fire upwards, from underneath the bomber. In addition, the Beaufighter was the only aircraft in service to readily accommodate the introduction of the new Airborne Interception 10cm radar, so vital to increasing target detection at night and in poor visibility. The faster de Havilland Mosquito took over the night fighter role from the Beaufighter, starting at the end of 1942, but there was more Beaufighter to come.

The Type 156 Beaufighter became a successful multi-role aircraft, used in maritime reconnaissance, anti-shipping torpedo and free-fall bomber roles, rocket-firing ground attack and as long-range interdiction aircraft, in many different theatres of operations. This was so successful that many Beauforts were converted to Beaufighters. In total, 5,928 Beaufighters were built. The grand total derived from the original Type 142M was over 12,000 (Blenheim, Beaufort and Beaufighter, plus 626 Canadian-built maritime patrol versions of the Blenheim, the Bolingbroke, the original name of the 142M Blenheim).

Aircraft Production by British Industry, 1930 to 1939

The early 1930s remained a poor period for British airliner production but a reasonable and fairly improving environment for utility/trainer aircraft. By the middle of the decade a rapidly escalating rearmament situation increased requirements for all kinds of military aircraft. The successful result of submissions and specimen prototyping of military aircraft in the mid-1930s sometimes overwhelmed the originating winning company factory capacity, especially as rearmament intensity increased. Until then, some aircraft companies, with their woodworking and metalworking skills and equipment, made furniture and like sideline products, and motor vehicle body panels, as the general economic depression persisted.

Air Ministry-directed contract build of the aircraft of other manufacturers became both a route to sustaining workload in those companies without much work and aircraft delivery rates to meet the imminent threat, often obviating the need for the fortunate "parent" company with a large contract having to invest time and money in increased factory capacity with only an uncertain future beyond the present contract. For example, 47 per cent of the total UK Hawker Hart production of 962 aircraft between 1934 and 1936 was carried out in the Armstrong Whitworth Aircraft factories (by the end of 1935, in the same Hawker Siddeley Group as Hawker). Sweden built forty-two more under licence. Although preparations for a possible war increased in intensity from the mid-1930s, gross industrial activity in the UK did not fully recover to the levels of 1914 until very close to the start of the Second World War.

The list in Appendix 9 includes all British military and civil types which were first flown in the years 1930–1939. In the event, total 1930s pre-September 1939 output of both civil and military aircraft which were first flown and entered service in the 1930s (all types, military and civil) exceeded 22,000, of which only about 10 per cent could be classed as "civil".

For the coming war, the RAF planning was based on an expected aircraft loss rate of 40 per cent overall, unlike the actual 62 per cent of the First World War (as described in section 2.4). The real unknown was the duration of this looming second major world conflict. Just like the earlier war, it would actually turn out to be far longer and more extensive than anyone anticipated.

2.8 British Aircraft Company Formation and Consolidation, 1908 to 1939

Introduction

The changes in the British aircraft industry started "immediately" after the first company was registered (Short Brothers in November 1908). Handley Page Company was registered in June 1909 and the competition began. There were eighteen independent aircraft companies active by the start of the First World War in 1914, with twelve more created during that war. There were aircraft companies which "crashed" after the end of the First World War, as aircraft production almost ceased completely for a while. By the end of 1920 , seven of the overall total of thirty which had started up had ceased trading in the aircraft design and manufacturing business, but two more started up before the end of the same year.

The immediate 1918 post-Armistice low level of the British (and other) government's interest in developing advanced aircraft for military use was only one of the factors not helpful to the aircraft manufacturers in the dozen or so years after the war. A major financial blow was the UK government legislation on "war profits" made by any manufacturer. Britain was one of several of the belligerent nations to use such a taxation principle, applied retrospectively. The wartime rules for acceptable company profits on British government contracts had been a 9 per cent normal maximum profit margin, plus a wartime intensive effort allowance of 6 per cent (15 per cent total). The new war profits tax was soon labelled as an "Excess" war profits tax by politicians, gaining acceptance from the public as "a tax on war profiteering". The taxation was solely based on ill-defined pre-war and during-war profit levels, taking account of a statutory maximum allowance of 6 per cent, plus 3 per cent for war risk (the 9 per cent), and allowing tax relief for investment in new plant and machinery. Defining the exact accounting basis for payment of the tax was challengeable in a legal sense but, in the climate of patriotic fervour pertaining immediately after the war, any challenge could generate extremely adverse publicity and even anger in the populace. The British government fixed the war profits tax at 80 per cent of the amount by which profits exceeded the pre-war standard of profits, according to the rules established by the government, to be paid immediately. This ruined the financial status of many companies, not least in the British aircraft industry, and several companies were forced to cease trading.

On top of such financial difficulties, the whole aircraft supply market (especially civil) between the end of the First World War and the early/mid 1930s was a "quagmire" which threatened the survival of many British aircraft companies. The aircraft industry in much of the world at large seemed to have nowhere to go but "down", if not "out". Something had to give!

Early British casualties were the collection of businesses which had been created by Samuel Waring. These were the British Aerial Transport Company, formed in 1917 and closed down in 1919, the Alliance Aircraft company, formed in 1918 by taking over Ruffy, Arnell & Baumann (established 1915) and closed in 1920, and the Nieuport and General Company, formed in 1916 and closed in 1920, assets acquired by the Gloucestershire Aircraft Company (which became Gloster). The Norman Thompson Flight Company (started as White and Thompson in 1912) also ceased trading in 1919.

The business situation for aircraft design and manufacturing organisations after the end of the 1914–18 war through to the early 1930s often led to one of three different places; merger, takeover or ceasing to trade. The attrition of numbers of independent aircraft companies, since 1908 up to the end of the 1920s, totalled nineteen companies. Added to these were the closures of aircraft design and production in the government establishments of the Air Design Department of the Admiralty in 1920 and the change of the Royal Aircraft Factory into a research-only establishment (the Royal Aircraft Establishment, RAE) in 1918. One or two others were financially restructured and renamed.

How did it all actually happen?

There were unequal successes in aircraft companies. Unsurprisingly, the empire-building aspirations of certain company proprietors and leaders often resulted in survival of the powerful at the expense of the weak (possibly irrespective of the quality of their product). Somewhat surprisingly (and precariously), eight new enterprises started aircraft design activity in the 1920s and a further twelve started in the 1930s. One or two "subcontract manufacture only" aircraft companies converted themselves (or split off from a parent) into a new aircraft design-and-manufacture establishment.

The timeline list below briefly describes the most prominent parts of the sequence, beginning with the established companies still trading in Britain after the "immediate closures" at the end of the First World War:

1919–29   Between the end of the war in 1918 and the end of 1919, eight British aircraft design-make organisations ceased trading. From the start of 1920 to the start of 1930, thirteen more aircraft companies ceased trading, as previously listed in Table 2.6. This included the seemingly successful Martinsyde company, which had turned to building motorcycles in 1919 but declared bankrupt after a disastrous 1922 fire in the main factory at Woking.

1919   After manufacturing aircraft during the war, George Parnall and Company split from original shopfitting company Parnall & Sons, to form an independent aircraft company, based in Bristol.

1920   At the suggestion of John Davenport Siddeley (Chairman and Managing Director of the Siddeley-Deasy motor company), Sir W.G. Armstrong Whitworth & Company acquired Siddeley-Deasy Motors, to form Armstrong Siddeley Motors and the separate Sir W.G. Armstrong Whitworth Aircraft (formerly the Aerial Department of Sir W.G. Armstrong Whitworth and Company). John Siddeley became chairman of the holding company for these two businesses.

1920	The Aircraft Manufacturing Company (trade name Airco) had supplied 30 per cent of all aircraft used by Britain and the United States during the First World War. After the end of the First World War, Airco (as the world's largest aircraft design and manufacturing company) was sold to BSA (a Birmingham gun, motorcycle and bicycle company which also owned Daimler cars). After the BSA acquisition (within days!), Airco was found to be insolvent and had to be liquidated. The original founder of Airco, George Holt Thomas, was accused of misrepresentation (by omission) of the true financial state of Airco, but no serious checks had been made by BSA before agreeing to the purchase.

Notwithstanding, investing their own money, Geoffrey de Havilland (who had started his career with the Royal Aircraft Factory as the designer of the BE.2 and was Chief Designer at Airco), George Holt Thomas and two others purchased Airco intellectual assets and its outstanding orders, forming a new company named de Havilland Aircraft. This commenced operations in modest premises at the Stag Lane Aerodrome, Edgeware, London. Geoffrey de Havilland was to continue the series of aircraft type numbers with the DH prefix which had been previously applied to Airco aircraft in their "DH" aircraft type numbers.

1920	Wealthy sportsman (yachting and motor racing) T.O.M. ("Tommy") Sopwith had set up the Sopwith Aviation Company in 1912, initially at Brooklands. In 1920 he persuaded Sopwith shareholders to liquidate Sopwith Aviation, ostensibly to enable "excess war profits" to be paid back. This was achieved in full with a fair return to shareholders. With his ex-Sopwith Aviation comrades, Australian Harry Hawker (Sopwith test pilot, aircraft designer-engineer and racing driver), Fred Sigrist and Bill Eyre, "Tommy" Sopwith bought up Sopwith patents and other assets and formed a new company, H.G. Hawker Engineering, which based itself in Kingston-upon-Thames in a redundant ice rink facility. Sopwith and Sigrist were joint managing directors. Harry Hawker was was killed on 12 July 1921, crashing in his Nieuport Goshawk in a practice flight in preparaton for an air race around London (the Aerial Derby).
1920	When Nieuport and General Aircraft ceased trading, Chief Designer Henry Folland transferred to the Gloucestershire Aircraft Company (GAC) which, until then, had only made propellers and aircraft under licence. After adapting Nieuport designs and building a single light aircraft, the first series production all-GAC aircraft was the 1923 Grebe trainer, of which the RAF took 123.
1920	The family-owned Bristol and Colonial Aeroplane Company was liquidated and assets transferred to a new Bristol Aeroplane Company. During this time, under ministry pressure, Bristol acquired the bankrupt aircraft engine company Cosmos Engineering (also based in Bristol) to form the Bristol Engines division of the Bristol Aeroplane Company. Bristol paid £15,000 (equivalent to about £700,000 in 2019) for all assets and intellectual property and received the "free transfer" of Roy Fedden, later to be knighted in 1942 for his contribution to aircraft engine design.
1920	Crossley Motors took a controlling interest in Avro (Avro started to make car bodies).
1921	George Parnall moved his new aircraft company to Yate, several miles north of Bristol.
1924	The Grahame White Aviation Company had been founded in 1911 by Claude Grahame White, at Hendon, London. As an early aviator and

aviation publicist, he was a famous personality in Britain. During the First World War, the company mostly assembled the designs of others, such as examples of the French Farman F.30 biplane and 600 Avro 504s. Post-war, the company designed several different aircraft but produced them in very small numbers. A dispute with the government over materials supply for a 1917 contract to build 700 Airco DH.6 trainers delayed production and depleted financial reserves, from which the company never truly recovered. After the war ended, the Air Ministry refused to return the company Hendon Aerodrome (requisitioned in 1914). Eventually, in 1924, the Air Ministry appointed receivers to recover debts.

1924   The English Electric Company had been formed in 1918 at the end of the First World War from the amalgamation of five companies involved in electrical power equipment. Two of these, the Phoenix Dynamo Manufacturing Company of Bradford and Dick, Kerr & Co. of Preston, had built aircraft during the war. William Oke Manning was part of Phoenix Dynamo and designed the Phoenix pusher seaplane in 1917 (not built). Manning had started out as an electrical engineer but had also been chief designer for a number of different pre-war aircraft, alongside Howard T. Wright, a prominent aircraft designer and constructor. Manning's Phoenix P.5 Cork flying boat prototype failed to take off from the estuary of the River Ribble, due to hitting some flotsam (almost sank) during the first attempt to fly in May 1924. With some relatively minor changes, the aircraft was modified and flown in November 1924, as the English Electric P.5 Kingston. Six were built. After three Wren motor-glider aircraft had also been built, as the last Kingston was delivered, English Electric closed its aviation department in 1926. (No further aircraft-related business at English Electric was carried out until allocated production of Handley Page Hampden and Halifax bombers during the Second World War – see section 3.2.)

1926   Cierva Autogyro Company was founded in Britain when designer-founder Juan de la Cierva moved his activity from Spain (see section 5.9). The G & J Weir Company (which had built aircraft for Airco during the First World War) financially supported the venture. Deputy Chairman and majority shareholder James Weir was an aviation enthusiast and had been the twenty-fourth person in Britain to obtain a pilot's licence. He had become interested in autogyros as a type of flying machine (he eventually had one of his own, to commute to his office).

1926   The Gloucestershire Aircraft Company changed its name to the Gloster Aircraft Company, to ease pronunciation difficulties experienced by overseas customers. Gloster was originally founded in 1917, by Airco Managing Director Hugh Burroughes and Airco H.H. Martyn & Co. (50 per cent between them) and G.H. Thomas (owner of the other 50 per cent and owner of Airco) to licence-build Airco aircraft. A.W. Martyn was a founder-director.

1927   Conglomerates Vickers Engineering Ltd. and Sir W.G. Armstrong Whitworth and Company merged. This created two different "Armstrong" aircraft companies, Vickers-Armstrong (Aircraft) and Armstrong Whitworth Aircraft. The Armstrong Whitworth aircraft business was "split away" from the merged Vickers-Armstrong business and bought by John Siddeley's organisation. The Vickers aircraft business was retained by Vickers Armstrong.

1928   Vickers took over Supermarine, which continued to trade independently as a wholly-owned subsidiary.

1928   Avro aircraft design employee Basil B. Henderson formed the Hendy aircraft company with H.A. Miles (ex-Avro stress office), operating in a shed at Shoreham. They designed two monoplanes, one of each built by George Parnall and Company. The Hendy Company was dissolved as a separate entity in 1935 and merged with the (renamed) Parnall Aircraft Company, with Basil Henderson remaining as aircraft designer.

1928   Crossley Motors sold their 65 per cent majority shareholding in Avro to Armstrong Siddeley Motors (in Tommy Sopwith's Hawker Engineering group of companies), to pay off debts of a partnership company with USA Willys Overland[8] (Willys Overland Crossley). The Crossley factory in Stockport had been used as a National Aircraft Factory during the First World War (see section 2.2) and was sold to Fairey Aviation in 1934.

1928   Oliver Simmonds designed the Spartan biplane in his spare time, whilst working for Supermarine (ex-Pemberton-Billing). The Spartan had interchangeable wings and tailplane. Following a disagreement, he left Supermarine and founded Simmonds Aircraft to build the aircraft, the first one at his home near Southampton. This company was refinanced in 1930 as Spartan Aircraft Ltd.[9] and Oliver Simmonds left, the company relocating to an airfield at Somerton, Isle of Wight, formerly used for flight testing by the J.S. White-owned Wight aircraft business until the end of the First World War.

1929   A.V. Roe sold his shares in A.V. Roe and Company (Avro) and resigns.

1929   A.V. Roe used cash from selling Avro shares to join Avro-based John Lord in taking over boat and aircraft builder S.E. Saunders at Cowes, Isle of Wight, forming Saunders-Roe Aircraft (Saro), aimed at producing flying boats. Prior to 1929, S.E. Saunders had produced the word's first amphibious aircraft and some unsuccessful (no sales) land planes and flying boats.

1929   John Kenworthy, previously an aircraft designer/chief designer with the Royal Aircraft Factory, Austin Motors, Westland and the Aircraft Disposal Company, co-founded the Robinson Aircraft Company at Croydon to build his "Redwing" light aircraft design. Twelve aircraft were produced. Company renamed Redwing in 1931 and moved, only to move back to Croydon. The company ceased aircraft design in 1933.

1929   Nicholas Comper established Comper Aircraft at Hooton Park Aerodrome (Ellesmere Port, Cheshire), moved to Heston, London in 1933. Ceased trading in 1934, re-established as Heston Aircraft same year under new management.

1929   Swiss-born William Beardmore Company designer Helmut John Steiger (1927 "monospar" wing structure patent) founded "The Monospar Company". After successful (Gloster-built) experimental aircraft of the "Monospar-winged" Steiger-designed ST-3, the General Aircraft Company was established in 1931 by Stieger at the London Air Park, Hanworth near Feltham, Middlesex, to build monospar winged machines (total of forty-five aircraft of eight variants eventually built). General Aircraft Ltd. went on to build aircraft of other companies as well as their own (not too successful commercially) designs.

1929   In 1929, James Martin started to design and build a two-seat sports monoplane, in Denham, Buckinghamshire. At that time, most contemporary

---

8. Willys Overland and Ford between them later produced the bulk of the 653,568 ubiquitous "Jeep" army vehicles of WW2 (the "Jeep" trademark eventually awarded to Willys Overland).

9. Not to be confused with the USA Spartan Aircraft Company, founded in 1928 as the Mid-Continent Aircraft Company, taken over by J.Paul Getty in 1935 and renamed as the Spartan Aircraft Company.

aircraft companies (big and small) stuck to biplane designs. The first aircraft – M.1 – was a sound design but sales did not materialise. In 1935 he was joined by Captain Valentine Baker, the company becoming Martin-Baker.

1930   With two other persons, C.H. Lowe-Wylde formed the British Aircraft Company (BAC) based at Maidstone, Kent (became a "limited" company in 1931). C.H. Lowe-Wylde had changed his name from T.H. Lowe since (at 20-years-old) privately designing and building the Lowe Marlburian Sports monoplane, which flew in 1922. BAC intended to design and build gliders. Around thirty sales were achieved, with a series of nine variations. In 1932, the BAC Planette appeared, as conversions of a BAC two-seat glider with a small (600cc) engine driving a pusher propeller. The company also built the prototype Percival Gull in 1932, for Edgar Percival's company. In May 1933, Lowe-Wylde was killed in a Planette accident. Austrian Jew Robert Kronfeld, a champion glider pilot and glider designer in Germany (and 1933 refugee from the Nazi regime) took over the company as the British Aircraft Company (1935) Ltd., moving the company to the London Air Park at Hanworth, Middlesex. He modified the Planette design into a more practical single-seater, calling it the Drone. The company was renamed as Kronfield Ltd in 1936 but closed down in 1937.

1930   Aircraft Disposal Company wound up.

1931   Aircraft Disposal Company re-constituted, as part of Redwing (the renamed Robinson Aircraft Company company).

1931   Gliding club founder member Frederick Slingsby built a German-designed glider, going on to found a glider design and manufacturing business at his furniture manufacturing business in Scarborough, Yorkshire. Later, the glider business moved to a new facility in 1939, at Kirkby Moorside thirty miles away.

1931   Phillips & Powis Aircraft established by Charles Powis and Jack Phillips, based at Woodley near Reading, Berkshire. In 1932 Frederick George Miles and Charles Powis agreed that Phillips and Powis would build a cheap light aircraft designed by F.G. Miles, resulting in the Miles Hawk design, which sold forty-seven examples plus sixty-four more of a development (the Miles Hawk Major). F.G. Miles became technical director of Phillips & Powis Aircraft in 1933.

1932   Percival Aircraft Co. was founded by Australian Edgar Percival in Gravesend (no production facility). He was joined by Lieutenant Commander E.B.W. Leake in 1933 and the company moved to Luton with production facilities (company name adjusted to Percival Aircraft Ltd.).

1933   Airspeed Limited established in York by Alfred Hessell Tiltman and Nevil Shute Norway (the aeronautical engineer and novelist under the pen-name Neville Shute) and with Alan Cobham as a founding director.

1933   H.G. Hawker Engineering renamed as Hawker Aircraft Ltd.

1934   Boulton & Paul sold their "Aircraft Department" (which had built more Sopwith Camel aircraft during the First World War than any other manufacturer). Established as Boulton & Paul Aircraft Ltd., a move from Norwich to Wolverhampton was planned, to a new-build factory (600 workers transferred from Norwich by 1936, when the new factory became fully operational).

1934   Rolls-Royce invested in Philips and Powis, making it a limited company.

1934   Swan Hunter purchased a controlling interest in Airspeed.

1934   Gloster Aircraft acquired by Hawker Aircraft.

1935   Hawker Aircraft merged with the John Siddeley (by then, Sir John) group of companies. Armstrong-Whitworth Aircraft, A.V. Roe and Company,

Hawker Aircraft and Gloster Aircraft all became part of the "Hawker Siddeley group of companies", alongside Armstrong Siddeley Motors and the Air Training Services companies. John Siddeley retired, leaving Tommy Sopwith as Hawker Siddeley overall group chairman. At first, the aircraft group of companies was formed under the Hawker Siddeley Aircraft Co. banner, but this became amalgamated into Hawker Siddeley Group Limited in 1938, recognising the diversification beyond aircraft design and manufacturing. The original four aircraft companies retained their separate identities.

1935   George Parnall acquired Hendy Aircraft, renamed combined company as "Parnall".

1935   Spartan Aircraft taken over by Saunders Roe.

1936   Short Brothers (Rochester and Bedford) join with Harland and Wolff (shipbuilders in Belfast) to form a new company Short Brothers and Harland, to build aircraft.

1936   Five brothers founded Moss Brothers Aircraft Ltd. in Chorley, Lancashire. Designed and built one example each of two different sports/light aircraft.

1936   Two separate companies, Wrightson Aircraft Sales and Malcolm and Farquharson, combined in 1936 to establish R. Malcolm Ltd. as a supplier of parts to the aircraft industry. At the beginning of the Second World War the company needed financial support, which was given by the Mobbs family. The company continued to trade as R. Malcolm Ltd. via the holding company Malcolm and Farquharson. Belgian national Marcel Lobelle left his position as chief designer of Fairey Aviation in 1940 and joined the R. Malcolm company. The holding company financial instrument was dispensed with in 1943 and Eric Mobbs became managing director with Marcel Lobelle as chief designer, appointed as a director in 1944. In 1946, the company split its operations between the parts-production site at Slough (ML Engineering) and the design, development testing, and assembly site at White Waltham (ML Aviation). ML continued business in aircraft-related products and expanded rapidly, becoming a supplier of underwing unguided rocket and (eventually) air-to-air guided missile launch rails. In 1954 the company was contracted to supply three inflatable-winged utility aeroplanes (inflatable in the field, for army use in communications and reconnaissance). Designed by Marcel Lobelle and known as the Inflatable Wing Mk.1 (or the M.L. Utility), three were supplied, the only aircraft ever supplied by ML Aviation. The aviation business of the ML group was eventually taken over by Cobham plc, in 1997.

1936   British Marine Aircraft formed at Hamble, on the bank of Southampton Water, to make Sikorsky flying boats under licence. Restructured financially in 1937 (see below) and named Folland Aircraft.

    British Marine Aircraft liquidated in 1937 and re-established under new management the same year, as Folland Aircraft, named after the new owner/ Managing Director and Chief Designer Henry P. Folland (ex-Gloster). The new company's first new design to fly was in 1940.

1937   B.A.O.T. Ltd. formed as a subsidiary of British American Tobacco Ltd., ostensibly to build Burnelli flying wing aircraft under licence (one only assembled), but really established as a shadow factory for nearby Supermarine (mainly built Supermarine Seafire). In 1938, company renamed as Cunliffe-Owen, after British American Tobacco chairman Sir Hugh Cunliffe-Owen. After the Second World War, the company designed and built two of their one and only design, the Concordia small airliner, which flew in 1947 but did not achieve any sales.

1937   Reid & Sigrist (aircraft instrument makers founded in 1927 by George Reid & Frederick Sigrist) formed an aircraft division. Sigrist was also joint managing director of Hawker Aircraft. After designing two different three-seat pilot training aircraft (a single RS.1 and a single RS.3), aircraft design activity ceased in 1945, due to lack of RAF interest. The RS.3 was converted in 1951 by RAE, to the RS.4, for a single prone pilot operation, with the purpose of investigating low speed controllability of aircraft from such a position (thought to be useful physiologically for high speed/high 'g' flight). The Reid and Sigrist instrument and optical equipment business was taken over by Decca in 1954.

1937   Two former de Havilland Technical School students (Old Etonians Andrew Dalrymple and Alexander Reginald Ward) formed Chilton Aircraft Ltd. The company designed and built four D.W.1 aircraft before the start of the Second World War. Three more were built post-war by amateurs, one of which first flew as late as 1987. Elliotts of Newbury constructed the prototype of the Chilton last design (the post-war Olympia glider, which was a redesigned version of the pre-war German glider intended for all gliding competitors at the 1940 Olympic games). Elliotts refused to sell the jigs which they had created to Chilton, and Andrew Dalrymple was killed in a flying accident in 1945. As a consequence, Chilton ceased to operate in 1946. The Olympia design was sold to Elliotts, a long-established furniture company which became involved with making Airspeed Horsa troop-carrying "war production" gliders during the Second World War. Elliotts branched out into glider manufacture and design in 1946, starting with the EoN Olympia glider.

1938   Taylorcraft Aeroplanes (England) Ltd. established, to build USA Taylorcraft Air Observation Post (AOP) aircraft designs for the UK army, under licence, at Thurmaston in Leicestershire. In 1946, it was renamed Auster Aircraft Ltd.

     AOP aircraft helped lay battlefront telephone lines, map and plot front line troop and gun positions, evacuate wounded soldiers and photograph enemy troop movements (sometimes under fire, occasionally "friendly"). By the 1950s, the AOP role was taken over by helicopters.

1938   Westland Aircraft absorbed into John Brown engineering conglomerate (final John Brown shareholding disposed of in 1980).

1940   Swan Hunter sold shareholding in Airspeed to de Havilland, Airspeed retaining identity.

1941   Rolls-Royce sold its Phillips and Powis shares to F.G. Miles, who became chairman and managing director and whose brother and wife also became directors.

1943   Phillips and Powis became Miles Aircraft Ltd.

1943   Short Brothers nationalised (much later denationalised and sold, in the 1980s).

1943   Weir Group revived Cierva activity as wartime aircraft parts maker, then full revival at the end of the war as a Weir-Cierva helicopter company, Cierva Autogyro.

1944   Percival Aircraft Ltd. acquired by the Hunting group.

     Founder Edgar Percival left the company when Hunting took over. In 1954, he founded Edgar Percival Aircraft Ltd. and designed one aircraft, the E.P.9. Twenty-one aircraft were built before he sold the engineering rights to Samlesbury Engineering Ltd. The new company changed its name to Lancashire Aircraft Ltd. but only built six more E.P.9, as the Lancashire Prospector E.P.9

There were obviously significant economic, political and personality forces in all these changes, and the financially strongest companies were obviously best-placed to survive. Those with "big parents" seemingly had an advantage, but some "parents" soon also suffered more widespread reduced post-war business levels in the 1920s and early 1930s. The surprise is that *any* new aircraft companies were formed in the 1920s and 1930s. The lure of aviation attracted more "triers", few of which would survive into the post-1945 age. The thirty British aircraft companies which still survived at the end of the Second World War are listed in Appendix 1, with dates of founding and principle aircraft. The further consolidation of the British aircraft industry in the latter half of the twentieth century is described in Chapters 6 and 8.

Geoffrey de Havilland's self-confidence (and staking his own money) enabled the acquisition of essential designs, patents etc. from the insolvent BSA-Airco business in 1920. A series of de Havilland civil passenger aircraft were sold in small numbers during the early years, but the DH.60 Moth series of utility aircraft (over 1,900 aircraft between 1925 and 1935) eventually stabilised the precarious financial situation of de Havilland. The Moth series of aircraft and the establishing of overseas subsidiary de Havilland companies, in Canada and Australia, enabled the new de Havilland company to rise above the rising tide of the looming Great Depression. Geoffrey de Havilland held on to the reins of all the de Havilland businesses until the extensive government-instigated industry mergers in 1960.

Success of the 1928 Hart aircraft and its 1930s variants Hind/Audax/Osprey developments, and the Fury aircraft, eventually helped Hawker to prosper. Avro's 504N and Avian aircraft successes helped in the late 1920s somewhat, but the 1929 shock resignation of A.V. Roe himself was a blow to business confidence.

It was the confidence of the Siddeley-Deasy shareholders in John Siddeley, and his self-belief, which enabled the successful merger of the Siddely-Deasy motor company with the motor and aircraft elements of Armstrong Whitworth. In 1935, the opportunity was seized to join the John Siddeley organisation to T.O.M. ("Tommy") Sopwith's Hawker Aircraft company, to form the Hawker Siddeley Group of companies. John Siddeley is often implicitly implied to be "father" (rather than mid-wife at the birth) of the famous resulting large British engineering conglomerate, the Hawker Siddeley Group. Tommy Sopwith, in charge of Hawker Aircraft, also must have had a very strong input to the Hawker Aircraft merger with John Siddeley's group. Sir John Siddeley retired as the merger was settled, leaving Tommy Sopwith established as the chairman of the whole of the new group of companies. Sir John Siddeley retired "with £1 million and benefits". The Hawker Siddeley Group added further aircraft related and non-aircraft businesses during the next twenty-five years.

By 1939, the two biggest aircraft empires in Britain were the Hawker Siddeley Group (containing Hawker, Avro, Armstrong-Whitworth and Gloster aircraft companies, plus Air Training Services and Armstrong Siddeley Motors) and the de Havilland Company, the latter designing and making aircraft propellers and aircraft engines, as well as aircraft. Tommy Sopwith was chairman of all Hawker Siddeley business, each constituent element continuing to trade, more-or-less independently, under their own name. Sopwith remained in charge until the 1960 reorganisation of the aircraft industry as a whole led to his retirement. By then, he was 72-years-old.

In 1937, the Air Ministry had encouraged Rolls-Royce and Bristol Engines to join their aircraft propeller activities in a venture to licence-build USA Hamilton Standard variable pitch propellers (which enabled propeller aerodynamics to be adjusted in flight to match engine thrust requirements at different phases of flight: taxi, take-off, climb, cruise). This became the Rotol propeller business (Rolls-<u>RO</u>yce-Bris<u>TOL</u>), taken over by the Dowty Group in 1958 and now part of the USA General Electric-owned GE Aviation Systems by their acquisition of the aviation business of Smiths Industries in 2007.

Variable pitch propeller work was eventually also taken up by de Havilland, in a factory at Lostock in Lancashire, built in only nine months, as a "shadow factory" (see section 3.2). At the same time (1935), de Havilland formed the DH Propellers Division. This later became the DH Propellers Ltd. company, which later moved into electronic equipment, guided weapons and space business in the 1950s (see section 6.1).

TIMELINES FOR BRITISH AIRCRAFT DESIGN-MANUFACTURING COMPANIES, 1908 TO 1945 (26 continued after 1945)

1908	1914	1918	1925	1930	**1935**	1940	1945

#	Company (span)
1	Aero'l Syndt.
2	Admiralty:- Air Design Dept.+RNAS
3	Airco
4	Air Navigation & Engineering
5	Airspeed
6	Ruffy etc. | Alliance
7	Armstrong Whitworth
8	Austin (aircraft)
9	A.V. Roe & Co. (Avro)
10	Beardmore
11	Blackburn
12	Boulton & Paul
13	Bristol and Colonial (Bristol 1920-on)
14	Br.Ae.Tr.
15	British Aircraft Company
16	British Marine/Folland
17	Central
18	Chilton
19	Cierva
20	Comper (insolvent) | Comper reformed as Heston
21	Cunliffe-Owen
22	de Havilland (acquired intellectual assets of Airco from Birmingham Small Arms)
23	Phoenix/English Electric | E.Elec
24	Fairey
25	F. Sage
26	General Aircraft
27	Gloucestershire (1926 changed name to Gloster)
28	Grahame-White
29	Handley Page
30	Hawker (acquired assets of wound-up Sopwith)
31	Hendy (Parnall t-over1935) | Parnall
32	London & Provincial
33	Man.Egtn
34	Moss Brothers
35	Martin Baker (last aircraft 1944)
36	Martin & Handasyde (renamed Martinsyde 1915)
37	Nieuport & Gnrl.
38	Parnall (last aircraft from 1935 Hendy takeover, in 1939)
39	Pemberton-Billing until 1916, then name changed to Supermarine
40	Percival
41	Philips & Powis, name changed to Miles 1943
42	Reid & Sigrist (no aircraft post-1945)
43	Rob/Redwing
44	Army Balloon/Royal A/cft. Factory
45	S.E. Saunders (Saunders-Roe from 1929)
46	Short Brothers
47	Siddeley-Deasy
48	Simmonds/Spartan
49	Slingsby
50	Sopwith (assets to Hawker)
51	Sunbeam
52	T'crft/Auster
53	Vickers (Vickers Armstrong 1927)
54	Westland (Petters Westland Aircraft works until 1935)
55	White & Th'pson/N.Th'pson

Summary:

The bar chart opposite records the main changes in the UK aircraft industry, between 1908 and the Second World War (1939–1945). Fifty-five companies were successfully formed (some "only just"), as illustrated in the bar chart and listed below. A further fifty-seven quite short-lived attempts to form partnerships/companies designing and building aircraft were made between 1908 and 1939, as described in items 1 to 79 on the pages immediately following the bar chart list.

UK Aircraft Design Organisations 1908 to 1945: Key to "Bar Chart" of British Aircraft Company Dates

1. Aeronautical Syndicate	1909–1912	Syndicate assets sold to H.Page
2. Admiralty – Air Dept. (incl. RNAS)	1910–1920	ceased aircraft design 1920
3. Aircraft Manufacturing Company (Airco)	1912–1920	sold to BSA (Airco found insolvent)
4. Air Navigation and Engineering	1919–1926	ceased aircraft design (closed 1927)
5. Airspeed	1931–1951	1940 de Havilland buy-out, name dropped 1951
6. Ruffy, Arnell & Baumann (Alliance 1918-on)	1914–1920	ceased aircraft design 1920
7. Armstrong Whitworth	1912–1963	into a division of Hawker Siddeley Aviation 1960
8. Austin Motor (aircraft)	1916–1920	ceased aircraft design 1920
9. A.V. Roe (Avro)	1909–1963	into a division of Hawker Siddeley Aviation 1960
10. Beardmore (aircraft)	1913–1928	ceased aircraft design 1928
11. Blackburn	1910–1963	into a division of Hawker Siddeley Aviation 1960
12. Boulton & Paul	1915–1961	ceased aircraft design, focused on hydraulics
13. Bristol & Colonial (reformed in 1929 as Bristol)	1910–1960	absorbed into British Aircraft Corporation 1960
14. British Aerial Transport	1917–1919	ceased trading
15. British Aircraft Company	1930–1937	renamed Kronfeld 1936, ceased trading 1937
16. British Marine/Folland	1936–1963	into a division of Hawker Siddeley Aviation 1960
17. Central	1916–1926	ceased trading 1926
18. Chilton	1937–1946	ceased trading 1946 (inoperative during WW2)
19. Cierva	1926–1948	reformed under Weir, taken over by Saunders-Roe
20. Comper/Heston	1929–1947	reformed as Heston 1934, ceased aircraft design 1945
21. Cunliffe-Owen	1937–1947	ceased trading
22. de Havilland (started by acquiring Airco assets)	1920–1963	into a division of Hawker Siddeley Aviation 1960
23. English Electric (design dept. closed 1926–1944)	1918–1960	absorbed into British Aircraft Corporation 1960
24. Fairey	1915–1960	aircraft business taken over by Westland 1960
25. Frederick Sage	1915–1918	ceased aircraft design 1918
26. General Aircraft	1931–1949	(merged with Blackburn 1949)
27. Gloster	1917–1963	into a division of Hawker Siddeley Aviation 1960

28. Grahame-White	1911–1920	ceased aircraft manufacturing (receiver, 1924)
29. Handley Page	1909–1970	acquired Miles assets 1946, ceased trading 1970
30. Hawker (acquired assets of wound-up Sopwith)	1920–1963	into a division of Hawker Siddeley Aviation 1960
31. Hendy	1928–1935	sold to George Parnall 1935, last aircraft 1939
32. London & Provincial	1913–1918	absorbed with Ruffy, Arnell & Baumann in Alliance
33. Mann Egerton (Engineering Co. 1899 to 1986)	1916–1918	WW1 only:1 new design + improved Short 184
34. Moss	1936–1940	two aircraft only, ceased design start of WW2
35. Martin Baker	1934	aircraft design turned to ejection seats after 1945
36. Martin & Handasyde (Martinsyde 1915)	1908–1922	1922 disastrous fire caused financial failure
37. Nieuport and General	1915–1920	closed with Alliance Aeroplane (item 32 above) 1920
38. Parnall (after 1935 merger with Hendy)	1916–1939	George Parnall 1921, no new a/c design post-1939
39. Phillips & Powis (name change to Miles 1943)	1932–1960	Miles bankrupt 1946. "Re-formed" as F.G.Miles 1948
40. Pemberton-Billing/ Supermarine	1913–1960	Supermarine 1916, bought by Vickers in 1928
41. Percival (later Hunting Percival)	1933–1960	absorbed into British Aircraft Corporation 1960
41. Reid & Sigrist (instrument makers)	1928–1945	started aircraft design 1938, ceased 1945
43. Robinson/Redwing	1930–1933	ceased aircraft design 1933
44. Army Balloon/Royal Aircraft factory	1908–1918	ceased aircraft design (Royal Aircraft Establishment)
45. S.E. Saunders/Saunders-Roe	1911–1960	aircraft business taken over by Westland 1960
46. Short Brothers	1908–1988	added joint venture Short. & Harland 1947
47. Siddeley-Deasy (engines 1912, aircraft 1917)	1917–1919	absorbed into Armstrong Whitworth 1919
48. Simmonds/Spartan (refinanced 1931)	1928–1935	assets bought by Saunders-Roe 1935
49. Slingsby	1931–1969	absorbed by Vickers Group 1969, later Marshalls
50. Sopwith Aircraft	1912–1920	wound up, assets acquired by Hawker 1920
51. Sunbeam (aircraft works)	1915–1918	WW1 only: 647 aircraft, only 1 own-design
52. Taylorcraft/Auster	1938–1960	merged with F.G. Miles to form Beagle 1960
53. Vickers (aircraft)	1911–1960	absorbed into British Aircraft Corporation 1960
54. Westland	1915–2000	joint merger into Augusta-Westland 2000
55. White & Thompson/ Norman Thompson 1915	1912–1919	ceased trading 1919 (Dr. White joined RAMC 1915)

Appendix 1 gives a brief history of the twenty-seven established British aircraft companies which had entered the Second World War (as shown on the bar chart) and continued to be involved in aircraft afterwards, plus Elliotts of Newbury, Hants & Sussex Aviation and Scottish Aviation, each of which built and/or repaired and maintained aircraft during the war and started designing them also, as war production ended.

Other (short-lived) Aircraft Design-and-Manufacture Partnerships etc. Between 1908 and 1940

From the earliest days, interest in designing, building and flying aircraft captured the imagination of enthusiasts in Britain, to the extent that many different individuals tried their hand at forming an aircraft company, in order to realise their own ideas. Sometimes, the design was "an idea" which required the help of an expert to detail the design, and/or to build the aircraft. The resulting companies and informal partnerships were often one design/one aircraft mayfly wonders. Others actually made and sold a few aircraft over a few years. In order to present a fuller picture of the early aircraft scene in Britain, the list below is mostly a collection of the attempts which failed to endure, over and above companies listed on the timeline chart. It also includes a few of the many more examples of "amateur enthusiasts only" with no overt attempt to create a business. It is worth remembering that most of those wishing to create a business started from simple aviation enthusiasm, in the same way as many of the better-known companies which had been involved in aircraft design and build, before, during and after the First World War:

1. In 1908, Naval Lieutenant John Wilfred Seddon and A.G. Hackett designed and built a tandem biplane (based on a paper model aeroplane), the Seddon Mayfly. The builders were Accles and Pollock, steel fabricators. The fuselage structure was based on intersecting (uncovered) hoops of steel. At the time, it was the largest aircraft in the world, had a fully loaded weight of 2,600lb, aiming at carrying five people plus a pilot. It had two 65HP engines. It failed to fly.
2. Harry George Ferguson (later, inventor of the modern agricultural tractor and founder of the company which became the Massey-Ferguson tractor company) and his brother designed a monoplane. They built it in their bicycle and car repair facility in Belfast. Harry flew it in 1909 at Hillsborough Park a few miles north of Belfast. He was the first Irishman to fly his own aircraft, in 1910, winning a £100 prize for being the first to fly in Ireland over two miles.
3. Wallis brothers Horace and Percival (respectively, father and uncle of Ken Wallis, of autogyro fame, see Appendix 12 – Civil Utility Aircraft) designed and built the Wallbro monoplane. This flew in 1910 (hopped) and was damaged on several occasions. Originally conceived to compete to be the first aircraft to win the prize for a British aircraft to cross the English Channel, the aircraft was damaged beyond repair when a storm blew down the shed in which it was kept and the brothers returned to the family motorcycle business.
4. The government ceased aeroplane activity at the Army Balloon Factory in 1909. This was re-instated at the end of 1911, with Geoffrey de Havilland as the new chief aircraft designer – the establishment changed to a civilian activity, with a name change to Royal Aircraft Factory in 1912. The employment of the previous chief designer, John William Dunne, was curtailed in 1909 and he became independent. His designs were then commissioned by the specifically-formed Blair Atholl Syndicate (see section 2.1) and constructed by Short Brothers at Eastchurch on the Isle of Sheppey (their first dedicated aircraft establishment). Before the start of the First World War, Dunne ended his participation and the syndicate was wound up.

5. Between 1909 and 1911, Frank Sowter Barnwell and his brother (Robert) Harold Barnwell designed and built three aircraft in Scotland, the first failing to fly but the second achieving the first powered flight of an aircraft in Scotland (crashing after a flight of 80 yards). The third won a prize in January 1911 for the first aircraft to fly over one mile in Scotland. Soon afterwards, Frank joined the new Bristol and Colonial Aeroplane Company, where (interrupted by a year in France in the RFC) he became chief designer. Frank Barnwell was responsible for the Bristol F.2B Fighter (see section 2.2) and the initiation of the Beaufighter major adaptation of his previous Blenheim/Beaufort (see section 2.7). Harold went on to become chief test pilot with Vickers (Aircraft Division) and was killed whilst testing the Vickers F.B.26 Vampire in 1917.

6. Howard Theophilus Wright designed and flew a biplane and a monoplane (built by the company founded by himself and his brother Warwick during 1909–1911). The business was taken over by Coventry Ordnance Works, who wanted to get into aviation. Howard and William Oke Manning briefly led the new enterprise and designed a biplane for the 1912 War Office competition. T.O.M. Sopwith was their test pilot. Coventry Ordnance Works soon merged with Dick Kerr, later included in the 1918 formation of the English Electric Company.

7. After brothers Howard and Warwick Wright split up in 1911, Howard went on to be associated with designing aircraft for shipbuilder J. Samuel White's aircraft company (Wight Aircraft, named for its location at Cowes, Isle of Wight), 1912–1919. J.S White built seventy-one aircraft with Howard T. Wright as chief designer and a further sixty-eight Short 184 float plane torpedo bombers under licence. J.S. White closed the aviation department after the end of the First World War.

8. In 1909, Christopher Pride built a tandem monoplane "with propellers front and rear", reportedly achieving a creditable flight of 2,928ft (891m). The flight terminated on hitting a tree.

9. The Scottish Aeroplane Syndicate was formed by Alan Boyle in 1909 and Howard T. Wright designed and constructed the Avis monoplane for the syndicate. Successfully flown in 1910, five examples were built.

10. With electrical engineer William Oke Manning and investor Horatio Barber, Howard T. Wright was also a founder member of the Aeronautical Syndicate Ltd. (ASL) between 1909 and 1912. Two aircraft were designed and built (in Battersea, adjacent to Short Brothers' balloon establishment) with the second achieving flight. The syndicate moved to Salisbury Plain, then back to London (Hendon). For a short while, the syndicate became a successful aircraft manufacturer, the first three designs having a canard wing configuration. Some eleven of the third design (the Valkerie) were built and sold (a significant number, for the time) but only one of the fourth design was constructed (a more conventional tractor biplane which successfully flew). The syndicate was wound up in 1912 and most of the assets were acquired by Handley Page. After joining the RN Reserve in 1914, Manning was posted to Phoenix Dynamo in Bradford as technical electrical engineering representative for the navy. Due to his aviation background, he was approached by the company and released from RN service in 1916 to become chief designer for a new aircraft part of the business. Phoenix Dynamo was later absorbed into the English Electric company, which pursued the newly-acquired aviation interest until closing the activity in 1926.

11. Robert Francis Macfie (American-born) came to England and designed and flew a Bleriot-style monoplane in 1909 (possibly two more aircraft also). Macfie went on to be involved in army tank development.

12. Between 1909 and 1913, the Sanders Aeroplane Company built at least two versions of a foreplane biplane (not untypical of the time) and advertised as suppliers of aircraft for naval and military purposes.

13. In 1910, Edwin Rowland Moon designed and built the Moonbeam I monoplane (only hopped) but, in 1911, the Moonbeam II monoplane flew successfully. Flying was from a field eventually war-requisitioned in 1917 and which now forms part of Southampton Airport. Moonbeam Ltd. was taken over by the Canute Airplane Co. in 1916 but there is no record of any successful aircraft design by that company.

14. Between 1910 and 1912, aviator Paul George Leon Jezzi designed and built two successful biplanes, the second of which could carry a passenger.

15. In 1910, Herbert Spencer designed, built and (after flight testing by French pilot Henri Pecquet) flew the Spencer-Stirling biplane at Brooklands. This aircraft is sometimes referred to as a Spencer-Farman, as it was similar in design to Frenchman Henri Farman's aircraft. Flown at various public displays for over one year, the aircraft crashed in early 1912 and was not rebuilt.

16. Engine manufacturer J.A. Prestwich (JAP) derived an aircraft from the Bleriot monoplane design for H.J. Harding, who was a motorcycle racer and agent for JAP engines in France. The JAP-Harding monoplane was the result. This had its first flight on 10 April 1910 and is now in The Science Museum, London.

17. Cecil Compton Paterson designed a biplane and had it built for him by Liverpool Motor Company, first flight being in 1910. He designed an improvement, both versions flew successfully.

18. Originally founded in 1829 in London as boat builders, Luke and Co. moved to Hamble, near Southampton in 1895. They became aircraft constructors by building an aircraft for T.O.M. Sopwith in 1910 (Sopwith amphibious biplane, BAT Boat type 1). They built a floatplane in 1913, to a design of F. Murphy, shown unfinished at the Olympia exhibition centre in London in May 1914. Later finished, it was tested by Gordon England but was not a success. Luke and Co. went on to build parts of more aircraft, one being the second Sopwith BAT Boat (a flying boat), which was subsequently assembled at the Sopwith Factory in Kingston-on-Thames and delivered to the Royal Navy in 1914, before the start of the First World War.

19. W.P. Thompson persuaded Handley Page to design and build a biplane aircraft incorporating ideas of his own. Given the Handley Page Type B designation, Handley Page disowned the aircraft during (unsatisfactory) trials. Thompson's company Planes Limited completed the aircraft and went on to design and build the Mersey monoplane, which first flew in 1911. The designers bought the monoplane and set up the Mersey Aeroplane Company. The monoplane crashed in 1912, was rebuilt but it crashed again in 1913, killing one of the two designer-owners of the new company.

20. John Gaunt designed and built two unsuccessful biplanes (1910 and 1911) but his third attempt was successful. A crash in 1912 destroyed the aircraft.

21. In 1911, the British Deperdussin Aeroplane Syndicate Ltd. was established in Britain, with a sales office in London and a flying school at Brooklands. The aircraft used were the products of the French company *Société Pour L'Aviation et ses Derives* (SPAD). To facilitate this, the British Deperdussin Aeroplane Co. Ltd. was established in 1912 to produce the aircraft in Britain. Dutch aircraft designer Fredereick Koolhoven was moved from the French parent to take charge in Britain in 1912, where the monoplane Seagull seaplane aircraft design was created in response to a British government requirement for a reconnaissance aircraft. The single example constructed and flown in January 1913 demonstrated poor performance and was not accepted for service. The Deperdussin parent company founder Armand Deperdussin was charged with fraud in 1913 and subsequently incarcerated, all causing the parent company to

enter administration. It was refinanced by a consortium headed by the celebrated Louis Bleriot, Société Provisoire des Aéroplanes Deperdussin (preserving the SPAD acronym). After failure of the wing structure of two monoplanes in RFC service, with fatal consequences (a Bristol Coanda, eventually ascribed to detachment of a bracing wire, and a French-built Deperdussin monoplane) the RFC banned all use of monoplanes for a while. This all caused British Deperdussin to close down. Koolhoven soon moved on to Armstrong Whitworth (aircraft division), as chief designer, later working for the short-lived British Aerial Transport aircraft company until they ceased trading in 1919 (Koolhaven returned to the Netherlands).

22. Lakes Flying Company added floats to three Avro-built land planes in 1911–12, to produce Lakes "Water Bird", "Water Hen" and "Sea Bird" aircraft, to give visitors to Lake Windermere "flights round the lake". E.W. Wakefield (Lakes proprietor) designed floats, had them built and sent to be added by Avro. The Lakes Flying Company was bought by Northern Aircraft Company in 1914 and operated as a flying school.

23. Richard Leonard Howard Flanders, an assistant to A.V. Roe, formed a company and designed and built the monoplanes Flanders F.2 in 1911, a two-seater/larger wing version the F.3 in 1912 and, also in 1912, four of the F.4 version of the F.3 for the RFC. Due to accidents with two other monoplane designs, the RFC soon barred the use of monoplanes and scrapped them. Howard Flanders also built the Flanders B.2 biplane, bought by the Admiralty in 1914. Following a serious motorcycle accident in 1913, Flanders' company went bankrupt. In August 1914 he joined Vickers as chief designer, designing the E.F.B.7 and the F.B.11.

24. In 1911, designer Eric Gordon England left Bristol and Colonial Aircraft and joined up with aviator James Radley to build the Radley-England Waterplane, a racing biplane with floats large enough to accommodate passengers. After a successful first flight in 1913 it was later damaged by running over a buoy during landing. Rebuilt and replacing the three 50 HP engines with a 150 HP single engine, it was entered in the 1913 circuit of Britain seaplane race but engine trouble prevented participation. Gordon England went on to be factory manager for the (short-lived) Frederick Sage aircraft company.

25. Between 1911 and 1914, Cedric Lee and George Tilghman Richards developed several "annular" wing and circular wing biplanes and monoplanes (annular = biplane with top wing joined to bottom wing by continuing top wing "bent in a curve at each tip to join bottom wing (which formed the annulus), and circular = complete circle around pilot, no separate tailplane). Experiments with gliders had a little success but the idea soon died out. Lee joined the RNVR in the First World War and was subsequently killed in action. Richards was commissioned in the RNAS but was allowed to resign in 1916 to design aircraft for Beardmore. As the war ended, he moved to Martinsyde as general manager, who were changing their business to motor cycle manufacturing as the post-war aircraft market collapsed.

26. George Miller Dyott designed his own monoplane aircraft, had it made and flew it in 1913.

27. In 1913, ex-Royal Aircraft Factory designers E.W. Copeland Perry and F.P. Hyde created Perry, Beadle & Co. and designed and built the Perry Beadle T.1 single engined biplane, first flown in 1913. As a modified T.1 (a more powerful engine), the T.2 flew in 1914. Requisitioned by the RNAS, it was found to be impractical and was broken up in 1915. The company partners split in 1914 but the business carried on as Perry Aviation for a short while. On 16 August 1914, Perry was killed in a flying accident in France, the first British officer to be killed on active service in the First World War.

28. In 1913, with the help of British investor-directors, Australian-born of Chinese parents Tsoe K. Wong founded his company T.K. Wong Ltd., based in Shoreham, Sussex, to design and build aircraft. His ultimate intention was to be first into China to offer aircraft for sale. The Tong-Mei single seat tractor biplane was built and tested in 1913 and soon modified into a two-seater with an increased-power engine. As an interim step into the Far East, the aircraft was dismantled and sent to Kuala Lumpur on the Malaysian peninsula. After successful reassembly and a couple of test flights, he demonstrated the aircraft on 14 July 1914. Unfortunately, a bad landing resulted in repairs being necessary. During the next demonstration on 18 July, the engine stopped in flight and the resulting crash caused sufficient damage to make it impossible for repairs to be effected from local resources. Lack of funds and the looming world war seems to have prevented further progress.

29. Originally founded by F. Bernard Fowler in 1909 as a flying school, the Eastbourne Aviation Company designed and built four aircraft from 1913: a monoplane, a civil (the Hunt) biplane to the order of a pupil, a second biplane offered for sale to the government, and a floatplane. The outbreak of the 1914–18 war caused further design activity to be curtailed, to concentrate on pilot training, and the business ceased activity a few years after the end of that war.

30. In 1911, schoolboy Reginald F. Mann formed a company with his teacher Robert T. Grimmer, initially as model aircraft suppliers. At the outbreak of war they designed a prototype two-seat fighter aircraft. First flight was on 15 February 1915, which demonstrated inadequate performance. After fitting a more powerful engine and other improvements, the aircraft finally crashed and was damaged beyond repair.

31. The London and Provincial Aviation Company was established in 1913 as a flying school at Stag Lane (later, the first home of de Havilland) and built French Caudron aircraft for training. In 1916 the company produced a two-seat biplane with a square-section fuselage in plywood with two separate cockpits, known as the "Fuselage" biplane and designed by A. Fletcher (previously at Martinsyde). Only one set of flying controls were fitted but the design was revised to create a dual-control version in an enlarged single cockpit. This was deemed to over-weaken the fuselage and the aircraft was refused a Certificate of Airworthiness. The business closed in 1920.

32. In 1913 the Commercial Aeroplane Wing Syndicate took over the previous attempts of the Varioplane Company to exploit the Alula wing concept. This was patented by Dutchman A.A. Holle. This implemented a wing design with an interior mechanism to vary camber in-flight, (rather than use trailing edge devices) and it had a curved leading edge planform. The wing was anticipated to have high lift but only useable at low speeds. Mounting the wing high above the fuselage of a DH.6 biplane (to place it out of the propeller slipstream) and fitting a 200HP engine, an experimental aircraft was created. The construction was carried out by Blackburn Aeroplane and first flight was in January 1921. The intended application was the ability to carry a four-ton load. After the tests by Blackburn, to investigate higher speeds a version of the wing was mounted on the fuselage of the record-breaking (161mph) Martinsyde Semiquaver biplane, which used a 300HP engine. Flight was achieved but nothing commercial came of the venture.

33. In 1917, the Wright Forge & Engineering company built and offered for sale a two-seat biplane designed by W. Westwood.

34. Robey & Co Ltd. (originally founded before 1849) were an engineering company required to build aircraft under licence for the RNAS during the First World War. In 1916 they built the Robey-Peters biplane with a pilot and two gunners sitting in "canoe nacelles" (one each on the top of port and starboard upper wings, with

the Admiralty-specified recoilless Davis machine gun). The pilot was in the rear fuselage just in front of the fin, with a very poor view forward! J.A Peters was the aircraft designer. The Robey-Peters Gun Carrier aircraft had its first flight in May 1917 from Bracebridge Heath. It crashed and was not repaired and a second machine under construction was not completed.

35. Chessborough J.H. Mackenzie-Kennedy went to Russia in 1908 at 18-years-old. He became involved in aircraft design in Russia, working with Igor Sikorsky. Back in the UK when the First World War started, he talked with the War Office, then formed Kennedy Aeronautic Company with three others, to design the "Giant" (142ft span bomber of 19,000lb empty weight, 4x 200HP engines), assembled in a field in Hendon (too big for any hangar). It was the only completed Kennedy aircraft, built by Fairey and The Gramophone Company – "only hopped, in 1917".

36. In 1917, the Siddeley Deasy motor company (which had subcontract-built Royal Aircraft Factory RE.8 aircraft) designed and built a new reconnaissance aircraft. With the end of the First World War, no orders beyond the initial three aircraft materialised and aircraft activity ceased (but see also Armstrong Whitworth Aircraft of the Hawker Siddeley group of companies, noted earlier, including the absorbed Siddeley-Deasy motor company within Armstrong Siddeley Motors aircraft and motor car engines).

37. In 1917, F.C. Nestler Ltd. a London-based aircraft hangar builder and builder of aircraft to Admiralty designs, established a design facility under Frenchman Monsieur E. Boudot. The Nestler Scout fighter biplane was designed and built as a PV. First flying January 1917, it crashed in March 1917 due to wing failure in turning flight. No more aircraft were developed by Nestler.

38. Walter George Tarrant, an established house builder and pre-fabricated wooden hut supplier to the army, built the Trabor bomber (designed by Walter Barling). This was a 37ft 3in high six-engined triplane with a 131ft span and an empty weight of 24,750lb (11¼ tonnes). In May 1919, it crashed and killed the two pilots at the first attempt to take off (never left the ground).

39. In 1920, George Handasyde left Martinsyde (partnership he formed with Helmut Paul Martin in 1908) to start his own aircraft company Handasyde, which, after designing a glider and a motor glider, ceased trading in 1923. Sydney Camm (much later, chief designer at Hawker) worked for George Handasyde as a draughtsman, having started with Martinsyde as a qualified carpenter interested in aircraft.

40. In 1921, F.W. Lowe designed and built the Marlburian monoplane.

41. In 1923, the RAE Aero club designed and built the Zephyr light aircraft competition aircraft. After trials it was "cannibalised" into a monoplane (Hurricane, not the Hawker variety).

42. In 1924, John Leeming, Tom Pine and Clement Wood (founder members of the Lancashire Aero Club) designed and built a glider from surplus parts of the Avro 504 biplane.

43. In 1924, G.T.R Hill and his wife built and flew his Pterodactyl tailless swept wing glider design, seeking to improve stall-resistance (aimed at pilot training). Hill did not seek to start his own company but the Air Ministry sponsored Westland for ten years to create his powered designs, culminating in a two-crew powered sesquiplane (biplane with lower wing of shorter span than the upper) as a fighter. The Mk.V was assessed at RAE as "OK, but not as good as the types emerging" (such as the latest Hart variants and its Gloster Gladiator replacement). Hill had joined Handley Page after the First World War, as test pilot and aerodynamicist. Subsequently, he became a Professor at the University of London and, after the Second World War, he helped Shorts in the design of the SB.1 and SB.4 tailless swept wing aircraft.

44. Based on the ideas of N. Woyevdosky, the Air Ministry asked Westland to build the Dreadnought mailplane/airliner flying wing experimental aircraft. Of all-metal construction, it crashed on its first flight, control being lost after reaching 100ft.

45. In 1925, the self-taught Frederick George Miles, son of a laundryman, designed and built his "Gnat" (never flew), followed in 1929 by an aerobatic adaptation of the Avro Baby called the Martlet (designed by F.G. Miles and brother George). Six built, under the company name "Southern Aircraft Ltd", established in 1928.

   F.G. Miles married divorcee Maxine Freeman Thomas (known as Blossom) with whom he designed the Miles M.1, built by George Parnall & Co. He then engaged in designing a light aircraft for Phillips & Powis at Woodley Reading, eventually taking over and renaming the company as Miles Aircraft in 1943.

46. In 1928, Harold Boultbee, a former Handley Page designer, established the Civilian Aircraft Company with a factory at Hedon (near Kingston-upon-Hull). The company produced one design, the two-seat civilian cabin monoplane Coupé. Only six aircraft were built and the company ceased trading in 1933.

47. In 1928 the Desoutter Aircraft Company was founded by well-known English-born aviator (André) Marcel Desoutter. He had had one leg amputated after an air accident in 1913, but returned to flying with a duraluminium prosthetic from a company he founded in 1914, simultaneously forming the Desoutter pneumatic tools company (still operating but now based in France). His aircraft company was licenced to produce aircraft based on the designs of the Dutch Koolhoven range, particularly the three-seater F.K.41 monoplane. Desoutter engaged G.H. Handasyde (ex-Martinsyde and ex-Handasyde aircraft companies) as works manager. Slightly modified after the first six aircraft were completed, the production aircraft became known as the Dessouter, a total of forty-one being produced. The initial Desoutter was later known as the Desoutter Mk.1 when a re-engined and improved version was created as the Mk.2. Six basic F.K.41s and forty-one Desoutters were built (twenty-eight Mk.1 and thirteen Mk.2). The business folded in 1932 after the main customer (National Flying Services) went into liquidation.

48. In 1929, William Lancelot Manuel, originally a Vickers employee and subsequently a corporal in the RAF, designed and built a biplane glider for the RAF gliding club at his station. He left the RAF in 1933 and went on to design and build more gliders (monoplanes) from a workshop in Dunstable, Bedfordshire, selling them and also copies of the designs for self-build, at £5 each. He later co-founded Luton Aircraft Ltd. at Barton-le-Clay (see item 65 below).

49. In 1929 ABC Motors (makers of cars, motorcycles and aircraft engines) had the ABC Robin designed (by A.A. Fletcher) to use one of the engines which ABC manufactured. One example built, no sales, scrapped in 1932.

50. In 1930, H.J. Hinkler (Australian Bert Hinkler, the Avro test pilot and record-breaking pilot) designed and built the Hinkler Ibis high-wing tractor-pusher two-engined monoplane, (wing designed by Basil Henderson, founder of the Hendy Aircraft company). The aircraft was stored in Hinkler's garden in Britain, found semi-derelict and scrapped in 1959.

51. In 1930, brothers R.F.T and R.J.T. Granger designed and built one Granger Archaeopteryx, with the intention of learning to fly. This was inspired by the Westland-Hill Pterodactyl series (see item 43 above), which were intended to be a stall and spin-resistant aircraft. The Archaeopteryx was the same design configuration as the Pterodactyl (tailless and swept wing) except that it had a tractor instead of a pusher propeller.

52. In 1930, K.N. Pearson (a Hawker aircraft designer) designed the D.W.2 biplane for Dudley Watt, intended as a competitor to the DH.60 Moth family of aircraft. Dudley Watt flew it for a few months, after which it was dismantled.

53. In 1930, Leslie Everett Baynes and F.W.J. Grant founded Brant Aircraft Ltd. to produce an aircraft using a Sidarblen (patent) diesel engine. Nothing came of this but Baynes designed his Scud glider, built at the Brant factory. In 1931 Baynes joined up with Edward Abbott to form Abbott-Baynes Sailplanes Ltd to build Scud gliders for sale. By 1935 and trading as Abbott-Baynes Aircraft Ltd, the company designed a glider with a retractable engine (effectively a glider with powered take-off capability) for Sir John Carden of Carden Aero Engines Ltd. Following Carden's death in an air accident, Baynes formed Carden-Baynes Aircraft at Heston in 1936. Out of this came the Carden-Baynes Bee aircraft, but the company failed in 1937. A venture joining Carden-Baynes to Kay Gyroplanes (see item 47) was promoted by Lord James Weir (chairman of the family company G & J Weir, supporters of Cierva Autogyro interests (see section 4.9) and ex-President of the Air Council) this caused the creation of Scottish Aircraft Construction Ltd. with the rights to both the Bee and the Kay Gyroplane. Nothing came of this. Baynes had carried on with the design of the B.4 three-seater light aircraft and formed Baynes Aircraft Ltd. in November 1937, but the imminent Second World War prevented development. In 1939 Baynes joined Alan Muntz & Co. as chief designer in the Air Division. In 1940, Baynes, along with Richard Becker and Viv Billings, was responsible for the Baynes Carrier Wing, known colloquially as the Bat. The 100ft wingspan flying wing was intended to fly a tank to the forward battlefield as a towed glider (automatically detachable wing on landing). A piloted one-third scale model was approved by the Air Ministry (built by Slingsby Sailplanes) and flight trials in August 1943 proved the practicality of the project. However, it was overtaken by the General Aviation Hamilcar tank-carrying towed glider and a full scale trial was not pursued. After the war, Baynes developed a special research aircraft design in collaboration with Robert Talbot Youngman of Fairey aviation, using large elements of the Percival Proctor but adding Youngman's novel high lift slotted wing flap system. This aircraft was built by the Heston aircraft company and first flight was in February 1948. Thereafter, Baynes investigated various aeronautical subjects, including swept wing aerodynamics and supersonic flight and he set up a new subsidiary of Alan Muntz – Baynes Aircraft Interiors Ltd. A whole series of new aircraft companies (five in total) but really different versions of "Baynes Ltd."

54. During 1930–31, Arthur Leighton Angus designed, built and flew his Angus Aquila lightweight single seat monoplane. In March 1931 Arthur Angus was killed when the aircraft crashed.

55. In 1931, the RAE Aero club designed and built their third (and last) aircraft, the Scarab, a monoplane which had a DH.53 Hummingbird wing, with new (longer) fuselage and a Bristol Cherub III 1,228cc engine (the 1923 DH.53 had a Douglas 750cc motorcycle engine).

56. In 1931, Arthur Cecil Thornton (an ex-Blackburn aircraft designer) formed Arrow Aircraft in Leeds. Arrow designed and built two versions of the aerobatic Arrow Active. One was a differently-engined Arrow Active, intended to interest the RAF but ended as a sports aircraft (one still on UK register, after being rebuilt/restored in 1958).

57. In 1931, Norman Adrian de Bruyne established the Cambridge Aeroplane Construction Company, basing his ideas on using lightweight plywood monocoque bonded structures. The Snark four-seat cabin monoplane was designed as a technology demonstrator and was successfully flown in 1934, the same year the company name was changed to Aero Research. The Snark was followed by the single-seat monoplane Ladybird, sold prior to completion to a Dutch resident in England. First flight was in 1938. De Bruyne business success, however, came from development of the Redux metal-to-metal bonding process used for aircraft and

other applications, and the later development of the two-part epoxy resin adhesive Araldite (see section 9.1). This business was eventually absorbed by Ciba-Giegy.

58. In 1932, Austrian Raoul Hafner gave up his job in Austria and, financed by millionaire Jack A. Coates, brought his Revoplane R2 helicopter to Heston, with ambitions to produce a practical helicopter (the Hafner R1 had not been a success but the R2 managed a successful hover, a few inches above the ground). He met Juan de la Cierva and decided to concentrate on autogyros, forming his own company ARIII Construction (Hafner Gyroplane) Co. to build his third machine. Flight success was mixed but the initial version of the modern helicopter rotor hub, with cyclic and collective rotor pitch control, was developed by Hafner on the ARIII. There was no further progress. Hafner then worked for Pobjoy, makers of small aircraft engines and, after a short period of internment during the Second World War, he worked on government projects before becoming founder technical leader of the Bristol Helicopter Division in 1944 (see section 5.9).

59. In 1933, William Shackleton (an aircraft designer ex-Beardmore) set up a partnership with fellow-Australian Lee Murray. They designed and built one example of the Shackleton-Murray SM.1, a high wing pusher monoplane.

60. In 1933, British Klemm Aeroplane Co. was founded to licence-build the German Klemm L.25 three-seat light aircraft, renamed as BK.Swallow. A successful six-seat cabin re-engined adaptation of the L.25 flew one year later, the BK.Eagle designed by G.H Handasyde (ex-Martinsyde). The company changed its name to British Aircraft Manufacturing Co. in 1935 (not to be confused with the British Aircraft Company founded in 1930 by C.H. Lowe-Wylde, see bar chart). The last aircraft produced was completed in 1936.

61. In 1934, David Kay designed and built an autogyro (Kay Gyroplane). Only one reached flight standard, first flying in 1935.

62. German immigrants Frederick P. Zander & Alfred R. Weyl started Dart Aircraft Limited in 1935 (gliders, later powered aircraft), for private owners. Both founders were interned on the Isle of Wight after the start of the Second World War. After the war, Zander and H.E Bolton started Hawkridge "self-build glider company", 1946–1952.

63. In 1935, Pobjoy Airmotors (founded in 1928 by Douglas Pobjoy) decided to enter aircraft design with the Pobjoy Pirate (competing with de Havilland Leopard Moth). One aircraft built, Pobjoy taken over by nearby Shorts in Rochester in 1935 or 1936.

64. In 1935, Mervyn Chadwick and Raymond Gordon came together to develop low powered low cost single-seat light aircraft. The Belgian low-winged cantilever monoplane Tipsy Moth inspired the design of their Gordon Dove, built by their company Premier Aircraft Constructions Ltd., formed in 1936. After building three aircraft, the company ceased trading.

65. In 1936, Luton Aircraft was established at Barton-le-Clay, Bedfordshire (later moved to Gerrards Cross, Buckinghamshire). After the L.A.1 Buzzard, one L.A.2 ultralight built (rebuilt after trials into the L.A.3 Minor aircraft). The company built one L.A.3 Minor (redesigned as the L.A.4 Minor home-build design) of which twenty-nine more were built. The single L.A.5 Major became the L.A.5A developed by the original designer C.H. Latimer-Needham, in his new company Phoenix Aircraft (founded 1958), several of which were sold in kit and plans form.

66. In 1936, R.C. Christopheros and B.V. Leak formed Chrislea Aviation to build their LC.1 low-wing cabin monoplane. Company revived after the war to design and build one Chrislea Ace four-seat high-wing cabin monoplane and thirty-two Super Ace and Skyjeep production versions, eleven of which were either never flown (six) or never completed (five). Assets taken over and the eleven aircraft scrapped, in 1952.

67. In 1936, the Deekay Aircraft Corporation was established at Broxbourne, Hertfordshire, building the Deekay Knight cabin monoplane, which had a novel stressed skin wing construction in wood. The intention was to convert the design to use plastic material but the company became more involved with plastic technology. The business was eventually absorbed by Fairey Aviation.

68. In 1936, Australian Geoffrey N. Wikner formed Foster Wikner Aircraft with partners V. Foster and J.F Lusty. One design, the Foster Wikner Wicko, was developed and ten aircraft built (impressed into RAF service in the Second World War, they were named the "Warferry"). After the Second World War Geoffrey Wickner returned to Australia.

69. In 1936, Carl K. Chronander and James I. Waddington formed a partnership to design and build aircraft, based at Slough, Berkshire. They designed and built the C.W. Cygnet Minor, powered by a Blackburn Cirrus Minor engine. This was the first British all-metal stressed skin light aircraft to be built and flown in Britain. The design was revised for the Kings Cup race by incorporating the more powerful Cirrus Major. The design rights were sold to General Aircraft when a third project, the C.W. Swan, caused the C.W. Aircraft business to become insolvent (General Aircraft modified the Cygnet design from tailwheel to nosewheel and built ten aircraft). Chronander and Waddington then formed an engineering company Chronander Waddington Aircraft Ltd., as suppliers to the aircraft industry (ceased trading 1949).

70. In 1936, Edmund Hordern collaborated with the Duke of Richmond in designing the Autoplane low-wing monoplane and had one built by the aircraft manufacturer Heston Aircraft. The intention to manufacture more never came to fruition.

71. Between 1936 and 1939 F. Hills and Sons, a long-established wood-working company, built twenty-eight of the Czech Praga two-seat high wing monoplane under licence. This had a Czech Praga engine, licence-built in England by Jowett cars. The company also built the Hillson Pennine two-seat high wing monoplane designed by Norman Sykes, with the same engine. This had a single flight in 1937, demonstrated poor control characteristics and was dismantled. The company built one more aircraft, the faster more powerful Hillson Helvellyn mid-wing tandem open cockpit monoplane, which flew in 1939. The imminent war caused the activity to cease, although the Helvellyn continued in use as a company aircraft from the Barton (Manchester) airfield.

72. In 1937, J.R. Currie designed the Currie Wot home-build aerobatic biplane and two were built by Cinque Ports Aviation, Lympne, Kent (called the Wot after Currie became fed-up of being asked "What is it?").

73. In 1937, Errol Spencer Shapely designed and built two Shapely Kittiwake monoplanes. One was dismantled in 1938 and the other crashed in 1946.

74. From 1937, Percival Willoughby established his ideas of a flying wing airliner. After extensive wind tunnel model testing in both the UK and the USA, in 1939, the Willoughby Delta Company built the Delta 8 (sometimes known as the Delta F) as a scale twin-engined "experimental proof of concept" pre-prototype of a planned Delta 9 trimotor twin-boom flying wing thirty-six-passenger airliner. First flying in March 1939, Delta 8 crashed in July the same year (not attributed to the novel configuration), killing the pilot and the designer/owner. Nothing more was heard of the project.

75. In 1938, Morris Barley Airpin, a Fairey Aviation draughtsman, established M.B. Airpin & Co. to build and test his earlier private design of the A-1. This was an unconventional twin-boom pusher light aircraft, intended as a possible contender for a new Air Observation Post (AOP) aircraft for the army. First flight was on 7 May 1938. The company was renamed as the Airpin Aircraft Manufacturing

Company on 26 May 1939 but the onset of the Second World War in September 1939 prevented progress.

76. In 1938, E.T. Watkinson and C.W. Taylor formed the Taylor Watkinson Aircraft Company. They designed and built one example of the Watkinson Dingbat, an ultralight monoplane.

77. In 1938, Egyptian S. Helmy designed and built his thee-engined Aerogypt low wing four-seat monoplane. Modified three times, the third time in 1939 from three-engined to two engined, as Aerogypt IV.

78. In 1939, sports car designer/driver Donald Marendez established International Aircraft & Engineering. Without acknowledging the major contribution by G.N. Wickner (see item 68 above), he claimed to design and build one Marendez monoplane two-seat training aircraft, at premises in Barton-le-Clay, Bedfordshire. After his company was placed in receivership, he formed Marendaz Aircraft Ltd. and constructed a two-seat open cockpit monoplane, first flown in 1939.

79. In August 1939, Captain Gerald Fane established the Comper Fane Aircraft Company Ltd. incorporating the name of his former partner Nicholas Comper, who died in June 1939. (Nicholas Comper was founder of Comper aircraft in 1929, but this had been reorganised as Heston aircraft in 1934.) The Comper Fane name soon changed to C. F. Aviation and subsequently to Fane Aircraft. In a response to Air Ministry specification F.1/40 for an Air Observation Post aircraft, the Fane 1/40 aircraft was a rework and adaptation of the Comper Scamp design. First flight was in 1941 but no order was forthcoming and no further aircraft were produced. In 1944 the company became Fane Engineering Designs Ltd.

Additionally, "aeronautical experimenters" created and made/had-made-for-them individually designed aircraft. A few aircraft were designed and built by flying clubs, and by organisations such as RAF Cranwell College and the de Havilland Technical School, as student design-and-build projects.

Excluding items 2, 3, 5, 8, 14, 15, 16, 17, 25, 26, 40, 41, 42, 43, 44, 50, 51, 54 and 55 (no new company formed or intended), avoiding items 6, 10 and 36 as already on the bar chart and counting item 53 as "one", the total number of private companies and partnerships above added fifty-nine organised attempts to design and build aircraft to the commercially (mostly) more successful fifty-five companies shown in the bar chart. From 1908 up until 1939, this made a grand total of 112 different attempts at commercial ventures (in just thirty-two years) started in Britain to design and build aircraft. Only a quarter of the companies and partnerships survived as separate companies to participate in the industry effort during the Second World War. A half (thirteen) of these survivors had previously participated in the British First World War aircraft industry effort.

Chapter 3

The Second World War, 1939 to 1945

3.1 British Military Aircraft and Developments During the Second World War

From 1935, new British military aircraft designs were almost exclusively of monoplane wing configuration. This departure from the era of biplanes was facilitated by the wider use of new or improved structural materials and design techniques. Engines continued to become more powerful and fuel efficient. The general level of aircraft equipment technology was increasingly able to perform new functions as well as existing functions, accurately/efficiently/reliably and with lighter and less bulky equipment. More importantly, new and longer-range aircraft missions previously undreamt of could be planned. "More payload, heavier armament/more ammunition, flying faster, higher, further". Bigger bombs, more powerful guns, more accurate navigation but, of course, each new aircraft type was costing more time and money to produce than those of the wooden (or even metal) biplane era.

Table 3.1 below contains data on some of the well-known aircraft types designed and made by a British company. For each company, only one example is listed which was produced in the years 1934–1945 and served in the Second World War. The sample data in the table is for a mixture of "first and mid-production examples". As the war progressed, increased engine power and improved overall performance was developed.

Appendix 9 includes all two hundred and eighty-one UK military and civil aircraft types which first flew during the years 1930–39 (many did not reach production status). Excluding general and utility aircraft, sixty-two new military types were specified and flown between the start of 1930 and the end of 1934. Sixty-eight types were specified and flown afterwards, up until the outbreak of war in 1939. Appendix 10 lists the one hundred and six types of all kinds (civil and military) which first flew 1940–49, a 63 per cent reduction from the 1930s, with a similar reduction in total numbers of individual aircraft. This is a distorted view of actual production in each decade, given that new types designed in the 1930s were produced in large numbers after 1940, during the 1939–45 war.

Technical developments covered all kinds of inventive war equipment which became fundamental to the war effort, once developed into a service-ready standard. Prominent aviation examples immediately prior to the war were the Spitfire and Hurricane Battle-of-Britain fighter squadrons, controlled by the development of an effective air-defence total system which included radar coverage of airspace between Britain and mainland Europe and the approaches to UK Western (Atlantic Ocean shipping) sea ports.

Notable New British Aircraft Developed During the Second World War
De Havilland Mosquito: A radical concept resisted by the RAF for several years was the "fast, light bomber without defensive armament", able to outrun enemy fighters due to low weight and low drag (no gun turrets, consequently no gunners). Partly as a result of the successful de Havilland DH.88 Comet Racer prize-winning aircraft of 1934, from 1938 onwards Geoffrey de Havilland illustrated more than one unarmed bomber design outline to the RAF. He was asked to concentrate his company's aircraft manufacturing efforts on the DH.82 Tiger Moth and Airspeed Oxford training aircraft and supplying parts of other manufacturer's designs. In January 1940, de

Table 3.1: Some of the most well known UK designed aircraft of the Second World War (in service 1935–45)

Company	Aircraft	A'cft class	First Flt.	Number built (total)	Crew	Engine	Total T-Off HP/Thrust (all engines)	T-Off weight (max. lb)	Max Speed (mph)	Service Altitude Ceiling (ft.)
C = Communications B = Bomber F= Fighter T = Trainer R = Reconnaissance										
PROPELLER-DRIVEN (Total Engine HP)										
Airspeed	Oxford	TC	1937	8,856	3	2	700	7,500	192	23,550
Auster	Taylorcraft	TC	1940	1,630	3	1	130	1,850	130	-
Armst'ng-W'w'th	Whitley	B	1936	1,814	5	2	2,290	33,500	230	26,000
Avro	Lancaster	B	1941	7,377	7	4	5,120	68,000	282	21,400
Blackburn	Botha (RN)	BR	1938	580	4	2	1,860	18,450	249	17,500
Boulton Paul	Defiant	F	1937	1,064	2	1	1,030	8,600	304	31,000
Bristol	Beaufighter	FB	1939	5,928	2	2	3,200	25,400	320	19,000
Hawker	Hurricane	F	1935	14,583	1	1	1,185	8,710	340	36,000
de Havilland	Mosquito	B	1940	7,781	2	2	2,960	18,649	366	29,000
Fairey	Swordfish (RN)	BR	1934	2,391	2/3	1	690	7,580	143	16,500
Gloster	Gladiator	F	1934	747	1	1	830	4,594	253	32,800
Handley Page	Halifax	B	1939	6,176	7	4	6,460	65,000	282	24,000
Miles	Magister	T	1937	1,303	2	1	130	1,845	142	18,000
Saunders-Roe	Saro designs did not feature much in the Second World War but the company produced Supermarine Walrus and Sea Otter									
Slingsby	T7 (glider)	T	1935	376	2	N/A	N/A	513	-	-
Short Brothers	Stirling	B	1939	2,371	7	4	5,500	70,000	282	16,500
Supermarine	Spitfire	F	1936	20,351	1	1	1,470	6,700	370	36,500
Vickers	Wellington	B	1935	11,461	6	2	2,100	28,500	235	18,000
Westland	Lysander	C	1936	1,786	1/2	1	820	6,330	212	21,500
JET POWERED (Total Engine Thrust lb.)										
Gloster – post Second World War Mk.8	Meteor F.1*	F	1943	244*	1	2	3,200*	11,925*	446*	43,000
	Meteor F.8	F	1949	see below	1	2	7,400	15,700	600	43,000
de Havilland	Vampire	F	1943	6* (3,268)	1	1	2,700*	10,494	548*	42,800

* Only 244 of the F.1 Meteors served in the war. A total of 3,947 Meteors in all variants were eventually produced between 1943 and 1955. A Mk. 4 version established a new jet aircraft world speed record in 1946, achieving 616mph. The Vampire flew in 1943 but it did not reach service until 1946, partly due to engine availability and partly due to de Havilland being instructed to concentrate on their overcrowded other wartime production commitments. Approximately six production Vampire aircraft were complete by May 1945, out of an eventual total of 3,268.

Havilland's persistent badgering, allied to presentation of a secretly prepared twin Merlin-engined design, finally convinced the RAF to support a single prototype bomber-reconnaissance version of the "DH.98". The RAF insisted that there should be provision for mounting defensive armament (which would be ignored by de Havilland!). Target performance was a calculated speed of 397mph at 23,700ft, a ceiling of 32,100ft, a range

DH.98 Mosquito. (*Author's collection*)

of 1,480 miles at 24,900ft, and a capability of eventually carrying a 1,000lb bombload. With de Havilland Chief Designer R.E. Bishop leading the design, the first flight of the DH.98 Mosquito (as the aircraft would be named by the RAF) took place on 25 November 1940. Testing against a Spitfire Mk.II in February 1941, the Mosquito was 30mph faster. Mass production was authorised on 21 June 1941, for seventeen PR (photo reconnaissance) versions and 176 as fighters with four nose-mounted cannon, augmented within a few weeks to add fifty bomber versions. Much of the aircraft was made by the furniture industry.

The Mosquito was soon to appear also in fighter/bomber and nightfighter versions. The 1942 photo-reconnaissance Mosquito PR Mk.VIII, with 1,565HP Merlin 61 engines, had a maximum speed of 436mph. Another example where it turned out that industry did know better than the RAF, although Air Marshal Wilfrid Freeman was an enthusiastic supporter and the DH.98 Mosquito was known in most RAF circles at first as "Freeman's Folly". So much of a "successful folly" that a total of 7,781 Mosquitos were built, 6,710 of which were completed during the Second World War.

Avro Lancaster: The iconic British heavy bomber of the Second World War was the Avro Lancaster (apologies to the 1939 Handley Page Halifax aficionados!). It started from the 1939 Avro Manchester twin-engined bomber, which suffered from problems with its two 1,750HP Rolls-Royce Vulture engines (an 'X' configuration twenty-four cylinder 4,200cc. capacity design). The Vulture had to be de-rated to 1,500HP in service, due to reliability issues. This hampered the Manchester aircraft performance.

Eventually, Rolls-Royce advised that Vulture engine production was to cease. Roy Chadwick, chief designer at

Avro Lancaster (BBMF). (*Cupcakekid, CC BY-SA 3.0*)

Avro, had already surreptitiously started a design for a Manchester development, with a stretched wingspan and re-engined with the latest four Rolls-Royce Merlin XX engines ('V' configuration twelve cylinder, 2,700cc. capacity, 1,280HP, see section 2.7). The Merlin had proved a very good engine, on Hurricane and Spitfire fighters and on the twin-engined Armstrong Whitworth Whitley medium night bomber. Without Ministry approval, Avro's Managing Director Roy Dobson made private contact with Rolls-Royce's managing director Ernest Hives, to obtain the loan of four Merlins. First flight of the four-engined Manchester was on 8 January 1941. Avro was quickly able to demonstrate the impressive performance of the "Manchester III", soon to be renamed the "Lancaster". There was some initial "huffiness" over the unorthodox way in which the Lancaster development had happened, which had to be smoothed over, helped by an enthusiastic Wilfrid Freeman. An initial order for 1,070 was placed, the eventual Lancaster

Lancaster Dropping Grand Slam on Arnsberg Viaduct, March 1944. (*Author's collection*)

total reaching 7,377 aircraft. Most Lancasters used Merlin engines but, due to engine availability, 300 Mk.II aircraft used the Bristol Hercules air-cooled radial engine.

A famous UK single-raid "special" was the Lancaster/Bouncing Bomb raid on the dams in the Ruhr valley, in May 1943, followed up later by the 12,000lb Tallboy and 20,000lb Grand Slam "earthquake" bombs carried by Lancaster bombers on special raids, including the final sinking of the last and most modern German battleship *Tirpitz*.

Many "special" aircraft developments occurred during the Second World War, on both sides.

Airspeed AS.51 Horsa: A British "special" was the development of the Airspeed Horsa towed glider for air assault troops. This arose from remarking that the German airborne landing success in Belgium (May 1940) and Crete (May 1941) included the use of troop-carrying towed gliders. First flight of the Horsa was in September 1941. The British Army Air Corps was formed in 1942 (Winston Churchill again) and they (and the US Army) used

Airspeed Horsa Glider (embarking troops). (*BAE Systems*)

the Airspeed Horsa towed glider to land assault troops behind enemy lines in the Normandy landings in 1944, and in other major operations. The Horsa could carry thirty troops and could accommodate a Jeep (the ubiquitous four-wheel drive Allied army vehicle of the war) or an anti-tank gun. Famously, Horsas carried troops involved in capturing one of the first objectives of D-day, the 'Pegasus' bridge over the Caen canal at Bénouville. Being of all-wood construction, production of the Horsa was largely by the furniture industry. Over 3,600 Horsas were built, many by furniture makers Elliotts of Newbury.

General Aircraft Hamilcar: The GAL. 49 Hamilcar towed glider was developed to carry light tanks or other armoured vehicles, or anti-tank guns and ammunition, in airborne assaults. Twice as heavy as the Horsa, with an MTOW of 36,000lbs (over 16 tonnes) it needed a large four-engined aircraft to launch and tow it. "Stripped-out" Stirling and Halifax bombers were often used. First flight was March 1942. General Aircraft only managed to build twenty-two but a total of 344 were built by the many subcontract organisations involved in wartime glider production. These included AC Motors, Birmingham Railway Carriage & Wagon Company and the Co-operative

Wholesale Society, all co-ordinated by Harris Lebus of Tottenham "the largest furniture makers in the world".

Both the Horsa and the Hamilcar were part of three large allied air assaults; the D-Day Normandy landings in June 1944 (as Operation Tonga, an integral part of Operation Overlord), Operation Market Garden in September 1944 (to cross various branches of the lower Rhine river in the Netherlands) and Operation Varsity in March 1945 (the largest

GAL.49 Hamilcar Glider (unloading M22 Locust light tank). (*Author's collection*)

Allied airborne assault of the war, supporting the Operation Plunder amphibious assault across the River Rhine, near Wesel, in north-west Germany).

Westland Lysander: An often unsung "special" hero was the Westland Lysander SCW (Special Contract Westland) version, with extra space and fuel. These were used for "special" wartime missions, night-landing in dark French fields for the delivery and rescue of many SOE operatives ("secret agents") involved in intelligence gathering and liaison with resistance groups. The Germans knew little about the British aircraft and wished to study them. German troops captured one intact in March 1942, because its pilot was unable to destroy it after a crash, but a train hit the truck carrying the aircraft, destroying the evidence! 1,561 Westland Lysanders were built in the UK and 225 more were built in Canada.

Hawker Typhoon/Tempest/Sea Fury:
Typhoon: In 1937, before the Hawker Hurricane actually went into series production, Hawker Chief Designer Sydney Camm had already started the design of its successor. Told to wait for a government requirement, Camm nevertheless progressed ideas for two different variants, using two different twenty-four-cylinder high power engines then in development. One was the Rolls-Royce Vulture and the other was the Napier Sabre[1], the design of which was led by Frank Halford. In March 1938, the Air Ministry released specification F.18/37

Hawker Typhoon inspection by King George VI: (note 2 cannons each wing and rocket rails under). (*BAE Systems*)

for a fighter which could fly at over 400mph at 15,000ft. The Hawker Typhoon was conceived, using the under-development 2,000HP Napier Sabre engine. It was intended as a medium-high altitude interceptor/fighter to replace the Hurricane.

---

1. The Vulture engine development was discontinued after problems with it on the Avro Manchester bomber, Rolls-Royce subsequently concentrating on further development of the 12-cylinder Merlin. The Napier Sabre went on to be developed to give over twice the power of the Merlin XX (The Sabre had 37 litres cubic capacity compared with the Merlin's 27 litres, and weighed 50 per cent more).

By the end of 1941, the Hurricane was outclassed as an interceptor/fighter by the new German Focke Wolfe Fw.190. The new Typhoon first flew in February 1941. It was a heavier airframe than the Hurricane, using aluminium alloy extensively and able to carry a 2,000lb bomb load for ground attack. Because Hawker factories were full of Hurricane production, Typhoon series production was allocated to another Hawker Siddeley company, Gloster. Urgently needed to counter the Fw.190, the Typhoon was rushed into service in September 1941, powered by the Napier Sabre II engine – just in time.

However, early Typhoons suffered engine unreliability and unexpected crashes during high speed dives. The cause of the crashes was eventually identified as separation of the elevator anti-flutter mass balance at high speed, due to insufficient strength of attachment. This allowed tailplane flutter to develop and could (and did) cause the tail of the aircraft to break off. For a short while, complete cancellation of the Typhoon order was contemplated. After the identification of the problems and correction had been effected, the Typhoon proved a very stable and effective medium altitude and low-level performer but was outclassed as a high altitude fighter by the Spitfire Mk.IX. This was largely due to the thin wing of the Spitfire Mk.IX, less prone to aerodynamic compressibility effects at the highest (dive) speeds as flight entered the transonic flight régime (approaching supersonic flight). At lower altitudes, however, the Typhoon was the only Allied aircraft capable of catching the formidable German Fokke-Wulf Fw.190. Typhoons were built in large numbers, finally totalling 3,317.

By 1943, a fast, stable ground attack aircraft was a significant RAF operational need for raids on Northern France, the role to which the Typhoon was very well suited. With ground attack rockets and four 20mm cannon, the Typhoon became one of the Second World War's most successful ground attack aircraft. The aircraft could also be armed with a wing-mounted 2,000lb bomb load, as an alternative to rockets. The sheer firepower of one Typhoon was described as "equivalent to a destroyer broadside".

Tempest: Under the leadership of Sydney Camm, the Hawker design team planned a series of Typhoon design improvements. In response to OR.109, the Air Ministry issued specification F.10/41 for the revised Typhoon. A new, thinner, semi-elliptic planform wing was introduced, intending to create laminar boundary layer airflow for reduced drag. The new wing had a thickness/chord ratio which tapered from 14.5 per cent at the root to 10 per cent at the tip, with maximum thickness at 37 per cent chord (compared with Typhoon at 19.5 per cent, 12 per cent and 30 per cent values and the Spitfire Mk.IX at 13.2 per cent root thickness and 6 per cent tip thickness). Wing root maximum thickness of the Tempest was five inches less than on the Typhoon. Flush riveting was used on the wing skins, to maintain the laminar airflow. The thinner wing reduced fuel capacity, so an additional fuselage bay incorporated an extra fuel tank. There were other changes, including a longer undercarriage to increase ground clearance, to allow a larger propeller to be fitted. Originally designated as Typhoon II, the final result became a new type, the Hawker Tempest. First flight was on 2 September 1942. Difficulties with the development of the up-rated (2,400HP) Napier Sabre IV engine resulted in delays, the final production version being the Tempest Mk.V, which entered service in January 1944 and 1,702 were built. It was an effective counter at low altitude to the German Messerschmitt Me.262 twin jet powered aircraft introduced into the Luftwaffe in April 1944, but the German jet had a much higher top speed at altitude.

The Tempest II was a further development, with a 2,520HP Bristol Centaurus air cooled radial engine. The chin radiator feature was removed, engine oil cooling being relocated to the inner wing leading edge. First flight of the Tempest II was on 28 June

1943. Of the 1,702 Hawker Tempests built, 454 were Tempest IIs. One hundred and forty-two Tempest VI with an uprated engine were built. In mock air battles with veteran USAAF pilots, the Tempest was assessed as very akin in performance to the USA Republic P-47 Thunderbolt, although the heavier P-47 had more firepower and was able to carry a greater bombload.

Sea Fury: Flying first as the proposed new RAF Fury in September 1944, the RAF contract for a "Tempest Light" was for a shortened wing Tempest with a redesigned (monocoque) fuselage, a higher pilot position (better all-round visibility) and the Bristol Centaurus eighteen-cylinder air-cooled radial engine (as fitted to the Tempest II). Given the progress of the war, the RAF order was cancelled but the RN considered it formed the sound basis of a carrier fighter/bomber. Strengthening the undercarriage for carrier landings was one change and the Sea Fury had its first flight in February 1945 – 864 Sea Furies were built in total, many being exported.

The type was purchased for the British, Australian, Netherlands and Canadian navies and the Pakistan and Iraqi air forces. The RN Sea Fury saw action in the 1950–53 Korean War, mainly in the ground attack role. It performed well (even when intercepted by the MiG-15 jets operated by the Russian-Chinese "friends" of North Korea). Not to be confused with the 1931 biplane Hawker Fury, the type was one of the fastest piston-engined fighters Hawker ever produced and surviving examples are still used in air races.

Gloster Meteor: One of the significant British developments was the Gloster Meteor fighter, the only turbojet-powered fighter in the Allied inventory of aircraft which saw active service during the Second World War. At the start of the war, Gloster were busy producing aircraft designed by other companies but had none of their own designs in production. The Gloster design department therefore had the only significant design team with enough spare capacity to take on the design of the first UK jet-powered aircraft. This was to be the experimental single-engined Gloster E.28/39, which would use the new-concept engine designed and developed by Frank Whittle (later Sir Frank – see section 4.2). On 15 May 1941 the successful first flight of the Gloster E.28/39 proved the viability and potential of jet-powered flight to the RAF and orders were placed for twelve prototype twin-engined aircraft (later reduced to eight), to specification E.5/42.

The final type name "Meteor" was allocated in 1944. On 17 July 1944 the Gloster Meteor F.1 was cleared for service use, powered by twin Rolls-Royce Welland versions of the Whittle W2 engine (see section 4.2). The whole programme was a closely-guarded secret but, in fact, the German air force was first to fly a jet turbine powered aircraft on actual operational service, the twin-engined Messerschmitt Me.262 (in the same month that the Meteor F.1 was cleared for RAF service). The 1946 cost of a Meteor was £27,800, equivalent to £1.174 million in 2019 terms.

Between 1943 and 1955, 3,947 Meteors were built. As evidence (and as a reminder) that the Meteor was at the frontier of aircraft design in the 1940s, 890 Meteors were lost in crashes which killed 450 pilots. Many of these were attributable to pilot error but aircraft/engine failure or servicing errors were also major contributors. The fatality rate was exacerbated by lack of ejection seats in early models. Due

Gloster Meteor. (*Author's collection*)

to the supply problems with early Whittle engines (see section 4.2), the government also specified a single-engined jet fighter in E.1/44, able to use either the Rolls-Royce Welland or the H.1 Halford/de Havilland versions of the Whittle engine, or the in-development and more powerful Rolls-Royce Nene. Gloster designed and built three prototypes of their GA.2 to E.1/44 but the resolution of engine supply (transferred to Rolls-Royce as W.1, later the Welland) and superior Meteor performance prevented any Gloster GA.2 production.

In truth, the lighter de Havilland Vampire developed in parallel with the Meteor made better use of the new jet technology, being designed around the (single) jet engine, rather than the more conventional twin jet engines of (then) limited power added to the aircraft in place of twin pistons, as on the Meteor. Overall, however, the Meteor was to prove an adaptable aircraft as jet engine technology and associated power levels developed. The aircraft accommodated modifications to perform many different roles as an RAF front line aircraft into the 1950s. It sold to overseas air forces in significant numbers.

De Havilland Vampire: In January 1941, Sir Henry Tizard informally approached the de Havilland company to ask them to consider if they could develop a new fighter aircraft, using the new jet turbine technology then under development by Whittle's Power Jets company. Employing engine consultant Frank Halford once again (see section 2.4), de Havilland succeeded in creating a significant improvement in engine thrust to create the Halford H.1/de Havilland Goblin engine (see table 4.2 in section 4). Around this engine they created the single-engined twin-boom de Havilland DH.100 Vampire. Less heavily armed than the twin-engined Meteor, the Vampire in service had a lower top speed but greater range. Flying by 1943, the Vampire promise was high but the production capacity within de Havilland was fully taken

DH. 100 Vampire (*BAE Systems*)

with more immediately vital war production. Transferred initially to English Electric, Vampires were produced in quantity but not in time to see service during the Second World War. In 1946, in side-by-side tests with the Rolls-Royce Griffon-powered Spitfire Mk.XIV, depending on altitude the Vampire proved to be 70 to 100mph faster, tighter-turning, faster-climbing and diving, generally outmanoeuvering the older aircraft (the Mk.XIV Spitfire first flight was also in 1943). Eventually, 3,268 Vampires were built with extensive worldwide sales, the type eventually being used by thirty-one air forces. The only significant Western European air forces *not* to use the Vampire were those of the Netherlands, Denmark, Belgium, Spain and West Germany. The RCAF, RAAF, the Indian and Rhodesian Air Forces also used Vampires.

Examples of Wartime Improved Versions of RAF Combat Aircraft (Spitfire, Hurricane, Halifax)

Successful combat aircraft were continuously improved throughout the war. Typhoon-to-Tempest was a case in point. With several significant developments, the Spitfire transitioned to the Mk.XIV of 1944, with a top speed of 449mph, double the rate of climb and more range. Armour plating introduced in vital areas of enemy aircraft required heavier armament to be introduced to all British fighting aircraft. Importantly, from the 1941 Mark VB onwards, the Spitfire carried much greater weight of ammunition (normally fired from two 20mm (0.79 inch) calibre cannon and four 0.303 inch calibre Browning machine guns). Compared with the original eight 0.303 inch calibre Spitfire Mk.1A machine guns, the result fired a total of three or four times more the total weight of shot per second and hit the target with three-and-a-half times the total momentum energy, plus the destructive power of high explosive (HE) or armour-piercing cannon rounds. The number of ammunition rounds carried for each cannon was around half that of each machine gun. The cannon rounds each had a projectile weight of 0.3lb (0.13kg), which was over ten times the mass of a machine gun bullet, and fired with a slightly increased muzzle velocity but at half the rate of fire.

The Hurricane design was not as amenable to major aerodynamic improvement as the Spitfire and, by 1941, it was overtaken by the latest German fighters. However, it had an adaptable and sturdy basic structure. With the 25 per cent increase in engine power of the Merlin XX compared with the original Merlin II engine, the 1942 Mk.II Hurricane accommodated a 22 per cent weight increase caused by the introduction of cockpit, engine and radiator armour and four 20mm cannons, with slightly better aircraft performance overall. The Mk.IIc aircraft had four 20mm cannons and was effectively used against night intruders over Britain. Hardpoint provision was made for mounting a 250lb or 500lb bomb and 4,711 of this version were built. In the fighter-bomber guise, it was often referred to as the Hurribomber. The 20mm cannon did not have enough penetration power to knock out tanks in North Africa and it was difficult to achieve a direct hit with a bomb. A Vickers 'S' type pod-mounted 40mm cannon was mounted under each wing (1.57 inch calibre, 3lb projectile weight each round). These fired at two thirds of the original Browning machine gun velocity and one tenth of the firing rate, but tracer bullets from a machine gun in each wing assisted aiming. Compared with the firepower of the original Hurricane Mk.I, the target could be hit with over twelve times the momentum energy of shot per second, the much heavier cannon shot including the destructive power of HE or armour-piercing rounds. Fitted with hard points for two 250lb (later 500lb) bombs and upgraded as the Mk.IId, this version was very successful when used for ground attack in the North African desert campaign and resulted in the type becoming colloquially known as the "Flying Tin-opener", of which 296 were built. By early 1943, the last major Hurricane variant to see service (the Mk.IV) was introduced as a further improved version of the Mk.IId; 580 of this variant were built, used in both the Near East and the Far East, alongside the Mk.IId.

The Halifax bomber suffered from an aerodynamic interference problem between engine/propeller and wing. This limited performance, especially the ability to carry maximum bomb load at the safer heights (greater range from anti-aircraft flak guns) as achieved by the Lancaster. The Lancaster could fly missions as much as 8,000ft higher than could be achieved by the Halifax. Part of the problem was the Halifax's Bristol Hercules engine supercharger, which was not as effective as the Merlin XX engine two-speed supercharger in providing the planned increased engine inlet air mass flow at altitude. This issue was resolved in 1944, with the 1,800HP Hercules 100 engine, which had a redesigned supercharger. In a revised engine installation, this gave the Handley Page Halifax altitude performance comparable with that of the Avro Lancaster.

General Technology Development: The stories of all the significant Second World War aircraft developments, British, American, German, Soviet Union and others, cover an almost magical period of rapid technical progress in many areas. As in the 1914–18 conflict, the technology gains were often "leap-frog" efforts, some of which were quite radical, in different fields. In Britain, the cavity magnetron (the heart of airborne radar), and ASDIC technology (known as Sonar in the USA) for underwater submarine detection were prominent. ASDIC was supposedly named after the non-existent "Anti-Submarine Detection Investigation Committee", but, in reality named after the Anti-

Submarine Division of the Naval Staff – ASDic – like "supersonic". From North America came the Sherman tank and the ubiquitous Jeep light army vehicle (USA), the atomic bomb (USA, with a British contribution) and the walkie-talkie (Canada and the USA). The jet turbine engine was independently developed by Britain and Germany. The rocket-powered ballistic missile (V2) was developed in Germany. The first high-speed (560mph) swept wing aircraft was the rocket-powered Messerschmitt German Me.163 Komet, first flown in 1941. There were many, many more examples. Stories of all of them have been published in numerous specialist books. Suffice it to mention that the need for continued survival (aiming at eventual supremacy) in war drove all participants to strive to lead, in whatever branch of technology that was necessary. Airframe, engine and aircraft systems equipment development were all integral parts of the process.

3.2 British Aircraft Production During WW2

The British aircraft industry business activity developments during the Second World War were much associated with major increases in production capacity. There were other developments, notably the sale of the Swan Hunter controlling interest in Airspeed to de Havilland. The last few items in the timeline list in section 2.8 outline other company business changes during the war.

During the rearmament years immediately prior to the Second World War, the British government considered the likely factory expansion needed to meet production of large numbers of new aircraft, each of which had greater work content and occupied more factory space than earlier designs. Aircraft production technology and management, therefore, also had to improve from that which had largely remained little-changed since the early 1930s. More efficient production, in larger numbers of ever-increasingly complex and capable aircraft was to be one of the fundamental factors affecting the eventual outcome of the coming war in the air and, ultimately, of the war as a whole.

The different aircraft manufacturers were naturally reluctant to provide information to competitors but the government insisted that they must subcontract enough to ensure that the promised aircraft delivery schedules were met. In 1936, this was stipulated to be "at least 35 per cent of work to be subcontracted". Tooling information, manufacturing process knowledge, and education, as well as basic design drawings and parts schedules should be supplied to each subcontractor. If necessary, this should include providing the same work and assistance to competitors, if they had significant spare capacity. Due to these measures, introduced by Viscount Swinton's Air Ministry and supported by his successor Sir Kingsley Wood, during 1939 fighter production was three-and-a half times greater than in 1938 and bomber production was three times greater overall.

Aircraft production to match operational requirements (capabilities, quantity, and delivery to service) had to be planned well in advance, at the direction of the Air Ministry acting on behalf of the RAF. It was also being dispersed geographically, partly as a hedge against damage from air raids halting production of any particular aircraft type and partly to be as close as practicable to enough of the appropriate supporting infrastructure (airfield, transport of materials, adequately skilled labour, power, drainage etc.).

It took several months to establish the readiness of any new factory to make a particular aircraft, needing the correct machine tools and metal-working and treatment facilities, fixtures for some of the complex individual parts manufacture, materials and aircraft equipment stores and drawing stores. A fighter aircraft could perhaps have 50,000 to 100,000 drawings and manufacturing process sheets for individual parts and assemblies, a large bomber perhaps having two or three times that number. Special-to-type fixtures and jigs for sub-assembly and assembly would be needed, with functional test facilities for aircraft pneumatic, hydraulics and electrical equipment, possibly with type-specific specialised test equipment for the completed aircraft. A new factory would need internal distributed power supplies, water, drains etc., all to be connected to external services and (probably) with back-up emergency facilities, especially in areas such as fire suppression. Even an already established aircraft factory would take a significant amount of time to be changed to produce a new aircraft.

Hence, some aircraft continued in production for operational needs reasons after they had been superseded by an improved or totally new version (e.g. Cessation in making the Avro Manchester bomber delayed until the factory changeover to the Avro Lancaster was virtually complete, which was reasonably seamless only because there was much commonality of drawings, parts and sub-assemblies in making the improved product. Thus Manchesters continued to be produced after Lancaster production had started). Even changing from one mark of aircraft to another needed careful production planning for production efficiency and "speed of delivery".

Development of improved and new aircraft types (thereby disrupting production) could not be forgone, in the technological race for aerial supremacy. In the competition for allocation of resources, the Ministry of Supply had a most difficult path to establish, when setting priorities and timing of the introduction of important new developments, balanced with the need to deliver as many as possible completed aircraft to front-line service as soon as possible.

By 1938 the total number of new aircraft per month produced in Britain had risen to 236 and, by the end of 1939, to 660 per month. The peak rate rose to 2,205 per month in 1944 (the comparable German aircraft production rose from 690 per month in 1939 to 3,380 per month, the latter 1944 German production total coming partly from slave labour, in factories in both Germany and the occupied territories). Britain produced 131,549 aircraft between 1938 and 1945, nearly two-and-a-half times the number produced in the First World War. This was actually 22 per cent of an Allied grand total of over 600,000 (includes USA production prior to USA joining the war as a belligerent in December 1941). Such a large grand total number is due to the 357,655 aircraft produced by the might of the industry of the United States of America. Aircraft production of new USA designs (such as the Boeing B-17 Flying Fortress, with a first flight in 1935), had increased from the mid-1930s but soon underwent massive growth for wartime production.

Comparable numbers for the First World War had been 55,093 aircraft produced by Britain 1914–18, out of 132,000 total Allied production, with only 1,500 actually available for combat from the USA (1917–18).

Including aircraft produced prior to the war, ninety-two aircraft types of British origin served during the 1939–45 conflict. Of course, the new aircraft produced were markedly more sophisticated, heavier and capable than those of the previous world war, so the comparison of numbers produced needs to be tempered with consideration of the "state of the art" at the time.

The distribution of different classes of all aircraft in the British Empire forces during 1939 to 1945:

Total	Fighters	Surface Attack	Bombers	Recon.	Transport	Training	Other
177,025	38,786	33,811	38,158	7,014	12,585	46,256	415

The above figures include aircraft manufactured before outbreak of war and several tens of thousands were designed and produced in the USA (approximately one fifth of the aircraft produced during the war for the RAF/RN were supplied from USA manufacturers). Others were also produced in Canada and Australia. Most of the aircraft were those of the RAF or RN but the RAAF, RCAF, RNZAF and the RSAAF also made a significant contribution to the British war effort. It is interesting to note that the largest number of aircraft class used were training aircraft, although some of these might well have been types removed from front-line service during the early days of the war.

Clearly, 46,256 aircraft trained a lot of aircrew. Much of Britain was not a suitable wartime location for intensive air training, due to possible enemy attack, strain of other air traffic at many wartime airfields and unpredictable weather. In December 1939, the British Commonwealth Air Training Plan (BCATP) was agreed between the governments of Britain, Canada, Australia and New Zealand. The agreement called for the training of nearly 50,000 aircrew each year, for as long as necessary. Elementary training would be in various Commonwealth countries (including Britain) before travelling to Canada for advanced courses. BCATP was responsible for training nearly half the pilots, navigators, bomb aimers, air gunners, wireless operators and flight engineers who served with the RAF, RN Fleet Air arm, RCAF, RAAF and RNZAF during the war. In total, Canada trained 131,500 aircrew personnel by the end of the war. Under a parallel agreement (the Joint Air Training Scheme), South Africa trained 33,347 aircrew for the SAAF and other Allied air forces.

For an island nation, with no active local ally from May 1940, and alone except for the distant Empire and Commonwealth countries until the beginning of 1942, the aircraft production record was a magnificent achievement aided, of course, by raw material and other supplies, mostly obtained from USA and Empire sources. Most supplies had to come via the hazardous U-boat infested route of the Atlantic Ocean.

Not all the aircraft used by Britain were designed or manufactured in British factories. In 1939, the USA only acquired 2,100 new aircraft from its industry. The following year, President Franklin D. Roosevelt startled his government and industry, requesting a rearmament programme which included USA industrial expansion to produce 50,000 new aircraft per year. This caused new factories to be built, some of which were to be directly financed by British contracts for new aircraft. The USA being a neutral country at that time, USA aircraft would be available to Britain on a "cash and carry" basis, (later replaced by the Lend-Lease programme, see below). The Lend-Lease process, formally titled in the USA as "An Act to Promote the Defense of the United States", was enacted in March 1941 (i.e. before the USA entered the war). Over 38,800 aircraft were supplied to Britain by the USA as part of the lend-lease programme. Many arrived by sea transport, disassembled and packed, thus requiring reassembly by British companies on arrival.

Amongst the aircraft supplied were Lockheed Hudson long-range bomber/reconnaissance aircraft. An initial offer from Lockheed, to adapt their Electra 14 airliner in response to a British request for 200 machines for maritime reconnaissance, was contract-agreed within two days, in the spring of 1938. A total of 2,539 Hudsons were eventually supplied. Ordered by Britain as an all-new design to a British specification, an eventual total of 1,839 North American P.51 Mustang fighters were mostly supplied lend-lease (1,746 with supercharged Packard-Merlin engines were lend-lease supplied, see Rolls-Royce Experimental aircraft in Appendix 10). North American Harvard pilot trainers also were supplied (initial 1938 "cash and carry" order for 400 but 5,019 eventual total). Many Harvards were used in Canada as training aircraft in the BCATP programme and 3,512 Curtiss P-40 Kittyhawk lend-lease fighters were used in the Far East war theatre. The RN Fleet Air Arm had 1,132 Grumman Wildcat (RN name Martlet) and 1,172 of the later, more potent, Grumman Hellcat fighters. Lend-Lease included 1,790 Douglas Dakota (C-47) transports (military verson of

DC-3), Consolidated B-24 Liberator bombers (2,450) and PBY-5 Catalina flying boats (2,681). Made by de Havilland (Canada), 200 lend-lease financed DH.82C Tiger Moths were retained in Canada for the BCATP. In the total of 38,800 aircraft supplied Lend-Lease by the USA for RAF, the RN and British Commonwealth forces were sixty-five different types.

USA lend-lease was labelled by Winston Churchill as "the most unsordid act in the history of any nation". An eventual total of US$ 50.1 billion worth of supplies, or 17 per cent of the total war expenditures of the USA, was provided to other Allied countries of the Second World War. Equipment, aircraft and ships were supplied. This total would be equivalent to US $740 billion (£570 billion) in 2019. US $31.4 billion (63 per cent, equivalent to US $463 billion in 2019) went to Britain. There were reverse lend-lease items, over US $7 billion being from the UK to the USA. This included Spitfires for USAAF use until USAAF squadrons based in Britain and North Africa received their own Mustangs. Advanced technology transfer was a two-way process. The British jet engine founded the USA jet engine industry and the cavity magnetron transfer (heart of 10cm airborne radar and, ultimately, the heart of billions of micro-wave cookers) was described by James Phinney III, wartime Director of USA Office of Strategic Services (OSS, forerunner of the CIA) as "When the members of the (UK) Tizard Mission brought the cavity magnetron to America in 1940, they carried the most valuable cargo ever brought to our shores".

Lend-lease among the Allies was two-way, or sometimes "lend-give at no charge". A total of £126 million (equivalent to £5.6 billion in 2019) of war materials was supplied by Britain to the Soviet Union, all entirely free of charge. This included some 2,776 Hawker Hurricanes and some 4,000 other aircraft, 5,218 tanks, 5,000 anti-tank guns, twenty-seven ships, fifteen million pairs of boots and many other items.

To reach the necessary domestic British aircraft production levels, several government sponsored initiatives were taken to increase aircraft factory total capacity, many of which were started before the outbreak of war. The following are major examples of what happened:

a. Factory space used for Avro aircraft production rose from 280,000 square feet in 1935 to 6,293,802 square feet (145 acres or 58 hectares/0.58 million square metres) by 1943, in a total of twenty-four different locations. Two new large Avro factories, at Chadderton (near Oldham, Lancashire) and Woodford (near Stockport, Cheshire) were opened during 1939, with an area totalling 1.5 million square feet. Peak wartime employment at Chadderton alone reached 11,267 employees, producing parts and major assemblies for 3,000 Avro Lancasters by the end of the war. In 1939, authorisation was given to create a new 1.5 million square feet factory for Avro, at Yeadon aerodrome, Yorkshire. At the time, this was the largest single-building factory in Europe. Between June 1941 and the end of the war, it produced over 3,000 Ansons and over 600 Lancasters. Peak employment at Yeadon was over 10,000 and peak production rate was achieved between October 1943 and March 1944, when 135 Avro Ansons were produced per month.

b. In 1939 the government instructed the English Electric company to expand the factory and airfield facility (ex-RAF) at Samlesbury, near Blackburn. Samlesbury was initially used to build Handley Page Hampden bombers and, after a runway extension and further factory building, Handley Page Halifax bombers. During the Second World War, English Electric delivered a total of over 3,000 bomber aircraft from Samlesbury.

c. In Canada, National Steel Car Ltd. (maker of rail carriages) was a subcontractor on Handley Page Hampden, Avro Anson projects and Hawker Hurricane, and had been building 225 Westland Lysander aircraft for the Canadian Air Force (RCAF). In 1942, their Malton factory near Toronto was taken over by the Canadian government and expanded to produce Lancaster (Mk.X) bombers. Named as "Victory Aircraft Limited", by the end of the war the factory was to have built 430 Lancasters and 3,197 Ansons. In 1945 the facility was sold to Avro, to become Avro Canada.

d. Manufacturing companies with no prior experience of war materials were allocated production of armaments, including aircraft parts and sub-assemblies. A major grouping for aircraft production was based in the London area, known as the London Aircraft Production Group (LAPG). This was led by London Transport (the engineering facility) and included five other companies.

LAPG was created in 1941. The intent was to form a group collectively capable of building Handley Page Halifax heavy bombers in quantity. The various sections of Halifax bombers produced by LAPG were sent to the new (1940-authorised) de Havilland facility at Leavesden, Hertfordshire, for final assembly, flight test and delivery to the RAF. London Passenger Transport Board establishments at Aldenham, Chiswick and White City were used. The other participants were Chrysler Motors at Kew, Duple at Hendon, Express Motor and Body Works at Enfield and Park Royal Coach Works at Acton. LAPG produced a total of 710 Halifax. Other factories elsewhere were also involved in Halifax production, including the parent factory of Handley Page at Radlett, Hertfordshire, the Fairey Aviation Halifax output in Stockport, and Halifax production from the Speke shadow factory and English Electric at Samlesbury. Ultimately, total Halifax output rose to a peak of 200 aircraft a month.

As an illustration of the scale of effort to produce a 1940s heavy bomber:

> **Halifax Bomber:** It has been calculated that building one of these aircraft involved the making, inspecting and assembling of 254,000 parts and incorporating two thousand items of government-supplied equipment (known as embodiment loan equipment, which would include RAF service-wide standard aircraft fittings, engines, guns and gun turrets, standard instruments and radio, navigation and bomb-aiming equipment). Materials required to construct the aircraft were two-thirds of an acre of light alloy sheet, weighing seven tons, three miles of rolled or drawn sections and five miles of extruded sections, all of which had been cut, formed and variously machined. These components were then progressively assembled using a series of jigs and fixtures specific to the type. Lengths totalling three to four miles of electrical cable and one mile of pipework had to be installed, and between six and seven hundred thousand rivets closed during sub-assembly and assembly.

e. Part of increasing wartime production was establishing shadow factories, often managed by other than the "parent" organisation. Dispersal of production was also introduced, to guard against production of any single aircraft type being arrested by bomb damage at any one factory. The principal shadow and dispersal factories associated with aircraft and their engines are shown in table 3.2 below, with the site origins and eventual use.

Table 3.2: UK Government Shadow & Principal Dispersal Aircraft factories (1939–1945)

Location	User/Owner	Original Use	Wartime Production	Today (2020)
Acocks Green, south of Birmingham	Rover Aero	Westwood family market garden	Parts for Bristol Hercules radial engine	Redeveloped as housing
Banner Lane, Coventry	Standard Aero No. 2	Golf course	Bristol Hercules sleeve valve radial engines	(Massey) Ferguson tractors. Closed 2002, now housing
Belfast, N.I.	Short & Harland	?	Short Sunderland, Stirling	Spirit Aerosystems (ex-Shorts) aerostructures
Blackpool Lancashire	Vickers Aircraft	RAF Squires Gate	Vickers Wellington	Blackpool airport (closed 2014)
Blythe Bridge Staffordshire	Rootes Group (Chrysler)	?	Bristol Blenheim and Beaufighter	Mostly residential development
Hawarden, near Broughton, Flintshire, Wales	Vickers Aircraft	Farmland	Mainly Vickers Wellington, some Lancasters	De Havilland production post-war. HSA/BAe Airbus wings 1970–96, now Airbus
Browns Lane Coventry	Daimler	Farmland	Aircraft sub-assemblies	Jaguar-Land Rover museum, housing & other business
Burtonwood, Warrington	Fairey Aviation	Farmland ?	Assembly & modification of imported American (lend-lease) aircraft	Junction 8 M62 M'way, Modern Industrial & Retail Businesses
Canley, Coventry	Standard Aero No. 1	Vacant land on Standard Motor's Canley site	Bristol Beaufighter De Havilland Mosquito	Standard Motor Company, demolished after closure in 1980. Now housing
Canley, Coventry	H.M. Hobson	Vacant land on Standard's Canley site	Carburettors for aircraft engines	Standard Motor, closure in 1980. Now housing
Castle Bromwich West Midlands	Austin Motors, then Vickers	Farm/Sewage Works	Supermarine Spitfire, Seafire and Avro Lancaster	Jaguar-Land Rover cars
Christchurch, Hampshire	Airspeed	Christchurch Airport	Airspeed Oxford, Horsa gliders	Mixed housing and industrial estate
Clifton near Manchester	Magnesium Elektron	Magnesium Elektron Factory	Magnesium alloys	Magnesium Elektron (chemical manufacturing)
Coventry, Stoke Aldermoor Lane	Humber	?	Aero engines	?
Crewe, Cheshire	Rolls-Royce	Farmland	Rolls-Royce Merlin	Bentley, Crewe

Location	User/Owner	Original Use	Wartime Production	Today (2020)
Cwmbran, South Wales	Lucas	Farmland	Aircraft turrets	?
Distington Cumbria	High Duty Alloys	Farmland	Aircraft parts made of Hiduminium	Abandoned
Drakelow Tunnels, Kidderminster	Rover Company	Hills	Machining parts for Bristol Hercules and Rolls-Royce Merlin	Preserved as Cold War site: Regional Seat of Government Shelter
Heaton Chapel, Stockport	Fairey Aviation	Crossley motor works until 1934	Bristol Beaufighters then Handley Page Halifax bombers	Multiple use industrial site, incl. WFEL engineering
Hillington, Glasgow	Rolls-Royce	Farmland	Rolls-Royce Merlin engines	Closed 2005, redeveloped as an industrial estate.
Liverpool (East Lancashire Road)	Napier	Farmland	Napier Sabre Engine	Industrial estate
Lode Lane, Solihull	Rover	Farmland	Parts for Bristol Hercules radial engine	Land Rover Solihull manufacturing
Longbridge (Cofton Hackett, East Works)	Austin	Farmland in Groveley Lane	Aero engines:- Bristol Mercury and Pegasus Aircraft production:- Avro Lancaster, Fairey Battle, Short Stirling, Vickers Wellington	Redeveloped as housing
Lostock, Chorley Lancashire	de Havilland	?	Aircraft propellers (initially Hamilton-Standard licence-build)	Was part of MBDA guided weapons up to 2000, now?
Meir, Stoke-on-Trent	Rootes Securities	Airfield	N.American Harvard assembly & modificat'ns	Aerodrome, now housing
Newtown Powys, Wales	Accles and Pollock	Farmland	Tubular Steel: aircraft frames, gun barrels	Industrial estate
Ryton, south-east of Coventry	Humber	Farmland	Aircraft engines	Car production, now redeveloped
Speke Airport Liverpool	Rootes Group (Chrysler)	Airport	Bristol Blenheim and Handley Page Halifax	Liverpool airport.... old hangars now industrial estate
South Marston, Swindon	Phillips & Powis (Miles)	?	Miles Master	Honda car plant
Staverton, Gloucestershire	Rotol	Staverton Airport	Variable pitch propellers	Dowty Propellers & Safran's Messier-Bugatti-Dowty Landing Gear
Swaythling Hampshire	Cunliffe-Owen	Farmland	Supermarine Spitfire parts, Seafire assembly	Ford Southampton plant (closed 2008)

Location	User/Owner	Original Use	Wartime Production	Today (2020)
Trafford Park, Manchester	Metropolitan Vickers	Engineering works	Avro Lancasters (assembled in Avro factory)	Modern industrial uses
Trafford Park Manchester	Ford	Derelict motor assembly plant	Rolls-Royce Merlin aero engine	Modern industrial uses
Weston-Super-Mare	Bristol	Land next to RAF station	Bristol Beaufighter	Became industrial estate, now housing
Willesden North London	Freestone and Webb	Coach Builders	Wing tips for Supermarine Spitfire	Redeveloped as housing
Woodstock Mill Oldham	H.M. Hobson	Cotton Mill	Carburettors for aircraft engines	Logistics Distribution Centre

By September 1939, over 8 million square feet of additional aircraft factory space had been created.

One of the largest of the shadow factories (in total, around one million square feet of shop floor space) was near the Castle Bromwich aerodrome, near Birmingham in the county of Warwickshire. After a difficult start and delays in organising the work, the first Spitfire Mk. II left the new Castle Bromwich production line in June 1940. This factory became the largest single UK wartime aircraft producer and was the main manufacturing source of the Supermarine Spitfire (12,129 produced in Castle Bromwich out of the 20,351 total). The factory also produced some 300 Avro Lancasters.

Castle Bromwich Spitfire Assembly. (*Charles Edward Taylor Collection*)

There were many smaller examples of creating additional aircraft manufacturing facilities. After Shorts factory at Rochester in Kent had been bombed in August 1940, a complete temporary factory was created to manufacture Short Sunderland flying boats, at White Cross Bay on the shore of Lake Windermere, Westmorland, complete with a village for the relocated 1,500-strong workforce. After building thirty-five aircraft, the factory became a Sunderland overhaul and repair base. This no longer exists, the location now being the site of a holiday park.

As the war progressed, production methods needed to change, to increase output. In the 1930s, structural elements of major sub-assemblies and final assembly of complete aircraft were not necessarily pre-positioned in a completely shape-defining jig, especially for the smaller aircraft. Part-assembly "to measured dimensions" was still used, with some individual parts "made to measured dimensions". This level of adjustment took time and skill. Small variations in the finished assembly dimensions occurred.

Similarly, aircraft piston engine production sometimes used some "refined adjustment on assembly" to achieve the closer tolerances needed for acceptable machinery performance. "Adjusting/drilling/honing on assembly" (fettling) took skilled workers time. This "adjusting" was reduced in the motor car industry mass production methods introduced by Henry Ford in the USA in the late 1920s, for his mass-produced "Model T" motor cars. Close tolerance control and (expensive) jigs/tooling fixtures saved more than their cost in the thousands of cars and engines assembled more quickly and ensured consistency of parts dimensions. This enabled assembly by semi-skilled workers, ensuring economic achievement of repeatable high standards, with less need for "fettling" to make everything fit together. It was quick, neat and

Castle Bromwich Factory & Coal Dump. (*Charles Edward Taylor Collection*)

secure, to consistent dimensions and accurate clearances. It also facilitated in-service replacement of individual worn, damaged or broken items.

There was an infamous wartime example in the British aircraft engine industry, in the need for Ford of Britain to produce large quantities of Rolls-Royce Merlin engines for Spitfires, Hurricanes, Lancasters, etc. As told by Sir Stanley Hooker of Rolls-Royce, in his autobiography "*Not Much of an Engineer*":

> "One day their [Ford] Chief Engineer appeared in Lovesey's office, which I was then sharing, and said, 'You know, we can't make the Merlin to these drawings.' I replied loftily, 'I suppose that is because the drawing tolerances are too difficult for you, and you can't achieve the accuracy.' 'On the contrary,' he replied, 'the tolerances are far too wide for us. We make motor cars far more accurately than this. Every part on our car engines has to be interchangeable with the same part on any other engine, and hence all parts have to be made with extreme accuracy, far closer than you use. That is the only way we can achieve mass-production.'"

Revised closer-tolerance drawings were prepared for Ford manufacture of Merlin engines.

By the late 1930s, some of the motor industry's more rigorous and extensive jigging/tooling methods were being introduced by aircraft manufacturers, notably in the Manchester/Lancaster and Halifax bombers. Separately manufactured sections of the aircraft (nose, centre fuselage, inner and outer wings, rear fuselage etc.) could be interchanged between different assemblies, with little need for adjustment to incorporate into any individual aircraft. This eased wartime final assembly and allowing dispersed sub-assembly manufacturing (and aircraft repair after major battle damage, by complete replacement of a damaged section).

At the beginning of the war, in some cases the necessary increase in production capacity was coming on stream too slowly for the looming air battles. In the new factories, not everything went smoothly immediately, especially Castle Bromwich. By May 1940, Castle Bromwich had not yet built its first Spitfire, in spite of promises that the factory would be producing sixty per week starting in April 1940.

Partly as a political response to over-impatient media and parliamentary criticisms of the supply of aircraft, to the RAF in particular, in May 1940 the new-broom Prime Minister, Winston Churchill, established a new "Ministry of Aircraft Production" (MAP) to take over the aircraft responsibilities of the Ministry of Supply. He appointed Max Aitken (Lord Beaverbrook) as the Minister. This new ministry became the over-arching government department manager of both the Air Council research and development responsibilities and aircraft supply responsibilities, which had already been combined in 1938 under the command of Air Marshal Wilfrid Freeman, as Air Member for Development and Production (AMDP). The working relationship between Freeman and Beaverbrook would be far from easy, with Beaverbrook's narrow-minded focus on short-term aircraft production numbers success and Freeman's parallel intent to seek and also ensure RAF and RN enhanced aircraft, in the medium and far term of the next few years.

The Nuffield (Austin) organisation's ineffective control of Castle Bromwich had led to the delay in start of production at the factory. Management responsibility was immediately changed to Vickers, under which immediate production output improvement was achieved, especially when MAP influence helped overcome the truculence evidenced by some of the workforce's threatened strike action.

The Beaverbrook leadership of MAP was soon evident. This caused friction between political "headline" objectives and some of the armed forces' other actual operational needs. The Beaverbrook war cry was "more, ever more aircraft NOW please". As a "political appointee", Beaverbrook was most interested in headline numbers and concentrated his attention on "more, ever more of the same". His success was actually built on the careful preparations for increased factory capacity created before his appointment. He did not have too much regard for the ever-demanding need for improved, more advanced aircraft capabilities, whose "newness" would inevitably cause some slowdowns in deliveries. His mantra might be expressed as "we need more aeroplanes, not more gadgets for aeroplanes". For example, the development of Airborne Interception radar (a major improvement in the ability to intercept German bombers during night-time air raids) was deliberately kept from him, in case he intervened to try to stop its introduction as "unhelpful diverted effort from making more front-line aircraft available".

Notwithstanding, as leader of MAP, he did help enormously to reorganise control of some of the less co-ordinated production issues, for aircraft, their engines and other equipment. Beaverbrook overcame bureaucracy by ignoring it! It was soon discovered that, due to bureaucratic processes, of 1,000 new Spitfires delivered to RAF storage units only 650 had been delivered to active RAF squadrons. Another example is the "rescue" from internment camps of the experienced colleagues of refugee German Jew Ludwig Loewy, an expert in the design of metal presses for extruded metal sections. Beaverbrook simply sent a couple of German-speaking Jews round all the internment camps (on his own authority), to identify and remove the lost colleagues to join the war effort, regardless of security regulations.

The provision of spares (equipment and structural items) was initially ignored by Beaverbrook, as not contributing to the headline numbers of new aircraft supplied. Aircraft in service sometimes had to wait for an unserviceable item of equipment to be replaced, due to spares shortages (sometimes due to "over-hoarding in individual airfield/squadron stores against future needs"). Proper attention eventually recognised this as a major contributor to keeping the front-line squadron operational strength as high as possible.

The initiative to enhance aircraft and aircraft engine repair function for both battle and accidental damage was not well-enough established at the beginning of the war to cope with the much increased work due to the impact of actual war. After intensive briefing, Beaverbrook eventually did use his elevated position to actively support (rather than ignore) his AMDP efforts to expand this vital service, as a major contributor to the supply of aircraft to the front-line. The clear objective was to ensure appropriate expertise was used to help ensure that no aircraft was scrapped unnecessarily, materials and spares were made available and enough skilled and dedicated personnel were allocated. Relatively small repairs were normally carried out in RAF maintenance hangars. Significant battle damage to the much larger wartime aircraft fleet would have overwhelmed the pre-war RAF repair organisation. The use of civilian industrial expertise in a massively expanded Civilian Repair Organisation (CRO) was to achieve the return of 79,000 repaired aircraft to service, in the five years 1940 to 1945. At the height of the Battle of Britain, of all Hurricanes and Spitfires delivered to front-line service in August 1940, 35 per cent and, in September 1940, 40 per cent of the total, were all from the CRO.

The result of MAP's efforts, coupled with the expanded CRO aircraft battle damage repair units, was that, despite losses, the RAF fighters available for operations over England actually rose during the Battle of Britain air conflict in 1940, from 644 at the beginning of July to 732 at the beginning of October. Over the same period, German fighters available in the battle fell from 725 to 275.

Beaverbrook often tried to manage by sheer force of personality, declaring that, "I do not plan, I make decisions". He also tended to be vindictive towards those who dared to disagree. This all became a hindrance to progress. This became apparent, as the gains resulting from earlier production planning prior to his appointment were overtaken by some of his ill thought out directives. After a year as Minister of Aircraft Production, Lord Beaverbrook's mistaken focus on "aircraft numbers" without taking due account of RAF aircraft operational effectiveness improvements was exposed. He was effectively forced to resign his position, replaced by John Moore-Brabazon.

Extra factories were not just to increase production capacity, they also dispersed production as "insurance" against aircraft production disruption due to air raids. The Supermarine Spitfire "home" factory at Woolston, Southampton was extensively damaged on 26 September 1940 by the air raid noted earlier, when the Supermarine 317 prototype bomber aircraft were destroyed. An estimated seventy tons of bombs were dropped and one quarter of the work force present was killed. Fortunately, most of the precision machine tools at the factory were not destroyed. Production was resumed in dispersed sites, to twenty-eight sites around Southampton, five garages, a laundry, a bus station and soon, further dispersal sites in Salisbury, Reading, Hungerford, Winchester and Newbury. The design staff and facilities at Woolston were moved to the Hotel Polygon in Southampton. Despite the disruption and dispersal, over 8,000 "Woolston" Spitfires and Seafires (carrier-capable navalised Spitfires) were produced as a result of these measures, to be complemented by the production of over 12,000 at the Castle Bromwich shadow factory.

The most significant aircraft had significantly dispersed production sites. As an example of the degree of dispersion, the location of production of various combat aircraft is shown in table 3.3 below and overleaf:

Table 3.3: Examples of Dispersed Aircraft Production During the Second World War.

Company	Factory Location	Produced
Handley Page Halifax		
Handley Page	Radlett, Hertfordshire	1,589
English Electric	Preston & Samlesbury, Lancashire	2,145
Fairey Aviation	Stockport, Cheshire	662
London Aircraft Production Group	LAPG major assemblies: final assembly at de Havilland Leavesden facility, in Hertfordshire	710
Rootes Securities	Speke, Liverpool	1,070

Company	Factory Location	Produced
Avro Lancaster		
A.V. Roe	Woodford, Cheshire (parts, sub-assemblies & major assemblies at Chadderton, Oldham)	2,978
A.V.Roe	Yeadon, Yorkshire	695
Armstrong Whitworth	Whitley, Coventry	1,329
Austin Motors	Longbridge & Marston Green, Birmingham	330
Metropolitan-Vickers (MV)	parts, sub-assemblies & major assemblies Trafford Park, Manchester (with MV final assembly line also at Woodford)	1,080
Vickers-managed	Castle Bromwich, Birmingham	300
Vickers-managed	Chester, Cheshire	235
Victory Aircraft	Malton (Ontario, Canada)	430
de Havilland Mosquito		
de Havilland	Hatfield, Hertfordshire	3,326
de Havilland	Leavesden, Hertfordshire	1,476
Standard Motor	Canley, Coventry	1,066
Percival Aircraft	Luton, Bedfordshire	245
Airspeed Aircraft	Portsmouth, Hampshire	122
Vickers	Hawarden, Chester	96
de Havilland	DH Canada, Toronto	1,076
de Havilland	DH Australia, Sydney	212
Hawker Hurricane		
Hawker Aircraft	Kingston and Brooklands, Surrey	9,935
Gloster	Brockworth, Gloucester	2,750
Canadian Car & Foundrey	Montreal, Canada	830
Austin Motors	Longbridge, Birmingham	300
Short Sunderland		
Shorts	Belfast, Northern Ireland & Rochester, Kent	570
Blackburn	Dumbarton, Scotland	175
Shorts	Lake Windermere (White Cross Bay)	35
Supermarine Spitfire (incl. 2,646 Seafire)		
Supermarine	Woolston, Southampton	7,917
Vickers-managed	Castle Bromwich, Birmingham	12,127
Westland	Yeovil, Somerset	2,158
Cunliffe-Owen	Eastleigh, Southampton	504

Some production facilities were extensively camouflaged. For example, at the large new Yeadon (Avro) factory, grass-covered earth ramps disguised the walls and the rectangular shape of the building and grass was planted covering parts of the roof. The intention was to replicate the original field patterns as photographed from the air.

Imitation farm buildings, stone walls and a duck pond disguised it as an agricultural area. Artificial hedges and bushes were changed to match the changing colours of the seasons. Dummy animals were moved around daily, like props in a film or theatre set. The nearby Yeadon dam was drained so as to prevent it being used as a marker for the Yeadon site, which included an RAF station. The factory was never detected by enemy bombers and remained untouched throughout the duration of the conflict.

All these efforts to replace, increase and conceal factory space were fundamental enablers in the striving to produce all kinds of aircraft but the factories needed a lot of workers. Skilled and unskilled workers were directed to where they were best used. As in the First World War, women were recruited and trained into many different areas. Despite the previous experience of being displaced from work (including aircraft manufacturing) when the men returned from service in the armed forces in 1918, women willingly took up the challenge again, including shop floor manufacturing work. In many aircraft factories, women became three quarters of the workforce. Without the extensive contribution from these extra workers, war production of aircraft never would have approached the levels actually achieved. From a total workforce of 128,000 in 1938, the peak reached over 1,600,000 workers during the war. Alone against the German forces in the desperate months following the Dunkirk evacuation of the British army from France between 26 May and 4 June 1940, the aircraft factory and other armaments establishments workforces had a seven-day working week and hours rose to as high as seventy, eighty or even eighty-four per week.

At the height of the war, in 1943–44, the physical weight of aircraft produced was one hundred times the weight produced in 1935. This required the employment of about one third of the country's manufacturing industry labour force, about 8 per cent of employed people. The actual average working week in Britain's wartime factories was between forty-eight and sixty hours for men and between forty-eight and fifty-four hours for women, depending on the degree of physical effort involved.

The massive expansion of the capacity to produce aircraft, which started in the mid-late 1930s in preparation for the Second World War, had resulted in an industry too large to be sustained in a peacetime environment, just as at the end of the First World War. Internal discussions started within the Air Ministry in 1944, on what level of reduction in capacity should be considered and what would be the case for rationalisation of the industry to match future aviation needs. With an optimistic outlook, the government-appointed Brabazon Committee was expected to outline the major way forward for British civil aircraft (see section 5.2) which would replace some of the war-related work. Almost to the end of the war, the military aviation effort was still at full speed. The promised peace was expected to create major reductions in expenditure on all war materials for several years.

In the event, the unexpected "Cold War" which was to emerge in 1946–50, in a new and frightening nuclear-armed environment, overtook any true consideration of, and embryo planning for, a major rationalisation of the UK aircraft industry (see section 5.11).

Chapter 4

About Aircraft Engines – The Changes To Come

4.1 Powerful Piston Engines

Aircraft capability and good performance requires the availability of an appropriate engine. Ever since man attempted to fly, the availability of a powerful-and-light-enough aircraft engine has been a prerequisite for success. The Wright brothers had to design and have their own engine built especially for the aircraft which gave them the very first powered flight success.

As aircraft development progressed, improved aircraft engines were essential enablers. Different engine manufacturers led the way at different times, generally allowing or even leading the improvements in aircraft design. The "best" engine of 1908 was the 50HP French V-8 air-cooled Antoinette reciprocating piston petrol engine, used on the S.F. Cody "first flight of an aircraft built in England" biplane. A.V. Roe's 1909 first flight in his No.1 Triplane used a much less powerful 9HP English JAP V-twin air-cooled engine. These two aircraft had an overall power-to-weight ratio of just under 0.02HP/lb.

Through the 1920s, 1930s and 1940s, piston engine power increased further and fuel efficiency continued to improve, culminating in Britain in the 2,300+HP Napier Sabre and Rolls-Royce Griffon liquid-cooled engines. In the USA, the massive Pratt & Whitney R-4360 Wasp Major 3,500HP twenty-eight-cylinder air-cooled radial piston engine appeared. This was 8ft long, 4.5ft diameter: 3,870lbs dry weight (1¾ tonne) developed to power the four-engined Boeing 377 Stratocruiser of 1947.

Examples of piston engine power growth are illustrated in Table 4.1 opposite.

The Rolls-Royce Merlin V-12 piston engine made a major contribution to the Second World War air campaign in Europe, in the extent to which it powered many different Allied aircraft. These included the majority of Armstrong-Whitworth Whitely bombers, the Hawker Hurricanes, the Supermarine Spitfires, the de Havilland Mosquitos, the vast majority of the Avro Lancaster bombers, a few Vickers Wellington bombers, and, in USA Packard V-1650 Merlin guise, the long-range developed version of North American P-51B fighter-escorts. In total, 205,182 Merlins were built, plus engines for over 5,000 British tanks (called the Meteor engine in the tank application, not to be confused with the jet turbine aircraft of the same name). Aircraft were to see a major change in the years to come, as piston engines were replaced by jet turbine engines.

The Second World War was also a major turning point in the history of civil aviation and the engines used in transport aircraft. The demands of global war caused a massive expansion of global air transport traffic, especially across the North Atlantic and South Pacific Oceans. At the same time, dramatic improvements in aviation engine technology allowed increased aircraft range and capacity. The large radial piston engines on aircraft like the Boeing Stratocruiser (Stratocruiser four engines, each twenty-eight cylinders, virtually unsilenced) delivered a lot of thrust, by use of propellers of up to seventeen feet diameter, with the tips of the propeller blades at speeds not far below supersonic. This added up to significant engine noise and vibration, as experienced in the passenger cabin.

Table 4.1: Examples of the Growth in Aircraft Piston Engine Power, from the First World War to post-Second World War.

Aircraft	First Flight	Engine	Engine Config^n. & Cooling	No. of Aircraft Engines	Aircraft Weight (MTOW) lb.	Total Installed Power (HP)	Aircraft Pwr/Wt. (HP/lb)
Military UK							
Royal A/c Factory B.E.2c	1914	RAF 1a	V.8-A	1	2,350	90	0.0383
Bristol Fighter F.2B	1916	R.Royce Falcon III	V.12-L	1	3,243	275	0.0848
Airco DH.9A (USA engine)	1918	Liberty L-12	V.12-L	1	3,990	449	0.1125
Hawker Hart	1928	R.Royce Kestrel IB	V.12-L	1	4,596	510	0.1110
Gloster Gladiator	1934	Bristol Mercury	R.9-A	1	4,594	825	0.1796
Vickers Wellington Mk 1C	1937	Bristol Pegasus	R.9-A	2	28,500	2,100	0.0737
Supermarine Spitfire Mk VB	1940	R.Royce Merlin 45	V.12-L	1	6,700	1,470	0.2194
Hawker Tempest V	1943	Napier Sabre II	H.24-L	1	13,640	2,180	0.1598
Civil UK							
DH.60G Gipsy Moth	1928	DH Gipsy I	I.4-A	1	1,640	100	0.0610
Avro Avian IVM	1929	ADC Cirrus	I.4-A	1	1,523	105	0.0689
DH.89 Dragon Rapide	1934	DH Gipsy Six	I.6-A	2	5,500	400	0.0727
Bristol Brabazon	1949	Bristol Centaurus	R.2x9-A	8	290,000	21,200	0.0731
Civil USA							
Douglas DC-3A	1937	P&W R.1830-21	R.2x14-A	2	25,199	2,400	0.0952
Douglas DC-4 (post-WW2)	1946	P&W R.2000	R.2x14-A	4	73,000	5,800	0.0795
Boeing 377 Stratocruiser	1947	P&W R.4360	R.4x7-A	4	148,000	14,000	0.0946

Engine Cylinder Configuration Code:
I = in-line, V = in a 'V', H = horizontally opposed, R = Radial. Type of Cooling: L = Liquid, A = Air (so R.2x14 -A is radial configuration, two banks of fourteen cylinders, one bank behind the other, air-cooled)

4.2 The Jet Turbine Engine Story

The most important game-changing aircraft engine development was the jet turbine engine, developed in Britain by Frank Whittle's company Power Jets. Frank Whittle (later Sir Frank) was an RAF engineer. In 1930, he was granted a patent for his idea of a jet turbine propulsion engine, which dispensed with the use of reciprocating pistons and crankshaft driving a propeller. A jet turbine engine is (conceptually) mechanically simpler than the reciprocating piston engine. Air from the engine inlet is continuously compressed by a turning compressor and passed into a combustion chamber, into which fuel is continuously fed and burnt in the pressurised air. This causes a major increase in gas pressure in the combustion chamber, which in turn forces the burnt fuel/air gas mixture to rush out of the back of the engine

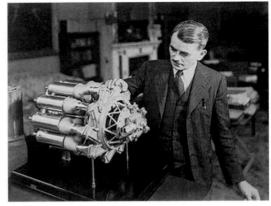

Frank Whittle and his Engine. (*Author's collection*)

in a continuous jet of hot gas, via blades on a disc (the turbine). The turbine acts like a fan in reverse, forced by the (very hot) gas to turn, turning the turbine central shaft which is the same shaft (in a central transmission tunnel) which turns the compressor. The jet exhaust behind the turbine provides the thrust.

When the patent came up for renewal in 1935, Whittle could not afford the £5 fee and the patent lapsed. In 1936 and with the help of two ex-RAF personnel, he founded Power Jets. With further support from the British Thomson-Houston Company, the first prototype engine ran in 1937.

After a successful demonstration to Air Ministry officials in 1939, Power Jets started to receive government financial support. By 1941 there was sufficient interest for Gloster to be contracted by the Air Ministry to design and build a flight demonstrator aircraft, using the W.1A model of Whittle's latest engine. This became the Gloster E.38/39, Britain's first jet turbine powered aircraft, which had its maiden flight on 15 May 1941. Whittle had postulated use of axial flow compressors but, at the time he started his detail design, materials technology was insufficiently advanced to allow this. His engines therefore had a centrifugal flow compressor, which was of larger diameter than the rest of the engine.

Gloster E38/39. (*Author's collection*)

Germany had flown the first jet turbine powered aircraft in the world, the experimental Heinkel He.178[1], on 27 August 1939. The German engine had originated as a development of the idea in Frank Whittle's first patent filing ten years previously, a copy of which was in a German library. The He.178 HeS.3 engine used a centrifugal

---

1. A jet propulsion engine had been developed in Italy, with the compressor driven by a conventional piston engine and the compressed air passed to a combustion chamber to produce a jet exhaust. This engine (classified as a motorjet) was developed in Italy by Secondo Campini. He cooperated with the Caproni aircraft manufacturer to produce the Caproni Campini N.1 aircraft, which first flew on 27 August 1940. The engine provided 1,550lbf thrust. At first, the N.1 was thought to be the world's first jet-propelled aircraft.

flow compressor like Whittle's engine but the follow-on Junkers Jumo 004 engines had an axial flow (i.e. straight through) compressor design, which offered a smaller engine diameter but overall length increased. The Jumo 004 engine entered service on the Messrschmitt Me. 262 fighter/bomber in April 1944 and on the Arado AR 232 twin jet/twin JATO rocket-engined bomber/reconnaissance in September 1944. BMW also produced a working jet turbine engine, the BMW 003, but this was not selected for production for either the Messerschmitt or Arado aircraft.

The Rover Company were tasked with "productionising" Whittle's W.2 engine (a revised version of the W.1A). Rover established a factory in a disused cotton mill, in Barnoldswick, Lancashire. Frank Whittle and Rover became frustrated with each other, partly because of misunderstandings, but the net result was threatening the availability of the new engine in time for a new Gloster jet fighter. Stanley Hooker of Rolls-Royce was in friendly contact with Whittle, and Rolls-Royce was on good terms with Rover. Aware of the clash, Hooker discussed the matter with Ernest Hives (a member of the Rolls-Royce management board, later chairman and ennobled as Lord Hives). In November 1942, Ernest Hives hosted a 5 shillings (60 old pence, now 25p) pub dinner in Clitheroe with Ernest Wilkes (Managing Director at Rover). Stanley Hooker was also present. During the dinner, with only a verbal agreement, Rover at Barnoldswick was simply "swapped to Rolls-Royce" in return for Rover taking over a factory in Nottingham producing the Rolls-Royce Meteor tank engine (a version of the Rolls-Royce Merlin aircraft engine). No "due diligence" or financial exchange was invoked but, quite simply, the ex-W.2 Whittle engine became the Rolls-Royce RB.23 Welland jet engine for the Gloster twin-jet fighter aircraft, in time for service entry in July 1944.

Stimulated by an approach in 1941 from Sir Henry Tizard, chairman of the UK government Aeronautical Research Committee (ARC), the de Havilland Aircraft engine division also started investing effort on an aircraft incorporating Whittle's invention. De Havilland sought the advice of Frank Halford, the engine designer of the Cirrus and ubiquitous DH Gypsy piston engine series of the many DH "Moth" and other aircraft types. Under his guidance, the Halford H.1 jet engine was the result, basically with improved airflow and more thrust than the Whittle W2. The Halford engine first ran in April 1942. The H.1 became the de Havilland Goblin, more powerful than the Rolls-Royce Welland and used in the single-engined de Havilland Vampire, first flown in September 1943. The Goblin was, however, seven inches greater in diameter than the Rolls-Royce Welland. When his company was purchased by de Havilland in 1944, Frank Halford joined de Havilland as chief designer of engines.

The first flight of the Gloster Meteor, in March 1943, was powered by H.1 engines, temporarily substituted for the intended W.2 (Welland). An H.1 engine supplied by Britain also powered the first flight of the prototype Lockheed P.80 Shooting Star (first USA operational jet fighter), on 9 January 1944. The second prototype Meteor was the first to fly with the Whittle engine and the third flew in November 1943 with the axial-compressor UK Metropolitan Vickers F.2 in underslung wing pod installations. This engine was 50 per cent heavier than the W.2 but delivered twice the thrust. Compared with the later DH Goblin, it was about the same weight (1,500lbs) but eight inches lower diameter, with nearly the same thrust capability and better fuel consumption.

Via contacts and relationships established during the 1940 British Scientific and Technical Mission to the USA (the Tizard mission), in 1942 the UK transferred early W.1 Power Jets engines and associated drawings to the USA, as developed by Frank Whittle's team. The USA transfer was to enable the production investment to produce the engine in quantity for the joint UK-USA war effort. The task was allocated to the US General Electric Company (GE) and two other USA companies, specifically chosen by Britain as "non-competitors to the Rolls-Royce aircraft engine business".

Before the GE involvement in this new type of aircraft engine, they had not been involved in internal combustion engine design but had designed and built the rotary centrifugal compressor superchargers for aircraft piston engines. Initially successful in producing these new jet engines, after periods of uncertainty GE were the only survivors of the original chosen three USA companies still in the military and civil jet engine business. Others started later, Pratt & Whitney in particular. GE established themselves as a major supplier of the technology. Much later, GE formed a subsidiary company GE Aviation in 1968, which now provides half of the total $120 billion (2017) annual revenue of the parent General Electric Company.

The progress in thrust level and fuel economy was dramatic and the effect on military and civil post-war aircraft design was equally dramatic. Development of the axial compressor by RAE and Metropolitan Vickers for the F.2/4 Beryl jet engine led to a first flight in June 1943. This was a test installation at the tail of a Lancaster bomber and realised 4,000lbf thrust, compared with the Rolls-Royce contemporary centrifugal compressor Derwent engine 2,450lbf thrust. In 1946, two F.2/4 Beryls were fitted as primary power in the Saunders Roe SR.A/1 jet fighter flying boat (the only floating aircraft designed with this engine as the only power source). The emergence of metal alloys able to withstand higher and higher temperatures (increasing combustion efficiency) and ingenious turbine blade cooling methods were starting to permit ongoing growth in engine power and thermodynamic efficiency.

Having a common turbine and compressor rotational speed (i.e. a single shaft engine) means a compromise in the efficiency of both compressor and turbine. If the compressor and the turbine are split into two independent sets of stages (called the Low Pressure and High Pressure pairs), each set running at different rotational speeds driven by their own turbine sections, the design speeds of the pairs of compressor and turbine elements can be more closely matched to an optimum.[2] The drive from the two turbine sets to the

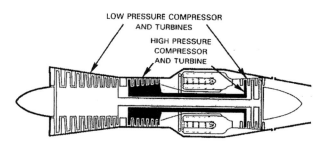

Two-Spool Jet Turbine. (*Author's collection*)

two different compressor sets is achieved using concentric shafts. In 1953, the practical realisation of a two-spool jet turbine engine emerged, as the Pratt & Whitney J.57 engine (zero per cent bypass), which entered service in 1954.

In 1947, Metropolitan Vickers stepped out of turbojet activity and their engine design team moved to Armstrong Siddeley. Continuing from the Metropolitan Vickers Beryl development, the Armstrong Siddeley Sapphire axial-flow turbojet was produced. This was the most powerful jet turbine engine available until the advent of the later developments of the Rolls-Royce Avon in the mid-1950s.

To improve fuel efficiency, letting part of the compressed air from the first stage(s) of compression bypass the combustion process reduces average jet exhaust speed, spread over a larger area exhaust. Efficient thrust generation happens when total jet exhaust speed is not too much higher than the aircraft forward speed. Initially, bypass ratio was set around 25 per cent of compressor air mass flow bypassing the combustion

---

2. Diagram based on Loftin (NASA) diagram in Ch. 10 of "*The Quest for Performance – The Evolution of the Modern Aircraft*".

chamber. The first commercial bypass engine, the Rolls-Royce Conway engine of the 1950s, started at this value, later increased to over 50 per cent when mounted free of the confines of the wing, in dedicated pods on the rear fuselage of the 1962 Vickers VC.10 airliner.

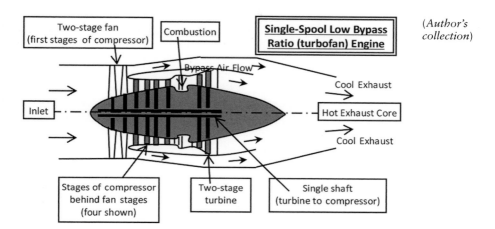

(Author's collection)

As bypass ratios increased, the modern term for this type of engine has become the "turbofan". A beneficial by-product of the turbofan is the partial containment of noise in the high-speed hot exhaust by the surrounding slower and cooler bypass (fan) air. The largest modern turbofans (GE, Rolls-Royce and Pratt & Whitney products, with bypass ratios of around 10:1 (i.e. 1,000 per cent) and fan diameters of around 10ft) are capable of powering a twin-engined large airliner carrying several hundred passengers, non-stop half-way round the world. Typical sale price for a large modern turbofan is US$25million to US$30 million.

Rolls Royce Trent XWB. (*Rolls-Royce PLC*)

For reasons of compressor efficiency, some turbofans are of a three-spool design, where there is an "Intermediate Pressure" compressor-turbine pairing. This is the configuration used in the Rolls-Royce RB.211 and Trent series of turbofans.

The development in jet engine technology, from the first (1942) production jet engine to twenty-first century large turbofans, is illustrated in table 4.2. Examples of developments in both the USA and UK are included. Engine specific fuel consumption (sfc = lbs of fuel per lb of thrust per hour) has improved along the way. Other than a rocket, the jet turbine engine is the only possible powerplant for any high subsonic/supersonic bomber or fighter and, in turbofan form, currently is also the only possible powerplant which can economically provide power for the high capacity long-range airliners at the speeds consistent with current airline schedules.

Table 4.2: Jet Engine Development over seventy years.

Company	Engine	First Run	Compressor Type	Dry Wt. (lb)	Bypass	Maximum Continuous Thrust* (lb)	cruise sfc (lb/lb/hr)
Rolls-Royce	Welland	1942	Centrifugal	850	nil	1,600	1.12
de Havilland	H.1/Goblin 1	1942	Centrifugal	1,550	nil	2,700	1.18
Metro-Vick rs.	F.2	1941	Axial	~1,500	nil	~2,400	1.07
GE (USA)	J31	1943	Centrifugal	850	nil	1,650	1.20
Rolls-Royce	Derwent 1	1943	Centrifugal	975	nil	2,000	1.17
Rolls-Royce	Nene	1944	Centrifugal	1,600	nil	5,000	1.06
de Havilland	Ghost	1945	Centrifugal	2,218	nil	5,000	1.02
Rolls-Royce	Avon (RA.26)	1956*	Axial	2,890	nil	10,000*	0.93
*first Rolls-Royce Avon ran in 1946 at 7,500 lb thrust							
Rolls-Royce	Conway	1956	Axial	~4,500	25%	18,000	0.87
P & W (USA)	JT3D (J-57 developed)	1958	Axial	4,605	25%	17,000	0.78
Example high bypass ratio turbofan (Rolls-Royce Trent on Airbus A350 XWB, 315 to 369 seats)							
Rolls-Royce	Trent XWB-97	2010	Axial	16,640	9.6:1	97,000*	0.51

* Thrust capability is measured on a test stand (i.e. "Static Thrust"). Trent XWB-97: 97,000lbf = 44 tonne static thrust. Trent XWB maximum continuous thrust fuel consumption would exceed 100 imperial gallon per minute per engine but, at cruising speed, thrust required and associated fuel consumption is significantl lower than the maximum continuous rate (which is set lower than the take-off power, which in turn is time limited, for reasons of engine life).

4.3 The TurboProp Engine

The jet turbine engine driving a propeller (turboprop engine) requires the engine turbine to provide most of its energy as shaft power to a propeller, allowing maximum gas flow for the propeller drive turbine, consistent with taking enough gas energy to drive the compressor shaft. The drive to the propeller is achieved via an integral gearbox on the same shaft as the power turbine, geared to slow the rotational speed of the propeller shaft from the high turbine speed, for reasons of propeller efficiency. Illustrating progress in turboprop engine power development, Table 4.3 opposite shows a few of the improvements in turboprop engine performance and weight reduction, in terms of power delivered to the propeller gearbox. Power output is measured as Shaft Horse Power (SHP), with a relatively small amount of additional thrust available from the jet turbine exhaust. For flight speeds lower than the high subsonic of the jet thrust type of aircraft, the propeller is more efficient.

The development of efficient low-weight small turboprop engines, such as the Pratt & Whitney Canada PT6 series (e.g. PT6A-6 with 580SHP, dry weight 270lb first version first run in 1960), enabled turboprop-powered aircraft designs eventually to dominate in parts of the general aviation market, as well as in short and medium range regional airliners, where fuel economy is more relevant than pure speed.

It is interesting to compare the 11,000SHP of the Europrop TP400-D6 engine with the 3,500HP of the P&W R.4360, the most powerful piston engine to enter service some sixty years earlier. The R.4360 had an engine power/weight ratio of a little over 0.9000 and weighed 84 per cent of the TP400-D6 (see table 4.1 in section 4.1). A piston engine

Table 4.3: Turboprop Engine Development, first 50 years.

Company	Engine	First Run	Compressor	Dry Wt. (lb)	Power (SHP)	Power/Weight (SHP/lb)
Bristol	Proteus 600	1947	Axial+Centrifugal	2,805	2,500	0.891
Rolls-Royce	Dart RDa.1	1946	Centrifugal	1,122	1,250	1.114
Rolls-Royce	Dart RDa.7	~1965	Centrifugal	1,207	2,280	1.889
Allison (USA)	T56 501-D13	~1955	Axial	~1,900	3,750	1.974
Rolls-Royce	Tyne Rty.11	~1955	Axial	2,219	5,095	2.296
Pratt & Whitney (Canada)	PW 125	~1984	2x Centrifugal	~1,000	2,400	2.400
Allison (USA)	T56-A-14	~1965	Axial	~1,900	4,590	2.416
RR Allison (USA)	AE2100-D2	1994	Axial	1,727	4,637	2.685
Example of 2017 large turboprop (four on Airbus A.400M Atlas, 81,600lb payload)						
Europrop*	TP400-D6	2005	Axial	4,617	11,000	2.382

* Europrop International is a joint venture company between four European aircraft engine companies, MTU Aero Engines (Germany), Safran (France), Rolls-Royce (Britain) and Industria de Turbo Propulsores (Italy). The company's sole product is the Europrop TP-400-D6 turboprop engine developed for the Airbus A.400M Atlas (see section 7.4).

to drive a propeller at a power level of 11,000HP would be "impossible" on an aircraft, due to actual engine size, weight and cooling limitations, and fuel consumption would be another barrier. The turboprop can be the most fuel-efficient and very satisfactory powerplant for almost any aircraft where high speed (approaching transonic) is not an operational requirement.

Chapter 5

The Post-Second World War Years, 1946 to 1959

5.1 UK Government Input to Aviation Technology Research and Aircraft Development

From the earliest days, in countries with an aircraft design and manufacturing industry, the governments concerned had been keen to provide support and research assistance. From 1919 in the UK, fundamental aerodynamic research[1] and the development of technology for aircraft and their engines were in part supported by the Royal Aircraft Establishment (RAE) and the National Physical Laboratory (NPL, established in 1900). The Royal Aircraft Establishment had its name updated to Royal Aerospace Establishment in 1988 and was eventually absorbed into the government agency Defence Evaluation and Research Agency (DERA). This was later split into the privatised company QinetiQ and the government agency Defence Science and Technology Laboratory (DSTL).

Just as in 1918, the end of the conflict in 1945 caused the abrupt arrest of much of the frenetic industrial activity in Britain. To scale the likely reduction, in terms of military aviation, the RAF had started with 173,858 personnel in 1939 (which was significantly more than most of the 1930s). The number had grown to 1,079,835 personnel by May 1945. This time, there was a common desire to proactively move forwards into the new aviation technologies and to "kick start" the virtually moribund British civil airliner industry. Fundamental and application research for aviation technologies needed stimulation, but the parlous domestic financial position would limit the effort. Nevertheless, there was a determination to progress civil aviation in Britain, exemplified by the formation of the Brabazon Committee (see section 5.2).

In 1946, Frank Whittle's Power Jets company was nationalised and amalgamated with the "gas turbine engine" design technology and test division of the RAE. The resulting organisation was established as the National Gas Turbine Establishment (NGTE), aimed at creating jet engine research and development test facilities. This finally closed in 2000.

In the frantic scramble between the victorious Allies for access to advanced technology in the conquered Germany, Britain persuaded aerodynamicist Dr Dietrich Küchemann to move to Britain, to work at the RAE. RAE and industrial research was to reap rewards for Britain (see sections 6.4 [VC.10], 7.1 [Concorde] and 7.4 [Airbus]).

The British government exercised a level of controlling authority over most aviation matters (including research) from before 1914. In January 1918 the Air Ministry had been established, to co-ordinate *all* air matters between the War Office, the Admiralty and the Army. In 1922, a new post "Director of Civil Aviation" was established as part of the Air Ministry. The Air Ministry soon became responsible for recommendations on and implementing "air policy" (both military and civil), aviation

---

1. Very similar aeronautical research government support in the USA was the responsibility of the National Advisory Committee for Aeronautics, formed in 1915 (NACA). This was absorbed into the National Aeronautics and Space Administration (NASA) from 1958. A NACA-sponsored offshoot, the Aircraft Engine Research Laboratory, was established in 1935, now the (NASA) Glenn Research Center at Lewis Field, Ohio.

infrastructure developments, air transport regulation and creating requirements specifications for both civil and military aircraft procured for any government-owned organisation. This included the armed forces and the nationalised Imperial Airways (and its 1940 incarnation as the nationalised BOAC, see section 2.7). If procurement of a broadly unchanged extant aircraft type was to be undertaken, a "production-only" specification was prepared, outlining any customisation needs. The Ministry of Supply co-ordinated the supply of *all* equipment to all three British armed forces. Due to problems in establishing effective wartime control of aircraft supply, the separate Ministry of Aircraft Production (MAP) was also established (as previously described in section 3.2).

To the present day, the British government continues to influence (and has actually directly controlled, at times) the civil and military aircraft industry and the aircraft engine industry (as described in later sections). Since the last years of the twentieth century, it has, however, seriously reduced the level of government directly-controlled research effort. More often, the government now chooses to encourage research with industrial and/or academia participation, rather more than run its own totally independent research team. This is not always compatible with "blue sky ideas being developed into an application".

5.2 The Wartime UK Brabazon Committee and the Aircraft Which it Spawned
The reasons for forming a committee
Starting to plan for a future peace, the government established the Brabazon Committee in August 1942, chaired by John Moore Brabazon (by then, Lord Brabazon of Tara). The committee remit was to consider the British domestic, Empire and other British international future civil aircraft transport needs, and the associated British industry aircraft and engine projects, after the war ended. It was feared that the parlous national financial position by the end of the war would not be conducive to several manufacturers producing different solutions to the market requirements (whatever they would turn out to be) and there was growing awareness of how far ahead in transport aircraft design the USA had already become. After the devastating effect of war expenditure, just paying for the import of the necessary materials for creating new airliners in peacetime would be a problem. The most important objective was to define the airliner needs, the aircraft engine development needs, and any aviation infrastructure/policy changes to be contemplated after the war. The committee needed to report in time for industry to be able to have responses ready to implement, especially forestalling a USA airliner industry "walk-over" in the post-war decade.

Initially, there were six members of the Brabazon Committee under the chairman, three each from the Air Ministry and the MAP. Terms of reference were quite general, abridged as follows:

1. To prepare outline specifications of the several aircraft types that would be needed for post-war air transport and which firms should be invited to tender designs.
2. To consider, in consultation with the aircraft firms involved, which existing military aircraft could be usefully converted to air transport purposes whilst new civil types were being produced.
3. To prepare a plan for the immediate utilisation, in the interests of post-war air transport, of spare design and production capacity whilst the aircraft industry made its transition from war to peace.

Specific planning assumptions for the Brabazon committee *may* have started along the lines:

- The USA was already well advanced and likely to "look after itself" for passenger aircraft, unless and until some major exclusive aircraft technology advance was developed elsewhere (an example which might have been considered would be the use of turbine engine technology). This was introduced into committee thinking later, with a significant impact.
- If Britain does not address the lack of an indigenous airliner design and build capability, post-war it will have no option but to "buy American, using dollars it does not have", or purchase the right to build USA designs under licence and thus losing its transport aircraft design capability forever.
- New British airliners need to be competitive in price, performance and operating cost with those likely to be available from the USA by the end of the war.
- Europe would be industrially and financially devastated by the war and it would be some while before a competitive aircraft industry would be recreated in continental Europe, but this will be rectified in due course.
- The next few years. This should focus on communication requirements between many (and far) regions of the Empire, on government needs and on catering for travelling members of the public. Domestic, European and long distance air travel and air freight each needed separate consideration, of necessity using crude estimation in the first place but to be refined further before the end of the war and before new designs are fully authorised.
- Places where wilderness and isolation made air transport the only viable physical communication option should be considered, but not as an immediate priority.
- Given the aircraft production capacity which had already been created for the war, no additional aircraft production facilities would be needed in Britain after the war to build passenger and freight aircraft.
- Post-war, public air transport was likely to remain largely limited to passengers on business or with some personal financial means.

The committee's first report did produce initial information consistent with much of the above but it is not clear whether any such (or completely different) assumptions were explicitly formulated. The MAP overall drive appears simply to have been "Britain is behind the USA in transport aircraft, we had better get our skates on".

The outline early recommendations were prepared by February 1943, divided into interim airliner adaptations of four (bomber) aircraft then in development or production for the war effort, and the design and development of five new airliner types as soon as practicable. Likely quantities were estimated. The initial thoughts turned out to be wildly overenthusiastic For example, the recommended Avro Lancaster bomber-derived Avro York, with a new fifty-six-passenger fuselage (already flying), was expected by the committee to result in 1,300 aircraft. After the presentation of the first report in August 1943, the Brabazon committee was reformed, to include representatives from BOAC and industry (notably, Geoffrey de Havilland). A co-ordinating Committee on Air Transport was formed under Lord Beaverbrook and the initial recommendations were reviewed. The USA air transport aircraft developments already in war service and USA airline service were known but "what was in the USA pipeline" was unclear at first. After a conference involving British Empire countries and a visit by individuals to the USA, much of a revised Brabazon Committee report was available by November 1943. A couple of aircraft industry chief designers had been authorised to visit the USA (Lockheed, Boeing and Douglas particularly). They shared what they had seen and heard and advised the committee. The final Brabazon report (the fifth) was not complete and issued until November 1944.

One consequence was a new Ministry of Civil Aviation was created within the Air Ministry, in November 1944.

The Wartime Air Transport Aircraft Supply

During the Second World War there had been (supposedly) an agreement, between Britain and the USA, that Britain would concentrate production of large aircraft entirely on heavy bombers and would use large transport aircraft supplied lease-lend by the USA. One statement (by a conference speaker from de Havilland in 1951, well after the war) was that:

> "Because we were ahead of the Americans in turbine development, we saw in the jet airliner an opportunity to re-establish British leadership on the airways of the world, which had been denied us from the middle thirties when British airline operations had not been encouraged to anything like the degree enjoyed by American airlines. The leeway had been increased by the war periods in which, by agreement, America concentrated on heavy bomber and transport aircraft while British effort was devoted to fighters and other combat types."

This has caused some to claim that this demonstrates that the existence of such an "agreement" was at least one of the reasons behind the Brabazon Committee's formation and, maybe, *the* cause:

- If the "we" in the conference statement refers to "de Havilland the company" only, it is quite reasonable to take the statement as representing "the truth for de Havilland". This would be logical as, during the war, de Havilland had not designed heavy bombers but had established their turbojet engine business. They had employed Frank Halford's engine design consulting firm in 1941, to improve the engine layout and internal airflow from that in Frank Whittles' early prototype jet engine design. Developed into the de Havilland "Goblin" turbojet engine, flight standard was achieved in 1943, used for the first flights of prototypes of both the new de Havilland DH.100 Vampire single-engined fighter and the new Gloster Meteor twin-engined fighter. De Havilland bought Frank Halford's business in late 1943, employing him as their engine chief designer. Rolls-Royce began developing the Dart turbo-prop engine in that same year (1943). The outcomes of both the de Havilland and Rolls-Royce moves into turbine engines turned out to be major influences in the post-1946 British aircraft industry story.
- If the "we" is taken to be the Brabazon Committee (or at least the British aircraft industry), the conference statement could imply that post-war piston-engined large airliner development would not be pursued in Britain. This is patently misleading, witness the Brabazon-inspired forty-seven passenger Airspeed Ambassador and the forty to eighty-two passenger Handley Page Hermes civil airliner development.

So the statement can have ambiguous alternative interpretations.

The inference "imparted" by the statement *could* be that, towards the end of the war, "Britain was to concentrate airliner efforts on defining (and eventually producing) the de Havilland Comet jet airliner and the Vickers Viscount and Bristol Britannia turbo-prop airliners *because of* such an agreement and its effect on the Brabazon Committee deliberations and, therefore, the consequences in the aircraft industry". Such an inference is totally speculative; unless and until authentic documentary evidence is available.

For warplane development, it is an obvious fact that the Americans not only built transport aircraft, they also built *very* large numbers of fighter, dive bomber, light, medium and heavy bomber aircraft during the war. Many were used in the Pacific war theatre. The North American P.51 Mustang fighters and Boeing B-17 Flying Fortress bombers served with the USAAF Europe in significant numbers, flying from British airfields, and RAF P.51 Mustang fighter squadrons had been formed.

It is also a fact that the RAF used a large number (over 2,000) of USA lend-lease supplied Douglas C-47 Dakota transports, militarised versions of the DC-3, built in thousands as transport, logistics and paratroop aircraft for the Allies. Even if there had been a British aircraft design of comparable size and capability, there were no spare wartime resources to produce such and, between 1939 and 1945, such an aircraft was not authorised to be developed, specified, or even seriously debated in Britain.

Paratroops boarding a Douglas Dakota, 5 June 1944. (*Author's collection*)

So, was there any truth in the existence of "a transatlantic agreement", or was it just a post-war retrospective assertion? In practice, with or without any agreement, Britain had had no choice but to concentrate most of the aircraft wartime efforts on production of large numbers of bombers and fighters. Given the state of the war's progress in 1942, this is not a surprising out-turn, whether or not there was any agreement about the USA producing all the transport aircraft. Given the knowledge of the USA airliner capabilities already in existence by 1942–43, it seems extremely likely that the Brabazon Committee (or something like it) should have been formed in any event, as a sensible stage-setting effort for the country after the war. If there really had been some kind of "wartime only" agreement concerning transport aircraft, it merely would have re-enforced the urgency of the Brabazon Committee deliberations. Perhaps too narrowly (as it turned out), the committee specifically considered the air passenger likely market in Britain, alongside the air travel needs to/from Great Britain, the British Commonwealth and Empire and Europe, without considering in any detail air transport needs not having British Empire involvement and the associated market for new aircraft. Overseas market needs therefore did not receive any real separate attention.

What happened in airliner development, immediately before and during the Second World War?

Well before the USA entered the world conflict in December 1941, for internal North American trans-continental passenger transport reasons the USA industry developed largish long-range airliners. The geographic size of the USA alone meant coast-to-coast or north-to-south travel took over three days by sleeper train, by car a couple of days or more longer, and by Greyhound bus a little longer than a train (if passengers took the extremely uncomfortable option of "sleeping on the bus"). Even in eight stages, by air in a 1936 DC-2 it would take a little less than a day flying (depending on wind direction and strength), allowing for intermediate en-route stops for crew changes, passenger pick-up and put-down and refuelling/passenger refreshment. Most USA internal passenger traffic in any case would be between population centres in the eastern states, in 1936 perhaps two or three hours by air compared with five, ten or even twelve hours by train, bus or car. From the middle 1930s onwards, the USA started with the two-engined fourteen-passenger 1934 Douglas DC-2 metal monoplane (range 1,085 miles, cruise speed 174mph). This was soon upgraded to the thirty-two-passenger DC-3 in 1935, cruising at 207mph.

There was also the Lockheed Electra model 10/12/14 airliner and the four-engined thirty-eight-passenger 1938 Boeing 307 Stratoliner (the first pressurised-cabin passenger aircraft in the world and first ordered by Pan American airways in 1937).

This was a technology leap in cabin environmental comfort and in the ability to fly higher, with an achievable range of 1,500 miles.

The Boeing 307 was soon joined by the four-engined (but unpressurised) forty to eighty passenger Douglas DC-4 (maximum range 4,250 miles) which commenced design in 1938. The introduction of the DC-4 would see trans-USA flights taking around twelve to fourteen hours, with a couple of intermediate stops. The four-engined and pressurised 1943 Lockheed L-049 Constellation (range 4,000 miles) could accommodate sixty-two to 109 passengers. The Constellation prototype was completed in secret (kept from even the US Army) by Lockheed before the USA entered the war. These latter projects were subsumed into the USA war effort after 1941. By this time, the USA aircraft industry was well ahead of the rest of the world in large airliner design. The ubiquitous and reliable DC-3/C-47/Dakota eventually would be available in large numbers as war surplus, sold off to civil operators after the end of the war. The original DC-4 would be improved and available for civil use after the war (and would be developed into the pressurised DC-6) and further developments of the Constellation would be similarly available.

The pre-1939 generally inward-looking USA had responded to internal requirements (USA airmail and slowly-growing civilian passenger needs). This was to eventually include services to Canada, Central and South America, all resulting in a market for the DC-4 and the Constellation. By happenstance, this also largely coincided with the medium and long-range post-war commercial land-plane capability needs worldwide. The USA airline Pan American trans-Pacific routes were a notable exception, resulting in the ordering of twelve of the seventy-four-passenger Boeing 317 Clipper flying boat, built specially for Pan Am. Air transport in the Americas was becoming "accessible" to more and more people (a chicken-and-egg serendipity situation).

Meanwhile, the British aircraft industry had also looked mostly "inward", in their case to the requirements of Imperial Airways. Unfortunately, Imperial Airways version of the European scene was seen as secondary to the onwards routes to Egypt and South Africa and to India, to Singapore and its connection to the Qantas services out of Australia. An Imperial Airways transatlantic multi-stop flying boat service was established shortly before 1939 but the real focus was essentially "Empire routes". This did not create a requirement for world-beating long-range landplanes. It took long-range passenger aircraft design in Britain down the single blind alley of large flying boats, in tune with the "no-runway environment" of the dispersed Empire destinations. The "best" (only) British landplane pre-war reasonably-sized airliners might be seen as either the 1931 Handley Page HP.42 Hannibal biplane (range 500 miles, cruise speed a leisurely 100mph, able to carry twenty-four passengers), or the 1938 Armstrong Whitworth Ensign (range 1,370 miles, cruise speed 180mph, able to carry up to forty passengers), or the 1938 de Havilland DH.91 Albatross monoplane (range 904 miles, cruise speed 210mph, able to carry twenty-two passengers). The very good 1934 de Havilland DH.89 Dragon Rapide biplane had a short range of 700 miles, cruised at 135mph and was small, only able to carry eight passengers.

The best pre-1939 European landplane offering could have been the German four-engined metal monoplane Focke Wulf Fw.200 Condor, which first flew in 1937 (with twenty-six passengers it had a range of 2,012 miles, cruise speed

Fw.200 Condor arrives in New York, 11 August 1938. (*Author's collection*)

208mph). Excluding four prototypes, only twelve were built as airliners, all subsequent production of 272 aircraft being militarised for service as an armed reconnaissance or military transport aircraft. The Condor served as an armed reconnaissance aircraft, particularly over the North Atlantic. The Condor airliner astounded the world in August 1938, by flying non-stop across the Atlantic from Berlin to New York (without passengers and with extra fuselage fuel tanks and against the prevailing westerly wind direction) in twenty-five hours. The shortest distance Berlin-New York is 3,965 miles (6,381 km) but the air miles actually flown by the aircraft (against the prevailing wind) were over 5,200.

The Brabazon Committee Report and the Aircraft Which Resulted

By 1943, the only large British transport landplanes with significant range were the "interim" nine passenger/troop carrier 1942 Avro Lancastrian adaptation of the Lancaster bomber (4,150 miles range) and the twenty-six to fifty-six passenger Avro York. The interim Lancastrian adaptation was first engineered during the war, in Canada (at the Victory factory, eventually to become Avro Canada), by modifying Lancaster aircraft, mainly as a freighter/air mail carrier for the RCAF, with most freight (often air mail, at least in part) carried in bomb bay areas converted to panniers. Later, a less wartime utilitarian cabin interior with seating for only thirteen passengers was engineered by Avro, for Lancastrian aircraft adapted in Britain to Lancastrians and delivered to BOAC. However, the fuselage above the bomb bay was limited and not really suitable for other significant commercial passenger air transport solutions. The York was a Lancaster redesign, with a new low-slung passenger cabin replacing the bomb bay, under the original mid-fuselage position of the Lancaster wing, with 3,000 miles range. After the war, the York did enter airline service, quite suitable for use on European routes but a fair way behind the range and capacity capability of the larger airliner products available from the USA (but there were no US dollars to spare in Britain's Treasury, in any case).

As the final (November 1944) Brabazon report was being prepared, the government announced that certain "interim" transport aircraft would be allowed to be quickly developed, for use until the country had produced new purpose-built airliners. The four "interim" transport aircraft were:

- Pressurised transport based on Avro Lincoln bomber, for non-stop transatlantic use (became Avro Tudor I).
- Avro York (already in production, derived from Lancaster bomber).
- Civil version (new fuselage) of Handley Page Halifax III bomber (became Handley Page Hermes airliner and RAF Hastings troop and cargo transport).
- Civil version of Short Sunderland maritime patrol flying boat (became Short Sandringham).

A fifth interim airliner was ordered in 1944 from Vickers: the Viking, a new (civil passenger) fuselage with the wings revised and the undercarriage and engines of the Bristol Hercules-powered version of the Wellington bomber. Interestingly, one Viking aircraft was to be powered by two Rolls-Royce Nene turbojet engines, ordered by the MoS as an experimental machine. This was the world's first pure jet-powered transport aircraft. On London-Paris (and same-day return) flights in 1948 commemorating the 39th anniversary of Louis Blériot's original 1909 first-ever aircraft English Channel crossing, a maximum speed of 414 mph was reached.

The final outcome of the Brabazon report on new types of aircraft that would be required after the war:

- **Type I**   Very large transatlantic airliner, particularly serving the London-New York route, seating (or sleeping) its passengers in luxury (became Bristol Brabazon).
- **Type II**   European-destination transport (split into two alternatives):-
  - **IIA**   A piston-powered aircraft (became Airspeed Ambassador).
  - **IIB**   A new turboprop-powered aircraft, engine to be developed (became Vickers Viscount *and* Armstrong Whitworth Apollo. Apollo reached prototype stage).
- **Type III**   Medium-range aircraft for various multi-hop routes serving the British Empire (became Avro type 693, originally four-engined turboprop, amended to jet propulsion, cancelled 1947, still on the drawing board, replaced by Bristol Britannia project in 1948).
- **Type IV**   Initially conceived as a modest mail plane powered by jet turbine engines, this became an airliner specification, growing to somewhere around forty passenger seats.

    This jet-turbine aircraft was added at the personal urging of one of the committee members, Geoffrey de Havilland, whose company was involved in development of both Britain's first jet fighters and jet engines and who persuaded the committee that...

    > "If the Type IV could be made to work, the whole concept of a jet airliner might be able to replace the Type III outright, and many of the duties of the other aircraft on shorter routes."

- **Type V**   Feederliner, to fill original feederliner specifications, when Type II evolved into larger designs.
  - **VA**   short range, sixteen to twenty passengers (became Miles Marathon*).
  - **VB**   light transport, eight to ten passengers (became de Havilland Dove, eventually also stretched to fourteen-passenger de Havilland Heron).

* Miles Aircraft were declared bankrupt in 1947 and the business was taken over as a Handley Page subsidiary, formed as Handley Page (Reading) Limited (HPR).

The intention was to blend quick re-entry potential into parts of the civil market and a "technology leap ahead" as the medium term aim for British transport aircraft. Air Ministry specifications were prepared and the Ministry of Supply started the process for agreeing contracts for the aircraft. This was carried out in the then normal way for UK government aircraft production. The Air Ministry Specifications were progressively issued and aircraft companies provided outline design proposals. Eventually, one (maybe two) of each type could be approved as prototype versions. Six of the seven different prototype aircraft reached production status and went into service.

Notionally, a fleet of two **Type I** might offer a six-days a week six-times faster journey (at least 600 passengers a week each way, in three-quarter day journeys), against a 2,000+ passenger Atlantic ocean liner one-way crossing of four, five or, occasionally, six days per crossing). In the committee stage and at the urging of the destination first customer (BOAC), the **Type I** Brabazon was seriously mis-specified as "super-luxury travel for 100 passengers," aimed at attracting what was thought by BOAC to be the most dominant (in numbers) of transatlantic air passengers, transferring from transatlantic ocean liner first class travel.

The **IIA** piston-engined Ambassador was well-liked (but soon outclassed by the new-technology IIB turboprop Viscount passenger comfort and economy).

The **Type III** Avro 693 as a jet was evaluated as superfluous, given the type IV development (DH Comet). The **Type III** Britannia turboprop was, unfortunately, too delayed to succeed in other than niche applications.

The **Type VA** Marathon was beset by the Miles Aircraft bankruptcy and was also "twixt the expanding post-war market", between the **Type VB** Dove/Heron and the **Type IIB** Viscount.

The sad overall result was that only two of these aircraft were to become truly commercially successful – the **IIB** Viscount and the **VB** Dove/Heron. A total of twenty-three proposals from twelve British aircraft companies were made for these all-new "Brabazon Committee types"..

5.3 The Bristol Type 167 Brabazon

"The biggest aircraft in the world? (in the 1940s)". The Brabazon, with a wing span of 230ft (17.5 per cent bigger than the 1970s Boeing 747 "Jumbo" and with a 25 per cent larger fuselage diameter), had an MTOW of 290,000lbs (132 tonnes) but cruised at a modest 250mph at 25,000ft. The Brabazon was the first aircraft to have 100 per cent powered flying controls, electric engine controls and the first to have high pressure hydraulic systems.

Bristol 167 Brabazon, landing at Farnborough, 1949 or 1950. (*BAE Systems*)

The first model was powered by eight 2,650HP Bristol Centaurus radial piston engines, coupled in pairs to four sets of contra-rotating propellers.

At the time, there were three "super-large" aircraft designs in the world. One was the American Lockheed R6V Constitution 168-passenger four-engined piston-propeller aircraft (MTOW 184,000lbs, first flight 1946, two prototypes built), the second was a six-engined 204 proposed passenger version of the American Convair XC-99 military freighter flying in 1947 (MTOW 320,000lbs one prototype built). The Bristol Brabazon (Type I in the Brabazon report) was the third, flying in 1949. An eventual fourth was the British Saunders Roe Princess flying boat, flying in 1952 (MTOW 345,025lb with only three prototypes built ...see section 5.6).

At BOAC request for their envisaged "wealthy and important" transatlantic air passenger, extreme luxury was to be created in the Brabazon. Space allocated per passenger was to be 200ft^3 (equivalent to the volume of the whole interior of a modern four-passenger family car) or 270ft^3 for super-luxury, sleeping berths, cinema, dining room. Halving the space used per passenger would allow at least 200 passengers to be accommodated but that was not BOAC's intention. The aircraft was mistakenly completely mis-specified to compete with the transatlantic ocean liner first class traffic but crossing the Atlantic non-stop in about fifteen hours (subject to wind speed and direction). To improve performance, the second Brabazon prototype was to use the Bristol Proteus turboprop engine (under development), which promised an increase in cruising speed to 330mph and a 10,000lb reduction in weight. The ten production aircraft standard planned were to be the turboprop-powered version.

The London-New York transatlantic faster American airliners soon appeared (and non-stop capable, at least west-to-east) with the Lockheed L-1049 Super Constellation in service in 1951 and entering transatlantic service in 1953. By this time, nearly £6 million (equivalent to over £200 million in 2019) had been spent on the Brabazon design and development. Flight testing with the single prototype was still in progress, without any customer serious interest, not even the British airline BOAC. Roomy and luxurious for all passengers, the piston-powered Brabazon fifteen-hour (± weather effect) London-New York might possibly be improved to about eleven or twelve hours, if/when the Proteus turboprop engine being developed for the second Brabazon could be introduced. This would be similar to the L-1049 Constellation 1953 flight time, which could carry about fifty to sixty transatlantic passengers (maximum capacity with reduced range, 106 passengers). For the moment, the piston-powered Brabazon would use almost twice as much fuel as the L-1049. Hangar space at airports or maintenance units for Brabazon-sized aircraft did not exist.

With the second prototype incomplete and no orders, in 1953 the Brabazon project was cancelled by the government. In part, this was due to design changes being needed to overcome an inadequate projected inner wing fatigue life. The total cost included a new large assembly hangar at Bristol's Filton factory and an essential runway extension (which demolished the nearby village of Charlton). Overall, this had been equivalent to some £400 million in 2019 terms. The runway extension and large hangar eventually proved to be valuable for the next Bristol aircraft project, the Britannia.

5.4 The UK-USA Race for Trans-Atlantic Airliner Market and the de Havilland DH.106 Comet

The Transatlantic Airliner "Big Pistons"

As discussed in section 5.2, by 1941 long-range airliner development in the USA was much further advanced than anywhere else, with the Lockheed L-049 Constellation and Douglas DC-4, each able to cruise around 4,000 miles in still air, with more passengers than the 1942 Avro York's maximum capacity. These American airliners were each powered by four large air-cooled radial-configuration piston engines. At the USA entry into the war in 1941, the US military requisitioned the first batches of Constellations and DC-4s, designating them as the C-69 and C-54, but the aircraft were still wanted by the USA airlines. Even though they did not have non-stop transatlantic capability, they would be fine for trans-America flying.

The map shows the land plane air routes used for USA military North Atlantic air traffic during the war, for both medium and long-range aircraft. The USA 1942 Douglas DC-4 (as the military type C-54 Skymaster) was the most advanced transport aircraft at this time. For UK civilian passengers (VIPs on government business) use during the war, BOAC (the new incarnation of the UK national airline and flying under wartime strictures) used a shuttle from Bristol to Shannon airport (on the west coast of Ireland). Passengers were transferred to a large flying boat in the adjacent Shannon estuary (at the seaport of Foynes) and flown via Gander to the USA. Immediately after the war the best (only) long-range

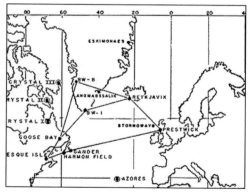

(USAAF) WW2 North Atlantic Air Routes. (*Author's collection*)

British landplane airliner available was the 1942 Avro York reconfigured adaptation of the Lancaster, with a twenty-one to fifty-six passenger capacity, a cruising speed 238mph and a maximum still air range of 3,000 miles. This generally required at least two refuelling stops for a New York-London flight (Gander, Newfoundland and Prestwick, Scotland), maybe three or four stops (adding Reykjavik, Iceland and a Greenland refuelling stop, inevitably when flying east-to-west).

The York had passenger-carrying capability slightly less than the DC-4. In 1946 the Lockheed L-049 Constellation and Douglas DC-4 airliners entered commercial service. These also did not have non-stop transatlantic capability, needing two refuelling stops when flying against any significant wind, often encountered London to New York. The DC-4 was faster than the York, with similar maximum range carrying more passengers.

Avro York. (*Author's collection*)

The L-049 included cabin pressurisation, an option on the DC-4 which was not taken up, thus limiting DC-4 useable altitude to less than 8,000ft. The DC-4 was soon to be stretched to become the pressurised DC-6, entering commercial service in the USA in 1947. Transatlantic DC-6B services started in 1952 and the Lockheed Super Constellation L-1049 entered transatlantic service in 1953.

BOAC also chose to operate the Boeing 377 Stratocruiser, a two-deck airliner with a pressurised cabin, derived from the military C-97 Stratofreighter, which was in turn derived from the B-29 Superfortress, the aircraft which had dropped the first atomic bomb on Hiroshima in 1945. The Stratocruiser carried sixty-four to 100 passengers with a cruising speed of 301mph. This fairly spacious two-deck aircraft was a favourite with passengers (space and extra sound insulation). The maintenance crews were not so enamoured, because of a poor reputation of the massive 3,500HP engines for in-flight fires, and requiring more maintenance effort than the other "big radial engines" of the Douglas DC-6 and Lockheed Constellation aircraft. There were also reliability problems with the electrically-controlled propeller of the Boeing aircraft. Britain did not have a home-produced aircraft comparable to any of these USA "big-piston" airliners.

Once Shannon airport was further developed (with a long hard runway, first opened to civilian traffic in 1947), this gave a single-stop New York-London transatlantic capability to the new American land planes although, when flying from London, Amsterdam or Paris to New York against the prevailing westerly winds, refuelling at Shannon and Gander was needed. The Douglas DC-6B was available with slightly less passenger capacity than the Boeing 377 Stratocruiser but with a slightly higher cruising speed. With less than maximum payload, both of these had westbound one-stop trans-Atlantic range.

Boeing 377 Stratocruiser. (*Author's collection*)

After the Lockheed L-1049 Super Constellation entered service, BOAC were forced by the Stratocruiser high operating costs to lease more of the

Lockheed Super Constellation. (*Author's collection*)

Super Constellations, taking in routes other than transatlantic. The ultimate Lockheed "big piston" airliner was the L-1649 Starliner, a further enhanced version of the Super Constellation. This became available in 1956. The jet airliner was to curtail the life of this last Lockheed large-piston airliner.

Meanwhile, the up to 105 passenger Douglas DC-7C was "in the wings", with a maximum still-air range of 5,600 miles (4,635 miles at maximum payload) and able to cruise at 346mph. The DC-7C was a stretched fuselage and larger-winged longer range version of the DC-7, which was an extension of the DC-4/DC-6 legacy. The DC-7C "Seven Seas" appeared in BOAC and other European airline colours in 1957, truly able to routinely fly to New York non-stop from London, Paris, Amsterdam etc., against normal westerly wind strengths.

Despite cabin sound insulation, all these "big-piston" four-engined USA airliners had noisy passenger cabins, approaching 105 to 110 decibels[2] immediately opposite the engine. The two inboard engine propeller tips passed the cabin only inches away and the poorly-silenced exhausts were only about the length of a large car away. The "smallest" big piston airliner (Douglas DC-6) had propellers 13½ feet (4.1 metres) in diameter on four eighteen-cylinder radial engines, each engine 46 litre displacement, total power per aircraft of 7,600 HP. The largest (Boeing 377 Stratocruiser) had 17 feet (5.2 metres) diameter propellers on four twenty-eight-cylinder radial piston engines, each engine 72 litre displacement, total power per aircraft of 14,600 HP.

The American aircraft totally outclassed the moribund Bristol Brabazon and the ex-wartime Avro York. What else could the UK do to respond to the challenge? Could the Brabazon Committee Type III or the Type IV airliners be developed enough? Bristol were to develop the **Type III** as the Britannia, based on new (turboprop) technology engines. The **Type I** Brabazon aircraft giant, however, had occupied Bristol's attention and resources and the airline specification for the **Type III** was in flux as the customer (BOAC) requested enhanced capability from that first envisioned. This was sufficient to delay the go-ahead for Britannia development until the middle of 1948.

With a range limit at 1,500 miles, due to the relatively immature jet turbine technology, this made the first version of the Brabazon Type IV, the de Havilland type 106 Comet 1, a complete non-starter as a transatlantic contender. The Comet held out some promise as a potential transatlantic challenger, because of the high speed and comfort (flying above the weather and very low engine noise in cruise, although higher frequency jet noise as heard inside the cabin could add a little to the air conditioning and the aerodynamic "hiss" as outside air passed the fuselage). After BOAC belatedly requested an increase in the capacity from twenty-four to thirty-six passengers (sic), de Havilland started serious additional development of the **Type IV** before the Comet 1 entered service, emerging as the Comet 2 with a 3ft fuselage stretch. Chief Designer R.E. Bishop substituted the "to be developed" higher thrust Rolls-Royce Avon jet engines for de Havilland's own Ghost jets of the Comet 1. Although much greater than the Comet 1, the Comet 2 range of 2,600 miles still remained an issue needing further improvement.

The struggles of the British aircraft industry to enter the world airliner market, between the end of the Second World War and the days of the first widebody (twin aisle) airliners of the 1970s, began with "the Brabazon Committee types." The rest of this section and sections 5.5 and 5.6 cover those aircraft and the subsequent British airliners post-Brabazon, in the years up to the end of the 1950s.

---

2. Petrol lawn mower noise is around 90 dB; prolonged exposure to anything above 85 dB can damage hearing.

The turbojet Comet 1 first flight was preceded by the first flight of the turboprop Vickers Viscount in 1948 (see section 5.5). After a visit to Britain in the spring of 1950, to see the British aircraft, John Herlihy (later, to become Senior Vice President of Engineering for his company, USA United Airlines) commented:

"The inescapable conclusion is that medium and large transport aircraft of the near future will be powered by gas turbine engines. The principle controversy is whether the propeller turbine or the jet turbine is the more suitable and it is seen as a difficult question to resolve. All gas turbines bring to transport aircraft the advantages of low weight and drag, negligible oil consumption, higher operating speeds and quiet, vibrationless flight. I do not consider that our company can safely undertake the financial risk of buying new additional types of conventional piston engined aircraft, insomuch as they are already rendered technologically obsolescent by these turbine powered transports"[3]

The de Havilland Comet Type 106 Story

The prototype of the Brabazon **Type IV**, the de Havilland Ghost-powered type 106 Comet 1, took to the air for the first time on 27 July 1949. What promise! Cruising speed of 420mph, 42,000 feet maximum altitude, thirty-six to forty-four passengers. A vibration-free and generally much quieter cabin than the "big pistons", flying above the weather and, if range could be increased enough in the future, ten hours London-New

DH.106 Comet Prototype. (*BAE Systems*)

York against the prevailing wind (including a one-hour refuelling stop like all other North Atlantic airline services of the early 1950s).

Introducing jet propulsion and the associated speed required several leaps forward in aircraft technology; for example, powered flying controls with multiple-redundant hydraulic power sources, and high altitude cabin pressurisation. Some six months ahead of schedule, the first production Comet 1 received its Certificate of Airworthiness and went into service on 2 May 1952. The limited range of the Comet 1 confined the aircraft to certain multi-stop "Empire" routes, via the Mediterranean area with passenger put-down/pick-up needs en route. Flights on the Comet 1 were almost 50 per cent faster than on advanced piston-engined aircraft, such as the Douglas DC-6B, as a faster rate of climb further cut flight times. The much higher flight altitude required a pressurised cabin with twice the pressure difference (between inside and outside) of the "big piston" airliners, which cruised at around 20,000 to 25,000ft.

The Comet 1 exceeded economic expectations, too. Although it was 50 per cent more expensive to buy than large piston-engined airliners, and consumed twice as much fuel overall, it was 20 per cent cheaper to operate. Distance flown each hour was clearly greater, with a 50 per cent higher cruising speed than piston-engined airliners. The jet engines required less frequent maintenance and jet speeds allowed increased utilisation in terms of air miles. After the first year of operations, BOAC reported that five Comets could do the work of eight conventional [piston] airliners.

In August 1953, BOAC scheduled nine-stop London to Tokyo flights by Comet for thirty-six hours, compared with eighty-six hours and thirty-five minutes using their

---

3. as noted in "*Evolution of the Airliner*", Ray Whitford

Argonaut piston airliner. The nine stops were dictated as much by passenger traffic considerations as by aircraft range limits, which suited the Comet 1 maximum range of just over 1,500 miles. The BOAC Argonaut was a Rolls-Royce Merlin-powered Canadair development of the Douglas DC-4, raising the cruising speed by 60mph or more, depending on altitude.

If range could be increased and the cabin stretched, instead of being just a "winner" with passengers the Comet would become an airliner "superstar". Along came the Rolls-Royce Avon-powered and stretched Comet 2, with a higher-lift wing section, planned to be in service by 1954. Disaster intervened.

Between October 1952 and May 1953 there were three Comet 1 hull-loss accidents (two with associated fatalities). As a result of accident investigations, two were eventually attributed to an aerodynamic and control system issue, accentuated by pilot response, and the third was attributed to extreme turbulence, in climb-out after take-off. Profile changes to the wing leading edge and the engine intakes resolved the aerodynamic problem and the control system had speed-sensitive feel ("Q" feel) replacing the simple spring loaded pilot controls. The aerodynamic and control problem had been magnified by insufficient line pilot awareness of the differences in handling between propeller-driven aircraft and the new jet-powered airliner.[4] Three accidents in the first year of service was, however, an inauspicious beginning.

On a flight from Rome to London in January 1954, the first production Comet (registered to BOAC as G-ALYP) crashed into the sea close to the Italian island of Elba, with the loss of all thirty-six on board. Among other potential causes, a bomb was one postulation. BOAC volunteered to ground their Comet fleet, pending the outcome of investigations. In April 1954, another unexplained crash of a BOAC Comet 1 aircraft (G-ALYY) into the Mediterranean resulted in grounding of all Comets. The crash of the first disappearance was in a relatively shallow part of the Mediterranean but this second disappearance was over much deeper water. Using grabs, Asdic (sonar) ultrasonic detection and underwater cameras, several parts of G-ALYP were recovered. Investigations focused on this wreckage, including reconstruction of the aircraft in the RAE laboratory at Farnborough, Hampshire. BOAC donated one of their new aircraft, G-ALYU, for further examination.

During the design phase of the Comet 1 there had been exceptional precautions taken in testing the fuselage structure, which was to experience much higher levels of pressurisation loading, because of the higher altitude capability than any previous pressurised passenger aircraft. The entire forward fuselage section was tested for metal fatigue, by repeatedly pressurising to 2.75 pounds per square inch overpressure and depressurising through more than 16,000 cycles, equivalent to about 40,000 hours of airline service. The windows were also tested under a pressure of 40 per cent above expected pressure differential (cabin-to-outside atmosphere) at the normal service ceiling of 36,000ft and one third higher than the maximum pressure differential at the absolute ceiling of 42,000ft. One window frame survived 1,250 per cent over the maximum pressure it was expected to encounter in service.

Nevertheless, RAE Director Arnold Hall decided to test the whole fuselage of G-ALYU in a dedicated water tank (water rather than air pressure, for safety), built at Farnborough specifically to accommodate the full length of the fuselage.

Under pressure, stresses around the corners of the cabin cut-outs for aerials, windows and hatches were found to be much higher than expected and stresses on other parts of the fuselage skin were a little more than previously expected. The square shape of the

---

4. The new generation of jet aircraft would all be found to require a different approach to aircraft handling, especially taking-off and landing. Pilot training would be modified in the years to come.

cut-outs caused stress concentration, generating local stress two or three times greater than across the rest of the fuselage. On 24 June 1954, after 3,057 pressurisation cycles (1,221 actual and 1,836 simulated in the water tank), the skin of G-ALYU burst open. When the water tank was drained it was revealed that a fuselage panel had ripped open at a corner of the forward left escape hatch cutout. A further test reproduced the same kind of result. Based on these findings, Comet 1 structural failures of the fuselage could be expected at anywhere from 2,000 to 6,000 pressure cycles. Even today, this degree of fatigue life prediction "scatter" from fatigue test results is a not unexpected normal assessment, when dealing with fatigue in aluminium alloy structures.

From examination of the actual remains of G-ALYP, the culprit was initially identified as growth of a crack in the pressure cabin, leading to explosive failure and cabin decompression. As a theory, it was suspected that the crack might have originated from the corner of the re-enforced square aperture on top of the forward fuselage which accommodated an ADF (radio navigation) aerial. The sections of fuselage wreckage so far recovered did not include this cut-out. Meanwhile, inspired analysis and scale modelling had enabled "blind trawling" to be directed to specific deeper parts of the sea, to likely areas to find more pieces of the very distributed wreckage. Miraculously, by late August 1954, more pieces of fuselage from G-AYLP were brought to the surface. This included a large piece of the top and port (left hand) fuselage, forward of the wing front spar, including the suspect aerial cut-out and a passenger cabin window section. Overall, 70 per cent of the empty weight was recovered. Examination suggested that probably (but not certainly) it was the structure at the corner of the ADF aerial cut-out which had failed as the initial cause of the almost instant crack propagation, causing explosive decompression and the subsequent complete break-up of the aircraft. The decompression theory had been suggested as a result of autopsies on the victims. It had taken a massive investigative effort to find the root cause. The detailed investigation had created a model for all future aircraft crash investigations. Without recovery of any actual wreckage of G-ALYY, the investigation also concluded that the accident to this aircraft was very likely due to the same cause.

An underlying probable contributory cause of cracking was identified as the method of punch-riveting used in construction of all the square-aperture re-enforcing elements of production aircraft, causing microscopic cracks in the skin and consequent built-in very local stress concentration points under load. Retrospectively, modern fracture mechanics analysis suggests that the "initiating" manufacturing-induced concealed crack at one of the rivet holes fastening the re-enforcing plate around the culprit cut-out was less than one tenth of one millimetre in length. Accentuated by the stress build up at that point during each flight and cycled through pressurisation/depressurisation each flight, the tiny cracks grew as a result of metal fatigue, until sudden explosive decompression occurred. It became clear that the true nature of metal fatigue in lightweight metal alloy structures was not a well-enough understood phenomenon. A structural redesign was necessary. The longer-fuselage Comet 2s which had been completed were strengthened and the windows changed, from square (heretofore a common shape used in many aircraft, pressurised or not) to rounded. Other aircraft manufacturers took note. The modified Comet 2 was an interim solution without the full thicker skin strengthening of the final Comet 4 (therefore the Comet 2 had lower pressurisation limits and was assigned to the RAF and limited to a reduced maximum altitude).

In 1954, the (only) Comet 3 first flew. The Comet 3 was a further stretch from the Comet 2, with an 18½ft (5.63m) longer fuselage compared with Comet 1, added wing pod fuel tanks and the new Rolls-Royce Avon engines giving twice as much power as the Comet 1 DH Ghost engines.

The effect of the Comet disasters and grounding, and the consequential loss of orders, over-stressed de Havilland's financial position. The de Havilland company was a major aircraft, propeller and engine business, with an additional number of overseas establishments in the British Commonwealth.

In 1955, the British government stepped in to help with a £10 million financial restructuring package, equivalent to £260 million in 2019 terms. Consequently, the De Havilland Aircraft Company founded in 1920 became De Havilland Holdings Limited (est. 1955), owning the aircraft, engine and propeller businesses and several overseas divisions, each individually re-established as individual companies. Founder Sir Geoffrey de Havilland became president of the new business.

The Comet 4 full fuselage modifications were proven by actual water tank fatigue testing of a redesigned fuselage, to permit restoration of the full pressurisation capability. The Comet 4 had an increased wing area and the latest Rolls-Royce Avon axial compressor engines (10,500lbs thrust, compared with the 5,000lbs of the original de Havilland centrifugal compressor Ghost engines of the Comet 1). The cabin was now capable of carrying fifty-six to eighty-one passengers, depending on layout and, with the improved fuel capacity and consumption the aircraft had a typical operating range of 3,225 air miles. On 30 September 1958, a forty-eight-seat BOAC Comet 4 aircraft inaugurated the first-ever transatlantic commercial jet service. London-New York first flight total time was ten hours twenty minutes (including a seventy minute refuelling stop at Gander) and the non-stop return flight of six hours twelve minutes was three hours shorter than the non-stop piston flights.

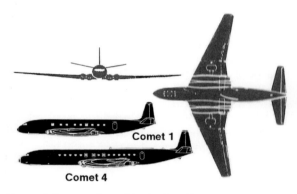

Comet 1-4 comparison. (*Author's collection*)

RAF DH.106 Comet 4. (*BAE Systems*)

Overflying the weather, a fast, comfortable and quiet service, totally outclassing the opposition. The very latest Lockheed and Douglas piston-engined offerings cost less than a Comet 4 and used half as much fuel per air mile (but quite frequently flew far more air miles per journey, in adverse weather), had non-stop London-New York capability but took longer than the one-stop Comet 4. The big pistons' significantly lower ceiling flight altitude could make their flights more subject to atmospheric turbulence (enough to quite often cause motion sickness for some passengers, an enduring scourge of air travel from the very earliest days).

The Transatlantic Airliner Race is Lost

In the meantime, Boeing had decided to really challenge the airliner market. Other USA airliner manufacturers had started post-war new airliner development ideas, either with large radial piston engines (with the idea that conversion to turboprops would follow in due course), or with turboprops in mind from the start. Turboprop propulsion at the speeds of the fastest piston-powered airliners held the promise of being the most fuel-efficient and with a significant reduction in the high cabin vibration and noise problems caused by piston engines. Lockheed's L-1249 Super Constellation experimental aircraft flew with turboprop power in September 1954, sponsored by the USN and the USAF, eventually leading Lockheed to proceed with the L-188 Electra turboprop airliner (rather than jet-powered), with a maximum range of 2,200 miles (not intended for the Atlantic crossing).

However, by the early 1950s Boeing had gained large jet aircraft experience with military jets, first with the B-47 Stratojet long-range strategic bomber, which went into USAF service in 1951 (combat radius over 2,000 miles with 20,000lb bomb load:- a total of 2,032 were eventually built, the last bomber version being withdrawn in 1966). In 1954 Boeing started deliveries of the first production-standard eight-engined B-52B Stratofortress bomber, capable of 600mph and an initial combat radius over 3,000 miles without the need for aerial refuelling (eight years later, the last of the upgraded turbofan-powered B-52H version was delivered, with ultimate unrefuelled combat radius extended to over 4,400 miles).

Boeing decided to "get ahead of the game" in long-range airliners, to try to break the Douglas and Lockheed USA airliner dominance. In 1952 they commenced the design of a large proof-of-concept four-jet aircraft, the 367-80 (known as the Dash 80), as a first step towards their bid for what was to become the new USAF aerial refuelling tanker. The Dash 80 flew in July 1954, only two years from go-ahead. Boeing also hoped to use the Dash 80 to develop their ideas for a new jet airliner, similar in size to the tanker but in a four abreast passenger layout (in a narrower fuselage than the Dash 80, at 11ft wide (3.35m), and a bit faster than the Comet). A four abreast cabin seating layout was typical for long-range airliners of the day, with wider seats and greater legroom than is usual today. Comet was wide enough for five abreast but was four abreast in first class configuration. As a result of competition developments at the drawing board stage (notably the UK Vickers V.1000/VC7 six abreast layout announced in 1953, see section 5.8, also adopted by the Douglas DC-8 for their new jet airliner), Boeing widened the fuselage design of the new airliner. At first, this was to five abreast (allowing common production tooling with the KC-135 tanker contract obtained in 1954) then, before detail design commitment, a further increase in fuselage diameter to accommodate six abreast. Douglas, having decided to await the turboprop developments being contemplated to mature a little, before deciding on the "turbojet or turboprop" question, were playing catch-up, having been caught napping by the early USAAF decision not to dual-source between Boeing and Douglas on the new tanker.

Amazingly, USA Pan American Airways placed orders for both the Boeing 707 and the Douglas DC.8 totally unproven new jet airliners in October 1955, well before the first flight of the first version of either (December 1957 and May 1958 respectively). Two different and absolutely new technology civil airliners, ordered well before anyone had imagined. The future outcome was to be that both Douglas and Lockheed would eventually lose their pre-eminent positions as suppliers of long-range airliners, never to be recovered. These new USA airliner projects were expensive investments. Boeing's 707 eventually became the runaway success (including the shortened 720, over 1,000 aircraft built). Reportedly, however, a $30.8 million write-down (equivalent to $267 million in 2019 terms) was made by Douglas against the DC.8 programme in

1960. Douglas eventually built 556 of these aircraft by the time production ended in 1972. General Dynamics-owned Convair had to write off over $150 million in 1962 (equivalent to $1,270 million in 2019 terms) against the smaller and range-limited Convair 880 and 990 jet airliner programmes, last aircraft completed in 1963 with a total of only 107 aircraft built.

The de Havilland Comet had required an inspired and massive aeronautical technology leap of faith. It was the first to use a radically new type of engine and powered flying controls driven by multiple hydraulic systems (with no direct manual reversionary control, because manually operated control loads would have been too high at the high airspeeds used), and cabin altitudes pressurised to the equivalent of 8,000 feet, all the way up to aircraft altitudes of 42,000 feet (35 per cent higher than the "big piston airliners"). It was "a brave, giant leap", overtaken by tragic events. The problems had eventually been overcome, but too late to prevent the USA industry catching up and overtaking. Excluding production of the Hawker Siddeley Nimrod (see section 6.3), seventy-five Comet 4s were built. The newer USA designs, soon to have more powerful and/or improved fuel economy engines, had learned from the early Comet problems, to become dominant in the market for intercontinental jet airliners, a burgeoning market of the 1960s and beyond. The only significant downside would be that much longer runways of 12,000ft (2¼ miles) would be needed, all over the world.

The comparison of the "best piston" and the new jet long-range airliners flying by the end of the 1950s is shown in table 5.1 below.

Table 5.1: Transatlantic Airliners.

	"Best Piston"	UK Jet	The USA Jet Competition		
First Revenue Flight	1956 (USA) DC-7C	1958 (UK) Comet 4	1958 (USA) B.707-100	1959 (USA) DC.8-12	1961 (USA) B.707-320
Maximum Take-off Weight (lb)	143,000	156,000	257,340	276,000	312,000
Passengers	105	56–81	110–179	110–176	147–219
Maximum cruise speed (mph)	361	556	620	601	605
Maximum range (still air miles)	up to 5,635	3,225	4,100	4,608	5,800
Wing area (ft²)	1,637	2,121	3,046	4,608	3,546
Maximum altitude (ft)	28,400	42,000	42,000	42,000	42,000
London-New York (avge flt hrs)	10 ± wind	7¾ ± wind	7 ± wind	7 ± wind	7 ± wind
Transatlantic Operation	**non-stop**	**E-to-W, had to have refuelling stop**			**non-stop**

5.5 The Other Brabazon Committee Aircraft

The Airspeed Ambassador and the Vickers Viscount

The Type IIA and IIB Brabazon aircraft were the "safe option" piston-engined Airspeed Ambassador and the "adventurous option" turboprop-powered Vickers Viscount. The Ambassador turned out to be a high-winged (providing low-sill passenger easy-entry doors) twin-engined and elegant forty-seven-passenger design, with a tricycle undercarriage and a pressurised cabin.

The prototype first flight was in July 1947. Capable of actually seating up to sixty passengers, the Ambassador was appreciated as a significant step forward from the "interim" post-Second World War Vickers Viking. British European Airways (BEA, split out of BOAC in 1946) was the first Ambassador operator, ordering twenty. Unfortunately for the type, the immediate passenger and crew popularity of the Viscount, once it made it into service, prevented further sales. A contributory factor might have been the same negative assessment from Airspeed owners de Havilland, who pulled the Sales Director out of Australia in the middle of a negotiation to sell to an Australian airline.

Airspeed Ambassador. (*Author's collection*)

The four-engined Viscount first appeared as a thirty-six-passenger prototype which first flew on July 1948, entering service in 1953. The first production model seated between forty and sixty-three passengers (depending on seating class). The low cabin noise and vibration associated with the turboprop engines (relative to piston engines) was much liked by

BEA Vickers Viscount 700. (*RuthAS, CC BY-SA 3.0*)

passengers and crew alike. Turboprop fuel efficiency made the aircraft popular with airline management. It was also appreciated by many overseas airlines and a total of 442 were eventually sold. The last authorised Viscount commercial service ceased in the late 1990s. Interestingly, the Rolls-Royce Dart turboprop Viscount was soon to face competition in parts of the market place, with the 1955 French Sud Aviation twin-jet (Rolls-Royce Avon) eighty-passenger Caravelle, which sold 280 worldwide.

The Bristol Britannia

Meanwhile, the Type III Brabazon aircraft (the Bristol Britannia turboprop) began development. First flying in 1952, optimism that there were good prospects for success seemed justified.

1952 was five years before the first new large turboprop airliner flew in the USA, (the Lockheed L-188 Electra, which commenced design with a seventy-five passenger maximum capacity, eventually finalised as ninety-five passengers). The Britannia was initially specified with a forty-eight passenger capacity but this was revised to seventy-four seats in late 1948, with a larger wing span. Development issues with the Bristol Proteus engines in particular delayed completion of trials and the Comet crashes caused the Air Ministry to require extra structural testing on all new pressurised aircraft. An engine fire (caused by a propeller reduction gear failure) resulted in the forced landing (and loss) of the second Britannia prototype on the mud flats of the Severn River estuary. In an attempt to create transatlantic capability, rather than just satisfy the medium range Empire route requirements originally envisaged by the Brabazon Committee, Bristol revised the design into a larger airliner. This resulted in the fuselage stretch of the Series 200 and 300 designs, the first of which went into service with the RAF nearly two years after the initial 100 series Certificate of Airworthiness was awarded. Such changes in requirements caused project cost escalation and delay.

Resolving easily avoidable inlet icing issues (discovered at the last minute as the first aircraft were being delivered to BOAC at the end of 1955, and which then were exaggerated by BOAC in public), seriously damaged the Britannia's sales prospects. During the first eight months of operational trials, a total of sixteen in-flight engine failures and forty-nine unscheduled engine changes punctuated the ongoing engine dilemma and delayed the eventual in-service date until February 1957. The L-188 Electra went into service in 1959 and 170 were sold. It was also adopted by the USN as the basis of heavily-adapted versions, as the P3 Orion maritime reconnaissance aircraft (of which, 795 were eventually built). Britannia airliner sales total was eighty-three aircraft, plus 112 more of the piston-powered RCAF Argus maritime reconnaissance and the thirty-nine Rolls-Royce Tyne turboprop CL-44 cargo versions of the Britannia, both adapted and built under licence by Canadair.

Eventually well-liked by passengers as quiet and comfortable, the Britannia was nicknamed "The Whispering Giant". The series 300 version carried up to 139 passengers at a cruising speed of over 350mph, a ceiling of 24,000ft and a maximum range capability of over 4,400 miles.

Canadian aviation historian Peter Pigott summarised his view of the impact of Britannia delays:

> "Had the Britannia first appeared in 1950, when it was faster than every American aircraft, it would have put the British at the forefront of commercial aviation sales. Now, competing with the 707, the turboprop airliner had become passé."

Apart from the obvious over-optimistic date quoted, this is only partially true, with the benefit of "hindsight". Although the sentiments expressed above have some inherent truth, it is also true that the original Britannia concept was smaller than the late 1940s "big pistons" of the three USA large airliner manufacturers and had less than two-thirds of their range. In 1949–50 Britain was not well enough prepared and ready to produce large pressurised aircraft at the same rate as the USA industry, even if companies other than Bristol were to have been allocated Britannia production (Shorts in Belfast, 15 per cent owned by Bristol, built several). A restrained build rate would have meant customers for large numbers would have to wait for the production facility and tooling investment necessary, or wait even longer due to the relatively slow rates possible in the Bristol facility alone. The Boeing 707 and Douglas DC-8 jets, and the Lockheed L-188 Electra turboprop, were available less than two years after the first (smallest) Britannia. Additionally, "turboprops are passé" as an expression is only appropriate in the case of intercontinental or other long-range air travel. In the twenty-first century there are new turboprop airliners still being produced, of modest size but with the fuel economy advantage of turboprop engines (compared with comparable turbofan engines), with more passenger capacity than the original forty-eight-seat Britannia concept and with ranges up to 1,000 miles.

The Miles Marathon and the de Havilland Dove

The Brabazon Type VA airliner project was awarded to Miles Aircraft, amongst much confusion. The MoS placed the contract but Miles were prevented from contacting the end-users. Despite a non-circular fuselage in the proposed design, a cabin pressurisation system was belatedly requested, then cancelled, then requested again, then cancelled again. The aircraft was eventually realised as the twenty-passenger Miles M.60 Marathon, which had four de Havilland Gypsy Queen piston engines and first flew in May 1946. Three prototypes were completed before Miles Aircraft went into liquidation in 1947. At the time, Miles also had orders for the Miles Gemini aircraft to complete. Handley Page aircraft bought the Miles assets at Reading, including the Marathon project and the UK supersonic Miles M.52 research aircraft project (see section 5.10). Keeping the Marathon activity separate, the Handley Page (Reading) business was created and the H.P.R.1 Marathon 1 first flew in 1949. Including the three Miles-built prototypes, forty-three Marathons were built, twenty of which were converted into navigation trainers for the RAF.

DH.104 Dove. (*Julian Herzog, CC BY-SA 4.0*)

The Brabazon Type VB airliner project was awarded to de Havilland. The aircraft was realised as the eight-passenger de Havilland twin-engined DH.104 Dove, with de Havilland Gypsy Queen piston engines. First flight was in September 1945, becoming the first new British civil aircraft to fly after the end of the Second World War. Eventually, 542 aircraft were built, the last one in 1967. In 1950 the aircraft was stretched as the DH.114 Heron, with a 40 per cent increase in wing area, four de Havilland Gypsy Queen piston engines and accommodation for fourteen passengers; 150 DH Herons were built.

5.6 1945–55 UK Transport Aircraft Which the Brabazon Committee Did Not Suggest

The Bristol Type 170 Freighter

The Bristol Freighter was not a response to a requirement identified by the Brabazon Committee. Designed to be a stop-gap product at the Bristol Company whilst the Bristol Type 187 Brabazon airliner was being developed, in December 1945, the type 170 Freighter was the second new UK civil aircraft design to fly after the end of the Second World War. The UK government provided some support, in order to help the aircraft compete against the many USA C-47/Dakota (Douglas DC-3) war surplus aircraft flooding the market at that time.

It was conceived as a military "large load carrier" using unprepared strips, having a wide track fixed undercarriage, with front-loading fuselage side-hinge clam-shell doors giving access to a large square section load compartment able to swallow a British Army 3-ton truck. Load compartment capacity was 2,020 cubic feet and could carry a heavy load to a maximum density of 350 cubic feet per ton. A loading ramp could be carried. In the Wayfarer passenger version, the clamshell nose doors were replaced with a sealed shell. It was a unique utility vehicle "doing what it says on the tin". By the 1950s, cross-Channel drive-on/drive-off car ferries were available, using the Dover-Calais route.

The Bristol 170 Freighter is iconically most often remembered as a cross-channel car transporter, for those wealthy enough to own a motor car and wishing to use them in continental Europe without the

Bristol Mk.32 SuperFreighter. (*Author's collection*)

inconvenience of the relatively slow Channel ferry crossing. The use of an air route could have car (or bulky cargo) from Britain to Brittany, the South of France, or in Holland, or in Switzerland, in a few hours, with relatively little actual driving, rather than the "drive to Dover-drive onto/off ferry-drive to destination" taking at least one whole day, for destinations significantly beyond Northern France.

First used by Channel Island Airways (loaned in 1946 by the aircraft manufacturer as a "marketing promotion"), a single Bristol Freighter (Wayfarer) with thirty-four passenger seats carried 10,000 passengers across the English Channel to/from Jersey in six months. The fly-away unit price of the Wayfarer was £47,000 in 1946, equivalent to just over £1.9 million in 2019 (the Freighter version was 30 per cent cheaper).

The piston-powered Type 170 looked ungainly and "unaerodynamic" but it was a simple design, easy to maintain and capacious. Production continued until 1958. A stretched version (the Mk.32 Superfreighter) was flown in 1953, capable of carrying three cars and twenty-two passengers (twenty built as new, two others converted from original). Including these, a total of 214 aircraft were built and delivered, sold to many countries in both military and civil applications. The last flying example retired in 2004.

The Portsmouth Aviation Aerocar

Portsmouth, Southsea and Isle of Wight Aviation, an air ferry operator, changed its name to Portsmouth Aviation in 1946 and designed and built the Portsmouth Aerocar, a five-seater (plus the pilot) light utility aircraft. It had a high wing and a twin-boom tailplane, with a tricycle undercarriage, and was first flown in 1947. It failed to attract financial support and was finally scrapped in 1950. Portsmouth Aviation did not design another aircraft.

A Speciality STOL Pair From Scottish Aviation

The Scottish Aviation Company was formed in 1935 as a flying school, based at Prestwick Airport in Ayrshire but, by 1938, was carrying out aircraft maintenance work. By the start of the Second World War they were operating in the 1938 Glasgow Empire Exhibition "Palace of Engineering" building, transferred to Prestwick airport. Between 1939 and 1945, Scottish Aviation were engaged in war work, modifying and maintaining USA Consolidated Liberator bomber aircraft, used as anti-submarine aircraft in the Atlantic. Scottish Aviation also removed armaments and converted Liberators to wartime trans-Atlantic personnel and equipment transports.

In 1945 the company decided to venture into aircraft design, responding to specification A4/45 for a three-seat light communication aircraft, with an unprepared strip short take-off and landing (STOL) capability. The 240HP de Havilland Gypsy Queen power plant specified was not powerful enough to provide the required performance and the aircraft was not accepted by the RAF.

A more powerful engine with about twice the power was needed. Converting two of the Pioneer I prototypes by fitting an Alvis 510HP Leonides radial engine, the Pioneer II first flew in 1950. The Pioneer concept was intended to produce a STOL capability (full span wing leading edge slats and

Scottish Aviation Pioneer II. (*BAE Systems*)

Fowler trailing edge wing flaps fitted). The revised aircraft was capable of a take-off run of only 225 feet and a landing run of 200 feet, using unprepared landing strips. This was a true STOL capability. Finally fitted with four passenger-plus-pilot capacity, the Pioneer CC Mk.1 entered RAF service in August 1953. It was used in the Malaya, Aden and Cyprus conflict zones in the 1950s and 1960s as communications and casualty evacuation aircraft – fifty-nine examples were built.

In 1955 the company flew the Pioneer wing-and-fuselage stretch as the twin-engined Twin Pioneer, with two pilot seats and thirteen troop seats and the same excellent STOL air strip capability of the Pioneer II. Including a single prototype, eighty-seven examples were built, nearly half of which served with the RAF. The civil-registered Twin Pioneer was sometimes used in areas without proper airfields, such as in remote mineral mining and as oil and geographic survey aircraft.

Percival Merganiser/Prince/Pembroke Family

In 1947, Percival designed the twin-piston Merganiser five-passenger light utility aircraft, which first flew on 9 May 1947. Unfortunately, the intended de Havilland power plant was not available in quantity and the first flight used engines loaned by the UK government. Nevertheless, useful flight data was obtained and an enlarged ten-passenger version with more powerful Alvis engines was developed as the the Percival Prince, first flown in May 1948. The Prince was largely intended to be used as a short range airliner, executive transport or air taxi aircraft. Seventy-five were built, several of which were naval navigation trainer versions known as the Sea Prince. In RAF service the Prince replaced the venerable Avro Anson (the last of which was actually only retired by the RAF in 1968).

On 21 November 1952, Percival flew the first example of a revised Prince with a larger wing span (to carry increased payload). Type named as the Pembroke, it was developed for the RAF, to be used as a transport/communications and survey/reconnaissance aircraft – 128 Pembrokes were built, fifty for the RAF, forty-seven for the RN, twenty-six for export to five countries and five configured as a civil transport (renamed as the President).

Percival Pembroke. (*Author's collection*)

RAF Pembrokes were to be used as the designated 'V bomber' air and ground crew dispersal aircraft (to remote 'V' bomber bases, when high nuclear alert status was declared, see sections 5.11 and 5.12). The aircraft so designated carried air filtration equipment and NBC (nuclear, biological and chemical warfare) clothing. Several RAF Pembrokes were based in Germany and flew "the Berlin air corridor" during the Cold War, eventually replaced by modified Hawker Siddeley Andover C. Mk. 1 aircraft (designated the E.Mk.3 version). The last Pembroke retired from service in 1988.

Saunders Roe Princess – the End of the Large Flying Boat Airliner Era

The Air Ministry issued a specification R.14/40 for a new large flying boat, as "faster and bigger than the Shorts Sunderland maritime patrol flying boat". They requested two flying boat manufacturers in Britain, Shorts and Saunders Roe, to collaborate in the design.

The Shorts Shetland emerged, basically designed by Saunders Roe (who also manufactured the wing). The rest of the aircraft and final assembly was provided by

Shorts. The first prototype first flew in 1944 but did not prove entirely satisfactory. It was burnt out when moored in January 1946, from a fire starting in the galley. With the end of the war, the second prototype was completed as a civil aircraft but no orders were forthcoming. Both Saunders Roe and Shorts were not enamoured of the basic Shetland design as a good foundation for a civil airliner.

In 1943, Saunders Roe and Shorts had privately collaborated to produce an outline design specification for an innovative large new flying boat to be the largest all-metal flying boat ever built, with a pressurised hull, a cruising speed of 340mph at 37,000ft altitude and a range of over 5,000 miles (reducing to less than 4,000 miles at maximum payload). Luxurious accommodation for 104 passengers was included. The two companies felt that this would be the right way to go about crossing the Atlantic non-stop and also re-establishing the "Empire" flying boat service for BOAC, the inheritor state airline of the pre-war Imperial Airways.

By 1945, the MoS were seemingly keen to see the establishment of a peacetime British transatlantic flying boat air service by BOAC, and the restarting of the pre-war Imperial Airways Shorts Empire flying boat service. They sought bids for a suitable aircraft from the UK industry. Strangely, the MoS were almost simultaneously party to the organising of contracts for the Bristol Brabazon, the Brabazon Committee-inspired land plane also intended to carry out the transatlantic passenger operation "with about 100 passengers in luxurious accommodation" (see section 5.3). It is therefore somewhat surprising that the Saunders Roe bid of the SR.45 Princess for the transatlantic flying boat envisaged by the MoS was agreed and contracted for in 1946, only two years after the order for two Brabazon prototypes had been initiated. This might have been the usual "hedging bets" government tactics, or it might just have been left hand and right hand lack of communication. It was true that the availability of long hard runways in the Middle East, India and the Far East was a bit hit-and-miss for large landplane operations (excluding the Pacific Islands used by the USAF large bombers). The growth of long-range travel would soon cause airfield facilities to improve.

At 345,025lb the Princess MTOW was 17 per cent greater than the Brabazon MTOW and it had nearly 20 per cent more installed engine power (ten Bristol Proteus turboprops compared with eight Bristol Centaurus radial pistons of the Brabazon, the Brabazon II was intended to have had eight Proteus). The Brabazon had the greater wing span (5 per cent more, giving 6 per cent more wing area) and was 20 per cent longer than the Princess. The Princess had a ceiling of 39,000ft and a 360mph cruising speed at 32,500ft, whereas the Brabazon I had only a 25,000ft ceiling and a cruising speed of 250mph at 25,000ft (Brabazon II with Proteus engines would have had a cruising speed of 330mph and higher altitude capability).

The Princess had a narrower fuselage than the Brabazon (Princess had four and five abreast in generous seats, on two decks, in a double-bubble fuselage). Dining areas and super-luxury lounges were on both aircraft. The Brabazon had 100 per cent powered flying controls whereas the Princess had power-assisted flying controls. Both giants of their time, both obsolescent in concept before the drawings were issued.

The age of the large flying boat was really over by the end of the Second World War. Nevertheless,

Saunders Roe Princess in flight test, circa 1952-1954. (*Author's collection*)

three Princess aircraft were ordered by the MoS, the first flight taking place in 1952. Only the first prototype took to the air. After completion of flight trials sufficient to prove performance capability, in May 1954 this aircraft and the two others almost completed were cocooned and stored until 1964. They were then purchased for potential use as heavy duty transports for Saturn V (Apollo moon rocket first stage) components for NASA. When de-cocooned, the Princess aircraft were found to be badly corroded and the aircraft were instead scrapped, in 1967. The Princess programme cost the government around £10 million, equivalent to over £270 million in 2019 terms.

Post-war Utility Aircraft and Sailplanes

Whilst most designers, politicians and barons of industry were focused on "Transports, Bombers and Fighters" (preferably with jet turbine engines), in the decade following the Second World War the utility and glider aircraft parts of British industry enjoyed some quiet success. This was particularly so for Auster aircraft, founded in 1938 as a company licenced to produce British-engined versions of the Taylorcraft high wing two-seat light aircraft. Coming out of the Second World War having supplied 1,630 of the Taylorcraft as an AOP aircraft to the RAF, the company changed its name from Taylorcraft UK to Auster Aircraft. Adaptations of the original Taylorcraft design became the basis of continuing business, until the 1960 amalgamation with Miles (see Section 6.1). Auster produced a range of high wing single-engined monoplanes, mostly using de Havilland engines and

Auster J/5 Aiglet. (*Author's collection*)

totalling some 953 aircraft, an example being the four-seat Auster J/5 Aiglet pilot training/tourer.

Furniture makers Elliotts of Newbury could not immediately return to furniture making when peace was declared, so the company decided to build on their wartime production of Airspeed Horsa gliders and their contribution of Supermarine Spitfire, Airspeed Oxford and de Havilland Tiger Moth parts. Their first attempt was a powered light aircraft, of which only one was completed and the business refocused back to gliders. Initially using design consultants Aviation and Engineering Products Ltd., Elliotts founded a continuing business, producing both training gliders and improved competition gliders. The gliders were initially based on German (pre-war) designs. Over 900 Elliott gliders were produced before the company ceased this activity, passing the ongoing support for the Elliott glider customers and any future new production business to Slingsby aircraft in 1966. No new Elliott glider was built by Slingsby.

Glider production by the Slingsby Company (founded in 1931) was reasonably stable after the war, with production for RAF training (Air Training Corps) and gliding clubs.

Slingsby T-41 Skylark 2. (*TSRL, CC BY-SA 3.0*)

They soon entered the high performance competition glider field. In total, over 1,000 Slingsby gliders had been produced by 1960 but the focus of glider building moved away from Britain. A disastrous fire in 1968 led to insolvency and a takeover by the Vickers Group (interested in the glass-fibre composite expertise of Slingsby). After several changes of ownership, Slingsby's last aircraft was the 1974 powered primary trainer T-67 Firefly, a composite structure complete rework of the French Fournier RF-6 design. Over 250 T-67s were sold before Slingsby aircraft design and build ceased completely. In 2006 the company became a dedicated composite structure specialist and was taken over by the Marshall Aerospace and Defence group in 2012.

5.7 The Shorts Move to Belfast and the Last Shorts Flying Boat

Originally founded in 1908, as the first commercial manufacturers of aircraft in the world, in 1936 at Ministry request, Short Brothers formed a new jointly-owned company, with Harland and Wolff (shipbuilders in Belfast, of RMS *Titanic* and HMS *Belfast* fame). The new company was Short and Harland Ltd. located in Belfast. Part of the reasoning was that Belfast would "be outside the likely attack range of German bombers" (until the fall of most of Europe, when German bombers were then able to operate from airfields in northern France and the Netherlands – German bombers did raid the Belfast facility, in 1941). Short and Harland built Handley Page Hampden and Short Sunderland flying boats and, later, Short Stirling bombers.

The original Short Brothers company was taken into government ownership in 1943, under wartime Defence Regulation 78. This was precipitously ordered by the new MAP minister, Sir Stafford Cripps, due to a perceived inadequacy of the Short Brothers company management in controlling cost and timescales. Trevor Westbrook, a forthright ex-Vickers manager, was chosen by Stafford Cripps to reorganise Shorts. His reputation had been made when, at the age of twenty-eight, he had been appointed by Vickers as general manager of Supermarine, following Vickers' 1928 take over. He had successfully modernised and reorganised the Supermarine factory for more efficient production but had not been popular due to his confrontational style. Not popular in his new appointment in Rochester, nevertheless, costs and timescales at Shorts factories were much improved after his arrival.

The factory facilities in Rochester had gradually become a little dispersed around the city, one facility being at Strood, a mile or so beyond the opposite (north-west) bank of the Medway river from the main riverside factory (between the river and Rochester Esplanade). Operating seaplanes from the winding Medway tidal river was sometimes problematical for (then) modern large seaplanes. Landplane sub-assemblies had to be taken a few miles by road, to the Rochester airport works, for final assembly and flying. Paraphrasing a 1946 Ministry of Supply report:- The main factory (on the sloping bank of the river) was a collection of several different workshops at different levels on a constricted strip of land, the whole having been erected progressively over a period of thirty years. The other company facilities were more modern but dispersed around Rochester. To replace just the main assembly shop with one large enough to accommodate (the expected) parallel assembly of several new large Short Shetland flying boats was estimated to cost £750,000 (equivalent to nearly £32 million in 2019 terms).

With the reduction in aircraft production as the war ended, something in the industry had to give. The Short and Harland facilities in Belfast had been used to assemble Stirling heavy bombers and Sunderland flying boat maritime patrol aircraft during the Second World War and the site facilities were suitable for efficient co-location of all Short Brothers activities. Northern Ireland was an economically deprived area of Britain and an Irish sectarian political hotbed of unrest, with consequential prominent political importance. In 1947, the government, as majority shareholder of Shorts, decided to consolidate all Shorts business in Belfast. Short Brothers (Bedford and Rochester) was to be liquidated, paying out any minority non-government remaining other shareholders. The intellectual property (design data), appropriate specialist manufacturing and other equipment would be owned by Short and Harland, renamed as Short Brothers and Harland[5], with the government as primary shareholder. The rather autocratic (but benignly intentioned) Oswald Short, one of the original Short Brothers founders, became life president of the new company. In 1948 Short Brothers and Harland relocated all operations in England to the Belfast site, at a total cost of over one million pounds but (eventually) disposing of the main (original) Rochester riverside site.

After the end of wartime activity, the passenger flying boats Sandringham (conversions of ex-RAF Sunderlands), Solent (sixteen new build, plus seven conversions from the RAF Seaford, the developed Sunderland) and the new build of the two Shetland large flying boats were the early post-war Shorts activities. The Shorts Sealand was a light (five to seven passenger) amphibious flying boat which had its first flight on 22 January 1948. Just twenty-five were built, the primary customer being the Indian Navy, which ordered a dual control version in 1952. The Sealand was the last Shorts flying boat design.

In the 1950s, most work became the building of aircraft (or major parts thereof) of other company designs, the most notable of which was the new English Electric Canberra bomber. In 1954, the Bristol Company took a 15.25 per cent share in Shorts. The cash injection was used to set up a Bristol Britannia production line in Belfast. Due to an unplanned shortage of work in Bristol, only fifteen complete Bristol Britannias and five sets of components were made by Shorts. Shorts were also allocated a part in government research programmes, designing and building the Short Sperrin (bomber candidate for a 'V' Bomber type – not pursued – see section 5.12), the SC1 vertical take-off experimental aircraft (see section 6.3) and the SB5 adjustable sweep research aircraft, built at RAE insistence to investigate the high sweep and low tailplane aerodynamic configuration of the English Electric Lightning (see section 6.3).

5.8 1955–60 UK Transport Aircraft

Vickers V.1000/VC.7

As the series 700 Viscount was being seen safely into service, with the improved series 800 established as the next variant in development, Vickers turned their attention to a UK government-specified new jet transport for RAF use, both as a replacement for the Handley Page Hastings four-engined piston troop carrier/logistics transport and as a fast deployment support aircraft for the new V-bombers, then in development. After many initial industry-Ministry discussions, the most promising submissions were from Bristol, de Havilland and Vickers. The Air Ministry were keen to allow the potential for a transatlantic airliner development larger than that of the Comet 4 to be included in the conceptual development of what was to be the new RAF logistics transport. The Vickers V.1000/VC.7 proposal was selected, intended to follow some of the basic ideas already incorporated in the Vickers Valiant, the new Vickers nuclear bomber soon to enter RAF service (see section 5.12).

Among the necessary differences from the Valiant would be an entirely new fuselage (capable of seating at least 100 passengers seated six-abreast), with the wing moved from the shoulder position to below the passenger cabin, combined with more powerful

---

5. The original company name, Short Brothers, was to be re-adopted in June 1977 and the company was privatised in 1984.

engines and high lift devices for RAF (and Empire routes) short field performance. The new engines were to be the new Rolls-Royce Conway[6] turbojet, with 25 per cent of compressor air bypassing the combustion chamber and turbine section. This much improved the fuel economy, allowed higher thrust and reduced jet exhaust noise (see section 4.2). Calculations by Boeing had shown that the improved fuel economy of the Conway would give the latest Boeing 707 proposal at least 8 per cent increased range. This proved to be an over-optimistic evaluation but the Conway would eventually become the first bypass jet engine in the world to enter commercial service.

After an RAF order for the V.1000 was placed in 1954, with declared interest from BOAC in the VC.7 potential, there was "panic in the USA" at rumours that Pan American were about to place an order for the British aircraft. This was partly because the VC.7 six-abreast fuselage had caused the world airlines to be very interested in the increased capacity, compared with the "then common" four-abreast passenger cabins in existing large airliners. Douglas, followed by Boeing, changed the designs of their new DC.8 and 707 jet airliners (still on the drawing board) to match.

Unfortunately, national airline BOAC became sceptical that the Conway bypass concept would deliver, declaring that "the Bristol Britannia will be OK for us across the Atlantic" (despite their earlier public criticisms of that aircraft), then (later) "we are waiting for Comet 4".

In November 1955, due to an RAF change in operational requirement and budget issues, the government cancelled the V.1000 project, with the prototype almost ready to roll out of the hangar. This also killed the VC.7. George Edwards, managing director of Vickers Aircraft, declared that the government had virtually "handed to the Americans, without a struggle, the entire world market for big jet aircraft". The final rub was that, after V.1000/VC.7 cancellation, less than one year later BOAC had to ask the government to allow them to buy the Boeing 707, which ironically materialised in BOAC service with an engine change to a more powerful Rolls-Royce Conway, repeated for four other national airlines.

In truth, the V.1000/VC.7 did have features which could be criticised. There was a question over VC.7 weight growth which could require more power (if not curtailed, leading to an increase in engine size and more fuel space being needed). Design flexibility was constrained by the "superior aerodynamic lines", the aerodynamically-clean burying of the four engines in the wing root (compared with using wing pods) allowed the fin size needed to be

Model of Vickers VC.7. (*Author's collection*)

reduced. However, the VC.7 engines occupied valuable internal wing space which could not be used for fuel, requiring fuel "pods" on each wing to achieve range. Engine access was also constrained and physically bigger engines would have required major wing structural redesign.

The supposedly less aerodynamically elegant "engines in wing pods" approach of the 707 and DC-8 required a larger fin to be designed but offered wing structure

---

6. The Conway was the power plant chosen for the UK Handley Page Victor B.Mk.2 nuclear bomber, which first flew in 1959. The term "bypass" was Rolls-Royce terminology. The industry later began to use the universal term "turbofan" engine, as compressor/turbine air bypass ratios increased.

advantages (wing bending load relief). Flutter speed was also improved, due to the engine positions being outboard, with weight cantilevered forward on the wing. The podded engine configuration also proved able to overcome undercarriage runway rain water spray and debris ingestion worries. Initial engine pod attachment structural integrity problems were soon overcome.

Vickers Vanguard

The Vanguard was not a "Brabazon-Committee" defined aircraft but grew out of the success of the Viscount, the problems of the Comet and the effect on Vickers of the cancellation of the V.1000/VC.7. The 139-seat Vickers Vanguard medium range four-turboprop (Rolls-Royce Tyne engines) project had twice the passenger capacity of the largest Viscount. It was inspired by a BEA-declared requirement and was aimed at enhanced operations in European and North American markets, compared with the successful and popular Vickers Viscount.

The Vanguard first flew in 1959 and remains one of the fastest turboprops ever built, able to match block times with 1960s jets on 500 mile stages, with better (less) block fuel. As a project, it failed to "break even" on orders from BEA and Trans Canada Airlines, with forty-four aircraft built. Most of the Western world market for large airliners became "jet orientated" (sometimes irrationally) just as the Vanguard was being introduced. Fairly soon, BEA had their remaining Vanguards converted to the "Merchantman", with a large freight door.

Rolls-Royce Dart Turboprop Power

As well as jet-powered large airliners, there was an emergent late 1950s-1960s market for replacing older fuel-thirsty short-range aircraft. At first, this would largely be to replace piston-engined aircraft, such as the Vickers Viking and the ubiquitous Douglas DC-3. The British company Handley Page produced an appropriate product first, the forty-four passenger HPR-3 Herald, designed at the ex-Miles Reading office (which had designed the Miles Marathon "Brabazon VA" small feederliner). Handley Page had consulted prospective customers (mostly DC-3 operators) before deciding on the power plant. They drew the conclusion that four small piston engines would be the customer airline preference, rather than use new (untried) turboprop technology. First flight was in August 1955. In the meantime, the 1950s emergence of the larger Vickers Viscount into service, importantly with four Rolls-Royce Dart turboprops, changed perceptions, such that the HPR-3 Herald's twenty-nine initial orders were cancelled by customer airlines, in favour of the new twin turboprop-powered (Rolls-Royce Dart) Dutch Fokker F.27 Friendship[7]. This forced a change by Handley Page, to a twin-Dart engine configuration, resulting in the stretched fifty-six passenger HPR-7 Dart Herald, the first production aircraft flying in 1959. The Handley Page lead was lost and only fifty Dart Heralds were built.

A third twin-Dart airliner competitor, the forty-four to fifty-eight passenger Avro 748, flew for the first time in June 1960. Avro had decided to re-enter the civil market as a direct consequence of the cancellations stemming from the 1957 "Duncan Sandys Defence Review" cancellations of most manned military aircraft programmes, (see section 5.15). Hawker Siddeley Aviation (into which Avro was fully absorbed in 1963) built 380 748s and eighty-six more were built under licence in India. Another thirty-one of the rear-loading 780 Andover C.Mk.1 logistics transport variant were built.

---

7. Fokker designed the 48-to-56 passenger F.27 "Friendship" from the start as a twin-Dart turboprop. This had its first flight in November 1955, three months after the piston-engined Herald. By the end of production, Fokker built 586 F.27 and USA Fairchild-Hiller built 206 F.27/FH.227 variants.

"Isolated" Handley Page (after the 1957 Defence Review consequences, see section 6.1) were unable to attract the government order, despite the more easily adapted high wing/low sill configuration of the Dart Herald.

The other significant British aircraft to use the Dart engine was the four-engined Armstrong Whitworth Argosy "wide" cargo aircraft, first flown in 1959. The initial 650 series Argosy had an Avro Shackleton wing (a mass-spar boom "safe life" design, like many aircraft of the 1950s era), and seventeen were sold to civil operators, including BEA. First flight was in 1959. The RAF ordered fifty-six of a modified version, the 660 series RAF Argosy

AW.650 C.Mk1 Argosy. (*RuthAS, CC BY-SA 3.0*)

C Mk.1, which dispensed with clamshell nose loading doors but had a rear loading facility with integral ramp, and other changes. The later revised 650-200 series was also ordered by BEA. This had a new "fail-safe" wing design which was lighter. Only six of the 200 series aircraft were delivered and the seventh remained unsold and was scrapped. The Avro 748 was the last Avro-named aircraft to fly and the Argosy 650-200 was the last Armstrong Whitworth aircraft.

Note:- Several non-UK aircraft also used the Dart engine, including the USA 1958 Grumman Gulfstream 1 twin Dart aircraft (200 built) and the 1962 Japanese sixty-four passenger NAMC YS-11 twin Dart aircraft (182 built). Most of the Gulfstreams were used as corporate executive aircraft (a few were configured as small airliners, with the stretched version accommodating up to thirty-seven passengers). Most of the YS-11 were sold in Asia. In total, more than 7,100 Rolls-Royce Dart engines were built in the forty years of production between 1947 and 1987.

5.9 The British Rotary Wing Aircraft Industry

First, a bit of history and definition of "Rotary Wing Aircraft":

The first recorded thoughts about a rotary winged aircraft are attributed to Leonardo da Vinci. His concept was a large "screw wing" with a vertical axis, shown in his famous sketch.

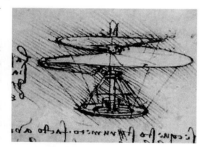

The helicopter (from the Greek "helix" and "pteron", spiral wing hélicoptère, a term coined by Gustave Ponton d'Amécourt in 1861) is an aeroplane "where the wings rotate". It has a rotor, a general term for a rotating device.

Leonardo da Vinci Sketch. (*Author's collection*)

There are two basic types of rotary wing aircraft:

1. The helicopter is an alternative casually used term for all rotary wing aircraft. It is more accurately used where the aircraft specifically has a powered multi-blade rotor pushing the air downwards, which provides lift and forward thrust by tilting the direction of thrust from the rotor a few degrees forward from the vertical, and...

2. The term "autogyro" (or "gyrocopter") is the differentiating term usually applied to rotary wing aircraft which have an unpowered rotor. The rotor axis is tilted slightly backwards from the vertical and a conventional propeller or jet engine provides thrust to move the aircraft forwards. The rotor provides only lift, rotation imparted by air moving up through the tilted rotor as the aircraft moves forwards, causing rotor rotation (called autorotation). This type of aircraft was invented by Juan de la Cierva, first flown as his C.3 model (unsteadily) in 1923. This was the first rotary-wing aircraft to fly in a truly controlled manner, from which the design of the practical helicopter started.

Several experimenters tried to design and build a helicopter, usually with multiple rotors revolving in opposite directions, to avoid "the aircraft rotating in the opposite direction to the torque applied to a single rotor" causing reaction torque. Between 1907 and 1909 there were some "uncontrolled very low and short hops/flights" by French brothers Jacques and Louis Breguét and by fellow Frenchman Paul Cornu. Cornu was "the first to leave the ground", in 1907. The British government funded more research by Argentinian Raúl Pateras-Pescara de Castelluccio, who had come to France with his family whilst a teenager. This resulted in his 1921 helicopter No. 3 which could fly for up to ten minutes and achieved groundspeeds of over 8mph.

Note: There is a short silent film available (2019) on the internet, accessible by searching his name.

In Britain, Irish-born Australian Louis Brennan conceived and developed the guided torpedo and, with his partner John Ridley Temperley, sold his patent to the government in 1884 for £100,000 (over £11.5 million pounds in 2019 terms). As this was being arranged, he started to think about helicopters but, without the availability of a suitable lightweight power unit, he accepted that the concept remained just that – a concept. With the advent of the internal combustion engine and practical aviation, by 1910 he became more enthused. Eventually, he persuaded the UK government that the idea was a sufficiently practical possibility that construction of his latest design could start (in great secrecy) in 1919, at the newly established Royal Aircraft Establishment at Farnborough.

The single rotor was driven by small four-bladed propellers at the tips of the two rotor blades, driven by a shaft running through the hollow spar of the rotor structure which was powered by a central piston engine. This arrangement was virtually free of any rotor reactive torque causing the main body of the helicopter to rotate. It was a significant machine, weighing 2,765lb with a rotor 61ft in diameter. Tethered flight inside the hangar was achieved but poorly controlled. Control was improved, but not really to a level acceptable for practical use. The Louis Brennan helicopter claimed the first successful flight of a helicopter in Britain. By 1924, free flights were regularly achieved outside the hangar. Testing continued, with a total of some seventy low-level flights (never higher than 10ft). However, in a free flight in the open air in 1925 the Louis Brennan helicopter suffered a non-fatal but terminal crash. By then, the government had become more interested in the progress made by Juan de la Cierva with his autogyro, and the Brennan helicopter was no more. Meanwhile, by 1939 the state of the art regarding the development of the helicopter became well advanced. Viable helicopters were flying in Europe and the USA.

In France, the Breguét-Dorand helicopter was demonstrating a high level of controllability, including an autorotative landing, and achieved 62mph (99.7kph). In Germany, demonstration of the Focke-Wulf Fw-61 in the Deutchlandhalle in 1938 and its subsequent achievements of speed and range were convincing evidence of progress.

Also in Germany, Flettner had flown his Fl 185 and 285, leading to production during the Second World War. In the USA, Hiller, Piasecki, Sikorsky and Young were all developing helicopters that would result in production aircraft. The age of the helicopter was nigh!

Cierva Autogyros and Helicopters

After several attempts at producing a practical autogyro in Spain, at Farnborough in 1926 Juan de la Cierva demonstrated his first "sustained and controlled flight" C.6 autogyro to the British government (Air Ministry). This aircraft used an Avro 504 fuselage as the basic airframe.

Cierva moved his activity to Britain in 1926, financially underwritten by G & J Weir at the instigation of their managing director James George Weir, who was also an aviation enthusiast. Within Britain, Cierva collaborated

Cierva C.6 Autogyro. (*CC BY-SA 3.0*)

mostly (but not exclusively) with Avro, using different Avro fuselage designs as basic airframe. The first autogyro built in Britain was the Cierva C.8, first flight in 1926. Three aircraft were built as progressively improved test machines and three sold (one to James Weir and two exported to the USA). The most-produced type was the Cierva C.30 autogyro, licensed for production to Avro (as the Avro C.30A Rota, first flight 1933), to Lioré-et-Olivier in France and to Focke-Wolf in Germany. Seventy-eight Rota were built, twelve of which were sold to the RAF. The other licenced builds produced twenty-five French C.30s and forty German C.30s, using different engines. Avro did not pursue further rotary wing opportunities.

In 1936, Cierva was killed in the Croydon KLM DC-2 airliner accident but the Cierva Autgiro Company continued to operate as designer-manufacturers until the outbreak of the Second World War. It produced the W.5 aircraft, considered to be the world's second practical helicopter (as opposed to an autogyro). The W.5 first flight was on 7 June 1938.

After producing parts and assemblies for aircraft of other UK aircraft manufacturers during the early years of the war, in 1943 the company was re-energised as the Cierva Autogyro Company, a division of G & J Weir, producing a twin-rotor helicopter design (the W.6), and two experimental helicopters (W.9 and W.11). The twenty-four passenger W.11 used three rotors with axes tilted so that torque and thrust from driving the rotors was "balanced" in a controllable manner. This avoided the more common helicopter design approach of using a separate tail rotor.

There was a single Rolls-Royce Merlin power plant in the fuselage driving all three rotors. The W.11 first flew on 7 December 1948. At the time, the W.11 was the largest and heaviest helicopter in the world. After the 1950 fatal crash of the W.11 prototype, the Weir Company started development of the W.14 two-seat helicopter. However, in 1951 the Cierva Autogyro Company rights to the Weir-supported developments were sold to Saunders Roe. James Weir did not lose his interest in helicopters and remained in contact with a J.S. Shapiro who, in 1951, started Servotech Ltd. to design and build "inherently stable" helicopters.

Servotech (Rotorcraft) Ltd and Cierva Rotorcraft Ltd

In 1951 J.S. Shapiro formed Servotech Ltd. to design and build "stable" helicopters (basically, a twin contra-rotating rotor design principle). James Weir "encouraged" Shapiro. F.G. Mitchell joined Shapiro to form a new company, Rotorcraft Ltd.

A prototype was designed (the Rotorcraft Grasshopper I) with construction subcontracted to Servotech, financed by Mitchell engineering. After hovering trials early in 1962 showed the need for more power, a second piston engine was added to make Grasshopper II, which made its first flight on 26 November 1962. Lack of finance due to death of the owner of Mitchell engineering halted further progress until James Weir became sufficiently interested to provide finance, via his "moribund" Cierva Autogyro Company, to develop the four-passenger Grasshopper III. This became a Cierva-Rotorcraft five-seater helicopter joint project, the CR Twin. First flight was on 18 August 1969 and three prototypes were built, but further financial backing could not be obtained.

Saunders-Roe Helicopters

Prior to the 1929 A.V. Roe/John Lord controlling investment in S.E. Saunders Ltd. (see section 2.8), the company had designed the first amphibian aircraft in the world (six supplied, just before the First World War), two different land planes and five different flying boats, all of which failed to get beyond the prototype stage. Saunders had also manufactured the designs of others. In 1928, Air Ministry Specification 2/28 was issued to S.E Saunders for the manufacture of a prototype helicopter of the Helicogyre No. 3 design of Vittorio Isacco. This was delivered (by road) but never flew. This was the first helicopter manufactured by Saunders-Roe, and the last until much later. After Saunders-Roe (Saro) was established in 1929, the new company concentrated on new landplanes and flying boats and, after the Helicogyre episode, did not pursue further any rotary wing activity until the 1950s.

The "Helicogyre" was the invention of the Italian Vittorio Isacco, basically an autogyro with separate small piston engines driving small propellers in the tips of each of the rotor blades until cruising speed is reached (fuel for each engine was in the blades of the rotor). The main idea was to avoid the usual autogyro design (for take-off) of needing a clutch in the main engine output to temporarily connect to "spinning-up" the rotor, or gaining forward speed with a conventional take-off run (usually quite short). A clear Helicogyre design disadvantage was the number of engines involved (five in total with the four-blade rotor of Isacco design No.3) and associated engine control problems, thrust balancing between each rotor blade engine and fuel feed/refuelling. Helicogyre No. 3 design never flew.

Saunders-Roe acquired Cierva assets (not the company name) in 1951, as Weir dropped out of the aircraft business. The acquisition of the helicopter activity was part of a conscious policy decision to expand into this new market. The Cierva (Weir) W.14 became the basis of the Saro Skeeter helicopter. Extended privately-funded development work (encouraged by ongoing Air Ministry interest) led to some four prototypes and eight pre-production evaluation models, before the aircraft finally entered service with the British army in 1957, almost ten years after the original prototype W.14 had flown. Some fifty Skeeters were

Saro Skeeter. (*RuthAS, CC BY-SA 3.0*)

used in different UK armed forces roles (Air Observation Post and Communications AOP.12 model and a training T.13 model). Overall, about seventy-four Skeeters were constructed, ten of these being exported to West Germany.

Design of the Saro P.531 helicopter was started in November 1957 as a private venture improvement of the earlier Skeeter. Two prototypes flew before Saro's helicopter business was absorbed into Westland Aircraft in 1960. (Under Westland, the P.531 project was to appear in a different guise.) In 1959 Saro had also demonstrated the first practical hovercraft, built under contract to the National Research Development Corporation to Christopher Cockerell's design, the SR.N1 ("Saunders-Roe Nautical 1"). The hovercraft business was also taken over by Westland (see section 6.8).

Fairey Helicopters

Fairey Aviation established a rotary wing aircraft division in 1945. In late 1945, Dr J.A.J. Bennett (ex-chief technical officer at the Cierva Autogiro Company, 1936–1939), joined them. In April 1946, Fairey announced a private-venture project for a rotary-wing aircraft, to be built to a design developed by Dr Bennett. This would be the Fairey FB-1 Gyrodyne. The concept had been part of a 1938 Cierva proposal for a Royal Navy helicopter requirement to Air Ministry specification 22/38, which had been put in abeyance on the outbreak of the Second World War. In June 1948, the FB-1 Gyrodyne first prototype set a rotary wing world speed record of 124mph. Competing against Westland and Bristol proposals for a post-war Air Ministry helicopter requirement, the FB-1 Gyrodyne proposal was selected over the rival Westland-Sikorsky Dragonfly and the Bristol Sycamore. The fatal crash of the first prototype (due to a manufacturing defect) delayed Fairey's development testing such that the Air Ministry ordered three Westland Dragonflys for immediate use by the army in Malaya, later ordering the Bristol Sycamore. No Gyrodyne order ever resulted.

The Gyrodyne is yet another version of an autogyro, where the cruising flight small rotational torque on the airframe (due to the asymmetric drag and central bearing friction on the free-wheeling rotor) is countered by two propellers, one each mounted on stub wings either side of the fuselage and set at pilot-controllable slightly different power (propeller pitch) levels.

The second prototype Gyrodyne was converted to the Jet Gyrodyne, which was actually a compound Gyroplane (rotary and fixed wing combined). First flight was in 1954. For takeoff, landing, and low-speed flight, the rotor was driven by compressed air extracted from the engine compressor stage and burnt with fuel in blade-tip mounted pressure-jets. This zero-torque rotor drive did not require a compensating anti-torque system, though the pitch of the propellers on each of the stub wing tips was controlled differentially by the rudder pedals to provide yaw control. As airspeed was gained, the rotor drive system was shut down, allowing the rotor to autorotate and provide most of the lift while the wing engine propellers provided the necessary thrust. For low-speed flight and landing, the rotor drive system was restarted to provide hovering capability. The Jet Gyrodyne was created as a flying research vehicle, to investigate the technology of the proposed Fairey Rotodyne.

The Rotodyne became a serious government-authorised project in 1953. A forty to fifty passenger Rotodyne version with more than 400 miles range was proposed, later envisaged as stretchable (with more powerful engines) to be capable of economically carrying fifty-seven to seventy-five passengers. In November 1957 the prototype maiden flight took place. Throughout the world, interest was growing in the prospect of direct inner city-to-inner city transport, and both the UK and USA military were also interested. The possibility of as many as 200 for the US army was rumoured.

The government-owned British European Airways would order "once the capability was proven". Government departments argued about whether the project should be financed via the defence budget or via the civil aviation route. As costs escalated, the Treasury eventually expressed their opposition to further finance.

The matter was raised with Harold Macmillan, the Prime Minister of the United Kingdom, who wrote to Aubrey Jones, the Minister of Supply, on 6 June 1958, stating that, "this project must not be allowed to die". Funding for the programme had been fifty-fifty between Fairey and the government. The penultimate nail in the project's coffin came when BEA chose to decline to place its own order for the Rotodyne, principally due to its unresolved concerns regarding operating costs and the high-profile tip-jet noise issue (which was significant during take-off and landing, but might have been amenable to noise reduction measures). Following a request for funding for eighteen production aircraft, in 1962 the government finally decided that, "for economic reasons" further government funding would not be provided. That was the final nail. Fairey Aviation had been taken over by Westland in 1960 and, in 1962, the Westland board decided that the total investment required to complete the programme as a PV would not be likely to show a return.

Fairey Rotodyne. (*Author's collection*)

About the same time as the Rotodyne project emerged, there was a British army requirement for a light helicopter "transportable by lorry" (which was a significant overall size restriction). Fairey developed their Ultra-Light Helicopter concept, the prototype of which first flew in 1955. The tip-driven main rotor was torqueless, driven by compressed air taken from the turbine engine and the Ultra Light used a boom-mounted tailplane with a fin/rudder combination for yaw control. The fin/rudder projected below the boom into the engine jet efflux, allowing directional control whilst hovering. The elimination of any tail rotor obviated the shafts, gears, and clutches associated with a tail rotor drive. The stub wing and associated propellers of the Gyrodyne were not needed.

Five more prototype and development aircraft were manufactured and flown but the army became more focused on the Saro Skeeter, ultimately making the Skeeter the final choice "as a matter of policy". Fairey attempts to market the Ultra Light for civil use did not result in any sales and the project was cancelled in 1959, Fairey then concentrating on the (doomed) Rotodyne.

Fairey lost the Great West Aerodrome in 1944, due to requisition by the Air Ministry (eventually used in the building of London Heathrow airport). No compensation was paid until 1964,

Fairey Ultra-Light, on a lorry. (*RuthAS, CC BY-SA 3.0*)

causing a severe financial shock to Fairey. This probably hastened the end of the Fairey Aviation Company part of the Fairey Group (see section 6.1), which had grown to range much further than its original aircraft design and manufacturing interests. A proud company which, by 1960, had designed thirty-seven aircraft types and produced 12,396 Fairey-designed aircraft over forty-five years (with only twelve types never proceeding beyond prototype), plus thousands of Fairey-produced aircraft not of Fairey design origin during the two world wars.

Bristol Helicopters

Raoul Hafner was an Austrian who had attempted to design helicopters in the 1930s (see section 2.8). He came to England in 1933, studied Cierva's autogyros and learned to fly them. He designed the A.R.III Gyroplane, built at the Martin Baker works in Denham and first flown in 1935. In 1940 he was interned as an alien until his naturalisation papers came through. Later in the Second World War, Hafner was responsible for

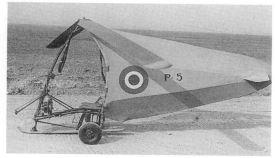

Hafner Rotachute. (*Author's collection*)

the design and development of the Rotachute (a man-carrying skeletal autogyro for air assault troop use) and the Rotaplane, a jeep-carrying equivalent of the Rotachute, known as the Rotabuggy.

In 1944 the Bristol Aeroplane Company formed a helicopter division and acquired Hafner's company and design rights, appointing Hafner as head of the division and, eventually, engaging some of his old team. Work started in 1944 on a four-seat helicopter for both civil and military use, resulting in the first flight of the Bristol 171 Sycamore in 1947. Three prototype aircraft were produced and a total of 154 Mk.4 production versions of the Sycamore were sold to the RAF, West Germany and Belgium. As civilian helicopters, fifteen more were sold as Bristol 171s. As such, this was the first British helicopter to receive a British Certificate of Airworthiness.

The Bristol Type 173 was a tandem rotor conceptual development of the earlier type 171 Sycamore single-rotor helicopter. The type 173 used two units of the Sycamore's engine and rotor, with a new "long" fuselage. The separated rotor gearboxes were connected by a synchroniser shaft which also enabled one engine to drive both rotors if an engine failed, a ubiquitous feature on separated twin-rotor helicopters such as the modern Boeing Chinook.

Designed originally for civilian use to carry ten passengers, it did not attract much airline interest but the RAF thought it showed significant potential as a troop carrier and casualty evacuation aircraft. Stretched, and with two new engines each more than twice as powerful as those in type 171, the type 191 was created.

First flight was in July 1958. After three prototypes and two evaluation machines, and some interest from the Royal Navy (which evaporated), twenty-six of

Bristol 192 Belvedere. (*Author's collection*)

the further developed version, type 192 Belvedere, were ordered for the RAF. This was able to carry up to nineteen fully equipped troops or twelve stretcher cases with attendants. First flight of the type 192 was in 1958. There were attempts to sell the type 192 on the civil market but no sales materialised. This was the last Bristol helicopter before the Westland takeover in 1960. Bristol Helicopter's Raoul Hafner became technical director for Westland Helicopters, until retirement in 1970.

Westland Helicopters

Westland Aircraft Works was established in 1915 (see section 2.6) and became fully independent of its founders Petters Ltd. in 1935. Control was acquired by the large engineering conglomerate John Brown in 1938, Eric Mensforth (later knighted) being made Westland managing director. Before and during the Second World War, Westland produced fixed wing aircraft of their own design and also produced Supermarine Spitfires and Seafires.

After 1945 they concentrated on the design of the Wyvern single-seater naval strike aircraft. This was the last fixed-wing project, a 500mph, long-range, torpedo/bomb-carrying carrier-based fighter of which 124 were completed between 1945 and 1956. Due to the unavailability of the intended engine, the Rolls-Royce Eagle 22 piston engine, which never entered series production, a change to various propeller-turbine engines were considered, eventually settled as the Armstrong Siddeley Python turboprop. Once described as "very nearly, a very good aeroplane", the Wyvern – and, in particular, its turbo-prop engines – suffered many serious difficulties. In all, there were sixty-eight accidents. Thirty-nine aircraft were lost with thirteen fatalities. The type was completely retired in 1958, only two years after production ceased.

Meanwhile, Eric Mensforth had been seconded for the last two years of the war into the Ministry of Aircraft Production, during which he came into contact with Igor Sikorsky, the Russian-born USA helicopter designer. He returned to become vice-chairman of Westland. During 1946 he was instrumental in negotiating an agreement between Westland and the Sikorsky helicopter company (signed January 1947), licensing Westland production of the Sikorsky S-51 helicopter.

As a result, its British equivalent, the Westland built WS-51 Dragonfly, flew on 5 October 1948. This was a successful venture, with a prototype and 133 production examples built and sold. A further fifteen improved versions (Westland Widgeon helicopter) were also produced (three of which were conversions from WS-51). Examples of the WS-51 and Widgeon were delivered to the UK airline BEA, the Royal Navy and the Royal Air Force.

Westland WS-51 Dragonfly. (*RuthAS, CC BY-SA 3.0*)

Before the end of Dragonfly production, in 1953, Eric Mensforth became Westland chairman. He decided that the Westland future would not include fixed wing aircraft and negotiated successfully to licence-build the Sikorsky S-55/H-19 Chickasaw, which became the Westland Whirlwind[8] (helicopter). Over 360 Whirlwind helicopters were built between 1953 and 1966, the majority of which were used by the RN and the RAF in various adaptations, as air-sea rescue, anti-submarine and transport helicopters.

In 1956, a Sikorsky H-34 (Sikorsky company designation S-58) was shipped to Westland as a "pattern" for the Westland-designed version as the Wessex helicopter. Westland changed the piston engine of the S-58 to produce the first helicopter in the world to be powered by a gas turbine engine. A total of 382 were built between 1958 and 1970, most of which were operated by the RN and the RAF, although over fifty were sold overseas. The last RAF Wessex in service retired in 2003.

The dramatic effect of the UK 1957 Defence Review on the aircraft industry is described in section 6.1. Even though the review did not directly affect helicopter

---

8. Whirlwind was also the name of the 1938 Westland monoplane heavy fighter.

projects in progress at the time, by 1960 the long-term rationalised future of the helicopter industry was clearly established, including the complete takeover by Westland of the helicopter businesses of Saunders-Roe, Bristol and Fairey. Eric Mensforth was a significant "mover and shaker" in this process. The company name was changed to Westland Helicopters.

The Saunders Roe hovercraft activity on the Isle of Wight was eventually joined to the Vickers Supermarine hovercraft activity at Southampton, under the umbrella of a new company British Hovercraft Corporation (BHC) jointly owned by Westland and Vickers (see section 6.8). In 1970, Westland bought out all other BHC shareholders. BHC became a fully absorbed part of Westland Aerospace in 1984 when hovercraft activity ceased.

All British Fairey facilities ceased involvement in aircraft engineering soon after 1960, ultimately including what would have been the Fairey contribution to the de Havilland DH.121 Trident airliner. The Bristol helicopter establishment at Weston-super-Mare airport became a Westland supply depot, until finally closed in 1987. The 1957 piston-engined Saro Skeeter P.531 project was to become the basis of the 1960 army Westland Scout (150 built) and the 1962 navy Westland Wasp (144 built) turbine-powered helicopters. The Westland helicopter business went on to further successes (see section 7.3 and 8.6).

Percival Helicopter

Percival Aircraft started a helicopter division in 1950. Their first (and only) helicopter was a response to an Air Ministry specification for an experimental helicopter with a rotor driven by tip air jets.

The P.74 was powered by twin Napier Oryx gas turbine engines beneath the cabin floor, which provided compressed air to the rotor tip jets. The engine exhausts passed through the cabin wall, which created a very noisy and hot cabin environment. As the P.74 was only intended as a "proof of concept" aircraft, this was accepted. Trials started in 1956 but the P.74 failed to take off. This was a potential "blessing in disguise", because the only exit was at the rear of the cabin, useless for the pilots in the event of any evacuation emergency! The primary test pilot was famously quoted as saying, "... the cockpit, flying controls and engine controls... designed without any input from a pilot". A ten-passenger design was on the drawing board when the aircraft industry rationalisation from the 1957 Defence Review caused the project to be abandoned and the Hunting-Percival helicopter division was closed down.

Firth Helicopters

Starting with just the fuselage of the incomplete second prototype of the (failed) Planet Aircraft Limited "Satellite" four-seat piston-engined aircraft (which, unusually, had a pusher propeller mounted in the tail), Firth helicopters designed the proof-of-concept Firth FH 01/4 Atlantic helicopter. In the interests of weight-saving, magnesium-zirconium alloy had been used extensively in the Satellite design.

The Satellite undercarriage collapsed after the first "low hop" in 1949. After repairs, the next landing (from only a gentle twenty feet-high "hop"), cracked the insufficiently-strong monocoque fuselage along the main "keel". The conclusion was that the whole design of the Satellite was not robust enough, not having anything like the correct amount of local re-enforcing and stiffening elements to take landing loads and other high local loads. The incomplete second Satellite prototype fuselage was incorporated in the design of the Firth Atlantic helicopter, with suitable modifications.

The Firth Atlantic helicopter concept was based on the patent of the American Fred Landgraf, involving two rotors (one each side) fitted on outrigger pylons (stub wings).

Directional control used ailerons at the trailing edge of the outriggers. Construction began in 1952. During ground tests, failure of parts of the rotor drive system curtailed activity and the helicopter never flew. There was insufficient funding to proceed. The aircraft was presented to the Cranfield College of Aeronautics in 1955, as a static specimen.

5.10 Quest for Faster-Than-Sound Flight

As the Second World War moved towards a close, the fastest warplanes (propeller driven and the new jet fighters) were starting to experience a range of significant flight control and structural problems as speeds approached the speed of sound. There was not enough power available to fly straight and level at these high speeds (especially in the denser air at low altitudes, where the sea-level speed of sound is 762mph). Diving from high altitude, however, could create severe buffeting, and a sense of imminent loss of control. It was known that fighter aircraft had sometimes got into control difficulties, or were even lost, when diving from altitude at high speed.

Ernst Mach (b.1838, d.1916) was a respected physicist. The ratio of the speed of an object in any medium to the speed of propagation of sound in that medium is called the Mach Number in his honour. Thus, an object moving at the speed of sound is at Mach 1. A "shock wave" is an abrupt, extremely rapid change of pressure, temperature and density, in a medium such as air.

Shock waves on aircraft flying control surfaces caused air loads to change rapidly and violent pitch control oscillations could occur. The actual physics of supersonic flight, however, were not known well enough in the field of aircraft design. The aircraft speeds during steep dives were

Bullet Shock Waves (*Mach/ Salcher, 1887*)

penetrating into the transonic range, above a critical Mach number (M_{CRIT}). At M_{CRIT} the aircraft drag coefficient C_D rises steeply[9], before falling above Mach 1. "Transonic" is generally defined as the range from about 20per cent under to 20 per cent over the speed of sound. It was clear that high flight speeds a little short of supersonic still caused very localised supersonic airflow over parts of the aircraft, changes in which contributed to the loss of control.

This particularly affected the flying control surfaces and associated structure. The so-called "sound barrier" became the populist term for accelerating through the point of highest drag at Mach 1. However, there was little detailed flight data to help scientific analysis of the phenomena. Both the USA and Britain started programmes to investigate. In the aftermath of the Second World War, it was discovered that, before the end, Germany had been well ahead. However, during 1943 and 1944, high speed controlled and instrumented experiments were conducted in Britain by the RAE, diving from high altitude using various RAF aircraft (Spitfire, Mustang, Tempest, Meteor and Vampire). The Spitfire PR.IX, with its thin wings, produced the fastest result, with a recorded maximum of Mach 0.9 during a dive from 40,000ft. Such experiments were highly dangerous, because of the lack of understanding of the problems associated with transonic flight.

In an attempt to eliminate the high risk to pilots, special purpose remotely-controlled unmanned rocket-powered aircraft were designed (built by Vickers) to explore further.

---

9. Although the drag coefficient C_D falls as airspeed passes Mach 1.0, the actual drag continues to rise, as a function of the square of the airspeed.

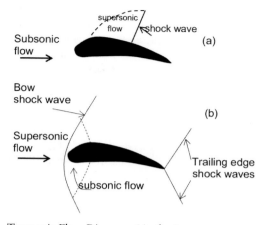

supersonic flow — shock wave

Subsonic flow → (a)

Bow shock wave

(b)

Supersonic flow →

subsonic flow

Trailing edge shock waves

Schematic of transonic flow over an airfoil.
(from The NASA History Series, NASA SP-4219. 1998)
(a) Freestream flow slightly below the speed of sound, typically a subsonic freestream Mach number from about 0.8 to 0.999.
(b) Freestream flow slightly above the speed of sound, typically a supersonic freestream Mach number from 1.0 to about 1.2.

Transonic Flow Diagram. (*Author*)

These models were carried to 36,000ft by a de Havilland Mosquito mother ship and released. In 1948, one reached a Mach number of 1.38 (930mph) in level flight. Because of the bulk of electronics equipment at that time, data telemetry was limited and manned flights continued in propeller-driven aircraft for some time, even though the propeller tips were clearly well into the unknown régime of transonic aerodynamics. In the meantime, jet-powered specially-built research aircraft were being considered and several were soon taking off.

The government launched a top-secret programme in 1942 to study the creation of a turbojet-powered manned aircraft intended to fly faster than sound. The British Miles aircraft company eventually proposed the M.52 with short-span thin straight wings which would not suffer shock wave interference on the wings from the aircraft nose shock (wing tips being inside the nose "shock wave cone").

The power plant was to be a specially enhanced Whittle W.2/700 jet turbine with an "augmenter" stage (conceptually, a ducted fan but mounted behind the turbine, with auxiliary air intakes) and the world's first jet turbine afterburner in the exhaust (fuel injection into the hot exhaust, now labelled "reheat"). This was intended to give the large increase in thrust needed to overcome the steep transonic drag rise. In 1944, with the design 90 per cent complete, Miles were given the go-ahead to build three prototypes.

Miles M.52 (artist's impression). (*Author's collection*)

Results from wind tunnel experiments and the one-third scale M.52 model tests had developed the idea that the rigidity of a power-controlled all-moving tailplane could avoid the violent aircraft pitching control oscillations often experienced in high speed dives (this was to be adopted later in the USA Bell X1 development and X1 testing confirmed that this resolved this particular problem). Due to budgetary constraints immediately after the war, and ignorant scepticism amongst some British officials that supersonic flight was even physically possible, the M.52 project was suddenly cancelled in 1946 by the new British government. The ability of the M.52 to have made a practical supersonic flight breakthrough remains unproven. Given the wartime German advances in supersonic aerodynamic technology and the immature new jet turbine engine technology of the time, in hindsight this now seems unlikely. An attempt to fly supersonically would, however, at least have enhanced the prestige of the previously secret advanced nature of late wartime and immediate post-war British aeronautical technology. The Miles Company went into administration in 1947, for reasons not associated with M.52 cancellation.

In the summer of 1945, the de Havilland Company had used a DH.100 Vampire jet fuselage to form the basis of the DH.108 tailless research aircraft. For a short while, it was thought that such a tailless configuration might show promise for the new "Brabazon type IV" (the DH.106 Comet-to-be), but that idea was soon abandoned. The idea of "no tail" was stimulated by the experience of extreme buffet/pilot control column shake in the high speed experiments with normal aircraft, which had direct manual control connection to the elevator hinged on to the fixed tailplane. An ultimate technical prediction of the phenomenon was an extremely rapid uncontrollable whole aircraft pitching oscillation "at up to three cycles per second", which would quickly cause pilot loss of consciousness and aircraft structural failure.

As a precaution, the DH.108 Swallow was to have the more rigid arrangement available with powered flying controls, but the power units were to be fitted later. After initial low speed trials with the first DH.108, the second aircraft started high speed trials, piloted by the de Havilland chief test pilot, son of Sir Geoffrey de Havilland. In steep dives from high altitude it achieved a Mach number of 0.895, with little sign of discouraging buffet as Mach 1 was approached. The aircraft was prepared for an attempt on the level flight world speed record. Just before the planned record attempt, the aircraft took off on 27 September 1946 for a high speed handling test. The aircraft broke up over the test area (the Thames Estuary) and Geoffrey de Havilland junior was killed. His body had a broken neck, possibly due to his head colliding with the cockpit canopy during the (predicted) pitching oscillation.

On 6 September 1948, the first British pilot "almost certainly" to have exceeded the speed of sound was de Havilland's John Derry, whilst diving from 40,000ft in the third and final version of the DH.108, registration VW120 (the recording equipment failed but a "loud sonic bang" was heard). All three DH.108 aircraft were lost in crashes in which the pilot was killed. John Derry was not one of these but he and his fellow crew

DH.108. (*Author's collection*)

member Tony Richards were killed later, when their DH.110 Sea Vixen prototype broke up during a display at the September 1952 SBAC Farnborough Air Show. As the wreckage plunged to the ground, twenty-nine people on the ground were also killed. Since transonic research testing started some ten years previously, twenty-four test flight crew were killed in Britain by the time of the 1952 tragedy, during the aeronautical research activities solely associated with aircraft development in the transonic speed régime. They were not the last to be killed.

Britain carried out test flying with twenty-three different transonic research and prototype jet aircraft throughout the decade after the end of the war, including pre-prototypes of the Supermarine Swift and the Hawker Hunter (see section 5.13). The flights yielded essential data helpful in creating several different transonic aircraft more capable than the first generation (wartime) jets, the Meteor and Vampire.

Meanwhile, in the USA, the Bell aircraft company were asked in March 1945 to commence the design of what became the rocket-powered XS-1 (Experimental Supersonic 1, later called the X-1), with the same objective of supersonic flight. Ideas from the cancelled M.52 programme were shared with the USA Bell aircraft company. In January 1946 the Bell X-1 commenced a series of gliding flights, being dropped at altitude from a B-29 Stratofortress "mother ship".

After modifications which included a tailplane change to "all-moving, powered", twenty-six powered flights were carried out by the Bell company during 1946–47. These were kept below Mach 1 by the Bell test pilot, who requested a bonus of $150,000 before attempting to fly that fast. The US Army Air Force became impatient and took over. On 14 October 1947, over the Mojave Desert in the USA, the Bell X-1 aircraft was released at 45,000ft and pilot Major Charles (Chuck) Yeager became the first man to exceed the speed of sound, reaching Mach 1.06.

Bell X-1. (*Author's collection*)

It could be done! Overcoming the so-called sound barrier had become an objective in itself. To create the ability to travel this fast was one of the objectives of aircraft designers, as a way of creating a new aircraft which could "outfly" older designs. The advent of the aircraft turbojet engine held out the promise of the motive power to do this, with an aircraft that could take off and land conventionally, as a much better alternative to using air launch and rocket power.

Progress was slower in Britain than in the USA, due to funding restraints. However, six British supersonic research aircraft were created. The 1954 first flights of the supersonic Fairey Delta 2 and the English Electric P1A yielded valuable actual flight data for supersonic flight (see section 6.3) and the subsequent P1B development became the pre-prototype for the Lightning. Two flying Bristol T.188 (maximum speed reached Mach 1.88) and two Fairey Delta 2 were also produced. Piloted by Fairey Chief Test Pilot Peter Twiss, the FD-2 became the first aircraft in the world to exceed 1,000mph, eventually setting a world record of 1,132mph on 10 March 1956. This was a massive 37 per cent (310mph) faster than the previous record, causing consternation in the USA and reshaping the French aircraft industry ambitions (see Marcel Dassault comment noted in section 7.2, under "AFVG"). The FD-2 later exceeded 1,300mph and the same aircraft became the BAC.221 as a supersonic research aircraft for Concorde wing development (see section 7.1). The 1950s development of high speed aircraft acceptable and capable of flying at high subsonic (transonic but less than Mach 1) speeds for RAF or RN service use[10], eventually produced aircraft like the Hawker Hunter, the Supermarine Swift and Scimitar, the Gloster Javelin and the de Havilland Sea Vixen (see section 5.13). The Avro Vulcan and Handley Page Victor 'V' bombers of the 1950s (see section 5.12) could also reach speeds as high as Mach 0.95 and the Victor once inadvertently exceeded Mach 1 in a shallow dive.

---

10. The first service aircraft capable of supersonic speed was the USAF North American F-100C version of the Super Sabre fighter, which entered service in 1954. The first British service aircraft cleared for supersonic flight (in a dive) was the RN DH.110 Sea Vixen (see section 5.13).

5.11 The Early Years of the Cold War

The Political Background to the Cold War

Hopeful of an enduring post-Second World War peace, the 1945 incoming new Labour government's initial stance on defence and military aircraft was that:

"No major conflict would occur for at least a decade, and thus there would be no need to develop or to procure any new [combat] aircraft until the middle of the next decade."

However, the end of the Second World War marked the beginning of a gradually increasingly aggressive stand-off, between the Soviet Union and the other allies which, together, had won the war against Germany and its Axis Allies. Winston Churchill's famous 5 March 1946 phrase: "From Stettin in the Baltic to Trieste in the Adriatic, an iron curtain is descending across the continent," (Europe) is a marker for the start of the "Cold War". The end of the Cold War is generally accepted as the end of 1991, when the Soviet Union (USSR) was dissolved nine months after the 1955 Warsaw Pact was finally and formally dissolved.

Immediately after the 1945 end of the war in Europe, the Soviet Union wartime ally increasingly adopted a slowly escalating confrontational political stance towards the USA and European non-communist countries. The invention (and actual use on Japan in August 1945) of the atomic fission bomb had clearly alarmed the Soviet Union, given that the USA were the "sole proprietors" of nuclear weapons and unwilling to share its secrets with them. The USA Atomic Energy Act of 1946 prohibited the export of nuclear technology outside the United States. This applied even to Britain, which had co-operated directly with the USA in the Manhattan project which resulted in the atomic nuclear fission bomb attacks on the Japanese cities of Hiroshima and Nagasaki.

Fearful of potential future conflict, the Soviet Union was known to be seeking to develop its own atomic weapon capability, as a strategic option. The Americans and the British knew that their erstwhile ally sponsored atomic (and other) espionage activity, which had actually started before the Manhattan project had been launched. In post-war nuclear research programmes, the Soviet Union made rapid progress, much aided by traitorous espionage.

Many West European nations felt that there was a new potential threat, in the escalating conflict of ideas between democratic freedom and the dictatorial communist control imposed on East European nations by the Soviet Union immediately following the end of the war. Not least of those affected was Britain, which, despite the economic ruin caused by the efforts of the Second World War, reluctantly felt that a new rearmament programme needed to be urgently addressed yet once more. There was a real fear that global conflict might once again break out in a few years, this time with the awful prospect of nuclear weapons being used. Any rearmament process would be a large consumer of industrial capacity, including the aircraft industry. Embryo ideas of amalgamating/reducing the number of different aircraft companies (which had been so essential to wartime efforts) had to be put in abeyance. Although facilities and workforces would see business prospects heightened during rearmament, this effort would not really benefit the country's Balance of Payments. Indeed, if war materials (commodities or finished products) were to continue to be imported (probably mainly from the USA) in any quantity for a significant period, the adverse long term effect on the economy would be severe.

The first Soviet atomic fission controlled explosion took place in 1949. The Soviet Union 1949 bomb demonstrated a real potential threat, the only real counter to which would be the ability to retaliate in kind. Britain had the science base and the ex-Manhattan experienced staff to be able to develop its own atomic bomb capability.

Prior to the 1949 dramatic demonstration of Soviet nuclear capability, Britain had already taken some action. Properly wary, the government had authorised a domestic atomic research programme in 1946, acknowledging also the need to develop a means of delivery of an atomic weapon to a distant target. On 3 October 1952, in the lagoon on the remote Monte Bello Islands in Western Australia, Britain exploded its first atomic device. France was the third and only other North Atlantic Treaty Organization (NATO) nation to develop atomic weapons, their first controlled test explosion taking place in 1960.

In 1946, Air Ministry specification B35/46 had been issued, requiring an aircraft capable of delivering a 10,000lb bomb (in reality, a nuclear bomb designed to OR.1001) to a target anywhere in the world 1,500 miles from the aircraft operating base. Eventually, this was to lead to the UK fleet of 'V' bombers (see section 5.12).

During the late 1940s, European nations and the pathologically anti-communist USA had become alarmed that the overt hostility of the Soviet Union could actually lead to another European war, intended to spread communist influence. The Russian isolation blockade of West Berlin from West Germany in 1948 (causing the June 1948– May 1949 "Berlin Airlift") was a stark pointer to the ruthlessness of Soviet intent. The Anglo-French-Benelux Brussels Treaty Organisation of 1948 was overtaken by the North Atlantic Treaty Organization (NATO) when the North Atlantic Treaty was signed in 1949 by the same countries, plus the USA, Canada, Norway, Denmark, Iceland, Italy and Portugal. By 1950, NATO was in place but the organisation could not be considered effective in a co-ordinated military sense, unless and until a centralised European military headquarters was established. In 1951, the "Supreme Headquarters, Allied Powers in Europe" (SHAPE) was established in Paris, later moving to Versailles in 1953 and to Brussels in 1967. The first NATO Secretary General (chief civilian) was appointed in 1952. This was the British Lord Ismay, an army general who had been chief military assistant to Winston Churchill during the Second World War.

NATO did not include countries under communist control. By the beginning of the 1950s, there had been several discussions about the reunification of occupied Germany and, in the west, the possibility of a German participation in NATO. The Soviet Union and the communist East European nations were understandably alarmed at the prospect of a "rearmed and unified" Germany. A "European Defence Community" (including a unified Germany) suggested by the principle NATO nations was unacceptable to the Soviet Union and the East Europeans. Some of the NATO member countries which had been occupied by Germany during the Second World War were also very unsure (eventually, the European Defence Community idea was finally formally rejected by France and others). The Soviet Union proposed a "General European Treaty on Collective Security in Europe", open to all European nations. This was unacceptable to the NATO nations, as it would exclude the USA. The Soviet Union eventually applied to join NATO but this was unacceptable to the USA, the UK and France.

An early major NATO concern was that insufficient modern military aircraft were being made available in Europe ready to counteract the perceived Warsaw Pact potential threat (see below). The USA acknowledged that it would be unlikely that European countries, still recovering from the economic effects of the Second World War, would be able to acquire large numbers of USA aircraft, exacerbated by the service support costs of American aircraft needing further scarce foreign currency (US dollar) expenditure. Accordingly, the USA offered financial assistance to help support plans for appropriate aircraft to be acquired from local European NATO sources. This would be "overseas procurement of USA-recognised armed forces assets". After several rounds of negotiations on "which aircraft, in which air force(s)", the European members of NATO were grateful to accept the American offer. The NATO announcement was made in Paris in April 1953, the full text of which is in Appendix 5. Included in the announcement was an agreement that the USA would contribute a total of US $550 million to an aircraft procurement programme for NATO Europe (in USA inflation terms, equivalent to over US $4,700 million in 2019).

In 1954, NATO agreed to admit West Germany into the organisation, noting that the West German constitution required the country to adopt a "defence-only" posture. The Soviet and East European response was to form an alliance, by an instrument dubbed "the Warsaw Pact", signed on 14 May 1955. This crystallised the political and geographic divide between former allies. The mere existence of these two alliances, each with nuclear warfare capability, created a final clear recognition that massive destructive capability (Mutually Assured Destruction) had forever entered the World political dictionary. This was made all the more alarming by the 1950s development of the more powerful thermonuclear fusion weapons (the hydrogen bomb).

As the emerging Cold War scenario began to unfold in the late 1940s, the RAF and others realised that the 1945 government "no more major conflicts for a decade" political analysis and decision might leave them increasingly incapable of effective air defence of the home country, or of prosecuting any overseas air counter-offensive against a sophisticated opposition. Without a British-controlled atomic weapon delivery capability as a deterrent, survival could depend entirely on the USA being prepared to act, even if only British interests were threatened.

"No More War For Ten Years"

In the event, the 1945 Attlee government "no need to develop or to develop and procure any new combat aircraft for ten years" stance turned out to apply only to fighter (interceptor) aircraft for the RAF. The 'V' bombers atomic weapon-carrying activity started in earnest at the same time as the atomic weapon development (see section 5.12).

Prior to the Second World War, Soviet engineers had independently developed at least two paper designs for possible jet turbine engines, the first one as early as 1937. Interrupted by the 1941 German invasion of Russia, the planned construction and bench tests of a third design (with axial compressor) were not carried out until 1945. With the aid of some copy-or-reverse engineering of German jet turbine technology, by 1947 Soviet jet-powered aircraft existed (e.g. MiG-9, first flight 24 April 1946). However, engine power levels, reliability and life remained low and fuel consumption was too high.

The British government received a 1946 request from the Soviet Union (USSR) to send a Russian delegation to Britain, to "see for themselves the latest jet turbine technology". The Soviets hoped to eventually obtain a licence to build their own version(s) of the new British jet engines or, at least, buy some. The opinion of Joseph Stalin, the Soviet leader, was that the approval for the visit would never be given .... "What a fool one must be, to sell one's own secrets" was his general view[11] ... but give it a try. The positive response agreeing to the request greatly surprised the USSR.

The delegation visit to Rolls-Royce was confined to the main factory in Derby (i.e. not Barnoldswick, the site where jet engine development was centred). Britain was nearly broke and desperate for cash and knew that the USA was already moving to take advantage of the donated British jet engine technology to completely satisfy whatever would be the USA's domestic needs. This meant that a major potential USA market for British engines would not materialise. It was also believed that the most advanced turbine engines then available (the Rolls-Royce Nene. the most powerful engine in the world at that time, and the Derwent V, an 85 per cent scaled down version of the Nene)

---

11. *"Early Russian Jet Engines – the Nene in the Soviet Union and the Evolution of the VK-1"*, Vladimir Kotelnikov and Tony Buttler.

were heading for an ultimate technology "dead end" in using centrifugal compressors. It was expected that this design type would be replaced in future for more powerful engines with the more efficient multi-stage axial flow compressor. This would be the route to much better overall performance. A near-term large market in the USSR for the sale of the then-current British engine might be anticipated. Russia did not have any very high temperature alloy technology (nickel-chrome "nimonic" alloys) and it was blythley assumed that it would take several years for the Russians to catch up, if/when they reverse engineered any of the existing British jet engines which might be supplied. It was thought that it would be a considerable while before Russia unlocked the high temperature alloy metallurgy secret. Sales of Vampire and Meteor aircraft to other foreign countries (Switzerland and Argentina) were being agreed, so new in-service engines eventually would be accessible worldwide, which would not prevent onward sale to the USSR. Sales of the latest British engines to the USSR would be ostensibly to the political (security) annoyance of the USA, whose jet turbine industry had yet to produce anything as reliable and powerful as the latest Nene and Derwent V engines. Part of the "annoyance" was very likely to be "economic envy" of the market being created. The Meteor, powered by the Derwent V, set a new world speed record in late 1945 and again in September 1946.

As a result of the Soviet visit, the British government was pleased to agree to sell thirty of the Derwent V and twenty-five Nene engines. Total sale price was £438,040 (equivalent to some £18 million in 2019 terms). Delivery of the first engine would be early in 1947. There was a supposed constraint "USSR not to use the engines for combat aircraft". Unbeknown to anyone in Britain, a member of the visiting Soviet delegation had slipped a turbine blade into his pocket. More subtly, another wore soft-soled shoes and deliberately trod on the floor where the parts of interest in the engine were being machined, to obtain samples of the metal swarf.

Contrary to British government and Rolls-Royce expectations, reverse engineering of the engine designs and materials was accomplished quite quickly, saving years of development effort and eliminating the need for the USSR to purchase any more engines from Britain. The RD-45, mostly used on non-combat aircraft, was the direct result of "exact copy" reverse engineering of the Nene. The RD-500 was a similar copy of the Derwent V. The essential high technology (e.g. turbine blade metallurgy) reverse engineering heavily influenced the Klimov VK-1 engine, which had started as a "remote" scaled-up copy engineering exercise nearly a year before the physical arrival of the British engines. The VK-1 target specification was actually for an engine 30 per cent more powerful than the Nene and the detail design was adapted to be more suited to Russian production techniques and facilities. The VK-1 finally achieved a 20 per cent thrust level higher than the Nene. It was used for the Mikoyan Gurevich MiG-15 and MiG-17 fighters and the Ilyushin Il-28 bomber (over 24,500 aircraft in total, including licenced production in USSR-influenced countries). The MiG-15*bis* (*bis* = second) with the VK-1 engine replacing the RD-45, went into service in 1950, the type going on to become the most-produced jet aircraft in the world (13,130 in the USSR and 4,180 under licence elsewhere).

Until the 1950s emergence of the USA North American F-86 Sabre and Russian MiG-15 fighter aircraft, there was "a little complacency" in British circles that, as the first nation ever to get large numbers of jet fighters into service (Meteors, followed by Vampires), improvements to engines etc. would enable these types to continue to match any operational need for several years ahead, and new swept wing fighter research would mature in time to produce replacements "when needed". The RAF were to continue to operate (improved) versions of the wartime-origin Gloster Meteor and de Havilland Vampire aircraft for some while, until replaced by the similarly unswept de Havilland Venom (in squadron service 1952) and, finally, by the swept-wing Supermarine Swift and Hawker Hunter (both in service 1954). The 1950–53 Korean War and the adverse experiences of the RAAF flying the UK Gloster Meteor aircraft in combat with the Soviet/Chinese MiG 15 had rapidly changed the priorities. The supply of new USA F-86 swept wing fighters was negotiated, as lend-lease war materials, pending the new Hawker Hunter and Supermarine Swift becoming available in quantity.

Although not at first intent on major armed forces re-equipment with the latest military technology, the British government had supported complete research compatible with a technically up-to-date capability for all military needs, specifically sponsoring several advanced research aircraft (see section 5.10).

As a result of ground tests of the Rolls-Royce Nene engine by the USA in 1946, at the behest of the United States Navy (USN), Pratt & Whitney of the USA purchased a licence to build it. Pratt & Whitney had not previously been involved in jet turbines but built 1,139 Nene (US designation J42, thrust 5,000lbs), used to power the 1947 Grumman Panther. Originally designed and tested by Rolls-Royce, the enlarged RB.44 Tay (not to be confused with later RB.183 Tay) was also licence-produced by Pratt & Whitney as the 7,250lbs thrust J48, used to power the 1951 swept wing Grumman Cougar. In his 1984 autobiography, Sir Stanley Hooker commented:

> "It is a sobering thought that the two great competitors [in aircraft jet turbine engines] of Rolls-Royce – Pratt & Whitney and General Electric – both started with British engines, the former with the Nene (1946) and the latter with the original Whittle F.1 (1941)."

The Gloster Meteor and the Korean War

The 1945 government "there would be no need to develop or to procure any new aircraft for ten years" chickens came home to roost in the Korean War. The Gloster Meteor F.8, the most capable RAF fighter aircraft in 1950, was outclassed in a real war. This war was initiated by a June 1950 unprovoked attack on the USA-supported South Korean region, from the communist-controlled North Korean dictatorship (tacitly supported by the Soviet Union and actively supported by the Peoples' Republic of China – Communist China). The United Nations declared this to be illegal and endorsed USA-led armed support to South Korea. Due to diplomatic disagreements and tensions, the Soviet Union had absented themselves from their position on the UN Security Council at the time the vote was taken supporting South Korea. There had been no possibility, therefore, of a Soviet veto on the UN Security Council. The Soviet Union never allowed such a situation ever to arise again.

During the intervention in the war in Korea, RAAF 77 Squadron (with some RAF pilots attached) found that their North American P.51 Mustang propeller engined aircraft became totally outclassed when, in October 1950, China intervened in Korea. North Korean/Chinese pilots ("unofficially", Soviet Union pilots) had Soviet Union-supplied MiG-15 aircraft (with swept wings), powered by the unlicenced derivative of the Rolls-Royce Nene engine. Unable to gain priority access to the new swept-wing North American F-86 Sabre, Gloster Meteor F.8 jet fighters were obtained by the RAAF. These were still found to have some limitations in one-on-one fighter combat with the MiG 15, especially in terms of maximum speed, rate of climb and altitude. This was partly due to the MiG-15 being swept-wing and two tons lighter, being single-engined. The USAF aircraft also in the Korean war zone were equally outclassed. Even the first version of the new North American F.86 Sabre swept-wing aircraft, introduced in Korea late 1950, still did not out-perform the MiG-15 opposition. The USAF introduced the F.86E in 1951, by which time an improved MiG-15 was in opposition.

The F.86F helped to re-establish air superiority for the USAF pilots in 1952–53. Learning the lesson, Britain obtained 430 USA North American F-86 aircraft. Between December 1952 and May 1953, 430 F-86 Mk.4 Canadian-built F-86F Sabres were ferried from Canada to the UK, effectively provided by the USA under the USA Mutual Defense Assistance Program[12]. The F-86 Mk.4 were not a permanent gift and were refurbished and returned in 1956, after the UK Hawker Hunter had been established in RAF service (see section 5.13).

Two New Aircraft For The RN Fleet Air Arm

Supermarine Attacker and Hawker Sea Hawk: In 1946 and 1947 respectively, two new jet aircraft for the Fleet Air Arm of the RN would take to the air. Both these aircraft used a single Nene jet engine. Production orders were quite modest, until accelerated with the advent of the Korean War. The RN Sea Hawk production received USA/NATO financial support (see Appendix 6). These new aircraft were also sold overseas; after the 1948 Indian partition Attackers were sold to the Pakistan Air Force. The Hawker Sea Hawk was also used by the Indian Navy, German Navy and Royal Netherlands Navy – 582 Sea Hawks and 182 Attackers were built.

The Sunderland Replacement

The RAF Short Sunderland armed flying boats had given sterling service, as anti-submarine maritime patrol aircraft in the North Atlantic and other theatres. The lend-lease USA Lockheed Hudson landplanes used by the RAF and other Empire countries had also been valuable maritime patrol assets (nearly 3,000 Hudsons had been built and a number were sold off for conversion to civil use).

Short Sunderland take-off. (*Author's collection*)

Starting in 1939, the RAF raised various specifications for the eventual Sunderland replacement, passing through the unsuccessful Short Shetland of 1944 (see section 5.6) to eventually create Operational Requirement OR.223 in 1946. A very large and long-endurance flying boat was envisaged (200,000lbs MTOW, with more than twelve hours endurance). After industry responses, OR.223 was replaced by OR.231 in 1947. This envisaged a simpler aircraft of around 90,000lbs MTOW, outlined the following year in basic detail in Air Ministry RAF Specification R.2/48. Shorts, Supermarine and Vickers had expressed interest and revised their proposals accordingly. Shorts preliminary design proposal (PD.2) was selected in 1950.

Many thought that this was not the best of the proposals but Shorts were a nationalised company based in Northern Ireland, where there was high unemployment. Without a contract, Shorts were reluctant to apply serious resources whilst, at the same time, the RAF and the RN argued about the effectiveness of different types of maritime patrol aircraft. Arguments were around land-based maritime patrol aircraft (operating from the long paved runways by then established around Britain, due to the recent war) and flying boats (which could operate in the distant parts of the British Empire

---

12. The Mutual Defense Assistance Program was authorised by the USA Mutual Defense Assistance Act of 1949, each assistance decision being a Presidential prerogative as to its use.

which did not have many such runways). The specification was changed several times, then R.2/48 was cancelled in 1953. Meanwhile Shorts had never held a contract for an actual prototype or production order of their PD.2 proposal. In 1954 there was even a government/RAF discussion about a nuclear-powered flying boat!

Based on a recommendation from Harold Macmillan (the newly-appointed Minister of Defence), the project was cancelled in January 1955. Ten years to get nowhere.

Except in very special scenarios, flying boats had passed their sell-by date, requiring calm water for turn-round servicing (imagine refuelling from a bobbing-about pontoon, rearming, or an engine/propeller change in similar circumstances). Beaching gear and/or dry docks in hangars would be needed for periodic servicing or major repairs. The deciding factor for cancellation probably was the fact that, from the late 1940s onwards, Britain was slowly pulling back from responsibilities "East of Suez", as much of the Empire moved towards independence from Britain, eventually to make British flying boat operations irrelevant.

Development of DH.112 Venom

In 1948, de Havilland carried out a major redesign of the 1943 Vampire, using the same twin-boom single engine configuration. However, it had a new thin wing and used the de Havilland Ghost 4,350lbf thrust development of the original Vampire Goblin engine. The aircraft was larger and heavier than the Vampire and had a maximum speed 100mph higher, with twice the maximum rate of climb. Range was slightly less. It was given the type number DH.112 and was known as the Venom. It first flew in 1949 and the first delivery to

DH.112 Venom. (*Tony Hisgett CC BY-SA 2.0*)

service was in 1951. In reality it was an interim between the first RAF jets (Meteor and Vampire) and the new swept-wing second generation of RAF jet aircraft introduced into RAF service in the mid/late 1950s. Venoms were sold to Iraq, New Zealand, Sweden, Switzerland and Venezuela. The naval (carrier-capable) Sea Venom served with the RN, the Royal Australian Navy and the French Navy (121 aircraft, built under licence as the Acquilon). In total, 1,431 Venom/Sea Venom/Acquilon aircraft were built.

The Long-lived English Electric Canberra Bomber

During the Second World War, the English Electric company re-established itself as an aircraft manufacturer, producing Handley Page Hampden and Halifax bombers (see section 3.2). Because of the high quality wartime workmanship, in 1943, Sir George Nelson, chairman of the company, was invited (with others) to Air Ministry discussions with industry, concerning production of a yet-to-be-designed replacement for the innovative Geoffrey de Havilland Mosquito "unarmed and fast" bomber (see section 3.1). The new aircraft was to be faster and higher-flying, which would mean employing jet turbine technology. Starting with Air Ministry specification E.3/45, upgraded to B.3/45 and then B.5/47, the jet replacement for the Mosquito was launched as a formal requirement for industry proposals in response.

Before this stage, Sir George decided to revive the English Electric aircraft design function (which had been closed in 1926, see section 2.5) and allow his company to produce its own aircraft.

W.E.W. Petter was recruited as chief engineer, with the remit to form his own aircraft design team. "Teddy" Petter had been the young technical director at Westland Aircraft, originally formed as a division of the family business Petters Limited. However, he was at odds with the Westland's forward plan to prioritise a fighter design over his own ideas for a bomber. He resigned in 1944. He had an offer from English Electric. Overlapping his last days at Westland with starting in his new position, and taking his bomber ideas with him, in 1945 Petter eventually recruited Frederick William Page, a 28-year-old senior aerodynamicist from Hawker, appointing him as chief stressman, with additional responsibility as an internal aerodynamic consultant. Frederick Page was eventually to succeed Petter and finally become Chairman and Chief Executive of British Aerospace in 1977 (knighted in 1979).

After iterations through several design concepts during the 1944–45 period, the "Petter influenced by Page" design was the chosen aircraft. It is not clear why bids from the established bomber aircraft designers were not chosen but it is likely that they were deemed to be busy with 'V' bombers (see section 5.12). During the extended preliminary design stages, the aircraft had grown from single-engined Rolls-Royce Nene to twin wing root engines and, eventually, the twin mid-wing Rolls-Royce Avon-powered aircraft, by then twice as heavy as the original Mosquito. Mission-creep had caused much of this change. Known as the English Electric A.1, the aircraft first flew on 13 May 1949. When an order from Australia was received the name was changed to "Canberra". The English Electric Canberra became a true classic.

The aircraft was a two-crew (pilot and navigator) unarmed, high-flying (pressurised cabin) and fast (580mph at 40,000ft Mach 0.88) tactical bomber. It could outfly the contemporary in-service fighter/interceptor opposition (as had the de Havilland Mosquito when it had entered service). It could carry a significant bomb load (6,000lbs internally). Without a heavy bomb load, maximum altitude capability exceeded that of contemporary opposition fighter/interceptor aircraft, sufficient for the Canberra to be used for flying reconnaissance flying over Soviet Union territory in the 1950s. Later, the RAF also flew UK-based and RAF-marked CIA-tasked North American RB-45C Tornado reconnaissance over Soviet territory. These were overtaken in 1956 by USAF Lockheed U-2 ultra-high altitude reconnaissance aircraft. The first USA-authorised U-2 overflight was in 1956 and four RAF pilots flew U-2 missions over Russia.

At the outbreak of the Korean War, Canberra production orders were increased, and production was also allocated to Avro, Handley Page

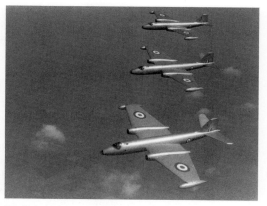

English Electric Canberra (RAF formation). *(Author's collection)*

and Shorts. Many different variants were produced, including under-wing bombs and multiple-rocket missile launchers, photo-reconnaissance capability, and electronic intelligence gathering capability.

One adaptation was for extensive use as a three-seat twin-jet trainer. The B.Mk.6 and B.Mk.8 interdictor versions had a low-altitude bombing system (toss bombing) capability which permitted a tactical (low energy) strike capability without overflying the target. By the mid-1960s, this included a tactical nuclear strike. The B.Mk.16 had the capability of mounting a four-cannon gun pack which occupied the rear half of the bomb bay (guns themselves in an external streamlined fairing).

Meanwhile, the USAF was urgently in need of a fast tactical bomber with photo-reconnaissance development potential. After a startlingly impressive impromptu flying display of manoeuvrability to a few senior USAF personnel in Britain, in 1951 the USA invited English Electric to demonstrate the Canberra prototype in a comparative fly-off display at Andrews Field, Maryland USA with four other aircraft of USA design and one of Canadian design. To participate in the demonstration, the Canberra made the first non-stop unrefuelled transatlantic crossing by a jet aircraft, on 21 January 1951. In all respects of handling and field performance, the Canberra outperformed all the other aircraft. The selection by the USAF of a foreign-built aircraft was a political "hot potato" which the convincing superior Canberra fly-off demonstration had been designed to "defuse". Eventually, the USA were to licence-build the aircraft with a change of engine from Rolls-Royce Avon engines to licence-built Armstrong Siddeley Sapphires (for hot climate operations). Known as the Martin B.57 in the USA, the Canberra served for many years with the USAF.

In later years, the B.57 had a number of USA-designed updates, including incorporation of a larger wing (42ft span increase) as the RB-57D specialised high-flying reconnaissance aircraft (photographic, SIGINT and ELINT). General Dynamics radically modified twenty-one B-57B versions with an all-new wing fifty-eight feet greater span than the original Canberra, a longer fuselage and a change of engine, plus two auxiliary engines used at altitude, to produce the 1963 RB-57F reconnaissance aircraft, which could achieve over 60,000ft altitude.

There were 900 aircraft built in Britain, forty-nine in Australia and 403 more were built by the Martin company in the USA. The type served with seventeen different nations, the last aircraft being retired in 2008.

The Canberra also established a succession of world flight altitude records. On 28 August 1957, a Canberra (RAF registration WK.163, fitted with a Napier Double-Scorpion rocket engine), set a new world record of 70,310ft. The last RAF operation using a Canberra was a photo-reconnaissance Canberra PR.9, on 28 July 2006. The Canberra aircraft type served in the RAF for fifty-five years.

5.12 The Three 'V' Bombers

Having made a significant contribution to the USA-led Manhattan atomic bomb project, nevertheless, Britain (as non-USA) were excluded post-war from the resulting data (and any further access to USA atomic energy programmes), as a result of the US Government passing the 1946 Atomic Energy Act (the McMahon Bill). Consequently, Britain established a research effort to build an atomic fission bomb of its own. The government also had to set about initial ideas-gathering for an aircraft to carry and deliver such a weapon. Soliciting aircraft industry responses to Ministry of Supply specification B35/46 created initial proposals from eight aircraft companies. Speeds of up to Mach 0.95 and operational ceilings of over 50,000ft were sought, out of reach of what was thought Soviet Union interceptor aircraft would be capable. A specific weapon load was outlined as "a single bomb weighing 10,000lbs with a diameter and length of the Second World War Grand Slam (20,000lbs) size" (see section 3.1).

Handley Page received an Instruction to Proceed (ITP) for two prototypes of the crescent-winged HP.80 (later to be named the Victor), soon followed by a similar request for two prototypes of the radical delta-winged Avro 698 (later to be named the Vulcan). The request for two alternatives was a "hedging bets" move, to guard against the event that one of these radical design proposals did not succeed. A further hedge was the ITP to Shorts for a prototype of their SA.4 response (later to be named the Sperrin) to a less demanding specification B14/46 and, finally, an ITP for the Vickers 660, for two prototypes of their more conventional design (later to be named the Valiant), which fell short of B35/46 requirements but seen as a lower-risk and more quickly developed option and, therefore, available earlier into service. These four aircraft types were reduced to three before production orders were placed:

Valiant: first flight 1951, in service 1955
Vulcan: first flight 1952, in service 1956
Victor: first flight 1951, in service 1957

As part of the development of the novel, ambitious and possibly risky Vulcan and Victor projects, some dedicated research aircraft were considered necessary, to be flown in time for flight results to influence the final designs before committing to initial production.

The Vulcan aerodynamic delta-wing research aircraft were the single-engined one-third Vulcan scale Avro type 707 series. Three versions were planned, in sequence, with differences which allowed the earliest exploration of the aerodynamics of delta wings at low speed first and, later, high speeds.

After initial testing had (crucially) identified the need for an increase in nose up ground attitude (for more positive aircraft rotation response on take-off), the first Avro 707 crashed on 30 September 1949, killing test pilot Eric Essler. The second (707B, first flight 6 September 1950), had different wing sweep and a longer nose and nose undercarriage leg than the first 707. This proceeded to

Avro 707B. (*Author's collection*)

provide more delta-wing aerodynamic data and also identified the need to have the Vulcan engine exhausts aligned slightly outwards and downwards, to make pitch trim changes due to changes in engine thrust less excessive. The next 707 to fly (707A) was aimed at higher speeds and had its first flight in 1951. It had the engine intakes moved from a dorsal position to the wing roots, discovered necessary from 707B flights due to the turbulence from the cockpit "bubble" disturbing airflow into the 707B dorsal intake.

After completing high speed investigations relevant to the Vulcan, the 707A was modified, with power units added to the flying controls and a pilot's ejection seat, before being transferred to Australia. This was under the technical sponsorship of the Commonwealth Advisory Research Council. Although originally constructed on behalf of a high speed aircraft research programme, the Australian career was almost entirely spent in low speed aerodynamic research. A second 707A was constructed for use in RAE research unrelated to the Vulcan programme. This first flew on 20 February 1953.

Originally conceived as a potential Vulcan pilot trainer, the two-seat 707C first flew on 1 July 1953. The Vulcan prototype had been already flying for ten months, showing the big delta not to need a special training aircraft, in turn causing the order for four 707C aircraft to be reduced to a single aircraft. The 707C was ultimately used on non-Vulcan research projects (notably, including fly-by-wire experiments at RAE in the 1960s).

Two research aircraft were created to support the Victor project. The intention of the Victor crescent-shaped wing planform was to keep limiting airflow Mach number constant from wing root to wing tip, reducing cruise drag, thus maximising range. RAE advised on the aerodynamic design. The Victor aerodynamic research aircraft were the HP.87 (a half-scale glider, to investigate the crescent-shaped wing low-speed aerodynamics) and the HP.88 (a Supermarine/Blackburn-engineered crescent shaped rewinging modification to a Supermarine Attacker). Unfortunately, after twenty-six flights the HP.88 was destroyed in a crash in 1951, due to instability in the control system. It would not have contributed much to Victor development, due to the eventual Victor wing design being changed from the first one designed which had been used as a guide for the HP.88 design.

It had been expected that only one of the Vulcan and Victor projects would be ordered for production, after performance of prototypes had been evaluated. However, development timescales had been extended, and waiting meant service introduction would not match the perceived urgent operational need. In 1955, the government contracted before development was complete, for twenty-five each of Vulcan and Victor. Twenty-five Valiants had already been ordered in 1951. Ultimately, the finally ordered quantities were:

3   Vickers Valiant prototypes built (1 crashed), plus:
    104 Production Valiant built as B.Mk1 with 57 converted to a tanker or bomber-tanker role
2   Avro Vulcan prototypes built (1 crashed), plus:
    45 Production Vulcan built as B.Mk1 (28 converted to B.Mk.1A)
    89 Production B.Mk.2 Vulcan built
    (6 B.Mk.2 converted to "emergency tanker roles" as a consequence of the 1982 Falklands war)
2   Handley Page Victor prototypes built (1 crashed), plus:
    50 Production B.Mk.1 Victor built (24 converted to B.Mk.1A)
    (8 converted to tanker role)
    34 Production B.Mk.2 Victor built
    (24 converted to tanker role by the ex-Avro part of Hawker Siddeley Aviation, after Handley Page went into liquidation)

The 'V' bombers were able to operate at up to 54,000ft (Valiant), 50,000ft (Victor) or 55,000ft (Vulcan), specified to be able to carry 20,000lbs of conventional high explosive (HE) bombs. The RAF cleared Victor maximum bomb load eventually became thirty-five 1,000lb bombs.

Handley Page Victor. (*Author's collection*)

Vickers Valiant. (*Author's collection*)

The prime reason for the 'V' force was, however, the first British free-fall nuclear bomb (Blue Danube, 62in diameter, 290in long [1.57 x 7.36m], weighing 10,000lb, delivered to stockpile before any aircraft capable of carrying it was in squadron service and only proof tested in 1956). This was replaced by the Red Beard weapon (28in diameter [0.71m], 144in [3.66m] long, weighing 1,750lb), which entered service in 1962.

However, intelligence-gathering by MI6 prompted the MoS to predict that, by 1960, the Soviet Union would develop a high altitude anti-aircraft missile capability. Such a development could compromise the 'V' bombers because it would make it impossible to successfully use high altitude bombing techniques on targets with such local air defence capabilities. Consequently, the development of a stand-off air-launched nuclear-armed missile capability for the 'V' force bomber fleet (the Avro Blue Steel missile) started in 1955. From 1963, Vulcan and Victor aircraft were modified to carry this nuclear-armed rocket-powered stand-off missile.

Avro Vulcan B.Mk.1A formation. (*BAE Systems*)

In 1956 the USA Lockheed U2 reconnaissance aircraft started flying missions over Russia, at altitudes in excess of 70,000ft. This was well beyond the reach of Russian air-launched or surface-launched anti-aircraft missiles. In May 1960, however, a U2 was brought down by a surface-launched missile in Russia, to the shock and surprise of many in the USA but as predicted by intelligence.

For the 'V' bombers, the Avro Blue Steel stand-off nuclear armed missile would be an essential counter.

The Blue Steel warhead was intended to be the "Green Bamboo" fission bomb but, in the event, this was changed to the "Red Snow", an Anglicised version of the fusion warhead of the USA Mk.28 weapon (heavier and less yield, but "safer"). Maximum stand-off missile range was 150 miles. Development of a Mk.2 version of Blue Steel was considered but overtaken by the decision to acquire the much longer range USA Douglas Skybolt stand-off missile. With the Red Snow warhead, a Skybolt stand-off range of 600 miles would be possible.

Partly due to serious development delays, Skybolt was cancelled in December 1963 by the USA, in favour of the submarine-launched Polaris nuclear-armed missile. Skybolt's cancellation caused a major crisis in British strategic military forward planning. After British Prime Minister Harold Macmillan and USA President John F. Kennedy had direct talks, the British strategic weapon was also changed to become the Polaris missile (with British nuclear warheads), launched from new British nuclear-powered long-range submarines. The RN Polaris submarine fleet became operational and took over the nuclear response responsibility in 1969. The 'V' force was retasked to reconnaissance and/or conventional bombing roles. The Valiant suffered early fatigue life problems which would have been further accelerated by the low-level nature of some of the new role(s) for the 'V' force. Consequently all Valiants retired by the end of 1964.

A B.Mk.2 version of the Valiant was developed by Vickers as a PV (prototype first flew in 1953), intended as a high-speed low-level penetrating "Pathfinder" target marker for the high-flying 'V' force bombers (as the Mosquito had been used as a target precision marking aircraft for Lancaster and Halifax bombers). Vickers Test

Pilot Brian Trubshaw said, "paint the ****er black", so it had the nickname "Black Bomber". The structure was designed to be more robust than that of the Mk.1 (due to the low-level high speed requirement) but, probably, it would still have suffered the basic design concept and material susceptibility vulnerability to fatigue, caused by air turbulence levels at low altitude. In the event, the RAF did not pursue the requirement.

Many of all three V-bomber types were progressively converted to the air-to-air refuelling role. This was to become a highly visible capability when the 1982 Great Britain-Argentina Falklands war started, with Argentina invading and capturing the South Georgia and Falkland Islands in the South Atlantic without prior warning, on 2 April 1982.

The UK soon sent a naval task force (including a troop-carrying land force convoy) charged to recover the islands. Meanwhile, the airbase on the British overseas territory of Ascension Island in the Azores, in mid-South Atlantic, between Africa and Brazil, became the base for an increasing number of RAF long-range reconnaissance and other aircraft. Starting just four weeks after the invasion, RAF

Victor K.Mk.2 Tanker. (*RuthAS, CC BY-SA 3.0*)

Vulcan bombers carried out seven raids from Ascension Island. The raids were code named "Black Bush" operations; two of the seven raids were aborted. The aircraft used were multiple Victor K.Mk.2 tankers "piggy-backing" refuelling formations, enabling a single Vulcan B.Mk.2 aircraft to reach and return from the target. For a single Vulcan bomber, these were sixteen hour missions flying nearly 8,000 miles. For the complete first Black Bush mission, a fleet of nine Victor K.Mk.2 tankers and one Vulcan B.Mk.2 bomber (not counting reserve aircraft also despatched) carried out a total of eighteen in-flight refuelling contacts (Victor tanker to Victor tanker, and Victor tanker to Vulcan), using a grand total of some 1.5 million pounds of aviation fuel (= 214,000 imperial gallons). The Vulcan received fuel in five of these air refuelling contacts.

The first Black Bush raid successfully targeted the only hard runway on the Falkland Isles, at the capital Port Stanley. This was soon repaired, but only enough to enable short-field Argentinian operations. There were longer-lasting strategic results. Runway damage and the implied threat of more raids were sufficient to prevent the establishing of an enduring and well-supported Argentinian fast-jet air defence/offence force based on the island (due to not enough runway). The uncertainty engendered in the Argentinian military command, and the diversion/retention of Argentinian military resources to/on the Argentinian mainland ("if the Falklands can be reached, so can Buenos Aires") had significant impact on the Argentinian conflict management. By 4 June 1982 the British Task Force had succeeded in retaking the islands.

5.13 Second Generation Jet Fighters and Naval Strike Aircraft

The immediate post-1945 government policy of "new fighter aircraft will not be needed for a decade" did not mean that research effort into high speed flight would not be supported (see section 5.10). The emergence of the Cold War also meant that the nuclear-armed high-flying high-speed jet bomber programme was soon started (see sections 5.11 and 5.12). The intended capability of these new bombers caused a rethink about the corresponding need for a British high altitude interceptor aircraft. After all, it was possible that the Soviet Union eventually would develop their equivalent to the UK 'V' bombers. The RAAF Gloster Meteor F.8 being outclassed by the Soviet MiG-15 in the Korean War was a salutary lesson to come. Accordingly, by the middle of the 1950s, five new British jet combat aircraft were in service and, beyond them, a new very fast interceptor fighter and a naval nuclear-capable strike aircraft would take to the air at the end of the decade (see section 6.3). For the mid-1950s, the five second generation jet aircraft were the Swift, Hunter and Javelin fighters and the Sea Vixen and Scimitar naval strike aircraft.

(1) **Supermarine Swift:** As part of the transonic research test programmes (section 5.10), Supermarine had provided a swept-wing research aircraft with a tail wheel undercarriage. This was the Rolls-Royce Nene-powered Supermarine type 510, which was a swept-wing adaptation of the straight-winged 1946 Supermarine Attacker, in service with the RN. The 510 was modified into the type 517, with a hinged rear fuselage to provide increased tailplane pitch trim range. For the second 510, the design was revised using an uprated Nene engine with afterburner, the type becoming the 528. As a penultimate step, a change to a tricycle undercarriage, a longer nose and an engine change to the new Rolls-Royce Avon created the type 535, which first flew in August 1950.

The new government of 1951 (Winston Churchill returning as Prime Minister) were convinced that the RAF required the urgent provision of a replacement for the Gloster Meteor. Rather precipitously, an off-the-drawing board order for an advanced and productionised version of the Supermarine 535 research aircraft was placed, including the new axial-flow Rolls-Royce Avon engine. This became the Supermarine Swift. (*RuthAS, CC BY-SA 3.0*)

type 541 Supermarine Swift, first flying in 1951. The change to the axial flow Avon would have allowed the original ex-Attacker fuselage cross-section of the Nene-powered 535 to have been reduced but, as an expediency, there was not enough time allowed for this change to be included in the new Swift. The Swift performance was therefore less than the optimum that could have been achieved. First flight of the first production Swift type 541 was on 25 August 1952 and a total of 197 aircraft were built, none of which were exported. Development issues delayed service entry until February 1954.

(2) **Hawker Hunter:** As part of the usual government "dual source" policy for advanced new aircraft, the possibility of developing the Hawker P.1052 high speed research aircraft (a swept-wing adaptation of the Sea Hawk) was considered simultaneously with the Swift. Almost at the same time as the Supermarine 510 research aircraft, Hawker had supplied their swept-wing

Hawker Hunter (prototype WB188). (*BAE Systems*)

P.1052 version of the in-service RN Sea Hawk. Having a single Rolls-Royce Nene as the powerplant, the aircraft was almost a "first cousin" of the Supermarine 510, except for a different wing sweep angle although, at first, only the 510 had a swept tailplane. Originally a Hawker PV, the P.1052 was supplied in response to specification E.38/46 for a swept-wing research aircraft. (A second P.1052 was developed by Hawker into the P.1081, with the tailplane also swept and which became of interest to the RAAF, but a purchase did not materialise. In the end, the P.1081 crashed, killing the pilot in the process.) As a PV, Hawker had started a new design with a fuselage to match the upcoming axial flow Avon engine. More or less at the same time as the Swift, this Hawker P.1067 version (later named the Hunter) was also ordered off the drawing board. The specification F.3/48 asked for an Avon-powered aircraft capable of 629mph at 45,000ft (Mach 0.95). First flight of the prototype Hunter was on 20 July 1951 but development issues delayed service entry until July 1954.

Part of the Hunter production was financed by the USA (NATO) offshore procurement contracting (see Appendix 5), enabled by the USA Mutual Assistance Program. This USA funding for UK Hunter production totalled US$140 million (£50 million) at the time, equivalent to £1,370 million in 2019. At the same time, US$42 million more was allocated by the USA towards licenced Hunter production in the Netherlands and Belgium, with prior British agreement to the granting of such a licence.

The Hawker Hunter became an iconic British aircraft of the decade 1955–1965, able to fly at speeds up to Mach 0.94 and heights of up to 50,000ft. The RAF eventually had eighteen versions and the Hunter eventually replaced the Swifts in RAF service. It remained in RAF service (in the two-seat training aircraft version) until 1994 and the last Hunter in military service anywhere only retired from the Lebanese Air Force in 2014. The aircraft was sold to many air forces (forty-four different export versions, some of which were refurbished aircraft). A total number of 1,972 Hunters were built.

The Swift and the Hunter each held the FAI absolute world speed record in 1953, the Hunter at 727.63mph (Mach 0.9556) on 7 September, overtaken by the Swift at 735.70mph (Mach 0.9662) on 23 September. The USA delta-winged fighter Douglas F4D-1 Skyray took the record back ten days later, on 3 October 1953, with 752.94mph (Mach 0.9888), overtaken on 29 October by the North American F-100 Super Sabre prototype at 755.15mph (Mach 0.9917), this was the last time the record was forced to be at low level for the record to be ratified by the FAI.

(3) **Gloster Javelin:** The potential threat posed by a future high altitude bomber was identified in 1944 and a night fighter counter was outlined in specification F.44/46. Altitude capability of 45,000ft and a speed at 40,000ft of 525 knots (604mph, Mach 0.91) was required, for a two-seat aircraft with airborne interceptor radar and night/all-weather navigation capability. Manoeuvring capability was not a major requirement, being limited to 4 'g' rather than the higher values associated with daytime "dog fighting" fighters. After protracted cost-cutting delays, the eventual choice came down to the Gloster Javelin T-tailed delta wing proposal, powered by twin Armstrong Siddeley Sapphire engines (12,000lbf thrust each), considered alongside the de Havilland DH.110 (twin Rolls-Royce Avon engines in a twin-boom proposal already under consideration as a carrier-capable aircraft for the Royal Navy). The Javelin was finally chosen and the DH.110 returned to its naval specification origins, to emerge later as the Sea Vixen.

Via the Mutual Assistance Program, the USA made a substantial cash contribution to the RAF acquisition of the Javelin, Hunter and Swift (see above). However, the hiatus of cost-cutting politically-inspired delays (due to vacillations between the Javelin and the DH.110 within the Air Ministry) caused the first Javelin prototype to be completed *after* the first production machine. In total, as cash and surplus equipment transfer to allies, the USA Mutual Assistance Program dispensed $37 billion between 1950 and 1967.

One unusual feature of the Javelin prototypes was opaque canopies over the two-man cockpits, because it had been believed that visibility was unnecessary and a hindrance to the navigator/radar operator role. His only external view available was via small 'portholes'. This complete lack of external view did not last long! The Javelin first flight was 26 November 1951.

One of the unwelcome characteristics of the Javelin was found to be the "deep stall", where the T-tail airflow could be "blanked" by the large delta wing at very nose-high stalling attitudes, preventing the elevator having enough effect to put the nose down to recover from the stall (the only safe option in this event was to eject). The Gloster test pilot Peter Lawrence was killed in the crash of the

Gloster Javelin (prototype). (*BAE Systems*)

prototype caused by the inability to recover from a deep stall. Automatic stall warning and stall prevention devices were engineered to compensate (the problem was to recur with T-tailed rear-engined jet airliners in the 1960s, again with fatal consequences). Javelin entry into service was on 29 February 1956 and 436 were built, the RAF being the only operator.

A thin-wing Javelin was proposed, capable of about Mach 1.6 and with a higher ceiling than contemporary USA designs. As the project started to develop momentum, the necessary changes would have created a very different aircraft which would only outwardly resemble the Javelin. The idea was not pursued further. The Javelin was the last Gloster aircraft design to fly.

(4) **De Havilland DH.110 Sea Vixen:** The RN requirement for a carrier-capable two-seat, twin-engined and radar-equipped interceptor originated in specification N.40/46, issued in 1947 (at the same time as F.44/46 which led to the Javelin).

Powered by twin Rolls-Royce Avon engines (11,000lbf thrust each), the first flight was on 26 September 1951.

Due to a structural strength issue, the aircraft suffered a catastrophic failure at the 1952 Farnborough air show (see section 5.10). Correcting this, and changing the tailplane-elevator to an all-moving tail on the second prototype, delayed progress. During the development, the

DH.110 Sea Vixen. (*Lmgaylard, CC BY-SA 4.0*)

concept of an "integrated weapon system approach" gained ground and the Sea Vixen design became the first British attempt at this. Introduction into service finally took place in July 1959 and 145 were built, the RN being the only operator.

Developments in service added a strike capability to the interceptor role, partly associated with the early withdrawal of the Supermarine Scimitar naval aircraft from the strike role. The Sea Vixen was the first British aerial combat aircraft to be armed only with missiles, rockets and bombs and the first Fleet Air Arm fighter not to be equipped with guns. It also had the distinction of being the first British two-seat combat aircraft to routinely be able to achieve supersonic speed, albeit not in level flight.

(5) **Supermarine Scimitar:** The Scimitar carrier-capable interceptor/strike aircraft stemmed from a number of different Supermarine naval aircraft designs. In 1947, specification N.9/47 resulted in a November 1947 order for Supermarine 508 research prototypes for evaluation. The objective was a twin-jet naval strike aircraft. The first two prototypes were straight-wing designs, limiting maximum speed. Unusually, Supermarine chose a 'V' butterfly tail, as combined fin/tailplanes. This 'V' arrangement was intended to keep the tailplane out of the fuselage-mounted twin new Rolls-Royce AJ.65 (early Avon) engine exhausts. The prototype aircraft were to diverge, the second becoming the type 529, with a revised fuselage and a third, with swept-wings and cruciform tailplane/fin, becoming the type 525 (an out-of-sequence number). Type 525 also had engine compressor bleed air blown wing flaps, to reduce landing and stalling speeds and catapult launch speeds, and variable (trimming) incidence was incorporated within the swept tailplane. Successful enough as the type 525 was in trials (but unfortunately crashing later), the final design became the Supermarine type 544 Scimitar, with a change to an anhedral tailplane and other refinements found to be necessary. The structure was strengthened to cater for high air loads in the low-level high speed naval strike role.

The Supermarine 544 Scimitar first flight was on 19 January 1956. Maximum speed was 640 knots at sea level (736mph, Mach 0.967) and service ceiling was 46,000ft. Introduced into service in 1957, for the older RN carriers of the day, the Scimitar was a large heavy aircraft (32,400lb). Thirty-nine aircraft were lost in accidents (51 per cent of total production of seventy-six aircraft). The strike role was taken on by the versatile (and heavier) Sea Vixen, but the Scimitar was kept on in service until 1969, modified to act as a top-up tanker for the early (underpowered) Blackburn Buccaneer S.1, a type which could not perform a carrier take-off at its maximum weight until the S.2 version was introduced (see section 6.3).

5.14 Two Small Pilot-Training Jet Aircraft

Introduction to UK pilot-training aircraft: From the days of the First World War, basic pilot training in the UK generally took place in biplane aircraft like the Avro 504 (first flight 1913), the DH.60 Moth series of the mid 1920s-early 1930s, the Avro 621 Tutor, 626 Prefect and 643 Cadet of the late 1920s-early 1930s and the DH.82 Tiger Moth, first flown in 1934. In 1937, the Miles response to specification T.40/36 resulted in the Miles Magister monoplane dedicated pilot training aircraft, 700 of which were in service by the beginning of the Second World War, with a total of 1,303 eventually being built. The Percival Proctor monoplane trainer was introduced in the RAF just as the Second World War was starting. All these aircraft were easy to fly and many were used in civilian aviation, for both instruction and for recreation, as well as by the RAF. In total, some 25,000 of all these different British types were built. They were not, of course, the only aircraft used for flying instruction. During the war, the RAF also used the USA North American T-6 Harvard as an advanced trainer, often based in Canada.

The RAF planned to have a new monoplane aircraft as their basic pilot trainer after the end of the war. Designed to meet Air Ministry Specification T.23/43 for a metal monoplane trainer, the Percival Prentice was selected and over 370 were delivered to the RAF between 1947 and 1949. The Prentice had side-by-side instructor/pilot-under-training seating, plus a third seat behind for "air experience" pupils. The RAF large fleet of de Havilland DH.82 Tiger Moths started to be sold off as surplus-to-requirements.

At the end of the Second World War, the de Havilland Canada (DHC) subsidiary of de Havilland designed the DHC-1 Chipmunk monoplane, as a new basic pilot training aircraft for the RCAF. In the UK, the RAF considered this potentially to offer a fine basic trainer, capable of modification to a fully aerobatic standard. A&AEE evaluated three examples of the aircraft, as a consequence of which the Air Ministry issued specification T.8/48. This resulted in selection of the Chipmunk as another aircraft which hastened the disposal of the RAF Tiger Moths. The RAF eventually acquired 735 Chipmunk aircraft (built by de Havilland in Britain), for use by RAF Training Squadrons, RAF Reserve Training Squadrons and University Air Squadrons.

The RAF Percival Prentice was a relatively docile aircraft to fly and there was little in the cockpit, which allowed the trainee to gain experience of the "real" environment of operating a service aircraft, such as flying in poor visibility, or experience of the manoeuvres and the manoeuvre rates closer to those of which a front-line aircraft needed to be capable. The Air Ministry issued specification T.16/48 to meet OR.257, for an all-weather (i.e. equipped for instrument flying in low visibility) two-seat training aircraft, with a single fairly powerful piston engine and significant aerobatic capability.

Contrary to the deliberate simplification of the cockpits of previous RAF pilot trainers, the new aircraft was required to provide a more representative operational task capability, as the student pilot advanced beyond basic flying skills. The next aircraft for the student pilot could then be a move directly to the trainer version of the then front-line de Havilland Vampire jet fighter. The Percival Provost was selected and the RAF received the first ones in 1953. Between 1953 and 1956, 461 Provosts were built, the majority of which were for the RAF, with sixty-eight also sold to overseas customer Air Forces.

Jet Provost

Percival Aircraft Company, having been in the Hunting Group since 1944, became Hunting-Percival in 1954. In early 1951, Percival Aircraft started to study the possibility

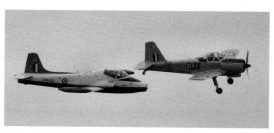

of an RAF jet-powered training aircraft, recognising that the new type of aircraft propulsion would need a like-powered pilot training aircraft in support. The design aim was to provide jet handling and performance experience but not at the expense of modest approach and landing speeds, with good low-speed handling characteristics for student pilots. Increasingly liaising with RAF Flying Training Command (a Percival Provost customer already)

Provost T.Mk.1 & Jet Provost T.5A. (*Author's collection*)

Hunting-Percival realised that the use of many existing items from the Provost would be a way of holding down production costs and help to gain RAF acceptance. Focused on "new fuselage and engine with existing Provost wings", by 1953 Percival's private venture received direct government support, in the shape of an order for a few "service test aircraft". The initial prototype flew on 16 June 1954, showing much promise.

After the first three of a pre-production batch of ten aircraft (Jet Provost T.Mk.1s) had been trialled at the RAF Central Flying School (with instructors and students), various improved aerodynamic features and systems design changes were made to produce the T.Mk.2 version. This version was first flown in September 1955. The pre-production batch was used for further development trials, including cold weather trials in Sweden and sales tours in Europe and North and South America.

A production order for thirty Jet Provost T.Mk.3 was placed by the MoS in June 1957, the same year that the company name changed again, to Hunting Aircraft. Eventually, the RAF received 509 Jet Provost aircraft (in various Mks.) and a total 731 were built. This total includes the export Strikemaster version. After Hunting Aircraft became part of British Aircraft Corporation (BAC, see section 6.1) in 1960, BAC continued to develop the aircraft into the Strikemaster, a Light Attack/Counter-Insurgency version, with underwing bomb-carrying capability, fuselage-mounted machine guns, wing tip fuel tanks and an up-rated engine – 146 Jet Provost Strikemaster versions were sold, all to overseas air forces.

Folland Gnat

Over several months in 1949, there had been growing disagreements between the manager of the English Electric Preston engineering works at Strand Road, Warton and Samlesbury and W.E.W. ("Teddy") Petter, aircraft chief engineer based at the company's Warton airfield on the River Ribble estuary. Eventually, in early 1950 a frustrated Petter resigned, later that year accepting the position of chief engineer and deputy managing director at Folland Aircraft, at Hamble near Southampton. This was only six years after Petter had been recruited by English Electric to lead their newly-created aircraft design team, when he had left his position of technical director at his family firm Westland Aircraft, in Yeovil (see section 6.3). Henry Folland was suffering severe ill health and had deliberately recruited Petter as his replacement. Within a year, Folland retired as managing director but remained on the company board until his death in 1954.

Theoretically constrained by an agreement with English Electric "not to poach", nevertheless Petter attracted a number of senior design staff at Warton to join him at Folland. Petter and his "poached" (ex-Canberra) staff gave Folland a boost, in terms of jet aircraft design credibility with the Air Ministry.

Petter initiated a study of the complexity, cost and time to produce the jet fighter aircraft which were emerging as a result of RAF/Air Ministry requirements placing (as Petter thought) "performance and quality" above "price and quantity" in the cost v. benefit equation. He concluded that, in a future war, lightweight simpler solutions in quantity were desirable, where any losses could be replaced more quickly. Heavily influenced by OR.303, which requested a lightweight fighter to intercept high flying Soviet bombers, he therefore commenced the conceptual design of a "simple jet fighter", called the Fo.141 Gnat, powered by a Bristol BE.22 Saturn turbojet with 3,800lbf thrust and a MTOW less than 10,000lb (compare this with the 7,000lbf thrust of the early Avon which powered the first flight of the Hawker Hunter with a MTOW more than 20,000lb).

Folland produced an unarmed proof-of-concept demonstrator using the structure and wings of the proposed Gnat design, called the Fo.139 Midge. However, the chosen powerplant, the Bristol BE.22 Saturn project, was cancelled in 1952. Eventually, the Saturn was able to be replaced by the Orpheus turbojet, specifically designed as a lightweight jet engine after a Petter-initiated late 1952 discussion with Stanley Hooker at Bristol Engines[13]. This promised something over 3,000lbf thrust (it eventually

---

13. Stanley Hooker had a major disagreement with Ernest Hives at Rolls-Royce and left in 1949, to become chief engineer at the Bristol Engine Company (wholly-owned by the Bristol Aeroplane

provided 4,705lbf thrust for the Gnat) but the Midge had to use the less powerful Armstrong Siddeley Viper engine (1,640lbf thrust at that time, later developed to be twice as powerful). On 11 August 1954, the Folland Midge took to the air. Although underpowered (but lighter than the planned Gnat), the compact jet could exceed Mach 1 in a dive and was extremely agile in aerobatic manoeuvres. Unfortunately a crash in September 1955 destroyed the aircraft.

The single-seat Gnat design was amended, with larger intakes for the Orpheus engine and mountings for twin 30mm cannon were added to the intake lips. The PV-funded Gnat prototype first flew at A&AEE on 18 July 1955. The MoS did not pursue the lightweight fighter requirement but orders for the Gnat F.Mk.1 were placed by Finland, Yugoslavia and India, for a total of fifty aircraft. The India purchase included a licence for production in India and 200 were built by Hindustan Aeronautics Limited (HAL). In the early 1970s, India decided to develop the Ajeet version of the Gnat and eighty-nine of these were built (including ten converted from the HAL Gnat) and the last one only retired in 1991.

Partly as a result of the creation of the Gnat and under the umbrella of the Mutual Weapons Development Programme, NATO raised NATO Basic Military Requirement NBMR-1 for a low-level strike/attack light fighter. The Gnat F.1 was the only contender under the target maximum weight and available by the required service date. However, the Gnat was not selected, mainly because Petter would not change the Gnat small undercarriage wheels, which were incompatible with the specified requirement for unpaved airfield operations. Wider wheels and lower-pressure tyres would involve creating more undercarriage stowage space, with knock-on fuselage structural design changes and a weight increase. The evaluation was eventually won by Italy's Fiat G.91, which was powered by the same Bristol Orpheus engine.

All was not lost. The RAF had hoped that a trainer version of the much heavier and more expensive Hawker Hunter (the T.Mk.7) would suffice, since the Hunter single-seat fighter was already entering service in large numbers in the RAF. However, in 1958 the RAF finally decided that a two-seat trainer version of the Gnat might be needed, to cover training in the aircraft performance capability area between the Jet Provost and the Hunter trainer, before pilots moved on to the the high performance new Mach 2 Lightning soon to enter service (see section 6.3). The new trainer requirement prompted Folland to create the two-seat Fo.144 Gnat, which included a new larger wing and more fuel capacity, space for more operational equipment in the fuselage and a more powerful variant of the Orpheus engine. Overall weight increase over the F.1 version was some 800lbs, including the wider wheels and tyres mentioned previously. The Fo.144 Gnat T.Mk.1 version was accepted and a pre-production order for fourteen aircraft was placed.

A full production order was held back because the MoS were not convinced that the small Folland company could be safely awarded an order for the intended 100+ aircraft. When the Hawker Siddeley Group took over Folland in 1959 (see section 6.1), confidence increased and further orders were placed for the Gnat T.Mk.1, to bring the eventual RAF total to 105 aircraft.

The Folland Gnat was used by the Yellowjacks RAF display team, informally created by a group of flying instructors at RAF Company).

Folland Gnat T.Mk.1. (*RuthAS, CC BY-SA 3.0*)

Valley (Anglesey). This arrangement was changed to become the RAF official Red Arrows display team, whose distinctive red Gnats performed public displays until the end of 1979, when the Gnats were replaced by British Aerospace Hawk aircraft (see section 6.5). Overall, 449 Folland Gnats were built (including the HAL Ajeet).

Petter developed the idea of a supersonic growth version of the Gnat as the Gnat 5, which weighed 20 per cent more than the basic Gnat T.Mk.1. However, the government-inspired 1959 Hawker Siddeley takeover of Folland was not to Petter's taste and, with his wife showing signs of a debilitating disease, he decided to retire completely at the end of 1959 and joined a religiously inspired faith healing commune in Switzerland. He was replaced by Maurice Brennan.

After resigning his well-established position of chief designer at the "stricken" Saunders-Roe in 1959, Maurice Brennan had had just ten months at Vickers/BAC, working with Barnes Wallis on variable geometry wings, before replacing Petter at Folland in 1960. Folland's new owners, Hawker Siddeley, were keen to use Brennan's recent experience of variable geometry wings to design the same feature into a new twin-engined version of the Gnat 5, called the Fo.147. It would have been 70 per cent heavier than the Gnat 5 and capable, in principle, of Mach 2. No RAF interest was ever expressed and Brennan soon moved on within Hawker Siddeley, succeeding Roy Ewans[14] as Avro chief designer and director.

In many ways, this shuffling around of experienced senior aircraft designers was a direct consequence of the uncertainties created by the government 1957 Defence Review (see section 5.15 following).

5.15 Government Control of Aircraft Projects and the 1957 Defence Review
UK Aircraft Project Government Control and/or Influence
Quite sensibly and reasonably, all industries wishing to export military or dual military/civil use goods, services or technology to someone based outside Britain has to have a government licence to supply anything on the UK strategic export control lists. Military aircraft and parts of aircraft come under such restriction and have always done so, as do civil aircraft or parts of civil aircraft which could be used or adapted for military purposes. This includes trade with British Commonwealth countries, with NATO countries and with European Union countries.

For sales of entirely non-military aircraft, overseas or domestic sales of aircraft with government-supported designs could be subject to a government restriction, payment of a fee of some kind, or even a complete veto, as part of arms control or other political decisions. The more all-pervading government direct influence on the actual industry management has had major impacts, sometimes welcome but, more often, not. Section 5.9 describes how financially powerful and politically influential the government was in the early helicopter industry activity in post-war Britain. This did not only apply to helicopters.

In the domestic aircraft industry, the government has always had control of the technical requirement setting for military aircraft of all types (see section 2.3). Strictly, they also have some "rights of use" of the designs of any aircraft for which they specifically pay to be developed. For a derivative of an independently-designed aircraft, the government technically would "own" any special design adaptation for which they paid. This ownership is not exercised to deny copyright and patent protection for the designing aircraft company but it could be used to "direct" domestic production to

---

14. Roy Ewans had been chief aerodynamicist at Avro, before becoming chief designer, responsible for the design of the Avro Vulcan B.2 revised wing, the cancelled Avro 730 and the new Avro 748 turboprop airliner. He joined BAC in 1960, later working in the USA aircraft industry.

any suitable facility if necessary (such as following the collapse of a particular aircraft company or, perhaps, preparation for war increased rates of production).

The government-supported Imperial Airways airline of the 1920s and 30s had been constrained to use British airliners. The government owned BOAC and BEA airlines were the target first customers of the Brabazon Committee recommendations for British civil types after the end of the Second World War. The Brabazon Committee airliner concepts finally recommended were converted into government sponsored actual development projects. Production orders would be the responsibility of airlines, of which, in Britain, the vastly dominant were the government-owned BOAC and BEA, later merged into one as British Airways (BA). The 1945 Civil Aviation act constrained BOAC and BEA to "buy British" unless there was no suitable UK airliner to suit particular operations *and* the Minister of Aviation used reserved special authority to allow "use of scarce foreign currency". BOAC and BEA (and their later merged identity BA) were managed by government appointed executives (but not government employed), until BA was privatised in 1987.

The 1957 Defence Review and Consequences

In February 1954, Denis Haviland, Under Secretary at the Ministry of Supply, issued a well-reasoned paper which argued that the number of aircraft and aircraft engine companies in Britain was unsustainable. Britain had more major airframe firms than the USA, an obviously unsustainable position. The point was made that spreading the work around the British industry (buggin's turn) weakened the overall industry capability, despite the many talented design teams which existed. Aircraft were becoming more and more complicated and expensive, military aircraft numbers accordingly being reduced due to budget constraints. Civil aircraft finance was also at levels where private industry in Britain could not even contemplate competing with the USA, with its large USA domestic and parochial market, without external financial support. The paper was discussed but no action emerged, a political "hot potato", until...

Under a new Minister of Defence (Duncan Sandys), the UK Conservative government eventually conducted an overall armed forces "Defence Review" covering Army, Navy and Air Force likely tasking, and associated personnel and equipment needs for the future. On 4 April 1957 the review and conclusions were published in a White Paper, the conclusions of which included the following effects.

For the RAF, future equipment needs would be based on the assessment that manned armed aircraft (defensive or offensive) would soon be overtaken completely by missile technology. The consequences were immediate and affected the following new aircraft programmes already in progress at that time:

- The Avro 730 Mach 3 supersonic bomber to specification RB.156T would be cancelled. (Originally the 730 was intended as a reconnaissance aircraft but was relaunched by the government in 1955, as a nuclear-capable high-level bomber with reconnaissance capability).
- The Air Ministry specification OR.329/F.155T for a high altitude supersonic interceptor to OR.329 would be cancelled. Fairey, working

Avro 730 (artist's impression). (*Author's collection*)

on the Fairey Delta III, were told by the MoS on 1 April 1957 that they were favourite to win the F.155T contract. Three days later, Duncan Sandys' announcement killed the whole idea.

Fairey Delta III (artist's impression). (*Author's collection*)

- Saunders Roe SR.177 (intended as a pre-prototype of SR.187) response to OR.329/F.155.T was an aircraft "rocket-powered to supersonic intercept, jet turbine engine to return to base", a drawing board study project. This would be cancelled and funding for the already-flying research jet and rocket-powered aircraft for the programme (the Saro SR.53) would be terminated.

Saro SR.177 (incomplete mock-up). (*Author's collection*)

There were eight responses to OR.329/F.155. As well as Fairey and Saro, there were three Hawker Siddeley Group responses and de Havilland, English Electric and Vickers responses:

(a) The Hawker P.1121 PV proposal had reached an advanced (full mock-up) stage as a single-engined Mach 2+ turbojet aircraft, having the predicted performance of what became the very successful USA MacDonnell-Douglas F-4 Phantom. The P.1121 reached the stage of completed major assemblies for the first aircraft. When OR.329 was cancelled the design was enlarged as a twin engined response to GOR.339, the Hawker P.1129 (contract won by BAC TSR-2, see section 6.3).

(b) The Avro 720 delta-winged project had been to the F.155T specification but had already been effectively terminated the year before. This was due to the belated RAF realisation that the use of liquid oxygen and kerosene in fueling the chosen Armstrong Siddeley Screamer rocket engine rocket would be a major operational inhibitor, complemented by government reluctance to continue to accept the escalating cost predictions.

(c) The Armstrong Whitworth AW.169.

(d) The de Havilland DH.117.

(e) The English Electric P.8.

(f) The Vickers Type 559 canard design.

- The English Electric P.1, as a supersonic research aircraft already flying, escaped cancellation (first flight P.1A in 1954, the much improved P.1B first flight coincidentally on the same day as the Defence Review was published). The P1 eventually matured into the English Electric Lightning (see section 6.3).

- The White Paper also insisted that improvements in the management of

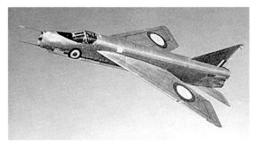

English Electric P1A. (*From Thunder & Lightnings*)

projects in the UK aircraft industry were desired by the government, to improve efficiency and control. Consequently, as an efficiency measure, government contracts would only be awarded in future to large "groups of companies" and the same would be expected of the guided weapons businesses and aircraft engine companies. Not much thought in the 1957 review went into considering improving the in-house government management oversight of their aircraft programmes.

Not in the White Paper, but advised privately to the industry leaders, was the promise that a suitably regrouped industry would receive government support for promising future new aircraft projects, as a balanced civil-military workload which recognised the need to save dollar expenditure and allow British industry to more effectively compete in the world aircraft marketplace.

At least one influential government appointee was the chief scientific adviser to government departments. From 1960, this was Professor Solly Zuckerman in the Ministry of Defence and, from 1964 to 1971, to the government overall. Zuckerman's scientific background was Zoology and wartime Operational Research. He did not have "hands-on" aerospace technical knowledge but was firmly of the opinion that Britain should satisfy all its aircraft needs "off the shelf" from the USA. The government "promise" of support was to be tainted!

The resulting reshuffling of the industry into larger groups would have short and medium term dramatic effects on the whole of the UK industry, but something along these lines had been essential for a while. There were too many aircraft companies with too little production to sustain them all.

The basis of the 1957 Defence Review, that "missiles will overtake manned aircraft in future conflicts", was the declared reason for the aircraft cancellations. It was also cover for an unpalatable political truth. Britain could not truly afford the updating of all of its RAF and RN aircraft fleets consistent with the expensive technology escalation which had become an integral part of the Cold War arms race. Britain had the talent and the expertise, but not really enough financial resource to "go it alone".

Britain's total worldwide defence posture commitments (as opposed to just the NATO European theatre of operations) added up to an enormous total expense for the public purse. Openly admitting that armed forces equipment funding needs were significantly higher than the country was actually able to afford was unacceptable to the government, because it would be likely to dismay (or at least discomfort) a large part of the British public, as well as NATO, other allies and many parts of the British Commonwealth. It would also diminish the perceived world position of Britain in general. In some senses, the defence "cull" consequence of the 1957 review could be interpreted as the first tacit admission from the government that Britain no longer was a major world power, but without the fact being openly stated.

In the event, the "all-missile" policy of the White Paper would soon be found wanting. The relentless ongoing evolution of the Cold War scenario ensured that the need for a variety of new manned aircraft would materialise. The continued existence of the 1956 GOR.339 (TSR-2) into the submission of responses stage and evaluation/selection in the 1960s and the subsequent events belied the "no new manned combat aircraft" policy. The policy was discredited almost as soon as it had been declared, but it existed long enough to cause the demise of very expensive advanced aircraft projects in Britain which were technically demanding, exciting and high risk. If these projects had been successfully developed, they may, or may not, have become (and remained) useful in their intended roles for longer. At the very least, the impact of the curtailment of much of the advanced aeronautical research programmes in Britain can be surmised as somewhere between "damaging" and "catastrophic". The effect on some of the companies was actually to lead to closure, which actually had already become necessary as part of an inevitable rationalisation of the industry. Fortunately, among all the ensuing mayhem, the resilience of some of the key technical and business managers in the British aircraft industry was sufficient to enable the successful achievements of the 1970s and 1980s, as described in later chapters.

How this all played out in the radical effects on the British aircraft industry, is described in section 6.1 following.

Chapter 6

Turbulent Years, 1960 to 1975

6.1 British Industry Mergers and the End of Original Aircraft Company Names

The 1957 Defence Review and resulting White Paper were very unwelcome in most of the UK aircraft industry. The reduction in new aircraft work due to the 1957 cancellations was a blow to the aircraft companies directly affected (Avro, Saunders-Roe and Fairey), but the "need to respond to the requirement to operate in large groups on future government work" was a significant organisational problem. The "fiefdoms" of the various companies were familiar with the sharing of military aircraft production work, either voluntarily or at government direction, but each company remained fiercely independent when it came to the design responsibility and testing for their own projects. The formation of groups for individual projects had already been occupying the individual "barons" of the industry for a while, to help mitigate rapid changes in numbers of in-house personnel, as new projects started and as they came towards the end. "Which company (ies) would come out on top?" was now a looming question.

The Hawker Siddeley Group was best placed, as it already included a loose collection of four companies (Hawker, Armstrong Whitworth, Avro and Gloster), with group chairman still Sir "Tommy" Sopwith from 1935, and managing director Sir Frank Spriggs. The loss of the Avro 730 project caused the company to consider a return by Avro to the civil market (the Avro 748 turboprop regional airliner was the result). Avro also had their Weapons Division (Blue Steel) and Avro Canada was a major contributor to group profits. Unfortunately, Avro Canada collapsed in 1959, with the cancellation of the Mach 2 interceptor project for the RCAF, the Avro Canada CF-105 Arrow. The Hawker Siddeley Group also contained the Armstrong Whitworth guided missile business and the Armstrong Siddeley engines company (luxury motor cars and aircraft engines).

The de Havilland Holdings Company was led by Chairman Sir Aubrey Burke. Company secretary Charles White also was a powerful influence. With some "parochial justification", they considered de Havilland to be the stand-alone supreme aerospace company in Britain (if not in Europe), as the holding company for four legally separate DH companies, producing aircraft, aircraft engines, guided weapons and space rocket launchers, plus subsidiary companies in Canada and Australia. They considered the de Havilland Aircraft part as one of the premier aircraft companies in the world. They were soon to gain the agreement of the Hunting and Fairey aircraft companies to participate in their new civil jet airliner (the DH.121, which became the Trident) and had also started work on defining a new business jet, the DH.125.

De Havilland Propellers activity had grown from "licence-build of USA Hamilton-Standard propellers" in pre-1939 days, to including the Comet aircraft undercarriage, electrical equipment and radar scanners. The company was also responsible for all air-to-air missile production in Britain in the 1950s and was also the producer of the British Medium Range Ballistic Missile (Blue Streak), which had been created in conjunction with RAE technical guidance. Blue Streak was first tested successfully in 1954 and went on to form the first stage of the Europa (satellite) launch system managed by the international European Launcher Development Organisation (ELDO). The Europa as a package proved unreliable and was eventually completely replaced by the Arianne series of space launchers, created by a new pan-European organisation in which Britain did not participate.

In negotiations, English Electric was led by main board director and managing director of the Guided Weapons Division, the second Viscount Caldecote (Robert Andrew Inskip) and the aviation business chief executive, Freddie Page. Vickers Aircraft were led by Chairman Lord Knollys and managing director Sir George Edwards, an aircraft designer to his roots and a longtime "Whitehall Warrior" with many senior MoS government contacts.

Westland, under Chairman Sir Eric Mensforth, were receptive to the idea of consolidation of the UK rotary wing industry, hoping that their strong connection to USA Sikorsky would work in their favour. The aircraft engine companies would also be affected. Only Rolls-Royce were large enough in aircraft engines not to really have any immediate worries.

The guided weapon businesses of the aircraft companies would also need to be "rearranged". The "then current" status of all the aircraft companies immediately after the 1957 Defence Review is shown in Table 6.1 below. The questions hovering were "how many takeovers, mergers or consortia would be formed?" and "how many of the UK aircraft companies would survive?"

Table 6.1: The UK Aircraft Company Business Positions, 1957–58.

Parent or Group	Aircraft Company	Other aviation activities	Aircraft Company 1957–58 position
Hawker Siddeley	Armstrong# Whitworth	Guided Missiles and sister co. Armstrong Siddeley Engines	Series 100 Argosy freighters "not really successful", small number of series 200 Argosy on order.
N/A	Auster	none	Struggling in a "niche" part of the light aircraft market.
Hawker Siddeley	Avro#	Guided Missiles	After Avro 730 cancellation, turned attention to civil aircraft market, whilst in the early days of Vulcan B.2 production.
N/A	Blackburn#	Aircraft Engines (Cirrus)	Producing Blackburn Beverley RAF transport and Buccaneer S.1 strike aircraft for RN. "As one of the smaller of the big companies", unsure about medium term future survival.
N/A	Boulton-Paul	Aviation hydraulics	Their last aircraft (Balliol) had been fully delivered and no new aircraft of their own design on the horizon. Had hydraulics expertise (from extensive aircraft powered gun turret experience).
N/A	Bristol (included helicopters & aircraft engines)	Aircraft Engines (Bristol Aero Engines) and Guided Missiles. Shares in Westland (10%) & Shorts (15%)	Concerned about end of production of Britannia. Designing/building T.188 supersonic research aircraft for cancelled Avro 730 project – wondering "what next".

Parent or Group	Aircraft Company	Other aviation activities	Aircraft Company 1957–58 position
N/A	De Havilland#	Aircraft Engines and Guided Missiles, Aircraft Hydraulic and Electrical Equipment, Space Vehicles & Propellers	After government financial rescue in 1955, DH were still recovering from Comet disasters. They had many broader interests than aircraft (engines etc). DH Sea Vixen in production for RN. About to form the Airco consortium, for the new DH.121 (Trident) jet airliner project. DH leading Fairey and Hunting, as partners.
N/A	Elliotts of Newbury	none	Building world-class gliders in modest numbers.
English Electric Company	English Electric#	Guided Missiles and sister company D. Napier aircraft engines	Canberra bomber new production still continuing (much contracted to Avro and Shorts licence-build), future conversion & refurbishment work in planning stage. P1 supersonic research aircraft programme on going.
N/A	Fairey# (included helicopters)	Avions Fairey (Belgium)	Completing licence-build production work (DH Venom) and hoping to join in new DH.121 (Trident) airliner. "Lost" Fairey Delta III (F.155T bid). Attempting to break into helicopter market (Fairey Rotodyne).
N/A	F.G. Miles	Structural Plastics, Aerial Mapping (plus non-aviation)	Established after 1947 bankrupcy of Miles Aircraft, struggling in a "niche" part of the light aircraft market.
N/A	Folland	none	Small company, with Folland Gnat F.Mk.1 ordered by Finland, India and Yugoslavia.
Hawker Siddeley	Gloster	none	Gloster Javelin in production.
N/A	Handley Page	none "active"	Handley Page Dart Herald in production Victor B.1 in production, B.2 planned.
Hawker Siddeley	Hawker#	none	Hawker Hunter in production. Diverted P.1121 effort into PV rework as P.1129, as bid for OR.339# (TSR-2 spec).
Hunting Ltd.	Hunting	none	Jet Provost pilot trainer in production. Hoped to join in new DH.121 (Trident) airliner. Early ideas on 30-seater twin jet airliner.
N/A	Saunders-Roe (included helicopters)	Black Knight Space Rocket (with RAE)	SR.53 & SR.177 (F.155T bid) just cancelled. Ex-Cierva helicopter business not yet succeeding.

Parent or Group	Aircraft Company	Other aviation activities	Aircraft Company 1957–58 position
N/A	Scottish Aviation	Aircraft maintenance	Twin Pioneer nearly at the end of production (25% redundancies threatened).
Short Bros. & Harland	Shorts#	Guided missiles	Design and test technical work with one-off research aircraft, production work for Bristol Britannia wing, English Electric Canberra.
N/A	Slingsby	none	Building world-class gliders.
Vickers	Supermarine	none	Supermarine Scimitar in production for RN (Fleet Air Arm).
Vickers Armstrong	Vickers#	Guided missiles	Vickers Vanguard in production, VC.10 on order "off the drawing board" (government instruction to BOAC).
N/A	Westland (included helicopters)	Moving entirely into helicopters as "own product", still able to produce fixed wing designs of others	Westland Westminster heavy lift helicopter "paper idea". Westland Whirlwind helicopter in production for RAF & RN (as adaptations of licence-build USA Sikorsky S-55).

Bidders for GOR.339 (TSR-2), issued March 1957: The only serious new military aircraft large programme to survive the 1957 White Paper was the aircraft defined in the operational requirement GOR.339, which was to lead to TSR-2. Nine different aircraft companies were to bid for this work (see section 6.3).

Some companies seemed to become resigned to losing their independence, some seemed to embrace the opportunity, while others steadfastly resisted any serious change, trying to opt for "the ability to arrange different groupings for different projects". All had to accept that the total number of significant new UK military aircraft projects would be reduced and that obtaining government financial support to new civil large-airliner programmes would also be unlikely to be possible for a one company project. The sparsity of aircraft programmes probably would also cause the number of new engine developments to be reduced as a consequence.

The other aircraft company businesses of "missiles" might anticipate an increase in production, of more and perhaps larger (and expensive) missiles. Space technology was about to emerge into the light, with the distant glimmer of potential for non-military business, and the opportunity was thought to be there for those already engaged, if the government supported the necessary research and development.

Rolls-Royce were in a fairly dominant UK position in the jet turbine (including turboprop) aircraft engine business but the future of piston engine development and projects in the UK was already shrinking fast.

The UK Aircraft Business Negotiations
Hawker Siddeley Group
The four Hawker Siddeley aircraft companies had been allowed by Group Managing Director Sir Frank Spriggs to compete with one another for new UK military aircraft work. Successful bids usually resulted in a sharing of sub-let design and production work amongst the group. A senior Hawker Siddeley Group director, Sir Roy Dobson (ex-Avro) actually favoured a closer integration, more working together from the

start, and tighter central management control. He and Chairman Sir Thomas Sopwith decided that this should happen. In 1958, Sir Thomas advised Sir Frank that "he should retire" and appointed Sir Roy in Sir Frank's place. In the event, Sir Roy took over the task of negotiating the group's way through the consequences of the 1957 Defence White Paper.

Encouraged by Ministry pressure on Folland, Sir Roy Dobson made an early move, by successfully negotiating for Folland to join the Hawker Siddeley Group in 1959. He also made three offers to purchase Handley Page, but founder Sir Frederick Handley Page was adamant in remaining independent, even after the last batch of twenty-one Victor B.Mk.2 bombers was cancelled during this time (before this batch of production had started).

There were discussions between Hawker Siddeley and Bristol, about joining up Bristol with Avro, with an offer to share in a Bristol proposal for a new airliner (Bristol Type 200, see section 6.4). The discussions were also partly stimulated by the existing contacts on the three Bristol Type T.188 high Mach number aerodynamic fundamental research aircraft in support of the Avro 730 just cancelled. These aircraft were already in progress (three more due to be ordered were cancelled as a result of the Avro 730 cancellation). If the Bristol 200 airliner project failed to gain traction, the Bristol business was really going to be an empty factory, unless the emerging supersonic transport study (in which Avro were participating) matured into reality. Hawker Siddeley would have liked to quietly take over Bristol, absorb the Bristol T.188 research aircraft effort into Avro (funded by the government) with an eye on possible future supersonic civil or military aircraft, sell the Bristol Engines business to Rolls-Royce and shut down or sell off the Bristol helicopter business and the rest of the company.

Avro, Gloster, Hawker and Armstrong Whitworth aircraft companies turned their technical attention to responses to the GOR.339 Tactical Strike and Reconnaissance aircraft requirement (eventually, three made formal submissions), as the only new military manned aircraft programme left with UK government support.

Blackburn Aircraft could sense their relative weakness and soon agreed to join the Hawker Siddeley team, thinking that they had acquired a "co-pilot" position in the group with their new Buccaneer aircraft programme, as a "good card" played. Their engine business was to have a different fate.

The Emergence of the British Aircraft Corporation

Vickers aircraft business was in financial problems after the failure of Vanguard turboprop airliner to attract large orders, other than from BEA and Air Canada, and their new VC.10 airliner project was not gathering orders at a rate which would recover the heavy development costs. Vickers were also suggesting the possibility of the VC.11, which was a smaller version of the proposed VC.10 and competitive with the DH.121 project. Eventually, the financial assistance needed by Vickers (for the VC.10 and the VC.11 combined,) was spelt out to the Minister of Supply, Sir Aubrey Jones. The total was some £309 million, equivalent to £6.8 billion in 2019 terms. English Electric and Vickers started to discuss merger possibilities. English Electric were adamant that they would not make any contribution to the current VC.10 and would reserve their position on the emerging Super VC.10 and the VC.11. Separately, Vickers (Supermarine division) had prepared a response to the only remaining new RAF manned aircraft requirement, GOR.339.

By 1959, the Minister of Supply had become a significant intermediary in three-way discussions between Vickers, English Electric and de Havilland. De Havilland were cautious and Chairman Sir Aubrey Burke and the company secretary Charles White had board backing "as the stand-alone premier totally independent aviation company in Europe". They expected the de Havilland company to be "top dog" in any new merger, or to remain independent with smaller companies (like Fairey and Hunting) participating in de Havilland projects.

De Havilland revived the Airco name (whence they had been founded in 1920), planned as a consortium of themselves, Fairey and Hunting, to produce a new three-jet airliner (DH.121, later named Trident). They were also soon to start (in 1961) a new business jet project, the DH.125.

Duncan Sandys moved from Defence to the new Ministry of Aviation, in the new government of 1959. He had become impatient of the lack of substantive progress and began to organise a "marriage bureau" for the industry. It became clear that Duncan Sandys had been given a specific remit and Cabinet authority to progress matters. It also became absolutely clear that a "two group" policy was non-negotiable, with Hawker Siddeley as one of the groups, and that "Groups" meant permanent association, rather than on a project-by-project arrangement.

English Electric urged Vickers to consider a joint bid to take over de Havilland (hostile if need be) to form the basis of the second group. Vickers sought a more peaceable approach. This particular arrangement (hostile or not) was well-favoured by Duncan Sandys, and would be founded by three well-regarded and capable aircraft companies. Arguments raged over the de Havilland DH.121 versus the Vickers VC.11 proposal and the parlous financial position of Vickers (seeking government aid).

The English Electric supersonic experience with the Lightning had caused them to believe they were best-placed to make a winning response to GOR.339. The government acknowledged the experience but, by 1959, definitely preferred the "total weapons system" response from Vickers/Supermarine (as opposed to "aircraft with weapon system added"). Requiring Vickers to lead English Electric within a joined-up proposal created Vickers-English Electric argument over their emerging joint TSR-2 winning proposal.

One of the major reorganisation difficulties was the clear definition of the level of exposure of each of the three companies (English Electric, Vickers and de Havilland) might acquire to each other's existing projects. Individual isolation from, or limited exposure to, any of the liabilities of the others, which either already existed or were committed to, were difficult issues to resolve. Duncan Sandys agreed that some measure of government support to airliner projects would be necessary to enable the UK to compete on a level playing field in world markets. It was also clear, however, that only one of the two competing new airliners (VC.11 and DH.121) would be supported.

Suddenly, the game changed. The de Havilland board of directors felt that they could not recommend to their shareholders joining what they considered to be an ill-defined Vickers-English Electric joint company, not least because the financial arrangements would be complex and the competitive overlap between the proposed Vickers VC.11 and the de Havilland DH.121 airliners remained unresolved. Sir Aubrey Burke and his board therefore negotiated to join the Hawker Siddeley Group, with the de Havilland chairman as chairman of a subsidiary company responsible for all aviation activity, to be named Hawker de Havilland. After initial agreement, this soon proved unacceptable to Hawker Siddeley. Instead, they offered de Havilland the deputy managing director position for the Hawker Siddeley group and deputy chairmanship of the combined "total aviation group" (including guided weapons and space) which would take over de Havilland, with Roy Dobson as overall chairman of the aviation group. Dobson would also be managing director of the whole Hawker Siddeley group. Inclined to reject this at first, the de Havilland board eventually accepted. This displaced Blackburn from a "co-pilot's seat" in the Hawker Siddeley group aircraft business. On this basis, de Havilland became the final addition to the Hawker Siddeley Group.

The English Electric-Vickers-de Havilland discussions had dragged on and Bristol were becoming accustomed to having to join up with Avro inside Hawker Siddeley.

When de Havilland suddenly jumped into the arms of Hawker Siddeley, the likelihood of Bristol joining up with Hawker Siddeley's Avro evaporated. This caused Bristol to get together with English Electric and Vickers to form the British Aircraft Corporation (BAC). Bristol were really forced into the arms of Vickers and English Electric within BAC, with Vickers and English Electric owning 40 per cent each and Bristol owning 20 per cent of the new company.

The Rest of the British Aircraft Industry

By 1959, Fairey Aviation in the UK was entirely confined to rotary wing aircraft, but the Fairey Group subsidiary, Avions Fairey (formed in Belgium in 1931), was still active in licence-build of (non-Fairey) aircraft for the Belgian government. Westland took over the total business of the Fairey Aviation activity in the UK, but Avions Fairey continued to operate in Belgium inside the Fairey group, much later being bought by the Belgian government when the Fairey group of companies collapsed in 1977.

The helicopter parts of Bristol and Saunders-Roe were also absorbed by Westland, including the hovercraft activity of Saunders-Roe. Thus the name Saunders-Roe was eliminated from the aircraft industry. In 1966 the Saunders-Roe hovercraft element was to be joined with others in a new Westland-Vickers company named British Hovercraft Corporation.

Percival Aircraft was a successful but relatively small aircraft company which had been in the Hunting group of companies since 1944. This activity was renamed Hunting-Percival in 1954, finally dropping the Percival connection in 1957 to become Hunting Aircraft Ltd. Not involved in the initial negotiations concerning the businesses making up the new Hawker Siddeley and British Aircraft Corporation (BAC) groupings, as soon as BAC had been established, the ex-Percival business was taken over by BAC.

Boulton Paul no longer had a "live" whole aircraft project but produced aircraft hydraulic system components (the Avro Vulcan and Blackburn Buccaneer Powered Flying Control Units in particular). A 1961 welcome takeover offer from the Cheltenham-based Dowty Group was accepted and Boulton Paul disappeared from the list of UK aircraft manufacturers.

Initially, Shorts had been teamed with English Electric in the GOR.339 response but, as a nationalised company since 1943, were not involved in group merger discussions (and were left out in the end).

Small fry glider companies Elliotts of Newbury and Slingsby were too small to be involved with government rationalisation policy for the industry, as were Scottish Aviation. These companies (happily?) resigned themselves to being "bit players", at least for a while, avoiding being completely crushed in the mêlée. Supermarine had to wait for Vickers to decide their future, which turned out to be the demise of the name (but not yet the factory).

In 1949 F.G. Miles (the former managing director of the bankrupt Miles Aircraft) had started a new company F.G. Miles Ltd. which included a small group of different engineering activities. This included building a few examples of Miles Aircraft designs, the design and construction of single examples of a new glider, modified versions of Miles aircraft and a brand new single-engined two-seat trainer (Miles Student). Peter G. Masefield, managing director of Bristol aircraft, approached the Pressed Steel deputy chairman A.H. Bellhouse (interested in aviation). Their ultimate objective was to form a British light aircraft company with the full range of light aircraft in one portfolio. The result was the Pressed Steel takeover of Auster in 1960 and the establishing of a technical and production liason with F.G. Miles. Peter G. Masefield was appointed managing director. By 1961, F.G.Miles had also been fully merged into the new company, British Executive and General Aviation Ltd (trading as BEAGLE). Soon reorganised, by 1962 this became Beagle Aircraft Ltd. Pressed Steel was taken over by British Motor

Corporation in 1962. Beagle Aircraft was loss-making and continued to require further investment, so was sold to the UK government in 1966, which provided financial aid as the only alternative to closing down the business. When further aid was needed in 1969, the company eventually went into receivership. It was wound up and assets disposed of, including the prototype and the design of the Beagle 121 Pup, eventually adopted by Scottish Aviation and developed into the Bulldog trainer (see section 6.6).

The Aircraft Engines Businesses

The British aircraft engines business was dominated by Rolls-Royce, followed by the engine businesses of Armstrong Siddeley, the aircraft companies' Bristol, de Havilland, and Blackburn engines, plus independent Napier and Alvis engines. The dominance of Rolls-Royce was felt to be an anti-competitive situation. A rationalisation process was a sensible way forward. The government made it clear that the suggested engine for the upcoming GOR.339 project could not be the Bristol Olympus 320 (developed from the Vulcan engine) unless Bristol and Armstrong Siddeley merged their engines businesses. This tipped the scale and precipitated wholescale merger moves. First, the Hawker Siddeley-owned engine businesses Armstrong Siddeley was joined with Bristol Aero Engines Company (from 1920 until 1956, the Bristol Engines Division of Bristol Aircraft Company) to form a new independent company, Bristol Siddeley Engines Ltd. in 1959. The Blackburn and de Havilland engines activities were added in 1961. The enlarged Hawker Siddeley Group thus became a 50 per cent shareholder in Bristol Siddeley Engines. Since 1942, Napiers had been owned by English Electric and the aircraft engines part of the business was absorbed into Rolls-Royce in 1961, only to be closed in 1963. Alvis ceased aircraft engine manufacture in 1966.

The Missiles and Other Businesses Owned by the "Aircraft Businesses"

The settling of aircraft company groupings and the aircraft engine businesses meant that the non-aircraft businesses of the aircraft companies could be sensibly grouped into single divisions or companies of Hawker Siddeley and BAC. The majority were formally listed as two groups; BAC Guided Weapons Division, alongside the BAC Aircraft Division and, in 1963, Hawker Siddeley Dynamics Ltd (HSD) alongside Hawker Siddeley Aviation Ltd (HSA). The Fairey missile activity was no longer active by 1960 and the Shorts missile business remained as part of the national majority-owned Short company.

The Final Groupings

By 1963, the post-Second World War company and division shuffles, mergers and takeovers resulted in the formation of an enlarged Hawker Siddeley Group (having absorbed the aircraft activities of Folland, Blackburn and de Havilland and the engines, guided weapon and space business of de Havilland). The engine businesses of de Havilland and Blackburn were added to the Armstrong Siddeley Engines company of the Hawker Siddeley Group and the agreed merger of Armstrong Siddeley's and Bristol's aircraft engine activity (plus other engine activities of the other aircraft companies) created Bristol Siddeley Engines, headquartered in Bristol and with Hawker Siddeley a 50 per cent shareholder. The chart below shows the final major aircraft merged company positions, including the effect of changes to their engine businesses.

The Armstrong Siddeley aircraft engine element of Hawker Siddeley Group businesses is shown grouped with Armstong Whitworth aircraft, to help illustrate the total change to both the aircraft and associated engine businesses owned by the UK aircraft companies.

In 1963, Hawker Siddeley Group reorganised its aircraft businesses into a new company, Hawker Siddeley Aviation (HSA), in divisions. At the same time, they placed their guided

Activity \ Company	Avro	A-Whit/A-Siddeley	Blackburn	Hawkr/Glos'r/F'lnd	de Havilland	Bristol	Vickers	English Electric	Hunting-Percival	Fairey	Westland	Saunders Roe
Fixed wing aircraft	H	H	H	H	H	B	B	B	B	C	C	C
Guided weapons	C	H			H	B	B	B				C
Helicopters					W					W	W	W
Aircraft engines		E	E		E	E						

Final company key:-

H Hawker Siddeley	**B** BAC	**W** Westland	**C** ceased activity	**E** Bristol Siddeley
"Aviation & Dynamics"	"Aircraft & GW"	"Helicopters"	"soon after"	"Engines"

weapons and space related businesses with other group engineering businesses in another new company, Hawker Siddeley Dynamics (HSD). The Gloster element of the Hawker Siddeley Group had initially been merged with the Armstrong Whitworth element to form Whitworth-Gloster Aircraft in 1960. When HSA was created in 1963, Whitworth-Gloster joined with Avro to form the Avro Whitworth division of HSA and the Gloster name disappeared. What had been Gloster was later hived off and joined with the remnants of Saunders-Roe, forming a separate business Gloster-Saro to focus on airfield equipment. Two more famous company names thus departed the UK aircraft industry. Constituent aircraft company names in HSA and BAC products also disappeared, all projects becoming "HS" or "BAC". Westland absorbed all helicopter business under the Westland Helicopters brand. As noted above, the light aircraft businesses Auster and F.G. Miles were collected together to trade as Beagle aircraft, but Handley Page, Shorts, Scottish Aviation, Slingsby and Elliotts of Newbury remained alone and separated. In 1966, at the request of the directors of Elliotts, Slingsby took over all Elliotts' glider responsibilities but not the production facilities.

Not long after these major upheavals in the aircraft industry, in 1968 Slingsby Aviation had a disastrous fire and went into liquidation the following year. Bought by Vickers, sailplane design and manufacture restarted as Vickers Slingsby in 1979 and absorbed within the British Underwater Engineering Group. Slingsby aircraft design finally ceased with the updating and licence build of French Fournier RF-6 1973 aerobatic training aircraft, as the 1982 Slingsby T.67 Firefly. Slingsby eventually passed to ML holdings in 1993, then Cobham in 1995 and finally ended as a specialist composite structures activity, owned by what is now the Marshall Aerospace and Defence group.

Appendix 2 is a timeline of the post-1945 significant government interventions of note in British aircraft industry, alongside aircraft and airline developments affecting the industry. UK government sponsoring of military and civil aircraft projects had differing characteristics.

6.2 Government Ministries, Airworthiness Regulation and the Influence of Rising Costs

Changes in Aviation Responsibilities in Government Ministries

The reorganisation of the industry was soon to be accompanied by major changes in the government departments involved with aviation. This continued to happen up to, and well after, the end of the twentieth century.

Except for the Second World War temporary expedient of creating the Ministry of Aircraft Production, from 1939 to 1959 the Ministry of Supply (MoS) was the government arm responsible for civil aircraft regulation, alongside the responsibility for the supply of government-controlled equipment (including all military aircraft and BOAC and BEA requirements). The MoS responsibilities for aircraft supply and civil aviation regulation were subsumed into a new Ministry of Aviation (MoA) in 1959.

The MoA was thus responsible for the supply of all military aircraft and civil aircraft for use by government agencies (this included BOAC and BEA national airlines). In 1967 the MoA aircraft supply responsibility was transferred into the Ministry of Technology (which had been created in 1964) and civil aviation regulation became part of the Board of Trade. In 1970 the Ministry of Technology was merged with the Board of Trade to create the Department of Trade and Industry, except that military aircraft supply became the responsibility of a short-lived revived Ministry of Aviation Supply, pending the outcome of a review of central government organisation.

From 1946 to 1964, five Departments of State had carried out the work of what became the modern Ministry of Defence:

- the Admiralty
- the War Office
- the Air Ministry
- the Ministry of Aviation, and
- an earlier form of the Ministry of Defence

These departments merged in 1964.

The defence functions of the Ministry of Aviation Supply merged into the Ministry of Defence in 1971, when a reform of central government created the Ministry of Defence "Defence Procurement Agency", known as MoD(PE). This agency became responsible for all government defence equipment procurement. This included the development of new weapons systems and equipment, such as warships, guns, tanks and military aircraft. The technology research initiatives at several government research establishments, (which could have civil or military application, such as fundamental aerodynamics at RAE Farnborough) also came under the wing of MoD(PE). Civil aerospace responsibilities remained with the Board of Trade.

MoD(PE) was replaced later by the Defence Procurement Agency, in 1999, as government supported research establishments, such as RAE, RSRE and NGTE, were privatised or closed down. In 2007 the Defence Procurement Agency was merged with the Defence Logistics Organisation to form Defence Equipment and Support, currently headed by a chief executive who can be either a 4-star ranking serving military officer or a civilian.

The UK aircraft industry working practices and reporting to government had to accommodate the effects of all these changes.

Civil Airliners for the UK, post-1945 until the mid-1950s

The general type requirements which were the outcome of the wartime Brabazon Committee were used as the post-1945 new British civil aircraft restart point. More detailed requirements specifications for each aircraft type were prepared by the government ministry responsible (the Ministry of Supply at the time) and issued to industry (in a "selective" manner). Assuming satisfactory responses, the associated contract to develop each of the aircraft was awarded (see section 5.2). The purchase of an aircraft from an overseas source would only be allowed where there was clearly no British aircraft which could satisfy the reasonable needs of nationally-owned airlines BOAC and BEA.

BOAC:

The first example of the acquisition of a new American airliner was a 1946 order by BOAC for six new Lockheed Constellations. More Constellations were added later. BOAC was permitted to spend further dollars on Boeing Stratocruisers for its key transatlantic routes from October 1949, offering a double-deck London-New York transatlantic service (see section 5.4). Another four Boeing Stratocruisers were taken over from a frustrated Swedish airline order and seven more were bought secondhand. The British medium range Handley Page Hermes (see section 5.2) was joined in the BOAC fleet by the Canadian Canadair Rolls-Royce Merlin-engined enhancement of the Douglas DC-4, the DC-4M Argonaut, between 1949 and 1950. This replaced the last of the non-pressurised types (such as the Avro York) on passenger services. When service entry of the Bristol Britannia was delayed in late 1956, BOAC was permitted to purchase ten new USA Douglas DC-7C (see section 5.4).

BEA:

British European Airways (BEA) was established in 1946 as a short and medium range airline, initially separated from BOAC as a division and soon converted to a nationally-owned separate company. BEA absorbed all other independent airlines in Britain. Except for early post-war operations with Douglas DC-3s (and ex-RAF Dakotas), the government ensured that the fleet of BEA fixed-wing aircraft remained all-British, from the 1946 formation until 1972, when BEA was merged with BOAC to form the government-owned British Airways. The Vickers Viking re-fuselaged adaptation of the Wellington bomber design was used by BEA (and later by new, short-lived independent airlines). The UK industry Vickers Viscount became the first new British post-war international airliner true success. The pre-war/wartime designs of the de Havilland Dragon Rapide and Avro York continued in service until replaced by other UK aircraft in the 1950s and 60s.

By the 1950s, there were independent airlines operating in Britain, mainly as charter companies. BOAC or BEA alone dwarfed all of them collectively. BOAC were to be allowed to continue to acquire non-British airliners (Boeing 707s in the 1960s and 747s in the 1970s). Just before the 1972 BOAC-BEA merger, BEA were to order USA Lockheed L-1011 Tristars with three British (Rolls-Royce) engines, as it was decided that there was no acceptable alternative UK product for their needs. Probably for totally political reasons, support to the nationalised Rolls-Royce which was rescued from bankruptcy in 1971 by the government, and the ignorance of both the government and BEA, the economic potential of the nascent alternative Airbus A.300 with American engines (described later, in section 7.4) was "not acceptable" to the nationally-owned BEA. The fact that the A.300B would have the much better aircraft fuel efficiency overall was not sufficient reason for BEA to be even interested in properly examining the potential offered by the Airbus, with its high British content. "Airbus was bound to fail" was the prevailing government opinion within the Ministry of Technology, clearly not the opinion of the British industry in the shape of HSA.

As airliner technical capability and capacity continued on an upward spiral, so did the cost of development and manufacture. Apart from airworthiness regulation and airline operations licensing and control, the influence of the government on the UK civil aircraft industry became focused entirely on financial support needs for new projects, without which that part of the industry would have expired. For all but the smaller projects, work-sharing with international partners would be the inevitable outcome. Almost inevitably, this would have to be within Europe, if the almost monopolistic dominance of the USA civil aircraft industry was to be challenged.

Military Combat Aircraft Spiralling Costs, post-1945

In the early years of the Cold War, UK military aircraft projects were founded on the perceived level of threat from, and capability of, the Soviet Union and its Warsaw Pact allies. The threat assessment mostly focused on Western Europe but did not exclude other potential areas with a perceived Soviet interest. Market forces clearly were less influential, although the ability to export UK military aircraft overseas was an important feature of assisting UK international influence and profit potential for the aircraft industry. As the 1960s dawned, the cost of developing and manufacturing advanced military aircraft started to rocket upwards and the number of aircraft actually built reduced accordingly. Just like the civil aircraft industry, work-sharing (mostly, but not exclusively, with European industry) would become an unstoppable feature of any of the high-capability aircraft projects.

By the early 1960s it had become a too frequent experience for large new equipment projects for the UK government to run into major cost and/or timescale problems. Advanced (and expensive) complex systems and equipment, such as a new military aircraft, were of concern in this regard. There were similar experiences in the USA and elsewhere.

Tools and techniques for managing such programmes were slowly developed, but the actual project management structure often was not always defined completely, with conflicting boundaries or gaps between the management responsibilities of the various participant organisations involved. Previously, it had not been uncommon for a project to be fully authorised with only an outline specification response to a defined requirement. The "old" method of paying for the development of different technology demonstrators and even prototypes from two (or more) different manufacturers[1] and "selecting a winning prime contractor" had clearly become inappropriate, too expensive for all concerned (customer and supplier). It was also far too time-consuming, in the emerging world of the development of increasingly complicated aircraft.

A way of staging the project was sought, with "decision points" at which measured progress and any revised cost estimates could be examined, before fully authorising the next stage. The information gathering to inform the "decision" would take place alongside the project, which might continue to run as planned unless and until a replanning was recommended by a decision to carry on, or mark time for a short time, or even to cancel due to a perceived too high a risk of failure emerging.

To address the project cost estimation and containment problems, the government organised a Steering Group on Development Cost Estimating, chaired by W.G. Downey of the Ministry of Aviation. Their report (the "Downey Report") was published in 1969. This expounded the need not to commit irrevocably to the whole of a project until a firm and detailed specification had been established, with a well-established development cost plan attached. For large and advanced technology programmes, alternative solutions should be examined in a feasibility study (with physical research and test demonstration as necessary) and some selection of solution decision made as a result. If the decision was to implement a chosen solution, the feasibility study should be followed by a project definition stage. To achieve this might mean spending between 10 per cent and 15 per cent of the total cost of the development programme, before the required degree of certainty could be established. The detail depended on how much new technology uncertainty and consequent development was to be needed. In the terms of 2019 money, for a really major project to reach this "End of Project Definition" stage the cost might be as much as several tens of millions (or sometimes

---

1. In USA military aircraft procurement, competitive fly-off of two differently-sourced demonstrators remains in force, last used for the Joint Strike Fighter contest won by Lockheed in 2001, with what became the F-35 Lightning II (section 8.8).

reaching near a billion) pounds, before enough confidence would be established to confidently authorise completion of full development and initial production.

In 1971, a Special Adviser to the UK government (Derek Rayner, a director of retailer Marks and Spencer) was seconded to government service. He prepared and issued a report which broadly endorsed the principles of the Downey report but suggested that, occasionally, spending 15 per cent of development programme cost might be increased to 25 per cent, before an acceptable level of certainty of success could be established. He also severely criticised the lack of clear definition of the lines of authority and responsibility on UK large government projects. The issue was the level and clarity of control exercised, by those (in the government) responsible for procuring a defence system, the intended user (the RAF, Army or RN) and the supplier(s) of the various parts of the total system. Examples might be separately developed major sub-systems, such as an engine or complete radar system, perhaps to be fitted on more than one different aircraft platform. This report led directly to the establishment of the integrated Ministry of Defence and its Procurement Executive (MOD(PE)). Unfortunately, failure to fully implement the principles was to contribute to future project cost and timescale escalation, and even become a main contributing cause of total failure.

Civil Aircraft Airworthiness Regulation

The airworthiness of civil aircraft and the licensing of pilots, airlines and aircraft maintenance in the UK was controlled by the Air Registration Board (ARB) from 1937, under the terms of the Civil Aviation Act 1936 (see section 2.3). Each type of aircraft (UK sourced or overseas sourced) had to be demonstrated to be in conformity with ARB "design and testing rules" and also demonstrated to comply with the performance and operational capability "regulations". This gains a "Type Approval". Each example of a Type-approved aircraft is examined for its individual build standard and satisfaction of quality requirements and given an individual Certificate of Airworthiness, valid for as long as it can continue to be shown that the manufacturer's inspection and maintenance requirements have been complied with.

In 1972, the Civil Aviation Act created the UK Civil Aviation Authority (CAA) which took on the responsibilities of the ARB. Later, in 1982, another act moved the air traffic control element to be the responsibility to the National Air Traffic Services (NATS).

In 1970, the European Economic Community (EEC) member nations created the Joint Airworthiness Authority (JAA), to harmonise airworthiness certification codes and practices between the European individual nations. They were seeking the ability to certify the airworthiness of civil aircraft in Europe to be a single-compliance process, covering all the EEC nations, rather than having to certify in each country individually. Part of the objective also was to establish equivalence with the USA Federal Aviation Authority (FAA) aircraft certification requirements, such that the likelihood of additional design work due to differences in requirements would be minimised (if not eliminated) when sold for operation under different (FAA or JAA) jurisdictions. Although not a member of the EEC, the British CAA collaborated with the process from the beginning and the country formally joined the EEC in 1973.

The resulting requirements were established as the European Joint Airworthiness Requirements (JARs). Satisfying the single set of codes and processes was to be recognised by each member nation so as to award one JAR Certificate of Airworthiness for an aircraft type, rather than apply different national codes and practices for each country where the aircraft was to be registered. By 1987 this had been achieved. During the five years 2003–2008, a restructuring allowed a new organisation, the European Aviation Safety Agency (EASA), to take over all JAA functions. Each national Airworthiness Authority acts as a local agency office of EASA. In March 2020, the

British government position was declared to be that Britain's planned 2021 exit from the European Union will result in British withdrawal from this arrangement, returning airworthiness regulation and certification in Britain wholly to a national responsibility (to an enlarged CAA in all probability). This will duplicate pan-European certification processes. As described in section 8.6, there is no longer any complete airliner production by a British company, making this decision seemingly just gesture politics.

Military Aircraft Airworthiness Regulation

Most military aircraft in the world have operational needs and actual equipment not covered by civil regulation. Obvious examples are armaments and ejector seats but, very often, the military equipment itself remains entirely "military only" and not qualified to civil standards. A couple of simple examples are rear-facing passenger seats on RAF military transports, not normally fitted to civil transport aircraft (greater seat back crash strength needed and aft-facing disliked by the general public), and communications and navigation radios (operating on military-only frequencies).

Until 1953, the Controller (Air) in the Ministry of Supply (MoS) was responsible for the "release to service" of all aircraft for the UK armed forces established within the MoS. In 1953, the position of Controller (Air) was established in the Ministry of Aviation, moved into the Ministry of Technology in 1971 and later into the Ministry of Defence. It is Controller (Air) responsibility to confirm that compliance has been established with the rules and regulations governing the design and operation of military aircraft. These requirements are established in UK ministry publication Defence Standard 00-970 (pre-1983 using Aviation Publication Av.P 970, and its antecedents going back to First World War days). Controller (Air) service release is established as a result of assured conformance with these requirements and "suitable-for-service use" acceptance by the government aircraft trials authority. The Aircraft and Armament Evaluation Establishment (A&AEE) are this "service ready" authority. A&AEE were originally established as the Experimental Flying School part of the RAF Central Flying School (founded 1912) at Upavon, Wiltshire. A&AEE was transferred to Boscombe Down, Wiltshire, from the start of the Second World War. In 1992 the Aircraft and Armament Experimental Establishment was renamed as the Aircraft and Armament Evaluation Establishment.

In 2010, a dedicated and independently staffed Military Aviation Authority was established as part of the Defence Safety Authority within the UK Ministry of Defence. The MAA is, in principle, the UK military equivalent of the Civil Aviation Authority. The MAA is headed by a three-star serving officer and the MAA independence from the chain of armed forces and government command is protected by a formal charter established by the government. In 2015, the MAA came under the umbrella of the Defence Safety Authority, alongside the Military Air Accident Investigation Branch and all other military safety regulators.

Plowden Committee

The new Labour government of 1964 declared concern about the way that the cost of military aircraft programmes consumed too large a portion of the defence budget and very often had cost out turns far exceeding original estimates. A committee, under the chairmanship of Lord Plowden, chairman of Tube Investments, was established, to consider the future place of the aircraft industry in Britain and what organisational or restructuring change might be appropriate. Remarkably, the committee members failed to actually visit any establishments other than one of the smaller ones, the government-owned Shorts factory in Belfast. They were particularly intent on future cost-cutting and re-enforcing the government agenda concerning national direct control of this expensive activity. Even so, the chairman, Lord Plowden, felt it necessary to ask the

Prime Minister if the exercise continued to have real merit, given that TSR-2, P.1154 and AW.681 aircraft projects were all cancelled well before the committee reported (see section 6.3).

The report was published at the end of 1965, the summary of which is shown in Appendix 4. It recognised that Britain could no longer afford to embark on major aircraft projects on a go-it-alone basis but did not remark on the long-term cyclical nature of designing and building aircraft. In the eyes of many, both inside and outside the aircraft industry, the report did not demonstrate understanding of how to balance the dollar cost of "buying American" with British financial restraints. There was also the inconvenient fact that "expenditure in pounds would be partly recovered in taxes, but expenditure in dollars left nothing to be recovered". Correctly identified was the need for pan-European collaboration, if complete dependence on American industry and purchase in dollars were to be avoided. Either naively (unlikely), or not thought through, it suggested a European government collective initiative without any (preliminary) consultation with the industrial businesses or the sources of finance which would be involved in implementing such a move. The whole tone of the report was that the British aircraft industry "was finished", rather than the fact that it had the broadest technical background in Europe, extensive research, development and production facilities (albeit decentralised and fragmented) and would have the most experience and expertise in Europe to offer in any collaborative project.

As a follow-up, Mr. St. John Elstub, a Plowden committee member and managing director of Imperial Metal Industries, was asked to chair another committee which primarily examined efficiency and productivity within the British aircraft industry, compared with other countries. The potential advantages and disadvantages of collaborative international projects were also addressed. The Elstub report included remarking on the poor productivity of the British aircraft industry, compared with the USA (measured as financial output per employee). The much greater USA capital investment in facilities per employee was noted and the greater level of control of production in USA factories was also remarked. An identified major British problem was the tailoring of both civil and military aircraft design too finely to domestic requirements as specified by BOAC/BEA and the RAF/RN. Another issue was identified as the lack of continuity and consistency of government decisions, which therefore inhibited major long-term investments by individual aircraft companies in Britain. If the government were to adopt a more active and prominent involvement in the industry decision-making as well as providing project launch aid, Elstub argued that "the industry might just as well be nationalised".

Overall, it seemed that the Plowden committee terms of reference or allocated timetable may have been too constrained, probably in the interests of speed, which in any case would be much slower than any industrial enterprise could readily accept in any similar investigations of its own. The Elstub report identified real problem issues but could not produce specific remedies. In truth, however, the *raison d'être* for eventual government ownership (nationalisation) of the British aircraft industry might be seen to be openly supported and become a consequence of the Plowden report (see section 8.1).

6.3 1960s New Military Jets and Cancelled Projects

(First flights: (1) Buccaneer – S.1, 1958: S.2, 1965 (2) Lightning – pre-production 1959)

Blackburn Buccaneer

The Buccaneer was designed in response to the extremely demanding Naval Staff requirement NA.39 of 1953. This requested a two-seat (pilot and navigator) transonic strike aircraft which could be conventionally or nuclear armed and operate catapult-launched from then current carriers, with a combat radius of 400 nautical miles at low level, or twice that with high altitude cruise.

The Blackburn Buccaneer aircraft design response included using engine compressor bleed air fed to leading edge aft-facing slots on the wing, wing flap and tailplane, for boundary layer control* during take-off and landing, thereby reducing stalling speed and increasing lift. The technique was not new (Supermarine had used it on the Scimitar flaps and a version was engineered for the wartime Messerschmitt Me.109) but the Buccaneer used it on all surfaces.

Boundary layer control reduces wing stalling speed and permits the wing to be smaller than it otherwise would have needed to have been (folded wing size actually limited by aircraft lift dimensions, down to the hangar deck beneath the flight deck). It also allows wing size to be reduced without unduly penalising the achievable aircraft high speed capability and range. Fuselage "area ruling"** was also incorporated in the Buccaneer, to minimise the overall aircraft transonic drag rise.

Boundary Layer
Control. (*Author*)

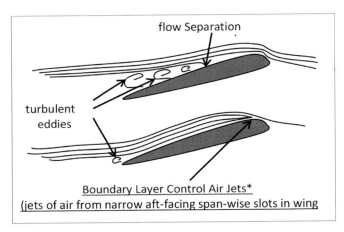

flow Separation

turbulent
eddies

Boundary Layer Control Air Jets*
(jets of air from narrow aft-facing span-wise slots in wing

* The boundary layer is the thin layer of air immediately adjacent to the actual skin of the aircraft. It is the "breakaway" of this layer from the skin which causes the air behind the breakaway point to become very turbulent and separate from the skin, creating a large wake with loss of lift (and very large increases in drag), as in a wing stall. Boundary layer control air jets "energise" the boundary layer to postpone the breakaway to a point nearer to where the skin surface ends.

** Area ruling means that the fuselage was waisted (like a famous "coke bottle shape") as it passed the wing root, to give a smooth *total* aircraft cross-section area change from nose to tail, rather than a rapid rise/fall as the swept wings added-to/left the total cross section, as air flow passed the wing leading edge.

A rotating bomb door allowed weapon carriage internally. This reduced drag until the door rotated about a longitudinal central hinge line close to the fuselage skin line, to place the weapon(s) mounted (with "crutch and release mechanism") on the inside of the rotating door into the airstream, immediately prior to release. The design enabled the "toss bombing" of a tactical nuclear bomb from a low height (a technique allowing the delivering aircraft to escape the blast area before detonation). External wing mounting points for pylon-carried weapons (missiles and rocket launchers) were also provided.

The prototype Buccaneer S.1 first flew in 1958. The first of forty production Buccaneer S.1s entered RN service in 1962, with twin de Havilland Gyron Junior engines (7,100lbf thrust each). These were not powerful enough to allow the Buccaneer S.1 to take off at maximum take-off weight (MTOW) from the RN carriers of the period. To enable full fuel-with-full weapon load missions, the RN were to use its Supermarine Scimitar ex-strike aircraft, as post take-off top-up buddy tankers for the Buccaneer S.1s from the same carrier. In fact, the Gyron Junior turned out to be prone to serious faults, sufficient to cause at least two Buccaneer S.1s to be lost. This eventually caused the S.1 to be grounded very soon after the S.2 version became available at squadron strength.

Derived from the Spey Mk.1 of 1959 as used on HS.Trident and BAC 1-11 airliners, the Rolls-Royce Spey Mk.2 redesigned turbofan engine first ran in 1964. It offered 40 per cent more thrust and much better fuel consumption than the pure turbojet Gyron Junior. Incorporating these new engines required slightly larger wing root spaces, which meant the design change included revised centre fuselage structure and engine intakes. Ten aircraft ordered as S.1s were converted to S.2 standard during initial build. Including a later order for the RAF, 120 were built from scratch as S.2s. Three of the new S.2s were also built specifically for weapons development research flying by the Ministry of Defence. The upgraded S.2 unrefuelled ferry range was significantly increased, becoming 2,300 miles. The use of a buddy-buddy refuelling capability was retained (a Buccaneer S.2 configured in tanker role refuelling one with weapon load) as a means of a major combat range extension.

Starting in 1965, a total of eighty-four Buccaneer S.2 aircraft entered service with the RN and forty-six more new-build aircraft finally entered service with the RAF as the S.2B, which included role-change additional fuel tankage. In 1979, as the UK's last large aircraft carrier *Ark Royal* was decommissioned[2], some of the RN S.2 aircraft had equipment changes to convert them to the S.2A, as additional land-based RAF strike aircraft. The last

Blackburn Buccaneer S.2. (*BAE Systems*)

Buccaneer retired from RAF service in 1994.

South Africa obtained sixteen Buccaneer S.2 (denoted as the S.50, adding underwing fuel tank capability and rocket-powered take-off assistance for South African high ambient temperature operations). This was part of the UK-South Africa Simonstown agreement, which gave the UK use of the Simonstown naval base on the Atlantic coast in the South African Western Cape. The US Navy also expressed some interest in the Buccaneer – allegedly one USN admiral was later heard to comment; "We should have gotten Buccaneers to do the job we are trying to with the Intruder" (the equivalent USN aircraft, the USA Grumman A-6), but this did not result in any USN Buccaneer acquisition.

English Electric Lightning

The Miles M.52 supersonic aircraft research project had been cancelled in 1946 (see section 5.10). "Teddy" Petter, the impetuous and recently-recruited Chief Engineer/Chief Designer at English Electric, felt strongly that the UK should be at the forefront of "supersonics". In 1947/48 he sketched several early ideas for a supersonic aircraft, including the concept of a pair of vertically stacked Rolls-Royce Derwent jet engines

---

2. The first of two new large aircraft carriers (HMS *Queen Elizabeth*) was commissioned in 2017, re-establishing RN fixed wing aircraft carrier capability after a gap of ten years.

(an attempt to reduce supersonic shock wave drag by keeping the fuselage span-wise size down and therefore reducing the overall wing span (for the same wing flying surface area) of heavily swept back wings, sufficient to keep the whole of the wing behind the fuselage nose shock wave front). By 1947, Air Ministry experimental aircraft specification ER.103 had already been issued for a single research aircraft, to be capable of Mach 1.5 and an altitude of 50,000ft. This eventually led to the Fairey Delta 2 (see section 5.10). In the same year, Petter approached the MoS with his supersonic proposal. After some discussion, the requirements of ER.103 were modified into a specification F.23/49, to which Petter promised a response.

OR.268 and associated specification F.23/49 were reissued to include fighter-level manoeuvre capability in the proposed research aircraft. On 1 April 1950, a contract for two flying aircraft and a static structural airframe test specimen was issued to English Electric. After setting out his ideas and commencing work, several months later Petter had suddenly left English Electric for Folland, in February 1950 (see section 5.14). "Freddie" Page, the protégé whom Petter had seduced to English Electric from Hawker, replaced him.

Page kept the "stacked" engines but the Rolls-Royce Avon axial flow turbojet was then planned to become available, more powerful and with lower cross section than the centrifugal compressor Derwent. In order to achieve the target speed of Mach 2, the design included wings swept at 60° and ailerons were placed on the aft-facing squared-off tips. All flying controls were powered and a conventional 60° swept all-moving tailplane was included, set quite a bit lower than the wing to avoid wing-wake downwash detected in wind tunnel testing. The aircraft had the company designation P.1 (Project 1).

The RAE was concerned about the high sweep and the use of a low-set tailplane. A separate order for a low speed research aircraft was placed with Shorts for an aircraft (the SB.5) which could have wings adjustable to various sweep angles and alternative tailplane locations. First flight was on 5 December 1952. After eighteen months of trials, the use of 60° wing sweep and the low-set tailplane were proved to be effective.

The first P.1s were hand built at the English Electric Samlesbury facility before being transported to the government flight trials facility at the A&AEE, Boscombe Down. The aircraft were powered by Armstrong Siddeley Sapphire (unreheated) turbojet engines. The planned Rolls-Royce Avon engine was still undergoing development trials. On 4 August 1954 the first P.1 took to the air for the first time. During subsequent flight trials a maximum speed of Mach 1.51 was imposed due to stability issues. Significant trials data was generated by P1 flight trials which allowed improvements to be designed into the three P1.B versions subsequently ordered (the original P.1 being redesignated as P.1A). Powered by Avon engines, the first P1.B flew on 4 April 1957, effectively as pre-prototype of the true Lightning. By 25 November the same year, the P1.B had achieved a maximum speed of Mach 2. This research aircraft was potentially faster than the record-breaking Fairey Delta 2 but lacked sufficient fuel capacity to perform the necessary flight profile required by FAI rules for official records.

Meanwhile, twenty pre-production versions of the Lightning-to-be were ordered early in 1954, the first of which flew on 3 March 1958. In the event, the availablity of a large number of pre-production machines greatly accelerated the flight trials process and clearance for service entry.

The P.1s (and the pre-production batch order) survived the 1957 Defence White Paper, but any export prospects of a future production version were severely compromised by the "no more manned combat aircraft" UK government policy, which indicated that a significant production run would be unlikely. After serious attempts to interest the West German Luftwaffe in the aircraft, English Electric discovered that a government representative had advised the Germans not to pursue any move to acquire a production aircraft.[3] Later, the UK government eventually ordered series production aircraft for RAF use.

"Lightning" was the service name for the aircraft, established in 1958. The F.1 version first flew in 1959 and entered RAF service at a pre-production standard the same year, the longer range F.6 variant becoming the final definitive version in 1966. The Lightning F.6 had Air Interception Radar information displayed on an early head-up display and the radar featured several operational modes which included autonomous

English Electric Lightning F.6. (*BAE Systems*)

search, automatic target tracking, and ranging for all weapons; the pilot attack sight provided gyroscopically-derived lead angle aiming and backup ranging for gun firing.

Armed with HSD (ex-de Havilland) Red-top infra-red homing missiles, it was a potent air defence platform of its day. With a Mach 2 top speed, a level-flight ceiling of 54,000ft and "zoom" ceiling greater than 70,000ft, the aircraft had been conceived as a "rapid response" aircraft for high altitude interception protection from Soviet bombers heading towards 'V' bomber airfields. This was to allow the RAF 'V' bombers to get "up and away" with their nuclear weapons. The achilles heel of the Lightning was the limited combat range and very limited patrol endurance. It was designed as an inteceptor, "scrambled from the runway", with targets already identified, rather than a patrol-interceptor.

The Lightning was a spectacular machine to hear and watch taking off, famous for climbing away vertically on its tail (not the fastest way to high altitude). It was a jet-jockey's joy to fly, provided he could handle certain sensitive control issues in certain (high altitude) flight regimes. However, with the engines stacked one above the other (with a removable fuel tank underneath) this meant that it was not the easiest aircraft to service. The F.6 had greater range than the first examples into service and the type was later developed to have a ground attack capability for export markets.

Including prototypes, 337 were built, forty-seven of which were supplied to the Royal Saudi Air Force and fourteen for the Kuwaiti Air Force.

BAC TSR-2

As an eventual supersonic replacement for the 1950s English Electric Canberra bomber/reconnaissance aircraft (see section 5.11), the Government/RAF had begun to discuss technical possibilities with English Electric in 1955. Initially, the Canberra had been too small to carry the original UK nuclear bombs, but the reduction in bomb size in new designs meant that a tactical nuclear strike became a Canberra capability. Not all air strike requirements were "strategic" and, at that time, a nuclear tactical strike was considered a viable "last ditch" option to counter a Warsaw Pact armoured breakthrough in Western Europe.

---

3. Eventually, 1,242 Lockheed F-104 Starfighters were produced in four different nations, for West Germany, Italy, Belgium and the Netherlands, all supported by the USA Mutual Assisstance Programme to European NATO nations.

Early studies for a Canberra replacement aircraft eventually settled on 2,300 miles (3,700km) ferry range (due to UK worldwide deployment needs), Mach 1.5 speed "at altitude" and 690 miles (1,100km) low-level range. A crew of two was required, one being the operator of an advanced navigation and attack system and a reconnaissance package. The maximum internal bomb load was to be 6,000lb (2,700kg) including tactical nuclear capability, and/or four 1,000lb (450kg) bombs. Additional/alternative weapons would be mounted on the wing, as required by particular operations.

A General Operational Requirement (GOR.339) was issued to various aircraft manufacturers in March 1957, with proposals in response to be available by 31 January 1958 or earlier. Nine aircraft manufacturers chose to respond. After the 1957 Defence Review it was almost the only serious new UK military aircraft programme still in existence (see section 5.15). One of the responses had been from the Blackburn company, with an uprated version of their Buccaneer carrier-capable naval strike (currently in production for the RN in 1958) which also had nuclear capability. This was heavily championed by the First Sea Lord, Lord Louis Mountbatten, at one stage dramatically claiming "two Buccaneers can do the job of one TSR-2 at the same cost".

The GOR.339 requirement was exceptionally ambitious for the technology of the day, requiring an all-weather reconnaissance aircraft that could also deliver tactical nuclear weapons over a long-range, operate at high level at close to Mach 2 or low-level at Mach 1.2. A short or vertical take-off and landing (STOL/VTOL) from semi-prepared strips capability was noted as "a very desirable feature". This requirement was to result in an undercarriage which became a significant weight issue and a source of development difficulties when flight trials started, taking some effort to resolve.

Meanwhile, in May 1958 the RAF organised a high-level seminar called "Exercise Prospect", in two parts. Prospect day 1 was service-only attendees and classified. Prospect day 2 was attended by the Duke of Edinburgh, the First Sea Lord, Generals, Admirals, MPs etc etc. The Minister of Defence Duncan Sandys accepted an invitation but did not attend. Basically, the seminar addressed the inadequacy of the "no more manned combat aircraft" policy (other than that expressed in GOR.339) in terms of the British obligations to NATO and the question of "are there any revisions required" to the expressed GOR.339 requirements. The RAF had deliberately publically crossed swords with the Minister of Defence. (Succeeding UK government administrations were to ensure that no such high profile and public dissenting gathering would ever again be allowed to happen.)

The acknowledged supersonic military airframe technology leaders in Britain were English Electric, with their P.1B (Lightning interceptor pre-prototype) success, and Fairey, with their record-breaking FD-2 research aircraft. English Electric's response to GOR.339 (the P.17A aircraft proposal) was well favoured and was, in fact, not very far from the final design adopted. However, the "Integrated Weapon System" approach propounded by Vickers/Supermarine in their response was also well favoured by the government. In January 1959, the Minister of Supply announced that the "Tactical Strike and Reconnaissance" aircraft TSR-2 would be built by Vickers, working with English Electric, provided that these two companies merged their TSR-2 activities[4]. Over the next few months, Vickers Aviation Technical Director H.H. Gardner and English Electric's Freddie Page had to establish the final joint response to GOR.339.

From the various responses and further operational thinking, the RAF started to revise the requirements in GOR.339. Changes included increased range and improved

---

4. Merger of the two aircraft companies into BAC eventually took place in 1960, see section 6.1.

take-off from rough strips. Maximum speed required at altitude increased from Mach 1.7 to Mach 2+. Radius of action remained at 1,000 miles but required ferry range on internal fuel increased from 2,000 to 2,750 miles. (If fuel economy of the engines remained the same, around 10,000lbs more fuel would be required to be carried, which would probably require an increase in wing size, requiring more power to achieve the same maximum speed.) Therefore, if achieved, these performance requirement increases would result in aerodynamic, engine power and weight changes. After several companies complained that the goalposts had been moved, an updated requirements document OR.343 was issued in May 1959, to replace GOR.339. The new requirement had 114 paragraphs compared with the forty-eight of GOR.339.

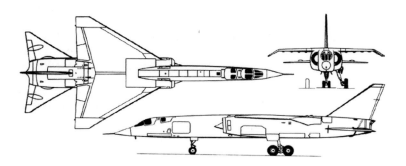

Requirement	GOR.339	OR.343	TSR-2 Spec.
Combat radius (miles)	1,000	1,000	860
Ferry range (miles)	2,000	2,750	2,877
Max. Mach No (High)	1.7+	2+	2.3
Max. Mach No. (Low)	1.2	1.2?	1.1+

The chosen TSR-2 Vickers-English Electric decision, however, remained in place, without significant renegotiation in cost and timescale allowed, despite the significant change in requirement to a "do everything" aircraft in bombing and reconnaissance roles and an associated cost increase was likely to ensue.

Given the vulnerability of the aircraft industry caused by the 1957 Defence Review and "no more manned combat aircraft policy", Vickers-English Electric did not overly protest or request significant time to consider in depth how the changes would affect the programme, when they most assuredly should have done so. This was not the last time such changes of mind were to happen in defence equipment specifications at a late stage in development of the programme. In October 1959, the retiring Controller (Air) advised the Chief of the Air Staff that the TSR-2 was now likely to cost twice as much to develop as originally anticipated in 1958. A worse programme management example was to happen some twenty years later, in the Nimrod AEW Mk.3 programme of 1976–86 (see section 8.2).

To achieve the required speeds, a simple small delta wing with 60° leading edge sweep was chosen, with no trailing edge ailerons. Roll control was by differential deflection of the all-moving tail sections, which combined with symmetrical deflection for pitch control. The small size of the delta improved the "ride" in higher-turbulence low altitude flight, at speeds up to Mach 1.1. For STOL performance, the delta had blown flaps (boundary layer control) along the whole wing trailing edge. With water injection into the engines for extra thrust, ground roll for a maximum weight (103,500lb) take-off was less than 1,800ft (550 metres).

The "Integrated Weapon System" contained electronic surveillance/reconnaissance equipment, combined inertial platform and Doppler radar navigation, supersonic (i.e. over 1,200 feet per second) autopilot low-level (200ft) terrain-following radar guidance, weapon aiming and weapon system management, using an innovative central digital computer control (with a pitifully small two kilobyte memory on hard disk). If the project had progressed, this computer would have needed development, to increase memory by a significant amount. It would still have been an extremely minute memory by modern computer standards, when capacity several hundred million times greater is commonplace in a twenty-first century domestic laptop.

Overall programme management was controlled by separate individual government departments responsible for each of various non-airframe system elements, with overall "co-ordination-by-committee led by the Air Ministry (Ministry of Defence, post-1964)", in conjunction with the Vickers-English Electric (BAC) team. The civil service proclivity for management by committee (and sub-committees) became an enormous burden on development decisions and change management, as the project progressed. Quarterly co-ordination meetings between all parties involved sometimes had as many as sixty people in attendance. At one infamous TSR-2 meeting, the chairman decided that far too many people had turned up, so he cancelled the meeting, with an order that only *essential* people were to attend the reconvened meeting. When the new meeting convened, it was found that *more* people were present than at the cancelled one! Co-ordinated technical development decisions could not be taken promptly. In other words, no single technically aware and experienced person was in charge of the total weapons system design, or the programme. BAC only had direct control of about 30 per cent of the total project. Effective overall cost management by the government (partly to prevent escalation due to RAF "mission creep" enhancements) hardly existed. Even the fundamental new engine choice was made by the government and contracted by them, not the airframe designer-manufacturer. The "Integrated Weapon System Development Programme" was not, itself, properly or efficiently integrated. This was a significant contributor to timescale and cost control problems for development of what was the most advanced combat aircraft platform with electronic navigation, weapon-aiming and surveillance capability ever attempted at that time, anywhere. Contract elements were delayed by the combination of government contracts department and the government project management in-effectiveness. For example, the first production batch of eleven aircraft was not formally contracted until 1963, causing factory preparations (tooling, space allocation etc. to be seriously delayed or done in advance of contract at the expense risk of BAC).

In the middle of TSR-2 design development, a serious attempt to uprate TSR-2 requirements to a strategic strike role was contemplated (by the RAF and the government). It was feared that the existing 'V' bomber high-altitude strike force would become ineffective due to new high-altitude missile defence systems going into service in the Soviet Union (see section 5.12). Just the contemplation of such a requirement change created uncertainty in the perception of the RAF commitment to TSR-2, which the army had supported for the tactical strike requirements in the

TSR-2 First Flight (Boscombe Down, 1964). *(Author's collection)*

event of a Warsaw Pact European land invasion. The RAF rethink may have been prompted partly as a result of the 1963 USA-UK agreement to supply USA Polaris missiles for a British submarine strategic nuclear force – eventually, the RAF was going to hand over its nuclear deterrent strategic role to the RN.

Given this vacillation over project objectives and the "fog and bog" of the project management process, it was amazing that the first flight of TSR-2 was achieved by 25 September 1964. If the initial flights could have started several months earlier, probably there would have been sufficient development progress which might have demonstrated the long-term performance aims of the aircraft were truly (if expensively) achievable. Overall, the aircraft itself showed initial promise of eventually becoming the basis of a fine, modern, long-range strike and reconnaissance package (but *far* more expensive than allowed for).

Cancellation: However, the 1964 incoming Labour party government had, in opposition, been openly unconvinced of the need for the overall level of defence expenditure. On 6 April 1965 the new Labour government announced the cancellation of the TSR-2 and a commitment to obtain an alternative, the USA TFX (which would become the General Dynamics F-111 aircraft). The new government believed that the rising cost predictions of TSR-2 were out of control and the change to the F-111 would save a significant amount, even after paying TSR-2 cancellation charges. Senior members of the Labour government of the day were actually keen to find a solution to the GOR.339/OR.343 needs, but more affordable than TSR-2. Defence Minister Dennis Healey's plan to procure the F-111 was intended to keep the RAF total strike capability relevant. The fact remains that British withdrawal from bases and operations East of Suez was eventually announced in 1968, following a sterling crisis. This seriously changed the TSR-2 long ferry range requirements *raison d'être*.

The Minister of Defence, Dennis Healey, made the following statement:

"The fundamental reason for our decision on the TSR-2 was the cost of the programme was out of all proportion to the aircraft's military value."

Sir Sydney Camm said of the TSR-2:

"All modern aircraft have four dimensions: span, length, height and politics. TSR-2 simply got the first three right."

Dennis Healey also said:

"The trouble with the TSR-2 was that it tried to combine the most advanced state of every art in every field. The aircraft firms and the RAF were trying to get the government on the hook and understated the cost. But TSR-2 cost far more than even their private estimates, and so I have no doubt about the decision to cancel."

As an example of the the lack of consistency of argument in political decisions involved in aviation, the former Conservative undersecretary of State for War (Julian Amery) at the time of the 1957 Defence Review (see section 5.15), which had actually cancelled advanced manned aircraft projects in favour of a move to guided missile technology, wrote in the *Sunday Telegraph* in 1965:

"There are jobs that missiles cannot do, they cannot reconnoitre enemy positions, they cannot be moved rapidly from one theatre to another, nor can they be switched from one target to another, only a manned vehicle can produce such flexibility."

Different versions of the cost of completing the TSR-2 programme abound. Government figures quote £750 million to develop and complete 150 aircraft. The BAC estimate was £400 million. In 2019 terms, these figures range from £13.5 billion to £7.25 billion.

The second Dennis Healey statement above contained several germs of truth about the technology and likely cost, although the company would have no doubt been responding to various RAF mission creep enthusiasms. The bigger problem was that the art of managing such a complex development programme did not exist within the Ministry of Defence, even though this was the requirement inherent in the concept offered by the chosen Vickers "TSR-2 leader". The idea of leaving the complete TSR-2 project in the hands of an independent *single* "knowledgeable, experienced and well-resourced full-authority Executive Project Management" had not even been considered from the outset and, even if it had, there was no precedent to follow in UK Defence System procurement. It can be argued that the Government's own project management ineptitude was the largest contributing factor to eventual TSR-2 cancellation.

TSR-2 cancellation meant some part of the recently formed British Aircraft Company (BAC) had to go. The axe fell on what had originally been Percival Aircraft (later Hunting) in Luton, absorbed into BAC in 1960. The ex-Hunting establishment (which had not been directly involved in TSR-2) was closed, due to the perceived need to preserve much of the ex-English Electric fast-jet design team in Warton as essential for any future military aircraft work. This was a painful but ultimately correct decision.

The next year, following the Defence White Paper, the Air Ministry formally decided on two aircraft to replace TSR-2:- the F-111K, a UK version of the USA variable geometry ("swing-wing") General Dynamics F-111 Aardvark, with a longer-term replacement being a joint Anglo-French new project for a variable geometry strike aircraft – the "swing-wing" Anglo-French Variable Geometry (AFVG) aircraft (see section 7.2). In a 1967 parliamentary debate on a motion of censure, the government noted that estimates forecast that the TSR-2 total programme cost (including fifteen years of operations) would have been £1.7 billion, compared with £1 billion for the combined F-111K/AFVG. These figures equate to £30 billion and £17 billion respectively in 2019.

The F-111 project in the USA was already in serious development difficulties (one example emerged as wing attachment cracks in 1968 in the fatigue test specimen, causing redesign, rework and retesting, another being the complex wing high-lift system which the USA asked experts in Britain to help sort out). Flight testing was to continue until 1973 and the end result was major time and cost overrun, with the aircraft costing twice as much as estimated when Britain placed their order. At the time of TSR-2 cancellation, the UK government were aware that there was a real danger that development, procurement and operations for the RAF F-111K version would have cost more than the likely actual cost of the cancelled complete TSR-2 programme. The initial orders of 1966 and 1967 for a total of fifty F-111K were cancelled within two years, in January 1968. An escalating British government financial crisis contributed to this decision. A fleet of fifty F-111K aircraft would have turned out to cost £450 million. With the £125 million spent on TSR-2 development and the TSR-2 cancellation cost of £70 million, the grand total for acquiring just fifty F-111K would have been around £650 million, equivalent to some £12 billion in 2019 terms (£240 million each aircraft), without including fifteen years of operations or the expected high cost of the (shared with France) AFVG development and production (see section 7.2).

To provide an alternative to the TSR-2/F-111K, the RAF had to settle on new HSA (Blackburn) Buccaneers (S.2B version, with RAF operational equipment added to the Buccaneer S.2A conventional weapon capability).

In the event, the Buccaneer S.2B proved to be a very capable low-level strike aircraft and remained in service with the RAF until 1994. The aircraft high altitude speed limit was less than Mach 1, compared with the TSR-2 Mach 2.3. Combat radius was less than TSR-2 specification but ferry range was good (demonstrated in a naval S.2 1965 flight across the Atlantic, Gander, Newfoundland to Lossiemouth, Scotland, in four hours without refuelling). In "Red Flag" exercises in 1977 in the USA, the Buccaneer outperformed *all* other low-level strike aircraft *and* the air and missile defence systems "defending" the practice targets. With autopilot control from Terrain Following Radar added, the Buccaneer might have done a significant part of the TSR-2 strike and reconnaissance job, but did not have the aerodynamics and power which could ever achieve supersonic "dash" speed.

The TSR-2 original operational requirement had not been properly satisfied, however. The Buccaneer was really a partial solution. It took a further decade for another aircraft development to match the TSR-2 operational task (see section 7.2).

Hawker P.1154 and the HSA Harrier
In a dramatic short period of cost-cutting in new military aircraft projects, two months before the cancellation of TSR-2 the still-being-designed Hawker P.1154 supersonic VTOL fighter/ground attack aircraft and the Armstrong Whitworth AW.681 STOL logistics/troop transport were also cancelled, eventually to be replaced by less capable but much less expensive alternatives.

This cancellation eventually brought the Hawker P.1127/Kestrel subsonic development VTOL aircraft into focus, as a potential less ambitious VTOL alternative to the P.1154. This was to lead to the HSA Harrier.

The availability of a suitable power plant was a stark problem for any proposed jet-powered VTOL aircraft – none had been developed. The eventual success came from a new engine concept and the willing integration of the engine and the aircraft design and development, and a combined airframe company/engine company team approach to the whole development programme. Most often (but not always), aircraft engine development precedes aircraft design, by a margin sufficient to ensure that at least prototype engines will have been ground tested and a single engine air tested on a multi-engined trials aircraft, before any flight of the new aircraft. The aircraft designer normally wishes to feel as certain as possible of engine performance and reliability before making an irrevocable selection. In the case of the P.1154, the aircraft design programme was almost in front of the engine!

P.1154: In the 1950s, NATO was interested in the idea of a vertical take-off and landing (VTOL) aircraft much faster and more potent than a helicopter. They were developing ideas on how to use VTOL ground attack and/or interceptor aircraft. The VTOL aircraft ability to avoid using airfields and hard runways vulnerable to air raids, and to disperse aircraft in camouflaged enclosures, or even hide them in small forest clearings not very far from a ground battle area, was a major attraction. An engine/airframe configuration to achieve this was not apparent. The NATO Mutual Weapons Development Agency (MWDA) was the means by which they hoped the technology development for this could become a reality. A NATO Basic Military Requirement (NBMR-3), for both a supersonic and a subsonic VTOL fighter, was issued in 1961. There were ten supersonic and eleven subsonic responses from the NATO nations.

Two joint supersonic winners were declared, as the HSA (ex-Hawker element) P.1154 and the French Dassault Mirage III.V proposals. British Aircraft Corporation (BAC) participated in this Dassault project proposal. International political disagreements over which was the better performer and which would benefit industry most was a difficult issue, because NATO did not have a budget of its own to procure aircraft, relying on member nations to actually respond "collectively" to NATO specifications. When the P.1154 was finally declared the technically superior proposal, the French proposal was withdrawn and was not heard of again. The German Vereinigte Flugtechnische Werke (VFW) VAK 191B was the winning subsonic proposal and a prototype was built, but did not result in a production model.

With the joint NATO idea moribund, in 1962 the British government was prepared to subdue any pretence of a "no more manned fighters and bombers" philosophy and gave go-it-alone approval for a detailed and costed proposal for the supersonic P.1154, as a common aircraft for use by both the RAF and the RN. The engine was to be the Bristol Engines B.100. This was similar in concept to the B.53 engine in development for the private venture P.1127 aircraft project (see below), but larger, and with Plenum Chamber Burning (PCB) to allow aircraft acceleration to supersonic speeds.[5]

Both services were initially interested but disagreements between the RAF and the RN, concerning role equipment and priorities, caused delays and confusion.

By August 1963, HSA was openly expressing the view that the range of changes being made to the aircraft requirements was damaging its potential for export sales. At the same time, the RN stated that it regarded the P.1154 to be a second-rate interceptor, and the RAF openly decried the loss of strike performance. By October 1963, the Ministry of Aviation was concerned with the project's progress. The Minister noted that the effort to combine a strike aircraft and a fighter in a single aircraft, and trying at the same time to fit that same airframe to both of the services was "unsound".

As a result of the inter-service bickering, the eventual P.1154 cancellation in 1965 was probably inevitable, with the publically declared reason of "cost". Cancellation of the P.1154 meant that a supersonic Hunter replacement still had to be found.

The USA twin-engined MacDonnell-Douglas F-4J Phantom II was the selected candidate, adapted for RAF use as a Hunter replacement, as well as for the RN as a DH.110 Sea Vixen replacement. The standard F-4J GE J79 engines (rated at 11,905lbf dry thrust, 17,835lbf with reheat) were replaced by developed Rolls-Royce Speys (rated at 12,000lbf dry thrust, 20,000lbf with reheat), to provide the extra take-off thrust for use on the UK aircraft carriers (smaller than USA's). The same change was applied to the RAF F-4M version of the Phantom. There were also changes to incorporate British avionics (which included differences between the RAF and RN operational needs). The larger engine required redesign of the rear fuselage. HSA were to be given the overall co-ordination of the total design changes but BAC designed and built the new rear fuselage. The RAF F-4M was conventionally armed, providing non-nuclear tactical strike (as a Hawker Hunter FGA.9 replacement), reconnaissance (Hunter FR.10 replacement) and close air support (Hunter FGA.10 replacement).

Initially, there was an intention to eventually buy 400 Phantom aircraft, for the RN and the RAF combined, but the development costs for the changes to the engines (and changes to incorporate UK avionics) raised the unit cost price for the first batch of 170 aircraft by a factor of three, compared with the standard F-4J. Because the government of the day focused on fixed price contracting, the development cost could not be spread on a later order of 230 more Phantoms and the total remained frozen at 170.

P.1127 and the Harrier: Sir Sidney Camm, chief designer at Hawker aircraft, had obtained board authorisation in 1954 to develop ideas for a supersonic replacement for the successful Hawker Hunter fighter of the 1950s (1,972 Hunters built). This resulted in a Private Venture (PV) by Hawker (as part of the Hawker Siddeley Group of companies) for project P.1121. By 1959 this had got as far as wind tunnel testing and completed major sub-assemblies of a prototype. Partly as a result of Hawker (among others) losing out to Vickers/English Electric for the TSR-2 contract in January 1959

---

5. PCB is similar to the jet exhaust fuel injection reheat process but applied also to the air jets from the "cold air" front nozzles, to generate the additional thrust for acceleration to a supersonic speed (see Harrier Pegasus Engine below).

and partly as a consequence of the 1957 Defence Review (no more manned armed aircraft, see section 5.15), the P.1121 activity was curtailed. Aware of the VTOL interest of NATO, Hawkers turned to responding to that requirement. This effort began life as the supersonic P.1150 but changing requirements had caused that project to become the P.1154. A subsonic VTOL PV study (P.1127) had also been initiated. The P.1127 (and P.1154) became "stalled" for a while, because the engine industry was pursuing two different approaches for generating sufficient vertical lift for VTOL. One was the use of dedicated lift engines and separate power plant(s) for in-flight thrust forward. Sidney Camm decided he did not like the idea (or the dead weight) of the dedicated lift engine approach, and sought alternatives.

Another (seemingly impossible) approach was directing part of a jet engine exhaust hot jet downwards (to provide lifting thrust for a STOL or VTOL capability). An alternative method for achieving directed jet lift had been conceptually developed and patented by the French engineer Michel Wibault.

In its initial form, the Wibault idea had cumbersome mechanical drives from a central turbojet engine shaft to a number of "big fans" (compressors) which could have their output air fed to the centre of rotatable "short spiral exhausts" (looked a little like a short spiral version of a snail shell), which could be rotated about an athwart-ship axis to point the compressed air jets either vertically downwards or fully aft, like a normal aircraft jet engine exhaust. In 1956 this idea was brought to the attention of Stanley Hooker, technical director at Bristol Engines. He also had been sceptical of the practicality of the use of lift engines separate from the engine providing forward thrust for wing-borne flight. He was therefore prepared to entertain the principles of the "directed jets of compressed air" inherent in the Wibault idea, albeit he found the proposed Wibault implementation "clumsy, heavy and inefficient".

One of Stanley Hooker's senior engineers, Gordon Lewis, was tasked with considering the idea in more detail. Through a series of interactive dialogues between Wibault and Lewis in Bristol, a new joint patent was applied for, concerning a turbine-powered engine with compressor bleed air fed directly to two rotatable nozzles taking part of the compressor stage air at the front of the engine into a directable nozzle and the usual jet pipe exhaust aft of the turbine providing forward thrust. The front nozzle motion would be synchronised to point down or aft, and all angles in between. This "compressed air jet lift" might offer at least direct vertical lift, to help provide a short take-off and landing (STOL) performance.

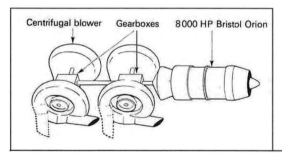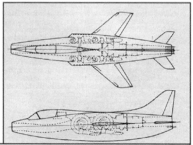

Wibault original concept for VTOL: "Gyroptere" aircraft, fitted with a British Bristol BE.25 "Orion" turboshaft engine in the rear fuselage with the shaft driving two sets of paired centrifugal blowers – Wibault original patent.

When a written request by Sidney Camm on 17 May 1957 asked if Bristol Engines could provide an engine for his VTOL P.1154 aircraft project, Stanley Hooker returned a short description of the Wibault idea on 3 June, as developed by Gordon Lewis, into a possible new engine. This was the first description of what was to become the Bristol Engines B.53. Stanley Hooker turned his attention back to some significant problems with the Olympus engine programme. After a terse message from the mercurial Sidney Camm (along the lines of, "Hooker, when are you coming to see me about your new engine?"), he and Stanley Hooker finally met face-to-face. They set Ralph Hooper (a senior project engineer at Hawker) to work with Gordon Lewis, to further develop ideas based on the proposed new engine, including how it might be integrated into a single-engined airframe as a lightweight fighter.

The Bristol B.53 (Pegasus) Engine: The jet-of-air lift concept had originally started to fly experimentally with the twin Nene engined Rolls-Royce Thrust Measuring Rig (TMR, nicknamed the "flying bedstead"). After tethered flights, TMR first flew freely in 1954.

Rolls Royce Flying Bedstead. (*Rolls-Royce PLC*)

More data about VTOL flight control was derived from the research aircraft Short SC.1 (funded by the UK government), which had five engines (four for jet lift and one for forward jet thrust, with the ability to swivel the four lift engines to contribute to forward thrust – very complicated). The SC.1 made its first vertical take-off in 1958.

A major disadvantage of a multiple lift engine concept is catering for a single engine failure causing uncontrollable asymmetric lift. Additionally, if the "lift engine swivel" cannot be engineered in an operational aircraft (rather than a research vehicle), the lift engines are dead weight after take-off. Vectoring thrust from a single central engine, between "down" for take-off lift and "backwards for forward flight", matured from the development of B.53 into a real prospect, the Bristol Siddeley Pegasus vectored thrust engine, to become the heart of the P.1127 and, thereafter, the Harrier.

The UK Bristol Engines company conceived the B.53 engine as a combination of existing elements of their Bristol Olympus (a 20,000lbf thrust large turbojet engine, as used in the Avro Vulcan nuclear bomber aircraft), combined with their Orpheus smaller turbojet engine (a 5,000lbf thrust engine used for the UK Folland Gnat and the Italian Fiat G.91 jet trainer aircraft).

Basically, the idea was that the large compressor of the Olympus could deliver air flow to the Orpheus compressor inlet, as a "supercharger" for the Orpheus jet engine. The large compressor of the Olympus would have enough "overkill" to have air to spare for two large outlet downward jets of compressed air just behind the compressor at the front, on the left and the right, promising a STOL (Short Take-Off and Landing) potential. An extra turbine stage of the supercharged Orpheus would drive a second shaft (concentric inside the hollow eight-inch diameter original Orpheus turbine-compressor shaft) forward to the Olympus compressor at the front. The supercharged Orpheus would deliver a hot jet exhaust for forward thrust in the usual way.

The design for the exhaust jet was soon to be bifurcated into two hot gas nozzle outlets on the left and right of the engine at the rear. With the cold front and hot rear air outlets both swivelable to "vector" (direct) their jets of air as balanced pairs, in front of and behind the aircraft/engine centre of gravity, air would be directed either downwards (to lift the aircraft) or backwards (to provide thrust to move the aircraft forwards). Control of all positions in between would provide transition from zero airspeed vertical flight (VTOL) to

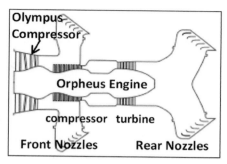

Pegasus Schematic, drawing. (*Author*)

and from high speed forward flight with no downward thrust. Pitch, roll and yaw control would be from wing tips, nose and tail small "down-pointing" nozzles fed with compressor air bleed, under pilot attitude control linked to his normal forward flight flying controls of elevator, aileron and rudder. Hence the "vectored thrust" descriptor for this method of jet propulsion.

The new Hawker private venture STOL/VTOL research aircraft project (the P.1127) was adapted to include the proposed Bristol "steerable" thrust engine idea. It seemed possible that the P.1127 could either be a technology-proving first-stage development vehicle for the engine for the NBMR-3 supersonic VTOL aircraft (the Hawker P.1154 as it became), or develop as a power plant for the NATO subsonic VTOL aircraft in NBMR-3. Following the cancellation of the P.1154, the P.1127 design, using the B.53, became the underpinning foundation of the HSA Harrier/Bristol Pegasus combination VTOL success.

With Sidney Camm encouragement and interactive co-operation with Bristol, the B.53 vectored thrust engine started design and development, mutually harmonised with the evolving design of the private venture Hawker P.1127 aircraft. In 1959, Bristol Engines was integrated with Armstrong Siddeley Engines, to become Bristol Siddeley Engines (under the same UK Conservative Party government pressure which caused HSA and BAC to be created). Under the 1957 Defence policy of "no more manned aircraft", government funding for new engine development for a new manned military aircraft would not be possible, so HSA and Bristol commenced actual detail design work as a PV. Proper funding for the B.53 eventually came from the NATO MWDA and Bristol Siddeley. MWDA funding rules limited their contribution to 75 per cent and necessitated Bristol agreeing to continue to provide the other 25 per cent as a PV.

The P.1127 first flight was in November 1960. After tests with several prototype aircraft, developing improving versions with improved flight control and ever-increasing engine performance, a viable VTOL aircraft started to emerge, albeit with limited payload.

A three-nation NATO evaluation squadron (Germany, USA and Britain) was planned, with uprated versions of the P.1127 known as the Kestrel. Hawker received an instruction to proceed for nine Kestrel aircraft in 1962. The evaluation by the three nations was to be for land-based operations, and (later) by Britain and the USN for aircraft carrier based operations. During this time, the RAF remained unsure of the value of subsonic fighter/ground attack aircraft which would be in front-line service in the 1970s but, when the preferred option of the larger and more sophisticated supersonic P.1154 was cancelled in 1965, RAF minds concentrated harder. For "Close Air Support" of ground troops from a forward aircraft deployment location, supersonic speed is not necessary to satisfy "maximum thirty minutes away from engine start to attack point" response time and the aircraft was often to prove able to do quite a lot better than that, clearly subject to actual forward base-to-strike distance.

Early in 1967, the government placed an initial order for sixty Kestrel, developed into a service-ready operational weapons platform. The service name allocated was "Harrier" and the B.53 engine had been developed to become the Bristol Siddeley (by then absorbed into Rolls-Royce) "Pegasus". The government purchase decision was probably partly based on the restoring of some credibility for having concern for the RAF defence of Britain and NATO interests in Europe. Alongside enough senior RAF officer support, they also anticipated favourable reactions from the industry trade unions, the public in general and the aircraft industry itself.

The aircraft handling of the transition from vertical take-off to horizontal wing-borne flight was difficult to master for some pilots. Natural selection by aptitude caused many of the most able fast jet pilots to be selected for Harrier squadrons, which started to convert to the type in April 1969. Tasking would be as a ground attack/infantry support aircraft. In 1968, the US Marine Corps (USMC) became very interested and purchased the aircraft as the AV-8A from the UK production line, entering service in 1971.

After the extensive licence production of the First World War de Havilland DH-4 day bomber (with USA Liberty engines) and the curtailed licence production of Bristol F2.B and Royal Aircraft Factory SE.5 aircraft, see section 2.2, and the 1960s Martin B-57 version of the English Electric Canberra (using USA licence-built Armstrong Siddeley engines), see section 5.11, this was to be the fifth time the USA had acquired a combat aircraft from outside the USA. The Harrier aircraft production for the USMC was sensibly (on economic grounds) selected to be completely by the originating company in Britain (HSA, with Rolls-Royce-supplied engines).

Later, a naval air defence/strike version was developed for the RN, as the carrier-borne Sea Harrier. The Sea Harrier FRS.1 was to gain fame during the Britain-Argentina Falklands war of 1982, "I counted them all out and I counted them all in" was a television reporter's line, direct from the "through-deck-cruiser" (small aircraft carrier) HMS *Invincible*, off the Falkland Isles.

A significantly improved version of the Harrier, the AV8-B, started development in the USA (McDonnell Douglas) in 1979, with a larger wing, increased fuel capacity, an uprated engine and more weapons capability. Britain joined forces with the USA in 1981, resulting in the AV-8B for the USMC and the HS.Harrier II for the RAF – 480 of these later versions were built. The RN Sea Harrier FRS.1 fleet was upgraded to the FRS.4 standard in 1988.

BAe Harrier II. (*Author's collection*)

In total, 824 Harrier aircraft (all variants) were built, operated by six different nations (the RAF, the RN, the USMC, and the Italian, Spanish, Indian and Thai navies).

AW.681 Cancellation and the Lockheed C.130 Hercules for the RAF

A STOL/VTOL supersonic interceptor/close support aircraft (the P.1154) was not going to appear. France had withdrawn their supersonic proposal and German and Italian attempts for the subsonic version showed no sign of becoming reality. However, a STOL/VTOL deployable logistics support aircraft for the STOL/VTOL armed aircraft had been described in a NATO Basic Military Requirement (NBMR-4). The British government had independently issued a requirement (OR. 351) for such a transport aircraft. In 1962 this resulted in the launch of the Armstrong Whitworth AW.681 project. The AW.681 long term aim was to develop a VTOL capability but STOL was the interim target. With VTOL developed, the 681 would have been operationally compatible with P.1154 VTOL dispersed operations (and with the eventual Harrier subsonic operations). The 1965 cancellation of the AW.681 created an overall operational logistics transport capacity problem for the RAF. For the industry, this cancellation meant the final closure of what had been Armstrong Whitworth, which, by 1965, had become part of the Avro-Whitworth Division of HSA.

The Short Belfast about to be delivered to the RAF was a large (four-engined Rolls-Royce Tyne turboprop) heavy lift logistics/troop transport, basically using the wing design of the Bristol Britannia airliner. It was not a short-field military transport aircraft with unpaved runway capability. It was really too large for other than strategic logistics operations and long-range transport. With only ten Belfast due to be delivered, the outdated 1950 Blackburn Beverley near retirement and the RAF

Blackburn Beverley. (*Author's collection*)

Armstrong Whitworth Argosy C Mk.1 with limited (compared with the Beverley) useful load and no real short/rough field capability. Without the AW.681 the RAF would become unable to provide airborne logistics support in all types of theatre, in Western Europe (NATO commitments) and in the Near and Middle East.

The only practical solution was to acquire the USA Lockheed C.130 Hercules aircraft, already in service with the US armed forces, which had STOL (but not VTOL) performance and could operate from semi-prepared strips. The first of sixty-six USA Lockheed C.130K Hercules aircraft was delivered to the RAF in December 1966. The in-country technical support to this American aircraft was awarded to Marshall's of Cambridge (now known as Marshall Aerospace and Defence Group), charged to liaise with the original designer-manufacturer Lockheed for all relevant in-service modifications. With the connection to Lockheed established, Marshall went on to provide the same service for the RAF Lockheed Tristar (L-1011) tanker/logistics aircraft in 1984 and the most recent second-generation Lockheed C.130J Super Hercules ordered for the RAF in 1999, alongside the C.130J project launch for deliveries to the USAF.

Maritime Patrol Aircraft

Pre-amble: In the late 1950s, there was an attempt to establish a requirement for a single maritime patrol/anti-submarine aircraft type, acceptable to all NATO nations. The requirement was described in NBMR-2. The twin-turboprop French Breguét Atlantic proposal was acceptable to some nations but not at all to others (such as the USA and Britain, who were concerned not to have less than three engines for long and distant patrols over deep oceans, such as the middle of the North Atlantic). For this reason (and industry-political issues), an all-NATO agreement could not be reached. Led by Breguét, a consortium of companies from the countries accepting the Atlantic (France, West Germany, the Netherlands and Italy) intended to develop the aircraft for their own use. The Atlantic first flew in 1961 and eventually entered service with NATO nations France, Germany and the Netherlands, which were parochially mostly concerned with the North and Baltic Seas and the Atlantic Ocean approach to the English Channel and the west coast of France. In 1968, Italy also acquired the Atlantic. The USA developed the Lockheed P-3 Orion, first flying in 1959. This was an adaptation of the Lockheed L-188 Electra airliner design, which had four turboprop engines. This was the aircraft eventually adopted by other NATO partners (Canada, the Netherlands and Norway) and several other nations.

In the UK, Air Staff Target AST 357 was issued, the RAF being very concerned to replace the ageing Avro Shackleton maritime patrol and anti-submarine aircraft with much more modern technology and capability. Time was short, because an Avro Shackleton out-of-service date of 1968 was being considered, due to wing fatigue life issues.

In response to AST 357, various alternatives were offered, based on the HSA (de Havilland) Trident airliner, the BAC (Vickers) VC.10 and 1-11 airliners and the HSA (Armstrong Whitworth) Argosy large transport, plus offers from overseas of the Atlantic and the P.3 Orion.

HS.801 Nimrod Evolution

The latest Shackleton version (MR.Mk.3) out-of-service date was to be brought forward to 1966, due to accelerated consumption of fatigue life. An interim aircraft was suggested in the UK, using the Breguét Atlantic as a "quick fix" pending the development of an aircraft to fully meet the requirements of AST 357. Almost as the aircraft contract for the "interim" Atlantic was about to be signed, the UK aircraft industry insisted that they should be asked if they could also respond to the "interim" requirement. Air Staff Requirement ASR 381 (actually written around the Atlantic's capabilities) was created and issued in response. Four UK responses, plus offers of the Lockheed Orion and the Breguét Atlantic, were received.

HSA made the winning submission, with "a Maritime Comet", using the ready availability of two new Comet 4 aircraft (nearly complete and still unsold) to use as prototype development aircraft and using some of the Shackleton MR.Mk.3 mission equipment as an interim fit. Because the Comet wing was situated at the bottom of the fuselage, a large pannier bomb bay could be fitted underneath without the need to incorporate a lengthened undercarriage (which would have needed larger bays in the wing when retracted).

A jet-turbine-powered aircraft with four engines, fast transit speed, a modest-sweep wing planform with good low-speed loiter potential to more than meet the patrol requirement, especially with a re-engining and a "patrol on two engines facility" to increase endurance. The Maritime Comet proposal was finally accepted, on 2 February 1965.

A fixed price contract of £100 million was agreed for thirty-eight maritime Comet aircraft (some £1.75 billion, or £46 million each aircraft, in 2019 terms), plus (quietly) a contract for three electronic intelligence (Elint) reconnaissance versions, with specialised (secret) electronics fitted subsequently by government agencies in the "empty cabin and bomb bay" of an as-delivered aircraft.

The Comet's four Rolls-Royce Avon engines were to be replaced by the more powerful and efficient Rolls-Royce Spey low bypass ratio turbofan, necessitating the wing root engine spaces having to be enlarged. A large pannier bomb bay was added under the original Comet fuselage. The RAF allocated "Nimrod" (The Mighty Hunter) as the name of the aircraft type.

Provision was made to include a nuclear depth charge capability and hard points were established on the wing and fuselage, for eventual carriage of externally-mounted guided weapons. The 1950s Shackleton mission sensor equipment would be transferred but new inertial and Doppler radar long-range navigation equipment was to be incorporated. The real time processing of acoustic sensor (submarine noise detector) data was to be passed to a new Central Tactical System real time (instant tracking) target plotting and display system, which used a 32k memory digital computer system which had been "born" in principle for the aborted TSR-2 aircraft development. On the Nimrod,

HS.801 Nimrod MR.Mk.1. (*Mike Freer GFDL 1.2*)

this became a "First" in airborne digital technology to enter service (and just about big enough!). The Mk.1 Nimrod entered service on time and on cost, in 1969. The RAF ordered eight more Nimrod MR.Mk.1 aircraft in 1972, to bring the grand total of Nimrods delivered to forty-nine (forty-six maritime plus three Elint versions, the Nimrod R Mk.1), plus the two Comets converted into the aerodynamic prototype and the systems trials prototype. The Nimrod external shape, including bomb bay, and wing changes to accommodate the Spey engines created the aerodynamic trials prototype from one of these Comets. The other Comet became the systems trials prototype but retained the standard Comet 4 Rolls-Royce Avon engines in a wing largely unchanged from its Comet ancestor.

Ex-Shackleton 1950s-era sensor equipment was to be part of the Nimrod MR.Mk.1 but, planned from the start, these Nimrods would return to HSA at Woodford for the conversion into the Mk.2 version, with the latest technology mission system equipment (essentially, fulfilling the original requirements of AST 357). The Nimrod MR.Mk.2 conversions started in 1975. A more powerful Central Tactical System computer system, a new surface surveillance radar, electronic emissions surveillance system (radio/radar signals classification and transmitter location), and upgraded navigation and acoustics (sonar submarine detection) data processing were introduced. Despite the "sophistication of the Central Tactical System", total numbers in the crew increased from the Shackleton MR.Mk.3's ten to the Nimrod MR.Mk.2's thirteen. There was more to do and achieve!

As an anti-submarine/anti-surface vessel and reconnaissance aircraft, the Nimrod MR.Mk.2 provided some thirty years of excellent capability to the RAF and proved adaptable to reconnaissance tasks over land as well as maritime duties. Unfortunately, in 2006 a total-loss fatal accident occurred during surveillance operations over Afghanistan. The accident was to the very first Nimrod aircraft handed over to the RAF in 1969, RAF registration XV 230. The most likely cause was ascribed to an original Nimrod MR.Mk.2 engine bleed air system feature, in juxtaposition with fuel leaks/spillage from the air-to-air Nimrod refuelling capability which originally had been introduced on Nimrods as a temporary emergency fit for the 1982 Falklands war (later, re-engineered to a permanent standard). In the 2006 accident, the starboard wing root area suffered a fuel-fed fire and the aircraft was seen to explode in the air.

After an intensive review of the cause of the accident by a government appointed independent QC, Nimrod aircraft were withdrawn from service in 2011, not to be replaced until ten years later (see section 8.11).

6.4 1960s New Civil Airliners

De Havilland DH.121 Trident

Due to the popularity and financial success of the Vickers Viscount turboprop airliner in service, British airline BEA established a preference for turboprop power fuel economy, at least on routes short enough where a pure jet speed advantage was not really a significant factor in scheduling aircraft utilisation (i.e. domestic and to and from Britian for Western Europe destinations). However, BEA issued a paper in July 1956 about needing a "second generation" (post-Comet) jet feeder-liner, to complement the in-service Viscount, to carry some seventy passengers in a two-class layout and with "more than two engines". The requirement was a recognition that future short/medium range airliners might not all be propeller-driven, despite a fuel economy advantage. Passenger perceptions might become "propellers equals old". This was stimulated by the emergence of the French Sud Aviation eighty-passenger twin-jet Caravelle short/medium range airliner (first flight 1955, in service in Europe by the end of April 1959).

De Havilland's own market research had led to a 1957 proposal for the world's first three-engined jet turbine airliner, with seating for 110 (mixed-class layout) or up to 140 passengers in a high density (single class) cabin layout. The engines were to be newly-developed Rolls-Royce Medway turbofan engines (low bypass ratio) rated at 13,790lbf thrust (the Medway would also be proposed later for the ill-fated Armstrong Whitworth AW.681 military transport project launched in 1962, see section 6.3). This engine would have its first run in November 1959. The three engines were mounted at the rear of the fuselage (centre engine air intake at the root of the fin). This permitted a clean wing design, improving wing aerodynamics and simplified the implementation of high lift surfaces (wing flaps). The project was the DH.121. Hoping to access the large American domestic airliner market, de Havilland approached Boeing in the USA to suggest co-operation (Boeing licence build) in the new proposal. Boeing listened carefully, visited de Havilland, took notes and added the de Havilland data to their own new jet airliner studies (which had started in 1956). There was a reciprocal visit exchange by de Havilland to Boeing but there was not a similar sharing of Boeing data. Out of these Boeing studies emerged the very successful rear-engined medium range Boeing 727 tri-jet, using a modified shorter version of the fuselage of their four-engined long-range 707 airliner. The 125-seat (single class) Boeing 727 had its first flight in February 1963. A later version was stretched to 155 seats.

In the middle of intensive discussions over the changing shape of the UK aircraft industry, Vickers belatedly became keen to compete for the aircraft outlined by BEA. They were financially committed, however, on the Vanguard turboprop (another project inspired by BEA, first flown in 1959). By this time, Vickers were also foreseeing the financial strain of their VC.10 airliner (detail design launch in 1958, totally based on internal PV funding, see section 6.4). Towards the latter stages of the protracted aircraft company group forming discussions (which turned into "forced merger" activity, see section 6.1) the Vickers VC.11 airliner proposal also emerged as potential business opportunity within the Vickers portfolio. This was to be an 80 to 140 passenger re-engined adaptation of the larger four-engined Vickers VC.10. However, the order for the DH.121 was placed before the VC.11 proposal could be sufficiently developed to be truly considered by BEA. There was really no chance that the UK government would financially help a second UK airliner almost directly competitive with DH.121. Without financial support to Vickers, the VC.11 had nowhere to go. In the event, BEA were soon to amend their DH.121 requirements with a reduction in size of the aircraft.

Avro had initially proposed their 740 design tri-jet to match the 1956 BEA requirement and Bristol had proposed their Type 200. Subsequently, Avro had joined with Bristol in the Type 200 bid, as part of the initial company "regrouping manoeuvres" following the 1957 Defence White Paper (see Section 6.1).

BEA had expressed some interest in acquiring the French Caravelle but this was totally unacceptable to the UK government. For political (maintaining employment in Bristol) reasons, the UK government actually preferred the Bristol 200 proposal but, in February 1958, they authorised BEA to begin negotiations to buy the DH.121. In April 1958 de Havilland slightly increased the diameter of the fuselage to accommodate six-abreast passenger seating (3-3, like the Boeing 727) and "froze" the DH.121 configuration.

Having failed to attract Boeing, de Havilland formed a consortium with Hunting and Fairey for the DH.121 project, using the old Airco name for the consortium. Both Hunting and Fairey had built aircraft for de Havilland in the past (Venom and Vampire).

In March 1959, however, BEA (and other airlines and airliner manufacturers) became concerned about a trend to high density seating becoming general. A reduction in the projected growth rate of air passenger traffic was also feared. BEA asked that their chosen DH.121 "ninety-seven seater mixed class, 111 seater single class", for which they were seemingly just about to place an order, be reduced in size to 100 single class seating. De Havilland were reluctant to comply but, with a relatively large potential launch order on offer, agreed. This resulted in accommodation for 101 passengers in a single-class layout and a change from the Rolls-Royce Medway to less powerful engines – three Rolls-Royce Spey – each rated at the time as 9,840lbf thrust. BEA placed an order (plus options) for thirty-six aircraft, in August 1959. First flight of the type (Trident 1) was in January 1962.

In the USA, Boeing considered the size of their tri-jet 727 airliner project and settled on a ninety-four mixed class passenger capacity. This flew in 1963 and was later available as a stretched version with a 155 mixed class cabin layout. Boeing and Douglas similarly considered the size of their slightly later new twin-engined projects, the six-abreast Boeing 737 and the five-abreast Douglas DC-9, which were to fly in 1967 and 1965 respectively. De Havilland recognised the dilemma and were already working on the design of larger versions of the Trident as the first flight of the Trident 1 took place. In the mid-1960s, BEA were actually to ask the UK government for permission to acquire the 155-seat developed version Boeing 727-200 but were "advised" by the government to pursue the stretched Trident versions.

From the beginning, de Havilland had included the provision of a complete blind landing (Autoland) capability in the aircraft specification, a major improvement to operational capability in European operations, not least into London Heathrow. This would be another "world first" in commercial air transport. The first Autoland with BEA fare-paying passengers actually in fog occurred on 4 November 1966 (after the first commercial flight Autoland in clear weather on 10 June 1965).

Hawker Siddeley Aviation (into which de Havilland was absorbed in 1960) built a total of 117 Tridents, the Trident 3 entering service in 1971 with accommodation for up to 180 passengers. Boeing built 1,872 of all versions of the 727

HS.121 Trident 1. (*TSRL, CC BY-SA 3.0*)

(varying from 125 to 155 single class seating) and Douglas/McDonnell-Douglas built 976 civil variants (90 to 130 single class seating) and forty-eight military variants of the DC-9. The Boeing 737 (much revised and re-engined) is still in production (2020) with seating for up to 184 in a high-density cabin.

BAC 1-11

In the meantime, Hunting Aircraft had separately conceived the H.107 thirty-seat twin jet airliner. After the Hawker Siddeley group bought de Havilland and Fairey (Aviation) had been acquired by Westland, Hunting were left holding only the small H.107, as a paper concept. When Vickers, English Electric and Bristol finally merged into the British Aircraft Corporation, Hunting was very quickly added to BAC. This led to a real project success, the BAC 1-11. Ironically, the first 1-11 delivery was to be the year of the BAC TSR-2 1965 cancellation, the consequences of which were to include closure of the ex-Hunting/Percival facility at Luton.

Newly-formed BAC adopted the Hunting H.107 idea and expanded the concept to fifty-nine seats, calling it the BAC.107. When the VC.11 airliner proposal (brought to BAC in the sublimation of Vickers) was finally abandoned, BAC stretched the BAC.107 idea further, to eighty-nine seats (five-abreast), with twin Rolls-Royce Spey engines mounted on the rear of the fuselage and the tailplane mounted on top of the fin (a T-tail, like the DH.121 Trident). The project was renamed as the BAC 1-11. It was not designed as a specific response to a declared particular UK airline need, it was aimed at the international market, including the USA, its capability directly competing with what was to become the Douglas DC-9. This was unlike the three-engined larger aircraft DH.121 (Trident), which had been inveigled by BEA in 1959 into shrinking to suit the immediate needs as perceived by that single airline, ultimately failing to attract the USA market, which became a Boeing 727-only province for that class of aircraft.

First flight of the 1-11 was in August 1963. During a test flight of the prototype aircraft (which, amongst many other tests, was intended to investigate stalling characteristics), the aircraft entered a stable permanent stall condition, with the tailplane blanked from the airflow by the wake from the stalled wing in front of it. This was a deep stall, or superstall, as had been seen on the T-tailed Gloster Javelin (see section 5.12). The 1-11 aircraft crashed because the tailplane/elevator on top of the fin was in the turbulent low energy airflow from the stalled wing, which prevented the tailplane from being an effective control surface to pitch the nose down, to remove the stalled wing condition.

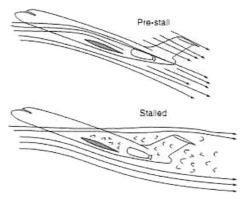

Superstall. (*Author's collection*)

In 1964, there followed a mandatory airworthiness requirement applied to all civil aircraft on the British register with a fin top T-tail configuration. The result was the introduction of stall warning devices, with automatic inputs to control column 'stick shakers' and 'stick pushers' (automatically causing the control column to physically shake *before* a stall started, followed by an automatic forceful movement to push the aircraft nose down if the pilot failed to respond). Initially, this involved all transport aircraft operating on the British civil register, irrespective of aircraft manufacturer. The BAC 1-11 incident prompted major reactions from all airworthiness authorities and manufacturers worldwide, especially concerning the Boeing 727 and Douglas DC-9 airliners. Superstall protection became a must-have feature of any susceptible aircraft, introduced retrospectively (and expensively) and in practice including mid-fin tailplane aircraft such as the Douglas DC-9.[6]

In May 1961, British United Airways ordered ten BAC 1-11 aircraft, formally launching the programme. In October 1961, USA airline Braniff ordered six aircraft and in July 1962 USA Mohawk Airlines concluded an agreement to order four aircraft. In October 1962, USA Bonanza Airlines tried to order three BAC 1-11. However, the USA regulator of aviation services, the Civil Aeronautics Board (CAB), denied Bonanza, on the basis that the airline would need subsidies to operate such an advanced aircraft (but there was a suggestion that there was a suitable USA alternative aircraft).

This CAB decision was seen as USA "protectionism"; there was a USA alternative aircraft, the very similarly configured Douglas DC-9, in design but not actually flying until February 1965. In 1963, BAC announced there would be two versions of the 1-11, the 300 and 400 Series. The 400 Series would have USA-supplied instruments and associated equipment. American Airlines ordered fifteen BAC 1-11 aircraft, with an option on fifteen more (later converted into firm orders).

The first flight of the DC-9 would not be until February 1965 and the USA CAB were unable to deny permission to use the BAC 1-11 by American Airways, Braniff etc.. The CAB had also denied Frontier Airlines, who instead went on to fly the slightly larger three-engined Boeing 727-100. Despite such obstacles, and the setback of the crash of the prototype, the success in achieving actual sales in the USA underlined both the market suitability and actual ability of the BAC 1-11 to penetrate the USA market.

For once, the British airliner industry was actually successfully ahead of the USA airliner industry. By 1965, a stretched version (the BAC 1-11 500 Series) was planned

but the programme was delayed by national British airline BEA taking time to make a firm commitment. The delay turned the original one year lead over American competition into a one year delay, which allowed the USA Douglas DC-9 and Boeing 737 time to catch up in development. The BAC 1-11 500 Series did not sell at all in America. As previously noted, Douglas went on to complete a total build of 976 DC-9 aircraft.

American Airlines BAC 1-11, *RuthAS, CCBT 3.0.*

Eventually, just 244 of all variants of the 1-11 were built, the largest (500 Series) version accommodating up to 119 passengers. Sales were declining rapidly by the late 1960s but, in 1968, six of the -400 series BAC 1-11s were ordered by the Romanian State Enterprise for Foreign Trade and, in May 1975 there was a further order for five series -500s. The Romanian airline TAROM became the first East European country to operate a new western-built airliner.

Despite Rumania's dependence on Russian air transport aircraft after the Second World War, the historic Rumanian aircraft industry produced Britten-Norman Islander aircraft (see later in this section), and gliders which were sold on the world market. These were built by Intreprinderea de Reparatii Material Aeronautic (IRMA), which

---

6. In 1972, the T-tailed BEA DH.121 Trident (fitted with stall detection and a stick shaker/pusher) on a passenger-carrying service flight was inadvertently forced into a superstall (deep stall) whilst the aircraft was climbing after take-off, by the premature selection (airspeed too low) of retraction of the wing leading edge high lift droop (lift augmentation and stalling speed-reducing devices). All on board were killed.

was reorganised and rebranded in 1991 to become known as Romaero. Part of the Romanian industry development plan was for IRMA to build another one hundred Britten-Norman Islander aircraft and construct parts for all future 1-11 production, such as wing trailing edges, elevators and stabilisers. This ultimately led to the Romanian BAC 1-11 agreement with the United Kingdom known as the "ROMBAC project".

In May 1977, a co-production agreement was signed between BAe and the Rumanian government. This intended to lead to the gradual transfer of technology and, ultimately, for IRMA to completely manufacture the BAC 1-11. A parallel agreement was made for Turbomeca to manage technology transfer for the Rolls-Royce Spey BAC 1-11 engines eventually to be produced in Rumania. Three aircraft were to be produced in the UK but assembled in Rumania. The first of these was rolled out on 27 August 1982 and flew on 18 September. The production rate never came close to the planned six aircraft a year and only one airframe was leaving the Romanian factory each year, 1-11 production in Britain having ceased. Only nine aircraft were completed and the whole ROMBAC 1-11 project collapsed when the "iron curtain" was opened, culminating in Rumania with a 1989 revolution which ended with the 22 December opening of a trial of the country's leader Nicolae Ceausescu and his wife (both executed three days later, on 25 December 1989). Various third party attempts were made to revive the ROMBAC project but nothing of substance was ever achieved.

Vickers VC.10

The 1955 cancellation of the V.1000/VC.7 (see section 5.6) left the USA long-range jet airliners well in front of the UK and everyone else, too far ahead to mount a direct challenge. The elegant 135-141 seat Vickers VC.10 (four Rolls-Royce Conway engines, rear-mounted and with greater power, using a 60 per cent by-pass ratio) was launched in 1959, as a "hot and high airfield" aircraft to a BOAC requirement for Africa and the Middle East, where very high airfield temperatures could seriously compromise take-off performance. Other niche operators in Africa also took a few aircraft.

The RAE aerodynamics expertise contributed to the efficiency of the VC.10 wing design. The VC.10 first flew in June 1962. It was later stretched to accommodate 163 to 210 passengers, as the "Super VC.10" (first flight May 1964); fully competitive with the contemporary Boeing and Douglas six-abreast jet airliners.

Until 2020, the VC.10 still held the trans-Atlantic crossing record for subsonic aircraft, at five hours one minute. It was a "fast and smooth" aircraft, well-liked by passengers. However, the January 1970 transatlantic Pan American service arrival of the Boeing 747 "jumbo" 360–400 seater wide-bodied airliner in the market place soon eliminated the narrow-bodied 707s; DC.8s and the Super VC.10s from much of the Atlantic air

Vickers Super VC.10. (*BAE Systems*)

travel market (see section 7.4). Before too long, the wide-body aircraft designs totally dominated long-range air travel on most of the worldwide airline major routes.

Only fifty-four VC.10 aircraft were built. In quantity, the main airlines of the world much preferred the Boeing 707, and, to a lesser extent, the Douglas DC.8 and, for a short while, the Convair 880 and 990.

Of all the VC.10s built, over one third were eventually modified into RAF aerial refuelling tanker/transport aircraft. In the early 1980s BAe converted nine ex-airline VC.10 aircraft to the aerial refuelling role for the RAF. The RAF later bought fourteen retired Super VC.10s of BOAC and stored them for ten years. In the 1990s BAe completely refurbished and converted five of these to the aerial refuelling and transport role, alongside adding an aerial tanking capability to the ten original VC.10.C.Mk.1s which had been supplied new to the RAF in the 1960s. The last VC.10 retired in 2013, the type having served in the RAF for forty-seven years.

The New Business Jet

Early in 1961, the new Hawker Siddeley Group member de Havilland started to seriously develop the idea of a twin turbojet-powered replacement for the twin piston-engined de Havilland Dove (see section 5.5), under the "Jet Dragon" title (shades of the pre-Second World War de Havilland DH.84 Dragon bi-plane). Range, speed and passenger comfort to outclass any equivalently sized turboprop potential competitor was the target specification. With a totally circular fuselage and a one-piece wing underneath, the physical size of the Bristol Siddeley Viper engines dictated a rear fuselage engine mounting. The rear engine made the cabin less noisy and left the wing clear for large double-slotted flaps for excellent landing field performance. The wing under the fuselage ensured no cabin floor obstruction and would allow a short main undercarriage. The unobstructed passenger cabin floor had 5ft 9in headroom (1.75m). Seating was typically arranged for six passengers in executive lounge comfort style.

Prototype build achieved a first flight in remarkably short time, on 13 August 1962. First production standard delivery was soon reached, on 10 September 1964. The type was to be progressively updated, re-engined, re-winged and stretched, over a production life of almost fifty years, the last aircraft being produced in 2012 by the fifth owner of the type design, Hawker Beechcraft in the USA.

The aircraft was manufactured as the Hawker Siddeley HS.125 but known for a long time in the North American market as the DH.125, where many sales took place.

As well as the usual small improvements (introduced almost on a regular and continuous basis in the business jet aircraft world), various significant upgrades were introduced from time to time, as a new series was introduced (nine times). An early special-purpose upgrade was for the RAF, when twenty aircraft were acquired by the RAF equipped as the Dominie T.Mk.1 Navigation Trainer. Other 125s were obtained by the RAF for

RAF 32 Squadron Dominie Mk.3 (125-700). (*Crown copyright, Open Government Licence version 1.0*)

the Royal (No.32) Squadron, where they were used as transports for Queen Elizabeth II and other members of the Royal family.

The major upgrades included more powerful engines on four occasions, two cabin stretches to eventually reach a maximum capacity of fourteen passengers, and a new wing design as the most significant changes.

The 125 is the only business jet to have been hi-jacked. In 1967, a chartered aircraft with the Prime Minister of The Republic of the Congo aboard was taken over by armed individuals and forced to divert to Algeria. It is also the only business jet to have been hit by an air-to-air missile, accidentally launched by a fighter aircraft of Angola in 1988 and hitting a BAe-owned 125-800 carrying the President of Botswana – one engine was destroyed, a fuel leak generated and the cabin depressurised, but the BAe pilot landed successfully.

The 125 also went to war with the USAF, as a specially adapted fleet of 125-800 aircraft. This version had extensive equipment installed for flight inspection (of ground-based radio navigation and landing aids, operated worldwide by the USAF at their military airfields). Designated as the C-29, the type served in the First Gulf war, August 1990 to February 1991 (Operations Desert Shield and Desert Storm).

Other military uses of the 125-800 are the U-125 and U-125A versions operated by the Japanese Self Defense Force, in a similar role to the C-29 (U-125) and a different adaptation (U-125A) as an air-sea rescue aircraft.

A sequence of ownership changes of the 125 aircraft project as a whole happened, commencing in 1993. In 1993, BAe (de Havilland type 125 inheritor-owners, after HSA nationalised in 1976) sold the project to Raytheon of the United States, although production of major sub-assemblies remained in BAe's Chester (Hawarden) factory in Britain until 2013. In 1994, Raytheon merged its Corporate Jets business with its other aircraft subsidiary Beech Aircraft, to form Hawker Beechcraft, when the largest version of the 125 became known as the Hawker 1000. Hawker Beechcraft became bankrupt in 2012, emerging from this state during 2013 as a new entity, Beechcraft Corporation, but having discontinued jet aircraft production. This ended 125 aircraft new build. In December 2013, the USA corporation Textron added Beechcraft to its portfolio, alongside its other aircraft company Cessna operating in the same city (Wichita, Kansas) as Beechcraft. However, the ex-DH.125 project was not revived, although spares and technical authority support are still provided by Beechcraft for the large number of the type still flying. In total, over 1,600 aircraft of the 125 type were built.

Britten-Norman and the Islander/Trislander

In 1953, two ex-de Havilland apprentices (Forester Richard John Britten and Nigel Desmond Norman) formed an aircraft company to convert and operate aircraft for agricultural purposes (crop-spraying). Having observed the rapid growth of the commuter airline activity, in 1963 they decided to design and build a shortish range light twin-piston airliner, where payload was more important than speed. They produced the Britten-Norman BN-2 Islander aircraft, first flown on 13 June 1965, able to carry up to nine passengers with a maximum range of over 800 miles. This was successful and it is still in small-quantity production

Britten-Norman Islander. (*Dale Coleman*)

(2020), with a larger airframe version with more powerful engines (the Britten-Norman Defender) being available for military/police/customs use, including surveillance and even armed missions. To keep up with demand, production and assembly was started at IRMA in Romania, initially assembling UK-supplied kits but eventually assembling aircraft from scratch. Over 500 Britten-Norman aircraft have been assembled in Romania.

In 1970, a three-engined stretched seventeen-passenger version, the Trislander, had its first flight. Seventy-two Trislanders were built between 1970 and 1980. Over 2,000 Islander/Defender/Trislander have been built. In 1972 Britten-Norman was sold to the

Fairey Engineering group, which had had otherwise ceased aircraft activity in the UK in 1960 (see section 6.1). Islander/Trislander production was soon moved to Fairey subsidiary Avions Fairey[7] in Belgium.

In 1977, the factory in Belgium seriously over-produced Islanders. The resulting cutbacks and associated redundancy payments in Belgium eventually led to the collapse of the Fairey group, which was taken over by the British government. The Belgian government bought Avions Fairey and transferred much of the Islander production to Romania. Islander sub-assemblies made in Romania were shipped to Belgium, whence finished aircraft were sent to the British Britten-Norman facility, for their acceptance for an individual Certificate of Airworthiness. More recently, Islander assembly was once again completed in Britain, with parts supplied by the original Britten-Norman factory on the Isle of Wight and using Romanian-built sub-assemblies. The Britten-Norman business in the UK was taken over in 1978 by the owner of the Pilatus aircraft company in Switzerland. Later acquired by Biofarm Inc. the B-N group was formed and the remaining Romanian production elements moved back to Britain. Biofarm was dissolved in 2014 and the B-N Group was declared bankrupt, but the business was taken over by the Zawawi investment company, owned by an Omani family.

After a dispute over access to the land on the Isle of Wight on which the company airfield was established, in 2011 the company started to move operations from the Isle of Wight to the British mainland, at Lee-on-Solent, Hampshire.

6.5 The Last All-British Military Fixed-Wing Aircraft

In 1964 Air Staff Target (AST) 362 outlined a new fast jet trainer to replace the Folland Gnat T.Mk.1.

The RAF had intended the two-seat Jaguar to be its fast-jet pilot training aircraft but this aircraft had grown in the design and development phase into a too sophisticated aircraft as a "pilot's first fast jet" (see section 7.2). In 1968, the ex-Hawker team at Kingston (in 1963 absorbed into Hawker Siddeley Aviation – HSA) began PV studies for a new fast jet trainer which would also have the optional capability of having a combat role added. This would have possible export potential as a light fighter, as well as a trainer. By the end of 1968, HSA were able to make a formal proposal to meet the original training objectives of AST.362, with a lighter and more suitable two-seat aircraft than the Jaguar. A revised AST.397 subsequently formalised the requirement for a new training fast jet aircraft based on the ideas in the HSA proposal. The HSA response to AST.397 became the single-engined HS.1182 aircraft project which was selected by the RAF in October 1971. The contract for 175 aircraft was signed in March 1972.

Power plant selected was an unreheated version of the Jaguar aircraft Rolls-Royce/Turbomeca Ardour turbofan (5,850lbf static thrust). First flight was on 21 August 1974 and the aircraft went into service in late 1976 as the Hawk T.Mk.1, replacing the Folland Gnat T.Mk.1 in RAF service. Eighty-nine of the Hawk T.Mk.1 were modified into T.Mk.1A standard, to carry

Red Arrows RAF Hawk. (*Author's collection*)

---

7. Avions Fairey was founded in 1931 as a subsidiary part of Fairey Aviation and had licence produced Fairey designs and other aircraft, notably Hawker Hunters and Lockheed F.104 Starfighters, in conjunction with SABCA, another Belgian aerospace company.

underwing air-to-air missile carriers and an underbelly gun pod for weapons training. In 1979, T.Mk1A Hawks were adapted to replace the Gnats of the "Red Arrows" display team (see section 5.14). The Hawk-50 export versions followed, having the dual role option of lightweight fighter and advanced trainer, with a greater weapons capability than the T.Mk.1A. Several upgrades and variations were developed from the basic Hawk T.Mk.1/50, including engine and other performance upgrades.

Sales to eleven different overseas customers were made before the Hawk won a US Navy competition in 1982, as the airborne element of a new pilot training system.

The USN version of the aircraft was designated as the T-45 Goshawk, to be a carrier-capable training aircraft. This required the Hawk to have revised wings with leading edge high lift devices, and to be strengthened for carrier operations (including a new undercarriage with catapult launch attachment and an arrestor hook), as well as being adapted to use US-supplied service equipment. The fuselage aft of the cockpit, the engine air inlets and vertical stabiliser (fin) were made in the UK, the remaining airframe elements and final assembly being carried out in the USA by McDonnell-Douglas (taken over by Boeing in 1997).

The engine is basically the same version of the Ardour as used by the Hawk 200 but has a unique USA designation. Of the total aircraft, 60 per cent is of UK origin. First flight of the T-45 was in 1988. All USN T-45 Goshawks now have the digital glass cockpit instruments, upgraded from the original analogue instrumentation.

The Hawk concept had always included a true combat-orientated single seat aircraft, capable of air defence/air supremacy and surface strike/close air support. In 1984 BAe started the development of the single-seat Hawk 200 light multi-role fighter. First flight was in 1986. The Hawk 200 can include air-interception radar and infrared sensors and weapon aiming, armed with gun, rockets, missiles and bombs (including air-to-air missiles and guided bombs). An air-to-air in-flight refuelling probe can be fitted. Sixty-two Hawk 200s were sold, the last one being delivered in 2002. If a Hawk 200 had been ordered in 2019, each would have cost around £25 million. (Note that a 1939 Hawker Hurricane would have cost around £10,000, equivalent to around £640,000 in 2019.)

In 1997 the Hawk was selected as the Lead-in Fighter (LIF) for Australia, some of which were licence-produced in Australia. India co-produce Hawk type 132 for the Indian Air Force and the Advanced Hawk is a recent joint venture between BAE Systems and Hindustan Aeronautics Limited. This latest Hawk had its first flight in June 2017. Other customers have repeat ordered the latest Hawk versions, including the RAF and the RN, who have ordered Hawk type 128 (T.Mk.2) versions. The T.Mk.2 has a digital glass cockpit and a significantly redesigned Ardour engine, compared with that of the Hawk 200/T-45, with 12 per cent more thrust and twice the service life.

Some fifteen countries currently operate Hawk aircraft and a grand total of nearly 1,300 have been produced to date (2019). The aircraft type is still available in production forty-five years after the first flight, although no orders are outstanding.

6.6 The Demise of Beagle and Handley Page Aircraft and the Revival of Scottish Aviation

Beagle

One of the several 1959–60 reorganisations in most of the British aircraft industry created British Executive and General Aviation Ltd. (BEAGLE) in September 1960, eventually combining aircraft companies F.G. Miles and Auster with the Pressed Steel aircraft drawing office, all under the ownership of Pressed Steel (see section 5.1). The company was based at Shoreham in Sussex, plus the Auster factory at Rearsby in Leicestershire.

The primary intention was to produce a comprehensive range of new modern light aircraft. The first was the seven-seat twin-piston Beagle 206, first flight of which was in August 1961. Beagle were eventually to produce seventy-nine. The RAF had twenty of these (RAF name Basset) as a light communications aircraft. As an interim, ex-Auster designs were also revised and Beagle made a total of 460 light aircraft of four different types, between 1960 and 1969. In the early 1960s Beagle also assisted Ken Wallis' business by constructing five of his lightweight autogyros. After Pressed Steel was taken over by British Motor Corporation, the UK government took ownership of Beagle in 1966 and refinanced the business.

The second (and last) all-new Beagle design, the four-seat tourer/two-seat aerobatic B.121 Pup, first flew in 1967. Beagle built 152. In 1968, the complete ex-Auster factory internal assets, including part-completed aircraft, were sold to Hants and Sussex Aviation, as a plan to create room for the new Beagle Pup production. However, the company was finally wound up by the government in 1969. Twenty-four more Beagle Pups were completed by various aircraft establishments after Beagle ceased trading.

The B.121 type was also assessed as an ab-initio pilot training aircraft and, as a prototype, the Beagle B.125 Bulldog trainer version flew before the company was wound up. An outstanding Swedish order for seventy-eight encouraged Scottish Aviation (see below) to take over the project. Eleven countries bought the aircraft, including 130 for the RAF. A total of 322 Bulldogs were built by Scottish Aviation.

Scottish Aviation Bulldog. (*Author's collection*)

Handley Page

The refusal of Handley Page to participate in the "mergers of 1960" (see section 6.1) had left that company isolated. Handley Page tried to enter the civil turboprop airliner market with the Dart Herald but without significant success (see section 5.8). A smaller airliner project was launched in 1965, for a twelve-seat twin-engined turboprop feeder liner. The project had promise, with interest from the USA and orders for twenty aircraft before drawings had been completed.

Scottish Aviation were to build the wings as subcontractors. Called the Jetstream, the first flight was on 18 August 1967. The prototype used the French Turbomeca Astazou XII engine. This was really not powerful enough and unreliability plagued flight trials. The engine for the type was soon changed to the Astazou XIV. In order to improve sales prospects in the USA, a change to an American engine was made on the fifth aircraft and a USAF order was received (but cancelled later). Including prototypes, thirty of the original design were built by Handley Page as the Jetstream 1.

A change of engines to the more powerful Astazou XVI created the Jetstream 2, but Handley Page went into voluntary liquidation, in March 1970. Handley Page was the first British aircraft company to be established by public subscription,

Scottish Aviation Jetstream T.Mk.1. (*RAF Museum, Cosford*)

on 17 June 1909, and had traded under the same name for sixty-one years. It was the last but two of the First World War aircraft company names to disappear from the British aircraft industry.

Scottish Aviation and a group of other investors took on the Bulldog project and also produced ten more Jetstream 1. The RAF ordered twenty-six Jetstream 2 (referred to by Scottish Aviation as the Jetstream 200 but as the Jetstream T.Mk.1 by the RAF), as multi-engine pilot trainers. Scottish Aviation (absorbed into British Aerospace in 1976) went on to develop the Jetstream design further (see section 8.4).

6.7 Shorts Last Independent Aircraft and Partnership with the Netherland's Fokker

In 1964, the first flight of the four-engined (Rolls-Royce Tynes) Shorts Belfast turboprop heavy-lift freighter took place. This aircraft had a maximum payload of 78,000lbs (over thirty-five tonnes) and a maximum range of 5,300 miles. The Belfast was designed for the RAF but only ten were built.

Short Belfast. (*Author's collection*)

After the Belfast, a successful small twin turboprop freighter aircraft, the SC.7 Skyvan, became the major new Shorts aircraft project. (Shorts also had a thriving missile system business, see section 8.9.)

Colloquially known as the "Flying Shoe Box", the ungainly square fuselage was an efficient transporter of many different loads. This utilitarian aircraft's first flight was in January 1973. With a maximum range of nearly 700 miles and, as a passenger aircraft, capable of carrying nineteen passengers, 152 Skyvan aircraft were built between 1973 and 1986.

Following on from the "Flying Shoe Box", Shorts developed the SD.330 airliner, first flying in August 1974. This retained the square fuselage shape but had a greater wingspan and a longer fuselage than

Short SC.7 Skyvan. (*Author's collection*)

the SC.7, and had more powerful engines. Affectionately known in aviation circles as "The Shed", the SD.330 had capacity for thirty passengers and had a maximum range of 770 miles. A version with a rear loading ramp was developed and eighteen of a militarised version became the Short Sherpa (not to be confused with the experimental SB.4 Sherpa). The Sherpa was purchased by the USAF as the C-23A (later, some transferred to the US Army and the US Forest Service), 125 Short SD.330 were built in total.

A further stretch created the Short SD.360. With more powerful engines, capable of carrying thirty-six passengers, this first flew in June 1981. A military version of this later development (the C-23B, with an air-openable rear ramp and inward-opening paratroop doors) was developed for the US Air National Guard. Sixteen of this version of the Sherpa were built, 165 Short SD.360 were built in total.

In 1962, Shorts agreed to become a risk-bearing partner company in a new project of the Dutch company Fokker, the F.28 Fellowship twin-engined regional jet airliner.

This was launched in 1963. Dutch Fokker, a German aircraft company (Messerschmitt-Bolkow-Blöhm), the Netherlands-German joint venture (Fokker-VFW) and Shorts were the risk-sharing partners. Eventually, the F.28 was to be made available in a "standard" version, and in a version with a stretched fuselage and wing, making maximum capacity variable between fifty-seven and eighty-five passengers. Maximum range of the lightest (smallest) version was 1,250 miles. Shorts took on the job of the detail design and manufacture of the F.28 outer wings and a total of 241 F.28s were built.

In 1983, Fokker announced a major stretch of the F.28 design, re-winging, re-engining and systems re-vamping, to create the 107-passenger F.100, with a maximum capacity of 121 passengers and a maximum range of 1,710 miles. First flight of the F.100 was in November 1988. Shorts took the same role as on the F.28, providing the outer wings of both the F.100 and the later "shrunk" fuselage F.70 version. Fokker built 248 F.100s and forty-eight F.70s (first flight of the F.70 was in April 1993). The F.100/F.70 project came to an end when Fokker became insolvent in 1996.

6.8 Hovercraft: Amphibious Vehicle, Boat or Aircraft?

The only certainty is that a Hovercraft is not an aeroplane! Strictly, it is a surface effect vehicle, included in this book because it is "something the British aircraft companies became involved with for a while".

Surface effect vehicles differ from ground effect vehicles and hydrofoils, in that they do not require forward motion to generate an air cushion to raise the vehicle off the surface. The concept was first remarked by a Swedish scientist in 1716. Several attempts to use the principle in a practical surface effect vehicle were made in the late nineteenth and early twentieth century. Sir John Thorneycroft (founder of Thorneycroft shipbuilders) patented a design in the 1870s, but a suitable engine was not then available. In the 1950s, Christopher Cockerell discovered that a simple ring of a downward jet of air flow around the periphery of a model created a surface effect vehicle.

The model consisted of two empty tin cans of differing size (one coffee, one cat food) one inside the other, with the resulting annulus supplied with air from a hair dryer) creating a downward air jet in a peripheral ring. He created working models demonstrating the principle and tried to interest the UK government, whizzing his models up and down various Whitehall carpets. The idea was quickly classified "Secret". However, no branch of the armed forces was interested. Cockerell later joked, "the navy said it was a plane not a boat, the air force said it was a boat not a plane and the army were plain not interested".

Eventually declassified, and with the financial help of the British National Research and Development Corporation and engineering support contracted from Saunders Roe, the first practical surface effect vehicle was developed. Called a "Hovercraft", this is a name trademarked by Saunders Roe and a name which has "stuck", to become generic for all such products, despite the trademark. The prototype SR.N-1 raised itself off the ground by using a cushion of air under slight

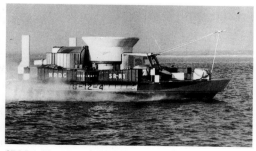

SRN-1 Hovercraft. (*Author's collection*)

pressure, contained under the vehicle by the peripheral ring from downward air jets. The lifting air cushion was maintained by a large engine-driven fan on a vertical shaft.

Forward motion was provided by bleeding off a small proportion of the lift fan air to blow past aircraft style vertical rudders, which could be rotated to provide steerable forward thrust using the bleed air. After eliminating some stability issues, the first flight (voyage?) proper was on 11 June 1959. On 25 June, SR.N-1 crossed a calm English Channel from Dover to Calais, in just over two hours.

Various improvements were developed, including a rubber skirt design based on a patent by Cecil Hugh Latimer-Needham (who had designed the L.A. series of light aircraft for Luton Aircraft in the 1930s, see section 2.8). With some further refinements, this made the craft more able to ride over waves and modest obstacles, and any bow wave would not be a limiting factor for normal operation in reasonable sea states.

As a versatile vehicle for land or water operation, several UK companies started hovercraft projects:

- Saunders Roe
- Vickers Armstrong
- Britten-Norman (B-N)
- William Denny
- Folland
- Slingsby

Hovermarine (solid sidewall hovercraft, with only peripheral air jets fore and aft establishing the air cushion) and Vosper Thorneycroft started a little later. Neither succeeded in establishing a commercial success. A government research company Hovercraft Developments Ltd. was active into the 1970s.

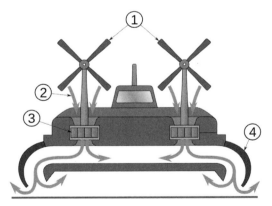

A Basic Hovercraft Schematic
1. Propellers (for propulsion)
2. Air
3. Fan
4. Flexible Skirt

Hovercraft Diagram. (*MesserWoland, CC BY-SA 3.0*)

Saunders Roe, by 1960 a division of Westlands, continued development from the SR.N-1 success, resulting in a series of hovercraft, including the SR.N-4, the world's largest hovercraft at the time (1968). It was used on channel crossings. Seven SR.N-4 were built, the Mk. 3 having a maximum payload of 110 tonnes, space for up to sixty cars and 418 passengers, a maximum speed of 80mph (subject to sea state) and the ability to climb a gradient of up to one in eleven (9 per cent), depending on total weight including any payload. SR.N4's first "flight" was on 4 February 1968. Hovercraft did get bigger; in 1988, the Russian Zubr-class military seaborne assault hovercraft was in service with a gross weight of 564 tonnes, able to carry tanks and troops.

Vickers Armstrong designed four hovercraft, the VA-1 and VA-2 being experimental, the third, the twenty-four passenger VA-3 going into a two-month trial service with British United Airways in 1962, as a commercial service between Rhyl in North Wales and Wallasey on the Wirral, on the mouth of the River Mersey opposite Liverpool. The fourth design remained as a proposal only. Like the original SR.N-1 before modification, the VA-3 did not have a flexible skirt, so could only operate in calm sea states.

A September 1962 storm caused the VA-3 to break loose from moorings and when being towed back, causing enough damage for it to be retired from public service. It was later used to trial hovercraft use as a mine detector by the navy (little actual draught a seeming advantage). It was blown up and sunk.

The hovercraft businesses of Westland-owned Saunders Roe and Vickers Armstrong were merged in 1966, into a new company, British Hovercraft Corporation (BHC).

Meanwhile, Britten-Norman formed a new subsidiary company, B-N Cushioncraft, in 1960, eventually designing six different hovercraft (of which only five individual machines were produced). The parent Britten-Norman Company ran into financial difficulties in 1972, which resulted in the B-N aircraft business being sold to the Fairey Engineering Group (see section 6.4) and B-N Cushioncraft being sold to the Westland-Vickers joint venture British Hovercraft Corporation.

William Denny and Brothers Ltd, a Scottish shipbuilding company, formed a subsidiary Denny Hovercraft Ltd. which designed the Denny D1 as an experimental machine. This was followed by the D2 "Hoverbus" as a prototype commercial hovercraft. This was launched (first flew?) in 1962. In 1963, the D2 voyaged (sailed/flew?) from Dumbarton to London, via the Caledonian Canal and the East coast of Britain, for trials and demonstrations on the River Thames. The parent company William Denny went into liquidation the same year and the project ceased.

Folland designed the GERM (Ground Effect Research Machine) hovercraft in 1961 but decided not to pursue business in that area (after being absorbed into the Hawker Siddeley Group in any case in 1959, see section 6.1.

A lot later, Slingsby established the separate company Slingsby Amphibious Hovercraft in 1988 and produced the SAH 2200 hovercraft, (seen in the James Bond film "*Die Another Day*"). Later, an American company acquired the SAH 2200 design and manufacturing rights.

The rest of the world were interested in hovercraft and formed other new ventures, in what turned out to be a niche market. As well as BHC, in Britain the Griffon hovercraft business was founded in 1976, eventually employing personnel much involved in the original Saunders Roe and subsequent BHC hovercraft businesses, the latter being closed down in 1984. Griffon Hoverwork Limited (GHL) was born out of the 2008 acquisition, by the Bland Group (an investment company based in Gibraltar), of Griffon Hovercraft Ltd. of Southampton and Hoverwork Ltd. and the subsequent 2009 merger of these two into GHL. Hoverwork included remnants of the B-N Cushioncraft activity on the Isle of Wight. The Bland merger united almost half a century of British hovercraft design and manufacturing activity.

Also Bland-owned, Hovertravel Ltd. is the only commercial passenger hovercraft operator remaining in the world, founded in 1965. Commercial operations started with Westland/Saunders Roe SR.N-6 fifty-eight passenger hovercraft. The GHL company now operates two 2016 GHL-supplied 12000TD eighty passenger hovercraft, providing a ten-minute commercial ferry service across the Solent up to seventy times per day, between Southsea near Portsmouth and Ryde on the Isle of Wight.

Griffon Hoverwork presently offer a range of hovercraft, ranging from five to 180 person capacity, used primarily by military organisations, lifeboat and other uniformed services. It is currently (2020) the largest producer of hovercraft in the world (by total number of units). An example is the eight fleet specially adapted 470TD, used by British coastal rescue service (RNLI) as particularly useful on mud flats and tidal estuaries.

Griffon GHL 12000TD Passenger Hovercraft. (*Stephen Foster for Hovertravel*)

At first, responsibility for safety certification of civil hovercraft, their design, maintenance and operation fell to the Civil Aviation Authority so, from 1959, "it is a plane" (or was). In 1996 this responsibility moved to be under the Civil Maritime Transport regulations for high speed craft, so "it is now a boat".

The UK military have not been as definitive! Christopher Cockerell's "joke" has remained true to life!

Chapter 7

International Collaboration, 1960 to 1975

7.1 Concorde – An International Joint Project

Introduction to the Supersonic Transport Aircraft

By the start of the 1960s, new long-range jet airliners were regularly flying at over 35,000ft altitude (i.e. in the stratosphere) at speeds of up to 90 per cent of the speed of sound (Mach number of 0.9). At 36,000ft, Mach 1 is 661mph (it is 760mph in the denser air at sea level), so high-flying airliners were flying at airspeeds of up to 595mph. The latest military jet interceptor aircraft of the day could fly even higher and faster, up to 60,000ft and almost twice the speed of sound, Mach 2 (over 1,200mph), but only at the expense of high fuel consumption.

The aviation transport world thought "the sooner long-range airliners can go supersonic, the better". This included both the large international airlines operating long routes and the technology-unaware general air traveller. If supersonic commercial flights could have started before the end of the 1960s, that may have been a successful strategy with a definite commercial return. It was not to be.

How did a British supersonic airliner project start? After the 1955 Vickers V.1000/ VC.7 UK airliner cancellation (see section 5.6), the enormous market lead of the USA large jet airliner manufacturers seemed too far ahead to challenge directly, by any other country. The UK Vickers VC.10 airliner launched in 1958 (first flight 1962, see section 6.4) was a "niche" long-range performer and not sufficiently far ahead of the market in capability to gather large orders against the established USA incumbents. The Boeing 747 and other "wide bodies" (see section 7.4) soon raised the bar further. In a move similar to the attempt to "leap ahead" with the Brabazon Committee Type IV immediately in the 1950s (the de Havilland Comet assault on the airliner market, see section 5.4), the industry in the UK started to study the possibility of a new, 1960s, "overtaking leap forward".

The Supersonic Transport (SST). In the late 1950s, it was felt that, to have any major impact, such a future aircraft would have to be at least capable of an either-way crossing of the Atlantic, at a speed ideally over Mach 2 (1,320mph at altitude), "with about 100 to 150 passengers". Such a speed would halve flight time and allow return trans-Atlantic trips every day by any one aircraft, without infringing on airport noise curfews by late night or early morning take-offs and landings. It could realise an improvement in aircraft utilisation, in terms of miles flown (and, therefore, revenue) per year. If the first supersonic airliner in the world was to be produced by Britain, there was some urgency, since at least the USA aircraft manufacturers had also "mused" on the possibilities since 1952 but had not yet planned a supersonic transport project.

From the late 1940s onwards, there was intensive British theoretical and experimental investigation into the fundamental aerodynamics of supersonic flight for large aircraft. More than one military aircraft capable of Mach 2 were in service by 1959 (the Mach 1.7 English Electric Lightning F.1 interceptor was introduced into RAF service in 1959, followed by the Mach 2 F.2 version in 1962). Wind tunnel model experiments and theoretical aerodynamic studies on larger aircraft were being carried out (or sometimes sponsored elsewhere) by the RAE and aircraft manufacturers. At the time, it was known that the drag at supersonic speeds was strongly related to the span of the wing. This had led to the use of highly swept or short span, very thin unswept wings, such as those seen on military aircraft like the 1956 prototype of the USA Mach 2 Lockheed F-104 Starfighter, or the planned Mach 3 Avro 730 supersonic bomber which commenced design in 1955.

Although the Avro 730 was cancelled in 1957 (see section 5.15), the aerodynamic research investigations were to have been supported by the Bristol T.188 Mach 2 research aircraft, 1953 design concepts of which had been converted into a UK government order for three. The Bristol T.188 (with a thin short wing of very little sweep) from the cancelled Avro 730 programme would eventually enter flight trials to provide more actual experimental data on supersonic aerodynamics. A thin straight wing concept would not, however, have sufficient fuel storage capacity in the wing for a trans-Atlantic SST. First flying in 1962, the T.188 maximum speed achieved was Mach 1.88 (co-incidentally)[1].

Bristol T.188. (*BAE Systems*)

Various configurations for an SST were explored by different parts of Britain's aircraft industry. An early SST baseline configuration looked like an enlarged Avro 730. The short span produced very little lift at low speed, which resulted in extremely long take-off runs and frighteningly high landing speeds. In an SST design, this would have required enormous engine power to lift off from existing runways and, to provide the fuel tank space needed, "some horribly large aeroplanes" resulted. Based on this, the concept of a transatlantic SST seemed to be either infeasible, or require the complexity and weight of a variable-sweep wing; low sweep (therefore large span) for take-off and landing and high sweep (therefore short span) for supersonic flight. However, after the end of the Second World War, in 1946, Dr Dietrich Küchemann, a German aerodynamicist well-versed in swept wing theory, had been persuaded to come to the UK and work in the RAE.

He soon persuaded another German aerodynamicist, a Dr Johanna Weber, to join him, in 1947. (They each became British citizens in 1953.) With others at the RAE they contributed much to aerodynamic knowledge, sufficient for the UK to become world-leading experts in wing aerodynamics.

Research at RAE in 1955 (Eric Maskell and Johanna Weber) demonstrated that a slender delta wing at high angles of attack generates strong separated flow vortices along its leading edges, which greatly increased the lift. This so-called

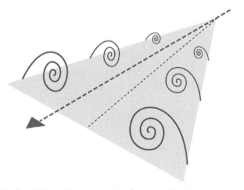

Delta Wing Vortices. (*Author's collection*)

---

1. BAC's Sir George Edwards later noted that "a major lesson from the T.188 was how not to design a high-supersonic aircraft".

non-linear lift gave a slender delta the possibility of achieving high enough lift at low speed for satisfactory take-off and landing performance, without the need for a variable geometry wing, while its slender configuration would potentially give it good supersonic performance. Küchemann recognised this potential of the slender delta.

The government established the Supersonic Transport Advisory Committee (STAC) in November 1956, chaired by Mr Morien B. Morgan, deputy director at the RAE. The STAC included ten aircraft companies, four aircraft engine companies, the airlines BOAC and BEA, and the two government Ministries of Aviation and of Supply.

The inclusion of the slender delta in STAC considerations was partly because the advocacy of Dietrich Küchemann had gained acceptance of the idea, as one of the realistic enabling possibilities for a supersonic airliner. At first, the investigation considered two versions of a supersonic airliner, a modest supersonic speed of around Mach 1.2 and a more ambitious Mach 2 or thereabouts. Such a two-step (or dual-pronged approach) might be less risky than a single Mach 2 project. The marginal advantage of Mach 1.2 (over the high subsonic speeds commonly used by existing jet airliners) might not be good enough, given the aircraft turnaround time at destination, the existing average seven or eight hour trans-Atlantic scheduled flight time and any night take-off and landing restrictions for reasons of noise.

The major aircraft companies in Britain were being reorganised during this time (see section 6.1) but the STAC remit included providing data to help companies develop and submit workable ideas for an SST. After a number of various options had been briefly evaluated, in March 1959 the STAC report recommended feasibility studies of two possible supersonic transports: a medium range M-planform wing aircraft cruising at Mach 1.2 and a long-range aircraft, cruising at Mach 1.8 minimum to Mach 2+. The Armstrong Whitworth part of the Hawker Siddeley Group of companies produced an M-wing planform design concept. A slim high-double sweep M-planform raised significant structural issues, such as possible susceptibility to wing flutter at high speed. Bristol Aircraft focused on the slim delta wing concept. Either a Mach 2.7 or a Mach 2.2 proposal for the long-range aircraft was requested.

One of the fundamental issues of supersonic flight is the dynamic heating of the leading parts of the aircraft structure, as the air is compressed and heated by the aircraft travelling faster than the air can "part" to let it through (the so-called sound barrier). Even the "sides" of the aircraft would reach close to 100°C and the SST would expand in length by several inches in flight. With sustained speeds of twice the speed of sound, the nose and wing leading edge temperatures would begin to exceed the sensible limits for enduring strength of even the best aluminium alloys, indicating that, beyond about Mach 2.2, titanium or steel alloys would be needed. Initially, a Mach 2.7 aircraft using stainless steel was preferred by STAC, but experience with manufacturing the Bristol T.188 steel alloy aircraft influenced Bristol towards a Mach 2.2 proposal, which emerged as the six-engined 130-seat Bristol type 198, maximum speed Mach 2.2 (Hiduminium[2] alloy construction). Bristol became part of the British Aircraft Corporation (BAC) in 1960.

The low speed handling characteristics of an aircraft with a slender delta wing was an unknown, mainly associated with the very high nose-up attitude required to generate the necessary lift at sensibly low landing speeds. The Avro Vulcan bomber, with a relatively thick delta wing of medium sweep, already used a high nose-up attitude on landing. The precise planform shape (and complex variations in wing twist for best performance at high speed) also needed further investigation. Partly due

---

2. Hiduminium is a high strength, high temperature aluminium alloy, originally developed by Rolls-Royce for the pistons of aircraft engines. Creep-resistance of the alloy is another major feature causing it to be appropriate for the SST wing and fuselage structure.

to the aerodynamic centre of wing lift (centre of pressure) moving aft as supersonic airspeed over the wing is reached, the management of the aircraft centre of gravity was a significant stability issue to be resolved. Some of this was to be achieved by advanced aerodynamic design, to restrain the amount by which the centre of pressure moved to less than two metres. The residual instability would be overcome by pumping fuel to an aft trim tank as the aircraft accelerated through Mach 1 and returning it forwards as the aircraft decelerated, in sympathy with the movement in the centre of lift. The optimum delta determined was the "ogee" reflex-curvature Gothic arch wing planform which was to become so familiar. The delta would have the necessary internal wing volume to accommodate enough fuel for transatlantic range.

It was clear that the slim delta aerodynamic theories would need validation by flight test. Both low speed handling and drag prediction validation at high speed would be needed. Two research aircraft were authorised in 1961, the low speed Handley Page HP.115 and the high speed BAC.221 (first flights 17 August 1961 and 1 May 1964 respectively).

The UK Fairey Delta 2* "straight triangular delta" was re-winged at Bristol with a new "ogee" narrow delta wing for STAC-sponsored flight research, becoming the BAC type 221.

BAC 221. (*Author's collection*)

*The Fairey Delta 2 had been the first aircraft in the world to exceed 1,000mph, setting a world record of 1,132mph (= Mach 1.73) on 10 March 1956, faster than the rotation of the earth surface at the equator (see section 5.10).

The selected configuration was a slim delta, of aluminium alloy construction, with a target maximum speed of Mach 2.2 (and not less than at least the psychologically significant "twice the speed of sound"). The estimates of timescale and cost were unusually high and an international collaborative programme would be needed, to share the work and reduce the overall market competition between different SST aircraft. The Mach 1.2 M-wing idea was quietly discontinued.

Meanwhile, in 1957 the Soviet Union had launched the very first space vehicle to orbit the earth (Sputnik 1). The USA suddenly became preoccupied with what became the "race to the moon" (committing to the Mercury-Gemini-Apollo manned spacecraft series of programmes, which succeeded in landing two men on the moon, on 20 July 1969). From 1958 onwards, however, the USA (especially Boeing) were also determined to try to launch an SST project. It took until 1963 before the USA president John F. Kennedy became convinced enough to allow state funds also to be allocated to the SST project. After the Anglo-French agreement on the SST, he also was reported as saying in private, "We have to beat that bastard De Gaulle" (Charles De Gaulle was the French president). It is noteworthy that the Boeing 747 "Jumbo jet" was a lower priority than a planned SST within Boeing, when the 747 project was launched in 1966. Supersonic passenger aircraft were expected to overtake and replace all others (including the 747) in the 1970s long-range airliner market (see section 7.4).

By 1960, the USA, France and the Soviet Union had all started serious studies for an SST. Before deciding how to proceed further, the British industry liaised with both the USA and the French aircraft industries, to seek possible collaborative agreement on a supersonic airliner project. The USA was very keen to have a maximum speed of more than Mach 2.5 and a passenger capacity of up to 300 passengers. Reportedly, they were also not keen "to give away or share what they thought was their lead in supersonic aircraft technology". The UK considered the USA performance target as "too ambitious, too soon".

Sud Aviation of France started to study a medium-range and smaller SST than Britain, with some sixty to seventy passengers and a range of about 2,000 miles, referring to it as "super-Caravelle". A politically inspired (and executed) "leak" of the STAC report (or parts of it) to the French government (inevitably reaching Sud Aviation) was effected during 1960. This was probably intended to allow the Sud Aviation supersonic team to become familiar with results of British research "so far", to help them to come to their own conclusions more rapidly and more certainly. Given the size, speed and range targets, the conclusion was seen by the British as "inevitable" from an aeronautical engineering point of view and the Sud Aviation/French government combination should come to a like conclusion, aided by having a supposed "sneaky view" of the STAC report. The effectiveness of such subterfuge might be challengeable but the outcome was, in fact, a "coming together".

At an exploratory meeting between the "Bristol" part of BAC and the French Sud Aviation, held in Bristol in the autumn of 1961, it seemed that two different supersonic airliners might be collaboratively created, with the same technology and significant commonality of production (*Quelle surprise!*):

- A Mach 2+ long-range aircraft with a slim delta wing, using six engines (long-range, 130 passengers) and
- A Mach 2 medium range smaller aircraft with a slim delta wing, using four of the same engines (medium range, sixty to seventy passengers)

In Britain, however, recent technical and sonic boom studies had gone against the Bristol type 198 130-passenger proposal and the smaller Bristol type 223 was now preferred, with 100 passengers and four engines. Bristol's Type 223 proposal was still larger than the French ideas for their "super Caravelle" but, unsurprisingly, the first substantive Anglo-French technical meeting in Bristol involved similar design concepts being tabled on both sides of the table. Meanwhile, the Bristol Siddeley engine company had started a dialogue with the French SNECMA engine company about collaboration on a possible engine for a supersonic airliner. Bristol Siddeley were already developing the Olympus 22R turbojet for the supersonic TSR-2, based on the Olympus 301 engine of the Vulcan B.Mk.2 RAF bomber. They were as aware as the aircraft manufacturers that an SST project involving a British company would need to be seen as an international collaborative project, from both an investment and a risk-sharing point of view.

Concorde

In December 1961 British and French government representatives met in Paris to discuss the whole concept of a joint SST project. After more discussions between senior engineers and specialists of both countries, the BAC and Sud Aviation company senior designers met in a closed three-day session in Paris in January 1962. Out of this session emerged joint project design proposals for two different versions of the SST, using much common structure, the same engines and inherent technology, except for a larger (longer) fuselage and bigger wing for the long-range 100-passenger version compared with the French medium range sixty to seventy passenger version. In the event, this smaller version was not to be pursued, mainly for lack of a market emerging.

The four engines would be a major upgrade of the Olympus turbo jet as used on the Vulcan B.Mk.2 bomber, to provide more thrust, with jet exhaust reheat useable for both take-off and for acceleration through the transitional drag rise, as the extra thrust needed to make the transition from subsonic to supersonic flight.

Table 7.1 below shows the engine performance enhancement finally achieved:

Table 7.1: Bristol Siddeley Olympus Turbojet Upgrade, Vulcan B.Mk.2 to Concorde.

	Vulcan Olympus 301	Concorde Olympus 593
Maximum Thrust	20,000lbf	34,000lbf (without reheat) 38,050lbf (with reheat)
Pressure Ratio	13:1	15:1
Length ("bare engine")	155.33in	159in
Diameter	44.5in	47.75in
Weight	4,290lb	5,600lb
Low Pressure Compressor	6 stage	7 stage
High Pressure Compressor	7 stage	7 stage

This represents an un-reheated thrust increase of 50 per cent and an 80 per cent increase in maximum thrust, for an 18 per cent increase in volumetric size and a 72 per cent increase in weight. In reality, it was largely to be a resdesign, development of which eventually consumed well over one third of total development costs for the Concorde as a whole.

The next few months were used to flesh out the whole project proposal, to the point where the French and British governments were prepared to commit. This was enshrined in a government-to-government treaty, signed in London on 29 November 1962. The treaty committed the go-ahead of a joint SST project and the terms included provision that, should either party withdraw, the penalty would be that all costs of the other party up to and including six months after the withdrawal date would be paid by the withdrawing party, a clause instigated at the request of the British government. Notwithstanding, the British government tried to pull out in 1968, but were baulked by French insistence on the use of this clause "in full" and the likely damage to prestige.

Since the bulk of the work on the engines would be with Bristol Siddeley, the other work was apportioned such that an equal share of the overall total was allocated to each of the two countries. The work share agreed allocated responsibility as follows:

British Aircraft Corporation	Sud Aviation
Nose, Cockpit and Forward Fuselage	Wing Centre Section/Integral Fuselage
Tail Fuselage, Fin and Rudder	Wing
Engine Intake and Engine Installation	Rear Fuselage
Rolls-Royce (took over B.Siddely 1966)	**SNECMA**
Engine	Engine Exhaust

The undercarriage and other systems responsibilities were also allocated on a national work-share basis.

The public announcement of the Anglo-French SST treaty set off something of a wave of panic in the USA industry, as it was then widely believed that almost all future long-range commercial aircraft eventually would be supersonic. It looked like the Europeans would start off with a huge lead. The director of the USA Central Intelligence Agency (and a former aerospace industry executive) expressed strong reservations to the British Prime Minister and the Minister of Defence, with a warning to the effect that, "the risks the United Kingdom are taking are far too great, you don't know what you are getting into". Dog in the manger? It also soon became known that the Soviet Union was also working on a design conceptually similar to the BAC-Sud Aviation project. The president of the USA announced the National Supersonic Transport programme, in June 1963. At first, the USA approach was focused on a Mach 3 aircraft with USA trans-continental range only, in an attempt to shorten the development programme but abandoning the trans-Atlantic competition to the British/French SST. However, in 1967 the USA selected the Mach 2.7 Boeing 2707 SST, with a maximum passenger capacity of 270 and transatlantic range.

As well as project cost growth issues, a vociferous (but not, at first, technically knowledgeable) "anti-SST sonic boom lobby" was starting to grow, the project eventually becoming a political football in the USA and elsewhere. Mainly due to cost and timescale growth predictions, the USA SST programme was finally cancelled in 1971, when the USA government discontinued funding, with two incomplete prototypes under construction after $1.035 billion had been spent[3] (equivalent to some $8 billion in 2019 dollars).

The first truly international joint production aircraft project (not just licence build) had been the Breguét Atlantic maritime patrol aircraft, first flown in 1961 (see section 5.4 – Nimrod). After a silly squabble over spelling, in 1968 the Anglo-French SST was eventually named "Concorde". It was to be the first truly international joint design *and* development *and* test *and* production *and* certification civil aircraft project. The final product specification was for a 100-passenger slender delta aircraft with trans-Atlantic range (London or Paris to New York at a cruising speed of Mach 2.04 (1,354mph).

A significant issue was that there were, at that time, no airworthiness regulations (in the world) which covered the safety, certification and operating regulations for a Mach 2 civil airliner, which would be flying over half-as-high again as the then current generation of high-flying jet airliners. Uniquely new civil certification rules and required regulatory test demonstrations for this very new type of civil transport aircraft had to be defined, before detailed project planning and definition of realistic and appropriate technical demonstration requirements could take place. The SST would be able to fly higher than, and cruise as fast as, the latest military interceptor aircraft "dash intercept speed" just entering service with either the RAF or French Air Force (*Armée de l'Air*) at the beginning of the 1960s. The SST would have to be able to maintain this speed without the use of fuel-guzzling engine exhaust reheat, if it was to fly non-stop across the Atlantic Ocean. Concorde would be the only civil aircraft to use the erstwhile military-only technique of engine exhaust reheat (but only for the high drag-rise phase during acceleration from subsonic to supersonic flight and for take-off).

The new technologies used on Concorde eventually were to include multi-channel fly-by-wire (analogue) flight control, 30 per cent higher pressure hydraulic power systems than previously used on civil aircraft, redesign of emergency oxygen equipment and facilities for use in the event of cabin pressure loss at 60,000 feet altitude, and the

---

3. Coupled with the ending of other USA military projects and a downturn in the commercial airliner market (temporary, due to fuel price rises as a consequence of the Arab-Israeli six-day war of 1967), Boeing were extremely vulnerable and laid off over 60,000 personnel. The 2707 became known as "the airplane that almost ate Seattle" (home town of Boeing). An air transport revival and the 747 "Jumbo Jet" into service in January 1970 (see section 7.4) eventually revived Boeing's fortunes.

first real-time digital computer control of anything on a civil aircraft, the engine intake (the control of the engine itself was electrical analogue).

Supersonic flight obviously involves supersonic air passing into the engine intake. The intake needs to slow down the air to below high subsonic BEFORE it enters the first stage of the engine compressor. The aerodynamics and associated gas (air) thermodynamics of the Concorde supersonic convergent-divergent engine intake (i.e. a large nozzle) achieves this. Precise control of the "nozzle" dimensions is necessary, if this is to be achieved efficiently. The intake control involves adjustable internal intake "ramps" to adjust the precise dimensions of the "nozzle", in accordance with airspeed, intake air temperature and pressure and demanded engine speed, ensuring shock waves do not reach the first stage of the engine compressor. This is the ONLY reason that the Anglo-French SST could hope for the necessary fuel economy to achieve transatlantic range, because (perhaps counter-intuitively) three-quarters of the thrust in Concorde supersonic cruising flight comes from the intake, not the jet exhaust. This "supercruise" (sustained supersonic cruise without engine exhaust reheat) at Mach 2+ has not been available on any aircraft other than Concorde, before or since (a few modern military aircraft can now "supercruise", but not in operations at speeds as high as Mach 2). The use of continuous reheat during cruise would have had a major adverse impact on fuel consumption, and on service life of the hot parts of the engine. After many development flight tests had resulted in several redesigns of the analogue computer system control of the intake ramps (safely, and balanced across all four engines), the radical decision was to accept that the multi-channel analogue computer control had to be replaced with multi-channel digital computer control, to carry out the task with the necessary precision, safety of operation and reliability. Given the relatively low level sophistication and miniaturisation of real-time digital computer control technology available in the mid-1960s, this was a bold but essential decision, involving major redesign and test proving but, without it, Concorde would have fallen well short of achieving Paris or London to New York range.

Fuel also cooled engine, hydraulic and generator drive oils, and the air conditioning air supply. At high temperatures and low ambient pressures, such as experienced by Concorde when cruising at Mach 2 as high as 60,000ft, conventional aviation fuel (kerosene) may be both highly supersaturated with dissolved air and near its boiling point. In-flight special measures were taken to de-aerate fuel in tanks not being used, preventing loss of fuel due to boiling-off, high transient pressures in the tank and loss of fuel due to a too rapid de-aeration of the fuel, and to ensure that the tank pumps would continuously provide the required pumping performance.

In the 1960s, the Soviet Union were also developing a supersonic transport, the Tupolev Tu-144. Although this project was not kept secret (technical liaison with the Concorde team did occur) the first flight occurred on 31 December 1968, surprising the rest of the world. The Tu-144 was not as technically sophisticated as Concorde but it was the first SST to fly. It was a "brute force" solution to an SST. During development it proved to be short of range, needed reheat for sustained supersonic flight, and was not really reliable enough for passenger service. Its reputation suffered badly when a development version crashed during a demonstration at the Paris air show (Le Bourget airport), on 3 June 1973. Thirteen production standard Tu-144 aircraft were completed. Between 1975 and 1978 the Tu-144 completed a total of fifty-five commercial passenger flights and forty-four more freight-only flights, all within the Soviet Union borders, before the type was withdrawn from commercial service.

The first of two Concorde pre-prototypes flew on 2 March 1969. As these revealed the actual characteristics of the first real supersonic airliner during testing, data was created to reveal the necessary improvements which could be incorporated into two prototype aircraft, the first of which flew on 17 December 1971.

The original world market size estimates for production aircraft had ranged between 120 and 500 aircraft, aimed at the "premium" traveller (especially across the Atlantic). A businessman would be able to take a Concorde flight from London at 9.00am GMT and land in New York by 8.00am EST (travelling "faster than the sun"). He/she might take off on the return the same day at 1.00pm EST and land back in London by 9.00pm GMT, having completed in one day perhaps four hours face-to-face business whilst in New York. This was well before i-phones and the internet became available! By the time of Concorde's first flight in 1969, the project had secured seventy-six "provisional orders" from sixteen world airlines.

It was thought that regular supersonic "boom" overpressure noise (shock wave, transmitted to ground level) from high-flying large supersonic aircraft would not cause any damage or even annoyance on the ground. However, test flights with military aircraft in the USA suggested that regular "sonic booms" from large aircraft (such as Concorde) might not be acceptable, to the extent that, by 1964, it was becoming clear that approval for regular supersonic large airliner overland flight might not be granted. The anti-SST lobby pressure became sufficient to cause the USA Congress and Federal Aviation Administration (FAA) to implement a ban on any supersonic civil flights over USA territory (such a ban was later adopted in Europe and elsewhere). There would not be a transatlantic (or transpacific) problem, but such restrictions would seriously affect the operations of many potential Concorde operators, because flying the aircraft subsonically for long periods would incur a large (fuel consumption) penalty and reduce maximum range dramatically, not to say almost completely negating the speed advantage. Consequently, it had to be tacitly accepted (before ever going into service) that the project would be likely to be a commercial failure.

The protracted development timescale which had eventually emerged allowed an extremely vociferous anti-Concorde lobby to develop, largely on the grounds of noise near airports, and a good deal of jealousy from parts of the USA after the USA SST programme had failed to deliver. The most difficult obstacle was the hostility of the Port of New York on unsubstantiated "environmental grounds". This was eventually overcome by actual take-off and landing demonstrations which the Port authority only permitted after a legal wrangle in the USA courts. All this "anti", and accepting that overland supersonic commercial flying would probably not be permitted anywhere in the west, caused all Concorde orders to be cancelled.

In the event, the total project costs had to be written off by the British and French governments, allowing the fourteen production standard aircraft actually finished to enter service with BOAC and Air France at a give-away initial price of some £20 million each. The first Concorde revenue flights took place on 21 January 1976. The British

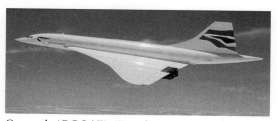

Concorde (G-BOAF). (*British Airways*)

and French national airlines went on to use the aircraft as their "flagships", with "VIP" treatment of all passengers, undoubtedly enhancing airline image and reputation because of this uniquely marketable "vision of the future" aircraft. Inventive "Mach 2 experience" flights over the Bay of Biscay and the very high premiums on fares between Europe and the USA enabled the undoubtedly high operating costs to be more than covered and profits were made for most of the aircrafts' thirty years of service. Withdrawn from service by the end of 2002, the last Concorde flight was to land at Filton (Bristol, UK) on 26 November 2003, to become a museum piece in the place where the project was born. The BA Concordes flew for an average of over 21,000 hours each and the Air France aircraft flew for an average of nearly 13,000 hours each.

Concorde programme costs are difficult to pin down exactly, partly because all of the costs of the extensive STAC-sponsored research and the French (ONERA and Sud Aviation) research prior to launch are not likely to have been included in the figures. Various estimates were made for the expected development effort. These varied from a predicted £75–£95 million in 1959 (STAC report for a Mach 2 trans-Atlantic range aircraft), to aeronautical technical media reports and government department revised final cost estimates as the aircraft was just about to enter service in 1979. The numbers varied between £1,300 and £2,000 million for the complete programme "to that date". Prior to abandoning efforts to sell the aircraft to any airline, unit sale prices of between $33.8 million (1972) and £23 million (1977) were also quoted.

Estimating "somewhere around the 1970s values" and escalating for inflation since, the post-launch fourteen-year development programme costs of £1 billion would equate to perhaps £10 billion to £11 billion in 2019 (14 billion US dollars, after accounting for historical exchange rate fluctuations and inflation). The 1959 STAC development cost estimate of £95 million would be equivalent to around £2.2 billion in 2019. Priot to abandoning efforts to sell the aircraft to any airline, the potential production cost (i.e. not including development cost recovery or profit) was calculated in 1974 at around £35 million each for the fourteen aircraft eventually delivered to national airlines BA and Air France, equivalent to over £400 million (500 million US dollars) each in 2019 terms. By way of comparison, modern 250-to-350 seat widebody airliners, such as the Airbus A.350XWB or the Boeing 787, have a 2019 list sale price of between 320 million and 370 million US dollars (depending on variant).

In the USA, NASA has a "Quiet Supersonic Technology" research aircraft being built by Lockheed Martin, (the X-59, labelled QueSST). This aircraft is designed to reduce sonic boom noise as heard on the ground and is due to fly in 2021. A sound economic case for a Concorde replacement has, however, so far failed to materialise. There are a number of start-up triers which are attempting to complete investigative steps towards creating a supersonic civil passenger-carrying business jet, and even a fifty-seat supersonic airliner. Boom Supersonics in the USA have a planned 2020 first flight technology demonstrator XB-1, as a technology proving step towards the Boom Supersonics "Overture" Mach 2.2 airliner. This has attracted "reserved position interest" from Japan Airlines and Britain's Virgin Group. Technology hurdles notwithstanding, the commercial business case for a new supersonic civil transport remains "unproven" but, in the eyes of those concerned, perhaps doable.

The lasting industrial legacy of Concorde is the international collaboration principle which eventually led to the creation of the Airbus business (see section 7.4). By the 1990s, Airbus became the head-to-head matching competitor with Boeing in the civil airliner business. The Airbus-Boeing "head-to-head" was a main contributor to causing USA Douglas and Lockheed (market leaders of the long-range airliner supply world in the decade immediately after the Second World War) to be completely overtaken and, eventually, eliminated from the supply of any civil aircraft.

7.2 UK International Collaboration in Fixed Wing Military Aircraft

Anglo-French Collaboration (Jaguar and the AFVG)

In the early 1960s, Air Staff Target 362 described a requirement for an advanced supersonic two-seat jet trainer aircraft, to replace both the Folland Gnat jet trainer and the trainer version of the Hawker Hunter, with the possibility of adding a strike capability later (replacing the instructor with a navigator). Training would include preparing pilots for transition to the supersonic TSR-2 and P.1154, then in the early stages of development. At the same time, the French Air Force (*Armée de l'Air*) were seeking an "inexpensive" subsonic two-seat jet trainer aircraft with (later) the addition of a light attack capability. Four design proposals were received in Britain and five were received in France. The British proposals to the RAF included variable sweep wings (strictly, only considered as a possible option because of the RAF supersonic performance requirement). The needs of each nation were quite pressing. However, committed procurement programmes for other aircraft in both countries had created financial constraints. France selected the Breguét Br.121 proposal but was unable to allocate the necessary funds.

In 1964, Anglo-French negotiations led to a collaboration agreement to jointly produce two aircraft to satisfy the requirement of both air forces and a Memorandum of Understanding was signed (not a Government treaty, as for Concorde). The two aircraft were a twin-engined trainer/light strike aircraft and a more advanced twin-engined aircraft with a variable geometry wing ("swing wing"). Eventually these became the trainer/strike aircraft (to be jointly produced by the newly-formed British Aircraft Corporation (BAC) and Breguét), and the Anglo-French Variable Geometry (AFVG) aircraft (to be produced by BAC and Dassault). The AFVG was intended to be a fleet defence (carrier-capable) interceptor for the French navy and an RAF interceptor and (after the TSR-2/F-111 hiatus), the future RAF tactical strike and reconnaissance aircraft (probably with different equipment fits relevant to each of the roles). The difficulty of reconciling several different roles for two or three different military operators into a single aircraft is a recurring problem for aircraft designers and manufacturers. The difficulties are illustrated by the TSR-2/Buccaneer (RAF-RN) controversy, the P.1154 for both the RAF and the RN, the AFVG interceptor-cum-strike both carrier and land based, the 1960s USA YF-16/YF-17 divergence between the USAF and the USN leading to the F-16 and F-18, through the MRCA (Tornado) strike/reconnaissance and air defence versions of the 1970s, right up until the twenty-first century of the three different variants of the Lockheed Joint Strike Fighter, the Lightning II.

SEPECAT Jaguar

As originally proposed, the Breguét Br.121 was agreed as the trainer-cum-strike "starting point". Breguét would be responsible for the nose, centre fuselage and undercarriage and the power plant preferred by Breguét was the Rolls-Royce RB.172; British Aircraft Corporation (in truth, the ex-English Electric team) would be responsible for engine intakes, rear fuselage, wings and tail. Each company would run identical domestic final assembly lines. The aircraft was to become the Jaguar. Overall responsibility was contracted by a new BAC-Breguét jointly-owned company, SEPECAT (Société Européene de Production de l'Avion d'Ecole de Combat et d'Appui Tactique – European fighter/trainer and tactical strike aircraft), which was established in May 1966. This was a sounder contract governance basis than the rather ad hoc approach use on Concorde. The French and the British Industry had both learned a little!

The British light strike/tactical support part of the trainer requirement was the most demanding, requiring more sophisticated electronics, a thinner wing for supersonic capability and high lift devices. This led to a more expensive aircraft, with three variants being planned ("B: British", "E: école" and "A: *appui*"). It also required an increased thrust afterburning development of the RB.172, to be shared between Rolls-Royce and the French engine company Turbomeca. The engine was to be called the Ardour, built in both France and Britain.

Initially, Britain was to buy 150 Jaguar "B" trainers, with its strike aircraft requirements being met by the more advanced BAC-Dassault AFVG aircraft. France was to buy seventy-five Jaguar "E" trainers (*école*) and seventy-five "A" single-seat strike attack aircraft (*appui*).

Because of the prospect of sharing the cost of the Br.121 development (now the Jaguar, up-specified to satisfy the RAF as a strike aircraft), the French government agreed to the interceptor/tactical strike/reconnaissance AFVG over the real *Armée de l'Air* desire for a single-purpose modern interceptor/fighter. The *Armée de l'Air* real desire, however, was in tune with the Dassault strong and parochial desire to become a major world supplier of dedicated fighter/interceptor aircraft.

In the meantime, the cancellation of two significant British strike aircraft (TSR-2 and P.1154, see section 6.3) and subsequent amendments to RAF planning caused a major rethink of the strike and interceptor requirements and the fleet mix of RAF Jaguar types changed. By October 1970 the original RAF requirement of 150 Jaguar "B" trainers had changed to 165 single-seat strike Jaguar "S" and thirty-five two-seat trainers. Meanwhile, France had decided to replace the carrier-borne Dassault Étendard IV with forty of a "maritime" Jaguar "M" version. Although the first prototype aircraft first flight was in 1968, these late changes in roles and requirements caused significant redesign into what became a supersonic (Mach 1.6 (1,056mph), ceiling 45,900ft) high technology aircraft, optimised for strike roles in a high-threat environment. The price escalated accordingly above a "trainer with light attack capability" and Jaguar M was cancelled. A single Jaguar "M" prototype for the French navy flew in 1969, but it had problems associated with control during emergency (single engine) landings and the landing high 'g' which is a natural part of carrier operations (12 "g" compared with the 9 "g" land-based design case). With some lobbying and encouragement from Dassault, the Jaguar "M" variant was cancelled in 1973, ultimately in favour of the Dassault Super Étendard. This entailed a major redesign of the Dassault 1958 Étendard IVM, with a new aircraft (redesigned wing, more powerful engine and impoved avionics. The 1974 Super Étendard became the Argentine Air Force operated aircraft which sank the British ship *Atlantic Conveyor* with a French (Aerospatiale) Exocet air-launched cruise missile, during the 1982 Falklands War.

After Dassault took over Breguét in 1971, the original Breguét enthusiastic support to the Jaguar slowly evaporated. Dassault would promote their Mirage aircraft in the international market and never supported their 50 per cent interest in SEPECAT Jaguar in ongoing sales efforts.

The first Jaguar entered service in 1973. Despite Dassault mounting an aggressive Mirage sales campaign, India also soon chose the Jaguar to replace its Canberras and Hunters. Including prototypes, a total of 569 Jaguars were built (not counting the continuation of production currently planned in India). In the early 1970s, a combined Belgium/Holland/Denmark NATO-supported requirement for a new mixed ground strike/interceptor fleet could be readily met by a mixed SEPECAT Jaguar/Dassault Mirage fleet. Dassault refused to give the Jaguar any support, actually inflating the French part of Jaguar pricing

SEPECAT Jaguar (French Air Force). (*Author's collection*)

to allow the Mirage to show as a single-aircraft more affordable solution. The orders went to a heavily-USAF supported offer of the USA General Dynamics F-16 eventually, for 350 aircraft in total. The British government positively declined to use diplomatic effort to bolster BAC attempts to sell the more affordable and effective Jaguar/Mirage package. So much for Dassault (and French government) co-operation and solidarity in European defence equipment procurement.

In service with the RAF for over thirty years, the Jaguar was an effective reconnaissance-cum-strike aircraft, in conflicts such as the Gulf wars and the Kosovo conflict of 1999. The RAF eventually took 200 Jaguars, 190 served with the French Air Force and a total of forty-nine were exported to Ecuador, Nigeria and the Oman. Britain built forty more for India and 130 more were licence built in India. India updated its Jaguars with indigenous system upgrades and progressively ordered thirty-seven new ones in 1999–2002, to be built entirely in India.

In RAF service the Jaguar released the McDonnell-Douglas Phantom II F-4M (FGR-2) from strike mission responsibility (allowing that aircraft to become dedicated to air defence roles in UK and NATO service, alongside the F4K (FG-1).

Anglo-French Variable Geometry (AFVG)

<u>Introduction to variable wing sweep</u>:- The idea of variable sweep was conceived by the UK designer Barnes Wallis (of Dam Busters "bouncing bomb" fame). Basically, the wings would be pivoted near the root, to be swept back for low drag at high speeds and fully extended for maximum span (maximum lift) during take-off and landing.

By 1965, the AFVG was defined as a variable wing sweep aircraft, larger and heavier than the Jaguar. It was to be a carrier-capable fighter for the French navy (Aéronavale) and fulfil the interceptor, tactical strike and reconnaissance roles for the RAF. It was to be supersonic at sea level (Mach 1.2+) and capable of Mach 2.5 at altitude. A minimum combat radius of 500 nautical miles (576 miles) and a ferry range of 3,500 nautical miles (4,030 miles) were required.

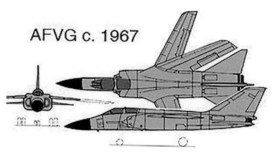

AFVG Outline. (*Bzuk, CC BY-SA 1.0*)

Marcel Dassault, founder of the French company sharing the project with BAC, was extremely uncomfortable with the BAC design leadership on the AFVG, feeling that it threatened his long term aims of being one of the world-leading producers of fighter aircraft. The Dassault Mirage III[4] was the focus of this ambition and, after several disingenuous discussions with BAC, he persuaded the French government to pull out of the AFVG in June 1967. This caused the project to fail. An alternative for Britain was needed once more.

Much later, it emerged that, after TSR-2, the French government had consciously decided on a long-term plan to try to wrest the aerospace leadership in Europe from the three times larger British industry than France's aerospace industry. The overall result would make Rolls-Royce the only major technical leadership aerospace company

---

4. The supersonic delta-winged Mirage III was a Dassault success, built in several sub-variants. A total of over 1,400 were built, used by the French air force and several other overseas operators, including licence-built aircraft for the RAAF and the Swiss Air Force. Marcel Dassault had been impressed with the 1956 world record-holding Fairey Delta 2 (see section 5.10) and later commented to British industry, "if it were not for the clumsy way in which you tackle things in Britain, you could have made the Mirage yourself" (but did Britain need the Mirage?).

in Britain, as an aircraft engine supplier. By encouraging the sharing of Rolls engine development with the French engine company SNECMA (renamed as Safran Aircraft Engines in 2016) for future French-led aircraft design and development, it would then be possible to ultimately take over the lead in European aircraft engine technology also.

Anglo-German-Italian Tornado

Just two years after TSR-2 was cancelled (see section 6.3), the demise of the AFVG forced yet another rethink about "if and how to replace the Canberra strike and reconnaissance capability" (taken over by the RAF Buccaneer S.2, as an interim solution when TSR-2/F-111 was cancelled). Although the AFVG was no longer a possibility, BAC still continued to develop the variable wing sweep configuration design. Determined to maintain a domestic capability to design and build advanced military aircraft, and in the climate of co-operation, other partnerships were considered.

In 1968, a working group involving West Germany, Italy, the Netherlands, Canada and Belgium started studies on the replacement for their licence-built USA-developed single-seater/single-engined Lockheed F-104G Starfighters (which, although fast, had quite limited capability). This group had a diverse range of operational requirements to satisfy and the project became the "Multi-Role Aircraft". Britain joined this group the same year, initially as observers. Britain and West Germany wanted strike and interceptor capabilities, other contributors wanted just "a Lockheed F-104 fighter replacement". The configuration of the aircraft remained open for a while but the final design selected was a two-seat (pilot and navigator) aircraft with variable wing sweep (the work previously carried out in the UK on the AFVG and since had imbued significant confidence in the advantages to performance this would offer). The aircraft project was called the Multi-Role Combat aircraft (MRCA).

Learning from the programme management improvements brought about by the SEPECAT "brass plate on the wall" contract management company used for the Jaguar programme (see section 7.2), in March 1969 the prime contractor companies in the three countries involved established Panavia GmbH, headquartered in Munich. This would be the complete management company for all MRCA programme activity, having executive control of the contract on behalf on the British, German and Italian companies. Senior staffing was by secondees from the three companies participating in the MRCA. Side-by-side in the same building, a NATO-recognised tri-national government management group NAMMO (NATO MRCA Development and Production Management Organisation) was established, with the day-to-day customer interface managed by NAMMA (NATO MRCA Management Agency). The setting up of dedicated programme and project management teams paid off handsomely, later adapted for the joint Britain-Germany-France-Spain Eurofighter project (see section 8.2).

Canada had departed, because they considered the project too focused on European operational needs and Belgium accepted an offer from France to participate in their Dassault Mirage 5 programme instead.

In June 1970, a separate multi-national company, Turbo-Union, was formed to build the RB.199 engine for the aircraft (40 per cent Rolls-Royce, Britain: 40 per cent MTU Aero Engines, Germany: and 20 per cent FIAT, Italy) to be headquartered in Derby, UK. In September 1971 the three governments signed an Intention-to-Proceed document for the MRCA programme. The MRCA was given the common service name "Tornado" in 1976. The Tornado involved British Aircraft Corporation (BAC, 45 per cent, Britain), Messerschmitt-Bölkow-Blohm (MBB, 45 per cent, West Germany) and Aeritalia (10 per cent, Italy).

The physical division of responsibilities for the airframe was as follows:

Britain	West Germany	Italy
Front Fuselage & Tail Assembly	Centre Fuselage	Wings

BAC's contribution was basically from the ex-English Electric team which had been absorbed into BAC in 1960. The MRCA would have a four-channel digital fly-by-wire (FBW) control signalling (continuous automatic stability augmentation mode, with reversion to "direct"). There was also a direct mechanical reversion capability. In 1979, Tornado was to become the second aircraft type in the world with digital FBW control to enter service, four years after the first, the USA McDonnell Douglas F-18.

The initial orders were for the IDS (Interdictor-Strike) version. The Tornado programme was to become the most significant military aircraft project, in terms of size, management complexity and level of technology in which Britain had been involved to that point.

In 1979 the Tornado IDS had its first flight. The RAF also needed an air defence capability to replace their ageing English Electric Lightning and USA McDonnell-Douglas Phantom interceptor capability (used regularly for interception of Soviet intrusion over the North Sea). The result was the Tornado ADV (Air Defence Variant). Italy requested similar capability and Tornado orders were suitably amended in 1976. A 1990 version was the Tornado ECR

German ECR Tornado (compare with AFVG, previous page). (*Author's collection*)

(Electronic Combat and Reconnaissance), operated by a reunified Germany and by Italy. The only other country to use the Tornado is Saudi Arabia.

Tornado strike performance was specified and demonstrated to be "better than TSR-2" in nearly all respects. In system upgrades, the Tornado aircraft went on to benefit from the technology improvements of the 1980s, resulting in a "significantly better than TSR-2" strike capability.

Table 7.2 below compares the aircraft capabilities of the 1965 cancelled TSR-2, the USA F-111, which was ordered in 1966 instead of TSR-2 then cancelled in 1967, the Buccaneer S.2, eventually adopted by the RAF in 1969 as a "stop-gap" (see section 6.3) and the service cleared Tornado GR.1 (RAF designation of IDS version) delivered to the RAF in 1979.

The Buccaneer is included in the table above to point out that the "reasonable" performance of this decade-older design *might* have been improved (to S.2* standard), matching much of the TSR-2 requirement. However, less than 100 of the enhanced Buccaneer S.2* would have been built, no "Air Defence Version" possible and therefore a total build nothing like the total number of Tornados. The systems performance of the Buccaneer clearly would not be capable of managing the sophistication of that afforded by the much later updated Tornado GR-4, which entered service at the end of the twentieth century.

The various versions of the Tornado brought the eventual total to 992 aircraft (compared with the initial TSR-2 order of thirty aircraft and the total unlikely to reach 100, even if it had ever gone into service). The original Tornado IDS development cost was US $13 billion (UK share would have been 45 per cent, equivalent to around US $25 billion in 2019 terms).

The definitive RAF Tornado GR-4 of the late 1990s was a mixed new-build and an upgrade of existing 1979 GR-1 aircraft. Including the original GR-1 acquisition, the total GR-4 unit cost is estimated to have been equivalent to £18 million at the time, or £31 million in 2019 terms. Capability of the GR-4 Tornado (with its twenty-first century communications, navigation and weapon-aiming systems and actual armament) is considerably greater than that of the TSR-2 of 1965, except for maximum range. The last RAF Tornado was retired in 2019; both the fighter and strike/reconnaissance roles in the RAF being taken over by the Eurofighter Typhoon (see section 8.8). Tornado aircraft are, for the time being, still operated by other nations.

Table 7.2: Comparison of RAF Alternatives for Tactical Conventional and Nuclear Strike Aircraft.

Aircraft	First Flt.	Service date (USAF for F-111)	Max. Speed (Mach No.) lo-level & hi-level	Max. Weapon Load (lb)	Max. Take-off Weight (lb)	crew	Max. Range a. ferry b. combat radius
TSR-2 *nuclear strike capability*	1964	N/A	M 1.10 lo M 2.30 hi (no extnl. wpn.)	6,000* (internal) plus 4,000 (external)	103,000	2	a. 2,877 miles b. 860 miles
F-111 *nuclear capable*	1964	1967	M 1.20 lo M 2.50 hi	31,000 total (internal & external)	100,000	2	a. 4,000 miles b ~1,120 miles
Buccaneer (S2)# *nuclear capable*	1965	1969 (RAF (RN earlier)	M 0.93 lo M 0.93 hi	8,000 total (internal & external)	62,000	2	a. 2,300 miles b. ~ 470 miles (RN S.2 standard)
Tornado GR.1 *nuclear capable*	1974	1979	M 1.30 lo M 2.20 hi	12,000* (external)	61,700	2	a. 2,400 miles b. 860 miles

* The nuclear-capability tactical strike no longer considered relevant by the late 1990s.
# During the earlier 1957–59 studies to satisfy the TSR-2 requirement (GOR.339), the existing Royal Navy carrier-borne strike aircraft (the Blackburn Buccaneer) was actively promoted by the Admiralty/RN as a suitable aircraft which could have satisfied much of the requirement. The Buccaneer S.1 would need significant modification to increase range, some of which the S.2 version provided in 1965. The Admiralty/RN motive was reducing navy logistics costs of operating the Buccaneer (and a little pride in their latest aircraft) but, for Blackburn (absorbed into HSA in 1960), this was clearly a business opportunity. From the beginning, the RAF were openly disdainful, refusing to consider an even further enhanced proposal (known as the Buccaneer S.2*) as a remotely viable solution to the actual TSR-2 operational requirement. The RAF probably feared that allowing the Buccaneer even into the argument would mean the "top of the range" TSR-2 would be seriously delayed, or even abandoned, by the politicians of the two major political parties (Conservative or Labour, whichever was in power). It was so, in the end, but for very different reasons (see section 6.3).

7.3 Westland Helicopters in the 1960s and 1970s

After the consolidation of the British helicopter businesses under a single roof as Westland Helicopters (see section 5.9), Westland's 1960s success with the ex-Saunders Roe Skeeter (developed into the Westland Wasp and Scout duo) was soon complemented by a successful adaptation of the USA Sikorsky S-61, as the Westland WS-61 Sea King for the Royal Navy. The engines were changed to twin Rolls-Royce Gnome turboshafts and various systems enhancements were introduced, including an Automatic Flight Control System and a search radar. The RN anti-submarine warfare (ASW) concept was an autonomous mission, rather than the USN practice of direction of the helicopter from the parent aircraft carrier, so the crew stations and equipment were quite different, with the mission command from one of the observer stations. The carrier-borne Sea King required folding rotor blades for aircraft stowage below the flight deck of the RN carriers. First flight of the WS-61 Sea King was on 7 May 1969.

Missions other than ASW were planned, requiring different equipment and layouts. These included Search and Rescue (RN and RAF) and a secondary RN anti-surface vessel role requiring missile armament. A commando version of the Sea King was developed, with an enlarged cabin able to carry up to twenty-eight armed troops. As a result of experience in the 1982 Falklands War, an Airborne Early Warning (AEW radar) capability was hurriedly introduced, to give the fleet radar warning coverage on any deployment (see section 8.2).

Overall, Westland built 344 Sea Kings, operators being the RN, the RAF, the RAN, the German Navy, the Royal Norwegian Air Force, the Belgian Navy, the Indian Navy, the Egyptian Army and Navy and the Qatar Emiri Air Force.

In 1967 France and the UK agreed a "quid pro quo" concerning helicopter purchase. The UK would acquire the Sud Aviation Puma "troop transport/utility" and Gazelle "scout/light communications" helicopters and, in return, the French army and navy would acquire the Westland Lynx helicopter. The agreement allowed the production of 292 Gazelles and forty-eight Pumas by Westland. 30 per cent of the production work on the Lynx would be allocated to Aerospatiale. The Puma and Gazelle were successful programmes for Sud Aviation (absorbed in 1970 into Aerospatiale), 697 Pumas and 1,775 Gazelles being produced in the end.

First flight of the Lynx was in 1971. It was a military vehicle, fundamentally designed as a battlefield-capable support helicopter, with a basic capacity of eight troops. The Westland 30 civil version, with an enlarged cabin having a passenger capacity of nineteen, had a production run of forty-one. The Lynx was unusually manoeuverable for a helicopter, being capable of loops and 360° rolls. In 1986 a specially prepared Lynx set a new world speed record for helicopters at 249.09mph, which still stands (2019).

There have been several model changes and upgrades, incorporating different types of mission equipment, including arming with torpedoes, air-to-surface missiles, gun and/or

Westland Lynx. (*Author's collection*)

rocket platform, fitting with radar and electro-optic surveillance equipment, casualty evacuation equipment and so on. There are several different airframe/engine versions in worldwide service. In the event, seventeen nations have operated the Lynx in army and navy roles. Including the forty-one civil Westland 30, 491 Lynx were built. The Lynx design was to become the 1990s foundation of the AugustaWestland AW.159 Wildcat helicopter (see section 8.7).

7.4 In and Out of Airbus

Origins of Wide-Bodied (twin aisle) Airliners

In 1964 the US government concluded studies for a "superlarge" strategic logistics transport aircraft for the USAF (USAF designation the CX-HLS). The cargo deck had to be 17 feet wide, 100 feet long and 13.5 feet high. The major USA companies making large aircraft, Boeing, Lockheed and Douglas, submitted proposals. The two major USA aircraft engine companies, General Electric and Pratt & Whitney, competed to supply the aircraft power plant. Lockheed was awarded the contract in 1965, to supply their proposed aircraft (USAF designation C.5), powered by four new (to be developed) large turbofans, the "20-tonne" (44,000lbf) thrust General Electric TF39. Almost at the same time, due to air traffic overcrowding at some major airports, USA Pan American Airways (Pan Am) had become interested in a new very large passenger aircraft "twice as big as the Boeing 707" and asked Boeing what might be done.

After considering "two 707s joined one above the other (with a larger wing)", Boeing chose to adapt their losing C.5 proposal and presented their ideas to Pan Am in 1965. After consultation with several more airlines, in April 1966, Boeing launched the 747 "Jumbo" airliner with just one actual customer, with a contract for twenty-five aircraft "off the drawing board" from Pan Am. By then, a significantly reconfigured version of the original Boeing submission to the USAF had evolved. The wing position had moved from high-wing to low-wing, the "cockpit hump" retained on top of the fuselage being a legacy of the front-loading USAF requirement. Boeing thought (at the time) that they would sell more 747s as freighters than as passenger airliners. The nose-loading facility could be reintroduced in that event, allowing freight containers to be passed straight along the fuselage under the cockpit. The main passenger compartment was a twin-aisle ten-abreast seating configuration. The first 747s would have new "20-tonne" thrust (actually 43,300lb) Pratt & Whitney JT9D turbofan engines, partly because GE were just a bit too occupied at the time developing the TF39 engine for the Lockheed C5 to develop another (civil-qualified) large turbofan to the 747 timetable. (GE would later develop the CF6 large turbofan version of the TF39 for civil wide-body airliner use.) Under the terms of the Pan Am contract, Boeing offered delivery of the first 747 to Pan Am by the end of 1969. This only allowed twenty-eight months to complete all details of the design, about two-thirds the normal time. Boeing had virtually "bet the whole company's future"

Pan American Boeing 747-100. (*Aldo Bidini, GFDL 1.2*)

with this commitment. Price per aircraft was US $21 million, equivalent to about US $125 million in 2019 terms. Development cost was US $1 billion, equivalent to about US $6 billion in 2019.

"The Boeing 747 changed the world"

The introduction of jet airliners at the end of the 1950s and early 1960s radically changed the long distance travel experience for those able to afford it, flying on de Havilland Comet, Boeing 707, and Douglas DC-8. Just over ten years later, the Boeing 747 (and subsequent wide-bodied airliners) changed the world even more, making long distance travel economically accessible to a large proportion of the western world population. Arguably, the overall impact changed social attitudes and world political relationships as much as the massive change in travel afforded by the Victorian railway system development changed Britain; or the digital communications revolution of the last thirty years changed the world in which we now live. The effects of the change eventually drifted down to impact almost everyone on planet earth.

Douglas (merged with McDonnell in 1967 to form McDonnell-Douglas) and Lockheed obviously noted Boeing's 747 launch, and discussed new wide-bodied airliners with other airlines (USA and overseas), many of which who did not wish for an aircraft quite as large as the 747. This ultimately led to the McDonnell-Douglas DC.10 and Lockheed L-1011 Tristar wide-bodied three-engined airliners, each with about three quarters of the Boeing 747 passenger capacity and intended to be in service about eighteen months after the Boeing 747. Both these aircraft first flew in 1970 but the Tristar service entry was delayed due to development problems with the 19-tonne thrust Rolls-Royce RB.211 turbofan engine. American Airlines also had previously announced their intention to have Rolls-Royce RB.211 engines in their fifty DC.10s. This all caused a furore in the USA and questions in Congress (foreign engines on USA airliners, costing jobs and loss of revenue, "un-American" arguments, and so on) but the American Airlines announcement proved to be a stalking horse, aiming to get a better price for a "civil TF39" from GE, in the shape of the CF-6. The first models of the DC.10 actually had three GE CF-6 engines. Longer range later models had versions of the Pratt & Whitney JT9D. This "created" the competitive three-supplier scenario for large turbofans that still persists today (GE, Rolls-Royce and Pratt & Whitney).

The original Lockheed request for an engine proposal first resulted in a December 1968 Rolls-Royce engine offer rated at 15 tonnes thrust but, by the time all negotiations with Douglas and Lockheed came to rest, the RB.211 finally agreed with Lockheed was to be rated at 19 tonnes thrust. The deal with Lockheed was sealed in March 1968. Unfortunately, a serious technical development issue with the RB.211 caused major redesign and delays, and, in 1971, the bankruptcy of Rolls-Royce. The company had to be financially rescued by the UK government, causing nationalisation which lasted until re-privatisation in 1987.

Airbus and the UK

In Europe, aircraft manufacturers were equally interested in the wide-bodied concept, anticipating that all significant large airliner business was likely to move in that direction due to continuing passenger traffic growth. At the same time, European aircraft manufacturers and their governments had finally come to realise – and reluctantly accept – that they could never compete with USA manufacturers, the USA domestic market size and operating scale advantages, unless they collaborated and pooled their individual resources. The 1965 government-sponsored Plowden Report on the United Kingdom aircraft industry clearly expressed this need (see Appendix 4), although this report was commissioned "to inform the government", rather than actually be a statement of government policy. Pooling of resources would have to be not just within one country, but include major players of the aircraft industry in Europe as a whole.

One of the promising wide-body aircraft studies was carried out by a joint team from Hawker Siddeley Aviation (Britain), Breguét[5] (France) and Nord Aviation (France), producing the HBN 100 200-passenger outline proposal in 1965. The proposal was aimed at short/medium range operations. At the same time, an alternative 250-seat proposal (the Galion) was unveiled, from Sud Aviation (France) and BAC (UK), the two aircraft companies already involved in a joint project, the Concorde SST (see

---

5. Breguét was an independent French aircraft company, later taken over by Dassault in 1971. Nord Aviation was a French nationally-owned aircraft company.

section 7.1). These (and other) proposals were originally termed by the industry as "airbus" aircraft, as a generic label.

Alongside the airframers, the French SNECMA engine company was being suggested as partnering Bristol Siddeley Engines (UK) and Pratt & Whitney (USA), as large high bypass ratio turbofan engine suppliers, as an alternative to Rolls-Royce (UK). Bristol Siddeley had taken out a licence to produce the Pratt & Whitney JT9D large turbofan. Feeling threatened by being left out of the emerging "wide-body" market, Rolls-Royce made a successful takeover bid for Bristol Siddeley engines in 1966. This made Rolls-Royce the largest aerospace business in Europe at the time. When Rolls allowed the Bristol-Pratt licence agreement on the JT9D to lapse, it apparently made a Rolls engine "a given" for British participation in a "European airbus" aircraft project. The Minister of Aviation stated, "it would be absolute nonsense to build a European airbus and then fit it with an American engine". Rolls put forward the RB.207 "21½-tonne (47,500lb thrust)" engine proposal (more powerful than the JT9D) for the airbus, which was emerging as a twin-engined 300-seat airliner concept, rather than using three engines.

West Germany was keen to revive its fragmented aircraft industry and a "co-operative group" of German aircraft companies joined the study. On 9 May 1967, the French, British and German governments agreed the compromise of a new Rolls-led engine programme in return for French leadership of the airframe design. The RB.207 engine would use the high-efficiency three-spool design concept which the smaller RB.211 was also to adopt for the Lockheed 1011 Tristar aircraft. However, France insisted that Sud Aviation would be the French airframe company and Breguét and Nord Aviation[6] from the foundation HBN 100 study would both be replaced. It seems likely that this was because government-owned Sud Aviation, with the Concorde connection and the successful Caravelle jet airliner in its past, was already being thought about by the French government as "central" in a new merger of French state-owned aircraft companies. This was soon to be Aerospatiale (estalished 1970), which would be designated as the French company to have responsibility for civil airliner design and manufacture in France.

Eventually, the three governments signed a Memorandum of Understanding on 26 September 1967, formally committing to an "airbus" project for a 300-passenger airliner, with just two turbofan engines and with total airframe and engine costs, work and responsibilities shared roughly in equal proportions. The Rolls-Royce RB.207 engine for the aircraft would remain a predominantly British project, with the British government providing 75 per cent of the engine development costs. The whole project would depend on orders of twenty-five aircraft from each country, to be confirmed by the end of June 1968 and none of the participants supporting any indigenous project which would be in competition with the "airbus". The MoU was not a binding commitment to produce the aircraft. Any party could withdraw unilaterally from the programme, subject to a notice period of six months, during which the agreed share of the costs incurred would continue to be the liability of the withdrawing party.

This was all in harmony with the second British application to join the European Economic Community (the first one in 1963, had been vetoed by Charles de Gaulle, president of France). On 27 November 1967, Charles de Gaulle again announced a French veto of Britain's latest attempt to join the Common Market. In 1972, Spain joined the consortium, taking a 4 per cent share (France and Germany giving up 2 per cent each).

Meanwhile, during 1967, BAC had revealed their 200-seater 2-11 airliner narrow-body proposal aimed at BEA's declared need for a 200-passenger aircraft. This was

---

6. Nord Aviation was finally merged with nationally-owned Sud Aviation in 1971 and a nationally-owned nuclear ballistic missile company, to form the group which eventually became known as Aerospatiale. Sud Aviation had been established on 1 March 1957 by the merger of Sud-Est (which had designed and manufactured the successful Caravelle jet airliner, first flight 1955) and Sud-Ouest.

an updated/re-engined wider-fuselaged airliner compared with the 1-11, (a similar capacity to the eventual 1982 Boeing 757 220-to-280 seater, derived from a lengthwise stretch of the Boeing 727 six-abreast fuselage, with a new wing and two wing-mounted engines). As conceived, the BAC 2-11 was not a proposition obviously in competition with the airbus 300-seater, by then designated as the A.300; the BAC 2-11, however, might have eventual "further stretch potential". The BAC 2-11 was to be powered by twin RB.211 engines mounted on the rear fuselage, at that time sized at 15-tonne (33,000lb) thrust. The Plowden report of 1965 (see section 6.2) had strongly advised that in-country aircraft programmes which might compete with each other for resources or market share should not be started. This sound principle was to be (partly) the declared reason for the government reluctance to support the BAC 2-11 project, when they were already scheduled to support the A.300.

The A.300 had, at that time, made little progress towards the original MoU goal of seventy-five aircraft confirmed on order by the middle of 1968. In that year, European financial houses made a run on the French gold reserves that depleted them by 30 per cent in a short period of time. This caused not just the collapse of the French franc, but contributed to the collapse of President Charles De Gaulle's government, amidst much political unrest in the country. As economic uncertainty spread through Europe, European airlines began to have doubts about the viability of the A.300 and its original 300+ seating capacity.

In December 1968 the A.300 partner companies proposed to reduce the size of the aircraft from 300 to 250 passenger seats (the A.300B), apparently fearing that 300 seats would make an aircraft too large for a significant number of potential operators. Was this a move by A.300 partners to head off the BAC 3-11 (proposed in 1967, see below) or was it just good sense? Too much money was at stake not to believe that it was, in fact, the latter. The proposal meant that the Rolls-Royce RB.207 engine might not be needed. The RB.211 (with a development to increase thrust), the American GE CF-6 and P&W JT9D engines would all be candidates for the twin-engined 252-seater A.300. The engine cost would therefore be reduced, compared with the all-new RB.207. The continental partners asked the British government to support the RB.211 development to meet the revised requirement. The government was not inclined to provide more money than that needed to complete RB.211 commitments for the three-engined Lockheed 1011 Tristar programme, which was a similarly sized aircraft (and which they had persuaded a reluctant USA government to underwrite for Lockheed because of the RB.211 delays which they (Britain) were separately taking responsibility).

BAC had proposed the BAC 3-11 airliner in 1967, as an alternative project. This was a twin-engined 245 passenger wide-bodied passenger aircraft with two up-rated RB.211 engines, again mounted on the rear fuselage. The French government became concerned that the likelihood of an A.300 programme success was less certain, with BEA showing preference for the BAC 3-11. The RB.211 engine clearly had the potential to grow into more powerful versions capable of satisfying any perceived requirement for further development of the 747/DC.10/1011, or any other wide-bodied aircraft which might be launched in the next few years. The government refusal to back an RB.211 stretch for the A.300B did not please the French and German A.300 partners. HSA, the British aircraft company involved in the A.300, had suspected that Rolls-Royce was hoping to "ditch" the dual nature of the RB.207-RB.211 programme. They raised the issue to senior Rolls-Royce management level. HSA quickly determined that their suspicions were the likely truth and knew that the A.300 partners would seriously have to consider using one of the new American 20-tonne engines for the A300B as an alternative (reneging on the Britain led engine programme principle in the Airbus inter-governmental MoU).

When the revised 252-passenger A.300B formal proposal was revealed, possibly to be offered with a choice of engines other than Rolls-Royce, the British government cried "foul". In the House of Commons the Minister of Technology declared that the A300B had created a new situation, requiring detailed study, whereas the French and German governments maintained that it was a logical development of the A.300 project, revealed as necessary by the market studies so far.

The French (predictably) refused to consider joining the BAC 3-11 as an alternative. By March 1969, the French and German patience over the internal United Kingdom debate ran out and declared that the A.300B would go ahead, sharing the costs amongst themselves. The British Government withdrew support to the A.300 project on 10 April 1969.

There were British suspicions (possibly unfounded) that the French in particular had "engineered the situation to their own advantage". This is not surprising, given the history of the French 1967 disengagement from the 1965 Anglo-French AFVG military aircraft (see section 7.2). It was also a truism, however, that changing to USA engines would enhance sales prospects to USA airlines, an Airbus "must-penetrate" section of the market. There were some in Britain who felt that there were persons in the government who were prejudiced against the A.300 itself, in any form, and even (King Canute-style) a few against the general idea of Britain having to collaborate with Europe (or anyone else) in a high-technology programme.

HSA had invested PV funding for their wing design contribution to the A.300 project and decided that they wished to continue to use their own money on the A.300B. With a supportive loan (to HSA) for new tooling from the West German government, this could be managed financially. To produce the aircraft, the Airbus GIE[7] business was established in 1970, as a consortium of government-sponsored French (50 per cent) and West German (50 per cent) aircraft businesses. HSA were accepted as a preferred subcontractor to the new Airbus business, "designing and supplying the A.300B wings, and to provide expert input to the A.300 marketing effort". This eventually became a lucrative position for HSA in Airbus business, equating to some 20 per cent of the whole programme of the A.300B and later Airbus aircraft. However, it did not give HSA any real say in Airbus policy, overall management or sales philosophy. Only after the later nationalisation and the subsequent privatisation of the bulk of the aircraft industry, as British Aerospace, had been completed, did the relationship between the British aircraft industry and Airbus change. (see sections 8.4 and 8.6).

BAC continued to try to gather launch orders for the 3-11. The marketing campaign did not, however, generate enough interest to provide the necessary certainty to start the project without outside support. With the previous success of the earlier BAC 1-11 in world markets, including airlines in the USA, BAC still believed that the 3-11 showed sufficient promise to be worth being considered for government launch aid. With continuing support from BEA, there was a company view (shared by some in the Labour government, which nevertheless prevaricated for a while) that the aircraft would prove a better proposition than the A.300B. The Airbus project, however, was not considered by everyone to be moribund, having the experienced HSA (ex-de Havilland) airliner team and the French ex-Sud Aviation team from the successful Caravelle airliner project involved. In the end, following the change to a Conservative-led government caused by the results of the June 1970 general election, the new Conservative government soon formalised the Labour government's 1969 putative decision, that launch aid for the 3-11 would not be provided.

It took Rolls-Royce twenty more years to become involved in another Airbus aircraft programme (the Rolls-Royce one-third share in the International Aero Engines V.2500, on versions of the Airbus A.320) and nearly ten years after that to have their own

---

7. Groupement d'intérêt économique (GIE), a French legal business construct for a consortium.

complete engine (the later Rolls-Royce Trent development of the RB.211) powering an Airbus aircraft (a post-launch developed version of the Airbus A.330).

"After the Dust Had Settled"

The decision to reduce the capacity of the original A.300 (to the A.300B) had opened the window for revised engine proposals from the major manufacturers. The GE CF-6 proposal had the requisite thrust and improved economy, compared with the alternative on offer from the Pratt & Whitney JT9D. Without further British government financial aid, bankrupt Rolls-Royce were too financially constrained to try. Critically, the Airbus had two (higher thrust) engines, whereas the other wide-bodies used three (Lockheed L-1011 and McDonald Douglas DC-10) or four (Boeing 747). The A.300B only needed two engines because, at the time, long-range route-flying[8] requirements for continued flying after a single engine failure needed frequent diversion airfields reachable within sixty minutes of an engine failure. Flying over large expanses of ocean was not included in the Airbus operational capability. First flight of the Airbus A.300B was on 28 October 1972 and the first operator was Air France in 1974.

Combined with the advanced aerodynamic techniques used by HSA for the wing (building on the subsonic/transonic aerodynamic work done at the RAE by Dietrich Kücheman's team (see section 6.4), the twin-engined A.300B had an overall fuel economy nearly 30 per cent better than the three-engined Lockheed L-1011 Tristar and Douglas DC-10. A speculative trial Eastern Airlines lease in 1977 demonstrated this and an order was placed for twenty-three A.300B in 1978.

Airbus A.300B. (*Author's collection*)

As a result, the Airbus reputation in the USA moved from "unfamiliar" to "good". As a small but important issue, Frenchman Roger Béteille (the Airbus technical director and experienced on Concorde) had insisted from the start on imperial measurement standards, rather than European metric standards, and English as the project language (like the majority of the Western commercial aviation world). This allowed the new Airbus to "fit in" the market as "just another aircraft", acceptable in the USA.

Ironically, well before the three-engine configurations of the DC-10 and L-1011 wide body were fixed, the concept of a wide-body two-engined airliner (still with sixty minute diversion rules) had been energetically promoted in 1966 by Frank Kolk, chief development engineer at American Airlines. He wrote to other major USA domestic airlines and all three USA large airliner manufacturers (Boeing, McDonnell-Douglas and Lockheed), pointing out the likely economy of operation of a wide-body twin, with twice the Boeing 727 capacity. Given the "brush-off" from most quarters in the USA (250 passengers with only two engines!... you are joking), when Roger Bétielle later

---

8. For transport category multi-engined aircraft, the ability to maintain a safe altitude after an engine shut-down is an operational requirement mandated by civil airworthiness authorities. When the necessary engine reliability improvements could be actually demonstrated in service, and aircraft systems assessed for other flight-essential reliability/redundancy improvements, Extended-range Twin-Engined Aircraft Operational Performance Standards (ETOPS) were promulgateded. Initially defined as EROPS (Extended Range Operations), ETOPS operations approval applied to twin-engined aircraft on routes with time to a diversion airfield from any en route position no more than 120 minutes flying away, at one engine inoperative speed, compared with the previous sixty minute rule.

went to talk to potential American customer airlines about the nascent European Airbus, Kolk helped in the definition of the emerging A.300 twin-engined widebody concept. This was towards what he (Kolk) perceived as a fundamental USA domestic airliner need, for all routes where such operations would be permissible. Kolk was disappointed in the American Airlines enforced choice of the DC-10 with its three engines. Much later, after ETOPS rules had been established, in 1988 American Airlines took delivery as launch customer for an extended range version of the A.300, the A.300-600R.

Other than the modest successes of the BAC 1-11 (see section 6.4) and French Sud Aviation Caravelle in the 1960s, no foreign civil jet airliner had been able to achieve significant sales to USA airlines. The Airbus initial slow sales success prior to the first US sale did not disturb the three USA major airliner manufacturers Boeing, Lockheed and McDonnell-Douglas, until the Airbus programme first penetrated that American market with the sale of the A.300 to Eastern, as one of the USA's larger airlines, with a wide-body airliner which was clearly competitive with an American product (the McDonnell-Douglas DC.10). The Eastern Airlines A.300B purchase in 1978 rang alarm bells. The method of finance of Airbus was not transparent and, to Americans, smacked of "government subsidy". The USA concern was that their near-monopoly in large airliners for the previous thirty or forty years might be about to be attacked. Eventually, they were proved right! (see section 9.5)

BAe provided all Airbus wing design and manufacture, via the ex-de Havilland team at Hatfield and Hawarden (Chester) production until 1993, when the design responsibility was transferred to the ex-Concorde BAe team at Bristol (Filton). This was aided by some technical personnel transfers from Hatfield, joining those remnants

Table 7.3: Airbus Fixed Wing Aircraft Products (total delivered).

Aircraft Type	Date		Number of		MTOW~ (tonnes)	Number of Aircraft
	Launch	1st Flight	Engines	Passengers		
A.220 (ex-Bombardier)	2008	2013	2	100-150	34.9	113*
A.300	1967	1972	2	281-345	171.7	561°
A.310	1978	1982	2	237–265	164.0	255°
A.320ceo (family)	1984	1987	2	117–236	93.5	9,373*
A.320neo (family)	2010	2014	2	160-240	97.0	1,306*
A.330ceo	1987	1992	2	280-440	242.0	1,480*
A.340		1991	4	228–340	381.0	377°
A.330neo	2014	2017	2	260-440	250.1	46*
A.350 XWB	2006	2013	2	325-440	338.7	366*
A.380	2000	2005	4	544-868	575.2	244**
A.400M Atlas (military transport)	2003	2009	4	troops/ equipt. & vehicles	141.0	89*

A.220 is a Bombardier project launched and sold as the "C-series" but control taken by Airbus in 2018

A.320 & A.330 ceo = "current engine option", A.320 & A.330 neo = "new engine option"

~ Maximum Take-of Weight (MTOW) is for largest version of each type

* still in production (2020)

** On 14 February 2019, Airbus announced production of A.380 would end in 2021

° out of production

of the BAC 1-11 team which had transferred (rather than retired) from BAe Weybridge when closed in 1988. BAe continued to design and build all the wings of Airbus projects until 1996, when they exchanged that part of the business (Filton-based wing design and parts manufacture) and the whole of the Hawarden (Chester) wing assembly facility to Airbus, in return for 20 per cent of the equity in Airbus (see section 8.6). In 2008, Airbus sold the Filton manufacturing facility to GKN (joining the GKN acquisition of the Westland facility at Yeovil, see section 8.7).

The current Airbus comprehensive range of transport aircraft is (in 2020) as listed in Table 7.3. Airbus have delivered over 12,000 aircraft since their first in 1974 and have a total outstanding order book of another 8,000 aircraft.[9]

Airbus A.380. (*Maarten Visser, CC BY-SA 2.0*)

9. A comprehensive account of the complete story of Airbus, with its exhaustive product definition, technical excellence and the political in-fighting which surrounded the company formation and development, is given by Bill Gunston in his book "*Airbus: The Complete Story*" (see bibliography).

Chapter 8

More Turbulence, 1976 to 2010

8.1 Nationalisation and Government Influence on UK Aircraft Industry

It was clear that the post-1945 British aircraft industry would have far too much production capacity for peacetime needs, even when "shadow" factory facilities were decommissioned and wartime-only employees redeployed or laid off. Several of the different design and manufacturing companies operating as the war ended (see Appendix 1) were really "surplus to requirements". One or two candidates seemed to "self-exterminate" quite quickly and even the well established companies would be competing for too little work for all to have truly sufficient work. The government, in the shape of the Ministry of Supply (after re-absorbing the wartime Ministry of Aircraft Production), had the authority to direct aircraft work, shared if appropriate between different companies. Aircraft companies were quite used to working on the designs of others, so a level of subcontract sharing of work could continue.

Nevertheless, rationalisation of the UK aircraft industry was discussed in government department circles as early as 1944. Government part or whole ownership of more than one company was thought about. The Short brothers company had been nationalised in 1943 under the wartime "Control of Industrial Undertakings" Defence Regulation 78. By the 1950s, the "Cold War" was keeping military aircraft work levels higher than had been thought would be necessary in the immediate aftermath of the war. Much of the civil aircraft industry, however, failed to prosper. The need to earn foreign revenue by selling British aircraft was to have mixed success (Brabazon failure, Viscount success, Dove success, Britannia semi-failure, Vampire success, Canberra success, Hunter success and so on). A major rationalisation was forced by the consequences of the 1957 Defence Review (see sections 5.15 and 6.1) but there was still over capacity.

The government established a "Committee of Inquiry into the Aircraft Industry, 1964–1965" which reported in December 1965 (the Plowden Report, see Section 6.2). This concluded that British aircraft programmes which competed with one another should not be supported by any form of government aid and that international collaborative programmes would give access to a larger market which should actually increase total work. In the military aircraft field, this was a fundamental change of approach, as the armed forces and the government often had been accustomed to being able to select an aircraft from at least two competing prototype responses to a particular operational requirement, or even ordering different aircraft for the same job (e.g. Vulcan/Victor and Swift/Hunter).

In 1966, the Labour government clearly stated in parliament that it intended to negotiate to take a significant financial stake in the aircraft industry. Negotiations did take place, but agreement could not be reached at a price which the directors and owners of HSA and BAC felt were true value, but the government was not prepared to afford. After a period of fluctuation in the composition of the government, in October 1974 a Labour government was elected with a majority of only three, a difficult majority for the forcing of radical reform of the aircraft industry.

Nevertheless, on 30 April 1975 the "British Aircraft and Shipbuilding Act" to take into public ownership (nationalise) the assets of Hawker Siddeley Aviation, Hawker Siddeley Dynamics, British Aircraft Corporation and Scottish Aviation had

Table 8.1: Timeline of Major Political Decisions on the Shape of the Aircraft Industry 1945 to 2000.

Years in Office	Party of Government	Prime Minister(s)	Government "Business" Action on UK Aircraft Industry
1945–1951	Labour	Clement Attlee	MoS controls which aircraft (civil and military) are built and which company "gets the job".
1951–1952	Conservative	Winston Churchill	
1952–1959	Conservative	Anthony Eden Harold Macmillan	1957: Defence Review aircraft cancellations and "aircraft industry to form into groups". *(Hawker Siddeley Aviation (HSA) and British Aircraft Corporation (BAC) established in response).*
1959–1964	Conservative	Harold Macmillan Alec Douglas-Home	1962: Government treaty with France launches Concorde project.
1964–1966	Labour (4 maj)	Harold Wilson	1964-65: Plowden Committee of Enquiry. 1965: TSR-2, P.1154 & AW.681 cancelled. Harrier development go-ahead, Nimrod agreed. 1966: "Nationalisation intent declared".
1966–1970	Labour	Harold Wilson	1967: UK agreement to join Airbus A.300 airliner project with France and West Germany. 1969: UK pulls out of Airbus A.300 project.
1970–1974	Conservative	Edward Heath	1970: new UK government confirms no support to Airbus A.300 project. 1971: R.Royce collapse, rescue by nationlisation. 1973: Government support to HS.146 airliner.
1974 Feb–Oct	Lab. minority	Harold Wilson	"Failure to agree" on nationalisation terms.
Oct 74–Mar 77	Labour	James Callaghan	1975: Bill to nationalise aircraft and shipbuilding industries:- First reading in parliament.
Mar 77–Apr 79	Lab. minority	James Callaghan	March 1977: Bill to nationalise passed into law.
1979–1983	Conservative	Margaret Thatcher	1980: British Aerospace converted to plc. 1981: British Aerospace privatised.
1983–1987	Conservative	Margaret Thatcher	1984: Government RLI support to Airbus A.320. 1984: Shorts converted to a limited company. 1985-86: "Westland affair" (see section 8.7). 1987 BA privatised. 1987: Government RLI to Airbus A.330/A.340. 1987: Rolls-Royce reprivatised.
1987–1992	Conservative	Margaret Thatcher John Major	1989: Shorts sold to Bombardier (Canada)
1992–1997	Conservative	John Major	1995: UK joins USA F-35 fighter aircraft project.
1997–2001	Labour	Tony Blair	2000: Government RLI in Airbus A.380.

its first reading in parliament. The act included ship building, in a separate group "British Shipbuilders", with twenty-seven major shipbuilding and marine engineering companies to be nationalised. The Harland and Wolff shipyard in Northern Ireland was at first excluded from the new group but was taken into public ownership in 1977. After considerable amendment and delay, the act received the Royal Assent on 17 March 1977. British Aerospace (BAe) was created as a wholly-owned government aircraft and other aerospace activities company.

After the 1979 general election resulted in a change of government to Conservative, the "British Aerospace Act" was presented to parliament, to convert the nationalised British Aerospace into a public limited company. This received the Royal Assent on 1 May 1980, coming into force on 1 January 1981. One month later, the government sold a majority of its shares and, in 1985, disposed of its minority holding except for a single "golden share" retaining the power of veto over any future take over.

Table 8.1 above illustrates the timeline of the government post-Second World War twentieth century direct involvement in the management of the aircraft industry. Returnable Launch Investment (RLI) in Airbus projects is noted. The timeline for major government interactions with the UK aircraft industry between the end of the Second World War and the end of the twentieth century is given in Appendix 2, including the events leading to the nationalisation, rationalisation and subsequent privatisation of most of the industry.

8.2 UK Airborne Early Warning Aircraft

Pre-amble:

The Airborne Early Warning (AEW) function is normally associated with an aircraft-based radar (and other sensors) for advance detection of threats to any particular area of operations. This includes air defence of the British Isles but first materialised in defence of Navy (USN) aircraft carrier forces towards the end of the Second World War.

The Skyraider AD-4W was an AEW adaptation of a 1945 USN Douglas Skyraider A-1 dive bomber/torpedo bomber, with a single piston engine. It was fitted with the American AN/APS-20 radar. As carrier-capable aircraft, these were supplied post-war to the RN by the USA, under the umbrella of the USA Mutual Defense Assistance Programme. The Skyraider was becoming obsolete by the end of the 1950s (although continued to serve as attack aircraft in the USN and the South Vietnam Air Force (RVNAF) during the USA assisted 1959–63 war in Vietnam).

The British decision was taken to develop an AEW version of the RN twin-engined UK Fairey Gannet turboprop fleet antisubmarine (carrier-borne) aircraft, first flown in 1949. In cruise/surveillance, one of the twin Armstrong Siddeley Mamba engines (gearbox interconnected to drive a single pair of contra-rotating propellers) could be shut down to give the Gannet endurance of five or more hours on patrol.

With significant aircraft fuselage changes (including eliminating the bomb bay), the AN/APS-20 radar system was transferred to the Gannet airframe. The Gannet AEW.Mk.3 was intended as an interim step, pending the introduction of a completely new solution.

Fairey Gannet AEW. (*Mike Freer, GFDL 1.2*)

With the retirement of both of the RN aircraft carriers (HMS *Eagle* in 1972 and HMS *Ark Royal* in 1978) and no replacement ship capable of operating a conventional fixed wing aircraft, the Gannet AEW aircraft fleet was wound down. Their radar was transferred to suitably modified Avro Shackleton MR.Mk.2 airframes, redesignated as the Shackleton AEW. Mk.2. The Shackleton Mk.2 already had wing spar replacements due to metal fatigue issues, being re-lifed accordingly.

Shackleton AEW Mk.2. (*BAE Systems*)

This deprived the RN Fleet Air Arm of indigenous fleet-borne AEW capability, proving to be a disastrous government decision during the Falklands war of 1982. (After several UK South Atlantic RN task force ships were lost to enemy air attack, hastily modified RN Westland Sea King helicopters were in service in the Falklands, one month *after* the end of that two and aa half months war[1].)

The Shackleton AEW.Mk.2 went into RAF service in 1972, with the intention of soon being replaced by a modern system. Several different options were examined, including purchase of either the already flying USAF Boeing E-3A AWACS, or the established carrier-borne USN Grumman E2-C Hawkeye aircraft, or the latter's APS-125 radar system "grafted" on to UK Nimrod aircraft. By this time, simple detection of threat(s) had grown into the directed control of threat interception (AWACS = Airborne Warning *and* Control System), with the British requirement focussed on a large land-based aircraft.

Nimrod AEW.Mk.3

An industry-based feasibility study considered the alternatives of acquisition of the USA Boeing E-3 AWACS aircraft, grafting the USA Grumman E-2C aircraft radar system (with a large "mushroom" antenna housing above the fuselage) on to the BAe Nimrod airframes, or a completely new UK-designed system with radar scanners fore and aft (FASS, to give all-round 360° coverage) on Nimrod airframes. The provision of nose and tail scanners on the Nimrod was selected by the government, with a "to be developed" new British one mega-watt (peak pulse) microwave radar transmitter. A new four-station situation display and control system would be included. The project as a whole was intended to assist British technology development and preservation. The result would be known as the Nimrod AEW.Mk.3, ordered in 1974. The radar system, digital computing system and operators' multi-function displays, digital data links with co-operating forces and a complete new multi-channel radio and intercom communication system were to be developed and provided by GEC Marconi. The intention was that the progamme would be managed by MoD(PE) in the manner advised by the Downey and Rayner reports (see section 6.2). Converted from low-flight time and the last of some incomplete surplus Nimrod MR.Mk.1 airframes, this was to create an all new airborne system providing and air/ground/sea surface target surveillance and "battle co-ordination" capabilities. The airframe, its systems and its interior needed significant modification.

---

1. New Queen Elizabeth class RN aircraft carriers (in service 2018) will have new AEW helicopters, based on the AW.101 Merlin helicopter design which entered RN service in 2014.

The aircraft changes to accommodate the new AEW system (called the Mission System Avionics – MSA) included a complete new tail fuselage and new large nose and tail radomes, wing tip electronic emissions sensor and surveillance pods and a new electrical generating system for the increased total electrical load. So much internal heat was generated by the new system that a heat exchange system was required, to use wing fuel as a heat sink. These basic airframe changes were developed using the first development Nimrod AEW aircraft, before incorporating the radar equipment. The prototype radar and the prototype new communications system were initially trialled separately, in two specially adapted Comet aircraft.

Nimrod AEW Mk.3. (*Mike Freer, GFDL 1.2*)

Because of frequent changes in the MSA design mostly caused by development difficulties, over 1,000 further changes to the aircraft design had to be engineered during the development programme, many before a complete MSA was fitted to the second development aircraft (the first to have the MSA fitted). Some of these were due to continuing changes to the radar specification by the government. Some changes were driven by the Royal Signals and Radar Establishment, some were MSA hardware issues and some stemmed from significant MSA development problems. Project timescales and cost predictions were increased several times. The change management process for aircraft and MSA became a tangled web.

One of the main programme issues was the management structure imposed by the MoD. The responsibilities for airframe and AEW (MSA) system were separately contracted and managed within the government, with separately managed contracts to the airframe contractor (HSA) and the MSA contractor (GEC Marconi). The airframe changes to provide the required airborne platform capability were completed successfully but the MSA itself got "bogged down" in development issues. The management structure provoked four-way finger pointing throughout, with no clear overall programme executive control. Quarterly project co-ordination meetings (with as many as sixty attendees) were held, co-chaired by the MSA government project manager and the airframe government project manager, with the MSA and airframe contractors in attendance, plus the several RAF and government departments involved, many of which hardly ever made a contribution to discussions but seemed to attend only to ensure that their department "got a copy of the minutes". Shades of TSR-2 (section 6.3), only worse.

Airframe modifications for all eleven production Nimrod AEW aircraft were complete but, after several postponements to the end of the MSA trials, the project was cancelled in 1986, after incurring a cost of £1 billion overall (equivalent to about £2.3 billion in 2019 terms).

An order for seven new Boeing E-3s was placed. Designated as the E.3 Sentry AEW.1 by the RAF, service entry was in 1991 and the 40-year-old Shackleton finally could be retired. The original APS-20 radar served for forty-one years in RN/RAF aircraft.

A project "post-mortem analysis" concluded that the principles of good project management promulgated by Downey and Rayner had not been adhered to in the Nimrod AEW.Mk.3 project management structure.

In March 2019, the government announced that the USA Boeing 737NG-based E-7 AEW aircraft would eventually replace the E-3 in RAF service. British company

Marshall Aerospace & Defence will be responsible for modification to incorporate changes to RAF-defined special requirements. (The Boeing 737NG is also the base airframe of the P-8A aircraft already ordered for the new maritime patrol aircraft, see section 8.11.)

8.3 European Collaboration Efforts on a New Single-Aisle Turbofan Airliner

By the early 1970s, there were several competing airliner proposals testing the market for the 100-to-200 passenger size. Turboprop-powered airliners dominated the smaller (less than seventy seats) short-range types, because turboprop fuel economy was the bigger attraction than the marginal advantages of jet speed, at least over routes with all stages or routes less than 500 miles. The new single-aisle jet (turbofan) studies ranged from "above the turboprop forty to sixty seaters", to just below the emerging new aircraft typified by the 200+ seaters (200-to-280 seater Boeing narrow-body 757 (in service 1982) and the "shrunk from A.300" 220-to-265 seater Airbus A.310 wide-body, which went into service one year after the 757). The jet airliners actually available in the eighty to 120 passenger range in the late 1970s were the 1967 USA Boeing 737, the 1965 USA McDonnell-Douglas DC-9, and the UK 1967 stretch of the 1963 BAC 1-11. As ageing designs, their replacement was an urgent consideration, by all three aircraft manufacturers and by major airlines desiring more modern and more efficient short-medium range aircraft.

Establishing the "right" passenger capacity, range capability, with the "right wings and engines" and other equipment etc. has always been a part of launching any new transport project. After satisfying the intended operational route requirements, aircraft operating costs are the prime airline interest above absolute technical performance. The technology has to show a return. For airliners, there is significant uncertainty in forecasting operating costs, due to the long project timescales (fluctuation and escalation in fuel prices, for example) and the financing cost of the investment levels needed by the aircraft manufacturer (see section 9.3). Aircraft selling price directly influences operating cost, via the purchase financing cost, or the leasing cost for those airlines leasing from either the manufacturer or an aircraft leasing company.

Competition from the more firmly established USA manufacturers was certain, either with new designs and/or further major upgrades of existing designs.

In Britain, BAC off-loaded the existing BAC 1-11 aircraft project to Romania (see section 6.4), hoping that their ideas for developing a 176-to-219 seater, to be known as the BAC 2-11 (see section 7.4), would find favour but, in parallel, joining in various collaborative 1970s studies with other European aircraft manufacturers. Meanwhile, Hawker Siddeley entered the lower end of the market with the smaller 70-to-100 seater fan-jet powered HS.146. This was conceived by the ex-de Havilland team after being merged into Hawker Siddeley, with the aircraft flying by 1981 (see section 8.4).

Throughout the 1970s, the market pressures among European aircraft manufacturers created various collaboration study groups for a 120 to 180 seat airliner, as the "most common interest" product between nine different manufacturers, as shown in table 8.2 below.

Various groupings of these companies assembled, made preliminary proposals, dispersed and reformed in different mixes. There were also single-company ideas. One of these was the BAC 2-11 200 seater, not built, see section 7.4, and another was the go-it-alone French government supported 1971 162-seater short range Dassault Mercure, only ten built. BAC, CASA, MBB and Saab studied various sizes of aircraft, under the "Europlane" group name, presenting four different options at the 1972 Farnborough Air Show. These were refined to a definitive 180-to-200 seater twin rear-engined layout, presented at the 1973 Paris Air Show. Under the group name "Civil

Aircraft Study Team" (CAST), Dornier, HSA and VFW-Fokker studied a number of 150 seat alternatives. In 1975, Aerospatiale led one joint proposal, for a twin-engined airliner, the AS.200, seating up to 160 passengers. The other companies involved in the AS.200 were British Aircraft Corporation, Dornier, Hawker Siddeley Aviation, MBB and VFW-Fokker. Other groupings made other proposals.

Table 8.2: European Aircraft Companies in 1970s New Single-aisle Airliner Studies (with historic background in turbine-engined transport aircraft; dates are "1st flight").

Company	Country
Aerospatiale (1955 Caravelle airliner and 1969 Concorde share with BAC)	France
British Aircraft Corporation (post-Second World War airliners, incl. 1962 VC.10 and 1968 1-11)	Britain
Construcciones Aeronauticas SA (1971 C-212 Aviocar cargo & 1977 Aviojet jet trainer)	Spain
Dornier (1966 Do.228D Skyservant STOL cargo/airliner)	West Germany
Fokker (1955 F.27 & 1967 F.28 airliners and joint venture 1971 VFW-Fokker VFW 614)	Netherlands
Hawker Siddeley Aviation (DH.121 Trident and DH.125 bus.jet and A.300 participation)	Britain
Messerschmitt-Bölkow-Blohm (with its new A.300 participation)	West Germany
Saab Scania (mostly military aircraft background, hoping to diversify into airliners)	Sweden
Vereinigte Flugtechische Werke VFW (joint venture 1971 VFW-Fokker VFW 614)	West Germany

The penultimate grouping in 1977 involved the ex-BAC part of the newly-nationalised BAe (Britain), Aerospatiale (France), VFW-Fokker (West Germany and Netherlands joint venture) and Messerschmitt-Bölkow-Blohm (West Germany). Labelled the Joint European Transport (JET) study, the group was established at Weybridge in Britain, the former Vickers/BAC site. The output of this study was a twin-jet (turbofan) airliner with underwing engines and a passenger capacity (in two variants) of 130-to-180 economy class passengers, with a maximum useable range of 2,000 to 3,000 miles (depending on the variant). This would be principally targeted at the European airline routes and traffic densities but, clearly and essentially, also applicable worldwide, especially the large American market segment.

The JET group members were employees of companies all involved (to a greater or lesser extent) with the Airbus consortium. Eventually, the study was re-established within Airbus. The JET study leader was a BAe Weybridge employee, later transferred to Airbus to continue in that role for the Airbus series of Single Aisle studies SA1, SA2 and SA3, joining other twin-aisle future airliner project studies[2]. Although Airbus were studying possible new variants of the much larger aircraft (the wide-body twin aisle A.300 and alternative possible all-new alternatives), in terms of total numbers

---

2. After the initial Airbus A.300B (B1 and B2 studies) had been launched, ongoing development studies were given further number suffixes (up to B14). Those which actually became new projects in their own right were derived from B9, B10 and B11. The B10 became the second Airbus aircraft, the A.310 launched in 1978, and B9 and B11 were later incorporated in the Twin-Aisle Studies (TA9, TA11 and TA12) which eventually matured as the twin-engined A.330/four-engined A.340 "common wing" airliners, jointly launched in June 1987, see section 7.4.

of aircraft and total market value the 120-to-160 seater sector (the so-labelled Single Aisle sector) was the greatest.

The revised Douglas DC-9 was first off the blocks for this class of airliner, redesignated as the McDonnell-Douglas MD-80, 143 to 155 passengers, first flight 1979, developed later into two variants, ranging from 120 to 170 seat capacity. Boeing launched a major update of their 737 as the 737-300, first flying in 1984 and ultimately available in three variants, also ranging from 120 to 170 seating capacity.

The Airbus SA3 proposal (derived from the JET) became the foundation of the Airbus A.320. Building on the philosophy of "using advanced technology" incorporated in the A.310 derivative of the A.300, Airbus decided to incorporate major technology advances in the A.320, the most radical of which was to be digital computer-controlled fly-by-wire. The project was finally launched as a 150 to 190 seater in April 1984, after protracted discussions about Returnable Launch Investment support from the French, West German, Spanish and British governments, but this took time to arrange.

With the aircraft definition finally settled, the A320 project required four-government financial support to each of the Airbus industrial participants (Spanish company CASA took a 4.2 per cent share in Airbus GIE in 1971). None of the individual Airbus partner companies could raise sufficient capital to self-finance the whole of their anticipated share of the multi-year, multi-billion dollar total investment required, the total design and development cost alone being 1.7 billion dollars US (equivalent to some four billion dollars US in 2019). The French government declared "in" after a short interval but the German industrial position at first focused more on wishing to launch a larger aircraft (which materialised later as the Airbus A.330/340 widebody pair project). The Spanish small minority position in Airbus was insufficient to influence the A.320 outcome. The British contribution (for the wing design and manufacture, BAe still as a subcontractor) was very important. Airbus GIE very much wanted this to continue but, theoretically, the work could be awarded to any willing and capable other company in another country. In government departments and at Cabinet level, the British government was sceptical about European new airliner projects, Prime Minister Margaret Thatcher declaring; "The last thing I want to do is encumber myself with another Concorde".[3]

The 1981 privatisation of BAe had resulted in a new, industrially-experienced chairman being appointed, Sir Austin Pearce, previously Chairman and Chief Executive of Esso UK. He had been involved also with the committee formed in the 1970s to discuss the nationalisation of the UK aerospace industry. French, German and Spanish governments each eventually agreed to provide Returnable Launch Investment (RLI) as part-contributions towards their country's share of the A.320 project. In 1984, after discussions with the British government stalled, Pearce was advised directly by a member of the German government that, if Britain had not decided on participation "within a few weeks", they (the French, German and Spanish governments) were prepared to support the other Airbus industrial partners in creating the wings themselves (or maybe seeking an alternative partner elsewhere).

Pearce was fully aware of the poor state of the BAe civil aircraft business. Apart from Airbus A.300 and A.310 widebody wings, BAe only had the ageing HS.748 turboprop project, the recently relaunched smaller Jetstream 31 turboprop and the (then) slow-selling BAe 146 regional jet in production. The A.320 project had been worked up with the input of likely customers of this class of airliner and had a good market case, despite a 700 aircraft break-even prediction, because it targeted the largest aircraft market in the world, with several thousand older designs with much

---

3. Stephen Aris: "Close to the Sun", page125.

higher operating costs in service and wearing out. The acknowledged supercritical aerodynamics wing design expertise of Britain made a strong case for including BAe but finance was needed.

Despite some personal reservations, without reference to his company executive management (some of whom had other ideas about future project investment) Pearce quickly requested a one-to-one meeting with Mrs Thatcher. The request was made directly with the British Prime Minister's office, to the fury of the British Secretary of State for Trade and Industry, Norman Tebbit (later, Lord Tebbit). On the Friday of the same week, Pearce was advised he had a slot with Mrs Thatcher at ten o'clock the following Monday morning. Pearce was used to negotiating at senior government level when at Esso and also knew that going "through channels" would take time, would be leaked in the process and, eventually, most likely result in a "No". On the Sunday, Tebbit telephoned Pearce and called him "several different kinds of bastard", partly because he, Norman Tebbit, believed the aircraft would not sell well. Pearce just replied that he was talking about the survival of his business, protocol was irrelevant here. When he arrived on the Monday morning, he found a thunderous-looking Norman Tebbitt also present. Pearce was advised he had just twenty-five minutes to make his case. He advised that he was talking about the actual survival of BAe and outlined the facts in three key matters, "the impact on the [BAe] commercial position, on the workforce and on the worldwide reputation as an aircraft manufacturer, without the money BAe was going down the drain", and a reminder that BAe had been the first company privatisation of Mrs Thatcher and her government in 1981. Site closures and thousands of redundancies were looming, a PR disaster for the British government's privatisation agenda.

After a few questions and answers, it is reported that Mrs Thatcher said, "Give him the money, Norman".[4]

Mrs Thatcher's decision, to support the A.320 project, was not actually all solely in response to the BAe Chairman's direct appeal. Prior to a Franco-German-British government summit meeting early in 1984, the French gogvernment had persuaded the German government to finally agree to support the SA3/A.320. At the summit meeting, the French and German leaders bluntly advised the British leader exactly the same warning given to Pearce, to the effect, "join in the A.320 or we will seek partnership elsewhere". In truth, by 1984 Airbus as an entity was balanced on the cusp of becoming financially stable. The supporting governments were each so heavily invested in the organisation's aircraft programmes by this time that there would not have been much sense in "pulling the plug" and causing the collapse of Airbus. The A.320 programme was formally launched in March 1984, with orders for ninety-six aircraft.

Would the A.320 pay for itself? After a 1987 first flight (and two reputation-disturbing early crashes, which were not the fault of the design or manufacture), the answer turned out to be yes, "in spades". Including all four variants ranging from 120 to 200 seating capacity and, with recent new engine options, over 9,000 aircraft of the total A.320 family had been built by the beginning of 2020. At that time there were outstanding orders to take the total to over 14,500 aircraft (see section 7.4, table 7.3). The underlying main reasons for success have been reliable advanced technology, competitive operating economics and build quality, sometimes offset to some extent by a higher initial sales price to airlines (but, at least initially, often on attractive financial terms). Everyone "has got more than their money back".

---

4. Stephen Aris: "Close to the Sun" page 126.

8.4 The Last All-British Airliners

BAe Jetstream

Scottish Aviation had absorbed the ex-Handley Page Jetstream project in 1970 (see section 6.6). In 1976 the nationalisation of the majority of the British aircraft industry into the single company British Aerospace (BAe) included Scottish Aviation in Prestwick, Scotland. As part of BAe, the re-engining and upgrade of the original Handley Page Jetstream turboprop feeder liner commenced in 1978. Known at first as the Jetstream 3 (became the BAe eighteen passenger Jetstream 31), the engines were changed to higher power USA Garrett TPE-331 units, maximum take-off weight allowed was increased by 22 per cent and a revised cockpit (digital electronic instruments) and cabin layout introduced. First flight was in March 1980 and the first BAe Jetstream 31 went into service in June 1982. In 1988 a further upgraded engine version was introduced, known as the Jetstream 32. In total, 386 Jetstream 31/32 were produced.

BAe Jetstream 32. (*Josh Beasley, CC BY-SA 2.0*)

In November 1992 the first flight of a significantly stretched model took place. Known as the Jetstream 41, this aircraft had seating for up to thirty passengers, 75 per cent more engine power and the MTOW was increased by 56 per cent to 24,000lb; 100 Jetstream 41 were produced.

In 1993, due to negotiations concerning the use of the BAe Woodford site in a joint venture with a Taiwanese aerospace company to take on the BAe 146 regional jet project (see section 8.6), the responsibility of the BAe ATP (a sixty-four seater turboprop project based at Woodford) was transferred to the Prestwick site. The ATP was re-branded under the generic "Jetstream" label as the Jetstream 61. However, the 146/Woodford joint venture was not established and the Jetstream 61 programme was curtailed before any aircraft were sold.

HS/BAe 146

The original Hawker Siddeley Aviation 146 regional jet airliner concept was intended to fit the passenger seating capacity gap between the HS.748/Fokker F.27 size turboprops and the smaller jet airliners, such as the BAC.1-11/Boeing 737. The aircraft needed to be well-suited to smaller regional airfields (i.e. airfields which had short runways, terminals not necessarily equipped with passenger air bridges and/or long passenger steps, or mobile power-driven baggage loading ramp facilities). A short runway take-off and landing performance was therefore specified, to widen the choice of regional airports which could be used. The "unsophisticated" airport compatibility meant low sill height for baggage bay loading, leading to a high wing configuration, in turn most compatible with a T-tail. There was not a turbofan engine available to provide the resultant aircraft with the right amount of power from two engines, so a wing-mounted four-engined configuration (using relatively simple USA Avco Lycoming ALF-502 turbofans) was selected.

The project was launched in 1973, with 50 per cent financial support to the development costs from the UK government in return for a share in the revenue from each aircraft sold. The same year, the 1973 world oil crisis resulted from the oil export embargo as a result of the" Yom Kippur" Arab-Israeli war, causing air transport cost escalation and traffic reduction. The air transport world contracted, one casualty result being the 1974 suspension of the 146 programme. Some low-key work on 146 design continued, but it was not until 1978 that BAe (having absorbed Hawker Siddeley Aviation), with government agreement, restarted the project, just as the Joint European Transport airliner study project was winding up (see section 8.3).

The BAe 146 design was a deliberate attempt to simplify, to hold down cost and to ease maintenance. Due to four engines improving short runway performance, there was no need for wing leading edge high lift devices. Full span wing flaps and spoilers/ lift dumpers enhanced the short field performance and obviated the need for engine thrust reversers. Three sizes of aircraft were eventually produced: Series 100, (seventy to eighty-two passengers), Series 200 (eighty-five to 100 passengers) and, in 1988, Series 300 (ninety-seven to 112 passengers).

Production was distributed, the nose manufacture and final aircraft assembly at the ex-de Havilland Hatfield site, centre fuselage at the ex-Bristol Filton site, the rear fuselage at the ex-Avro Chadderton site, the fin at the ex-Blackburn Brough site and the engine pylons at the ex-Scottish Prestwick site. Overseas suppliers were to build the wings (Textron, USA) and the tailplane (Saab, Sweden), later repatriated to BAe sites. First flight was 3 September 1981. The four turbofan engines made the aircraft quiet on both take-off and landing and, for some time, the 146 was the only jet airliner allowed to operate at airfields with vociferous particularly noise-sensitive communities nearby, notably John Wayne airport in Orange County, Southern California, USA. The large "petal" airbrake on the rear fuselage could be deployed during descent to the runway, enabling steep approaches to difficult airfields. This was a major performance advantage when, in 1992, the 146 became the first (and only, for a while) jet-powered regional airliner to be cleared to use London City Airport with its very short east-west runway (4,900ft = 1,500m), surrounded by a city landscape and almost in line with and less than three miles from Canary Wharf and its high rise buildings. London City Airport was thus opened up to European inter-city jet airliner operations, prompting further sales of the BAe 146.

A second 146 assembly line was opened at BAe Woodford in 1986, becoming the only production line when the Hatfield site was closed by BAe in 1993. Updates to the aircraft and its engines were carried out on more than one occasion (as is usual in an airliner project, to maintain competitiveness) and, as production at Hatfield finished, the aircraft was re-branded as the

Avro RJ.100 (= 146 Series 300). (*Julian Herzog, CC BY-SA 4.0*)

Avro RJ (-70, -85 and -100 denoting capacity). The final update, to an RJX standard, involved a revised engine and cockpit update. This commenced in 1999 but BAE Systems (as BAe had become) curtailed development in 2002. The last Avro RJ (née HS.146) left the Woodford site in 2003 (see section 8.6) after 387 aircraft "of the 146 type" in total had been produced, the largest number of jet airliners produced in Britain.

BAe ATP

From its first flight in 1960, the original Avro/HS 748 twin turboprop forty to fifty-eight passenger airliner (see section 5.8) had been upgraded several times with improved engines and systems. It remained in production until 1988, with 380 produced in total.

By the early 1980s it was clear that an increased size replacement was needed. The sixty-four passenger BAe Advanced TurboProp (ATP) was launched in 1984. The decision was made to create a newly-certificated 748 derivative (i.e. redesigned to be certificated to the latest airworthiness requirements). This contrasted with the "prototype modified" less expensive approach adopted by its main competitor, the imminent upgrade and re-engining of the (1955 first flight) Dutch F.27 Friendship, to become the Fokker F.50 version of the F.27. Part of the BAe reasoning was the additional competition from the all-new Franco-Italian ATR.42 forty-eight passenger twin turboprop, which would have its first flight in 1984 and would clearly be capable of stretching to at least ATP capacity.

More fuel-efficient engines and a slow-revving six-bladed propeller, a stretched fuselage (with a revised nose, more closely-spaced windows and accommodating sixty-four passengers), new engine-propellers, a small increase in wing span and a raked fin were the most noticeable external changes from the 748 to the ATP. Internally, all systems were completely changed. First flight was on 6 August 1986 (at 10.05 am, five minutes late to the original date and time set at programme launch). Only sixty-four aircraft

BAe ATP. (*Radoslaw Idaszak, GFDL 1.2*)

were built, the curtailed production being due to slow sales and the 1988 emergence of the ATR.72 turboprop with a capacity of up to seventy-eight passengers.

The ATP was rebranded by BAe as the Jetstream 61 in 1993 but this did not prolong production, because BAe decided to cease all indigenous airliner activity by the start of the twenty-first century (see "BAe Jetstream" above and section 8.6).

8.5 After Britten-Norman

John Britten

John Britten left the board of Fairey-owned Britten-Norman (the company he had co-founded) in 1976, see section 6.4. In 1979, he formed a new company Aerospace Designs (Bembridge) Ltd, within which he organised the creation of the Britten Sheriff light aircraft design. Britten's project team included his brother Robin Britten as Sheriff Aerospace chairman, Jim McMahon and Frank Mann (fellow founder-directors of Britten Norman), Dennis Berryman (former chief designer for Britten Norman), John Mills (former chief production engineer at Vickers) and Maurice Brennan (former Saunders Roe chief designer and subsequently at Folland and Avro within the Hawker Siddeley Group, see section 5.14).

The Sheriff was a twin piston-engined light low wing monoplane aircraft, with a cabin which could be configured as a two-seat trainer or a four-seat tourer. It was deliberately created with overseas licence production in mind, aimed at undercutting other equivalent aircaft. Production was to be financed via a dedicated new company, Sheriff Aerospace. John Britten died in 1977 but, by 1983, an agreement to produce in Romania seemed imminent. Lack of finance prevented this before the prototype under construction could be completed. Sheriff Aerospace ceased trading in 1984. Aerospace Designs (Bembridge) continued as a consultancy in all aspects of light aircraft design.

Nigel Desmond Norman

When co-founder Nigel Desmond Norman left Britten-Norman in 1976, he took the last Britten-Norman design with him. This was the BN-3 Nymph, a high wing single piston-engined four-seat monoplane design, intended for overseas licence production (the prototype first flew under the B-N banner in 1969).

Norman founded NDN Aircraft Ltd. at Sandown, on the Isle of Wight. NDN designed the NDN-1 Firecracker, a single-engined trainer, aimed at replicating the low speed handling of a jet trainer. The first aircraft flew using a piston engine, on 26 May 1977. Revising the design, during 1983–84 three NDN-1T Turbo-Firecrackers were produced for Specialist Flying Training of Hamble (who contract-trained foreign military student pilots). An upgraded version, with a more powerful engine and ejection seats, was proposed for the RAF Jet Provost replacement, in collaboration with the Hunting Group, via a specially formed company Hunting Firecracker Aircraft Ltd. In March 1985, the proposal lost to the Shorts-Embraer Tucano (see section 6.7).

NDN moved from Sandown to Barry, near Cardiff in 1985, encouraged by financial support from the Welsh Development Agency. Around the same time it was renamed as the Norman Aeroplane Company (NAC). Hunting handed responsibility for the Firecracker back to the new company (NAC) in 1986.

A reworked version of the BN-3 Nymph, with a lengthened cabin accommodating the pilot and three passengers, was designed. The first example flew before the move to Wales, in September 1984, appearing with the type designation NAC-1. Parts were built for five more aircraft but NAC ceased trading before any more could be assembled.

NDN had previously designed and built a new agricultural aircraft (crop sprayer), the NDN-6 Fieldmaster. This was later known as the NAC-6 Fieldmaster. The prototype first flew at the NDN facility at Sandown, Isle of Wight, in December 1981. As part of the 1985 company move to Wales, series production of the Fieldmaster was planned. It was intended that parts would be produced in Yugoslavia and the aircraft assembled in Cardiff. The series of ethnic wars in Yugoslavia prevented this. Only five more production Fieldmasters were completed before NAC went into receivership in 1988. A Fieldmaster revival was attempted in Turkey but only four aircraft were completed, two without engines.

After the collapse of NAC, Norman was associated with several different light aircraft projects and consultancy roles, including the creation of the Skylander light cargo aircraft, based on an enlarged version of the BN-2 Islander configuration. This was a project of the specifically-created Sky Aircraft subsidiary of the French company GECI Aviation, announced in 2001. Desmond Norman died in 2002. The Skylander went on to progress as far as producing a mock-up and production and financing discussions with several potential partners, which petered out. Sky Aviation finally went into receivership in 2013.

8.6 British Aerospace Reformed

BAe was much more than an aircraft company as the last decade of the twentieth century opened, more than even an aerospace company: 1991 had dawned with BAe Airlines Division, BAe Military Aircraft Division, BAe Dynamics (Missiles and Space & Communications) and the ex-UK government privatised Royal Ordnance Factory (ammunition and light weapons business). As a diversification policy, BAe had also acquired a car business (Austin Rover), a Dutch construction company (Ballast Needham) and had a legacy shareholding in the Hutchinson telecommunications company. The diversification policy of the chairman (Professor Sir Roland Smith) had not solved the financial issues facing the company. Concerned about the cash demands of some of the acquired businesses (for essential new product development) a majority of the directors of the company wanted to reverse some of the diversification, continue to rationalise parts of the aircraft and missiles businesses and re-establish a more stable financial position. Allegedly, in September 1991, Professor Smith went into a board meeting and asked what was being done about the first item on the agenda. The senior director present advised the chairman that there was a new first item and passed over an unsigned letter of resignation, with Sir Roland's name at the bottom. The professor looked round the table, saw the mood, signed and left.

One main financial problem was that BAe had to make a balance sheet provision in 1992 for a £1 billion potential liability to 146 airliner lease-sales (any of which theoretically could be returned to BAe in what had become a difficult airline transport market). The Rover Group car business (control controversially acquired by BAe in 1988 for £100 million) also needed heavy financial commitment, in order to modernise its range of cars by creating new models.

An "Asset Management" facility was created specifically to manage the re-lease of any 146 regional jet airliners which might be returned. As the airline industry mini-recession receded, the value of retaining such an in-house proactive management of the BAe airliner fleet (all types) became more attractive, helping financial arrangements to aid new aircraft sales and onward sales of second-hand models.

The company had actually started to reconstruct its aircraft businesses in 1982, one year after privatisation. BAe as a whole now began changing direction. In 1992, the 80 per cent shareholding in the Rover Group was sold to the German company BMW for £800 million (the 20 per cent owned since 1980 by the Japanese car company Honda was later also sold to BMW). Ballast Needham was sold off and the telecommunications shareholding was reduced.

In June 1997, British Aerospace Defence managing director John Weston commented, "Europe… is supporting three times the number of [defence] contractors on less than half the budget of the U.S.". The company had clearly decided that the business had to grow its presence in the USA, to compete more effectively with Boeing, Lockheed and Northrop-Grumman for the systems integrator role which new projects demanded. The basic objective was to gain better access to the large USA budget for defence systems acquisitions. BAe had no stamina, heart or cash for the cost of continuing on their own in commercial aircraft design, and they had only a minority say in Airbus when confronted by a seemingly stacked Franco-German alliance.

British Aerospace "Aircraft Change Direction" Decisions, 1982 to 1999	
1982	Close Bracebridge Heath in Lincolnshire (ex-Avro) support site and the test airfield facility site (ex-Blackburn) at Home-on-Spalding Moor
1983	Close Bitteswell (ex-Armstrong Whitworth) aircraft repair & support site
1984	Close Hurn, near Bournemouth (ex-Vickers), test and assembly site
1987	Close Weybridge (ex-Vickers) manufacture and assembly site
1987–90	Widening of business base (defence and non-defence) (Royal Ordnance, Austin-Rover cars, Ballast Needham Construction acquired)
1990	Close Preston "Strand Road" (ex-English Electric) manufacturing site
1992	Close Kingston (ex-Hawker) design and manufacturing site
1993	BAe 125 business jet project (ex-de Havilland) sold to Raytheon (USA)
1994	Close Hatfield (ex-de Havilland) design, manufacture, assembly and test site. Airbus wing design responsibility moved from Hatfield to Filton site
1996	BAe take 20 per cent stake in Airbus Company in exchange for BAe Filton (ex-Bristol) and Hawarden (ex-de Havilland) facilities, as "Airbus UK"
1999	Close Dunsfold (ex-Hawker) assembly and test site

The BAe Chester (Hawarden) site was, and remains, the facility where Airbus wings were and are assembled. Transfer of the Hatfield element of parts manufacture and design responsibility for Airbus wings to the Filton site allowed the combined Filton-Chester sites to become the BAe Airbus Division. In 1996, BAe exchanged the division in its entirety for a 20 per cent equity stake in Airbus. For the BAe aircraft business, the programme of change would continue well into the twenty-first century, as described later, in section 10.2.

Other BAe 1990s changes not involving "aircraft" site closures were:

- In 1992, BAe Defence Ltd. was created as a wholly-owned subsidiary, containing BAe (Dynamics) Ltd., BAe (Military Aircraft) Ltd., Royal Ordnance plc. and BAe Systems and Services Division.
- In 1993, Ballast Needham construction was sold to a Dutch consortium for £175 million.
- In 1994 the BAe Defence subsidiary Space Systems business within BAe (Dynamics) Ltd. was sold to Marta-Marconi Space. The ex-BAe Dynamics 25 per cent share in Matra-Marconi Space would be returned to BAE Systems with BAe's acquisition of Marconi Electronic Systems in 1999 (see section 10.2).
- In 1994, the BAe 80 per cent stake in Rover Group cars was sold to BMW (Germany) for £800 million (within a month, the remaining Honda 20 per cent stake was also sold to BMW).
- In 1996 BAe merged the remaining guided weapon business of BAe Dynamics Ltd. into a half-share in the Anglo-French Matra-BAe Dynamics guided weapon and UAV business (MBDA).

BAe/BAE Systems Ceases In-house Complete Airliner Activity:

By the start of the 1990s, British airliner manufacturing activity had become confined to two turboprop types (the sixty-four passenger ATP and the smaller Jetstream) and the turbofan BAe 146 70-to-112 passenger family (see section 8.4). These were all essentially in the regional airliner market.

The emergence of a regional jet (as opposed to turboprop) really began with the French twin turbojet-engined eighty-passenger Sud Aviation Caravelle, which entered service in 1955. Although its Rolls-Royce Avon engines were a quite thirsty compared with the more modern ones since developed, this was partially offset by fuel prices being relatively low. Jet speeds did not offer any significant total travel time advantage over turboprops on shortish range operations but passengers liked the further reduction in cabin noise and vibration in cruise, even when compared with the new turboprop Vickers Viscount. In the eyes of most manufacturers and operators, until the 1980s short-medium range operations with forty to sixty-five passenger seats mostly remained the domain of Rolls-Royce Dart turboprop powered aircraft (see section 5.8). For routes with more passengers, three newer twin (low by-pass) turbojet-powered airliner families went into service. These were the British eighty-seat BAC 1-11 and the American ninety-seat Douglas DC-9 (both into service in 1965) and the Dutch sixty-five to eighty-five seat Fokker F28 (into service in 1969), as more fuel-efficient airliners than the earlier pure turbojet Caravelle. Except for the spikes due to the short Arab-Israeli armed conflicts of 1967 and 1973, until 1974 fuel prices overall remained low enough for these aircraft to continue to make overall business sense for airlines. A five-times basic crude oil price rise in 1974–75 and a three-times further rise 1979–82 created a very difficult economic challenge for all modes of transport, not least jet turbine-engined commercial airliners. From 1982 to 1999, oil prices fluctuated but dropped by 75 per cent overall, then rose dramatically in a spiky volatile manner for the next fifteen years, declining again in the last few years before 2020. That is why fuel efficiency has become a major economic issue, especially for internal combustion engined transport such as airliners.

A re-engined and enlarged Fokker successor to the F28, the 97-to-122 passenger F100 with medium by-pass engines, went into service in 1988. A smaller version, the Fokker F70 seventy to eighty-five seater, entered airline service in 1995. The Fokker F100/F70 two-airliner family was intended as the main competitor to the BAe 146. These two manufacturers competed in the section of the market for jet turbofan airliners under the the DC-9 size, which had had a variant stretched to 135 passenger seat capacity by 1974. Despite turboprop fuel economy, which still pertained, from the mid-1980s more of the world's airlines gradually "changed gear". They wished to respond to the fact that fuel prices overall dropped in the 1980s and regional jets rather than turboprops were more "what the passenger liked" (quieter and quicker). Passengers also felt (inaccurately) that "propeller-driven aircraft are passé old technology", despite their fuel economy (seat-mile cost) advantage. Newer airframe technology and the use of ever more fuel-efficient turbofan engines would begin to challenge Fokker and BAe in parts of their turboprop market areas.

By the early 1990s, the regional jet airliner maximum size potential was seen to be progressively "capped" by the 120-to-130 seat McDonnell Douglas MD-87 developed version of the DC-9 (first delivery 1987), the 135-seater twin turbofan Airbus A.319 (launched in 1993 as a shortened version of the A.320,[5] first flight 1995), the slightly larger in-service Boeing 737-500 (first delivery 1990), the 120-to-130 seat McDonnell Douglas MD-87 developed version of the DC-9 (first delivery 1987) and a further development of the DC-9, the 106-to-117 seat MD-95/Boeing 717-200 (first delivered in 1999).

So what happened in the 1990s to the regional airliner market and the British business of airliner design and manufacturing?

(1) During 1992–1993, BAe attempted to set up a joint venture for the three-variant (70 to 112 seats) 146/RJ regional jet (turbofan-powered) airliner project (soon to be marketed as the Avro RJ). This was to include transfer into joint ownership of the BAe Woodford site with the Taiwan Aerospace Corporation (TAC), with an implied commitment to develop a twin-engined and re-winged version of the 146 called the New Regional Airliner (NRA). The Woodford ATP turboprop project was not part of the proposed agreement and was transferred to the BAe Prestwick site, the ATP being renamed as the Jetstream 61 alongside the Prestwick-based Jetstream 31 and 41 turboprop projects. TAC and BAe were, however, unable to cement the proposed deal. This was partly because there was failure by TAC to obtain the necessary financial guarantees and partly because there was no agreement established concerning intellectual property rights transfer.

(2) After the curtailment of the BAe-TAC joint venture discussions, the BAe airliner design and marketing functions carried out a fifteen-month study during 1993–94, with actual market testing. This produced the outline of an all-new twin turbofan engined regional jet, known as the RJX. This internal study result was a low-winged airliner with five-abreast seating (3-2) and a capacity of 90 to 135 passengers, depending on variant. Maximum range was to be 2,000 miles. A high speed model was tested in the Aircraft Research Association (ARA) transonic wind tunnel at Bedford, showing real promise. Externally and technically

---

5. As a later market-defensive measure, Airbus launched an even smaller version of the A.320, the 100-to-130 seat A.318, first flight 2002.

(modern materials, fly-by-wire etc.), this all-new BAe RJX looked a lot like the later outcome of the Canadian Bombardier BRJ-X studies (see item (9) below).

In 1994 terms, the likely total development cost and investment in production for this all-new BAe RJX airliner in the last half of the 1990s would have approached around half the 2019 values shown graphically in section 9.3 (in 2019 terms, the RJX would have actually cost close to the same values, mostly due to the effects of inflation). Combined with the 1992 £1 billion financial "black hole" in BAe's accounts, in what was likely to be a crowded regional jet airliner future marketplace, senior BAe management were, however, unenthused about pursuing this RJX idea, even if the project could be shared with others. BAe instead focussed on continuing to trying to obtain a partnership in the market, as outlined in item (3) below.

(3)   During 1995–98, a further attempt in the rationalisation of the regional aircraft supply business arena was a joint venture between the Franco-Italian Avions de Transport Regional (ATR) and BAe, called Aero International (Regional), or AI(R). This joint venture recognised the overlap between the turboprop airliners ATR.72 and the BAe ATP/Jetstream 61. As a result, the ATP/Jetstream 61 project was ended. Further discussions did not lead to agreement on a new regional jet future joint project and the AI(R) joint venture was eventually dissolved. Parallel BAe discussions concerning the 146/RJ aircraft programme took place in Asia (China, 1995–96 and Malaysia, 1997), with a view to sharing in regional aircraft supply. These did not result in any agreement. At the end of this period, the last BAe Jetstream 41 turboprop airliner was delivered in 1998.

(4)   After the 1986 Bombardier takeover of Canadair, in 1989, a relatively inexpensive fuselage stretch and re-engining development of the Canadair Challenger large business aircraft was launched by the new owners. This created the CRJ twin turbofan powered regional jet series of aircraft, with four-abreast seating. The resulting fifty-seater CRJ-100 was in service by 1992. Including the uprated later CRJ-200 version, 1,021 were built. The further stretched CRJ-700/900/1000 series (66 to 104 seats) was launched in 1997 and achieved sales of over 850 aircraft in total.

In 1996, Bombardier briefly considered acquiring a majority stake in the Dutch aircraft manufacturer Fokker. After a month, Bombardier withdrew. This contributed to Fokker having to declare bankruptcy and F100/F70 production ceasing in 1997. Bombardier started their own all-new regional jet aircraft studies (labelled BRJ-X) but, due to market conditions, these were suspended in 2000.

(5)   The twin turbofan powered Brazilian Embraer ERJ.145, with around fifty seats in a four-abreast interior layout, entered service in 1997. Later, the ERJ.145 became available in the smaller variants ERJ.140 and ERJ.135. Success (over 1,000 ERJs eventually sold) led to further development. The all-new Embraer regional jet, the E-jet family series with 66-to-116 seats, was launched in 1999 and flying by 2002. By the middle of 2019, 1,500 of the E-jet family of aircraft had been delivered with some 350 more on order.

(6)   During the 1993–94 BAe RJX study, the Japanese Mitsubishi regional jet study team visited BAe and expressed a little interest. Mitsubishi's own Japanese government-sponsored regional jet studies only actually launched as a significant study project much later, in 2003, becoming the seventy-five to ninety seat Mitsubishi Regional Jet (MRJ) launched as a real two-variant project in 2008. Vacillation over the incorporation of high technology delayed detail design such that the MRJ first flight was only in 2015. Protracted testing delayed delivery, such that orders for fifty aircraft of the 167 total received were cancelled. Subsequently, in May 2019, Mitsubishi specifically targeted the individual airliner capacity-limited

part of the USA regional market, by limiting the smaller version of the MRJ to less than seventy-six seats and renaming the project as the Mitsubishi Space Jet. Mainly in order to capture a well-developed and established worldwide technical support organisation for its new aircraft, Mitsubishi purchased all rights to the Bombardier in-service CRJ project, also in 2019. Almost 1,900 CRJ aircraft in total had been delivered by Bombardier by then and there are outstanding orders yet to be delivered in a Mitsubishi-managed process. By the start of 2020, MRJ deliveries had not commenced but firm orders for 167 were in place, with 180 more as "options".

(7)   Russian Sukhoi company regional jet protracted studies started in 1993. After procrastination and over-extended development, these finally led to the 90-to-100 seat Sukhoi Superjet 100 (first flight 2008). Net orders of over 300 aircraft were achieved by the start of 2020, with half of these delivered.

(8)   After gaining experience of Western aviation technology, by licence building McDonnell-Douglas developments of the DC-9, the government-owned Chinese Aviation Industry Corporation (AVIC) decided to produce a new regional airliner. Forming a subsidiary Commercial Aircraft Company (Comac), the ARJ 21 project was eventually started in earnest in 2002. This was a two-variant product, seating seventy-eight to 105 passengers and used twin rear fuselage mounted USA GEC turbofan engines. The declared intention was a first flight in 2005 but this did not take place until 2008. Protracted development problems (including wing failure during static load testing) and certification difficulties causing service introduction to be delayed until 2016. As of the end of 2018, just six aircraft were in service out of eighty-two confirmed on order and twenty-five options, with another reported 378 on order (later data suggests that forty-eight more deliveries had been achieved by the end of April 2020). The outstanding orders are all for service with Chinese airlines, except for five speculatively on order for a USA aircraft leasing company.

(9)   Bombardier had started an all-new regional jet study under the BRJ-X label in the early 1990s. Overtaken by the CRJ project (item 4 above), the BRJ-X resurfaced in 2004. This was under the freshly-appointed leadership of a senior ex-Boeing executive who had led the 737NG (Next Generation) programme (the third generation of this ubiquitous Boeing type) which first flew in 1997. The new project became the Bombardier C-Series 116-to-160 passenger airliner two-variant family, finally launched in 2008. This is a fly-by-wire high technology aircraft, taking much more development effort and time than planned but finally achieving the first delivery in 2016. Absorbed into Airbus in 2018, there were 100 C-Series deliveries by the end of 2019, with 430 more on order and the project reidentified and marketed as the Airbus A.220.

(10)   "E2" updated variants of the Embraer E-Jet family, with improved aerodynamics, Pratt and Whitney geared turbofan engines and fly-by-wire technology, were launched by Embraer in 2011, with the first delivery taking place in 2018. The 120-to-130 seat E195-E2 (the largest variant) totalled eight deliveries by December 2019 with 160 more on order. This model is a head-to-head competitor with the smaller of the two variants of the Bombardier C-Series (see item 9 above).

(11)   In 1999, BAe and Marconi Electronic Systems merged to become BAE Systems (see section 10.2). The 1999-authorised jointly sponsored BAE Systems-Honeywell-GKN re-engined upgrade of the 146/RJ (as the 146-RJX) was cancelled by BAe at the end of 2001. This was in the middle of the flight test programme and with committed orders for ten aircraft. The cancellation, which included compensation to the other partner companies and affected customers, was excused as the consequence of the reduction in world airline activity following the 2001 World

Trade Centre 9/11 terrorist atrocity in New York. The last 146/RJ was delivered from Woodford in 2003. The reasoning for project complete termination might have had some validity at the time but there was no visible BAE Systems subsequent attempt to consider any airliner alternative for the future.

All this study and business activity at the small-size end of the world jet airliner market was taking place when the world was often in economic turmoil amongst greater world events. The break-up of the Soviet Union and its after-effects, the ethnic wars in former Yugoslavia, other military confrontations in places like Kuwait and Iraq and the emergence of major terrorist activity in the Western world were prominent. Significant variations in the price of oil-based fuel in the 1970s, 1980s and 1990s, the subsequent twenty-first century oil price rise and fall and the 2008 world financial crisis were other economically destabilising influences on the world.

Both Embraer and Bombardier sought external partnership participation in the early stages of their respective regional jet programme studies. BAe did not make any move to try to join any of these programmes on a collaboration basis, even those launched after the end of 146/RJ production in 2003. As well as Airbus taking a controlling share in the C-Series, Boeing were expecting to complete an 80 per cent buy-in to the Embraer E2 regional jet programmes by mid-2020. Amicable negotiations were derailed in April 2020 (see section 9.5).

In 2003, thus ended the British design and manufacture of complete new airliners, which had been continuous since the end of the First World War but never achieving more sales of one type than the 442 Vickers Viscounts delivered between 1953 and 1964, well before the airliner market "extravaganza years". Of the airliner industry, only the design and manufacturing of the Airbus wings, the wings for the Bombardier C-series (now the Airbus A.220) and the small Britten-Norman Islander aircraft family remain as active British production airliner products.

8.7 Westland Helicopters in the 1980s and 1990s

Subsequent to the 1960 regrouping of all British helicopter design and manufacturing activity under Westland Helicopters (see section 6.1), the company enjoyed some success with the Westland Scout and Wasp derivatives of the former Saro P.51 Skeeter and adaptation of the USA Sikorsky S-61 design into the Westland Sea King. Collaboration with the French company Aerospatiale on helicopter production had also been good business (see section 7.3), although not every element had been strictly adhered to by the French implementation, in failing to take delivery of Lynx helicopters as promised.

By the early 1980s, however, business had started to decline and the company was making losses. The British government, led by Margaret Thatcher, declined to provide any support, bluntly advising, "Westland was a private sector matter and it was on its own". In November 1985, USA Sikorsky were invited (by Westland) to consider taking a stake in Westland, via the Sikorsky parent company USA United Technologies (UTC). Sikorsky (UTC), later joined by the Italian Fiat aviation and automobile company, made a formal offer of a capital injection, in return for what would become a 22 per cent share of the ordinary shareholding. Westland were prepared to put the Sikorsky/Fiat offer to their shareholders. With a possible conversion of preference shares which the bidders owned, this would potentially increase the joint Sikorsky/Fiat voting shareholding in Westland to just under the 30 per cent level at which the British take over code would have forced a complete take over offer. Investment company Hanson also acquired shares totalling a 14.6 per cent stake in Westland.

Because the British armed forces helicopters all came via Westland (even the French-designed ones noted previously), the British government became involved with evaluating this, against a counter-proposition supported by the Secretary of State for Defence (Michael Heseltine). This involved a European-centered investment consortium of BAe (Britain), Augusta (Italy), Aerospatiale (France) and MBB (Germany). Concerning Westland, officially the government was neutral, the decision being in the hands of Westland shareholders. However, a proposed British, French, Italian and German government joint agreement to "buy European helicopters" would probably collapse if Westland were to become part-owned by an American helicopter company. Westland preferred the Sikorsky connection, which included placing work in the Westland factory. The Sikorsky connection had been well established over many years, with adaptations and improvements of Sikorsky designs (under licence).

The government (Cabinet) discussions on the subject were disharmonious and one or two of the details were leaked to the media, including confrontations involving the Prime Minister (Margaret Thatcher), the Secretary of State for Defence (Michael Heseltine) and the Secretary of State for Trade and Industry (Leon Brittan). By January 1986, the argument had polarised opinion sufficiently that the government "collective responsibility" was being invoked on a matter which, legally at least, was not actually the responsibility of the Cabinet. At a Cabinet meeting on 9 January 1986, Michael Heseltine dramatically resigned. Subsequently, Leon Brittan was forced to resign, due to supposed misrepresentation of the Prime Minister's position emerging after the protracted "Westland Affair".

The link to Sikorsky went ahead, with an injection of capital and work into Westland by the Sikorsky parent company United Technologies. In 1988, British engineering and services company GKN bought the Fiat and Hanson shares in Westland, giving GKN a 22 per cent share of Westland. In 1995, GKN then bought out other shareholders to take control, taking full ownership and naming the company as GKN Westland.

European Helicopter Industries and AugustaWestland

Previously, in 1980 the joint venture European Helicopter Industries (EHI) was established by Westland and the Italian helicopter manufacturer Augusta, specifically to respond to a British and Italian requirement to develop a replacement for the Sea King naval helicopters (which were based on the USA Sikorsky S-61, adapted and built under licence both in Italy and Britain and operated by both countries). In June 1981, the British government allocated £20 million to develop nine pre-series examples of a new helicopter. In 1984, the British and Italian governments secured the full funding of the development for a new aircraft. The supply of forty-four helicopters to Britain was contracted in 1991 to a consortium led by US management company IBM, which had the necessary financial resources to underwrite the contract.

Between 1984 and 1987, Westland separately investigated and proposed a design for a low-observable (stealth) attack helicopter, with motive machinery features derived from the Westland Lynx. Joining in with other European helicopter manufacturers, this culminated in the confidential WG47 as a response to army staff target GST.3971 for a "Light Attack Helicopter", which did not proceed.

Techniques used in the stealth studies were applied to the European consortia NH.90 helicopter project and the separate and larger Westland and Augusta (Italy) EHI joint venture design for a basic helicopter adaptable to ASW, air-sea rescue and troop transport roles. Given the type name EH.101, the first flight of the new Westland-Augusta helicopter was on 9 October 1987. In February 1995 Britain placed its first order for sixteen aircraft and Italy placed an order for sixteen more, later in the year.

When Westland and Augusta merged in 2001 to form AugustaWestland Helicopters, the EH.101 was re-branded as the AW.101. In UK army and navy service the AW.101 is known as the Merlin. Three turbine engines provide the power and, as the RN

Merlin HM.1 version, the helicopter has an MTOW of 32,188lbs, a maximum speed of 192mph and a range of just over 500 miles.

A total of over 145 AW.101 have been built so far, in service with ten different nations and in versions for naval and army use. The total does not include Canadian orders which were cancelled due to customer internal procurement political controversy. The Canadian Armed Forces (CAF) eventually acquired fifteen AW.101, all configured for use as search and rescue helicopters. CAF designated the type as the CH-149 Cormorant. Separately, nine specially adapted AW.101, (supplied to the USMC and known as the VH-71 Kestrel), were delivered as the winning offer for the USA VIP (Presidential) Helicopter Replacement project. Political controversy in the USA over "use of a foreign import for the President" caused the aircraft to be sold on to Canada, who used them to support their CH-149 version. AugustaWestland also produced two individual special civil versions of the AW.101. In April 2019, Poland signed an-offset deal to enable purchase of four AW.101s for the Polish navy.

Westland WAH-64 Apache Longbow
In 1986, the governments of Italy, the Netherlands, Germany and Spain agreed to study a new light attack helicopter. Between 1988 and 1990, Westland supported this study, which looked like becoming a scaled up development of the Augusta A.129 Mangusta (Mongoose). This was intended to be the pan-European light attack helicopter development. The British version was intended to respond to GST.3971 noted previously. The project also involved Fokker (Netherlands), MBB (West Germany) and CASA (Spain). In 1990, however, the Netherlands and Britain decided to acquire the USA Boeing AH-64 Apache instead and Westland and Fokker left the study.

Changes to the AH-64D Apache (Longbow) were made for Britain, including changing the two engines from the USA GE T700 to the more powerful Rolls-Royce-Turbomeca RTM 322, and adding a folding blade facility needed to adapt the helicopter to seaborne (RN) use. The first eight of the sixty-seven WAH-64D Apache aircraft ordered by the UK were built by Boeing, the remaining fifty-nine being built at the Westland factory in Yeovil (by 2001, the Yeovil facility of AugustaWestland).

In 2016, a UK-USA agreement was signed for Britain to acquire the upgraded AH-64 Apache Guardian built in the USA. Re-manufacture of fifty of the existing UK aircraft to the same standard will be included.

Lynx Becomes AW.159 Wildcat
In 1995 a project to replace the original Westland Lynx (see section 7.3) began to be discussed with the UK armed forces.

As the concept developed, Westland merged with Augusta of Italy to form AugustaWestland. The Lynx replacement became Future Lynx then, eventually, the Lynx Wildcat. By this time there were major design changes such that, although the overall shape was still recognisably a Lynx derivative, only 5 per cent of parts were common. Much of the change was caused by "monolithic" design, with far fewer separate piece-parts making up the airframe, reducing assembly costs considerably.

AW.159 Wildcat. (*Photo: PO(Phot) Si Ethell/MOD*)

First flight was in November 2009. AugustaWestland relabelled the new product as the AW.159 Wildcat in April 2009 and sixty-eight have been ordered to date, in versions for the British army and navy and the navy of the Republic of Korea.

8.8 New International Fighter/Strike Collaborative Aircraft

European Collaboration: Eurofighter Typhoon

The development effort for the Eurofighter Typhoon really started in 1972. It took twenty-two years from initial ideas to first flight in 1994, formal (committed) launch as a project of substance not taking place until 1986.

Starting with Air Staff Target (AST) 396 in 1971 for a Jaguar/Harrier replacement, rethought in 1975 as AST 403, the RAF initiated a requirement for a new air-superiority fighter, as an eventual replacement for RAF Jaguar and Phantom aircraft (then just entering service). HSA and BAC responded with a total of twenty single-engined and eight twin-engined alternative proposals, which outlined the trade-offs between performance, timescale and cost. Some proposals were insufficiently advanced beyond the USA McDonnell-Douglas F/A-18 Hornet, which would have its first flight in 1978. Six of the suggested designs merited further study. There was government doubt that the project would be affordable unless it was shared with another country. Meanwhile, a parallel West German Air Force initiative had led to the Messerschmitt-Bolkow-Blohm (MBB) TKF-90 fighter aircraft proposal. By 1978, Germany was also looking to find another partner-country to share in such a project, possibly using an international company such as Panavia, which had developed the Tornado (in service by 1979, see section 7.2). In 1979 BAe and MBB jointly presented to their respective governments the "European Combat Fighter" proposal. In October the same year, the French company Dassault joined in, to form a tri-nation study, as the European Combat Aircraft (ECA).

National designs were pursued and jointly discussed. All were aimed at relaxed stability aircraft (giving more manoeuvrability under pilot control), augmented by computer-controlled automatic stabilisation inputs allowing this relaxation.

Of the several alternative configurations studied by the BAC/HSA teams (by then combined in BAe), two alternative proposals were put forward:

- P.106 (single-engined, bifurcated fuselage side intakes, delta wing with canard*) (superficially resembling what became the Swedish Saab JAS 39 Gripen)
- P.110 (twin-engined with separate fuselage side intakes, delta wing, with canard*)

West Germany (MBB) refined their earlier ideas:

- TKF-90 (twin engined with chin intakes, cranked delta wing, with canard*)

France (Dassault) based their proposal on a development of their earlier ACT92 concept studies:

- ACX (twin-engined with separate fuselage side intakes, delta wing, with canard*)

The RAF rejected P.106 as "half the effectiveness of twin-engined at two-thirds the cost".

---

* in aeronautical terms, a canard wing is a small aerofoil (wing) ahead of the main wing, causing a reduction in pitch stability but giving a beneficial reduction in overall drag and improved aircraft manoeuvrability.

Ostensibly due to differences over operational requirements, such as the French requiring carrier-capable operational capability, plus French insistence on using the yet-to-be-developed French SNECMA M.88 engine (rather than the Anglo-German choice of a further developed version of the Tornado engine, the RB.199 made by Rolls-Royce-Britain/MTU-Germany/FiatAvio-Italy), France pulled out of the ECA in 1981. A more dominant and more likely main reason for the French departure was Dassault failing to successfully insist on design leadership for the ECA.

As a consequence, the existing Panavia (Tornado) partners BAe, German MBB and Italian Aeritalia launched the Agile Combat Aircraft (ACA) study programme in April 1982. The ACA was very similar to the P.110 proposal, in both configuration and overall size, but with chin engine intakes. However, the West German and Italian governments belatedly withdrew funding. Britain's MoD offered 50 per cent funding continuation for project development, if the other 50 per cent would be provided by industry. Industry partners MBB and Aeritalia signed up to join BAe in building two pre-prototype demonstrator experimental aircraft, one by BAe and one by MBB, known as the EAP (Experimental Aircraft Programme). In the event, only one EAP was built (by BAe) and flown (at the BAe Warton facility) at a cost of £80 million to the British government and £100 million to BAe, MBB and Aeritalia combined.

The front fuselage contained innovative materials, including carbon fibre composites and a new light alloy, aluminium-lithium. The other fuselage elements used conventional alloys and a modified Tornado fin was employed. The starboard (right hand) wing was a BAe co-bonded carbon fibre composite (developing the manufacturing tools and techniques used later on Eurofighter Typhoon),

BAE EAP. (*BAE Systems*)

whereas the port (left hand) wing was made in Italy. Canard foreplanes were also carbon fibre. Two standard Tornado RB.199 engines were installed. First flight was 8 August 1986.

The EAP and the eventual Typhoon bear a very strong external resemblance. The main differences are that the EAP cranked delta wings have been replaced by a straight delta, fin size is less and the rectangular chin engine intakes have been replaced with a curved ("smiling") shape. EAP was retired on 1 May 1991. Without the production techniques development and aerodynamic research and systems trials of the EAP, the Typhoon would not have become a reality. Meanwhile, in 1983 Italy, West Germany, France (again), Britain and Spain launched the Future European Fighter Programme (FEFA). STOL performance was included and combat capability beyond visual range (BVR) was an essential requirement. In 1984 France once again tried to insist on design leadership and a carrier operations capability. West Germany and Britain opted out and established a new European Fighter Aircraft (EFA) programme, joined by Italy on 2 August 1985. Initially remaining outside EFA, Spain joined one month later, despite French industrial and political pressure. France returned to its indigenous ACX/Rafale project.

A new international company was established in Munich in 1986 (Eurofighter Jagdflugzeug GmbH), to manage the Eurofighter project. EuroJet Turbo GmbH (headquartered in Hallebergmoos, near Munich) as an alliance of Rolls-Royce, MTU, FiatAvio and Industria de Turbo Propulsores (in Spain) were to develop the new EJ200 engines. The EJ200 is a production-developed version of the Rolls-Royce XG-40 advanced technology demonstrator turbojet, developed with British government support beginning in 1984 (first run 1991). The new aircraft was initially known as the Eurofighter EFA. Similar to the Tornado (MRCA) project, (see section 7.2) a four-nation NATO-recognised customer government agency (NATO EFA Development Production and Logistics Management Agency) was established, later absorbed into the joint NATO Eurofighter and Tornado Agency (NETMA), as responsible for both Eurofighter and Tornado.

All hiccups and delays were not yet over:

- Selection of the radar became an extremely contentious issue until the British government reassured the West German government that the British Ferranti company radar proposal would become part of the (then) much larger company GEC and receive British government backing after allowing the proposed GEC takeover. (West Germany had preferred a Hughes(USA)-GEC-AEG(Germany) proposal.)
- West and East Germany were reunited as a single country in 1990, requiring a general election for a new government for a united Germany to be held. The expected financial consequences[6] of German reunification caused the West German Chancellor Helmut Kohl to make an election promise for the December 1990 election, to cancel Eurofighter. In the early months of 1991 the new united Germany Minister of Defence tried to action this election promise but, because of the money already spent and committed, and the binding commitments on each partner government, Germany was unable to withdraw. Perhaps Helmut Kohl privately knew this would be the likely outcome when he made the promise!

First flight of the prototype Eurofighter Typhoon was on 27 March 1994 and the first production contract was signed on 9 December that same year. The originally intended aircraft production delivery totals were Britain 232, Germany 180, Italy 121 and Spain 87, with production work allocated as BAe 37.42 per cent, DASA (into which MBB had been merged) 29.03 per cent, Aeritalia 19.52 per cent and Spanish CASA 14.03 per cent. Production orders for the partner countries were not to be placed 'en bloc'; they would be split into batches called Tranches 1, 2 and 3. The Tranche 3 unit fly-away cost is approximately £98 million (2019 value). There are four separate assembly lines, where each partner company assembles its own national aircraft but each company builds the same parts for all aircraft (including export models to non-partner countries). To date (2019) 623 Typhoons have been ordered. The parts division of responsibility for major assemblies is as follows, based on the number of aircraft originally to be acquired for each national air force:

BAE Systems (Britain, ex-BAe)	Premium AEROTEC (German Airbus)	CASA (Spanish Airbus)	Leonardo (Italy, ex-Aeritalia)
Front & Rear Fuselage Foreplanes & Canopy Dorsal Spine & Tail Fin Inboard L.Edge Slats	Centre Fuselage	Starboard Wing L.Edge Slats	Port Wing Outboard Flaperons Rear Fuselage Sections

Weapons system responsibilities are similarly divided. The cockpit has three multi-function Head-Down Displays and a Head-Up Display, a helmet-mounted sight target designation (with fire and forget missiles), voice-recognised direct vocal command input (but *not* "missile shoot", for which a physical action is required), a computer-controlled Defensive Aids Sub-System (sensor-stimulated chaff, flares, towed radar

---

6. One estimate has totalled these costs at two trillion Euros over twenty years.

decoy and Electronic Countermeasures (ECM), plus target data fusion to enhance situation awareness). Data fusion is the computer-driven rationalisation and precision-enhancing combination of multi-sensor target detection data (radar, ESM, Infrared, plus data transferred from other friendly forces). This eliminates clutter (confusion between different sensor data creating more apparent targets than are actually present). Data fusion more precisely locates actual targets and threat identification.

Eurofighter Typhoon technology is a single-seater advanced twenty-first century fighter/strike aircraft, in that it is not naturally stable (computer-stabilised and fly-by-wire, therefore highly manoeuvrable with high agility (+9G/-3 'g')). It has a low radar signature (although not a true Stealth airframe design). Performance is Mach 2+, 65,000ft maximum altitude, thrust/weight ratio 1.15, with a maximum range (no drop tanks, unrefuelled) of 2,300 miles. It is a versatile aircraft, able to be an air superiority interceptor or to be armed to act in the strike role and/or surface reconnaissance.

RAF Eurofighter Typhoon FGR4. (*By Photo: SAC Tim Laurence/MOD, OGL v1.0*)

After the project launch in 1986, first flight was in 1994 and entry into service was nine years later, with front line squadron operational service starting two years after that. Compare this with the Supermarine Spitfire four years from the 1934 design launch, with a 1936 first flight and 1938 entry into service. The 1939 Spitfire fully armed export cost quote to Estonia (never fulfilled) of £12,500 each (see Section 2.7) would be equivalent to nearly £1 million in 2019 terms. The 2019 Eurofighter Typhoon new-order offer price was £125 million each, but the capabilities of the Eurofighter Typhoon and the Spitfire cannot be compared meaningfully.

Transatlantic Collaboration: The Lockheed-Martin Joint Strike Fighter, Lightning II
(A USA project in which Britain took a 15 per cent design-and-build share.)
The Joint Strike Fighter grew out of an early 1990s joint USN/USMC and the USA Defense Advanced Research Projects Agency (DARPA) Common Affordable Lightweight Fighter (CALF) ambition. The objective was to create a single aircraft intended as a replacement for both the Lockheed-Martin F-16 Fighting Falcon and the VTOL Boeing (ex-MacDonnell Douglas) and BAe AV-8B (BAe Harrier II), see section 6.3. Another *extremely* expensive programme was already in progress, producing the "best fifth generation interceptor in the world", the Lockheed-Martin twin-engined F-22 Raptor, which would be delivered to the USAF at a unit production cost of US $150 million (2009 price, equivalent to US $176 million in 2019). Aware of "the true (very high) cost of aiming at maximum performance", the US Congress directed that early studies for a future eventual F-22 Raptor replacement (the Joint Advanced Strike (JAST) programme) must be merged with CALF, to create the Joint Strike fighter (JSF) programme within a more overall cost restraint.

This created an immense technical challenge, because satisfying the advanced ambitions of the JAST programme, which was nominally for a conventional take-off and landing (CTOL) aircraft, could be compromised by the CALF VTOL requirement. The weight and, therefore, performance penalty of incorporating a direct lift system for VTOL would be an issue. The VTOL capability would have to be removable, to permit weight reduction for Raptor-like JAST aerodynamic performance, without fundamental redesign of whatever the JSF would turn out to be. Very interested in the VTOL capability, at an early stage (in 1995) Britain signed a Memorandum of Understanding to join the programme, offering to pay 10 per cent of the research costs in return for participation.

To satisfy the VTOL requirement requires a multi-point balance of vertical thrust. The replacement for the F-16 did not need this, as a conventional take-off and landing aircraft. In this respect, this formed some commonality of divergent complexity in JSF, as between the original CALF and JAST requirements. A competitive concept demonstrator programme was planned and, by 1996, the chosen two conceptual solutions to proceed to flight demonstration were the Boeing X-32 and the Lockheed-Martin X-35. For the X-32, Boeing chose a thrust vectoring set of nozzles along the lines of the principles of the AV8B/Harrier II/Pegasus engine combination (see section 6.3). The physical diameter of the engine compressor needed to provide sufficient compressor-bleed front nozzle air would be a problem, when trying to achieve supersonic flight.

The provision of vectoring jet engine exhaust thrust direction changing from horizontal to vertical, balanced with a vertical thrust ahead of the aircraft centre of gravity (to provide VTOL), was conceptually to be implemented differently on the Lockheed X-35. This was a large fan with air flowing vertically down, mounted forward of the engine and driven (via a clutch) by a long shaft, this shaft being driven (via a bevel gearbox) by the two low pressure turbine stages of the turbojet engine. Fan inlet and exhaust doors would open during VTOL operations. The VTOL balancing aft vertical lift is provided by the jet turbine exhaust being swivelable from directly aft (in normal flight) to vertically down (and moderately side-to-side once down, for yaw control). This was a new approach. The shaft-driven lift fan idea was a Lockheed-Martin patent and the twin blisk[7] contra-rotating lift fan assembly was to be designed and developed by Rolls-Royce in the UK.

The whole Lockheed vertical direct lift concept can be thermodynamically viewed as the same as a modern high bypass turbofan but with the low-pressure stage of the compressor (i.e. the fan) mounted remotely from the engine and driven by a shaft, exhausting fan air vertically downwards (providing direct lift) rather than around (i.e. bypassing) the engine. The lift fan does not contribute to engine forward thrust, as in a conventional turbofan. The Lockheed inventor of the lift fan concept persuaded the USAF that the simple "omission" of the lift fan would provide the weight reduction relief for non-VTOL versions and actually allow more fuel to be carried in some of the space vacated. The VTOL capability would actually be revised into Short take-off/Vertical landing (STOVL) by the time all the design and performance compromises were settled. Supersonic acceleration is achieved by use of reheat. The X-35 was declared the winner of the demonstration programme and a contract for the F-35 System Development and Demonstration was awarded to Lockheed-Martin in 2001.

As a twenty-first century fifth generation fighter, the F-35 design incorporates extensive radar and infrared stealth concepts, some of which have been derived from (and improved upon) the F-22. It has many of the most advanced systems technologies available, not dissimilar from those described for the Eurofighter Typhoon latest models described earlier in this section. The aircraft is intended to supersede a number of other types in service, including the original CALF objectives of the F-16 and the AV-8B/Harrier II/Sea Harrier, plus some of the Boeing F/A-18 Hornet and Panavia Tornado roles. To cater for the several different requirements, the F-35 has to be a single-engined, single seat all-weather multi-role air fighter-cum-reconnaissance aircraft, capable of ground attack and air superiority missions, operating from main bases, forward deployment locations and aircraft carriers.

---

7. A blisk is a shorthand term applied to a disc with fan or turbine blades integral to the disc (i.e. made as a single-piece item, not with separately-attached blades). Blisks can be castings, machined, 3D-printed or of welded construction.

The F-35 therefore had to become a three-member family of aircraft:

		Expected Unit Fly-Away Cost (2018)
F-35A	Conventional take-off and landing (CTOL), no direct lift system	US $85 million
F-35B	Short take-off, Vertical/Landing (STOVL*) with lift fan etc. direct lift system	US $110 million
F-35C	USN Carrier-based (larger, folding wing), no direct lift system with Catapult-Assisted Take-Off But Arrestor Recovery (CATBAR)	US $110 million

* Vertical take-off would not be possible except at unusable light weights (payload/ fuel sacrifice).

Composed of a lift fan, drive shaft, two wing tip roll posts and a Three-Bearing Swivel Module (3BSM), the engine direct lift system provides 42,000lbf thrust (19 tonnes) of controlled and balanced lift to achieve STOVL capability. The 3BSM acts as a thrust vectoring nozzle, allowing the engine hot exhaust jet to be directed downwards, with a small degree of controlled lateral direction for zero/ low airspeed yaw control. The blisk lift fan up thrust is balanced by the rear jet 3BSM up thrust. Unheated engine bypass compressor air is also diverted through downward facing nozzles mounted on the wings of the aircraft, called roll posts, in order to allow roll control.

Lockheed F-35 Lightning II. Left to right: F.35C, F35B & F.35A. Note larger wing on F-35C. (*By Photo: Harland Quarrington/MOD, OGL v1.0*)

There are three levels of participation in the whole programme. These reflect the levels of financial contribution, the amount of technology transfer permissible and the subcontracting open for bids from the different national suppliers and the order in which countries can obtain production aircraft. Alongside the USA, Britain is the only Tier 1 participant in the project, signing a Memorandum of Understanding as early as 1995. Britain has contributed some US $2.5 billion to the development programme and become responsible for 15 per cent of the airframe design and production work. Up to 30 per ceent of the complete aircraft (depending on model) is supplied from Britain, including the rear fuselage, vertical and horizontal stabilisers (fins and tailplanes) from BAE Systems, the actual Lift Fan from Rolls-Royce (the drive shaft and gearbox are from Rolls-Royce subsidiary Allison in the USA), and the pilot's ejector seat from Martin Baker. BAE Systems Inc. in the USA supply the electronic warfare (EW) system.

There are also Tier 2 and 3 participants, with their development programme contributions:

Tier 2: Italy (US $1 billion) and Netherlands (US $800 million)
Tier 3: Turkey (US $195 million), Canada* (US $160 million), Australia (US $144 million), Norway (US $122 million) and Denmark (US $180 million)

* Canada has been considering not proceeding with procurement (since 2015).

In June 2007, the F-35 family was named Lightning II, in salute to the USA Lockheed P.38 Lightning fighter of the Second World War and the British English Electric Lightning of the Cold War era. The Lightning II is a NATO-wide aircraft and beyond. Several nations have contributed to the programme and presently are taking/intend to take delivery. Currently planned are the following units:

F-35A	Number	F-35B	Number	F-35-C	Number
Australia	100	Italy	30	USMC	80
Denmark	27	Turkey	32	USN	260
Israel	75	Great Britain	138		
Italy	60	USMC	340#		
Japan	42	Singapore	12		
Netherlands	37				
Norway	48				
Poland	32				
South Korea	40				
Turkey	120*				
USAF	1,763				
TOTAL	2,304	TOTAL	540	TOTAL	340

\# In March 2020, the USMC announced a review of its future equipment strategy. The review is to include assessment of more extensive use of new developments in Unmanned Air Vehicles (UAVs), to the extent that a 120-to-130 reduction in the total number of USMC F.35B and F.35C might be the result.

* Turkey may not be permitted to acquire the F-35, due to an embargo by the USA government following Turkey's 2019 order for a Russian ground-to-air missile system.

The Republic of South Korea is considering ordering twenty more F-35As, with an additional purchase of the F-35B being mooted. Procurements by several other countries are in discussion. The end date of production as defined by the current plan is 2035, but it remains open to amendment if further orders are received.

During the operational work-up testing phase in the USA by RAF pilots prior to delivery of Lightning II to British bases, comments by the RAF pilots involved include:

> "We don't actually even need to carry a weapon, albeit we can. I can track targets, identify them all, after having turned cold [nose away from targets] then datalink that information to my Typhoons. The Typhoon pilots can then carry their ordnance to bear against the targets. In the F-35, I can generate a wormhole in the airspace [hostile Missile Engagement Zone] and lead everyone through it. There isn't another platform around that can do that. This isn't all about height and speed – it's the ability to not be seen."

8.9 Collaboration Difficulties

Why Collaborate?

International collaboration in significant military and civil aircraft projects takes place for a few main reasons:

- To share the project development investment cost and to reduce head-to-head competition in the market place.

- As a customer country, to offset foreign reserve expenditure with compensating economic activity.
- The transfer or injection of technology into a (potential) customer country.

The sharing of expense and/or market is practised by all countries having major OEM companies in the aircraft design and manufacturing world. The biggest current examples are the Airbus A.320 assembly factories in China and the USA, supplementing those in France and Germany. Boeing sub-assembly design and manufacture for a number of Boeing projects exist in Italy, Japan, Brazil and Britain. The establishing of customer in-country assembly facilities for acquiring new military aircraft (particularly fighters, such as the F-16, Hawk, Rafale and Jaguar) has been/is quite common, where economically "not too much of a penalty" (saving foreign currency expenditure by the customer).

For aircraft projects with customer government involvement, there are also many examples of "offset", using reverse trade of non-related goods produced in customer countries to offset aircraft acquisition costs.

The use of Western suppliers or partners in civil aircraft programmes in China, India, Indonesia and Russia are examples of satisfying the technology transfer/injection ambitions and, in selected places, even military aircraft programmes (Belgium, Netherlands, Turkey and South Korea Lockheed F-16 manufacture, and Britain's Lockheed Lightning II project involvement are examples).

How is Collaboration Negotiated?

The most difficult issue is the negotiation itself, which eventually and inevitably leads to the ongoing technical involvement in in-service support. A great deal of the aircraft technical capability is now "embedded in on-board software" in modern aircraft. The OEM wishes to partition software and intellectual property, such that the OEM can only be bypassed by customer countries for those elements of operational software associated with new or updated customer-selected mission equipment. Software elements affecting basic aircraft performance or safety must remain the domain of the OEM, with no customer direct access to changes or upgrades, without regulated OEM authority and approval. Customer-selected mission equipment needs borders which interact with aircraft physical installation borders (mounting, electrical connectors, etc.), but the interaction of aircraft and mission equipment software also has to remain fully qualified for the intended use and basic airworthiness and safety. In a fully-integrated weapon system such as a twenty-first century sophisticated computer-controlled military aircraft, partitioning between aircraft supplier and customer user of responsibilities and computer hardware and software requires a very careful and controlled approach, plus extensive integration testing.

There has to be a willingness on all sides to compromise; the difficulties are "How much?" and "Where might this lead in the future?" and "Will it create a new or emergent competitor and can we stay ahead?" and "Can international politics sometimes override industry intellectual property rights, reservations or enthusiasms?"

Each company/country involved will have its own reasons and levels to which compromise is possible. Some are more assertive than others and the political dimension often intrudes.

Particular Perspective: There is a temptation to use self-serving subtly perfidious negotiating tactics on international collaborative ventures. Nowhere has this been more evident than in Anglo-French discussions involving collaborative military aircraft proposals with, in particular, the Dassault company. Even after project agreement and commitment has been established, there have been occasions where commitment has been retrospectively withdrawn or seriously modified. Any inter-company and international collaboration discussions have participant reserved positions which are revealed late in the day, but the Dassault reserve position sometimes seems to be the default "we will take our ball home if we don't win and this may be *after* we have signed up!"

This difficulty has ranged through simple French subterfuge during the NATO maritime patrol (NBMR-2) 1957–58 evaluation, the 1962 withdrawal from the NATO supersonic VTOL (NBMR-3) evaluation when the Dassault Mirage IIIV proposal lost to the embryo Hawker P.1154 proposal, the dissembling, "France has reached the same conclusions as you", during early Supersonic Transport technical discussions in 1961, and the imposition of nationalised Aerospatiale (displacing independent previous partner Nord Aviation) in Airbus initial discussions of 1968. There was nil Dassault support in the 1970s to Anglo-French SEPECAT (Dassault-BAC) Jaguar sales efforts, (with Dassault Mirage aircraft counter-bids in the marketplace). In 1967, Dassault withdrew unilaterally from the AFVG strike aircraft project two years "in" and subsequently built-up the Dassault Mirage as a competitor. Dassault withdrew again, in 1981, from the Advanced Combat aircraft (ACA), re-entered into the Future European Fighter Aircraft (became Eurofighter Typhoon) but Dassault would not agree to continue if they (Dassault) would not be allowed design leadership. Subsequently, there was French pressure on Spain to leave Eurofighter and join the Dassault Rafale project, but this tactic was unsuccessful.

Not all Anglo-French collaboration has encountered such difficulty. The Concorde programme, once agreed, was a co-operative engineering success, as was the Jaguar, and the 1967 Westland-Sud Aviation agreement on co-operation in helicopters had a limited but successful jointly agreeable outcome. Overall, from a national perspective, the French approach has generally succeeded for the French. This is consistent with the French ambition to "lead in Europe", as described previously in section 7.2 (AFVG).

8.10 Shorts Partnership with Brazil's Embraer and Canadian Bombardier Takeover

Embraer Partnership

In 1984, Shorts agreed to partner with the Brazilian company Embraer, to submit an adapted version of the Embraer EMB-312 Tucano as a replacement for the RAF Jet Provost trainer (see section 5.14). Competition was from the Pilatus PC-9 (Switzerland), an upgraded version of the NDN1-T Firecracker, from the company started by Nigel Desmond Norman (one of the two original founders of Britten-Norman, see sections 6.4 and 8.5), and the A.20 Wamira II (from the Australian Aircraft Consortium, proposing a new-design turboprop trainer, RAF aircraft to be built in Britain by Westland). The Wamira project foundered when not selected for the RAF, never getting beyond the mock-up stage.

Shorts Tucano. (*Andrew P. Clarke, CC BY-SA 2.5*)

The Tucano was selected, with an updated engine control system and a cockpit layout change to make it similar to the RAF Hawk jet trainer. With other changes

(900 modifications from the EMB-312 standard) this reduced the commonality with the original by 50 per cent. The RAF ordered 130 Shorts Tucano, built in the UK. The Kenyan Air Force ordered twelve and the Kuwait Air Force ordered sixteen more, modified with underwing armament for weapons training and light strike aircraft use.

Bombardier Takeover

In 1989, Short Brothers was sold by the British government to the Canadian Bombardier Company (producer of the Canadair Challenger[8] corporate jet, having taken over Canadair in 1986). In 1990, Bombardier would also take over the USA Learjet light business jet aircraft activity.

Short Brothers was the first aircraft founding company name in Britain (in 1908) and became the last but one truly independent name to disappear. The last name to disappear would be Westland, a business started by the Petter family-owned company but established as an offshoot division during the First World War, becoming the independent Westland Aircraft in 1935. The name did not disappear completely until 2016, see section 10.2.

The ex-Shorts Belfast factory became the Bombardier manufacturing location for the Learjet 45 business jet fuselage and empennage. This aircraft had its first flight in 1995 and production ceased in 2012. The same factory now supplies the wings for the Bombardier C Series regional jet, launched in 2008, first flight 2013, and, from July 2018, 50.01 per cent owned as a project by Airbus, renamed as the Airbus A.200.

Short Brothers had become successfully involved in guided weapons in the early 1960s. In 1993, Bombardier-Shorts formed a joint venture with the French company Thomson-CSF, Shorts Missile Systems. In the same year, Thomson-CSF went through a series of mergers to become part of a new French-listed multi-national, the Thales Group, buying out the Bombardier interest. Shorts Missile Systems became Thales Air Defence Ltd., headquartered in Belfast. This completed the separation of all the guided weapons businesses in Britain from the British aircraft businesses which spawned them, beginning at the start of the 1960s with the formation of Hawker Siddeley Dynamics and the BAC Guided Weapons Division (see section 6.1).

8.11 Replacement of the Nimrod MR.Mk.2

The British maritime patrol aircraft requirements include long endurance at both long and short range, over deep ocean areas and shallower seas over the continental shelf. Prime mission requirements are submarine and surface vessel detection (and prosecution with missiles, depth charges or torpedoes, as necessary), reconnaissance and intelligence gathering (including electronic surveillance), counter-people trafficking and contraband activity, off-shore asset patrol, and air-sea rescue/distressed mariner location, with rescue mission co-ordination capability. The Hawker Siddeley Nimrod maritime patrol aircraft of 1969 was a design conversion of new-build Comet 4 aircraft, with significant modifications (see section 6.3, Maritime Patrol Aircraft, Nimrod). As operated by the RAF, it proved to be among the very best at contributing to the Cold War NATO Soviet naval vessel (submarine and surface vessel) detection, surveillance and tracking task. Britain was well-served for thirty years by the fleet of Nimrod MR.Mk.2, not confined to the oceans and seas around the British Isles and actually including intelligence and communication missions covering Kosovo, the Persian Gulf and landlocked Afghanistan.

---

8. The Challenger was later stretched by Bombardier and developed into the CRJ Series of regional jets.

In the late 1980s, the RAF started initial thinking about a more modern and improved replacement maritime patrol aircraft capability, knowing that this was likely to take up to ten years from contract to create a service-ready twenty-first century capability. In the very earliest days of this planning, the RAF were interested in the proposed Lockheed new-build Lockheed P-7 for the US navy. This would involve new engines and systems in what was, underneath, a stretched fuselage and increased wingspan version of the 1950s Lockheed Electra airframe design originally used for all versions of the P-3 Orion of the USN, also sold to several other nations. In 1990, USA government cancellation of the P-7 project on cost grounds took that aircraft out of the RAF considerations.

BAe had independently considered many options for a new MR aircraft since the mid-1980s, including an optimisation study labelled the "Next Generation Maritime Reconnaissance" aircraft (NGMR). The outline design of an optimum aircraft size for the intended task was established. Of all existing aircraft designs, the original Comet-derived wing/fuselage size of the Nimrod was found to be nearest to the optimum general size of fuselage and general arrangement for this role. Four engines were considered "optimum", with the same ability as the Nimrod MR Mk.2 to shut down two engines once on patrol and fuel (weight) reduced by the time arriving on station, with the ability to maintain a minimum altitude on one engine while restarting a shut-down engine. The confidential NGMR study was circulated to the RAF and MoD.

One of the difficult mission requirements to satisfy is the need to be able to patrol fairly slowly at low and medium altitudes for long periods but to be able to have a high speed transit at high altitudes. Low drag during low speed patrol conserves fuel, making the increased drag of high-lift device deployment unattractive. Given the relatively small numbers of aircraft envisaged, however, an all-new maritime patrol airframe design with four engines was out of the question. Modern jet airliners have relatively high aspect ratio (high span-to-chord ratio) and significantly swept wings, very suitable for the high speed economic transit capability at altitude. However, when flying at low-ish speeds they would need some lift generation augmentation (wing flap partial deployment, say) to fly slowly, causing increasing drag and fuel consumption. Additionally, modern airliners of the nearly-right general fuselage size for possible conversion to the maritime role have only two engines. Given the high reliability of modern turbofan engines (see note on Extended Range Twin-Engined Operations (ETOPS) for airliners in section 7.4), BAe did consider a modified Airbus A.310 as the basis of a possible modern maritime patrol aircraft (A.310 type first flight 1982) but, in reality, the A.310 fuselage was basically too big.

By the late 1990s, on average each Nimrod aircraft had only completed less than a quarter of the airframe expected maximum flying hour life and the original Comet development history had ensured a very robust and corrosion-resistant fuselage design. The basic Nimrod fuselage had a long life remaining but basic aircraft systems and some of the older elements of the Nimrod's mission equipment began to suffer reliability and spares availability issues. Despite various ad hoc equipment changes on the aircraft, more modern equipment in all areas would give higher performance.

The MoD outlined a Replacement Maritime Patrol Aircraft (RMPA) programme, aimed at meeting Air Staff Requirement (ASR) 420, first released in 1993, with a target in-service date early in the twenty-first century. In the event, three generally acceptable technical bids to satisfy the requirement were submitted, based on either new-build of existing maritime aircraft designs (updating engines and systems) or rework and re-engining of existing, significantly older maritime aircraft airframes actually flying:

- Lockheed offered an all-new P-3 build, with a stretched fuselage-wing combination and with four modern turboprop engines replacing those of the current P-3 Orion maritime patrol aircraft.
- BAe offered to salvage and completely refurbish the basic Nimrod fuselage (known to be in extremely good condition) and add a completely new wing with four modern turbofan engines. The existing Nimrod bomb bay doors and the empennage would be reworked/replaced, as found necessary. The result would be a 95 per cent all-new package, which BAe named the Nimrod 2000.
- A less expensive bid from Loral (USA) of refurbished and re-equipped existing P-3Cs (Loral was taken over by Lockheed in 1996, making this an alternative second Lockheed submission).

Two further bids were made:

- Dassault offered a radically updated version 3 of the updated Atlantique 2 version of the twin-engined Breguét Atlantic (see section 6.3, Maritime Patrol Aircraft). With only two engines, the Atlantique was again considered unfavourably, despite the reliability of modern engines. Even with a major and expensive change to a four engine configuration, the proposed Atlantique 3 would still have been unlikely to attract the RAF.
- Russian industry offered new-build Beriev Be-42 twin-jet amphibian aircraft. A twin-engined (plus two take-off boosters) design, the Russian contender was "excused", because "the RAF had lost the means of operating flying boats in the 1950s". There was no mention of security problems!

All these proposals included completely updated mission systems. The new-build Orion and rebuild Nimrod proposals included all-new two-pilot cockpits with computer-controlled electronic displays (dispensing with a flight engineer on the flight deck and a dedicated routine navigator station in the main cabin).

In 1995, a contract valued at US$ 3.5 billion for twenty-one aircraft to replace the Nimrod MR.Mk.2 was awarded to BAe. The aircraft was named the Nimrod MRA4 (Nimrod Maritime Reconnaissance and Attack, Mk.4). The scheduled introduction into service was to be 2003. The refurbished fuselage and empennage of existing Nimrod MR.Mk.2 aircraft would be mated to an all-new wing/engine combination and all systems would be replaced by modern equipment, in a completely refurbished and rearranged cockpit, main cabin outer shell and under-fuselage weapons bay. A new cabin floor would be fitted. The four engines would be Rolls-Royce BR.710 modern turbofans providing 15,500lbf thrust each, compared with 12,000lbf thrust of the Nimrod MR.Mk.2 engines. The improved fuel consumption would be sufficient to add 80 per cent to the range of the MR.Mk.2 with two hours on station at long-range (e.g. Britain to Canada, at Baffin Bay and over the Labrador Sea).

As well as new engines, electric and hydraulic power generators and undercarriage, completely new aircraft basic systems and aircraft flight control and mission avionics were to be provided. The new mission systems were to be incorporated to the latest technology standards (some not available in any form on the Nimrod MR Mk.2).

Systems Power, Flight Control and Flight Management Avionics:

1. Electronic Flight displays (EFIS and EICAS) in a two-crew cockpit
2. Automatic Flight Control including Autothrottle
3. Digital Air Data
4. Navigation

5. Traffic Collision Avoidance (TCAS)
6. Flight Management
7. Maintenance Management
8. New electrical power and hydraulic power systems
9. New auxiliary power unit

Mission Avionics:

1. Infra-red and TV optical surveillance (EOSDS)
2. Enhanced surface surveillance radar with target classification and overland capability
3. New acoustics (sonobuoy) data processing
4. New ESM
5. Defensive aids threat countermeasures
6. Improved magnetic anomaly detector for submarine magnetic field detection from low level
7. Digital crew intercom and new radio communications equipment
8. Advanced mission data recorders (for post-mission analysis)
9. Eight tactical crew stations in the main cabin, each able to display the complete tactical situation as well as the individual sensor control and display (one radar, two acoustic (sonobuoy) data, one ESM and Threat Warning, one Information and Communications manager and two Tactical Co-ordinator stations)

Four wing hard points in the new wing were included (two more than the MR Mk.2) to enable up to eight air-to-air missiles to be carried. The combined wing-bomb bay weapon capability included torpedoes, depth charges, mines, anti-ship missiles and cruise missiles. Four 'ten-shot' rotary launchers at the rear of the cabin allowed patterns of sonobuoys[9] to be launched through the rear cabin floor (cabin unpressurised) and the two Nimrod MR Mk.2 pressurised flight sonobuoy launchers were refurbished to be fitted to the MRA4. Storage for 350 sonobuoys was provided, adjacent to the launchers.

BAe collaborated with Boeing to provide the co-ordination control and display of all sensor data, including data fusion (similar in concept to that described for Eurofighter Typhoon in section 8.8, but for all eight tactical crew members at the individual operator stations in the main cabin, and an overview to the pilots in the cockpit). All equipment operators could see their individual sensor data displays and the data fusion enhanced overall picture, much reducing crew intercom voice exchange when the MRA4 would be trying to detect and locate (and prosecute as necessary) any targets. The vastly increased and integrated on-board computer-based sensor data processing capability (and there were more sensors than were available on the MR.Mk.2), together with the modern display and control facilities meant that the three flight deck crew of the Nimrod MR.Mk2 (two pilots and a flight engineer) could be reduced to two on the MRA.4, and only eight MRA.4 mission system operators were needed instead of the MR.Mk.2's ten.

A difficulty to be accommodated was that, although the original Comet (and Nimrod) fuselage keel was originally created in a jig (to ensure consistency of dimensions and shape), the fuselage frames had been "hand-assembled" to the keel with drill-on-assembly tolerance allowance, rather than the much closer tolerance standards of fifty years later associated with computer-defined jig design and jig manufacture. This

---

9. Sonobuoys are devices dropped into the sea, set to float at a predetermined depth. They have a radio transmitter connected to a floating aerial, transmitting detected underwater acoustic signals back to the patrolling aircraft.

tolerance issue surfaced in the design of the joint of the new 1990s-designed Nimrod MRA4 wing to the (refurbished) 1950s designed original Comet fuselage. A revised approach had to be introduced, to accommodate the differences between the as-drawn wing geometry attachment dimensions for mating the original Nimrod (Comet) fuselage to the original wing and the variations from drawing as built. This variation was slightly different for every individual original fuselage/new wing combination.

BAE Systems Nimrod MRA.4. (*BAE Systems*)

The new avionics suite and mission system equipment integration did not proceed completely without development problems but this element of the aircraft was the most complicated flying integrated computer system ever produced. Development problems are to be expected in any new programme and time and effort allowance is programmed in, but not enough in the case of this programme.

All in all, by the start of the twenty-first century the programme had slipped by a couple of years. In 2002 the contract was renegotiated to deliver eighteen aircraft and BAE Systems took a loss charge of £300 million. A further charge of £500 million was taken in 2003. In July 2004, the Secretary of State for Defence announced a reduction to sixteen aircraft and suggested that only twelve might actually be needed. In July 2006 BAE Systems received a revised contract, for just nine production MRA4s with three development aircraft (eventually to be refurbished to full production standard). After further disputes on cost and delivery, the number was further reduced to nine aircraft in total. In December 2009, the minister announced that defence spending cuts would delay Nimrod MRA4 introduction into service until 2012.

As a result of the 2010 Strategic Defence and Security Review of the UK armed forces, the Nimrod MRA4 was cancelled on 19 October 2010. All existing Nimrods were withdrawn from service by the end of 2011, leaving the UK without any fixed wing long-range maritime patrol capability[10], which had been continuously available until 2011 since before the Second World War (see section 2.6).

The total cost to the government of the cancelled Nimrod MR4A programme was reported as £3.2 billion, but nearly £1 billion of the actual total project investment had been at BAE Systems expense. Without serious discussion, the government ordered the immediate scrapping of all Nimrod MRA4 aircraft, even the three production aircraft completed (one of which had been delivered). BAE Systems were not given a chance to make an offer to complete more aircraft and possibly sell them to an overseas customer, at least recovering their costs. The government were not prepared to suffer

---

10. Other strategic assets were withdrawn from all armed forces as a result of the same review, including all Harrier aircraft. Only one of the three Invincible class aircraft carriers (of Falklands fame) remained, HMS *Illustrious* used as a helicopter carrier, until that ship was decommissioned in 2014, leaving the UK with no long-range maritime airborne capability (reconnaissance, intelligence gathering or strike) whatsoever.

the slightest possibility of being mightily embarrassed if the aircraft were seen to be any kind of success after all!

The likelihood of another large military or civil transport, or a multi-sensor surveillance aircraft original airframe design and manufacture revival in the UK is therefore virtually a non-starter, the skills and capabilities now having retired. Possibly inevitable, but certainly another nail in the coffin of the British aircraft industry.

Postscript:

In 2016 the British government announced that the RAF long-range maritime patrol capability would be restored by the (phased) purchase of nine Boeing P-8 Poseidon aircraft, as developed from the twin-engined Boeing 737NG airliner for the USN. The RAF finally had to accept that this two-engined solution would be the only option, based on the modern high-reliability of aircraft turbofan engines (evidenced by trans-atlantic civil twin-engined ETOPS operations as described earlier, in section 7.4). Subsequently, the delivery of the first aircraft was agreed to be in 2019, with the nine aircraft delivered over a ten year period. The range capability of these two-engined aircraft is not as great as that of the Nimrod MRA4 and the sophistication of the mission system (as currently available) is less than that intended (and almost completely developed) on the MRA4. The total project cost was forecast to be £3.9 billion, 2016 value, which includes training and support and £132 million for physical infrastructure at RAF Lossiemouth (which had been created for the MRA4 at the RAF Kinloss Nimrod base but was decommissioned when the Nimrod MRA4 were scrapped). It could have been significantly less expensive overall to continue to complete the nine aircraft Nimrod MRA4 programme, but there was a suggestion of a hidden agenda, see below.

Hidden Agenda? Nimrod MR.Mk.2 Accident Consequences on Nimrod MRA.4

Following an RAF Board of Enquiry into the 2006 total-loss fatal accident to Nimrod MR.2, registration XV 230 (see section 6.3 – Nimrod), the cause of the crash was further investigated by an independent review. This was conducted by Charles Haddon-Cave QC, as appointed by the government (Minister of Defence) in December 2007. The 587-page report from the independent investigation was submitted in October 2009.

This report ascribed the likely reason for the accident to the combination of features of the original Nimrod MR Mk.1 design, a modification to the engine bleed air system (as part of the fleet conversion to MR.Mk.2 standard) and a modification introduced later, to add in-flight refuelling capability to the aircraft in 1989. The in-flight refuelling modification was introduced as a direct result of the 1982 Falklands War. (A temporary-fit modification to provide this facility for a number of Nimrod MR Mk.2 was engineered, fitted and cleared in eighteen days, at the start of that war. This temporary fit was later replaced with an improved installation, derived from that engineered for the Nimrod AEW Mk.3.)

The independent review concluded that, in combination, these features, combined with an actual in-flight refuelling, could create a fuel-fed fire risk situation in the wing root, and was the most probable cause of the accident.

A 2001 to 2005 safety review of the Nimrod MR Mk.2 had been carried out as a new process (i.e. retrospective, after many years in service), due to new safety assurance standards promulgated for *all* British military aircraft in 2002. This safety review had not identified the potential hazard which the independent review considered to be the most likely cause of the XV 230 accident. The independent review report clearly stated that this was due to a failure to take enough care in the establishing of the safety review process and in the execution of the safety review. The independent review of the XV

230 accident thus identified a failure in the duty of care responsibilities of the RAF, the aircraft contractor BAE Systems and the government technical advisors QinetiQ (privatised elements of what had been parts of the RAE and A&AEE).

Instead of conducting a thorough consequences review, which could have included considering the need (and likely expense) to design out any such potential hazard from the Nimrod MRA4, the government were accused of using the issue to contribute unduly to the decision to cancel the seriously over cost and overrunning MRA4 project. Despite all the mistakes and problems, this project had been about to deliver to the RAF the most advanced and capable maritime patrol aircraft in the world.

The public disclosure of the independent report and resulting public discussions were also the likely trigger for the 2011 grounding of the Nimrod MR Mk.2 fleet and the three Nimrod R Mk.1 aircraft. Combined with the MRA4 cancellation, it also conveniently overtook media attention on the aftermath of the tragic accident situation and, equally significantly in the eyes of the UK Treasury, caused cessation of near-term significant government expenditure on any maritime patrol capability, using either/both of the Nimrod MR Mk.2 and the MRA4. This would persist until (eventually) the 2016 decision to acquire nine Boeing P.8 maritime patrol aircraft recreates the necessary RAF capability, after a complete service gap of ten years or more.

Chapter 9

Industry Technical Progress and Commercial-Political Issues

9.1 A Century of Technical Progress in the World of Aircraft

The progress in the world of aeronautical achievement since the first flight of 1903 has been stupendous. This is just as it has been in many fields of human scientific and engineering endeavour, in many different branches of engineering, in physics, chemistry, cosmology, medicine, computing and telecomunications, agriculture and so on. A simple way of illustrating the level of progress in world aeronautical performance is a table of the Fédération Aéronautique Internationale (FAI) officially-recognised world level-flight speed records for air-breathing ground-launched aircraft. An abridged form of this is shown in Table 9.1 below, with the dates of UK aircraft holding the record also shown.

Table 9.1: Sustained Level Flight World Airspeed Records (as recognised by the FAI)

End of Decade	Aircraft	Speed (mph)	UK Aircraft Holding Record in Decade	Date	Speed (mph)
1901–10	Antoinette Monoplane	48.21			
1911–20	Nieuport Delage	194.53			
1921–30	Supermarine S.6	357.75	Supermarine S.6	12–09–1929	357.75
1931–40	Messerschmitt Bf 109	462.22	Supermarine S.6B	29–09–1931	407.02
1941–50	North American F-86A	670.98	Gloster Meteor F.4 Gloster Meteor F.4	07–11–1945 07–09–1946	606.38 615.78
1951–60	Convair F-106A Delta Dart	1,525.95	Hawker Hunter F.3 S'marine Swift F.4 Fairey Delta 2	07–09–1953 25–09–1953 10–03–1956	727.63 735.70 1,132.00
1961–70	Lockheed YF-12A	2,070.10			
1971–80	Lockheed SR.71 Blackbird	2,193.16			

Many more aircraft held the record successively during each decade. The records listed here are the ones standing at the end of the decade. From 1920 onwards, all these particular record holders were military or government research aircraft operations. The USA Lockheed SR-71 Blackbird set records for both sustained level flight speed and altitude in 1976, at 2,193mph and 85,069ft (over 16 miles high and not the same flight as the speed record). There are other aeronautical achievements, a few of which have not been able to be FAI-recognised, largely due to military secrecy preventing independent observation and verification.

The brief description of engine developments in Chapter 4 is another fair indication of progress. The improvements in engine power and efficiency allowed lightweight metal structures to be introduced which, in absolute terms, soon became generally more substantial (therefore heavier) than their ancestral wood, fabric and string forebears. The newer aircraft structures were designed to carry greater payloads, often much further, and had to carry their own greater weight, plus heavy systems such as hydraulics and electrical equipment, conditioning equipment needed to allow bombers and fighter crews to fly in the stratosphere, with heavier armament and so on, usually faster and further. Transport aircraft needed to carry more passengers faster and further in greater comfort. For all aircraft types, there was always the desire to create greater range potential, ultimately implying increased fuel tankage and complexity of fuel management systems.

Of course, speed and altitude records do not tell the whole tale of aeronautical progress. Payload and range are extremely important and cruise speed and fuel economy are important parameters. These are major factors in any aircraft operations, ranked alongside direct operating costs (amortised actual aircraft purchase (or lease) cost, fuel cost, airfield/airway charges, maintenance cost and crew cost). This is especially true for civil operations. Development of costly technical sophistication is still a *raison d'être* for some aircraft (such as smart weapon load, low radar signature or aerial reconnaissance resolution of detail for military aircraft, or payload-range and passenger amenities/entertainment for civil airliners).

Another way of illustrating general progress in the capability of aircraft is to compare the changes in aircraft power-to-weight ratios (for different classes of aircraft), as a function of time. The aircraft classes chosen here are propeller-driven British fighters, bombers and military and civil airliner transports[1].

The ratio of maximum power to maximum take-off weight (HP/lb) is a reasonably simple numerical way of comparing different piston-powered fighter aircraft, because engine power and aircraft weight dominate fighting capability (speed and rate of climb). Broad comparison can be made using just this ratio, recognising that aerodynamics, weight of armament and aircraft manoeuvrability are also clearly important, but all influencing power requirement and overall weight. Fighters are generally interceptors and, for the UK, range is not often a major factor for the air defence of Britain. Speed (time) to intercept is more value (except when a fighter has another role, such as ground strike). Speed is heavily influenced directly by engine power and aircraft size. So power-to-weight ratio multiplied by maximum speed (scaled up by a factor of ten for presentation purposes, as shown in the second of the columns in the following graphs) is a reasonable capabilty comparator between different piston-engined fighter design eras.

The next two graphs are derived from the data in Appendices 7 to 10, for those aircraft which actually entered service. They illustrate how the average power/weight ratio and the "average capability" of the British piston-engined propeller-driven aircraft which actually entered service improved, from 1910 to 1950. The change from biplane to monoplane configuration resulted in the 1934 Gloster Gladiator biplane having a slightly higher power/weight ratio than the monoplane early 1935 Hawker Hurricane and 1936 Supermarine Spitfire aircraft but, in terms of maximum speed, the lower drag configuration of the monoplanes gave a significantly superior overall performance. By the end of 1940, the Hurricane and Spitfire Merlin engine maximum power had been improved by almost 25 per cent and all biplane fighters were totally obsolete.

---

1. The jet turbine-engined aircraft, first introduced in the 1950s, make direct engine-related comparison with the previous piston-powered years numerically misleading, having to be based on maximum thrust-to-weight ratio for the turbojet and turbofan, rather than the piston-engined aircraft horsepower-to-weight ratio. It would be misleading to try to directly compare modern jet turbine powered aircraft with piston engined types in such a simplified way, although modern jet aircraft are clearly more efficient and capable than earlier aircraft.

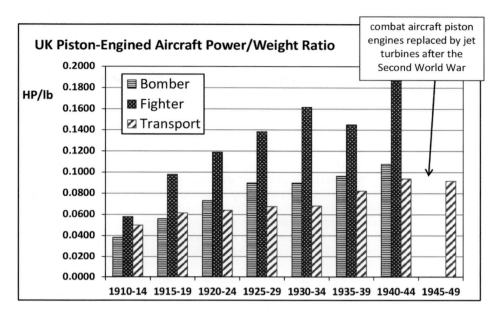

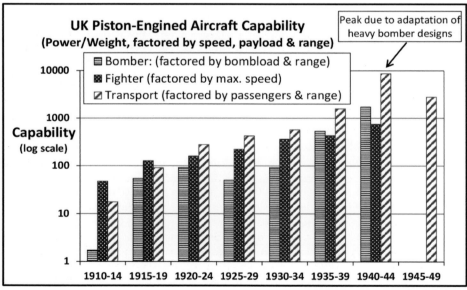

For bombers, including the light day bombers of the 1920s and 1930s alongside the medium and heavy bombers of the 1930s and 1940s, as time went by the increases in engine power went along with range and speed increase, greater bomb loads and greater fuel weight, larger crews etc. Physical size increase was not so marked (wing span of the 1917 Handley Page O/400 was 100ft, the 1918 V/1500 span was 126ft and the 1941 Avro Lancaster span was 102ft). The comparison for bombers between decades is therefore better illustrated by multiplying the power-to-weight ratio by the maximum bomb load (in thousands of pounds) and the maximum range (in hundreds of miles), noting that maximum bomb load is not in practice compatible with achieving maximum range. This results in a "capability" value which more realistically allows capability improvement to be compared over time, for each class of aircraft but without explicitly being concerned with differentiating between light/short range, medium/medium range and heavy/long-range types.

In a similar manner to bombers, military transport and civil airliner capability comparisons are illustrated by using maximum power-to-weight ratio (HP/lb) multiplied by maximum number of passengers and by maximum range (in hundreds of miles). Like bombers, maximum range is not compatible with a maximum payload. For interest, an early version (in service 1953) of the British turboprop Vickers Viscount airliner is also included in the figures (Viscount 700: 0.0948 power/weight ratio, capability value 10,715).

Fighter aircraft values clearly illustrate that, as time passed, greater engine power has been extremely important. For bombers and transports since the end of the First World War in 1919, the power/weight ratio has increased by a smaller amount, the weight of payload and range achievable being increased to take advantage of greater, more efficiently-generated power.

Overall, the diagrams demonstrate that the general performance of these three different classes of aircraft were impressively improved in the first half of the twentieth century, facilitated by much improved engines and the increasing sophistication of the aeronautical technology.

Comparing the "best" pre- and post-Second World War British airliners actually entering service, the actual (rather than artificially factored) capability of British airliners in the table below illustrate the development over fifteen years, alongside pre-war and 1940s airliners of USA origin.

Entry into Service	Airliner	pwr/wt (HP/lb)	Maximum Passenger	Max. Range (miles)	Cruise Speed (mph)
British Airliners					
1935	de Havilland DH.89 Dragon Rapide	0.0727	8	573	~135
1938	Armstrong Whitworth AW.27A Ensign	0.0667	40	1,370	180
1938	de Havilland DH.91 Albatross	0.0712	22	1,040	220
1951	Airspeed AS.51 Ambassador	0.1000	60	550	260
1951	Vickers Viscount p'type (turboprop)	0.0857	36	~1500	275
1953	Vickers Vicount 700 (turboprop)	0.0948	64	1,650	310
USA Airliners					
1933	Boeing 247	0.0806	10	745	188
1936	Douglas DC-3	0.0873	32	1,600	170
1937	Lockheed Model 14 Electra	0.1029	14	850	250
1940	Boeing 307 Stratoliner	0.0978	38	1,750	215
1946	Douglas DC-4 (civil DC-4A)	0.0795	80	4,250 (30 passengers)	227
1947	Douglas DC-6	0.0988	68	4,588 (~40 passengers)	311

Despite the improvement in capability over time, there was no room for complacency in the immediate post-Second World War years regarding the levels of British airliner capabilities, as the USA airliners of the 1950s were to reveal (see sections 5.4 and 5.8).

A few "aeronautical engineering examples" from the world aircraft industries may help to further illustrate the technical achievements inherent in modern aircraft:

Example 1: During the first forty years of powered flight, propulsion was basically by piston-engine/propeller combinations. The engine power required for this kind of propulsion can be shown to be related to the cube of aircraft speed (V^3). It can be shown that the high drag characteristics and wing area of the 1903 version of the Wright Flyer (which had a 12HP engine, specially designed by the Wright brothers) would have required an engine power of about 10,000HP to achieve a maximum speed of around 300mph (but it would have disintegrated first, at engine start!). That such a speed was achieved in a service aircraft by the late 1930s with engine powers around a tenth of that power (e.g. Supermarine Spitfire Mk.1A, 367mph with 1,000HP from the engine) is a tribute not only to engine designers but also to the application of new (amazing, in reality) aerodynamic improvements. These aerodynamic improvements, to increase lift and reduce drag, stemmed from the development of theoretical and experimental understanding of fluid dynamics as the century progressed, especially concerning air flows around wing shapes.

Example 2: Section 2.2 briefly alludes to the survival issues associated with the environment when flying at altitudes above 10,000ft. At typical modern turbofan long-range airliner cruising heights (several thousand feet higher than Mount Everest's 29,000ft) the outside air is at -54°C and air pressure is one third of that at sea level. Even insulated and breathing oxygen, the human body starts to slowly die in these conditions. By the time Concorde speeds (1,340mph, Mach 2.02) and altitudes (ceiling 60,000ft, two-thirds towards the edge of space) are reached, the outside air temperature has stabilised at -57°C and the atmospheric pressure is just one tenth of that at sea level. Even in a pressurised cockpit, at these heights military aircrew wear flight suits with pressure-breathing oxygen available (via a regulator and mask) in these conditions. On Concorde, passengers and aircrew sit comfortably in a shirt sleeve environment, having to wrestle with smoked salmon and champagne in a relaxed social environment. How was this all achieved reliably and in safety? On turbine engine powered passenger aircraft (turbojet, turbofan or turboprop), upstream of the fuel-burning stage the engine compressor is bled of some of its air (typically at temperatures up to 350°C and up to two or three times sea level pressure) to feed into the cabin conditioning system, known generically as the environmental control system (ECS). The ECS cools, filters and conditions the air and distributes it to the cabin, to make it always equivalent to being on a mountain top of never more than 8,000 feet high, on a warm day.

Example 3: Mentioning Concorde, in Mach 2 supersonic cruise the very nose of the aircraft is heated to 125°C by dynamic heating due to the airspeed. The passenger cabin external skin is at 90°C. This means the cabin conditioning system has to continuously cool the aircraft in supersonic flight, using the fuel in the tanks to absorb the heat and conveniently dispose of it when the fuel is burned in the engines. On the way up to cruising altitude, Concorde cabin outer structure would be several tens of degrees below freezing (as with subsonic airliners) and the conditioning system still has to provide warm air to the cabin.

Example 4: After working in conjunction with de Havilland aircraft on bonding layers of lamination in propellers, a urea formaldehyde synthetic glue product called Gordon Aerolite was developed by Norman de Bruyne, in his own company Aero Research

Limited. This was used in furniture making and, subsequently, in de Havilland Mosquito aircraft and Horsa gliders. Aerolite, however, did not bond to metal. The bonding of aircraft primary structure metal-to-metal or metal-to-wood with a Phenol-formaldehyde/PolyVinyl-Formal combination as adhesive is called Redux bonding (from the **Re**search at **Dux**ford in Britain, the place where it was developed by de Bruyne). The Redux process was developed by 1941 and the first practical use was as a better alternative to riveting-in tank clutch plate assemblies. At the end of Second World War, Redux bonding was used extensively in the de Havilland Hornet aircraft, the Dove and the Comet jet airliner, and in many post-war aircraft of British and other manufacturers. Used mainly on flat and single (low) curvature stringer-skin assembly and re-enforcing skin doublers, the process obviated drilling and riveting as it was light, strong, durable and low drag. The same de Bruyne company developed the epoxy resin Araldite.

Example 5: The machining of aluminium alloy aircraft fuselage and wing skin, complete with integral stiffening stringers and thickness variation, are a current manufacturing technique developed for use in the aircraft industry. The capability was first developed in Britain in the late 1950s for the Blackburn Buccaneer strike aircraft and the Vickers VC.10 airliner wing skins. Acid etching/chemical milling to reduce skin thickness in skin areas with (relatively) low loads was another development.

Example 6: The gradually increased use of non-metallic lightweight materials in modern aircraft, culminated in the current use of carbon fibre for primary main load-bearing structure such as wings, tailplanes and fuselage. The high-strength carbon fibre is made in a process developed by the RAE and patented by the British Ministry of Defence in 1963. Carbon fibre itself is a five to ten micron-thick filament of very high tensile strength (a micron is one thousandth of a millimetre). When used embedded in a resin medium, in multiple layers of carbon fibre "woven" sheets, a very high strength composite material is created with designed-in directional strengths, becoming a very superior material compared with the earlier fibreglass composite material.

Example 7: The stable flight of most fixed-wing aircraft generally comes with a naturally stablising position of aircraft centre of gravity forward of the centre of lift from the wings, counteracted by a balancing downforce provided by the tailplane. The margin between stability and instability needs to be sufficiently large to allow human pilots to react to disturbances as well as control the range of manoeuvres to suit the range required. Tailplane downforce reduces total aircraft lift, requiring the wing incidence to be increased to increase lift accordingly, and this causes an increase in the "lift-dependent drag" (sometimes labelled "induced drag"). Reduced stability margin allows increased maneuverability of the aircraft and flight with less drag (less tailplane downforce) but with less ability to be adequately controlled by the unaided pilot. For the fighter aircraft, reduced natural stability can also offer advantage in the extreme manoeuvres associated with interceptor "dogfighting". To allow a reduction in the natural stability, "artificial" stabilisation needs to augment the reduced stability. The first military aircraft to go into service with a system to allow this reduction was the USA Lockheed F-16 Fighting Falcon. It originally employed a multi-channel analogue computing system[2] to input instantly-stabilising augmentation control of the tailplane and/or elevator, using data input from multiple sensor inputs such as speed, attitude (pitch, roll and yaw angles) and associated angular rates, acceleration forces in all

---

2. Later models of the F-16 (C and D versions from 1988, at block 40) changed to a digital fly-by-wire control system

three axes (up/down, left/right and forward/aft). The first aircraft to be able to use digital computing stability augmentation were the USA McDonnell-Douglas F/A.18 Hornet and the European Panavia Tornado. Augmented or artificial stability allows the aircraft-balancing aerodynamic trim forces to be reduced, thus reducing drag. Later, the idea extended into the civil airliner arena with the fly-by-wire Airbus A.320, certificated for service use in 1988. The commercial airliner advantage is the reduced effort on inspecting and maintaining the flying control system:

Reduced drag = reduced fuel use = less operating cost (or more range).

Digital computer processing also provides enhancement to safety, from the ability to advise (and autonomously act upon) potential traffic conflict, accurate navigation irrespective of visibility, the need to ascend to avoid unseen high ground, as well as help to improve safety by physically preventing aircraft handling errors by the pilot beyond the aeroplanes aerodynamic and structural limits.

Example 8: Aeronautical engineering has to overcome many and various issues like the examples above, large and small, for the whole aircraft and its systems. Safe, consistent and reliable aircraft performance is required, in a manner *proven* for each aircraft to be compliant with all the regulatory safety and certification standards. For commercial passenger aircraft, the safety record has continuously improved since the first airlines started to operate. In terms of airline accident rate per year, the worst year on record per mile flown was 1929, with fifty-one fatal accidents in some 50 million miles flown. The present total of all the world's commercial aircraft miles flown per year (large and small, intercontinental airline to single-engined "prop. hop"), is about 45,000 million. At 1929 accident rates, this would equate to around 47,000 fatal air accidents per year in the present day!

Of course, average flight lengths are currently very much greater than in 1929 but, even re-estimating on a "per flight" basis, aircraft accident rates of 1929 would be totally unacceptable in the twenty-first century. In fact, the world all-region present fatal accident rate for commercial jet airliners is one for every 16 million flights.

By way of comparison, table 9.2 illustrates the gross statistics for individual UK travel in the decade 1990 to 2000, noting that external factors contribute most (particularly human error).

Table 9.2: Individual Travellers' Safety (UK).

Transport Type	1990–2000, Deaths per		
	Billion Journeys	Billion Hours	Billion miles
Bus	4.3	11.1	0.644
Rail	20	30	0.965
Air	117	30.8	0.080
Water	90	50	4.183
Van	20	60	1.931
Car	40	130	4.988
Foot	40	220	87.208
Pedal Cycle	170	550	71.761
Motor Cycle	1,640	4,840	175.220

9.2 UK Industry Jet Aircraft Production since the Second World War

Britain designed and built the first military and civil turbojet aircraft to be delivered "commercially" – the Gloster Meteor F.3 evaluation model in 1946 to the RAAF and the de Havilland Comet airliner in 1951 to BOAC. There was great anticipation that the country could become a major player in the world aircraft market, with the parallel success of the world's first turbo-prop airliner (Vickers Viscount), first delivered as a production model to BEA in 1953 and the first overseas sale of the de Havilland Dove in 1948. The other civil aircraft defined by the Brabazon Committee were hopes which were not to build on this promising start.

As an illustration of the eventual sales out-turn for the industry, the specific market results for jet airliners and jet fighter aircraft are summarised in the following charts.

Jet Airliners

Britain delivered the world's first jet airliner (de Havilland Comet) in 1951 and delivered its last-build jet airliner (a BAE Systems 146, as an Avro RJ100) in 2003.

To illustrate the influence of the British aircraft industry on the Western world jet airliner market, the graph below shows the annual jet airliner deliveries by Britain, other European single companies, USA Boeing, USA "other" (Douglas, Lockheed, Convair), Airbus, Bombardier (Canada) and Embraer (Brazil).

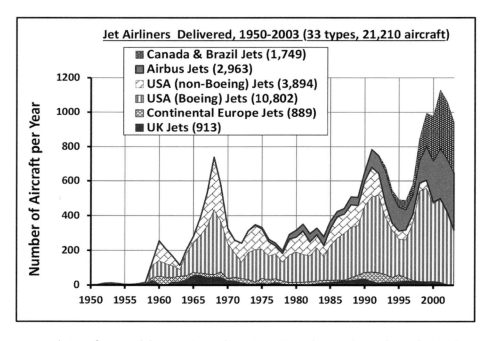

Despite being first to deliver a jet airliner in 1951, the total number of British jet airliners has been a very small fraction of the total built worldwide, the USA clearly dominating until the end of the twentieth century approached. The downturn in sales overall from 2002 (stimulated by the New York World Trade Centre terrorist atrocities of 2001 on the 9 September, causing major reduction of traffic predictions) was the reason given for BAE Systems to cease airliner production of the last British airliner. A new civil aircraft for the future was not being planned by BAE Systems. As it turned out, the world total airliner delivery turn-down at the start of the twenty-first century was to be reversed by 2005 and total delivery rates for the companies in the graph peaked at over 1,700 aircraft in both 2018 and 2019.

Jet Fighters (including armed trainers)

In military jets, Britain has had more success, having provided some 45 per cent of all western jet fighter aircraft types. Excluding experimental-only types, total production over the period was:

Numbers of New Fixed Wing Jet Combat Aircraft Produced, 1943 to 2000.

Britain	France	Italy	Sweden	W.Europe Total	USA
19,357 (3 types collaborative)	3,319 (1 type collaborative)	885	1,348	24,909	67,930

The two charts below illustrate the numbers of types successfully developed and built in the UK, the USA and by continental Western European countries.

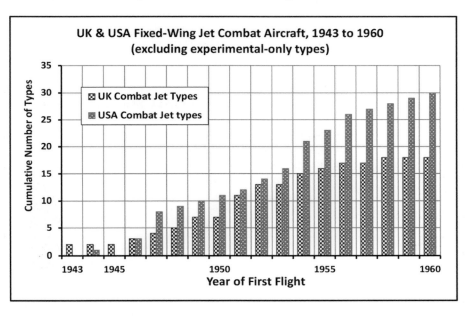

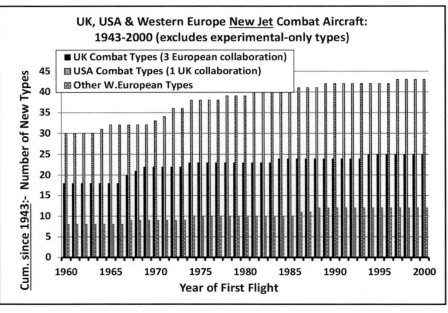

The influence of the USA on NATO countries acquisition of jet combat aircraft is partly as a result of the generosity imparted by the USA Mutual Defense Act of 1949, which resulted in European acquisition of European assembly of USA aircraft in projects partly financed by the USA. Sometimes, this generosity extended to financing European aircraft acquisition (see Sea Hawk, section 5.11 and Hunter and Javelin, section 5.13). Excluding experimental and prototype-only aircraft, of 92,839 jet-powered combat/armed trainer aircraft produced in the twentieth century, 27 per cent were produced to European designs. Over 75 per cent of these European jet combat aircraft involved the British aircraft industry.

9.3 The Cost of Developing Modern Aircraft and Recovering That Cost

Except for light and other general aviation aircraft, the development costs of new civil and military aircraft are likely to absorb billions of pounds, dollars, or euros, in non-recurring costs. The additional investment in work-in-progress, to enable sales to be completed as soon as type development is complete to a certificated standard, absorbs more heavy investment. Usually, complex military aircraft cost more to develop than even the largest civil aircraft. Some examples for recent aircraft are given below in table 9.3. Note that the aircraft industry in Britain is currently involved in all Airbus (20%), Eurofighter Typhoon (45%) and Lockheed F-35 (15%) aircraft projects.

Table 9.3: Recent New Advanced Aircraft Developments, Currently in Production.

Aircraft	Launch Year	Year of 1st Delivery	Development* Cost (US $)	Unit fly-away Price* (US $)
Civil Airliners: (excluding engine development costs)				
Boeing 787	2004	2011	39 billion	300 million
Airbus A.350XWB	2006	2014	11 billion	317 million
Boeing 737MAX#	2011	2017	1.6 billion	117 million
Airbus A.320neo#	2010	2016	1.3 billion	111 million
Military Aircraft: (including engine development costs)				
Lockheed F-35 Lightning II	2000	2011	58 billion	110 million
Eurofighter Typhoon	1986	2003	30 billion	120 million
Airbus A.400M Atlas	2004	2013	30 billion	130 million

All figures adjusted to 2019 equivalent

*Development costs are estimated total for all variants current in 2019. Fly-away price is not list price. Airliner launch customers/large fleet orders gain major price reductions from list price and National governments usually pay "a full price" for first orders of a new (national) military type. Note that US$120 million is roughly six times the equivalent 2019 unit price of a British Vulcan or Victor bomber of the 1950s.

#Airbus A.320neo and Boeing 737MAX are new-engined new-build derivatives of earlier models.

The illustrated costs and prices in Table 9.3 are not derived directly from historical company actuals. They are estimates from published information and commentators opinions, updated to relate to 2019 dollars. The table mereley indicates only the overall scale of new aircraft project costings with which the world industry has to contend.

These significant amounts mean that financing a new project often requires external investment. International work sharing has become normal for significant new aircraft projects. Even in the USA, the domestic industry mergers and rationalisations and the invasion of the USA home market by Airbus and others, has persuaded two of the

USA aircraft industry Titans (Boeing and Lockheed-Martin) to seek project production sharing and development investment from international partners.

To illustrate the financial demands associated with a new airliner project, the following (hypothetical) simplified example is an illustration:

Basic assumption:
After a market research effort over several years, including extensive interaction with potential customer airlines, initial orders are received sufficient to launch an all-new medium size new single-aisle twin-engined airliner project (initial model 140 to 175 seats, say).

Based on representative (*but not actual*) USA/Europe values of 2019–2020:

- World market size 6,000 aircraft, target market share to be 25 per cent (1,450 aircraft after fifteen years; market share extendable when updated variants developed, within a few years of first delivery)
- Projected true development timescale: six years to first delivery
- Projected total research and development cost: out-turn twelve billion dollars US (new engine/equipment development costs recovered in engine/equipment purchase costs)
- Projected peak production rate: 250 per year
- Projected unit production cost (average): 55 million dollars US (assuming no new production facility required)
- Projected average achieved fly-away sale price: 115 million dollars US, no deposits in advance
- Financing cost: 5 per cent net project debt per year

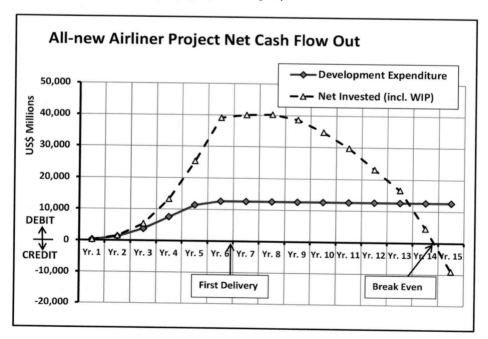

The resulting cash flow chart above shows a predicted peak investment of 40 billion dollars US, project break-even after about fourteen years, with some 980 aircraft delivered, with a project profit of around 10 billion dollars US fifteen years after the start. If development timescale is held to only five years and at a development cost of 10 billion dollars US (instead of six years/12 billion dollars US), peak investment is reduced to 33 billion dollars US, break even in just over twelve years with 880 deliveries, with the same market and with a project profit of some 40 billion dollars US after fifteen years. (These values are representative of the scale of investment, timescale and profit potential and do not refer to an actual project.) However, an upgrade or new version would be likely to be needed at some stage, probably emerging as an active derivative project starting serious design before, at the same time, or not long after the initial first versions entered service, so successful aircraft companies need access to very extensive financial reserves, patience, persistence, consistent, bold and brave decisions, over decades. These are not well-known government political virtues!

The shorter the development timescale, the less the peak investment and the greater the potential for project profit, provided that the development is not curtailed too soon, before some significant unsatisfactory feature has been revealed and corrected before delivery. For example, this might be as "simple" as a too fragile cabin trim for actual in-service durability. Rework/modification in service is very expensive for the manufacturer. If safety is affected, payment of damages, fines and even criminal proceedings can result, as well as the cost of the corrective action and loss of reputation.

The costs and timescales involved in modern civil and military aircraft programmes are clearly a major investment barrier. The British civil aircraft industry record of the 1960s and 70s did not present a convincing-enough argument to obtain unreserved British government ongoing support to the growth of the European collaborative Airbus Industrie venture. British confidence to invest whole-heartedly in large civil aircraft projects was not, therefore, engendered. Pointedly, Airbus has received continuous support from the French and German governments.

The peaks and troughs of both military and civil aircraft major programmes are generally complimentary but are now stretched over long periods (ten, fifteen or even twenty years). Government ministers (and even aircraft company management and shareholders) find this hard to accept without shivers of uncertainty and not a little apprehension!

With the benefit of hindsight, it is clear that both the British government and the inheritor of the British share in Airbus (BAe/BAE Systems) made choices which ultimately eliminated Britain as any kind of major world player in civil aircraft. It is worth noting that the current UK Airbus aircraft wing business in Britain supports 9,000 jobs directly and many more in the supply chain. The result of leaving civil aircraft business also threatens the future involvement of Britain in military aircraft, in the longer term. The non-aircraft parts of the total British aerospace business will not necessarily share the same fate, but even the Rolls-Royce aircraft engine future position is now less assured than it might have been.

9.4 Vacillation in UK Civil Airliner Projects

UK Government and Industry Investment

When Imperial Airways had been formed in 1924 as the sole British airline, the original government policy was that the airline should use British-sourced aircraft (see section 2.4). It meant that the nationally-owned airlines were still restrained to prefer domestically-produced aircraft. This most often meant that Imperial Airways (and BEA/BOAC later) had undue sole-launch customer influence on the design of any new UK large commercial aircraft. The government did not seem to challenge Imperial Airways/BEA/BOAC, except to restrain the purchase of aircraft not of home origin, and did not seem to seek alternative (market) opinion on BEA/BOAC influence on UK aircraft designs.

This had sometimes limited overseas aircraft sales potential of the earlier twentieth century British civil aircraft, although nationalist preferences (in France, Germany and the USA particularly) were to blame as often as not. The exceptions for the airliners were the "clearly superior", such as the Vickers Viscount in the 1950s, or the smaller airliners able to be wholly financed by the individual companies, like the pre-1939 de Havilland Dragon Rapide, the post-1945 de Havilland Dove, the 1960s Avro/HSA 748 and the BAC 1-11.

In the late 1940s, the Viscount airliner and its engines, the Rolls-Royce Dart turboprop, were developed using government support. Viscount sales reached 442, which still represents the best-selling post-Second World War British civil airliner. The Dart engine continued to develop sufficiently to remain in production until 1987, used on many, many different aircraft worldwide and had sales in excess of 7,000 engines. The government return on the Viscount and the Dart investment (and other projects) would have been real but very "indirect", through the corporation tax paid by Rolls-Royce and their suppliers and the income and other taxes paid by Vickers and Rolls-Royce employees. From the 1920s to the end of the 1980s, there is no record of any net positive *direct* return on government direct investment in British civil aircraft programmes. Returnable Launch Investment (RLI) for some of the Airbus programmes of the 1990s would eventually redress this, due to the sales successes of the Airbus A.320 and later projects.

The British government had insisted on maintaining overall control of the flag-carrying national airlines BEA and BOAC, formed during the Second World War. This continued when BOAC and BEA were merged into British Airways (BA) in 1974 (together with two regional airlines, Cambrian Airways and Northeast Airlines). The government direct control of the British airlines only finally evaporated when BA was privatised in February 1987. This fully exposed the home civil aircraft industry to worldwide market forces and, at the same time, released them to respond freely. By 1987, however, the British civil aircraft industry had become quite weak, offering only three regional turbo-propeller airliners: the BAe Jetstream 31 (later stretched to the 41) and the BAe ATP, plus one regional turbofan airliner (the BAe 146 regional jet), a business jet (BAe 125), the light transports Britten-Norman Islander/Trislander and the Shorts SD.330/360. Significant new all-British civil aircraft products were not being planned, with energy and investment mostly focused on sharing in Airbus developments.

BAE Systems Leave Airbus

Having participated from the beginning (despite the Government) as HSA, and having "bought into" Airbus in 1996 (see section 8.5), in September 2006 BAE Systems decided to exercise its "put" option to sell its 20 per cent stake in the Airbus commercial aircraft business. Airbus finally offered €2.75bn (£1.9bn), though this was set quite a bit lower than BAE Systems originally hoped for. Even the Airbus company (in 2000 reorganised as part of the European Aeronautic Defence and Space company, EADS, including businesses other than Airbus, such as Eurocopter) had valued the stake "conservatively" at €3.5bn. The low valuation was put on BAE Systems' stake by investment bank Rothschild, after a specially-commissioned audit pointed to a cyclical downturn in Airbus profits and cash, and the need for substantial investment to maintain its position in the market against a resurgent Boeing.

At the time, it appeared that BAE Systems feared that Airbus could require significant cash injections in the next few years, already having been hit by production and technical problems which seemed likely to cost the Airbus business €2bn in earnings between 2007 and 2010. First flown in April 2005, by September 2006 the A.380 (world's biggest airliner) had secured only 159 orders, short of the 250-300 thought to be required to make a profit. BAE Systems is thought to have had insufficient faith in the development of a new A.350 long-haul, 250-to-300 passenger airliner (which eventually developed into the A.350XWB, to compete with the Boeing 787 Dreamliner project).

In reality, some of the real (undeclared) reason for the BAE Systems decision probably was to raise capital to help acquire a substantial stake in the on-shore USA defence business area. A further significant background reason was the 20 per cent minority position of BAE Systems in Airbus management control, which meant actual business control was in the hands of the other Airbus combined majority stakeholders.

Subsequently, the Airbus SAS commercial aircraft group within EADS was created in 2001. The overarching company "Airbus SE" for *all* activity (including helicopter, space and defence activities) was established in 2017.

Consequences of Britain's Failure to Fully Participate in Airbus

From 1945 until the late 1980s, the Western world market for front-line airliners had been dominated by the USA Boeing, Douglas and Lockheed companies. By 1984, the European Airbus Industrie organisation had created a slight inroad into this dominance. After the "in-out" British government dalliance with the first Airbus product (the A.300), the launch of the 150-to-180 seater Airbus A.320 in 1984 was the point at which Britain's government rejoined the other Airbus country governments in granting "Returnable Launch Investment" for a new Airbus airliner project, approved because of the BAe 20 per cent involvement in the project (wings design and manufacture, (see section 8.3). The investment was to be returned with a profit-share as a result of sales. The project adopted new technologies, notably the first civil airliner to have flight control entirely "digital computer fly by wire". The A.320 was a head-to-head competitor with the Boeing 737 airliner family and it became a spectacular success, so successful for Airbus that the financing of other competitive airliner projects could be achieved in the 1990s (see table in section 7.4).

As well as becoming a mature competitor with Boeing, the rise of Airbus eventually hit USA Lockheed and Douglas companies hard in their airliner businesses. The last Lockheed airliner (the L-1011 Tristar) ended production in 1984. Douglas airliners (DC-10, soldiering on after merger with the McDonnell company as the derivative MD-11) made a last wide-body final delivery three years after Boeing took over McDonnell-Douglas in 1997. The Boeing 717 "revived version" of the twin-engined narrow-body Douglas DC-9, as the MD-80/MD-90 airliner series, ceased production in 2006.

By the end of the twentieth century, only Boeing and Airbus were left as front-line medium and large airliner suppliers in the world. There were signs that Russia, China, and Japan were trying to enter the smaller regional jet part of the market. Canada (Bombardier) and Brazil (Embraer) created successful new airliners, at the fifty to 100 seater end of the market and both were to eventually create a new 130–150 seater challenge. There was no attempt from the only significant British incumbent civil airliner player (BAE Systems) to challenge, that company having abandoned – in the early years of the twenty-first century – any attempt to remain involved as a "prime contributor" to commercial aircraft design and/or manufacturer. From 2011, the Russian United Aircraft Company actively studied how to break into the exclusively USA-European wide body airliner manufacture. Joining up with the Chinese Comac company in 2012, this led to a 2017 joint venture, the China-Russia Commercial Aircraft International Corporation Ltd. (CRAIC) with the aim of building a 250-seat wide body modern airliner. The "as yet imprecisely defined" target is a 2025–2028 maiden flight and a total investment of US$13 to US$20 billion.

The costs and timescales involved in modern civil and military aircraft programmes are clearly a major investment barrier (see section 9.3). The United Kingdom civil aircraft industry record of the 1960s and 1970s did not present a convincing enough argument to obtain unreserved British government ongoing support to the growth of the European collaborative Airbus Industrie venture. This contrasted with the unreserved (almost) financial support of the French and German governments. British commercial confidence in large civil aircraft projects was not engendered.

So the BAe/BAE Systems-controlled part of the aircraft industry abandoned any ambition to be directly involved in the commercial airliner business in the twenty-first century. As a consequence, enthusiasm for future British government financial investment in Airbus developments may be reduced, even if this would help the Airbus industrial activity still in Britain. With the benefit of hindsight, both the government and the inheritor of the share in Airbus (BAE Systems) made a sequence of choices which inevitably led to the final elimination of Britain as any kind of world player in significant civil aircraft. The British decision to "opt out" of participating in civil airliner project launch decision making has to have been based on a deliberate political/commercial judgement that the investment level required for new large civil aircraft is either too great, and/or too risky, and/or not profitable enough.

…A medium or a long term view?…A wise or a flawed decision?
Boeing and Airbus have a definite business view! Other countries also have a view!

The consequences of those same choices *also* threaten the future involvement of the United Kingdom in military aircraft, in the longer term. The businesses of the domestic aircraft supply chain are affected, from major aerostructures and major elements such as undercarriages and engines, to smaller parts such as fasteners, transparencies, hydraulic equipment and the like. Even future military aircraft mission equipment business such as airborne missiles and sensors could be seriously affected. Without a successful British aircraft project reputation to headline, good British suppliers which are not "the true, well-in-front leaders" in their field, both technically and commercially, would not be even considered for non-UK aircraft projects. It would be at least as hard as it currently is for suppliers in countries like India to become a prime supplier involved in a Boeing or Airbus new aircraft project.

The non-aircraft parts of the total aerospace business in Britain will not necessarily all share the same fate, but even the Rolls-Royce aircraft engine future position is now less assured than it might have been.

9.5 International Trading Practices (as Affecting the Aircraft industry)

Direct government financial and unconditional support to the civil aircraft industry competing in international markets is inconsistent with "free international market trading principles", in any export situation. However, all governments of any nation which has any kind of aircraft industry have been adept at using government support to their industry. Sometimes military procurement is employed, as a means of indirectly financing a civil project launch process, or there can be an indirect subsidy using advanced technology research programmes, or there may be regional investment grants or tax incentives. Occasionally, direct investment in, and/or control of a project (or even the industry itself) happens. In the direct investment case, it can be constructed as a commercial investment with a profitable return generated on the basis of profits from future sales. Thus, investment in a commercial project by a government is not precluded. It is often referred to as Returnable Launch Investment (RLI). Table 8.1 (in section 8.1) notes UK government RLI in Airbus projects.

From time to time over the last hundred years or more, the British aircraft industry has enjoyed and experienced all of these methods of financial support. Not necessarily always openly admitted and so have all the others in the world – and not just in the aircraft industry.

Historically, international trade agreements came to be important to more and more nations (for trade in manufactured, mined and agricultural products). Almost as soon as the United Nations was formed in 1945, there was an attempt to create a world trade agreement agency (the International Trade Organisation). This was to have included issues other than trade (such a business practices, employment and investment agreements) but the United States declined to ratify their participation. With a less all-encompassing arrangement (not including anything other than "tariffs and trade"), the General Agreement on Tariffs and Trade (GATT) was signed by twenty-three nations in 1947, coming into effect 1 January 1948.

The World Trade Organisation (WTO) officially commenced to operate in 1995, wholly absorbing the GATT wording. The WTO has since been involved in resolving international trade disputes.

The most recent dispute associated with the world aircraft industry concerns a 2005 filing by the USA (Boeing) about foreign airliner projects (Airbus) financing by European government subsidy, said projects being sold in the USA. A counter-file action by Europe (Airbus) argues that Boeing has received indirect support through government-funded technology research programmes and tax incentives from individual USA States. The British aircraft industry is involved by virtue of the Airbus wings built in Bristol, Hawarden, and Belfast, and in the equipment of British origin included in the completed aircraft. This dispute has yet to be finally resolved (see Appendix 6) and the Sino-Russian state-funded competition in airliner supply is due to arrive in the 2030s, which could result in an even more contentious situation.

It is worth noting that a 2017 entirely separate but similar trade dispute, between Boeing and Bombardier (Canada), concerned the Bombardier C-Series airliner sales to a USA airline. The initial decision by the USA Commerce Department ruled in favour of Boeing but this was overturned on appeal by the US International Trade Commission. The British aircraft industry is involved by virtue of the C-Series (A.220) wings built in the UK (Belfast, Northern Ireland). This dispute and its outcome do not have a direct bearing on the Boeing-Airbus WTO dispute. In July 2018, Airbus completed a 50.01 per cent majority benign takeover of the Bombardier C-Series, the programme becoming the C-Series Aircraft Limited Partnership (CSALP) programme. The airliner is now presented as the A.220 in the Airbus portfolio. Subject to the outcome of trade negotiations, the departure of Britain from the European Union (Brexit) may create another international trading difficulty affecting the whole aerospace industry in Europe.

After an outline agreement in July 2018, followed by a protracted (twelve-month) challenge by the Brazilian government and other Brazilian indigenous organisations, Boeing and Embraer were expecting to sign an agreement for Boeing to acquire an 80 per cent stake in the direct A.220 competitor project, the Embraer E-jet series airliner. Boeing were to pay Embraer $4.2 billion. On 24 April 2020, Boeing declined to cement the deal, stating that the financial values used to evaluate the transaction had become null and void. The financial arguments for the deal had been overtaken by two world events. The dire financial consequences of the enforced 2019 grounding of the entire new Boeing 737MAX 160-180 seater airliner fleet (and the need for re-certificated modification of each aircraft before flying and deliveries can resume) was one issue. The 2020 Covid-19 coronavirus world pandemic and its dramatic effect on the travel industry was a second influencing issue. Embraer have challenged the validity of the Boeing pull-out decision.

9.6 A Century of World Aircraft Industry Amalgamation

In 1908, the British aircraft industry's first aircraft design and manufacturing organisation "opened for the business of selling aircraft". The industrial growth, mergers and collapses, from 1908 to the end of the Second World War in 1945, are described in section 2.8. Thirty UK aircraft companies emerged from the Second World War. The number of aircraft factories operated by the industry as the war ended far exceeded 100 (Avro alone controlled twenty-two). Many were either wartime shadow factories or were in dispersed facilities used for war production only. Aircraft parts during the Second World War were made in a great number of subcontract businesses, contributing extensively to aircraft war production rates.

After the war, more change was to come, as described already. Summarising all the changes in Britain since 1945, the following two diagrams are self-explanatory. Not shown are the Britten-Norman business changes, which was owned for a while by Fairey and is now based at Lee-on-Solent, Hampshire. Britten-Norman manufacturing was basically subcontracted from 1977 to Romania but was later repatriated to Britain (see section 6.4). The 2019 takeover of GKN by Melrose is also not shown.

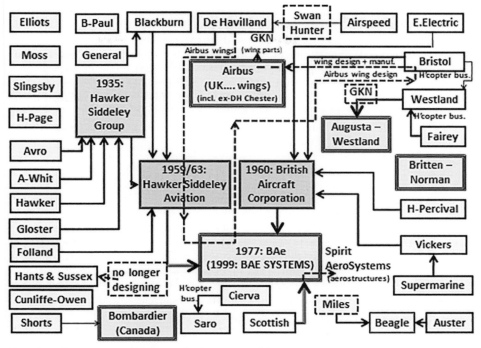

See also diagrams available on the internet, address:
http://britishaviation-ptp.com/timeline.html

Clarifying the mergers and takeovers in the helicopter part of the British aircraft industry:

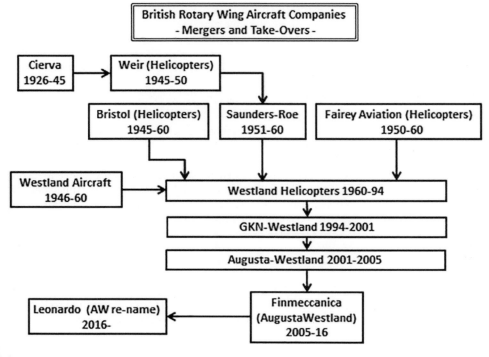

The current situation is that five significant organisations in the UK are responsible for aircraft design and manufacturing activity: BAE Systems, Airbus (UK), Leonardo (ex-Westland), Bombardier (ex-Shorts) and Britten-Norman. These five companies currently operate their aircraft businesses in a total of ten actual establishments.

Since the 1950s, the world aircraft industry has consolidated into ever-larger groups. Several companies disappeared completely. The British industry was no exception, as described in section 6.1 and the diagrams above. For comparison, the dominant USA industry of the 1950s also went through major rationalisation and consolidation, as illustrated below.

1959 Onwards. USA Aircraft Industry Consolidation	
1961	Chance Vought taken over, renamed as "Ling-Temco-Vought" (LTV)
1964	Fairchild buy Hiller
1965	Fairchild take over Republic
1967	McDonnell and Douglas combine as McDonnell-Douglas Rockwell International buy North American Aviation
1992	Northrop and Carlyle jointly buy Vought (LTV aerostructures) (in 2000, Carlyle buy out Vought from Northrop-Grumman)
1993	General Dynamics sell Fort Worth Jet Division to Lockheed
1994	Northrop and Grumman combine as Northrop-Grumman
1995	Lockheed and Martin Marietta combine as Lockheed-Martin
1996	Boeing take over North American Aviation (from Rockwell group)
1997	Boeing absorb McDonnell-Douglas under Boeing name
1999	Fairchild bankrupt, assets sold as aircraft component and assembly manufacture capability only ("aerostructures")
2015	Lockheed-Martin buy Sikorsky from United Technologies

The consolidation of businesses into larger groups has become a common worldwide occurrence, including many cross-border international mergers and takeovers. The world aircraft industry has not been exempt from this process. Using the start date of the 1959 "forced" mergers described in section 6.1, Table 9.4 below illustrates the current status of significant aircraft in-country companies (such as Airbus UK and Leonardo (ex-Westland) in the UK). Excluded are companies specialising solely in motor gliders, ultra-light aircraft, sports sailplanes and the like.

Table 9.4: SIGNIFICANT European and North American Aircraft Industry Company Consolidations, 1959 to 2018.

Geographic Region	Aircraft Companies Operating		percentage change
	1959	2018	
United Kingdom	27	5	-81%
Rest of Western Europe	21	9	-57%
USA and Canada	34	14	-59%
Soviet Union and "Warsaw Pact"	16*	6*	-63%
TOTAL	98	34	-65%

* Soviet Union design and manufacturing often separately located. Nationally "dispersed" in the 1990–1991 break-up of the Soviet Union into twenty-four independent states.

In all except the split-apart Soviet Union, the "romance" of many of the old company names has inevitably been lost but, without consolidation, the majority would have been lost in any case.

Chapter 10

Late Additions, Even More Turbulence, the Mistakes

10.1 Late Additions to the British Aircraft Industry

Edgley Optica

The Edgley Optica company was originally formed in 1971 by John Edgley, to build his Optica design. The Optica is a ducted fan two-seat and very light and quiet aircraft concept. After initial success, first flying in 1979 and gaining airworthiness approval in 1985, the project faltered after some ten aircraft had been delivered (an arson attack on the factory destroyed eleven). Earlier, as a result of the company going into receivership, John Edgley had been forced out. By 1988 the company foundered and went through various administrations until, in 2007, it was offered back to John Edgeley, who formed a new company AeroElvira Limited. Although one Optica has been refurbished as a company demonstrator, the revival progamme was still dormant early in 2020. The availability of financial support has been noted in the form of a June 2017 Letter of Intent from Interflight Global (a USA international consulting, brokerage and financial partnership organisation). Subject to due diligence investigations, the programme may restart by the end of the decade (2020).

Edgley Optica. (*Author's collection*)

The Little Fast Business Aircraft

A speculative attempt to capture a small portion of the light business jet-cum-sports aircraft market was made by an individual, Ian Chichester-Miles, retired Head of Research at BAe Hatfield. He formed Chichester Miles Consultants (CMC) and designed and financed the mainly-composite 500+ mph CMC Leopard four-seater twin jet. A prototype was completed, first flying in 1988. The original engine supplier ceased operations and a revised prototype flew in 1999. Both of the prototypes were withdrawn from flying when Ian Chichester Miles died in 2009 and the enterprise folded.

Hybrid Air Vehicle

The concept of hybrid air vehicles (wing body shape inflated by a lighter-than-air gas, the shape generating a percentage of total lift when in motion) was established as the technology principle behind the Aerospace Developments Ltd. company founded in the UK in 1971. Between 60 per cent and 80 per cent of total lift is aerostatic, from the helium gas-filled shape, the remainder is aerodynamically generated from forward motion. After the assets passed through six changes of ownership (including a joint venture in the USA), Hybrid Air Vehicles Ltd. (HAV) are the present owner/

designer company (founded in 2008). After cancellation as the US Army Long Endurance Multi-intelligence Vehicle (LEMV) HAV 304 development aircraft (built in Britain but first flown in the USA in 2012), the Airlander 10 hybrid air vehicle is the flying asset. This is the HAV 304 reassembled modified and renamed in the UK by HAV during 2012-16. First flight as the Airlander 10 was on 17 August 2016. Development is ongoing, using "the largest flying aircraft in the world" description in the press releases about the project: the Airlander 10 is 302 feet (92 metres) long.

HAV Airlander 10. (*Philbobagshot - Hybrid Air Vehicles, CC0*)

Electrically-Powered Aircraft

A lot of interest in recent years has been focused on the potential for "More-electric", "Hybrid-electric" and "All-electric" aircraft. There are a number of British-based research initiatives and even start-up all-electric aircraft companies in Britain:

- PHASA-35/BAE Systems Solar Powered Long Endurance UAV
  British technology company Prismatic and BAE Systems expect to trial the PHASA-35 high altitude long endurance (HALE) UAV, intended to be able to stay aloft for up to a year. The PHASA-35 is the latest vehicle after three previous designs developing HALE technologies. The intended use of the technology is as a surveillance and communications relay facility. In September 2019 BAE Systems announced an agreed decision to acquire the Prismatic activity as a subsidiary company.
- Rolls-Royce "Accelerating the Electrification of Flight" (ACCEL)
  This Rolls-Royce sponsored project intends to produce a single-seater 300mph/200 mile range battery powered aircraft, flying by 2020. Project partners are recently-formed Oxford based YASA, providing the electric motor, and London-based Electroflight. It is a technology development demonstration programme, aiming to capture the 217mph all-electric powered speed record previously set in 2017 by the hybrid diesel-electric Magnus eFusion aircraft with a Siemens electric motor.
  Rolls-Royce is also in a joint technology development project with Siemens and Airbus, to adapt a BAe 146 regional jet to a hybrid-electric aircraft, and a third project involving Rolls-Royce is the Cranfield University/Aston Martin Volante Vision Concept hybrid-electric VTOL vehicle. In June 2019, Rolls-Royce agreed to buy Siemens eAircraft division for some £50 million.
- Loganair Electrically-Powered BN-2 Islander
  "Fresson" is a Cranfield University project aimed at converting a BN-2 Islander of the airline Loganair, to either all-electric power or hybrid-electric power. The target is CAA/EASA certificated approval by 2021 to carry fare-paying passengers, on Loganair's short Scottish Island air routes.
- Samad e-Starling
  A start-up company based in the UK with a direct interest is Samad Aerospace. The company has plans to build more than one version of a hybrid-electric VTOL aircraft, able to carry between five and ten persons up to 1,500 miles, at speeds over 400mph. Either diesel or low-cost gas turbine engines are planned, as integral means of charging the main source of power, the batteries used to power the several large

electric motor-driven lift and thrust fans. Unveiled in January 2018, the e-Starling Jet project has the ultimate objective of becoming all-electric in the 2030s, subject to necessary improvements in battery technology.

A one-fifth scale version of the initial design is currently undergoing trials. The preliminary design review of the first aircraft proper was targeted for early 2019. The stated aim is to achieve a first flight in 2020, with the smallest version of the aircraft in service by 2022. Practicality of such ambitious timing remains open to question and requires immediate financial backing which, if not obtained from UK sources, Samad has declared may cause the company to try elsewhere. Letters of intent for 109 aircraft have been received by Samad, but that is the easy part.

AERALIS (modular approach to fast jet training)

A new venture started in 2015 was the Dart Jet aircraft project for a new adaptable light jet design for pilot training. By 2018 this had morphed into the AERALIS start-up project of a three-pronged modular approach to a design for a basic single engined jet-powered training aircraft, a twin-engined advanced jet trainer and a more adventurous aerobatic machine.

It has technical support from respected British aerospace establishments such as ARA and investment from Thales (a

AERALIS Twin-engined Trainer. (*Copyright Aeralis Ltd*)

major French defence contractor with a significant guided missile business, originally founded by Shorts in Belfast, and an avionics business presence elsewhere in Britain).

Swift Aircraft

Swift Aircraft was founded by David Stanbridge in 2004 and is part of the Swift Technology Group. Located at a former RAF base (RAF Coltishall at Badersfield, a few miles north of Norwich), the declared business objective is the revival of the British light aircraft industry, in the training and touring section of the General Aviation market. The first aircraft is currently under construction.

10.2 The Twenty-first Century and Even More Turbulence

By the closing years of the twentieth century, the thirty British aircraft design and manufacturing companies listed in Appendix 1 which existed at the end of the Second World War had been consolidated into five remaining active elements. The progress in company consolidation and mergers, from the start of the Second World War to the end of the twentieth century, is shown in the diagrams in section 9.6.

To summarise the state of play at the start of the second millennium:

1. The helicopter business of Westland Helicopters, based in Yeovil.
   Control taken by the UK company GKN in 1995. In 2000 Westland became part of a GKN joint venture with the Italian Finmeccanica-owned Augusta helicopter company.
2. The Canadian Bombardier company facility in Belfast (ex-Shorts).
   The 1943 nationalised Shorts aircraft company, privatised in 1984, and sold in 1989 to become part of Bombardier's aviation business.

3. The 1954 founded light aircraft company Britten-Norman, on the Isle of Wight, owned by Pilatus of Switzerland and aircraft produced almost entirely overseas (Romania and Belgium, see section 6.4).
4. The Airbus (UK) wing design and manufacturing at Filton (Bristol) and wing assembly at Hawarden, near Chester.

   This had been British Aerospace (Airbus Division) until exchanged in 1996 for a BAe 20 per cent equity share in the Airbus aircraft company. Airbus later sold the Filton wing parts manufacturing facility to GKN.
5. The largest British element (by far) remained the aircraft part of British Aerospace (BAe).

   The BAe (renamed BAE Systems in 1999) remaining aircraft establishments were located in Warton and Samlesbury (ex-English Electric, both near Preston), Brough (ex-Blackburn, near Hull), Woodford and Chadderton (ex-Avro, both near Manchester), Prestwick (ex-Scottish Aviation, Scotland) and a new Farnborough (Hampshire) design centre (housing ex-Hawker Kingston personnel) and company administration services centre in leased office development, with a senior company executive HQ office in London.

Twenty-first Century British Aircraft Industry

As shown in the diagram in section 9.6, in 2005 GKN sold their interest in AugustaWestland helicopters to Finmeccanica (owner of Augusta). Finmeccanica changed its name to Leonardo in 2016 and now brands the complete AugustaWestland helicopter business as Leonardo Helicopters of Italy. The original Westland site in Yeovil (named by Mrs Petter, see section 2.1) is now part of Leonardo.

The Bombardier ex-Shorts factory in Belfast (Northern Ireland) presently participates in the Airbus A.220 (ex-Bombardier C-Series) airliner programme, as wing manufacturer. In May 2019, Bombardier announced its intention to sell the ex-Shorts facility. Possible buyers included Airbus and Melrose/GKN but the sale to USA company Spirit Aerosystems was announced in November 2019.

Britten-Norman, on the Isle of Wight, now under new Oman-based ownership, have not produced a new design for an aircraft for some time but probably remain capable of revival to do so. They continue to support their two basic products, one still in production. Basic airframe build, subcontracted to a Romanian company for several years, has been repatriated to Britain.

Global Industry and the Creation of BAE Systems 1999

As outlined earlier (section 9.6), a spate of USA aerospace company game-changing mergers took place in the mid-1990s. In 1993 Boeing acquired the ex-North American aircraft business from Rockwell International. In 1994 Northrop and Grumman became Northrop-Grumman. In 1995, Lockheed and Martin combined as Lockheed-Martin and in 1997 Boeing absorbed McDonnell Douglas. These "USA combined business strength" changes increased the pressure on European defence companies to consolidate. The BAe board were clearly wondering what the best available counter to the problem might be, which was almost certainly recognised as involving some kind of significant merging of resources and influence. Was the best option to merge with one of the USA companies, or should BAe look to Europe?

Exploratory dialogue secretly started in mid-1998, about a three-way tie-up between BAe, Marconi Electronic Systems (MES) and DaimlerChrysler Aerospace (DASA). UK General Electric Company (GEC, not the USA GE) as parent company of MES wanted to sell the defence company and use the capital raised to expand in the information technology and communications (broadband) world. MES was a respected defence systems business which included radar and navigation equipment, the fly-by-wire digital computers for the Boeing 777 airliner, a major defence electronics business in the USA and British shipyards building warships.

DASA was the business controlling the German industry contribution to Airbus, the German part of Eurofighter Typhoon aircraft activity, a 40 per cent share in the Eurocopter helicopter business (with the other 60 per cent held by French company Aerospatiale) and the German MTU aero-engine activity (as preferred partner on USA Pratt & Whitney aircraft engine programmes).

BAe contribution to the merger would have been activity in European collaborative aircraft programmes (especially in Airbus and in the Eurofighter Typhoon, both also involving DASA), the BAe involvement in the potentially huge USA Lockheed Joint Strike Fighter (the JSF programme, which became the Lockheed Lightning II), the legacy aircraft support activities for the RAF and in the Middle East (Tornado, Hawk and, Eurofighter Typhoon), and BAe Australia.

DASA decided to pursue discussions of a two-way merger with BAe. BAe remained hopeful that a subsequent merger with MES might be possible but MES withdrew completely, fearing a weakened negotiating position with a much larger BAe/DASA combined company. Daimler/Chrysler, as parent company of DASA, were also asking for fifty-fifty control of future product strategy of the combined BAe/DASA company, despite DASA being significantly less than half the size of BAe. This was unacceptable to BAe, because they were concerned about the possibility of the powerful Daimler/Chrysler group (heavily biased towards the automotive industry) having any control of the strategy of BAe's defence business. Nonetheless, an agreement at chairman level to try to merge BAe and DASA was announced, in December 1998.

GEC decided to offer Marconi Electronic Systems for sale on 22 December 1998, a possible situation about which BAe had been concerned. It might create an opportunity for an overseas defence business to make a competitive move in BAe home territory. BAe feared a "swoop" for MES, by a USA defence company or a similar opportunistic move by a French defence/electronics company (such as Thomson-CSF, which had recently acquired the UK defence electronics company Racal).

Keen to maintain "home" defence market dominance, BAe decide to acquire the MES business, deferring further merger discussions with DASA. Announced in principle on 19 January 1999, this was completed later that year. It brought into the merged company (soon named BAE Systems) UK surface and sub-surface warship business, UK-based aviation electronics (avionics) and other defence electronics in the USA. This was partly a "vertical integration", where both the airframe platform and a fundamental contribution to its effectiveness (electronics) became part of the same company business. Naval vessel design and construction activity could be advantageously integrated (the MES Yarrow (River Clyde) and the MES Barrow (ex-Vickers) shipyard building submarines) with the Kvaerner Govan shipyard leased by BAe in 1999, also on the Clyde river. The UK MES avionics business had a significant activity in civil aerospace and communications programmes but, focusing almost exclusively on becoming a large defence contractor, BAE Systems would later sell most of this to Selex, which in turn was absorbed in 2007 into the Italian Finmeccanica group (Leonardo). Most importantly, the USA Tracor defence systems electronics company part of the MES portfolio to pass into BAE Systems was seen as a "large jewel", giving significant direct access into the USA defence budget activity. This entry into the USA was something which BAE Systems wished to build on.

Partly as a result of BAe abandoning discussions with DASA, in 1999 DASA became a willing participant in the forming of the joint European Aeronautic, Defence and Space company (EADS). Just before this, Aerospatiale, the company which was the French partner within Airbus, was privatised by the French government and merged with the Lagardere Matra company. This was the kind of move which actually already existed on the confidential BAe "to do" list of possibilities! The EADS Franco-German-Spanish alliance included Aerospatiale-Matra, DASA (which took control of the CASA Spanish 4.2 per cent stake-holder in Airbus in 1999) and the Anglo-French Matra-Marconi Space businesses. EADS thus became the third-largest aerospace company in the world, with 96,000 employees and an annual turnover of £20 billion.

Further Changes to BAe/BAE Systems

The 1996 Matra-BAe Dynamics missile business had been merged with Alenia-Marconi Systems and Aerospatiale-Matra missiles in December 2001, to form MBDA, the second-largest guided weapon company in the world. LFK, a German missile company was added. Via the merger with Marconi Electronic Systems, BAE Systems thus acquired a 37.5 per cent share in MBDA.

In 2003 BAE Systems sold its interest in the space systems company Astrium, which also had been acquired by virtue of the BAe-MES merger. BAe had originally helped enlarge the Matra-Marconi half of Astrium in 1994, when they sold their Space Systems subsidiary, but the interest in Astrium had returned to BAE Systems with the 1999 acquisition of Marconi Electronic Systems.

In 2004, BAE Systems acquired the UK military vehicles company Alvis plc (in which BAE Systems already had a 29 per cent stake), paying £309 million to outbid the USA General Dynamics. This was a synergistic business move with the BAE Systems owned Royal Ordnance Factory business and had defensive overtones for the BAE Systems land systems business, by preventing a USA foothold in the UK market.

In 2005 BAE Systems strengthened its defence industry position in the USA by acquiring the armoured fighting vehicles business United Defense, for £1.1 billion. This was merged into a "land systems" subsidiary of BAE Systems, alongside the UK Alvis fighting vehicles business and the weapon-producing ex-Royal Ordnance Factory (ROF) business acquired when this had been privatised and sold to BAe in 1987.

The £1.95 billion cash from selling BAE Systems 20 per cent stake in Airbus in 2006 was used to help finance the acquisition of United Defense. Notably, BAE Systems felt that Airbus was, at the time, "a business in an airliner market which had started to decline" (wrongly, as it turned out later). The 2007 £2.275 billion acquisition of Armor Holdings in the USA, the United Defense business and the USA Tracor defence electronics business (which had been part of Marconi Electronics Systems portfolio) were brought together under the umbrella of BAE Systems Land and Armaments Inc., headquartered in the USA as a wholly-owned BAE Systems subsidiary, BAE Systems Inc. This created the largest company in the world in this type of defence systems activity.

The BAE Systems 2006 sale of its Airbus stake ended all significant British-owned company new commercial aircraft design activity in Britain with the exception of in-service support based at Prestwick, for legacy aircraft projects still in commercial operation but no longer in production. Still active are the remaining fringe light aircraft businesses, the largest part of which is Britten-Norman, near Southampton and on the Isle of Wight, owned by the Omani-owned Bland Group based in Gibraltar.

The BAE Systems aerostructures manufacturing facility in Prestwick (Scotland) and the small non-military part of the aerostructures activity at Samlesbury were sold to USA Spirit Aerosystems in 2008. GKN acquired the Airbus wing parts aerostructure manufacturing facilities at Filton from Airbus (the original Bristol aircraft site, including the large "Brabazon hangar", transferred from BAe to Airbus in 1996, as described in section 10.2). The entire GKN company was taken over by Melrose Industries in April 2018.

The 2008 aerostructures sales meant that BAE Systems only continued to own and operate aircraft parts manufacture/sub-assembly and assembly capability at the Samlesbury (near Preston) factory (currently used for the Eurofighter Typhoon multi-national project and Hawk jet trainer aircraft), and Brough (the old home of Blackburn aircraft near Hull), with a final assembly and flight test capability co-located with the major design and development capability at Warton (near Preston, the old home of Canberra, Lightning and TSR-2 in their flight test days).

The 2008 BAE Systems Prestwick aerostructures sell-off also left the small remaining civil aircraft design support activity "isolated" in the Prestwick site. 146/RJ design support responsibility had been transferred there from BAE Systems Woodford prior to the closure of the Woodford 146/RJ production line and associated design function, joining the ex-Scottish Aviation Jetstream and the earlier (1993) transfer of ATP and 748 technical support responsibilities. Technical authority design support to aircraft out of production is an essential airworthiness-maintaining activity which only ends when the last aircraft of a type goes out of service or has its type certificate withdrawn.

The ex-Avro/HSA sites at Woodford and Chadderton (both near Manchester) were closed in 2011 and 2012 respectively, as the Nimrod MRA.4 was cancelled and the last VC.10s retired from RAF service. As Hawk aircraft sales declined, manufacturing ceased at the ex-Blackburn factory at Brough (near Hull) in 2013.

As a result of the site closures, no significant technical skills pertaining to the ab-initio design, manufacture, test and certification of fixed wing transport aircraft, of any kind or style, civil or military, remain in the BAE Systems organisation.

The BAE Systems-EADS Merger Proposal, 2012

(Pre-amble) In February 2008, the winner in the KC-X tanker competition to replace older United States Air Force Boeing KC-135 Stratotankers, was declared as a joint European-American (Airbus and Northrop-Grumman) bid, based on an adaptation of the Airbus A.330-200 Multi-Role Tanker-Transport (MRTT). This was an adaptation of the A.330 airliner design. The KC-X version of the A.330 MRTT for the USA would be assembled in a newly-constructed plant in Mobile (Alabama, USA). A contract for the supply of an initial fleet of 179 aircraft was to be negotiated. Boeing, the other credible bidder, protested. Controversially, the bid technical requirements were then amended. Northrop-Grumman protested that the rule changes favoured Boeing and subsequently pulled out. EADS (Airbus) continued to compete alone. In 2011, the new bid from Boeing was selected, based on adaptation of the Boeing 767 civil airliner airframe. At the time, EADS and some neutral commentators felt that the A.330 MRTT bid was rejected unfairly. It is likely, therefore, that the EADS senior management felt "unfairly excluded" from a USA defence business opportunity.

This seems likely to have stimulated intensified EADS internal discussions on how they might further increase EADS business presence in the USA. One result was the 2012 decision to establish an Airbus A.320 airliner assembly facility in Mobile (the fourth A.320 assembly facility, after French, German and Chinese plants). Construction began in 2013 and the facility opened in 2015.

(The merger proposal) A big surprise surfaced in 2012. A merger between EADS and BAE Systems was being discussed. The proposition was a "dual company listing" of a merger between BAE Systems and EADS (each company still retaining their own identity but pooling overall management and resources).

An EADS objective would have been to become part of a larger business, able to match Boeing in more than just civil aircraft and space business, but also to take advantage of BAE Systems established position as an accepted USA defence equipment supplier.

BAE Systems motives were to become a major part of a world-leading company which would be able to fully match the USA aerospace companies' overall strength (particularly Boeing, in military aircraft capabilities), with the additional feature of a new aircraft factory presence in the USA. It would also give BAE Systems potential access to more involvement in space transport and communication satellite businesses and to the commercial aircraft business world after "getting completely out of" entirely new civil aircraft activity by selling its 20 per cent "ailing" Airbus stake in 2006.

(**Proposal termination**) On 12 October 2012, less than one month after the announcement of a possible merger, BAE Systems and EADS jointly announced termination of discussions, due to the impossibility of reconciling (quote) "the interests of the parties' government stakeholders with each other", or with "the objectives that BAE Systems and EADS established for the merger".

In other words, the different governments involved could not be convinced that their individual strategic and economic interests would not be compromised. Reportedly, this was especially true of the German government position, which was a little surprising, given the German participation in both Panavia (Tornado) and Eurofighter (Typhoon) aircraft projects. It was accepted that there were difficulties also in satisfying the interests of shareholders, including where control truly would lie and how dividend policy would be affected, but the merger talks did not seem to have yet progressed far enough to believe that such issues caused the project to be terminated at that early stage. One issue which might have been an eventual difficult obstacle would have been the expected USA government concern about unintended access to USA classified programmes or techniques "by an information leakage path, possibly enabled by personnel transfers involving BAE Systems personnel moving from USA programmes to European programmes". Might not the French or German participants have had the same concerns in reverse, since the EADS motive for a merger was partly to give better market access for their products to the USA defence business opportunities?

Another important problem also predicted to stand in the way was the likely reluctance and reservations of the European governments involved (Britain, France, Germany and Spain) and which the government of the USA also would have, concerning British-European-USA differences in arms control policy and issues.

10.3 A Century of Missed Opportunities and Mistakes

This is mostly a matter of opinion, to say the least! And those who have never made a mistake have never done anything; except doing nothing is sometimes a mistake! Risk-taking is absolutely necessary sometimes (and has to be *seen* to be considered and managed, and not massaged away "out of sight"). In the last 100 years the world aircraft industry has only made progress by taking financial risks (and sometimes personal career risks) to develop aircraft technology, and even greater risks when deciding to apply new technology developments to real aircraft. Britain has been connected to some total risk decisions in aircraft design and manufacture. Deciding "not to do" is sometimes as hard to justify as deciding "to do". Either can be the cause of success or failure. The "not to" which turns out to be a "to do" success for others (lucky or otherwise) is usually labelled as a missed opportunity and the "to do" failure is almost always inevitably labelled a mistake, no matter what the cause of failure.

These and all like decisions needed to be taken "by someone prepared to take the flak", either way. Opinion can be insightful, well-reasoned and wrong all at the same time. Personal bias may show, be unpopular, but still correct (as perceived at the time, and may or may not continue to be so viewed with hindsight). This did not stop this section from being written, it merely held it up for quite a while! So "dive in" to this small selection of "missed opportunities and mistakes" which are felt to have had a major impact in the UK. The preceding chapters are the evidence.

Missed opportunities:

- Civil air transport 1920s and 1930s *extensive* government support not offered (but might spoon-feeding have weakened further the proper manufacturer independence, and prevented *any* understanding of the embryo world airliner market during those decades?).

  This was an ongoing issue, right into the 1960s, when lack of independence allowed the government-owned BEA airline too much influence on the DH.121 (HSA) Trident tri-jet (launched before the USA tri-jet Boeing 727) to force HSA to reduce the aircraft size, then BEA later wanted a bigger one, even asked to be allowed to buy the larger 727!

- 1944 Brabazon transatlantic airliner over-specification of luxury standard, oversizing the aircraft as a consequence (and underpowered).

- Overlapping Brabazon AND Britannia projects at Bristol meant Britannia start was delayed (probably inevitable anyway, given the new Bristol Proteus turboprop engine development difficulties). Otherwise, the Britannia may have captured a slice of the US domestic airliner and long-range market, *if* it had "beaten 707/DC8/Convair 880 jets to market". As it was, the Britannia lost most of its lead over the USA turboprop Lockheed L-188 Electra.

- Neither "Fully-in" nor "Fully-out" government support to the aircraft industry.

  Sir Arnold Hall, when Chairman of HSA and giving evidence to a 1971 House of Commons Select Committee, stated that his company had been on the receiving end of changing government policy and expressed an opinion as "one of the difficulties we have to face is that moods change because ministers change but projects do not change, perhaps the inevitable price for democracy, but disruptive, not good for doing good engineering".[1]

- Despite any wartime profits, the British aircraft industry was apparently too under-financed (post-1945) to launch any civil large aircraft programme without government support (and therefore tied to the vagaries of government policy much more than market needs). However, the British industry world airliner market awareness was myopic at the time. Investment in any project would have needed government approval in any case, in the overall scenario of the post-war national financial weakness.

- Industry barons had "autonomous power" derived from their original company silos, which continued in the different ex-HSA and ex-BAC facilities after BAe formed in 1976. Although work-sharing was "reasonably sensible", the local Chief Executive/Managing Director and/or Chief Designer control rivalry was sometimes disharmony-making. Inside BAC, Preston (English Electric) and Weybridge (Vickers) vied for supremacy – especially on TSR-2 – Bristol "kept head down" within BAC in latter stages of Concorde. Inside HSA, ex-de Havilland Hatfield personalities vied with ex-Avro Manchester personalities, while ex-Hawker at Kingston tried to remain "independent" but had to learn to work with ex-Blackburn in Brough etc. etc. The Westland helicopter part of the industry seemed to fare better, by being rationalised into a cohesive whole as part of the 1959–61 formation of Westland Helicopters Ltd. (formally established in 1961). The helicopter integration was probably aided by the Bristol helicopter division chief designer becoming overall Westland Technical Director.

---

1. Government and British Civil Aerospace, Hayward 1983

- The murky world of British political party politics obscured both good business planning and the gunsmoke-and-sparks fog of industrial battles for supremacy (or "not losing out", "me too" individual leaders in industry attitude, preservation of employment and media influence, to name but a few issues). In reality, it was obvious that there were too many sites remaining in the British aircraft industry, even after the 1960 "government induced" rationalisation into BAC, HSA, Westland and Beagle. The position was understandable, given the prominent contribution of the industry to the Second World War effort, not to forget the subsequent Cold War, but the industry really needed hard-headed rationalisation and refocus earlier than the 1980s and 1990s. Partially dealt with as a result of the "forced" mergers of 1960, but only finally dealt with after BAe privatisation in 1981 (but too slowly, probably due to fear of likely government/media, employee and trade union reaction). This extends into discussion of the possibilities which might have been generated by an earlier nationalisation-rationalisation-privatisation sequence and final rationalisation.

What might have been done differently?

Aircraft industry consolidation and/or nationalisation was talked about within government departments in 1944. The new 1945 Labour government, however, was in a seriously austere economic financial position immediately post-war. Other priorities were financial stabilisation, other nationalisations (National Health Service, the coal industry, road and rail transport, steel-making) and earning foreign currency (rules to ensure that nearly all cars would be exported, to earn foreign currency, for example). Additionally, the Cold War soon forced Britain to wish to continue to have a credible self-contained defence position, deemed to include contributing to NATO with the deterrence of a nuclear weapon delivery system (the 'V bomber force, section 5.12) and the ability to defend their bases (the Lightning interceptor capability, section 6.3 and the Bristol Bloodhound surface-to-air missile capability). Without this commitment, it could have been possible to seriously contemplate radical consolidation and reorganisation of the UK aircraft industry as early as the end of the 1940s.

There was also the national post-1945 belief that "Britain was among the best at aeroplanes", with the world's first civil jet and turboprop aircraft (Comet and Viscount) and the first military jet fighters (Meteor and Vampire). However, there was never the production capacity investment to modernise (including centralise) production facilities for the larger aircraft, to respond to the scale required if the world market was to be properly attacked. Wartime facilities like Yeadon and Castle Bromwich might have continued to have been used, say for increased Viscount and Comet production (before the disasters of Comet 1 interfered). The capacity and facilities which the USA had created for wartime aircraft production of large aircraft enabled the post-war greater quantities overall of USA large aircraft (military and civil) deliveries to service be efficiently completed, in a timely manner. At the time, nowhere else in Europe could have competed but, even with product superiority and adequate production investment, would Britain acting alone have been able to overcome the USA preference for "Buy America" in the dominant USA domestic market for aircraft? Doubtful, except for unlikely volume production of "unique" aircraft for USA airlines, such as Viscount and pre-disaster Comet. Even then, co-operation with an on-shore USA player could have been the only possibility, probably as a USA-based European (probably British) final assembly facility (as for Airbus, Airbus-Bombardier and Boeing-Embraer today).

The change to a Conservative government in 1951 "probably never" would have resulted in aircraft industry nationalisation but they finally made a major move in 1957, by being prepared to force the 1960 mergers (see sections 5.15 and 6.1). They used a false military premise (no more manned combat aircraft) coupled to the aircraft project investment control "carrot and stick", and the financial support of civil aircraft project one-at-a-time rules approach, all coupled with the "you *must* group together" incentive. As a product of the later 1965 Plowden report on the aircraft industry commissioned by the next (Labour) government, there was a 1966 parliamentary "statement of intent to nationalise" (see Appendix 4). The (unwilling and protesting) industry actually had to wait until 1977 for nationalisation and wholescale merger of the bulk of the industry into the two organisations BAC and HSA, alongside the independent much smaller Westland helicopter business which was mainly dependent on military machines.

The right *business* time for major rationalisation (for the future) would have been much earlier. However, if an attempt to do this had been made in the 1960s (perhaps initially nationalisation and placing into large groups and the merged business(es) subsequently privatised), the political, financial and social consequences would have been "Blood on the floor" and severe depression all over the aircraft industry. Probably, this would have encouraged many prospective aircraft engineers to choose something different, or to go overseas just as "the old guard" were starting to retire in droves. This would have been alongside a problem labelled "the UK brain drain" in the 1960s, whereby young, highly qualified personnel of all kinds were leaving the country in the late 1960s and early 1970s, for much more lucrative opportunities overseas. Balancing long term business rationalisation against ensuring qualified talent retention on a national basis would have been a "square the circle" exercise!

On the plus side, less overlapping of aircraft projects would have happened and a more assertive world aircraft industry United Kingdom voice might have been established, as early as 1970, with more influence in international project discussions? ("Sick man of Europe" soubriquet applied to the Britain of 1969–79 might or might not have mitigated the level of influence. "Sick man of Europe" has also been used to refer to Germany for the ten years post-reunification in 1990, Italy since 2005 and, more recently, France since 2014. Did it/has it hurt their influence today?)

As a side issue, the 1960 merger of Auster and F.G. Miles into British Executive and General Aircraft Limited (Beagle), as an attempt to start a world-competitive general aviation aircraft business, was facing a massive challenge which would have required a risky and large investment and some faith to overcome. As it was, the attempt was probably doomed from the start, partly because the size of the risk versus the size of the opportunity was not dealt with "head-on", financially or otherwise, but mostly because of the hugely dominant size of the USA domestic general aviation market and its USA-based suppliers.

If nationalisation was the only possible way that a full-on industry merger and rationalisation scenario could actually occur (a la BAe), and if this had miraculously happened before the end of the 1960s, the privatisation could have been in place in time for final rationalisation to have been complete well before the start of the 1980s. The opportunity for a "more powerful international UK aircraft industry voice" could have been created or, perhaps, the British industry might have joined as an "equal share/equal voice" in Airbus (maybe by investing "sites plus cash") to gain 33 per cent or more, rather than the less authoritative 20 per cent actually obtained in 1996), or the British industry might even have joined with a USA aerospace company, such as Northrop Grumman, or might have been totally taken over by another US company? … Maybe not all fantasy?

Biggest Mistakes:
There are several to choose from, involving government, the aircraft industry and the government-owned airlines. A selection is made below:

- From the 1931 Handley Page HP.42 onwards, until the privatisation of British Aerospace in 1981, government-owned national airlines Imperial Airways and the follow-on BOAC and BEA were allowed far too much influence on British airliner design, tailoring aircraft to their own (and ever-changing mid-project) special needs, ignoring the wider potential world market requirements.
- Airbus was not joined wholeheartedly by Britain.
- Not developing the Rolls-Royce RB.211 engine to 40,000–45,000lb thrust for Airbus A.300B thus let USA General Electric back into large civil jet market, via the TF-39 41,000lb thrust turbofan of the Lockheed C-5 aircraft, the engine which was later developed into the CF-6 51,000lb thrust turbofan for A.300B. Easy to be right (or think you are right!) using hindsight 20-20 vision! Rolls-Royce collapse in 1971 and government rescue "should not have, but understandably did" prevent government financial support for further major development of a more powerful version at the time, although the RB.211 eventually was further developed. Given the late 1960s to late 1970s "sick man of Europe" economic woes, could the government have acted otherwise? Perhaps a risky opportunity with a big pay-off declined, mainly for political rather than business reasons. Rolls-Royce Trent 600 and 700 engine eventual development from the RB.211 has turned into success (Rolls-Royce is "one of the only three companies able to supply the really big turbofan engines" which power all the long-range wide-bodied transport aircraft).
- Government not overtly countering (and the industry deliberately ignoring, for the sake of government cash investment) the French history of aggressively putting France first, or French rejection of collaboration where they were not going to lead (e.g. Breguét Atlantique French dominance, French pull-out from Anglo-French agreement on the AFVG and the Future European Fighter joint projects). If the AFVG had not been stopped, the subsequent Anglo-German-Italian Tornado might have been the Anglo-French-German-Italian VG instead? A French AFVG continuation might have pulled the UK into French Anglophile territory and vice-versa, rather than increasing mutual mistrust. Following the Second World War, the French government did not always "trust" their own industry BUT almost always supported (and moulded) the aeronautical ambition. The British government neither trusted, nor consistently and durably supported, the domestic industry, and managed public money projects "by committee" inefficiently.
- Two "BAe regional jets" (the ex-HSA 146 and ex-BAC 1-11) just about overlap in the early 1980s. The 1-11 had made an excellent USA start but, by 1980, the airliner needed to change from the Rolls-Royce Spey engine and/or have a development upgrade to compete with the equivalent upgrades to the USA Douglas DC-9. The initial 1973 start of the 146 airliner project caused associated HSA v BAC conflict which continued well after the BAC-HSA 1976 joining together inside BAe or, *instead*, BAe might have bitten the bullet in the mid/late 1970s and developed the 1-11 into an ongoing success, with a revised wing and USA engines if need be? The 146 much better short take-off and landing capability and generally higher maximum range is a feature not really offset by the 1-11 higher cruising speed (but 1-11 range might have been increased with a change of engine). In 1987, due to its excellent short field capability, the 146 was the first aircraft to make jet regional aircraft operations feasible – and acceptably quiet – using London City Airport, which caused other regional jet airliner manufacturers to make design and procedure changes to allow them to share in the "London City 146 jet aircraft legacy", albeit not always at maximum payload. Both 146 and 1-11 made reasonable success in their slightly different markets. The question remains, "Would total business have been improved if one had been cancelled and the other developed more?", or "BOTH replaced by a single new regional product", in service in the early-mid 1990s?

- Despite all the programme and cost issues, the late cancellation of the Nimrod MRA4 in 2010 was a mistake with particularly adverse long-term implications.

Was Concorde an opportunity missed, or a mistake? Perhaps some might consider it both. Technically, it was a momentous success, the difficulties overcome being almost as challenging as the USA Apollo moon shots. The real problem was the massive leap into the technology, environmental and economic unknowns, with a complete underestimation of the time and money it would take. The much-delayed service entry allowed the myths of the populist adverse publicity to become dominant. There was a lack of understanding of the need to identify and deal with the truths concerning the environmental impact of supersonic commercial flying, right from the start of the programme (easy to say with hindsight but true, none the less). From this distance, it is easy to observe that this should have involved everyone in the SST melting pot, including France, Russia and the USA, *and* the airlines wanting an SST, as a global issue to be agreed upon. By taking as long as it did to reach delivery standard and not sufficiently proactively anticipating and dealing with the hysterical aspects of the anti-Concorde environmental lobby *before* the USA supersonic aircraft cancellation in 1971, Concorde became predestined to be another "brave try", like the Comet.

The USA made a bigger supersonic mistake, (too fast, too big), at nearly the same development cost as Concorde before cancellation and nothing to show. Russia tried to "bludgeon" a solution which did not start with any real hope of success other than speed, with insufficient attention to operating economics.

In Britain, what projects went right? Over a significant period, quite a lot! See the next chapter.

Chapter 11

"Glory" and Conclusions

11.1 Where was the Glory?

Ever since the beginning in 1908, the British aircraft industry has been a major innovator and contributor to progress in the world of aviation. Many research efforts have helped establish the fundamental physics of aeronautics to help explain (and exploit) the aeronautical engineering achievements of the industry worldwide.

In the aviation world, many initial aircraft ideas are developed on paper, only to be abandoned because the technology required to implement them is not available in a sufficiently well-developed form. Any aircraft company with several tens of years of activity has on file hundreds of paper aircraft[1], usually dominated in numbers by those with military requirements to respond to. As an example, the quest for faster-than-sound flight (described earlier) caused many one-off experimental aircraft to be built and flown, with disasters, near misses and successes all in the mix. Only relatively few of all the paper aircraft make it to flight, and only a few of these can claim "glory", either from their unique (at the time) performance, or from their outstanding commercial success.

Why "where *was* the glory in Britain?" and not "where *is* the glory?" Perhaps exclusive use of the past tense is too gloomy. Britain has ambition and talent enough to continue to contribute.

It is appropriate to regard "glorious" as pertaining to periods or products in which Britain has excelled and outperformed the rest of the field, or at least shared the peak with another. It is possible that some present activities, or consistent still ongoing performance over a protracted period, will also eventually qualify for the soubriquet "glorious". Clearly, the whole subject is judgemental. It still might be appropriate to express such judgement, if only for a personal satisfaction which might be consistent with a shared view of others. Hindsight does have a valid input!

For the category "nearly glorious", the choice is those notable, ambitious and prominent events or projects where implementation was inhibited by unknown (at the start) or uncontrollable external influences and truly memorable success "just missed".

As well as failure to fly well enough, "Absolute Failures" most often are associated with financial failure to be so labelled. The root cause might be an inadequate design or an overambitious or irrelevant specification, or inadequate management. Large projects wrongly specified for market requirements, or relying on an unfounded speculatively hoped-for technology development, and major business changes poorly thought through or without objectives defined in advance were the absolute failures. There were surprisingly few of any great size, but a few were big enough to truly qualify!

The industry rationalisation in Brtain was successfuly completed but took far too long and should have started earlier. It really started in the late 1950s, mostly completed by 1993. Starting with the national internal merging of some French and

---

1. Examples are in Tony Buttler's "British Secret Projects" (Vol. 1 & 2) and Richard Payne's "Stuck on the Drawing Board". (See the Bibliography.)

some German companies (respectively, to form Aerospatiale in 1970 and Messeschmitt-Bölkow-Blohm in 1968) full privatisation of the "adult" Airbus took place in 2000, as EADS in two subsidiary companies and is now formally constituted as the independent aerospace business group, Airbus SE. This group has interests in aeroplanes (including helicopters), guided missiles and space technology. The rationalisation and consolidation of the world aircraft-building community into large enterprises (as briefly described in section 9.6) has been a survival strategy. The investment levels required to stay in the game have forced this, just as in other manufacturing industries such as automobiles.

A "designer" perspective on British aircraft industry glory is likely to differ from a perspective solely focused on "business success". Hindsight may dictate that the merging and rationalisation of the aircraft industry in Britain should have been condensed into a period between the late 1940s and the late 1950s, rather than the protracted thirty-three years it took. For this to have actually happened, a complete dictatorial attitude from the British government would have been needed for the first ten years. Wholescale forced nationalisation and merger, faster closure of several existing facilities, investment in larger centralised facilities, followed by privatisation before industrially-led rapid completion of the rationalisation. Shortly after Britain had just fought a debilitating war, leaving the country heavily indebted and a Cold War to respond to and pay for? Not really likely.

The table below summarises a personal version of "the glory" and the evidence for the choices is the text in all previous chapters. Others may think differently!

"Glorious" British Success	Main Reason
UK aircraft design and production for and during the First World War *(Misleading to choose particular aircraft)*	Innovative, sustained and massive ingenious industrial effort
DH "Moths":Type 60 (1926–35) and Type 82 (1934–45) Type 89 Dragon Rapide (1935–45) Avro Anson, 1934–52	Quality products, continuously improved, sold well (helped by British wartime needs)
Hawker Hart total family of the 1930s	Quality product, UK govt./RAF backing
UK aircraft design and production for and during the Second World War *(especially persistence in creating Hurricane, Spitfire, Mosquito and Lancaster, against doubts in some RAF quarters)*	Innovative, sustained and massive ingenious industrial effort
Gloster Meteor and de Havilland Vampire jet aircraft	Game-changers and sold well
Vickers Viscount turboprop airliner	Game-changer and sold well
English Electric Canberra jet bomber	Game-changer and sold well
Hawker Hunter jet fighter	Capable, enduring and sold well
Handley Page Victor and Avro Vulcan V-bombers	Advanced technically, superb performers
English Electric Lightning jet interceptor	Very capable, fit for purpose and sold reasonably well
de Havilland 125 business jet	Sold well, in fiercely competitive market dominated by USA
HS. Harrier/Bristol-Siddeley Pegasus VTOL fighter/strike	Belief and investment by originators *(Unique capability – no competitor)*
SEPECAT Jaguar (joint project) fighter/strike/trainer	Despite politics, capable and sold well

"Glorious" British Success	Main Reason
HSA Hawk jet trainer and light fighter	Fifty years and still in production (over 1,300 built). Continuously improved
Panavia Tornado (joint project) "swing wing" strike	Capable and sold well, forty years' service
Westland Lynx multi-role helicopter	World's fastest helicopter, fifty years in production *(Now as AW.149 Wildcat)*
Wing aerodynamics of Concorde, VC.10 and Airbus airliners	World-leading technology of the day
Eurofighter Typhoon interceptor fighter/strike	BAe-UK government EAP/EFA faith, cash and persistence, for top performer still in production with 565 completed to date.
UK aircraft technology advances "as a whole"	112 years of continuous effort

"Nearly Glorious" British Success	Main Reason
Handley Page V/1500 bomber of 1918	Biggest and best, just too late
de Havilland Comet jet airliner	Technological leap, brought down by unforeseen (unknown) technology flaw
Blackburn Buccaneer tactical strike	Unsung top performer
TSR-2 tactical reconnaissance/strike	Over-ambitious, poorly managed
BAC 1-11 airliner	Successfully beat competition in USA but failed to invest in upgrades in time
HSA 146 airliner	Good success "but not good enough"
BAC-Sud Aviation Concorde (joint project) supersonic airliner	"Technically superb", too late and market not properly addressed

"Absolute British Failures"	Main Reason
Bristol Brabazon transatlantic airliner	Failure to assess emerging USA airliner competition or address true market
British Government Civil and Military Aircraft Industry Policies, post-1945	One step forward, half a step back, or change direction! Repeatedly!
Saunders Roe Princess Flying Boat	As Brabazon but also large flying boat airliners past sell-by date
Fairey Rotodyne forty-passenger gyroplane	Technology flaw and market not ready
Nimrod AEW Mk.3 and MRA.4	Mismanagement, by govt. & industry
BAE Systems twenty-first century Airbus disengagement	Mistaken significant cash-generating business decision. Has left the company "exposed"

Overall, the most glorious period probably was either the decade 1935 to 1945, or the post-war years 1946 to 1960. Most likely the latter, even though the end of those years included the start of some of the most traumatic and frustrating experiences, as the (necessary) economies and reorganisations loomed large on the political and business agenda.

Over the whole one hundred and twelve years of the British aircraft industry to the start of 2020, a total of 282,713 all-new aircraft have been built and flown, represented by 1,153 different aircraft types, seven of which have been joint international projects (Concorde, Jaguar, Harrier II/AV8B, Tornado, Eurofighter Typhoon, Lynx, Leonardo AW.101). These figures do not include the British involvement with Airbus aircraft (over 12,000 sets of wings delivered for all Airbus fixed-wing airliners and military transports, with nearly 8,000 sets of outstanding orders to complete) or the minority British contributions to projects initiated and led by other overseas companies (McDonnell Douglas AV-8B and Lockheed Lightning II).

In the fifty years between the end of the First World War and 1969, Britain has been responsible for the production of 200,787 aircraft whose first flight was in that period, represented by 749 types (two types being joint projects, the Jaguar and the Concorde). It is interesting to compare this total with the fact that, in the fifty years *since* 1969, the UK has been responsible for the production of 5,821 aircraft in total whose first flight was in that period, represented by seventy-three aircraft types (five of which were/are joint projects with other countries totalling nearly half of the total number built). The 12,000 sets of Airbus wings are also post-1969.

Of course, the impact of the Second World War distorts comparisons (with approximately 90 per cent of the 1919–1969 total produced being in preparation for and during that conflict). The complexity, capability and cost of each decade's aircraft have mostly been increasingly beyond fair comparison with the types of the previous decade. Some of the more recent most advanced military aircraft have taken considerably more than a single decade to develop.

11.2 Conclusions – The British Aircraft Industry Future
The Political Dimension to New Aircraft Large Programmes
Other than military adaptations of airliners for transport-only purposes, the direct involvement of government in starting new military aircraft programmes has always been an obvious "given". In countries with an indigenous aircraft industry, very few new military aircraft projects have been started without a "home" government initial requirement, specification and finance. Government levers on the aircraft industry in Britain have always been "long and strong".

These levers have often also been used on civil aircraft programmes. By virtue of the British government-owned monopoly Imperial Airways, the airliner part of the British aircraft industry was both assisted *and constrained* by this in the 1930s (as described in section 2.7). The 1940s de Havilland Comet and Dove and the Vickers Viscount were backed by the government, as aircraft arising out of the Brabazon report. Help was also given in the 1955 financial restructuring of the de Havilland company. This government control has had financial, domestic political and ever-increasing international political dimensions. In the 1960s, the forced restructuring of British industry, (as described in section 6.1), the financing of reconnaissance-bomber TSR-2 (as described in sections 6.3) and the de Havilland 121 Trident and the Vickers VC.10 airliners, (as described in section 6.4), are very prominent later examples of direct government influence.

As projects became evermore technologically advanced, they became more expensive. In Europe, they also became politically-charged, because of the level of government investment contribution needed, when pressing other non-aircraft (and non-defence) government programmes also required use of scarce financial support. For military programmes, it was part of the landscape but, for airliner programmes, it was not only government finance but active government support that also became essential in the civil aircraft marketplace, alongside attempts to sell military aircraft to overseas customers.

During and after the Second World War, USA levels of military spending on aircraft became far beyond the capability of any single European nation. The dominant USA airliner position of the post-1945 years of the twentieth century was also much assisted indirectly by the USA government, sometimes via procurement of early models of new transport aircraft for USAF use, sometimes by technology and technique developments in experimental projects, by military aircraft large projects with companies also involved in airliner design and manufacture, and by localised US state support for manufacturing facility development. The confidence so engendered, and the readiness to take risks by American industry, airlines and financial institutions, combined to produce iconic airliners, from the Douglas DC-3 and DC-6, Lockheed Constellation and Boeing 707, to the Douglas DC.10, Lockheed L-1011 and Boeing 747. By the mid-1970s, the only way to break into the near-monopoly USA dominance in airliners was direct home government support for the non-USA manufacturers, ostensibly limited only to the extent permissible by world trading rules pertaining at the time.

Government direct subsidy and repayable loan assistance (Repayable Launch Investment – RLI) has been needed to underwrite or assist (indirectly or directly) in the launch of several significant modern large airliner projects in Europe. This includes most of the British jet airliners noted previously and the Airbus airliner programmes, from the beginning. More recently, modest-sized airliner programmes in Brazil, Canada, Russia, China and Japan have received national government support, including efforts to sell in the North American market.

As well as the problem of finance, the industrial importance of the aircraft industry in several countries ensured that the political leaders of those countries also had to become personally involved from time to time, in both the domestic and international issues associated with the world market. This was especially so when new aircraft projects cost several billions of US dollars (just for design and development, and tens of billions more investment in work in production before sales revenue from deliveries could commence). Civil airliner projects often take ten or more years to actually show any kind of financial return (see section 9.3) and military developments can sometimes take longer to develop to an acceptable service standard.

From time to time, the personal involvement of political leaders in the attempt to make sales included Prime Ministers and Presidents, sometimes openly linking extraneous diplomatic issues to military aircraft and/or airliner sales campaigns in the target customer country. The international diplomatic dimension became a normal hazard, starting in earnest with Concorde and continuing with nearly every significant new sale of aircraft to an operator in a foreign country since that date. The domestic additional political dimension to airliner development internal to Britain is exemplified in sections 7.1 (formation of Airbus) and 8.3 (the A.320 and British Prime Minister Margaret Thatcher).

Since the first Airbus successful sale to an American operator in 1978, American airliner manufacturers have claimed that "the airliner market financial playing field is not level", accusing Airbus of "dumping" subsidised aircraft in the USA. The European counterclaim view is that USA manufacturers receive similar levels of financial support but often indirectly, through tax reliefs from USA states and from military-sponsored fundamental research and aircraft development. (See Appendix 6). This issue escalated as Airbus success grew over the next twenty years and became the subject of a World Trade Organisation review process in 2005. This yet remains to be fully resolved.

The British involvement in new medium and large airliner programmes is now confined to the Airbus wings connection. Will this endure? The answer is largely not in British hands, the only influence being efficiency and efficacy of any British design and production contribution to Airbus aircraft (currently, the wings) and, almost certainly, the British government's continued willingness to contribute RLI on future Airbus programmes. The size of any RLI contribution from any of the national governments for a future project may be reduced from the levels heretofore, by an eventual resolution of the World Trade dispute between the USA and Europe.

Including military aircraft, the following speculation about the British future aircraft industry is offered.

Short Term

For the moment, the UK involvement in ongoing aircraft projects is reasonably secure. The share in both the Eurofighter Typhoon and the USA Lockheed-Martin F-35 Lightning II, by BAE Systems at ex-English Electric in Preston (Warton and Samlesbury), plus the participation in Airbus with ex-De Havilland/Bristol at Chester (Hawarden) and Filton, the share in Leonardo helicopters with ex-Westland in Yeovil, and the Spirit Aerosystems wings of the Airbus A.220 airliner (renamed by Airbus as the A.220 in July 2018) and

Lockheed F-35A Lightning II. (*Author's collection*)

components for other manufacturers aircraft all have some certainties (orders).

There are, however, also some unknowns regarding the near future:

- Aircraft supplied in the recent past and in the future will enable aircraft support business (usually the source of most revenue on any particular project) to continue, but third parties sometimes secure the business of changes, such as future weapons system upgrades, cockpit or cabin interior upgrades or freighter conversions.
- For "niche" aircraft projects, will the demand for light aircraft be sufficient to maintain/revive the Britten-Norman facility, can the Edgley Optica project really be revived, and will the hybrid air vehicle of the Airlander style become a commercial success?
- Will Britain's departure from the European Union (Brexit) change the trading situation sufficiently to create real difficulties in the Airbus UK supply of wings to Airbus? (Always supposing that Airbus does not decide to eventually move to a continental European establishment or even a developing country like India, as the source for this part of the business.)
- Similarly, and assuming that the fierce competition in the helicopter world does not seriously intensify even further, will Leonardo continue with an ongoing helicopter sourcing policy which includes Britain?
- When will the next all-new Airbus aircraft programme be launched? ... and will there be a British content? To scale the product life cycle of a modern airliner, it is thirty years since the Airbus A.320 first flew and the latest version (A.321LR) only commenced deliveries in November 2018.
- Will the Airbus A.220 (ex-Bombardier C-series) airliner endure and will it succeed in its bid to capture an enduring slice of the regional jet airliner market, thus

supporting the present sourcing of wings from Northern Ireland? And will the Bombardier sale of the business lead to long-term continued support of the Northern Ireland factory?

Airbus A.220 (formerly Bombardier C-series). (*Airbus SE*)

- Are there still opportunities for further sales of the BAE Systems Hawk military trainer aircraft? The start-up Aeralis project (see section 10.1) implies that there may not be any more. The fact that a major European defence contractor (French company Thales) has been prepared to invest in this new venture indicates that this new approach may not be a "no hope of success" venture. With the right attitude and action, might this be a British-operated and financed opportunity instead? Inexpensive enough at this early stage to try?

Medium Term

Might BAE Systems seek new joint venture opportunities in the aircraft supply business? Transport aircraft (civil or military) would now fall in the "lost UK skills" category, except for the wing expertise currently resident in Airbus UK.

The extant BAE Systems expertise in the "fast military jet" environment might make the company an attractive partner in that area, but the use of manned (expensive) and/or unmanned (costs unclear) air vehicles is yet to be resolved. Over the last thirty years, various ideas have been examined by BAe/BAE Systems, under various acronyms such as FOAS (Future Offensive Air system) and others. These concerned what/how a future combat scenario might require new air vehicle developments, integrated in a way made possible by digital communications facilities of ever-increasing capacity. The unmanned aircraft can be directed in real time and controlled from afar, rather than be pre-programmed, and full autonomy post-launch is feasible, perhaps employing artificial intelligence.

Corax is a BAE Systems prototype Unmanned Air Vehicle (UAV) first flown in 2004 and another is the Mantis demonstrator UAV which first flew in October 2009. Another British UAV is the BAE Systems "Taranis", first flown in 2013.

In 2010 an Anglo-French government accord was reached on studies of what BAE Systems had generically labelled "the Future Combat Air System (FCAS)". BAE Systems and Dassault were the two companies involved, with an exclusivity agreement that neither would co-operate with other partners to develop UAVs. The Medium Altitude Long Endurance (MALE) Reconnaissance UAV capability required by both the RAF and the *Armée de l'Air* was the focus. The companies declared that there would be a competitive assessment during 2011 with a view to equipment delivery taking place between 2015 and 2020.

The BAE Systems-Dassault Telemos study UAV started with the Mantis concept and an overall BAE Systems design leadership. In 2012, this became another Anglo-French project which was cancelled, when Dassault pulled out. Dassault made a new agreement with Airbus in 2018, in a joint project later joined by Spain, labelled the Sixth Generation or New Generation Fighter (NGF). Airbus were already involved with a UAV project called Talarion, which also involves the Turkish aerospace industry. Airbus involvement brings in France, Germany and Spain, and, with Dassault, "more France". If this does not expand to include a British contribution (and perhaps other European countries, such as Italy, Sweden or the Netherlands) it would require either a UK/BAE Systems "go it alone", or British co-operation with European non-Airbus countries, or perhaps countries such as Australia (where there is a significant BAE Systems presence), Canada, Turkey, India or Japan. British collaboration with the USA would ensure market size but a junior role.

In a restarted beginning, in July 2018, the British government invited other countries to join a new initiative, the "Team Tempest" study and concept development for a future combat air system, which could mature into a future committed project. Sweden and Italy have since joined with the British government in supporting the initial study phase. The countries and companies presently involved are Britain, (BAE Systems, and MBDA – MBDA as a British, French, Italian

Tempest 6th Generation Fighter. (*Author's collection*)

and German multinational guided weapons company), Italy (Leonardo as a British-Italian multinational defence company) and Sweden (Saab). Other listed potential partner countries include Turkey and Japan. Without exploiting the capability of BAE Systems experience, from Panavia Tornado, Eurofighter Typhoon and Lockheed Lightning II, British creative competence in the fast military jet regime will slowly expire, possibly to join the complete extinction of commercial airliner competence.

The history of Anglo-French disharmony in military aircraft projects portends the possibility of significant obstacles, given the military aircraft projects from which France unilaterally disengaged (see section 8.8). The intransigent unwillingness of the French company Dassault concerning sharing design leadership has often turned out to be an issue. The uncertain consequences of Britain's exit from the European Union (Brexit) may eventually also cast significant doubt on the FCAS future international collaboration between the present major European aircraft companies. Could this all turn out to be a Dassault-inspired attempt to dominate, perhaps causing an AFVG or ECA (Eurofighter Typhoon – Dassault Rafale) style of unhelpful competitive duplicated rerun, as described earlier? This would be a market-dividing Tempest-NGF competition, really only helping the USA to continue to dominate this part of the world market.

Conceptually, FCAS could ultimately include both reconnaissance-only and armed combat UAVs, perhaps with some autonomous capability. The FCAS concept in Europe might lead to a system replacing both the Dassault Rafale and Eurofighter Typhoon aircraft. A new manned aircraft, or a modified version of the present design(s), could be accompanied by a controlled loyal wingman, pack, flock (or even a swarm?), of smaller pilotless fast combat UAVs, possibly released on command to "autonomous". As a result of initial thoughts of the "Tempest" initiative, a Sixth Generation Fighter Concept was revealed by BAE Systems in 2019. A ground-controlled flock of semi-autonomous armed UAVs could also be part of FCAS. Or? Or? The most sensible European approach would amalgamate the Tempest and NGF efforts. Presently, BAE Systems is the only British aircraft company likely to be able to take a large leadership or co-leadership role in such a programme, although Rolls-Royce is clearly capable of providing/developing suitable power plants. There is the possibility that new domestic and/or international suppliers of UAVs may emerge. Israel, China and Russia are already active in this field.

As far as other aircraft manufacturers with presence in Britain are concerned, might the Leonardo connection lead to more project work with both the Leonardo Italian arm and long-time USA helicopter collaborators Sikorsky (now owned by USA

Lockheed-Martin). There is no reason to believe aerostructures manufacturing work will not be obtained in Britain by a revamped Bombardier/Spirit in Belfast under new ownership, or by Leonardo in Yeovil, but aircraft design skills and testing/qualification skills need nurturing also, to be able to maintain a long-term future.

Long Term

The longer-term future is, however, even less self-evident. In terms of total aerospace business in Britain, the Aeronautical Technology Institute economic forecast of 2017 suggested the annual Gross Value Added (GVA) for UK aerospace as a whole will be around £15 billion in 2040. The forecast however ranges from as low as £5 billion to close to £30 billion, in 2017 terms, therefore ranging from stagnation (or even decline) to modest boom. An aerospace business boom in Britain in total may disguise an *aircraft* industry further decline. The GVA forecast will have included the value added in Rolls-Royce aircraft engines, several internationally-owned aerostructures UK businesses, major equipment suppliers such as landing gear, flight simulators, ejection seats, the British workshare in the MBDA guided weapons business, the Britain-based element of the Astrium satellites business, etc. etc. etc. The uncertainties and assumptions made in economic forecasts might be magnified by the final outcome of Brexit negotiations and future trade agreements. Despite the recent success of Eurofighter Typhoon sales for the medium term, what will be the longer-term military aircraft next generation project be, and with which company/country might the current domestically-controlled "big two" in United Kingdom aerospace (BAE Systems and Rolls-Royce) have a chance to be part of this longer term future? Extending the speculation, might a merger between Rolls-Royce and BAE Systems ever be considered? Partially, this could be a move to try to "bullet-proof" the bulk of the British aerospace industry from any single project failure (akin to the Rolls-Royce 1971 RB.211 issue), or create a high hurdle to forestall any foreign take-over threat and an associated intellectual property asset strip. To scale such a join-up, the April 2020 merger of USA GE and Raytheon created a combined business second in size to Boeing and worth well over BAE Systems and Rolls-Royce combined.

True success in this long-term and high-investment industry requires more than accurate market forecasting and a technically excellent response. It needs steady access to cash (billions of US dollars), resilience, management strength, faith and persistence, product continuous improvement and responsive customer interaction, and a little luck, from time to time. As a timely reminder of how world events influence industry, the economic effects of the 2020 Covid-19 coronavirus world pandemic will continue to be a major disturbing and re-alignment influence on all manufactured goods trade for some time.

Extending Sir Sydney Camm's comment on TSR-2 (see section 6.3), the British aircraft industry needs to ensure the correct size of the next military aircraft project in FIVE dimensions:

Span, length, height, politics, and affordability.

Overview, from the beginning in 1908 to 2020

After a slow start (compared with France and Germany), the necessities of the First World War made the British aircraft industry become the largest in the world. The political and industrial struggles of the two decades after the end of the First World War did little to promote the British industry, until the looming threat of war in the mid-1930s caused a major revival of military aviation. Apart from Germany (at first, forced to focus by the Treaty of Versailles on civil aviation, this stricture later ignored) the rest of Western Europe aircraft also made technical and industrial progress in aviation in fits and starts, during the first fifteen of the inter-war years. During the same period, Russia was similarly semi-progressive in aviation but mostly insulated and isolated by the new communist regime, led by the paranoiac Joseph Stalin. In the Far East, Japan started to develop their own aeronautical capability in the 1930s, prior to that relying entirely on imports of aircraft. From 1935, preparations for the looming war in Europe massively accelerated British aircraft industry activity and progress. Meanwhile, the sheer size of North American geography and demographics stimulated civil aviation in the USA and, by the end of the 1930s, had helped long-range transport aircraft development in that country to leap ahead of the rest of the world.

Throughout the twentieth century, the world continued to make great strides in the understanding of aerodynamics, structural design and other technical subjects related to aviation. Britain made a huge contribution to this progress, in government, academic and industrial research facilities.

The totality of the Second World War once again forced the intensive growth and technical development in the British aircraft industry but did not allow British (or any other Western European) civil aviation to make any serious progress. After the war, Britain and most of the rest of Europe were financially exhausted. The exigencies of total war had also forced Britain to give away the secrets of a number of aviation technical developments, such as the jet turbine engine.

In the decade after the Second World War, a government-planned revival of civil aviation in Britain aimed to give an emphatic world-beating restart in civil aviation, in both airframe and aircraft engine development. This foundered on the over-specified Brabazon, the Comet technical disaster and the inadequacies of investment in upgrade of manufacturing methods and facilities for more efficient production. The Viscount was the main innovative British commercial aircraft success. Stimulated by the Cold War following the Second World War, military aircraft design and development did prosper domestically for a while, in the shape of the Canberra, Hunter, Javelin, Sea Vixen, Buccaneer, Lightning, Harrier and the V-bomber force, backed by overseas sales of Meteor, Vampire, Hunter, Lightning and the Harrier. The difficulties of selling British military aircraft products directly to the USA worked against any chance of matching USA industrial access to the largest Western/NATO aircraft market in the world. To acquire British aircraft, the licence-build was enforced by the USA government for the English Electric Canberra and, later, the AV-8B updated version of the BAe Harrier. The manufacture of the later USA Goshawk version of the BAe Hawk also had to be shared with a USA company.

Until 1960, the whole process (mostly under government control) was hampered by sharing out work amongst too many aircraft companies, some of which were really too small to have the necessary strength to compete in the expanding post-1940s aviation world. Significant rationalisation of this started in the late 1950s, when the government finally "grasped the nettle" to force much-needed change.

Too often, new aircraft (and aircraft engine) project planning in Britain was based on intuition, unrealistic optimism and guesswork. Pressure "from above", to keep forecast cost and timescale as low as possible (to help achieve decision to proceed) sometimes overtook more mature evaluation. "Second guessing" that too big a forecast would "doom" the project can be a temptation some find hard to avoid, perhaps expecting decision makers to "double the forecast" in their decision making! In truth the shambles of projects started and cancelled was frequently due to a combination of initial over-specification, changes in specification after work began, ineffective programme management of the evermore complex programmes and/or, on occasion, sheer unhelpful and technically ignorant political dilatory behaviour by individual British government ministers. For new airliners, the parochial influences of government-owned BOAC and BEA were allowed to be far too intrusive, capricious and, sometimes, downright unhelpful, or even damaging.

Overtaken completely by the USA in civil aviation, the British military aircraft industry's technical excellence was not enough to counteract the might of the USA industry until, at last, Britain made positive moves towards international co-operation in aircraft design and manufacture. The British government support in this co-operative approach was mixed, sometimes being very helpful but, at other times, vacillating and inadequate. Government technical ignorance and vacillation were prominent contributors to lack of true success in airliners, with the single exception of the Viscount. Government support was, however, largely steadfast for the SEPECAT Jaguar, the Panavia Tornado, the Eurofighter Typhoon and the launch of Concorde (where, however, support did waver halfway through the project).

As a commercial venture, the Concorde project was doomed to failure almost at birth, by inadequate geo-political attention to growing environmental issues. The British government total political retreat from Airbus, before this consortium-cum-company properly started, and the later industrial (BAE Systems) retreat from their inherited minority share in Airbus, ensured the elimination of the British airliner industry. Of any substance, what remained in Britain by the beginning of 2020 was the foreign-owned diminished role as an expert supplier of just the wings of Airbus airliners, plus a very competent military aircraft capability desperately trying to generate a new project to ensure an ongoing commercially viable business beyond the 2020s. The industrial enterprises involved will have to fight fiercely to remain relevant and commercially sustainable during the next twenty or thirty years and almost certainly needing consistent government political support and concomitant investment.

As a final speculation ...

Will the current BAE Systems exclusively defence and security industry focus provide enough future business opportunity to maintain (preferably grow) BAE Systems total business levels? In the field of total actual work on aircraft manufacture, probably not, given the likely impact of future unmanned aircraft developments. The likelihood is that, in the future military world, aircraft design, development and manufacture will not be as dominant in terms of the expenditure of governments as it has been recently, except, perhaps, in the Middle East, India and (maybe) the Far East. However, the 2018 British government "Team Tempest" announcement on the next generation airborne interceptor/strike/reconnaissance capability is a clear signal of intent for the future. Words now need turning into action.

There are other opportunities emerging. The RAF wish to replace the E3 Sentry Airborne Early Warning aircraft in the not too distant future is formally scheduled to be satisfied with the Boeing E-7 (see section 8.2). The opening up of space activity within Britain (Spaceport etc.) would provide other new opportunities for the British aerospace industry.

Might it be desirable (and possible) for BAE Systems to redirect aircraft design skills and manufacturing facilities, to once again include civil and military transport aircraft? The BAe Military Aircraft Division of the 1990s certainly was involved with producing components and assemblies for Airbus aircraft. Unlikely though it may seem, an "about-face" could be attempted, with a massive reinvestment and patient rebuilding of expertise and relationships needed to effect such a manoeuvre. The task might be a mountain to climb, witness the documented protracted difficulties of building/rebuilding a transport aircraft industry in Brazil, China, India, Indonesia, Japan, the "separated states" of the ex-Soviet Union, etc. etc. The likelihood of British success other than via the Airbus connection is extremely low, if only for the fact that Airbus and Boeing are the only airliner producers with sufficient foundation and financial strength in the market. The exceptions are where political will, availability of massive and sustained government financial backing and domestic airliner demand are all strong enough, as seems eventually likely in China and (maybe) Russia.

In twenty-five years' time, if a BAE Systems-EADS (Airbus) type European merger has not happened, or a BAE Systems tie-up with (or takeover by?) a large USA Company (which one?) does not appear, as an alternative perhaps BAE Systems will have morphed into something which is no longer recognisably a significant part of the aircraft industry, or even part of the wider aerospace industry. A merger or partnership with a US company may need a cautious approach, due to the proclivity of the USA to try to insist on defence projects being based "on-shore", letting the USA-based BAE Systems Inc. USA "in" and keeping BAE Systems plc UK "out".

Is it likely that Airbus will establish its wing design and manufacture outside Britain, either as a commercial cost-cutting venture, or a direct result of Brexit? Additionally, if the outcome of Brexit negotiations and/or the "Trade War Scenario" stirred by the President of the USA, causes the surviving Italian-owned helicopter presence in Yeovil and the ex-Shorts/Bombardier Spirit Aerosystems aerostructures facility in Belfast to be closed, this might leave only aerostructures businesses like the recently ex-GKN Melrose facility in Bristol, American-owned Spirit Aerosystems in Prestwick (ex-Scottish Aviation) and fringe activities in (say) hybrid air vehicles or light aircraft in Britain. In such a scenario, it is possible that:

By the fourth or fifth decade of the twenty-first century, the British aircraft industry's ability to lead (or even share the lead) in the design of a significant complete aircraft might be no more.

BUT it will *always* have had a "glorious" past! ... (for some of the time, for some of the people.)

AND a future is still "there to reach"... *if* there can be found the foresight, the desire, the investment...

AND the will and the leadership... and the magic ingredients, the passion... with a helping of luck.

Post Scriptum

The 2020 coronavirus (Covid-19) world pandemic effect on world business activity has had, and will continue to have, short and medium term major effects on mass air travel. There have been major reductions in the number of commercial aircraft flights. This radically changes the financial strength and future revenues of airlines, ultimately impacting airliner manufacturing. The inevitable consequent reduction in new airliner delivery rates could last for a few years. All previous air traffic forecasts, confirmed airliner orders and forecast future sales therefore will be seriously revised. The total world airliner manufacturing industry position over the next five years will be radically affected. "Wait and see" will be the only thing which observers and commentators can do.

Index of Personalities

Aitken, Baron William Maxwell, 99–101, 114
Alcock, Captain Sir John William, 12
Amery, Baron Harold Julian, 201
Attlee, Earl Clement Robert, 43, 156
Austin, Baron Herbert, 16

Baker, Captain Valentine Henry, 51–2, 63
Baldwin, Earl Stanley, 43
Baynes, Lester Everett, 77–8
Barnwell, Frank Sowter, 10, 57, 72
Beaty, Admiral Earl David Richard, 29
Beaverbrook, Lord, *see* Aitken
Bétielle, Roger, 249
Bishop, Ronald Eric, 84, 123
Blackburn, Robert, 4
Bleriot, Louis Charles Joseph, 1, 7, 74, 118
Brabazon, Lord, *see* Moore-Brabazon
Brennan, Maurice Joseph, 174, 263
Brittan, Baron Leon, 271
Britten, Forester Richard John, 218, 263
Brown, Lt. Colonel Arthur Whitten, 12
Burke, Sir Aubrey Francis, 179, 183–4
Burroughes, Hugh, 62

Camm, Sir Sydney, 47–8, 76, 86–7, 201, 204–207, 328
Cayley, Sir George, 1
Chadwick, Roy, 56, 84
Chamberlin, Arthur Neville, 39, 54
Chichester-Miles, Ian, 307
Churchill, Sir Winston Spencer, 11, 17, 19–20, 28, 85, 94, 99, 154–5, 167
Cierva, Juan de la, 62, 142–3
Cobham, Sir Alan John, 27, 64
Cockerell, Sir Christopher Sydney, 223, 226
Cody, Samuel Franklin, 1, 4, 104, 366
Comper, Nicholas, 63, 81
Cotton, Frederick Sydney, 40
Cripps, Sir Richard Stafford, 137

Cunliffe-Lister, Viscount Philip (birth surname Lloyd-Graeme), 43, 91
Curtis, Glen Hammond, 12

Dalrymple, Andrew, 66
Dassault, Marcel (birth surname Bloch), 153, 239
de Bruyne, Norman Adrian, 78, 293–4
de Gaulle, Charles André Joseph Marie, 230, 246–7
de Havilland, Sir Geoffrey, 33, 61, 67, 71, 82, 84, 114, 119, 152, 160
Deperdussin, Armand Jean Auguste, 73
Desoutter, André Marcel, 77
Dobson, Sir Roy, 56, 84, 182–4
Dowding, Air Chief Marshal Sir Hugh Caswall Tremenheere, 48
Downey, W.G., 190
Dunne, John William, 4, 71
Dunning, Sqdn. Cdr. Edward Harris, 14

Eden, Earl Robert Anthony, 43
Edgeley, John, 307
Edwards, Sir George Robert Freeman, 139, 180
Ellington, Marshal of the RAF Sir Edward Leonard, 43
Ely, Eugene Burton, 13
Ewans, John Roy, 174
Eyre, V. William, 61

Fairey, Sir Charles Richard, 5, 42
Fedden, Sir Alfred Hubert Roy, 58
Ferguson, Harry George, 71
Fokker, Anton Herman Gerard, 14
Folland, Henry Philip, 20, 61, 65, 172
Freeman, Air Chief Marshal Sir Wilfrid Rhodes, 43, 48, 53–4, 56, 84–5, 100
Frise, Leslie, 57

Geddes, Sir Eric Campbell, 23
Gnosspelius, Oscar Theodor, 12, 403
Grahame-White, Claude, 61

Haddon-Cave, Sir Charles Anthony, 287
Hafner, Raoul, 79, 147
Halford, Frank Bernard, 27, 89, 107, 115
Hall, Sir Arnold Alexander, 125, 315
Haviland, Denis William Gordon Latimer, 175
Handasyde, George Harris, 76–7, 79
Hawker, Harry George, 61
Healey, Baron Dennis Winston, 201–202
Henderson, Basil B., 62–3
Heseltine, Baron Michael Ray Dibdin, 271
Hinkler, Herbert (Bert) John Lewis, 27, 77
Hives, Baron Earnest Walter, 84, 107
Hooker, Sir Stanley George, 99, 107, 158, 172, 205–206
Hooper, Ralph Spencer, 206

Inskip, Viscount Robert Andrew, 180
Inskip, Viscount Thomas Walker Hobart, 30

Johnson, Amy, 1, 27, 35
Jones, Sir Aubrey, 146, 183

Kennedy, John Fitzgerald, 165, 230
Kenworthy, John, 20, 63
Kolk, Frank, 249, 250
Koolhaven, Frederick, 6, 73, 74, 77
Kronfeld, Robert, 64
Küchemann, Dietrich, 112, 228, 229, 249

Leake, Lt.Cdr. E.B.W., 64
Lewis, Gordon Manns, 205–206
Lloyd George, Earl David, 19
Lobelle, Marcel, 65
Londonderry, Lord, *see* Vane-Tempest-Stewart)
Lord, John, 63, 164
Lowe-Wylde, Charles Herbert (born Thomas Harold Lowe), 64, 79

MacDonald, James Ramsay, 42–3
Mach, Ernst Waldfried Josef Wenzel, 150
Macmillan, Earl Maurice Harold, 146, 160, 165
Manning, William Oke, 62, 72
Martin, Helmut Paul, 76
Martin, Sir James, 51–2, 63

Martyn, Alfred Willie, 62
Masefield, Sir Peter Gordon, 185
Maskell, Eric, 228
Mayo, Robert Hobart, 37
McClean, Francis Kennedy, 2
McLean, Sir Robert, 48
Mensforth, Sir Eric, 148–9, 180
Meredith, F.W., 50
Miles, Frederick George, 64, 66, 77, 185
Mitchell, Reginald Joseph, 48–9, 56
Mollinson, James Allan, 27
Moore-Brabazon Baron John Theodore Cuthbert, 2, 101, 113
Morgan, Sir Morien Bedford, 229

Nelson, Sir George Horatio, 160–1
Norman, Nigel Desmond, 218, 264, 281
North, John Dudley, 7
Norway, Neville Shute, 64

Page, Sir Frederick Handley, 3, 16, 28, 180, 183, 198
Page, Sir Frederick William, 161, 196
Parker, E.B., 16
Parnall, George, 61, 65
Pearce, Sir Austin William, 259–60
Pemberton-Billing, Noel, 4, 19
Percival, Capt. Edgar Wikner, 35, 64, 66
Petter, William Edward Willoughby, 161, 172–4, 195–6
Phillips, Jack, 64
Powis, Charles, 64
Plowden, Baron Edwin Noel Auguste, 192

Rayner, Baron Derek George, 191
Reid, George Hancock, 66
Roe, Sir Edwin Alliot Verdon, 1, 3, 19, 63, 67, 104, 144
Roe, Humphrey Verdon, 3, 16
Roosevelt, Franklin Delano, 67

Sage, Frederick, 6
Samson, Air Commodore Charles Rumney, 13
Sandys, Baron Edwin Duncan, 175, 184, 198
Saunders, Samuel Edgar, 63, 144
Scott-Paine, Hubert, 5
Shenstone, Beverley Strahan, 49
Short, Albert Eustace, 2

Short, Horace Leonard, 2
Short, Hugh Oswald, 2, 138
Siddeley, Sir John Davenport, 60, 62,
    64–5, 67
Sigrist, Frederick Charles, 61, 66
Simmonds, Oliver, 63
Slingsby, Frederick Nicholas, 64
Smith, Professor Sir Roland, 264–5
Smuts, Field Marshal Jan Christian, 19
Sopwith, Sir Thomas Octave Murdoch,
    5, 61, 63, 65, 67, 72–3, 179, 183
Spriggs, Sir Frank, 47, 179, 182–3
Stanbridge, David, 309
Stieger, Helmut John, 63

Tebbitt, Baron Norman Beresford, 260
Tedder, Marshal of the Royal Air Force
Baron Arthur William, 54
Thatcher, Baroness Margaret Hilda, 259,
    260, 270–1, 324
Thomas, George Holt, 5, 21, 61
Thomson, Baron Christopher Birdwood,
    25
Tiltman, Alfred Hessell, 64
Tips, Ernest Oscar, 5
Tizard, Sir Henry Thomas, 89, 107
Trenchard, Viscount Hugh Montague,
    28–9, 48

Vane-Tempest-Stewart, Marquess
    Charles Stewart Henry, 43, 54

Wakefield, Edward W., 12
Wallis, Sir Barnes Neville, 55, 174
Wallis, Wing Cdr. Kenneth Horatio, 71,
    221
Ward, Alexander Reginald, 66
Waring, Samuel, 6
Weber, Johanna, 228
Weir, Air Commodore James George, 62,
    78, 143
Westbrook, Trevor, 137
White, Claude Graham, 7, 61
White, Sir George, 4–5
Whittle, Air Commodore Sir Frank, 88,
    105–107, 112, 115
Wibault, Michel Henri Marie Joseph,
    205
Wong, Tsoe K., 75
Wright, Howard Theophilis, 4, 62, 72
Wright, Orville, 1
Wright, Warwick Joseph, 4, 72
Wright, Wilbur, 1

Youngman, Robert Talbot, 78

Zuckerman, Baron Solomon, 177

Bibliography

This book is based on data and other information which has been derived from many sources. The main publications concerned are listed below. The internet has also been a very useful data source. As far as reasonably possible, internet sourced information has been cross-checked between different web sites, actual publications and copies of historical documents.

Particularly acknowledged useful data sources, attempting to cover all British aircraft first flown in each decade from 1900 to 2019, are the examples below. These have been augmented from, and cross-checked with, other sources to create the lists in the Appendices.

Examples:
"UK Aircraft 1920–29" Wikipedia (and similarly 1900–1909 .... 1930–39 etc.)
   https://en.wikipedia.org/wiki/Category:British_aircraft_1920–1929
(Can select military and civil aircraft as separate categories or individual types.)

"Military Factory – Global Defense Reference"
   https://www.militaryfactory.com/aircraft/index.asp
(Can select by type, country or manufacturer.)

Whatever the sources, the author accepts responsibility for any factual errors included in this book.

Published references used:

J.A.D. Ackroyd, Sir George Cayley: the Invention of the Aeroplane, near Scarborough at the Time of Trafalgar
   Journal of Aeronautical History, Vol.1, pp 130–181: Paper 2011/6
   The Royal Aeronautical Society, 2011
J.A.D. Ackroyd, The Spitfire Wing Planform: A Suggestion
   Journal of Aeronautical History, Vol.3, pp 121 – 135: Paper 2013/02
   The Royal Aeronautical Society, 2013
J.A.D. Ackroyd, The Aerodynamics of the Spitfire
   Journal of Aeronautical History, Vol.6, pp 59–86: Paper 2016/03
   The Royal Aeronautical Society, 2016
J.A.D. Ackroyd, Aerodynamics as the Basis of Aviation: How Well Did It Do?
   Journal of Aeronautical History, Vol.8, pp 1 – 62: Paper 2018/01
   The Royal Aeronautical Society, 2018
J.A.D. Ackroyd, B.P. Axcell and A.I. Ruban, Early Developments of Modern Aerodynamics, *Butterworth Heinemann, 2001. ISBN 0 7506 5133 4*
John D. Anderson Jr, From Engineering Science to Big Science – Pamela E. Mack (editor) The NACA and NASA Collier Trophy Research Project Winners (Ch.3: Research in Supersonic Flight and the Breaking of the Sound Barrier)
   NASA History Office, Washington DC, USA, 1998. ISBN 0-16-049640-3
An Official History, Airlines at War – British Civil Aviation, 1939–1944 first published under the title: "*Merchant Airmen: The Air Ministry Account of British Civil Aviation, 1939–1944*", *HMSO London 1946*
   Air World Books (an imprint of Pen & Sword), 2018. ISBN 978-1-47839-409-9

Stephen Aris, Close to the Sun:- How Airbus Challenged America's Domination of the Skies
First published in Great Britain by Aurum Press, 2002
reprinted by Agate in Canada, 2004. ISBN 0-9724562-4-4

Pierre Barbaroux and Blandine Laperche, Mergers Failure in the European Defence Technological and Industrial Base, in the Case of EADS/BAE Systems
Network on Innovation, Working paper No.33/2013

Roland Beaumont, English Electric P.1 Lightning
Ian Allan, 1985. ISBN 0 7110 1471 X

Patrick Bishop, Air Force Blue
William Collins, 2018. ISBN 978-0-00-743315-5

Tony Blackman, Vulcan Test Pilot: My experiences in the Cockpit of a Cold War Icon
Grub Street Publishing, 2019 (third reprint). ISBN 978-1-904943-88-4 (First published 2008)

Tony Blackman, Nimrod: Rise and Fall
Grub Street Publishing, 2013. ISBN 13 9781909166028

Paul Brickhill, The Dam Busters
Pan Macmillan Ltd., 1983. ISBN 978-0-330-37644-0

Brian Brinkworth, On the Planning of British Aircraft Production for the Second World War and reference to James Connolly
Journal of Aeronautical History, Vol.8, pp 233 – 299: Paper 2018/09
The Royal Aeronautical Society, 2018

Andrew Brookes, X Planes 5: TSR2 – Britain's Lost Cold War Strike Jet
Osprey Publishing (Bloomsbury Publishing), 2017. ISBN978 1 4728 2248 2

Tony Buttler, The 1957 Defence White Paper
Journal of Aeronautical History, Vol.8, pp 86 – 99: Paper 2018/03
The Royal Aeronautical Society, 2018

Tony Buttler, Britain's Secret Projects Vol.1: Jet Fighters Since 1950 (2nd edition)
Crécy Publishing, 2017. ISBN 978 1910809051

Tony Buttler, Britain's Secret Projects Vol.2: Jet Bombers Since 1949 (2nd edition)
Crécy Publishing, 2018. ISBN 978 1910809105

Tony Buttler, The Design and Development of the Hawker Hunter
The History Press, 2014. ISBN 978 0 7524 6746 7

Dougald Cameron and Douglas G. Thomson, Scottish Contributions to Rotary Winged Flight *64th Annual Forum, April 29th–May 1st 2008 American Helicopter Society International Inc. 2009*

Ian Castle, London 1914–17: The Zeppelin Menace
Osprey Publishing, 2008. ISBN 9-781846-0-324-55

Peter Caygill, Flying the Buccaneer: Britain's Cold War Warrior
Pen & Sword Aviation, 2008. ISBN 978 1 84415 669 6

Christopher Chant, Aviation (An Illustrated History)
Orbis Publishing, 1980. ISBN 0-85613-213-6

J.C. Chaplin, Safety Regulation – The First 100 Years
Journal of Aeronautical History, Vol.1, pp 75 – 96: Paper 2011/3
The Royal Aeronautical Society, 2011

Martin Chorlton, Hawker Hurricane Mk I–V
Osprey Publishing 2013. ISBN978 1 78096 602 1

Baron Cohen (Lionel Leonard Cohen), Report of the Court of Inquiry Into the Accidents to Comet G-AYLP on 10 January 1954 and Comet G-AYLL on 8 April 1954
HMSO London, 1955

Evan John David, Aircraft: Its development in War and Peace and Its Commercial Future
Charles Scribner's Sons New York (Curtis Publishing Co.) 1919
reproduced by Forgotten Books (FB&C Ltd.), ISBN 978-1-331-38090-0

Peter G. Dancey, British Aircraft Manufacturers Since 1909
  Fonthill Media, 2014. ISBN 978-178155-229-2
David P. Davies, Handling the Big Jets (3rd edition, 1977 printing)
  Civil Aviation Authority. ISBN 0-903083-01-9
Glyn Davies, From Lysander to Lightning: Teddy Petter, Aircraft Designer
  The History Press, 2014. ISBN 978 0 7524 9211 7
M.J.B. Davy, Aeronautics, Heavier-Than-Air-Aircraft, Part 1: Historical Survey
  Science Museum London, HMSO, 1949
Andrew Dow, Pegasus: The Heart of the Harrier
  Pen & Sword, 2009. ISBN 978-1-84884-042-3
David Edgerton, England and the Aeroplane: Militarism, Modernity and Machines
  Penguin Books, 2013. ISBN 978-0-141-97516-0
Günter Endres, British Aircraft Manufacturers Since 1908
  Ian Allan, 1995. ISBN 07110 2409 X
Mark Freshney, Robert Muller and John Wood, The Avro Vulcan – Celebrating 60 Glorious
  Years
  Vulcan to the Sky Trust, 2012. ISBN 978-0-9567880-1-6
Anthony Furse, Wilfrid Freeman: The Genius Behind Allied Survival and Air Supremacy,
  1939 to 1945
  Spellmount Ltd. 1999. ISBN 1-86227-079-1
Charles Gardner, The British Aircraft Corporation
  B.T. Bailsford, 1981. ISBN 0 7134 3815 0
Till Geiger, Britain and the Economic Problem of the Cold War: The Political Economy and
  the Economic Impact of the British Defence Effort, 1945–1955
  Ashgate, 2004. ISBN 0 7546 0287 7
David Gibbings, The Evolution of the British Rotorcraft Industry 1842–2012
  Journal of Aeronautical History, Vol. 2 pp 112 – 146: Paper 2012/07
  The Royal Aeronautical Society, 2012
Ron E. Gillman, Croydon to Concorde
  John Murray, 1980. ISBN 0-7195-3471-X
Chris Gibson, Nimrod's Genesis:- RAF Maritime Patrol Projects and Weapons since 1945
  Hikoki Publications, 2015. ISBN 978-19021-0-9473
C.V. Glines, Flying Blind
  Air Force Magazine, Airforce Association (USA), September 1989
John Godden (Ed.), Harrier: Ski Jump to Victory
  Brassey's Defence Publishers (Pergamon Press). ISBN 0-08-031167-9
R.G. Grant, Flight: The Complete History of Aviation
  Dorling Kingsley Limited, 2017. ISBN 978-0-24129-803-9
John Green, Obituary – Dr. Johanna Weber (b. 8 August 1910, d. 24 October 2014)
  Royal Aeronautical Society, 12 January 2015. www.aerosociety.com.news
Bill Gunston, Airbus: The Complete Story
  Haynes, second edition 2009. ISBN 978 1 84425 585 6
Bill Gunston, Buccaneer – An Outstanding Strike Aeroplane
  Flight International, Vol. 83, No. 2821, 4 April 1963, pp. 467–478
Charles Haddon-Cave, The Nimrod Review
  The Stationery Office HMSO, 2009. ISBN 978-0-10296-2-659
Bruce Barrymore Halfpenny, English Electric Canberra
  Pen & Sword, 2013. ISBN 978-1-78346-190-5
James Hamilton-Paterson, Empire of the Clouds: When Britain's Aircraft Ruled the World
  (Paperback edition) Faber and Faber, 2011. ISBN 978-0-571-2495-0
Keith Hayward, Government and British Civil Aerospace (A case study in post-war
  technology policy)
  Manchester University Press, 1983. ISBN 0-7190-0877-8

Keith Hayward, Government and British Civil Aerospace 1945–64
  Journal of Aeronautical History, Vol.8, pp 100 – 1366: Paper 2018/04
  The Royal Aeronautical Society, 2018
Keith Hayward, The British Aircraft Industry (British Industry in the Twentieth Century Series)
  Manchester University Press, 1989. ISBN 0-7190-2816-7
Keith Hayward, The Formation of the British Aircraft Corporation (BAC) 1957–61
  Journal of Aeronautical History, Vol 2 pp 222–99 Paper No. 2012/01
  Royal Aeronautical Society, 2012
Michael Hickey, The Korean War
  John Murray, 1999. ISBN 0-7195-55590
Harry Holmes, Avro, The History of an Aircraft Company
  Airlife Publishing Ltd., 1994. ISBN 1-85310-531-7
Sir Stanley Hooker, Not Much of an Engineer
  Airlife Publications, 1984. ISBN 0-906393-35-3
H. Montgomery Hyde, British Air Policy Between the Wars: 1918–39
  Heinman, 1976. ISBN 9780434479832
Vittorio Isacco, The Helicogyre
  The Aeronautical Journal, Vol 33, Issue 223
  Royal Aeronautical Society, July 1929
Philip Jarrett, Frank McClean: Father to British Naval Aviation
  Seaforth Publications, 2011. ISNN 978 1 84832 109 0
Philip Jarrett, Ultimate Aircraft
  Dorling Kindersley Limited. 2000. ISBN 0-7894-5961-2
Sir Richard Johns, Bolts From the Blue
  Grub Street Publishing, 2019. ISBN 978 1 911 621 09 6
Brian Johnson, The Secret War
  BBC Publications, 1978. ISBN 0-09-920790-7
Brian Johnson and Terry Heffernan, Boscombe Down, 1939–45 – A Most Secret Place
  Jane's Publishing, 1982. ISBN 0-7106-0203-0
Joint Engineering Team, An Introduction to the Joint European Transport
  British Aerospace, Messerschmitt-Bolkow-Blöhm,
  Société Nationale Aerospatiale, Vereinigte-Flugtechnische-Werk
  64th Annual forume-Fokker, 1978 (unpublished)
Barry Jones, British Experimental Turbojet Aircraft
  The Crowood Press, 2003. ISBN 1 861 26 621 9
Brian A.L. Jones, The London Aircraft Production Group
  Railway and Canal Historical Society (https://rchs.org.uk)
  Occasional Papers (2nd Series No.32), July 2016
David Kaminski-Morrow, Economic Calamity
  Flight International, 11–17 June 2019, pp74/75
Kenny Kemp, Flight of the Titans:- Boeing, Airbus and the Battle for the Future of Air Travel
  First published by Virgin Books, 2006
  Revised edition (paperback) 2007. ISBN 978 0 7535 1345 3
Anthony J. Kinloch, Norman Adrian de Bruyne, 8 November 1904 – 7 March 1997
  Biog. Mems Fell. R.Soc.Lond. vol 46, pp 125–143
  Royal Society, 2000
Vladimir Kotelnikov and Tony Buttler, Early Russian Jet Engines – the Nene and Derwent in the Soviet Union and the Evolution of the VK-1
  Rolls Royce Heritage Trust: Historical Series No. 33, 2003. ISBN 1 87922 25 2
Paul Lashmar, Spyflights of the Cold War
  Sutton Publishing, 1966. ISBN 0-07509 1183 2

Peter Lewis, The British Fighter Since 1912 (Third edition)
  Putnam, 1974. ISBN 0 370 10049 2
Laurence K. Loftin, Jr., Quest for Performance: The Evolution of Modern Aircraft
  National Aeronautics and Space Administration, 1985
Andrew Lorenz, GKN: The Making of a Business 1750-2009
  John Wiley and Sons, 2009. ISBN 978-0-470-74953-1
Matthew Lynn, Birds of Prey: Boeing Versus Airbus – A Battle for the Skies
  First printed by Reed International, 1995
  Revised edition published in United States by Four Walls Eight
  Windows, 1997. ISBN 1-56858-086-X
Peter J. Lyth (Business History Unit, LSE), The Empire's Airway: British Civil Aviation
  From 1919 to 1939
  Revue Belge de Philolologie et d'Histoire, 2000 Vol. 78–3 pp 865–887
Francis K. Mason, The British Bomber Since 1914
  Putnam, 1994. ISBN 0 85177 861 5
Tim McLelland, TSR2: Britain's Lost Cold War Strike Aircraft
  Ian Allan Publishing, 2011 reprint. ISBN 978-1-90653-719-7
Tim McLelland, The Avro Vulcan
  Crécy, 2007. ISBN 978 0 85979 127 4
Peter W.G. Morris, The Management of Projects
  Thomas Telford, 1997. ISBN 0-7277-2593-9
Kenneth Munson, Civil Aircraft of Yesteryear
  Ian Allen, 1967.
Kenneth Munson, Warplanes of Yesteryear
  Ian Allen, 1965.
Arthur W.J.G. Ord-Hume, Imperial Airways: From Early Days to BOAC
  Stenlake Publishing, 2010. ISBN 9781840335149
Richard Overy, The Birth of the RAF 1918
  Allen Lane, 2018. ISBN 978-0-241-27421-7
Kenneth Owen, Concorde, New Shape in the Sky
  Jane's Publishing Company, 1982. ISBN 0-7106-0213-8
Richard Payne, Stuck on the Drawing Board: Unbuilt British Commercial Aircraft Since
  1945. *Tempus, 2004. ISBN 0 7524 3172 2*
Arthur Pearcy, Lend-Lease Aircraft in World War II
  Airlife, 1996. ISBN 1 85310 443 4
Harald Penrose, British Aviation – The Pioneer Years 1903-1914
  Putnam & Company, 1967. ISBN 978-0-37000-122-7
Harald Penrose, British Aviation – The Adventuring Years 1920–29
  Putnam & Company, 1973. ISBN 0 370 10016 6
Colin Philpott, A Place in History: Britain's Headline News Stories Remembered. *Ammonite,*
  2012
Mike Phipp, The Brabazon Committee and British Airliners 1945–1960
  Tempus, 2007. ISBN 978-0-7524-4374-4
Peter Piggott, On Canadian Wings: A Century of Flight
  The Dundurn Group (Toronto) 2005. ISBN 1-55002-549-X
Carl C. Plehn, War Profits and Excess Profits Taxes
  The American Economic Review, Vol. 10 No.2 pp 283–289
  American Economic Association, June 1920
Baron Plowden, Chmn. (Edwin Noel Auguste Plowden), Report of the Committee of Inquiry
  into the Aircraft Industry: appointed by the Minister of Aviation under the chairmanship
  of Lord Plowden 1964–65. Command 2853.
  HMSO London, 1965

Alfred Price, Spitfire: A Documentary History
  Macdonald and Jane's (second impression 1978). ISBN 978-0354010771
Sebastien Ritchie, Industry and Air Power – The Expansion of British Aircraft Production, 1935–41
  Frank Cass, 1997. ISBN 0-7146-4343-2 (paperback)
Arthur Reed, Britain's Aircraft Industry: What Went Right? What Went Wrong?
  J.M. Dent & Sons, 1973. ISBN0 460 07850 x
Peter Reese, In Turbulent Skies: British Aviation Successes and Setbacks – 1945–1975
  The History Press 2020. ISBN 978 0 7509 0302 9
Peter Reese, Transforming the Skies: Pilots, Planes and Politics in British Aviation, 1919–1940
  The History Press, 2018. ISBN 978 0 7509 8410 2
Peter Reese, The Men Who Gave Us Wings
  Pen & Sword Aviation, 2014. ISBN 978-1-84884-8481-1
Kevin Renshaw, F-35B Lightning II Three-Bearing Swivel Nozzle
  Posted on the internet by Lockheed Martin on 12 August 2014
Brian R. Robinson, Aviation in Manchester: A Short History
  Manchester Branch of the Royal Aeronautical Society, 1977
Douglas Hill Robinson, The Dangerous Sky – The History of Aviation Medicine
  Foulis, 1971. ISBN 978-0-295-955-30-304-5
Andrew Roe, Air Power in British Somaliland, 1920: The Arrival of Gordon's Bird Men, Independent Operations and Unearthly Retributions
  RAF Centre for Air Power Studies: Air Power Review, Volume 21 Number 1, Spring 2018
Glen Segell, The Defence Industrial Base and Foreign Policy
  Glen Segell, 1998. ISBN 1-901414-12-4
Stephen Skinner, BAe 146/RJ: Britain's Last Airliner
  First published in 2005 by Tempus Publishing
  Reprinted by The History Press, 2009. ISBN 978 0 7524 3562 6
Stephen Skinner, Hawker Siddeley Aviation and Dynamics, 1960–77
  The Crowood Press, 2014. ISBN 978-1-84797-739-7
Stephen Skinner, British Aircraft Corporation, A History
  The Crowood Press, 2012. ISBN 978-1-84797-318-4
G. Geoffrey Smith, Gas Turbines and Jet Propulsion for Aircraft
  Flight Publishing, June 1943 (Second Edition)
Ron Smith, British Built Aircraft (Volume 1) – Greater London
  Tempus, (reprinted 2005). ISBN 0 7524 2770 9
Ron Smith, British Built Aircraft (Volume 2) – South West & Central Southern England
  The History Press, (reprinted 2010). ISBN 978 0 7524 2785 0
Ron Smith, British Built Aircraft (Volume 3) – South East England
  Tempus, 2004. ISBN 0 7524 2993 0
Ron Smith, British Built Aircraft (Volume 4) – Central & Eastern England
  Tempus, 2004. ISBN 07524 3162 5
Ron Smith, British Built Aircraft (Volume 5) – Northern England, Scotland, Wales & Northern Ireland
  Tempus, 2005. ISBN 0 7524 3487 X
Stanley Stewart, Air Disasters
  Ian Allan, 1986 (2nd impression 1988). ISBN 0-7110-1585-6
John Stroud, The Imperial Airways Fleet
  The History Press, 2005 (reprinted 2012). ISBN 978 0 7524 2997 7
Ray Sturtivant, British Research and Development Aircraft
  Haynes Publishing Group, 1990. ISBN 0-85429-697-2
Ted Talbot, Concorde: A Designer's Life, The Journey to Mach 2
  The History Press, 2103 (reprinted 2014). ISBN 978 0 7524 8928 5

Barrett Tillman, On Wave and Wing
  Regnery History (USA), 2017. ISBN978-1-62157-591-7
Timothy Walker and Scott Henderson, Silent, Swift, Superb: The Story of the Vickers VC10
  Scoval Publishing, 1998. ISBN 1-902236-02-5
Timothy Walker and Scott Henderson, The First Jet Airliner: The Story of the de Havilland
  Comet
  Scoval Publishing, 2000. ISBN 1-902236-05-X
Nigel Walpole, Swift Justice: The Full Story of the Supermarine Swift
  Pen & Sword, 2004. ISBN 1 84415 070 4
Rowland White, Vulcan 607
  Bantam Press (Corgi edition) 2007. ISBN 978-0-5522-1552-97
Ray Whitford, Evolution of the Airliner
  The Crowood Press, 2007. ISBN 078 1 86126 8709
P.A. Withey, Fatigue Failure of the de Havilland Comet 1
  Engineering Failure Analysis, Volume 4, Issue 2. pp 147–154
  Elsevier Science, 1997
Derek Wood, Project Cancelled – British Aircraft That Never Flew
  The Bobs Merrill Company, 1975. ISBN 0-672-52166-0
D.C. Wood et al., The Design and Development of the Avro Lancaster
  Manchester Branch of the Royal Aeronautical Society, 1991
General Chuck Yeager and Leo Janos, Yeager
  Century Hutchinson, Australia Pty Ltd, 1986. ISBN 0 09 157160 X

Fatal Flight Testing statistics in Chapter 5 (section 5.10) from
"The Test Flying Memorial Project" *https://www.thunder-and-lightnings.co.uk/memorial*

Appendix 1

The Thirty British Aircraft Industry Companies of 1946

Company	HQ Location in 1946
Airspeed	Portsmouth, Hampshire
Auster	Rearsby, Leicestershire
Armstrong- Whitworth	Coventry, Warwickshire
A.V. Roe	Manchester, Lancashire
Blackburn	Brough, East Yorkshire
Boulton-Paul	Wolverhampton, Warwickshire
Bristol	Filton, Bristol
Cierva	Southampton, Hampshire
Cunliffe-Owen	Southampton, Hampshire
de Havilland	Hatfield, Hertfordshire
Elliotts of Newbury*	Newbury, Berkshire
English Electric	Preston, Lancashire
Fairey	Hayes, Middlesex
Folland	Hamble, Hampshire
General	Feltham, Middlesex
Gloster	Brockworth, Gloucestershire
Handley Page	Radlett, Hertfordshire
Hants & Sussex*	Portsmouth, Hampshire
Hawker	Kingston, Surrey
Hunting-Percival	Luton, Bedfordshire
Martin Baker	Denham, Buckinghamshire
Miles	Woodley, Berkshire
Moss Brothers	Chorley, Lancashire
Saunders-Roe	East Cowes, Isle of Wight
Scottish Aviation*	Prestwick, Ayrshire
Short Brothers	Rochester, Kent
Slingsby	Kirkbymoorside, East Yorkshire
Supermarine	Southampton, Hampshire
Vickers-Armstrong	Weybridge, Surrey
Westland	Yeovil, Somerset

All of the companies which existed at the start of the Second World War survived until the war was over, although two had a change of ownership. In 1940, Airspeed was sold by Swan Hunter Group to de Havilland and, in 1944, Percival was acquired by Hunting Group.

* Elliotts of Newbury and Scottish Aviation did not actually design an aircraft until after the end of the war. Hants & Sussex, founded 1946 as "surplus aircraft engine parts salvagers", started aircraft maintenance and engine repair 1949...one-only aircraft design, one built 1953. (Hants & Sussex company renamed H+S Aviation in 1987).

The following pages of this Appendix outline brief histories of each company's founding, and their most prominent products in their existence, until most were absorbed in the 1960–63 consolidation into the large groups of Hawker Siddeley Aviation, the British Aircraft Corporation and Beagle, which submerged most of the original names.

Founding of the Thirty Aircraft Companies and Their Histories
(until 1960 rationalisation of the industry)

Company Name	Est.	Dates/Events	Significant Aircraft (numbers)
Airspeed	1931	founded in York, moved to Portsmouth 1933. 1934 bought by Swan Hunter. 1940 Swan Hunter sell Airspeed to de Havilland. 1951 Airspeed name dropped.	Oxford (8,500), Horsa Glider (3,800), Ambassador (23).
Auster (Taylorcraft)	1938	founded in Thurmaston, moved to Rearsby 1946. 1960 absorbed into Beagle, with F.G. Miles.	Redesigned Taylorcraft (1,630, various marks as "Auster")
Armstrong-Whitworth	1912	founded in Newcastle, moved to Coventry 1927. 1927 separated from Sir W.G. Armstrong as a result of Vickers-Sir W.G. Armstrong merger. 1935 bought by Hawker Siddeley Group. 1961 combined as Gloster-Whitworth.	AW.154 Argosy (7), AW.38 Whitley (1,814), AW. 650 & AW.660 Argosy (74).
A.V. Roe	1910	founded in Manchester in Brownsfield Mill. 1920 moved to Newton Heath, Manchester 1924 moved airfield to Woodford, Cheshire. 1935 bought by Hawker Siddeley Group. 1938–39 new Chadderton & Woodford factories.	504 (9,977), Avian (405), Tutor (606), Anson (11,020) Lancaster (7,377), Lincoln (624), Shackleton (185),Vulcan (134), 748 (380).
Blackburn	1914	founded in Leeds moved to Brough (Hull) 1916. 1949 absorbed General Aircraft. 1960 joined Hawker Siddeley Group,	Botha (580), Skua (192), Beverley – General GAL60 (49), Buccaneer (211).

Company Name	Est.	Dates/Events	Significant Aircraft (numbers)
Boulton-Paul	1915	1915 established in Norwich as "Aircraft Dept." 1934 moved to new factory in Wolverhampton. 1961 taken over by Dowty (aviation hydraulics)	Overstrand (21), Defiant (1,064), Balliol (229).
Bristol	1910	Est. in Bristol by Bristol Tramway & Carriage. 1919 started aero-engines division (ex-Cosmos). 1946 started helicopter division. 1960 merged into British Aircraft Corporation	Boxkite (75), F2 Fighter (5,329), Blenheim (4,422), Beaufighter (5,928), Brabazon (1), Britannia (85).
Cierva	1926	founded in Southampton at Avro (Hamble) 1932 moved to Hanworth Aerodrome (Feltham) 1946 re-established as Cierva Autogyro by Weir. 1951 assets bought by Saunders-Roe.	Cierva C.30 autogyro (78), Weir W.5 helicopter (1), Weir W.11 helicopter (2).
Cunliffe-Owen	1937	founded by Imperial Tobacco in Southampton to build "Burnelli lifting fuselage" designs. Built one (OA-1): Charles de Gaulle personal aircraft. 1947 company dissolved.	Mainly used as wartime "two-centre with Westland" focus of Seafire manufacture (2,334). One own-design, Concordia (2).
de Havilland	1920	founded in Edgware, London. 1934 moved to Hatfield. 1940 bought Airspeed (fully absorbed 1949). 1960 joined Hawker Siddeley Group.	Tiger Moth (8,868), Dragon Rapide (731), Mosquito (7,781), Dove (542), Vampire (3,268), Comet (114), type 125 (1,600).
Elliotts of Newbury	1870	furniture company, established in aircraft manufacturing during WW2. 1947 first indigenous glider (ex-German). 1966 taken over by Slingsby.	Eon Olympic (150), Primary Eon (80).
English Electric	1922	founded as English Electric Aviation in Bradford. 1926 discontinued aviation activities. 1940 wartime aircraft building of H.Page aircraft. 1945 re-established design function. 1958 established as English Electric Aviation. 1960 merged into British Aircraft Corporation.	Canberra (949), Lightning (337).
Fairey	1915	founded at Hayes, Middlesex. 1930–44 used Great West Aerodrome which govt. requisitioned in 1944 – became Heathrow. 1959 "aviation" became separate company, sold to Westland 1960.	Fox (231), Swordfish (2,391), Battle (2,185), Firefly (1,702), Fulmar (600), Barracuda (2,607), Gannet (348), Rotodyne (1), Fairey Delta 2 (2).

Company Name	Est.	Dates/Events	Significant Aircraft (numbers)
Folland	1936	Founded as British Marine in Hamble, Hants. 1937 name changed to Folland after Henry Folland becomes Owner-MD/Chief Designer. 1950 W.E.W Petter joins, becoming MD in 1951. 1959 bought by Hawker Siddeley Group.	mostly subcontract work until 1950. Fo.108 (12) as engine test bed aircraft for others. Gnat (449, incl. 89 Indian Ajeet).
General	1931	founded at Croydon Aerodrome, London. 1935 moved to Feltham, London. 1939–45 wartime subcontractor. 1949 merged with Blackburn.	"Monospar" series (45), GAL 60 prototype transferred to Blackburn, to become Blackburn Beverley (49).
Gloster	1917	founded at Brockworth, Glos. as Gloucestershire Aircraft, 1926 simplified name to Gloster Aircraft. 1934 bought by Hawker. (1961 combined as Gloster-Whitworth Division).	Gladiator (747), E28/39 (2), Meteor (3,941), Javelin (436).
Handley Page	1909	founded at Barking, Essex. 1912 moved to Cricklewood, Middlesex. 1929 moved to Radlett, Hertfordshire. (1970: voluntary liquidation.)	O/400 (554), V/1500 (63), HP.42 & HP.45 (8), Hampden (1,430), Halifax (6,176), Victor (86), Jetstream (50).
Hants & Sussex	1946	founded Portsmouth, Hants as WW2 surplus parts salvage service. 1953, one aircraft design.	H&S Herald (1, only "hopped").
Hawker	1920	founded in Kingston, Surrey (using Sopwith assets). 1934 bought Gloster. 1935 merged with John Siddeley group to form Hawker Siddeley Group (incl. Avro & Armstrong Whitworth.)	Hart (1,004), Hind (528), Hurricane (14,583), Typhoon (3,317), Fury/ Sea Fury (864), Tempest (1,702), Hunter (1,972), P.1127/Kestrel/ Harrier (404).
Percival	1933	founded in London (no manufacturing facility). 1934 moved to Gravesend, Essex, with hangar. 1936 moved to Luton, Bedfordshire. 1944 Taken over by Hunting Group. 1954 changed name to Hunting-Percival. 1957 became Hunting Aircraft. 1960 taken over by British Aircraft Corporation.	Gull (55), Mew Gull (6), Proctor (1,143), Prince/Pembroke (203), Piston Provost (461), Jet Provost (741).
Martin Baker	1934	founded in Denham, Buckinghamshire, soon included aircraft safety/escape equipment. 1943 Partner-Pilot Capt. Valentine Baker killed. 1944 Air Ministry contract "high speed aircraft escape facility, research & development"	MB.5 (1, 1st flt.1944) assessed by A&AEE as "better than best Spitfire", too late to enter WW2.

Company Name	Est.	Dates/Events	Significant Aircraft (numbers)
Miles	1932	founded as Phillips and Powis at Woodley, near Reading, Berkshire. 1933 first F.G. Miles aircraft design flew. 1936 Rolls-Royce buy share of company. 1943 Rolls-Royce interest bought out by Miles Aircraft. 1947 bankruptcy (F.G. Miles established 1948).	Magister (1,293), Master (3,250), Messenger (80).
Moss Brothers	1936	founded in Chorley, Lancashire by five brothers, mid-1950s, ceased operations.	MA1 (1), MA2 (1).
Saunders-Roe	1929	c. 1911 S.E. Saunders built boats and aircraft. 1929 A.V. Roe and John Lord bought controlling interest, name changed to Saunders-Roe (Saro). 1935 acquire Spartan Aircraft assets. 1951 acquired Cierva Autogyro assets (ex-Weir). 1959 aviation interests absorbed by Westland.	A.19 Cloud (22), London (31), Princess (3), SR.53 (2).
Scottish Aviation	1935	founded as a flying school in Prestwick, Scotland. 1939–45 wartime a/crft. repair/ maintenance. 1946 first indigenous aircraft design. (1969 took over Beagle Pup project.) (1970 took over H. Page Jetstream project.)	Pioneer (59), Twin pioneer (87).
Short Brothers	1908	1902 founded in Hove as balloon manufacturers. 1903 moved to Battersea, London. 1908 founded aircraft business. 1909 moved to Isle of Sheppey, Kent. !913 Rochester site opened. 1943 nationalised. 1948 joint venture Short Bros. & Harland, Belfast.	S.38 (48), Bomber (83), Type 184 (936), S.23/S.30 Empire Flying Boats (42), Sunderland (749).
Slingsby	1931	founded in Scarborough, North Yorkshire. moved to Kirkbymoorside, North Yorkshire. 1969 liquidated after disastrous fire, revived by Vickers, then others, dropped out of aircraft in 1995, finally taken over 2010 by Marshall Aerospace as a composite structures company.	>5,000 gliders total, incl: T.21B (226), T.31 (230), T.41 (200), T.59 (105), plus T-67 Firefly powered light aircraft (>250).
Supermarine	1913	founded as Pemberton Billing in Southampton. 1916 name changed to Supermarine. 1928 taken over by Vickers 1957 name dropped 1960 merged into British Aircraft Corporation.	Walrus (700), Schneider Trophy winners S.5, S.6 & S.6B Spitfire (20,351), Seafire (2,334), Attacker (185), Swift (197).

Company Name	Est.	Dates/Events	Significant Aircraft (numbers)
Vickers-Armstrong	1911	1911 new Vickers Company aircraft division in Weybridge, Surrey. 1927 merger with Sir W.G. Armstrong creates Vickers-Armstrong Aircraft. 1928 took over Supermarine. 1960 merged into British Aircraft Corporation.	Vimy (~776), F.B.5 Gunbus (224), Wellington(11,461), Viking/Varsity/Valetta (426), Viscount (445), Vanguard (44), Valiant (107), VC.10 (54).
Westland	1915	1915–17 Petters "Westland Aircraft Works" licence build of aircraft. 1935 founded as separate Westland Aircraft. 1960 absorbed helicopter businesses of Bristol, Fairey and Saunders-Roe (later, including British Hovercraft Corporation).	Wapiti (585), Lysander (1,786), Wasp/Scout (133/~150), Sea King (344), Lynx (450).

Appendix 2

The British Aircraft Industry/Government Interaction Timeline (1940 Onwards)

(With Significant Overseas Aviation Inter-active Developments)

Year	Decision/Action
1940	In June, British government authorises Henry Tizard (Head of UK Aeronautical Research Council) to lead a mission to USA to discuss exchange of secret scientific and engineering developments, partly as insurance against a feared imminent German invasion of the UK. Among other things, the Tizard Mission to USA (September 1940) discussed transfer of design details of the secret UK Frank Whittle turbojet aircraft engine (for Meteor aircraft).
1941	After a demonstration in the UK of the E38/39 experimental jet aircraft, USA accepted the Tizard transfer offer (including a complete working jet engine). USA General Electric company tasked to mass-produce a version of the engine.
1942	Brabazon first committee formed, to advise on likely British airliner needs after the end of the Second World War. Recommendations made February 1943: Committee asked to widen membership beyond government-only participants. 1 Oct 1942, first USA-produced experimental jet aircraft Lockheed XP-80 (became P.80 Shooting Star) first flew with British Halford H.1 version of UK Power jets (Whittle) engine.
1944	Brabazon Committee second report accepted by government, March 1944. In final report, seven new airliners recommended, from large transatlantic airliner to eight-seater feeder liner. One turbojet and two turboprop types included. Ministry of Supply issues specifications of Brabazon Committee types to industry.
1945	Ministry of Aircraft Production absorbed by Ministry of Supply.
1946	British European Airways (BEA) separated from British Overseas Airways Corporation (BOAC). Civil Aviation Act creates Ministry of Civil Aviation (includes responsibility for BOAC, BEA and British South American Airways (BSAA)). Act reiterates "Buy British" principle inherited from pre-war Imperial Airways mandate. Government cancels Miles M.52 supersonic research aircraft project.
1948	Avro Tudor crash: Court of Enquiry criticises centralised national procurement of civil aircraft. First flight of Vickers Viscount, world's first turboprop airliner.
1948–49	Minister authorised to direct aircraft purchase if "considered to be in national interest" (including purchase from foreign source, e.g. BOAC acquiring USA Boeing Stratocruisers). Minister authorised to continue sponsorship of civil aircraft development.
1949	British South American Airways merged into BOAC. First flight of de Havilland Comet, world's first turbojet-powered airliner. First flights of Bristol Brabazon, Vickers Viscount and English Electric jet bomber (Canberra).

Year	Decision/Action
1951	Government commits to reducing state's role in aircraft industry, with a Private Venture (PV) allowed for civil aircraft development.
1952	USA Pan American Airways (Pan Am) orders Comet 3 airliners. Boeing launches 707 jet airliner development. Vickers V.1000 large jet turbine aircraft project launch, for RAF troop/logistics deployment.
1953	Bristol Brabazon project cancelled, with the prototype the only aircraft to fly.
1954	Comet 1 disasters: subsequent crash investigations commence. Comet 1 grounded, all Comet orders cancelled. Bristol Aeroplane Company buy 15% share of Shorts (which had been nationalised in 1943)
1955	British government rescues financially stressed de Havilland company. USA Douglas launches DC.8 jet airliner development. USA airline Pan American order Boeing 707 and Douglas DC.8 jet airliners simultaneously. Government cancel V.1000 project, killing the VC.7 airliner version which was to follow.
1956	BOAC chooses Bristol Britannia medium/long rang turboprop airliner. BOAC orders Boeing 707 jet airliner. UK Supersonic Transport Aircraft Committee (STAC) formed. First flight of Vickers Vanguard medium range 139-passenger medium range turboprop airliner.
1957	UK "Duncan Sandys" government defence review published: • Avro 730 supersonic bomber and Saunders-Roe rocket-jet interceptor (SR.53 pre-prototype & SR.77) cancelled. • English Electric P.1 (prototype Lightning) supersonic programme preserved. • Government declares "future air warfare will be missile-based" and advise industry "all future government contracts for aircraft will only be awarded to large groups of companies".
1958	Re-engineered Comet 4 starts BOAC trans-Atlantic service. BOAC orders Vickers VC.10 for Empire routes. De Havilland forms "Airco" consortium with Fairey and Hunting for DH.121 Trident medium range jet airliner. Mergers of non-Rolls-Royce aircraft engine businesses start.
1959	BEA order de Havilland Trident, specifying 25% smaller version than that planned by de Havilland. Trident will be first passenger aircraft in the world to have "down to runway touch-down" blind landing facility with fare-paying passengers. Supersonic Transport Aircraft Committee (STAC) report, faster than Mach 2.2 discounted. Bristol Aero Engines and Armstrong Siddeley Motors merge into Bristol Siddeley Engines.
1960	Vickers reveal financial crisis in VC.10 development programme. Under pressure from UK government, mergers of aircraft and missile companies enlarge existing Hawker Siddeley Group, and create British Aircraft Corporation (BAC) and Beagle Aircraft. Government award Supersonic Transport (SST) study project to BAC (at Bristol). BOAC told by government to order Vickers VC.10, rather than enlarge 707 jet airliner fleet.
1961	Britain applies for European Economic Community membership. Discussions with USA on possible joint SST project break down, partly due to USA insistence on "Mach 3 and bigger" aircraft. De Havilland and Blackburn Engines businesses merged under Bristol Siddeley Engines. Supersonic Transport (SST) joint project discussions with France.

Year	Decision/Action
1962	Britain and France agree on joint SST, formal government-to-government treaty signed to launch Concorde project.
1963	BOAC financial crisis revealed, chairman and managing director resign.
1964	Government agrees to financially support BOAC, with the proviso that BOAC place an order for Super VC.10 airliner. Government-commissioned Plowden Committee of Inquiry on aircraft industry established.
1965	1 February Plowden report on aircraft industry published. HS. P.1154, BAC TSR-2 and HS. 681 cancelled, followed by HS. Nimrod ordered. UK-France MoU to develop new strike and fast-jet trainer aircraft (AFVG and Jaguar).
1966	Government publically endorses *parts* of Plowden report, approving the idea of eventual government ownership or part-ownership of major elements of the British aircraft and guided weapons industry. BEA requests permission to buy Boeing three-engined 727 and twin-engined 737 (refused). Rolls-Royce takes over Bristol Siddeley Engines. BAC announces 2-11 airliner project (slightly greater capacity than largest Boeing 727 tri-jet but with only two (Rolls-Royce RB.211) engines): BEA asks for reduced 2-11 size, with lower power RB.211 engines and requests permission to order.
1967	Failure of negotiations for government to purchase major part of UK aircraft industry (Hawker Siddeley Aviation, Hawker Siddeley Dynamics and British Aircraft Corporation). UK, French and German governments agree funding to help launch "Airbus Industrie" consortium to build A.300 twin-engined wide bodied airliner. Rolls-Royce launch RB.208 large turbofan project for Airbus A.300 wide-body proposal. Government refuse to give launch aid for BAC 2-11, BEA directed to buy de Havilland Trident 3 (180-passenger stretched version of Trident 1 and 2). Rolls-Royce offer RB.211 turbofan for Lockheed and MacDonnell-Douglas consideration for their proposed new three-engined wide body airliners. Government agrees to provide RB.211 launch aid. France withdraws from Anglo-French Variable Geometry (AFVG) strike aircraft project.
1968	American Airlines announce that they intend to order RB.211 engines for its proposed order of fifty McDonnell-Douglas three-engined DC.10 wide-body airliner – US senators object to "a foreign engine on a US aircraft in US airline service". Lockheed choose Rolls-Royce RB.211 for L.1011 Tristar three-engined wide body airliner. DC.10 ordered with GE CF-6 engines by American Airlines (25) and United Airlines (30) in USA.
1969	French, German and British governments voice concern over likely A.300 sales success but UK government are the only ones to pull out. Hawker Siddeley invited and agree to stay involved in A.300 as "wing subcontractor", using their own PV funding. UK Ministry of Supply takes on aviation responsibilities of Board of Trade. Concorde pre-prototype first flight. BAC propose 3-11, a 245–270 seat twin-engined wide body with up-rated RB.211 engines. UK, Germany and Italy create Panavia multi-national company to manage three-nation Tornado variable geometry strike aircraft project.

Year	Decision/Action
1970	New Conservative government refuses launch aid for BAC 3-11 and reaffirms previous Labour government decision not to be part of Airbus. Handley Page cease trading. Alternative co-operative civil aircraft study groups formed in Europe (short-lived): HSA (UK) and Dornier (Germany) in CAST (Civil Aircraft Study Team) and… BAC (UK), MBB (Germany), CASA (Spain) and SAAB (Sweden) in Europlane group.
1971	Collapse of Rolls-Royce, company rescued by government and taken into public ownership, with government as sole shareholder. Lockheed L.1011 Tristar RB.211 engine contract renegotiated (engine delivery delayed).
1972	First flight of Airbus A.300. Internal UK government report (Marshall Report) on "the state of the UK aircraft industry, including government spending on aviation" – not published outside government.
1973	UK government give launch aid to H-Siddeley Aviaton HS.146 regional jet airliner project.
1974	HS.146 new airliner programme suspended, due to predicted world airline recession. BOAC and BEA, together with UK regional airlines Cambria Airways and Northeast Airlines, merged into British Airways (BA).
1976	Concorde enters service with BA and Air France.
1977	Aircraft and Shipbuilding Industries Act – 1977 effects nationalisation and merger of HSA/HSD and BAC (plus Scottish Aviation) into single company British Aerospace (BAe). Concorde enters service from London and Paris to New York. Joint European Transport (JET) study consortium formed (re. future airliners, single-aisle): BAe (Britain), Aerospatiale (France), MBB (Germany), Fokker VFW (Germany-Netherlands). BAe study Multi-Role Support Aircraft (MRSA) concept, for maritime patrol, logistics transport and aerial tanker roles.
1978	Boeing offer BAe collaboration on Boeing 757 project, to be launched with Rolls-Royce higher power development of RB.211 engines. British government offers finance to develop RB.211 for 757. British Airways allowed to order Boeing 757. (BAe involvement in 757 not taken up, incompatible with BAe commitments to Airbus.) German government encourages British government to re-join Airbus programmes. Airbus A.310 launched. HS.146 project relaunched. Joint European Transport (JET) consortium project study result effectively transferred to Airbus (JET study result will be developed and re-emerge as Airbus A.320 in 1984).
1979	New Conservative government writes off British share of Concorde development and production costs (~£3 billion) and announces privatisation of BAe.
1981	BAe privatised. BAe, Aerospatiale (France), MBB (West Germany), Lockheed (USA), create study group for Future International Military Airlifter (FIMA), to replace and improve upon 1960s Lockheed C.130 Hercules and European Transall C.160. Italy and Spain join, group renamed as Future Large Aircraft Exploratory Group (FLAEG). (This absorbs and replaces BAe moribund Multi-Role Support Aircraft (MRSA) study started in 1977, and includes USA Lockheed).

Year	Decision/Action
1984	British, French and W.German governments make Returnable Launch Investment in A.320. Shorts in Northern Ireland privatised.
1986	Nimrod AEW.Mk.3 cancelled.
1987	British, French and W.German governments make Returnable Launch Investment in Airbus A.330/A.340 airliners. BA privatised and takes over British Caledonian.
1988	British GKN company buys into Westland Helicopters.
1989	Shorts sold to Bombardier (Canada). Due to FLAEG slow progress, Lockheed leave group, project becomes EUROFLAG (European Future Large Aircraft Group, eventually established in Italy as a limited company in 1991).
1994	GKN take overall control of Westland. EUROFLAG absorbed by Airbus, renamed as Airbus Future Large aircraft (FLA).
1995	Memorandum of Understanding signed making Britain 15% partner in Joint Strike Fighter (Lockheed Lightning II) project.
1999	Airbus FLA renamed as A.400M, with agreed European nations role definition. After "flirting" with joining up with DASA (German part of Airbus), BAe instead acquires Marconi Electronic Systems, to form BAE Systems.
2000	British, French and German governments make Returnable Launch Aid Investment in Airbus A.380 "super-jumbo".
2003	Airbus A.400M programme launched by European governments' orders, primary role military logistics, plus aerial tanker role. BAE Systems end last UK jet turbine airliner programme (HS/BAe 146). BAE Systems close their last complete civil aircraft production line.
2006	BAE Systems sells Airbus stake, leaving civil and military transport aircraft business.
2009	Airbus A.400M first flight.
2010	Nimrod MRA.4 cancelled by British government.
2011	BAE Systems close Woodford (last "large aircraft assembly" site, ex-Avro).
2012	BAE Systems close last "ex-civil aircraft" aerostructures site (Chadderton, ex-Avro). British Airways takes over British Midland airline.

Appendix 3

British Air Ministry Aircraft Specification Process

For the years 1917 to 1920, the Air Board, on behalf of the armed services – the Army (RFC), Navy (RN) and the RAF (after being formed in 1918) – prepared performance requirements/capability specifications for industry response. Industry, and agencies such as the RAE, would often be consulted beforehand. Outline design proposals, actual prototype design and development and/or production of British military aircraft might be requested by the issued specification.

From 1920, requirements specifications were prepared by the newly-formed Air Ministry in conjunction with the service(s) concerned. This included specifications for civil aircraft where the UK government would be financially responsible for any of the development (an example would be the R.100 and R.101 prototype airship developments). Other than special circumstances, these specifications were offered to several companies, from which a response in the form of a proposal was expected. Sometimes, the specification might be amended in the light of the proposals. One or more different proposals might be authorised for prototype actual aircraft to be produced, trials of which would lead to the selection of a winning design (or sometimes no selection, because of inadequate offers or, too often, a change of requirement!). From 1930, specifications for British military aircraft with different purposes were often prefixed B for Bomber, C for Communications, E for Experimental, F for fighter, R for Reconnaissance, T for Training etc. Specifications were numbered sequentially, from one in each year so, for example, Specification F.7/30 was the reference number for the seventh aircraft specification of 1930 and was for a Fighter and B.12/36 was the twelveth specification of 1936 and was for a Bomber.

Formally, in production contracts the Air Ministry competition rules included the purchase of a master tracing of the chosen type design drawings and the right to allocate production to one or more aircraft companies *of their choosing*, allowing the designer company always to make a bid to supply. This was very contentious from the aircraft company point of view but, from the government point of view, it prevented any monopoly supply situation arising. As aircraft became more sophisticated and (perhaps) type-special tooling for manufacture or assembly became more and more common, this could become too expensive or even impractical, except when originating company full co-operation with another contractor could be directed (as for times of war, or preparation for war).

Aircraft specifications were prepared for both new aircraft development and for production of a particular type. In all, there were at least 424 different requirements specifications for aircraft in the years 1920 to 1949. After 1939 the responsibility was transferred to the Ministry of Supply, soon transferred to the Ministry of Aircraft Production (MAP), then back to the Ministry of Supply (MoS) until 1959. Later, for military aircraft only, the responsibility was absorbed into the Ministry of Defence (MoD).

Up until the 1930s, the Air Ministry Specification was created on an internal assessment of the requirements of potential operators (armed forces or nationally-owned airlines). In the 1930s a service-originated formal "Operational Requirement" (OR) began to be raised, prior to an actual specification requirement document being prepared as a consequence. Immediately pre- and during the Second World War, the formal OR/Specification process became very abridged or sometimes bypassed, mostly without a formal OR being prepared. After 1949, most specifications for a military aircraft stemmed from a considered formal statement of an Operational Requirement from the armed service in question (General Staff for the army, Naval Staff for the navy and Air Staff for the air force). Occasionally, a specification might be issued retrospectively, as a result of an industry private venture (PV) investment realising an aircraft which the Air Ministry and the RAF belatedly recognised as already potentially capable of more than satisfying a requirement, or even offering a new capability previously not considered. A notable early example was Specification F.10/35 entitled "A prototype aircraft of R.J. Mitchell design", already several weeks into the detail design stage of the Spitfire, as a Vickers-funded Private Venture (PV).

From the 1930s, preparation of an aircraft "Specification" was often sometimes completed by the designer/manufacturer responding to the requirements of an "OR". For the later (post-1949) complex products which might involve significant advanced technology development effort, a more detailed product-related initial Staff Target (AST for the Air Staff, NST for the Naval Staff, or GST for the General Staff) would be issued by the Ministry of Supply/Defence. After considering the options proposed by industry, this might be followed by research contracts (to compare or reduce technical risks), followed by the finally issued Staff Requirement (ASR, NSR, or GSR). By the 1970s, a complete project definition, with firm cost and timescale predictions would be the expected response from the selected company. By the 1970s, preparation costs of the Project Definition could be "millions of pounds" and could be wholly financed by the government department concerned.

The "OR" led process was not always followed exactly. In particular, the Royal Navy and the Royal Air Force processes differed from time to time (e.g. the 1953 Naval Air Staff Requirement which led to the Blackburn Buccaneer strike aircraft project was NA.39, not NSR.39), resulting in specification M.148T (M= "maritime") and not NA.148/53.

Note: There are (in 2019) unclassified partial lists of Air Ministry specifications on the following web addresses:

https://en.wikipedia.org/wiki/List_of_Air_Ministry_specifications
www.theinfolist.com/html/en/list_of_air_ministry_specifications.html

There is also a book describing the evolution of pre-Second World War Air Staff Operational Requirements:

Author: Colin S. Sinnott, The RAF and Aircraft Design: Air Staff Operational Requirements 1923–1939

Routledge, 2014. ISBN 9780415761307 (264 Pages)

Appendix 4

Plowden Report* on the British Aircraft Industry, 1965

* Report of the Committee of Inquiry into the Aircraft Industry appointed by the Minister of Aviation under the chairmanship of Lord Plowden 1964–65." Command 2853.

Report Conclusions and Recommendations

The following extracts, taken from Chapters 40 and 41 of Plowden Committee's report on the aircraft industry, cover the committee's general conclusions and summary of recommendations.

General Conclusions

The picture presented in this report is of an industry in difficulties. The basic problem is that the British home market is small and does not call for the volume of production needed to bear the high initial costs of developing and producing aircraft. Because of this, the industry finds it difficult to compete with the United States industry on costs. In recent years the Government has supported the industry by paying relatively high prices for British military aircraft and by contributing to the development of civil aircraft. The Government is now finding the price of British military aircraft disproportionately high and, in some cases, is seeking cheaper alternatives abroad.

Thus the industry faces competition even in the hitherto sheltered home military market, which is the greater part of its total market. On top of the basic problem, there have been shortcomings in handling aircraft matters in Government and in industry. There is no predestined place for an aircraft industry in Britain. The economic justification for the industry receiving more Government support than other industries must rest on whether it provides particular benefits to the country. There are such benefits: to defence policy, technology, and the balance of payments. But the present degree of support is already higher than these benefits justify, and in future the value of the benefits seems likely to decrease. We consider, therefore, that the Government should adopt policies which will lead to paying relatively less in future for the aircraft it buys, and should be more discriminating in the assistance given to civil aircraft development.

The industry must adapt itself to this reduced level of support. The difficulties of adaptation, though arduous, can and must be overcome. Many of them are difficulties which, in a somewhat less acute form, face all technologically advanced industries in this country. Indeed, the aircraft industry may be conceived as today embodying the predicament, as it has long embodied the aspirations, of the United Kingdom in the world. If the aircraft industry's problems are not solved, they will simply have to be tackled again elsewhere, while in the meantime the nation will have lost much.

The main policies we recommend to deal with the problems confronting the industry are:

(a) Wholehearted collaboration on a comprehensive range of civil and military aircraft projects with European countries, with the aim of evolving a European industry to produce aircraft fully competitive [with USA].

(b) Concentration on projects for which development costs are not disproportionate in relation to the market.

(c) Purchase from the United States in cases where the requirement at *(b)* cannot be met by a European project.
   The Committee believe that this will mean meeting from American sources any future requirements for the largest and most complex weapon systems.

(d) A sustained drive to increase exports.

(e) Overhaul and improvement of the machinery in Government and industry for making and selling aircraft.

(f) Purchase by the Government of a financial share in the airframe companies in order to engage the Government more directly in the industry's affairs while at the same time enabling the existing duplicated system of control which impedes efficiency to be removed.

The industry faces a tremendous challenge. Radical changes of outlook will be needed for it to adjust to these policies. Ultimately the survival of the industry will depend on the success with which it does so. The difficulties, though great, are not insurmountable. We believe that the future for the industry lies in a recognition of some overwhelming economic realities on the one hand and an imaginative and wholehearted collaboration with Europe on the other. If the policies we recommend are implemented with vigour and determination the industry should emerge smaller but stronger, and make a valuable contribution not only to the British but to the European economy.

1965 has been for the industry a year of uncertainty and difficulty. Many issues have had to await the defence review and our report. Early decisions are now needed as a foundation for future plans. We trust that the Government will make these decisions as soon as possible.

Recommendations:

Guide Lines for Future Policy

(a) The level of support which the aircraft industry has been receiving from the Government is too high and should be reduced. The aim of policy should be to create conditions in which industry can thrive with no more support or protection than that given to comparable industries in Britain.

(b) The object must be to improve the relationship between sales [costs] and development and initial production costs.

(c) There is little prospect of substantially increasing the sales of products made by the British industry on its own.

International Co-operation

(d) Britain must turn to collaboration with other countries as the means of improving the relationship between sales and development and initial production costs. . .

(e) Britain should seek a comprehensive programme of collaboration covering a wide range of projects. No realistic prospect is seen of achieving this with the United States. The major effort in future should therefore be towards an association between the British and other European industries in a European aircraft industry ...

(f) In cases where the development and initial costs of a European project would be disproportionate to the total market, recourse should be had to purchase from abroad. The Committee believe that this will mean meeting by purchase from America future requirements for the largest and most complex types of military aircraft and guided weapons, or possibly their manufacture in this country under licence from American designs. Wherever it is technically and economically sound to do so, British engines and equipment should be incorporated in aircraft bought from the United States.

(g)   The present association in aviation matters with the United States can in some limited way be extended, especially if the political will is present in the United States.

Policy on Defence Purchases

(h)   Far greater thrust than in the past must be put behind the policy of collaboration within Europe. A maximum effort must be made to harmonise military requirements among the allies, and to this end they must be ready to sacrifice particular national military needs.

Exports

(i)   The industry's exports must be increased. Designs must be selected which will appeal to [a] wide range of customers.

Civil Aircraft

(j)   The world market for civil aircraft is continuing to expand. The short-term prospects for Britain are not favourable; but the possible future rewards make the effort . . . worthwhile.

(k)   On civil aircraft, as on military, Britain is handicapped by the small home market. There may still be scope for a few new smaller types made solely in Britain. But for all major civil types in future, an association with partners in Europe is likely to provide the only promising foundation on which to launch a project which could compete with the United States.

(l)   Manufacturers should be pressed to contribute at least 50 per cent of the launching costs of civil ventures. But the Government are likely for a time to have to provide more than 50 per cent of the funds in some cases.

(m)   The Government should in future play a bigger role in the country's civil aircraft programme than in the past.

Appendix 5

USA Offshore Procurement Contracts for Aircraft in Europe

NATO ANNOUNCEMENT, 23 APRIL 1953, PALAIS DE CHAILLOT
NATO announces $550,000,000 aircraft programme
Announcement by Lord Ismay, Secretary General

"Today, at the Minister's first meeting, I was able to report that, after 10 months study and hard work, contracts have been signed for the manufacture in Europe of more than $550 millions' worth of combat aircraft for the allied air forces. Practically all these aircraft will be delivered between now and June 1956. Let me explain how this has come about.

"At the Lisbon Conference, it was decided, as you all know, to create an International Staff, one of whose duties was to assist in the co-ordinated planning of defense production in Europe.

"In June last year, a bare two months after the International Staff had been assembled in Paris, the US Government gave them their first Opening. They said that, if a sound plan could be devised for the production of additional military aircraft in Europe they, for their part, would be prepared to place offshore procurement contracts in Europe on condition that European Government, for their part, would find sufficient additional finance to make the programme worthwhile.

"In July, the International Staff presented the result of their studies to the Council, who commended it to governments.

"This plan provided for the production of military aircraft in Belgium, France, Italy, the Netherlands and the United Kingdom. Prolonged bilateral negotiations followed, in which numerous financial, technical and productions problems arose. All these have happily been overcome and the United States Government have now signed offshore procurement contracts for military aircraft to the value of $281,540,000 with Belgium, France, the Netherlands and the United Kingdom. An additional contract with Italy is now in the final stage of negotiation.

"These United States offshore procurement contracts make provision for the delivery of substantial numbers of the British Hawker "Hunter" and the French "Mystère". The largest single order placed by the United States is for Hawker "Hunter" interceptor planes costing $140 millions, to be built in the United Kingdom. A contract signed with France valued at $86,540,000 is for the Dassault "Mystère" Mark IV, a jet interceptor fighter.

"The Hawker "Hunter" will also be produced on the Continent for the first time, under US offshore contracts with Belgium and the Netherlands totalling $42 millions. The United Kingdom has agreed to grant licences for this purpose. The US contract with the Netherlands, subject to final confirmation by the latter Government, is for $18 millions, and with Belgium for $24 millions.

"The Italian contract, when details have been completed, will call for the assembling in Italy of the American F86D all-weather fighter planes.

"In addition to these agreements, the United States Navy has signed a contract with the United Kingdom Government to buy a quantity of the Hawker "Sea Hawk" aircraft costing $13 millions under the off-shore procurement programme. It was designed and developed for use by the Royal Navy and will help replace obsolete carrier-based interceptor aircraft now in service.

"The Belgian and Netherlands Governments for their part have decided to purchase the equivalent of $117 millions' worth of Hawker "Hunter" interceptor aircraft, to be built in those two countries under a co-operative agreement. The Netherlands participation is subject to Cabinet approval.

"The French Government have placed orders equivalent to $91 millions for the Dassault "Mystère" Mark II and IV ground support and interceptor aircraft.

"The United Kingdom have let contracts for the production of $70 millions' worth of Vickers Supermarine "Swift" interceptor aircraft.

"In addition to the above contracts, Belgium, the Netherlands and Norway have agreed to buy a large number of all-weather fighters.

"It must be emphasised that the funds subscribed for this programme for the manufacture of certain types of military aircraft are only a proportion of the money being spent by European members of NATO on aircraft production. In certain of these countries extensive aircraft production programmes had already been adopted before this joint programme was proposed.

"The equipment of the air forces of some member states has hitherto been dependent to a certain extent upon US aircraft. This dependence is not only strategically unsound and logistically unwise, but the maintenance and replacement of United States-built aircraft imposes a considerable additional burden upon the limited dollar resources of European Governments. Now that six Allied Governments have decided to pool their resources, production facilities, technical skill, manpower and money in a joint enterprise, not only will the European aircraft industry be greatly strengthened, but the North Atlantic air forces will be equipped with the most modern aircraft and NATO will have taken a long step forward in furtherance of its planned force build-up.

"This is the first example of a major coordinated arms production programme based on an international plan devised by the North Atlantic Treaty Organization. It has now been put into effect and its existence is fresh evidence of the continuing determination of member governments to work together for their common defence. It is the intention that it should be the forerunner of many others."

Appendix 6

The Boeing-Airbus Dispute on Trade Subsidies to Aircraft Programmes

(a fifteen year ongoing dispute yet to be finally resolved)

In 2005, Boeing claimed to the World Trade Organisation (WTO) that Airbus had unfairly subsidised Airbus civil aircraft programmes, contrary to WTO principles of fair trade. Airbus soon counter-claimed that Boeing had received unfair tax breaks on its civil aircraft programmes. More than one statement has been made by the World Trade Organisation since 2005 but, fifteen years later, the dispute is yet to be resolved.

The disagreement between Boeing and Airbus reached a head in 2011 and 2012, when the WTO ruled that both had received unlawful financial assistance in support of their airliner programmes.

On Tuesday, 15 May 2018 the WTO ruled on the Boeing claim concerning unfair trading by Airbus:

> The WTO rejected 204 of the total of 218 claims by the USA. The WTO ruled that Boeing had not lost sales due to European Union (EU) governments preferential loans (returnable launch aid investment) on the A.320 and A.330 aircraft programmes. However, the WTO also ruled that the EU had failed to remove unfair support for the Airbus A.380 and A.350 projects. The EU Trade commissioner responded that the EU would take swift action to bring itself into line with WTO rules as regarding its remaining obligations.

On Wednesday, 2 October 2019 the WTO ruled further concerning unfair trading by Airbus:

> The WTO ruled that amount of punitive tariffs the USA may levy on USA imports from Europe would be $7 billion, rather less than the $22 billion Boeing claimed would be due.

On Tuesday, 13 October 2020, the WTO ruled further concerning unfair trading by Boeing:

> The WTO ruled that the amount of punitive tariffs the EU may levy on EU imports from the USA would be $4 billion, rather less than the $23 billion Airbus claimed would be due. The EU stated that a further $4 billion can be added, due to a previous WTO ruling.

Stalemate?

The following Appendices, 7 to 14 list all aircraft designed and manufactured in Britain, from 1908 up until 2019, in decades as below.

Appendix 7:   1900–1909 and 1910–1919
Appendix 8:   1920–1929
Appendix 9:   1930–1939
Appendix 10:   1940–1949
Appendix 11:   1950–1959
Appendix 12:   1960–1969
Appendix 13:   1970–2019
Appendix 14:   Experimental Aircraft

Aircraft included are in line with the definition of "industry-produced", thus specfically excluding micro-lights, home-build and human-powered aircraft designs. Aircraft types used in different roles are duplicate-listed in appropriate roles but only one entry records numbers produced and performance data.

The classification 'P' in the "numbers made" denotes prototype(s) intended for series production but failed to receive an order or was discontinued before any delivery to service for any other reason.

Dates are first (prototype) flight date, "numbers made" are to End of Production for all variants (often beyond end of listed decade). The records for these numbers conflict (between 0.1% and 1% different in different sources) but this is understandable, given that many factory original production records are no longer available.

Weight and performance values are mainly (but not exclusively) for early variant. Exact values for each mark or variant should be checked and verified elsewhere.

Appendix 7

British Military and Civil Aircraft 1900–1919

Data in this Appendix is representative of aircraft type, usually early model. For exact data, refer to original sources.

BRITISH "FINDING OUT HOW TO FLY" MILITARY AND CIVIL AIRCRAFT 1900-1909

pwr/wt ratio = power/weight ratio = [(total engine power) ÷ (max. weight)] = HP/lb

Manufacturer & Aircraft	First Flight	No. Made	M.pln B.pln T.pln	No. Eng.	No. Crew	Max. passenger	Max. mph	pwr/wt ratio (HP/lb)	service ceiling (ft.)	Max. wt. (lb.)	Max. Range (miles)
A	(ASL = Aeronautical Syndicate Ltd.)										
ASL Monoplane No.1	1909?	1	M	1	1	?	?	?	?	?	?
ASL No.1 first attempt to fly failed, sold off and modified, crashed on 1st flight.											
ASL Monoplane No.2	1910	1	M	1	1	-	?	?	?	?	?
B											
(Robert) Blackburn First Monoplane	1909	1	M	1	1	-	?	0.0438	?	800	-
April-May a series of "hops", crashed 24 May, Robert Blackburn survived											
Blackburn-Walker biplane	1909	Harold Blackburn-Albert Walker aircraft, not known to have flown									
British Army Aeroplane No. 1 (Cody 1)	1908	1	B	1	1	-	65	0.0169	?	2,950	?
Recognised as first British-built aeroplane to fly (used French engine), 16 Oct. 1908											
Br. Army Dirigible No. 1	1907	1		1	1	-					
Airship at Army Balloon Factory (later Royal Aircraft Factory)											
Br. Army Nulli Secundus	1908	1		1	1						
Airship involving Col. S.F. Cody, moved to Army Aeroplane No. 1											
D											
De Havilland Biplane No. 1	1909	1	B	1	1	-	?	0.0529	?	850	100ft.
DH Biplane No.1 wing failed in 1st flight, Geoffrey de Havilland injured climbing out											
Dunne D.1	1907	1	B	n/a	1	-					
"propeller-driven trolley part remained on ground"											
(Army Balloon Factory glider)	Dunne D.1 rebuilt as Dunn D.4 with engine added. A "few short hops" made										
F											
Ferguson Monoplane	1909	1	M	1	1	-	?	0.0461	?	760	2.5
H											
Howard Wright 1909 Biplane	1909	1	B	1	1	-	?	0.0313	?	1,600	?
Howard Wright 1909 Monoplane	1909	?	M	1	1	-	35	0.0588	?	600	-

"Finding out how to fly aircraft" 1900-1909 continued on next page

APPENDIX 7, 1900-1909

Manufacturer & Aircraft	First Flight	No. Made	M.pln B.pln T.pln	No. Eng.	No. Crew	Max. passenger	Max. mph	pwr/wt ratio (HP/lb)	service ceiling (ft.)	Max wt. (lb.)	Max. Range (miles)
H, 1900-1909 Finding out how to fly aircraft, continued.											
Humphreys Biplane	1909	-	M	1	1	-	?	0.0217	n/a	650	n/a
Humphreys Biplane failed to fly											
R											
Roe I Biplane	1908	1	B	1	1	-	?	0.0369	n/a	650	n/a
Roe I Triplane	1909	1	T	1	1	-	?	0.0200	?	450	0.3
("Roe" used before change to "Avro")	Roe 1 biplane short flights only (even with more powerful engine & wing changes)										
Roe I Triplane recognised as first all-British aeroplane to truly fly, 5 June 1909											
S											
Short No.1 Biplane	n/a	1	B	1	1	-	?	0.0250	?	1,200	n/a
Short Biplane No. 2	1909	1	B	1	1	-	45	0.0404	?	1,485	19
Short No.1 Biplane did not fly, Short Biplane No.2 first flight 27 September 1909											
W											
Willows airships (Nos.1–5)	Willows non-rigid airships listed below. Built and flown by Ernest Thompson Willows (b.1886, d.1926)										
No.1:	1905	1	No. 1:-6 flights, longest 2 hours								
No.2:	1909	1	122-mile cross-country flight. Later Flew across English Channel								
No.3:	1910	1	Modified No.2. Flew to France and "round the Eiffel tower"								
No.4:	1912	1	No.4: 2-person, max. speed 50mph. Sold to HM government as HMA No.2								
No.5:	1913	1	No.5: 4-person, a number of flights over London								

1910-19 Experimental military and civil aircraft on next page

BRITISH EXPERIMENTAL MILITARY AND CIVIL AIRCRAFT 1910-1919

APPENDIX 7, 1910-1919

pwr/wt ratio = power/weight ratio = [(total engine power) ÷ (max. weight)] = HP/lb

Manufacturer & Aircraft	First Flight	No. Made	M.pln B.pln T.pln	No. Eng.	No. Crew	Max. passenger	Max. mph	pwr/wt ratio (HP/lb)	service ceiling (ft.)	Max wt. (lb.)	Max. Range (miles)
A (ASL = Aeronautical Syndicate Ltd.)											
Aerial Wheel Syndicate Monoplane	Built for 1912 Military Aircraft Competition but never assembled										
ASL Valkyrie (different versions)	1910	~11	M	1	1	1	70	0.0555	?	900	?
ASL Viking	1912	1	B	1	1	-	55+	0.0500	?	1,000	6 hrs
Avro Burga	1912	1	M	1	1	1	?	?	?	?	?
Avro Type D	1911	7	B	1	1	1	49	0.0700	?	~800	?
Avro Type E (500 & 502)	1912	18	B	1	2	-	40	?	?	?	?
Avro Type F	1912	1	M	1	1	-	65	0.0438	?	1,400	?
B											
Blackburn Second Monoplane	1911	1	M	1	1	-	60	0.0400	?	1,000	?
Blackburn-Walker Biplane	Harold Blackburn and Albert Walker 1909 design. Not known to have flown										
Boulton Paul P.6	1918	1	B	1	1	1	?	0.0522	?	1,725	2⅓ hrs
Boulton Paul P.10	Never flew										
Bristol Monoplane	1911	2	M	1	1	-	55	0.0658	?	760	?
Bristol-Burney seaplane (X1,X2,X3)	1912-1914	X1 did not fly, X2 crashed in towed take-off, X3 abandoned									
C											
Cody Circuit of Britain	1911	1	B	1	1	-	58	0.0267	5,000	2,250	350
Cody Michelin Cup	1910	1	B	1	1	-	65	0.0203	?	2,950	?
Cody Floatplane	1913	1P	B	1	1	1	70	?	?	?	?
	During flight trials, Cody Floatplane crashed, S.F. Cody and passenger killed										
Cody Monoplane	1912	1	M	1	2	-	70	0.0667	?	1,800	?
D											
De Havilland DH.15	1919	1P	B	1	2	-	139	0.1048	20,000	4,773	?
	This was a standard Airco DH9A, converted as test bed for a new 500HP engine from Galloway Engineering.										
Dunne D.5	1910	1	B	1	1	-	45	0.0387	?	1,550	?

1910-19 Experimental military and civil aircraft continued on next page

APPENDIX 7, 1910-1919

Manufacturer & Aircraft	First Flight	No. Made	M.pln B.pln T.pln	No. Eng.	No. Crew	Max. passenger	Max. mph	pwr/wt ratio (HP/lb)	service ceiling (ft)	Max wt. (lb.)	Max. Range (miles)
D, 1910-19 Experimental military and civil aircraft continued											
Dunne D.7	1911	1	M	1	1	-	?	?	?	?	?
Dunne D.8	1912	4	B	1	1	-	56	0.0421	?	1,900	?
Dunne-Huntington triplane	1914	1	T	1	1	-	43	?	?	?	?
E											
Edwards Rhomboidal	Built 1911, never flew										
Eastbourne Aviation Co. Monoplane	1913	1	M	1	1	-	>50	?	?	?	25
F											
Felixstowe Fury	1918	1	T	5	7	-	97	0.0661	?	25,263	?
From Admiralty Air Design Dept. at Felixstowe. 5-engined Fury was largest flying boat in the world at the time.											
Flanders B.2	1912	1	B	2	1	-	56	0.0364	?	1,100	?
Flanders F.2 (2nd seat, F3 adaptation)	1911	1	M*	1	1	-	60	0.0480	?	1,250	?
Flanders F.4 (F.3 development)	1912	4	M*	1	2	-	67	0.0378	?	1,850	?
* After fatal crashes of two other monoplanes (1912 Bristol Coanda and a French Deperdussin), the Royal Flying Corps banned the use of monoplanes											
G											
Gaunt biplane no.2	1911	1	B	1	1	-	50	0.0375	?	~800	?
Graeme White VI	1913	1	B	1	2	-	70	0.0305	?	2,950	2¾ hrs
H											
Hamble River H.L.1 Seaplane	1914	1	B	1	1	-	65	0.0588	?	2,550	5 hrs?
Handley Page Type A only flew "a few straight hops"											
Handley Page Type B	1910	1	M	1	1	-	35	0.0444	?	450	?
1909 W.P. Thompson commissioned build by H. Page. Not H.Page design, damaged first flight attempt and disowned by H.Page. Returned to Thompson's assistant, modified/repaired. Flown by "Planes Limited" 1910.											
Handley Page Type D	1910	1	M	1	1	-	50	0.0806	?	620	?
Handley Page Type E	1912	1	M	1	1	-	60	0.0385	?	1,300	3 hrs
Handley Page Type F	1912	1	M	1	1	-	55	0.0483	?	1,450	?
Handley Page Type G	1913	1	B	1	1	1-2	73	0.0563	?	1,775	4 hrs
Handley Page Types H, K, L, M, N Types K, M and N unbuilt, Type L never completed											

1910-19 Experimental military and civil aircraft continued on next page

APPENDIX 7, 1910-1919

H, 1910-19 Experimental military and civil aircraft, continued

Manufacturer & Aircraft	First Flight	No. Made	M.pln B.pln T.pln	No. Eng.	No. Crew	Max. passenger	Max. mph	pwr/wt ratio (HP/lb)	service ceiling (ft.)	Max wt. (lb.)	Max. Range (miles)
HMA No.1	"His Majesty's Airship No.1": Rigid airship built by Vickers, wrecked by winds in 1911 before flight										
HMA No. 9r	1916	HMA No. 9r was a government experimental rigid airship built by Vickers									
Howard Wright 1910 Monoplane	1910	3	M	1	1	-	35+	0.0661	?	605	?
L											
Lakes Sea Bird	1912	1	B	1	1	1	62	?	?	?	?
Used fuselage of Avro Duigan (Avro 500 variant), float design E. W. Wakefield											
Lakes Water Bird & Water Hen	1911& 1912	1 of each	B	1	1	1	45	0.0422	800	1,130	?
(Water Bird first British seaplane to fly) Float plane based on Avro build of Curtiss type aircraft (front elevator), float design by E. W. Wakefield. Water Hen built when Water Bird destroyed by storm (lakeside hangar collapsed). Later, Hen had modified floats.											
M											
Macfie monoplane	~1910	1	M	1	1	-	?	0.0398	?	~880	?
Mersey Monoplane	1911	1	M	1	2	-	55	0.0391	?	1,150	6 hrs
P											
Paterson Biplane	1910	2	B	1	1	-	?	?	?	?	?
Perry Beadle T.1	1913	1	B	1	1	-	65	?	?	?	2 hrs
R											
Radley-England Waterplanes	1913	1	B	1	2	-	60+	0.0600	?	2,500	10 hrs
Waterplane data for rebuilt T.2 from damaged Radley-England T.1											
Roe Triplane II	1910	2	T	1	1	-	45	0.0636	?	550	?
Roe Triplane III	1910	6	T	1	1	1	?	?	?	750	?
Roe Triplane IV	1910	1	T	1	1	-	25	?	?	?	?
("Roe" used before change to "Avro")											
Royal Aircraft Factory F.E.1	1910	1	B	1	1	-	37	?	?	?	?
Royal Aircraft Factory S.E.1	1911	1	B	1	1	-	?	0.0500	?	1,200	?

1910-19 Experimental military and civil aircraft continued on next page

APPENDIX 7, 1910-1919

Manufacturer & Aircraft	First Flight	No. Made	M.pln B.pln T.pln	No. Eng.	No. Crew	Max. passenger	Max. mph	pwr/wt ratio (HP/lb)	service ceiling (ft.)	Max wt. (lb.)	Max. Range (miles)
S, 1910-19 Experimental military and civil aircraft, continued											
Saunders T.1	1917	1P	B	1	2	-	74	0.0560	11,100	2,650	3 hrs
Saunders T.1 was first aircraft built by S.E. Saunders company. Designer H.H. Thomas died in 1918-19 influenza epidemic, development abandoned.											
Scottish Aeroplane Syndicate Avis	1910	5	M	1	1	-	?	0.0635	?	630	?
Seddon Mayfly	n/a	2	2xB	2	1	4	?	0.0500	-	2,600	-
Seddon Mayfly had tandem biplane wings. It failed to fly.											
Short Improved S.27	1910	1	B	1	2	-	48	0.0347	?	1,540	?
Short S.26 to S.44 are serial nos. of individual progressive models, adapted from S.27, except for S.38 which had major modification from S.27 standard after a loading accident.											
Short S.39 Triple Twin	1911	1P	B	2	1	-	?	?	?	?	?
The S.39 was a three-propeller twin-engined adaptation of the S.27 (a pair of chain-driven outboard wing contra-rotating tractor propellers, driven by an engine in front of pilot, plus one pusher propeller direct driven by an engine behind the pilot). The S.39 was world's first twin-engined aircraft											
Short S.36	1912	1P	B	1	1	-	60	0.0538	?	1,300	6½ hrs
Short S.27 Tandem Twin	1911	1P	B	2	2	-	?	0.0580	?	~1,720	?
Short S.80 (floatplane)	1913	1	B	1	1	2	60	0.0444	?	3,600	?
Short S.81 (armed S.80)	1914	1	B	1	1	-	60	0.0444	?	3,600	?
Sopwith Bee	1916	1	B	1	1	-	?	?	?	?	?
Personal aircraft of Harry Hawker (Sopwith test pilot, name later used for Hawker Aircraft)											
Sopwith 1913 Circuit of Britain floatplane	1913	1	B	1	2	-	65+	0.0417	?	2,400	?
Spencer-Stirling biplane	1910	1	B	?	?	?	?	?	?	?	?
Vickers E.F.B.1	1913	1	B	1	2	-	70	0.0301	?	2,660	4½ hrs
Vickers E.F.B.7	1915	1	B	2	2	-	75	0.0626	9,000	3,196	2½ hrs
Vickers E.F.B.8	1915	1	B	2	2	-	98	0.0766	14,000	2,610	3 hrs
Vickers E.S.1	1915	3	B	1	1	-	112	0.0733	?	1,501	2 hrs

1910-19 Military aircraft on next page

BRITISH MILITARY AIRCRAFT 1910-1919

APPENDIX 7, 1910-1919

P = Prototype(s) Only   (NF) = Night Fighter   (TB) = Torpedo Bomber

pwr/wt ratio = power/weight ratio = [(total engine power) ÷ (max. weight)] = HP/lb

"Bomber aircraft 1910–1919"

Manufacturer & Aircraft	First Flight	No. Made	M.pln B.pln T.pln	No. Eng.	No. Crew	Max. bomb load	Max. mph	pwr/wt ratio (HP/lb)	service ceiling (ft.)	Max wt. (lb.)	Max. Range (miles)
A											
(AD= Admiralty, Air Design Dept.)											
AD Seaplane 1000 (TB)	1916	2P	B	3	5	?	84	0.0108	4,900	27,900	553
Airco DH.3	1916	2P	B	2	3	680	95	0.0413	?	5,810	700
Airco DH.4	1916	6,295	B	1	2	460	143	0.1080	22,000	3,472	470
Airco DH.9	1917	4,091	B	1	2	460	113	0.0607	15,500	3,790	4½ hrs
Airco DH.9A (with Fairey)	1918	1,997	B	1	2	740	123	0.0861	16,750	4,645	5¼ hrs
Airco DH.10	1918	258	B	2	3	920	131	0.0833	19,000	9,060	6 hrs
Airco DH.11 Oxford	1919	1P	B	2	3	920	123	0.0912	14,500	7020	3 hrs
Armstrong Whitworth F.K.8	1916	1,650	B	1	2	260	95	0.0427	13,000	2,811	3 hrs
Avro 504	see military trainer										
Avro 519	1916	4P	B	1	1	?	75	0.0500	?	3,000	?
Avro 523 Pike	1916	2P	B	2	3	224	97	0.0534	?	6,064	7 hrs
Avro 529	1917	2P	B	2	3	1,000	116	0.0645	17,500	7,135	5¼ hrs
Avro 533 Manchester	1918	3P	B	2	3	880	128	0.0866	17,000	7,390	5¾ hrs
Beardmore W.B.1	1917	1P	B	1	1	660	91	0.0411	?	5,600	7¼ hrs
Beardmore W.B.1a	?	1P	B	1	2	?	110+	0.0562	?	8,900	6½hrs
Beardmore W.B.VI (TB)	?	1P	B	1	1	?	102+	0.0621	?	5,637	3 hrs
Blackburn Blackburd (TB)	1918	3P	B	1	1	1,423	91	0.0614	11,000	5,700	3 hrs
Blackburn G.P. (TB float plane)	1916	2P	B	2	3	920	97	0.0442	11,000	8,600	8 hrs
Blackburn Kangaroo (TB)	1918	20	B	2	3	920	98	0.0624	13,000	8,017	?
Boulton Paul Bourges	1918	3P	B	2	3	920	124	0.1013	20,000	6,320	9¼ hrs

Boulton Paul Bourges was intended to replace DH.10 but end of WW1 caused 1918 DH.10 to remain in service

1910-19 Bomber aircraft continued on next page

Manufacturer & Aircraft	First Flight	No. Made	M.pln B.pln T.pln	No. Eng.	No. Crew	Max. bomb load (lb.)	Max. mph	pwr/wt ratio (HP/lb)	service ceiling (ft.)	Max wt. (lb.)	Max. Range (miles)
B, 1910-19 Bomber aircraft, continued											
Bristol B.1 Braemar	1918	2P	T	4	6	1,500	125	0.0888	17,000	18,000	1000+
Initial design had tandem-pair engines in fuselage, with shaft drive to propellers on wing.... design revised to place engines on wings in tandem pairs driving pusher and tractor propellers											
D											
De Havilland DH.14 Okapi	1913	3P	B	1	2	672	122	0.0848	?	7,074	5 hrs
Dyott Bomber	1916	2P	B	2	3	?	?	0.0308	?	7,800	?
G											
Grahame-White Ganymede	1919	1P	B	3	5	?	105	0.0506	?	16,000	9 hrs
H											
Handley Page Type O/100	1915	46	B	2	4-5	600	85	0.0380	7,000	14,013	~700
Handley Page Type O/400	1917	554	B	2	4-5	2,000	98	0.0513	8,500	13,360	700
Handley Page V/1500	1918	63	B	4	8-9	7,500	99	0.0500	11,000	30,000	1,300
K											
Kennedy Giant	1917	1P	B	4	3	-	-	0.0421	-	-	-
Kennedy Giant only hopped											
M											
Martinsyde G.100	1915	100	B	1	1	260	96	0.0488	14,000	2,458	450
Martinsyde G.102	~1917	171	B	1	1	260	108	0.0657	14,000+	2,458	?
R											
Royal Aircraft Factory F.E.2b	1915	1,939	B	1	2	517	92	0.0527	11,000	3,037	3 hrs
Starting in 1911 (first flight) of F.E.2, 2a, 2c, 2d ,2h redesign variants also produced											
Royal Aircraft Factory R.E.5	see military reconnaissance aircraft										
Royal Aircraft Factory R.E.7	1915	230	B	1	2	336	84	0.0435	6,500	3,450	6 hrs
Royal Aircraft Factory R.E.8	see military reconnaissance aircraft										
S											
Short Admiralty 166 (TB)	1916	26	B	1	2	?	65	0.0437	?	4,580	4 hrs
Short Bomber 184 (TB)	1915	83	B	1	2	896	77	0.0368	10,600	6,800	6 hrs

1910-19 Bomber aircraft continued on next page

APPENDIX 7, 1910-1919

S, 1910-19 Bomber aircraft, continued

Manufacturer & Aircraft	First Flight	No. Made	M.pln B.pln T.pln	No. Eng.	No. Crew	Max. bomb load (lb.)	Max. mph	pwr/wt ratio (HP/lb)	service ceiling (ft.)	Max wt. (lb.)	Max. Range (miles)
Short N.1B Shirl (TB)	1918	4P	B	1	1	1423	92	0.0647	10,010	5,950	6½hrs
Short Type 184	Float plane: see military reconnaissance aircraft										
Short Type 320(310) (TB)	1916	127	B	1	2	460	73	0.0456	3,000	7,014	6 hrs
Sopwith 1½ Strutter	see military fighter										
Sopwith B.1	1917	2P	B	1	1	560	119	0.0655	19,000	3,055	3¾ hrs
Sopwith Baby	1915	386	B	1	1	130	100	0.0641	10,000	1,715	2¼ hrs
Sopwith Cobham	1919	3P	T	2	3	750	?	0.0921	?	6,300	?
Sopwith Cuckoo (TB)	1917	232	B	1	1	?	106	0.0515	12,100	3,833	335
Sopwith Rhino	1917	2P	T	1	2	450	114	0.0641	12,000	3,590	3¾ hrs
Sopwith Two-Seat Scout.	1914	24	B	1	2	-	69	0.0555	?	1,800	3½ hrs
Sopwith Type 860 (TB)	1914	22	B	1	2	?	?	?	?	?	?
Sunbeam Bomber	1917	1P	B	1	1	300	113	0.0678	18,500	2,952	4½ hrs
T											
Tarrant Tabor	1919	1P	T	6	6	~4,600	110	0.1091	?	44,672	?
V											
Vickers Vimy	1917	~776	B	2	2-3	2,476	100	0.0388	7,000	10,884	900
W											
Wight Twin	1915	4P	B	2	2	1,000	80	?	?	?	5 hrs
Wight Bomber	1916	1P	B	1	2	448	89	0.0532	?	5,166	?

"Fighter aircraft 1910–1919"

Manufacturer & Aircraft	First Flight	No. Made	M.pln B.pln T.pln	No. Eng.	No. Crew	Max. bomb load (lb.)	Max. mph	pwr/wt ratio (HP/lb)	service ceiling (ft.)	Max wt. (lb.)	Max. Range (Miles)
A (AD = Admiralty, Air Design Dept.)											
AD Scout (Sparrow): anti-Zepplin use	1915	4P	B	1	1	-	84	?	?	?	210
Airco DH.1 (70 HP)	1915	~30	B	1	2	-	80	0.0342	?	2,044	?

1910-19 Fighter aircraft continued on next page

APPENDIX 7, 1910-1919

Manufacturer & Aircraft	First Flight	No. Made	M.pln B.pln T.pln	No. Eng.	No. Crew	Max. bomb load (lb.)	Max. mph	pwr/wt ratio (HP/lb)	service ceiling (ft.)	Max wt. (lb.)	Max. Range (miles)
A, 1910-19 Fighter aircraft, continued											
Airco DH.1A (120 HP DH.1)	1915	~70	B	1	2	-	90	0.0513	13,500	2,340	?
Airco DH.2	1915	453	B	1	1	-	93	0.0694	14,000	1,441	250
Airco DH.5	1916	552	B	1	1	-	102	0.0737	16,000	1,492	2¾ hrs
Alcock Scout	1917	1P	B	1	1	-	?	?	?	?	?
Armstrong Whitworth Ara	1919	2P	B	1	1	-	150	0.1658	28,000	1,930	3¼ hrs
Armstrong Whitworth Armadillo	1918	1P	B	1	1	-	125	0.1237	24,000	1,860	2¾ hrs
Armstrong Whitworth F.K.6	1916?	1P	T	1	3	-	99	?	?	?	?
Armstrong Whitworth F.K.10	1916	9	Q	1	1	-	84	0.0644	10,000	2,019	2½ hrs
F.K.10 was Quadruplane: numbers made include one F.K.9 as prototype											
Armstrong Whitworth Sissit	1914	1P	B	1	1	-	75	?		?	?
Austin Greyhound	1919?	3P	B	1	2	-	~130	0.1036	?	3,090	?
Austin Osprey	1918	1P	T	1	1	-	119	0.1218	19,000	1,888	3 hrs
Austin-Ball A.F.B.1	1917	1P	B	1	1	-	138	0.0964	22,000	2,075	2 hrs
Avro 508	1915	1P	B	1	2	-	65	0.0476	?	1,680	4½ hrs
Avro 521	1915	1P	B	1	1-2	-	95	0.0551	?	1,995	4½ hrs
Avro 523 Pike	1916	2P	B	2	3	-	97	0.0534	?	6,064	7 hrs
Avro 527	1916	1P	B	1	2	-	103	?	?	?	?
Avro 530	1917	2P	B	1	2	-	114	0.0746	?	2,680	4 hrs
Avro 531 Spider	1918	2P	B	1	1	-	120	0.0857	19,000	1,517	250
B											
British. Aerial Transport (BAT) FK.23 Bantam	1918	15	B	1	1	-	138	0.1500	20,000	1,333	3½ hrs
First prototype built as FK.22. Subsequent changed design became FK.23 Bantam											
BAT Basilisk	1918	3P	B	1	1	-	162	0.1535	22,500	2,085	?
Beardmore W.B.II	1917	2P	M	1	2	-	120	0.0755	?	2,650	2¾ hrs
Beardmore W.B.III	1917	100	B	1	1	-	103	0.0620	12,400	1,290	2¾ hrs
Beardmore W.B.III was adaptation of Sopwith Pup for shipboard use (jettison-able undercarriage)											

1910-19 Fighter aircraft continued on next page

APPENDIX 7, 1910-1919

Manufacturer & Aircraft	First Flight	No. Made	M.pln B.pln T.pln	No. Eng.	No. Crew	Max. bomb load (lb.)	Max. mph	pwr/wt ratio (HP/lb)	service ceiling (ft.)	Max wt. (lb.)	Max. Range (miles)
B, 1910-19 Fighter aircraft, continued											
Beardmore W.B.IV	1917	1P	B	1	1	-	110	0.0827	14,000	2,419	2½ hrs
Beardmore W.B.V	1917	2P	B	1	1	-	112	0.0800	14,000	2,500	2½ hrs
Blackburn Triplane	1917	1P	T	1	1	-	115	0.0666	?	1,500+	3 hrs
Blackburn Twin Blackburn	1915	9	B	2	2	-	86	0.0571	?	3,500	4 hrs
Boulton & Paul Bobolink	1918	1P	B	1	1	-	125	0.1155	19,500	1,992	3¾ hrs
Bristol Badger	1919	5P	B	1	2	-	142	0.2051	20,600	1,950	?
Bristol F.2B Fighter	1916	5,329	B	1	2	-	123	0.0848	18,000	3,243	369
Bristol F.3A	None completed										
Bristol M.1	1916	130	M	1	1	-	130	0.0816	20,000	1,348	1¾ hrs
Bristol S.S.A.	1914	1P	B	1	1	-	106	0.0667	?	1,200	3 hrs
Bristol Scout	1914	374	B	1	1	-	94	0.0669	16,000	1,195	2½ hrs
Bristol Scout F	1918	4P	B	1	1	-	145	0.1394	?	2,260	?
Bristol T.T.A.	1916	2P	B	2	2	-	87	0.0471	?	5,100	3½ hrs
F											
Fairey F.2	1917	1P	B	2	3	-	93	0.0779	?	4,880	3½ hrs
G											
Grahame-White G.W.19	1915	25	B	1	2	-	83	0.0529	14,110	4,158	6¼ hrs
Breguet Bre.5 Ca.2 escort fighters built in Britain as G.W.19											
M											
Mann & Grimmer M.1	1915	1P	B	1	2	-	85	0.0446	?	2,800	4½ hrs
Mann Egerton Type H	1917	2P	B	1	1	-	113	0.0860	16,800	2,326	3¼ hrs
Martinsyde Buzzard	1918	370+	B	1	1	-	146	0.1251	24,000	2,398	2½ hrs
Martinsyde F.1	1917	2P	B	1	2	-	110	0.0767	16,500	3,260	3¾ hrs
Martinsyde S.1											
Nieuport B.N.1	1914	60	B	1	1	-	87	?	?	?	?
Nieuport Nighthawk	1918	1P	B	1	1	-	127	0.1133	26,000	2,030	3 hrs

Original prototype made by Nieuport (unreliable Dragonfly engine). Gloster adapted design for several aircraft, including 1921 Sparrowhawk

1910-19 Fighter aircraft continued on next page

APPENDIX 7, 1910-1919

Manufacturer & Aircraft	First Flight	No. Made	M.pln B.pln T.pln	No. Eng.	No. Crew	Max. bomb load (lb.)	Max. mph	pwr/wt ratio (HP/lb)	service ceiling (ft.)	Max wt. (lb.)	Max. Range (miles)
N, 1910-19 Fighter aircraft, continued											
Norman Thompson N.1B	1917	1P	B	1	2	-	93	0.0880	12,600	2,273	3½ hrs
P											
Parnall Scout	1916	1P	B	1	1	-	114	?	?	?	?
Parnall Scout designed as anti-Zeppelin aircraft: declared unsafe to fly after initial flights											
Port Victoria (Isle of Grain) was RNAS experimental seaplane design and test facility											
Port Victoria P.V.1	1916	1P	B	1	1	-	77	0.0478	8,000	2,302	?
Port Victoria P.V.2	1916	1P	B	1	1	-	93	0.0588	10,000	1,702	?
Port Victoria P.V.4	1917	1P	B	1	2	-	81	0.0458	?	2,400	?
Port Victoria P.V.5	1917	2P	B	1	1	-	95	0.0611	9,900	2,456	?
Port Victoria P.V.7	1917	1P	B	1	1	-	85	0.0713	11,900	491	?
Port Victoria P.V.8	1917	1P	B	1	1	-	95	0.0597	14,900	586	?
Port Victoria P.V.9	1917	1P	B	1	1	-	111	0.0763	11,500	1,965	2½ hrs
R											
Robey-Peters Gun-Carrier	1917	1P	B	1	3	-	?	?	?	?	?
Royal Aircraft Factory A.E.3	1918	1P	B	1	2	-	95	?	?	?	?
Royal Aircraft Factory B.E.12	1915	601	B	1	1	-	102	0.0638	12,500	2,352	3 hrs
Royal Aircraft Factory F.E.2	see military bomber										
Royal Aircraft Factory F.E.3.	1913	1P	B	1	2	-	75	0.0481	5,000	2,080	?
Royal Aircraft Factory F.E.4	1916	2P	B	2	3	-	84	0.0383	12,000	7,825	?
Royal Aircraft Factory F.E.8	1915	295	B	1	1	-	94	0.0748	14,500	1,470	2½ hrs
Royal Aircraft Factory F.E.9	1917	3P	B	1	2	-	105	0.0806	15,500	2,480	?
Royal Aircraft Factory N.E.1	1917	6P	B	1	2	-	95	0.0679	17,500	2,946	2¾ hrs
Royal Aircraft Factory S.E.2	1913	1P	B	1	1	-	91	0.0707	?	1,132	3 hrs
Royal Aircraft Factory S.E.4	1914	1P	B	1	1	-	135	?	?	?	?
Royal Aircraft Factory S.E.4a	1917	4	B	1	1	-	90	?	?	?	?
Royal Aircraft Factory S.E.5	1917	5,205	B	1	1	-	138	0.1006	17,000	1,988	300

1910-19 Fighter aircraft continued on next page

APPENDIX 7, 1910-1919

S, 1910-19 Fighter aircraft, continued

Manufacturer & Aircraft	First Flight	No. Made	M.pln B.pln T.pln	No. Eng.	No. Crew	Max. bomb load (lb.)	Max. mph	pwr/wt ratio (HP/lb)	service ceiling (ft.)	Max wt. (lb.)	Max. Range (miles)
Sage Type 2	1916	1P	B	1	2	-	112	0.0647	16,000	1,546	308
Sopwith 1½ Strutter	1915	5,939	B	1	2	-	100	0.0640	15,500	2,150	?
Sopwith Bee	see Experimental aircraft category										
Sopwith Buffalo	1918	2P	B	1	2	-	114	0.0749	9,000	3,071	275
Sopwith Bulldog	1918	2P	B	1	2	-	109	0.0802	15,000	2,495	2 hrs
Sopwith Camel	1916	5,490	B	1	1	-	113	0.0895	19,000	1,453	300
Sopwith Dolphin	1917	2,072	B	1	1	-	131	0.1021	20,000	1959	195
Sopwith Dragon	1918	200	B	1	1	-	150	0.1689	25,000	2,132	?
Sopwith Dragon developed from Sopwith Snipe, difficulties with ABC Dragonfly engine (hence name) caused 200 aircraft to be stored, never issued to squadrons											
Sopwith Gunbus	1914	23	B	1	2	-	80	?	4,000	?	2½ hrs
Sopwith Gunbus landplane developed from floatplane (12) sold to Greek Navy & Royal Navy											
Sopwith Hippo	1917	2P	B	1	2	-	115	0.0772	17,000	2,590	?
Sopwith Pup	1916	1,770	B	1	1	-	112	0.0653	17,500	1,225	3 hrs
Sopwith Snapper	1919	3P	B	1	1	-	140	0.1644	23,000	2,190	?
Sopwith Salamander	1918	497	B	1	1	-	125	0.0916	13,000	2,512	1½ hrs
Sopwith Snail	1918	2P	B	1	1	-	125	0.0855	?	1,920	?
Sopwith Snark	1919	3P	T	1	1	-	130	0.1577	?	2,283	?
Sopwith Snipe	1917	497	B	1	1	-	121	0.1139	19,500	2,020	3 hrs
Sopwith Swallow	1918	2P	M	1	1	-	114	0.0775	18,500	1,420	?
Sopwith Triplane	1916	147	T	1	1	-	117	0.0844	20,500	1,541	2¾ hrs
Supermarine Baby	1918	1P	B	1	1	-	116	0.1177	10,700	1,699	3 hrs
Supermarine Nighthawk	1917	1P	Q	2	4	-	75	0.0325	?	6,146	>9hrs
Supermarine Nighthawk was a Quadruplane: specifically an anti-Zeppelin aircraft											
Vickers E.F.B.1	1913	see Experimental aircraft									
Vickers E.F.B.7	1915	see Experimental aircraft									
Vickers E.F.B.8	1915	see Experimental aircraft									

1910-19 Fighter aircraft continued on next page

APPENDIX 7, 1910–1919

V, 1910-19 Fighter aircraft, continued

Manufacturer & Aircraft	First Flight	No. Made	M.pln B.pln T.pln	No. Eng.	No. Crew	Max. bomb load (lb.)	Max. mph	pwr/wt ratio (HP/lb)	service ceiling (ft.)	Max wt. (lb.)	Max. Range (miles)
Vickers E.S.1	1915	see Experimental aircraft									
Vickers F.B.5	1914	224	B	1	2	-	70	0.0488	9,000	2,050	250
(Gunbus)	Vickers F.B.5 (Fighter.**B**iplane.**5**) Gunbus was world's first purpose-designed fighter										
Vickers F.B.11	1916	1P	B	1	3	-	96	0.0507	11,000	4,934	7½ hrs
Vickers F.B.12	1916	~22	B	1	1	-	86	0.0784	11,500	1,275	3 hrs
Vickers F.B.14	1916	100+	B	1	2	-	100	0.0615	10,000	2,603	3¾ hrs
Vickers F.B.16	1916	1P	B	1	1	-	135	0.1067	18,500	1,875	2¼ hrs
Vickers F.B.19	1916	62	B	1	1	-	102	0.0673	17,500	1,485	2¾ hrs
Vickers F.B.24	1917	5P	B	1	2	-	130	0.1038	23,000	2,650	3 hrs
Vickers F.B.25	1917	1P	B	1	2	-	86	0.0611	11,500	2,454	4 hrs
Vickers F.B.26 Vampire	1917	4P	B	1	1	-	121	0.0985	20,500	2,030	3 hrs
W											
Westland N.1B	1917	2P	B	1	1	-	107	0.0755	10,400	1,987	2¾ hrs
Westland Wagtail	1918	5P	B	1	1	-	125	0.1278	20,000	1,330	2½ hrs
Westland Weasel	1918	4P	B	1	2	-	131	0.1042	20,700	3,071	?
Wight Quadruplane	1916	1P	Q	1	1	-	?	?	?	?	?

"Patrol aircraft 1910–1919"

Manufacturer & Aircraft	First Flight	No. Made	M.pln B.pln T.pln	No. Eng.	No. Crew	Max. bomb load (lb.)	Max. mph	pwr/wt ratio (HP/lb)	service ceiling (ft.)	Max wt. (lb.)	Max. Range (Miles)
A (AD= Admiralty, Air Design Dept.)											
AD Flying Boat	1916	27	B	1	2	-	100	0.0561	11,000	3,567	4½ hrs
C											
C* (Star) class airship	1918?	10	Non-rigid airships: Coastal class replaced by revised version C* (more controllable). Western								
Coastal class airship	1916	35	approaches anti-submarine convoy protection, bombs/depth charge and Lewis gun armament.								

1910-19 Patrol aircraft continued on next page

APPENDIX 7, 1910-1919

Manufacturer & Aircraft	First Flight	No. Made	M.pln B.pln T.pln	No. Eng.	No. Crew	Max. bomb load (lb.)	Max. mph	pwr/wt ratio (HP/lb.)	service ceiling (ft.)	Max wt. (lb.)	Max. Range (miles)
F, 1910-19 Patrol aircraft, continued											
Fairey Campania (float plane)	1917	62	B	1	2	700	85	0.0468	6,000	5,329	4½hrs
Fairey Campania had fold-back wings, was first aircraft in world designed especially for aircraft carrier operation. (jettisoned undercarriage after deck landing, water landing, craned on board)											
Felixstowe F.1	1915	4	B	2	4	?	?	?	?	?	?
RNAS Felixstowe (Lt. Cdr. John Cyril Porte) adaptation of USA Curtis H-4 flying boat (new hull design)											
Felixstowe F.2	1916	175	B	2	4	460	96	0.0629	9,600	10,978	6 hrs
Felixstowe F.3	1917	182	B	2	4	920	91	0.0564	8,000	12,235	6 hrs
Felixstowe F.5	1917	163	B	2	4	920	88	0.0544	6,800	12,682	7 hrs
M											
Mann Egerton Type B	1916	15	B	1	2	?	?	?	?	?	?
Floatplane: improved (larger wing) Short Type 184 reconnaissance aircraft											
Norman Thompson N.T.2C	1918	2P	B	2	4	?	?	?	?	?	?
Norman Thompson N.T.4	1916	70	B	2	4	?	95	0.0618	11,700	6,469	6 hrs
The Norman Thompson N.T. 4, 4A and 2C were flying boats											
NS class airship	1917	14	Non-rigid airship (NS = North Sea)								
P											
Phoenix P.5 Cork (flying boat)	1919	2P	B	2	5	1,040	106	0.0621	?	11,600	?
P.5 Cork used as basis of 1924 English Electric Kingston											
R											
R31-class airship	1918	2	Rigid airship								
R33-class airship	1919	2	Rigid airship								
Royal Aircraft Factory C.E.1	1918	2P	B	1	2	?	92	0.0520	7,500	5,000	3¾ hrs
C.E.1 the only flying boat designed by Royal Aircraft Factory											
S											
Short S.38	1912	48	B	1	2	-	58	0.0450	?	1,500	5 hrs

1910-19 Patrol aircraft continued on next page

APPENDIX 7, 1910-1919

S, 1910-19 Patrol aircraft, continued

Manufacturer & Aircraft	First Flight	No. Made	M.pln B.pln T.pln	No. Eng.	No. Crew	Max. bomb load (lb.)	Max. mph	pwr/wt ratio (HP/lb)	service ceiling (ft.)	Max wt. (lb.)	Max. Range (miles)
SS class non-rigid airship	1915	8	To counter German submarine threat in waters surrounding Britain, an Admiralty-led consortia of Admiralty Air Design department, Royal Aircraft Factory & Vickers created armed SS, SSP, SST, SSZ class "Submarine Scout" airships. Single-engined SS class started with aircraft fuselage as under-slung" crew car. SST were twin-engined versions, SSZ had purpose-designed car and became standard.								
SSP class non-rigid airship	1917	6									
SST class non-rigid airship	1917	13									
SSZ class non-rigid airship	1918	77									

"Reconnaissance aircraft 1910–1919"

Manufacturer & Aircraft	First Flight	No. Made	M.pln B.pln T.pln	No. Eng.	No. Crew	Max. bomb load (lb.)	Max. mph	pwr/wt ratio (HP/lb)	service ceiling (ft.)	Max wt. (lb.)	Max. Range (miles)
A (AD= Admiralty, Air Design Dept.)											
AD Navyplane	1916	1P	B	1	2	?	64	0.0588	1,300	2,550	6 hrs
Airco DH.1 & D.H.1A	see military fighter										
Armstrong Whitworth F.K.3	1915	~500	B	1	2	?	89	0.0438	12,000	2,056	3 hrs
Armstrong Whitworth F.K.8	1916	1,650	B	1	2	260	95	0.0569	13,000	2,811	3 hrs.
Avro 504	see military trainer										
Avro 511	1913?	1P	B	1	1	?	~90	0.0687	?	1,165	?
Avro 523 Pike	see military fighter										
B											
British Army Airship Beta	1910	1	Non-rigid airship								
British Deperdussin Seagull (float plane)	1913	1P	M	1	2	?	63	?	?	?	?
Monocoque fuselage and metal tube braced wing, designed by Frederick Koolhoven											
C											
Cody V biplane	1912	2P	B	1	1+3	?	72	0.0218	?	5,512	336
F											
Fairey III	1917	964	B	1	2/3	500	120	0.0944	20,000	6,041	1,520
Fairey III configured as landplane or with floats. Later variants served in Second World War											

1910-19 Reconnaissance aircraft continued on next page

F, 1910-19 Reconnaissance aircraft, continued

Manufacturer & Aircraft	First Flight	No. Made	M.pln B.pln T.pln	No. Eng.	No. Crew	Max. bomb load	Max. mph	pwr/wt ratio (HP/lb)	service ceiling (ft.)	Max wt. (lb.)	Max. Range (miles)
Fairey N.9 (float plane)	1917	1P	B	1	2	224	90	0.0525	8,600	3,812	5¼ hrs
Felixstowe Porte Baby (flying boat)	1915	11	B	3	5	?	88	0.0556	8,000	18,600	?
H											
Handley Page HP.14 (also known as R/200)	1917	3P	B	1	2	?	95	0.0669	12,000	2,990	?
P											
Parnall Panther	1917	155	B	1	2	?	109	0.0886	14,500	2,595	4½ hrs
Pemberton-Billing P.B.9	1914	1P	B	1	1	?	78	?	?	?	?
Pemberton-Billing P.B.25	1915	20	B	1	1	?	99	0.0635	?	1,576	?
(RNAS) Port Victoria Grain Griffin	1918?	8	B	1	2	?	113	0.0805	16,500	2,858	5½ hrs
Royal Aircraft Factory A.E.3	1918	3P	B	1	2	?	95	?	?	?	?
Royal Aircraft Factory B.E.2c (total incl. B.E.2a to B.E.2e)	1914	~3,500	B	1	2(1)	(224)	72	0.0383	10,000	2,350	3¾ hrs
B.E.2a (first flight 1912) quite a lot different from (much improved) 1914 B.E.2c. With bombs, pilot sole crew											
Royal Aircraft Factory B.E.8	1913	~70	B	1	2	100	70	?	?	?	1½ hrs
Royal Aircraft Factory B.E.9	1915	1P	B	1	2	?	82	?	?	?	?
Royal Aircraft Factory B.E.10	never completed										
Royal Aircraft Factory H.R.E.2 (float plane)	1913	1	B	1	2	?	60	?	?	?	?
First flew as landplane, floats fitted and saw service, converted back to landplane											
Royal Aircraft Factory R.E.1	1913	2P	B	1	2	?	83	0.0443	?	1,580	?
Royal Aircraft Factory R.E.5	1914	24	B	1	2	60	78	?	?	?	?
Royal Aircraft Factory R.E.8	1916	4,077	B	1	2	224	103	0.0488	13,500	2,869	?
S											
Sage Type 4 (float plane)	1917	2	B	1	2	?	97	0.0696	13,700	2,875	2½ hrs
Short Admiralty Type 74	1914	7	B	B	1	2	65	0.0370	?	?	?
Short Admiralty Type 81	1913	9	B	1	2	112	78	0.0207	?	7,716	5 hrs
Short S.41 (+ S.51 & S.52)	1912	3	B	1	2	-	60	0.0625	?	1,600	5 hrs
Short Folder (wings fold back, patent)	Term for S.41, S.63(S.81), Admiralty S.74 and S.81, S.166, S.184, Short Bomber, S.827(S.830), S.310(S.320)										

1910-19 Reconnaissance aircraft continued on next page

APPENDIX 7, 1910-1919

S, 1910-19 Reconnaissance aircraft, continued

Manufacturer & Aircraft	First Flight	No. Made	M.pln B.pln T.pln	No. Eng.	No. Crew	Max. bomb load	Max. mph	pwr/wt ratio (HP/lb)	service ceiling (ft.)	Max wt. (lb.)	Max. Range (miles)
Short N.2B	1917	2P	B	2	1	460	92	0.0560	10,600	4,911	4½ hrs
Short Type S.166	1916	26	B	1	2	336	65	0.0437	?	4,580	4 hrs
Short Type S.184	1915	936	B	1	2	520	89	0.0485	9,000	5,363	2¾ hrs
Short Type S.827(830)	1914	126	B	1	2	?	62	0.0441	?	3,400	3½ hrs
Short Types N.2B ,S.74, 81, 41, and Folder types S.166, 184 & 187 were float planes											
Siddeley-Deasy R.T.1.	1917	3P	B	1	2	?	108	0.0739	18,000	2,707	?
Sopwith 1½ Strutter	see military fighter										
Sopwith Baby	see military bomber										
Sopwith Buffalo	see military fighter										
Sopwith Three-seater	1912	13	B	1	1+2	?	74	0.0442	12,900	1,810	2½ hrs
Sopwith Type 807	1914	12	B	1	2	?	80	0.0410	?	2,440	?
W											
White & Thompson N.T.3 (Bognor Bloater)	1915	12	B	1	2	?	?	?	?	?	?
Wight Converted Seaplane	1916	37	B	1	2	?	84	0.0580	9,600	5,556	3½ hrs
Straightforward floatplane adaptation of Wight Bomber											
Wight Pusher Seaplane	1914	11	B	1	2	?	72	0.0571	9,600	3,500	6 hrs
Wight Seaplane	1917	52	B	1	2	810	81	0.0468	?	4,810	?

"Military Trainer aircraft 1910–1919"

Manufacturer & Aircraft	First Flight	No. Made	M.pln B.pln T.pln	No. Eng.	No. Crew	Max. bomb load	Max. mph	pwr/wt ratio (HP/lb)	service ceiling (ft.)	Max wt. (lb.)	Max. Range (Miles)
A											
Airco DH.6	1916	>2,280	B	1	2	-	70	0.0443	?	2,030	2¾ hrs
Avro 504 (1915 504K data)	1913	9,977	B	1	2	-	90	0.0601	16,000	1,829	250

1910-19 Military Trainer aircraft continued next page

Manufacturer & Aircraft	First Flight	No. Made	M.pln B.pln T.pln	No. Eng.	No. Crew	Max. bomb load	Max. mph	pwr/wt ratio (HP/lb)	service ceiling (ft.)	Max wt. (lb.)	Max. Range (miles)
B, 1910-19 Military Trainer aircraft continued											
British Aerial Transport (BAT) F.K.24 Baboon	1918	1P	B	1	2	-	90	0.1259	?	1,359	2 hrs
Bristol Coanda Monoplanes	1912	37	M	1	2	-	90	0.0480	?	1,665	5 hrs
Bristol Coanda: 5 different versions, military version formed basis of Bristol T.B.8											
Bristol T.B.8	1913	54	B	1	2	120	70	0.0483	?	1,665	5 hrs
G											
Grahame-White Type XV	1913	135	B	1	2	-	?	?	?	?	?
Derived from type XII, this was a large variety of "different" aircraft, 1913 to 1917											
H											
HMA No.9r (r for "rigid")	1913	Rigid airship: see military experimental aircraft 1910-1919									
N											
Norman Thompson N.T.2B (flying boat)	1917	~79	B	1	2	-	85	0.0631	11,400	3,169	?
R											
Royal Aircraft Factory B.E.3	1912	~5	B	1	2	-	?	?	?	?	?
S											
Sage Type 3	1917	2P	B	1	2	-	76	0.0379	9,000	1,980	4 hrs
Sage Type 4 (flt.plane)	see Reconnaissance aircraft										
Short S.26 to S44	At first, Shorts numbered each aircraft. Starting with S.26 there were 13 individual aircraft (S.40 to S.42 missing). Improved S.27 typical, see 'Experimental' types										
Short S.45/48/49/50	1912	4	B	1	2	-	60	0.0467	?	1,500	5 hrs
Short S.80	1913	1	B	1	1	-	60	0.0444	?	3,600	?
Vickers 23-class airship	1917	4	Rigid airships: 23-class replaced by R23X.								
Vickers R23X class airship	1918	2	One R23X the only British rigid airship to engage the enemy (destroyed submarine)								

1910-19 Military Utility aircraft next page

"Military Utility aircraft 1910–1919"

APPENDIX 7, 1910-1919

Manufacturer & Aircraft	First Flight	No. Made	M.pln B.pln T.pln	No. Eng.	No. Crew	Max. passenger	Max. mph	pwr/wt ratio (HP/lb)	service ceiling (ft.)	Max wt. (lb.)	Max. Range (miles)
A											
Avro 500	1912	18	B	1	2	-	40	?	?	?	?
Avro 501 (float plane)	1913	1	B	1	1+1	-	55	0.0370	?	2,700	?
Avro 503 (float plane)	1913	4	Improved Avro 501: First aircraft to cross North Sea. Gotha licence-built further aircraft as WD.1, others built unlicenced during WW1.								
Avro Type G	1912	1	B	1	1+1	-	62	0.0355	?	1,792	?
B											
Bristol Gordon England biplanes	1912	5 total	B	1	2	?	68	?	?	2,000	?
	Gordon England designs for Bristol: G.E.1 (1), G.E.2 (2) & G.E.3 (2).....G.E.2 values shown. Designed for quick disassembly/assembly for ground transportation										
G											
Grahame-White Type XI	1914	1	B	1	2	-	80	~0.070	?	~1,350	5 hrs
S											
Sopwith Sociable	1914	1	B	1	2	-	90	0.0610	?	1,640	3 hrs
V											
Vickers Viking (amphibian flying boat)	1919	34+3*	B	1	1	3	113	0.0777	?	5,790	4¾ hrs
*Two other versions were Vickers Vulture (2 built) and Vanellus (1 built)											

Civil Aircraft 1910-19 next page

BRITISH CIVIL AIRCRAFT 1910-1919

APPENDIX 7, 1910-1919

pwr/wt ratio = power/weight ratio = [(total engine power) ÷ (max. weight)] = HP/lb

"Airliners 1910–1919"

Manufacturer & Aircraft	First Flight	No. Made	M.pln B.pln T.pln	No. Eng.	No. Crew	Max. passenger	Max. mph	pwr/wt ratio (HP/lb)	service ceiling (ft.)	Max wt. (lb.)	Max. Range (miles)
B											
British Aerial Transport (BAT) F.K.26	1919	4	B	1	1	4	122	0.0777	18,000	4,500	600
4th F.K.26 was the last aircraft produced by BAT											
C											
Central Centaur IIA	1919	2	B	2	2	-	90	0.0441	?	7,250	?
Central Centaur IV	1919	8	B	1	1	1-2	75	0.0714	?	1,400	3 hrs
G											
Grahame-White Type X	1913	1	1	B	1	4	51	0.0323	?	3,100	?
Grahame-White GWE.7	1919	1	B	1	2	4	116	0.0403	?	7,547	?
S											
Sopwith Wallaby	1919	1	B	1	2	-	115	0.0692	?	5,200	?
V											
Vickers Vimy Commercial (new fuselage on bomber)	1919	*(43)	B	2	2	12	109	0.0647	10,000	11,120	450
*Vimy Commercial numbers (43) included with Vimy military bomber of 1917											
W											
Westland Limousine	1919	8	B	1	1	4	118	0.0769	12,300	5,850	520

"Sports and Sailplane aircraft 1910–1919"

Manufacturer & Aircraft	First Flight	No. Made	M.pln B.pln T.pln	No. Eng.	No. Crew	Max. passenger	Max. mph	pwr/wt ratio (HP/lb)	service ceiling (ft.)	Max wt. (lb.)	Max. Range (miles)
1910-19 Sports aircraft											
A											
Alliance P.2 (built for transatlantic attempt, untried)	1919	2	B	1	2	-	140	0.0608	?	7,400	21 hrs

theoretically very long endurance, enclosed cabin. First aircraft flew 900 miles London-Madrid

1910-19 Sports aircraft continued on next page

APPENDIX 7, 1910-1919

Manufacturer & Aircraft	First Flight	No. Made	M.pln B.pln T.pln	No. Eng.	No. Crew	Max. passenger	Max. mph	pwr/wt ratio (HP/lb)	service ceiling (ft.)	Max wt. (lb.)	Max. Range (miles)
A, 1910-19 Sports aircraft, continued											
Austin Whippet	1919	5	B	1	1	-	95	0.0555	?	810	2 hrs
Avro 510 (float plane)	1914	6	B	1	1	1	70	0.0536	?	2,800	4½ hrs
Avro 539	1919	1	B	1	1	-	?	0.1437	?	2,119	2 hrs
Avro Baby	1919	9	B	1	1	-	80	0.0424	?	825	200
Austin Whippet	1919	5	B	1	1	-	95	0.0555	?	810	2 hrs
B											
British Aerial Transport (BAT) F.K.27	1918	1	B	1	2	-	142	0.1429	?	1,400	4¾ hrs
Blackburn Sidecar	1919?	1	not known ever to have flown								
Blackburn Type D	1912	1	M	1	1	-	60	0.0510	>4,000	980	2½ hrs
Blackburn Type D is oldest British aircraft still flying in UK (2019): Shuttleworth Collection											
Blackburn Type 1	1913	1	M	1	1	1	70	0.0533	?	1,500	4 hrs
Blackburn Type L(float plane)	1914	1	B	1	2	-	?	?	?	?	?
Blackburn White Falcon	1915	1	M	1	1	1	?	?	?	?	?
Bristol Babe	1919	3	B	1	1	-	107	0.0714	15,000	840	?
Bristol Prier monoplane	1911	34	M	1	1	-	68	0.0610	?	820	?
D											
Dyott monoplane	1913	1	M	1	1	-	75	?	?	?	3 hrs
E (EAC = Eastbourne Aviation Company)											
EAC (Hunt) Biplane	1914	1	B	i	i	1	>75	?	?	?	?
G											
Grahame-White Baby	1911	~6	B	1	1	-	55	?	?	?	4 hrs
Grahame-White Bantam	1919	3	B	1	1	-	100	0.0804	?	995	?
Grahame-White Type VII	1913	1	B	1	1	-	50	0.0583	?	600	2¾ hrs
Grahame-White Type XIII	1913	1	B	1	1	2	85	0.0555	?	1,800	5½ hrs
Short Sporting Type	1919	3	B	1	1	3	95	0.0647	?	3,554	270
Sopwith 1919 Schneider Cup Seaplane	1919	1	B	1	1	-	170	0.2045	?	2,200	?

1910-19 Sport aircraft continued on next page

APPENDIX 7, 1910-1919

Manufacturer & Aircraft	First Flight	No. Made	M.pln B.pln T.pln	No. Eng.	No. Crew	Max. passenger	Max. mph	pwr/wt ratio (HP/lb)	service ceiling (ft.)	Max wt. (lb.)	Max. Range (miles)
S, 1910-19 Sports aircraft, continued											
Sopwith Atlantic	1919	1	B	1	2	-	118	0.0610	13,000	6,150	?
Sopwith Bat Boat (flying boat)	1913	6	B	1	2	-	70	0.0641	?	3,120	?
Sopwith Gnu	1919	13	B	1	1	2	93	0.0328	?	3,350	300
Sopith Tabloid	1913	178	B	1	1	-	87	0.0588	7,000	1,700	315
(Schneider Trophy winner 1914)	Sopwith Tabloid among first of Sopwith aircraft. Schneider Trophy float plane variant data										
Supermarine Sea Lion I	1919	1	B	1	1	-	147	0.1522	?	2,900	?
	Built for 1919 Schneider Trophy race. Sea Lion I hull holed on first take-off by floating debris, sank on landing										
W											
White & Thompson No. 1 (flying boat)	1914	1	B	1	2	-	93	0.0880	12,600	2,273	3½hrs
White & Thompson No. 3 (flying boat)	1914	9	B	1	2	-	70	0.0500	?	2,400	6 hrs
1910-19 Sailplanes											
B											
Bristol Glider	1910	1	B	-	2				n/a		

"Civil Trainer aircraft 1910-1919"

Manufacturer & Aircraft	First Flight	No. Made	M.pln B.pln T.pln	No. Eng.	No. Crew	Max. passenger	Max. mph	pwr/wt ratio (HP/lb)	service ceiling (ft.)	Max wt. (lb.)	Max. Range (Miles)
A											
Alliance P.1 (Ruffy Arnell & Bauman)	1919	1	B	1?	2?	-	?	?	?	?	?
B											
Blackburn Mercury	1911	9	M	1	2	-	60	0.0500	?	1,000	?
Bristol Boxkite	1910	78	B	1	2	-	40	0.0435	?	1.150	?
	Bristol Boxkite was most-produced British aircraft in years prior to First World War										
Bristol P.B.8	Never flew										
E (EAC = Eastbourne Aviation Company)											
EAC Military Biplane	1914	1P	B	1	2	-	75	~0.067	?	~1,200	?

1910-19 Civil Trainer aircraft continued on next page

APPENDIX 7, 1910-1919

Manufacturer & Aircraft	First Flight	No. Made	M.pln B.pln T.pln	No. Eng.	No. Crew	Max. passenger	Max. mph	pwr/wt ratio (HP/lb)	service ceiling (ft.)	Max wt. (lb.)	Max. Range (miles)
E, 1910-19 Civil Trainer aircraft, continued											
EAC = Eastbourne Aviation Company)											
EAC Seaplane (floatplane)	1914	1	B	1	2	-	65	0.0479	?	2,809	?
L											
London and Provincial Fuslage Biplane	1916	1P	B	1	1	-	75	0.0571	?	1,400	?
Also four developed designs: Single seater not built, two-seater versions refused a Certificate of Airworthiness											
R											
Ruffy, Arnell & Bauman "Advanced"	?	1P	B	1	1	-	?	?	?	?	?
V											
Vickers R.E.P. Type Monoplane	1911	8	M	1	2	-	56	~0.048	?	~1,250	?
Licenced adaptation of French Robert Esnault-Pelterie shoulder-wing monoplane (hence R.E.P.)											

Appendix 8

British Military And Civil Aircraft 1920–1929

Data in this Appendix is representative of aircraft type, usually early model. For exact data, refer to original sources.

BRITISH MILITARY AND CIVIL AIRCRAFT 1920-29

MILITARY AIRCRAFT

APPENDIX 8, 1920-29

P = Made as Prototype(s) Only   (NF) = Night Fighter   (TB) = Torpedo Bomber

power/weight ratio = [(total engine power) ÷ (max. weight)] = HP/lb

"Bomber aircraft 1920–1929"

Manufacturer & Aircraft	First Flight	No. Made	M.pln B.pln T.pln	No. Eng.	No. Crew	Max. bomb load (lb)	Max. mph	pwr/wt ratio (HP/lb)	service ceiling (ft.)	Max wt. (lb.)	Max. Range (miles)
A											
Armstrong Whitworth Atlas	1925	478	B	1	2	448	142	0.1119	16,500	4,020	400
Avro 549 Aldershot	1921	17	B	1	2	2,000	110	0.0594	14,500	10,950	625
Avro 557 Ava	1924	2P	B	2	5	2,200	115	0.0653	?	19,950	?
Avro 571 Buffalo	1926	1P	B	1	2	1,560	135	0.0713	13,700	7,430	650
Avro Antelope	1928	1P	B	1	2	500	173	0.1058	22,000	4,538	580
B											
Blackburn Beagle	1928	1P	B	1	2	?	140	0.0752	16,000	6,120	3½hrs
Blackburn Cubaroo (TB)	1924	2P	B	1	4	2,200	115	0.0526	11,800	19,020	1,800
Blackburn Dart (TB)	1921	124	B	1	1	1,040	107	0.0705	12,700	6,383	356
Blackburn Ripon (TB)	1926	92	B	1	2	1,380	111	0.0783	10,000	7,282	356
Boulton Paul Bugle	1923	7	B	2	3	640	112	0.1010	?	8,914	?
Boulton Paul Bodmin	1924	2P	B	2	3 / 4	?	116	0.0818	16,000	11,000	?
Engines in fuselage, shaft drive to each wing. Propellers were contra-rotating . One engine tractor, other pusher											
Boulton Paul Sidestrand	1926	20	B	2	3 / 4	1,040	139	0.0902	20,800	10,200	520
Bristol Berkeley	1925	3P	B	1	2	500	120	0.0800	?	8,128	12 hrs
D (DH = De Havilland)											
DH.27 Derby	1922	2P	B	1	3	2,200	105	0.0563	12,800	11,545	550
DH.65 Hound	1926	1P	B	1	2	460	153	0.1115	25,500	4,934	870
DH.56 Hyena	1925	2P	B	1	2	?	130	0.1005	19,230	4,200	?
F											
Fairey Fawn	1923	2P	B	1	2	460	114	0.0802	13,850	5,834	650

1920-29 Bomber aircraft continued on next page

F, 1920-29 Bomber aircraft, continued

Manufacturer & Aircraft	First Flight	No. Made	M.pln B.pln T.pln	No. Eng.	No. Crew	Max. bomb load (lb)	Max. mph	pwr/wt ratio (HP/lb)	service ceiling (ft.)	Max wt. (lb.)	Max. Range (miles)
Fairey Fox (1934 VIR variant data, 860 HP Hispano Suiza s'charged engine). *1926 RAF Fox 450 HP USA Curtiss engine - later Fox mostly R.R. Kestrel.	1925*	231	B	1	2	220	224	0.1663	32,800	5,710	634
1925 Fox I designed as PV, attracted RAF attention (50 mph faster than Fairey Fawn), ordered by RAF. Rolls Royce Kestrel engine introduced 1929, made Fox IIM competitive with 1928 Hawker Hart. Sold to Belgium (Avions Fairey producing some). Updated Fox VIR operated in WW2 by Belgian air force											
G											
Gloster Goring	1927	1P	B	1	2	690	136	0.0814	16,500	5,650	?
H											
Handley Page Hanley	1922	3P	B	1	1	?	116	0.0698	15,500	6,444	?
Handley Page Hare	1928	1P	B	1	1	2,000	152	0.0698	20,000	7,243	1,000
Handley Page Hendon	1924	6P	B	1	1	460	116	0.0646	15,000	6,444	?
Handley Page Hinaidi	1927	36	B	2	4	1,450	123	0.0611	14,900	14,400	850
H. Page 28 Handcross	1924	3P	B	1	2	550	120	0.0823	19,250	7,500	500
H. Page Hyderabad	1923	44	B	2	4	1,100	109	0.0736	14,000	13,5950	435
Hawker Harrier (TB)	1927	1P	B	1	2	1,000	135	0.1031	20,000	5,656	?
Hawker Hart (1930s, add 2,656 Hart derivatives)	1928	1,004	B	1	2	500	185	0.1109	22,800	4,554	470
1930s Hart variants:- Audax, Demon, Hardy, Hector, Hind, Osprey; see Appendix 9											
Hawker Horsley	1927	124	B	1	2	1,500	125	0.0833	14,000	7,800	900
N											
Nieuport London	1920	2P	T	2	2	2,250	100	0.0740	18,000	8,650	4 hrs
P											
Parnell Possum	1923	2P	T	1	3	?	105	0.0714	?	6,300	?
Possum has fuselage-mounted engine, shaft-driving tractor propeller on each wing (conttrs-rotating)											
V											
Vickers 131 Valiant	1927	1	B	1	2	500	130	0.1089	19,650	4,519	?
Vickers Type 163 (scaled-up Vanox , 4 engines)	1931	1P	B	4	4	3,000	160	0.0747	25,200	25,750	1,000
Type 163 flight delayed to 1931: 4-engined heavy/long-range: Vildebeest selected											
Vickers Vanox	1929	1P	B	2	4	2,200	125	0.0594	23,000	15,400	920

1920-29 Bomber aircraft continued on next page

APPENDIX 8, 1920-29

Manufacturer & Aircraft	First Flight	No. Made	M.pln B.pln T.pln	No. Eng.	No. Crew	Max. bomb load (lb)	Max. mph	pwr/wt ratio (HP/lb)	service ceiling (ft.)	Max wt. (lb.)	Max. Range (miles)
V, 1920-29 Bomber aircraft, continued											
Vickers Vildebeest (TB)	1928	209	B	1	2 or 3	1,100	140	0.0741	19,000	8,100	1,250
Vickers Vincent	1932	197	B	1	2 or 3	1,056	142	0.0784	19,000	8,100	1,250
(also used as general purpose aircraft)	The first batch of Vincents converted from Vildebeest										
Vickers Virginia (Vimy development)	1922	124	B	2	4	3,000	108	0.0658	13,800	17,620	985
W											
Westland Wapiti	1927	585	B	1	2	580	129	0.0776	18,800	5,410	313
Westland Witch	1928	1P	M	1	2	?	138	0.0694	19,000	6,050	?
Westland Yeovil	1925	3P	B	1	2	?	120	0.0827	?	7,864	?

"Fighter aircraft 1920–1929"

Manufacturer & Aircraft	First Flight	No. Made	M.pln B.pln T.pln	No. Eng.	No. Crew	Max. bomb load (lb)	Max. mph	pwr/wt ratio (HP/lb)	service ceiling (ft.)	Max wt. (lb.)	Max. Range (miles)
A											
Armstrong Whitworth Siskin	1921	485	B	1	1	-	156	0.1278	27,000	3,012	243
Armstrong Whitworth Siskin replaced Bristol Fighter. 1924 Siskin III was first all-metal RAF aircraft											
Armstrong Whitworth Starling	1927	2P	B	1	1	-	160	0.1486	?	3,095	?
Avro Avenger	1925	1P	B	1	1	-	180	0.1717	22,000	3,220	?
Avro Avocet	1927	2P	B	1	1	-	133	0.0922	23,000	2,495	?
B											
Beardmore W.B.XXVI	1925	1P	B	1	2	-	145	0.0905	20,000	3,980	4 hrs
Blackburn Lincock	1928	7	B	1	1	-	164	0.1297	23,000	2,082	380
Blackburn Nautilus	1929	1P	B	1	2	-	154	0.1105	18,800	4,750	375
Blackburn Turcock	1929	1P	B	1	1	-	176	0.1636	27,500	2,726	1¾ hrs
Boulton Paul Bittern (NF)	1927	2P	M	1	1	-	145	0.1022	?	4,500	3¾ hrs
Boulton Paul Partridge	1928	1P	B	1	1	-	167	0.1421	28,950	3,097	?
Bristol Bagshot	1927	1P	M	2	2	-	125	0.1098	?	8,195	?

1920-29 Fighter aircraft continued on next page

Manufacturer & Aircraft	First Flight	No. Made	M.pln B.pln T.pln	No. Eng.	No. Crew	Max. bomb load (lb)	Max. mph	pwr/wt ratio (HP/lb)	service ceiling (ft.)	Max wt. (lb.)	Max. Range (miles)
B, 1920-29 Fighter aircraft, continued											
Bristol Bulldog	1927	443	B	1	1	-	178	0.1261	29,300	3,490	?
Bristol Bullfinch	1922	3P	M	1	1	-	135	0.1326	22,000	3,205	4 hrs
Bristol Bullpup	1928	1P	B	1	1	-	190	0.1684	?	2,850	?
Bristol Jupiter Fighter	Jupiter engine thirsty, airflow over pilot upset gunner position: see civil trainer										
Bristol T. 84 Bloodhound	1923	4P	B	1	2	-	130	0.1003	22,000	4,236	3 hrs
Bristol Type 101	1927	1P	B	1	1	-	160	0.1271	?	3,560	?
D (DH = De Havilland)											
De Havilland DH.77	1929	1P	M	1	1	-	204	0,1316	25,900	2,297	?
DH.42A & 42B (Dingo I & II)	1923	2P	B	1	2	-	128	0.1026	15,700	3,897	?
DH.42 Dormouse	1923	1P	B	1	2	-	128	0.1078	15,700	3,897	?
F											
Fairey Firefly I	1925	1P	B	1	1	-	185	0.1579	?	2,724	?
Fairey Firefly II	1929	91	B	1	1	-	175	0.1461	30,840	3,404	240
Fairey Flycatcher	1922	196	B	1	1	-	133	0.1321	19,000	3,028	310
Fairey Pintail	1920	6	B	1	2	-	125	0.1011	?	4,700	?
G											
Gloster Gamecock	1925	108	B	1	1	-	155	0.1486	22,100	2,860	365
Gloster Gnatsnapper	1928	2P	B	1	1	-	154	0.1420	24,500	3,804	490
Gloster Goldfinch	1927	1P	B	1	1	-	172	0.1391	26,960	3,236	?
Gloster Gorcock	1925	3P	B	1	1	-	164	0.1416	24,000	3,179	1¾ hrs
Gloster Grebe	1923	133	B	1	1	-	152	0.1530	23,000	2,614	2¾ hrs
Gloster Grouse	1924	1P	B	1	2	-	120	0.0873	18,000	2,118	3¾ hrs
Gloster Guan	1926	2P	B	1	1	-	175	0.1380	31,000	3,803	?
Gloster Nightjar	1924	22	B	1	1	-	120	0.1062	19,000	2,165	2 hrs
Gloster Sparrowhawk	1921	91	B	1	1	-	125	0.1062	16,900	2,165	300
H											
Handley Page Type S	1923	2P	M	1	1	-	147	0.1133	21,000	2,030	3 hrs

1920-29 Fighter aircraft continued on next page

H, 1920-29 Fighter aircraft, continued

Manufacturer & Aircraft	First Flight	No. Made	M.pln B.pln T.pln	No. Eng.	No. Crew	Max. bomb load (lb)	Max. mph	pwr/wt ratio (HP/lb)	service ceiling (ft.)	Max wt. (lb.)	Max. Range (miles)
Hawker Danecock	1925	15	B	1	1	-	145	0.1264	22,800	3,045	?
Hawker F.20/27	1928	1P	B	1	1	-	202	0.1651	?	3,150	?
Hawker Hawfinch	1927	1P	B	1	1	-	171	0.1546	24,000	2,910	?
Hawker Heron	1925	1P	B	1	1	-	156	0.1456	23,300	3,126	3½hrs
Hawker Hoopoe	1928	1P	B	1	1	-	197	0.1432	23,600	3,910	?
Hawker Hornbill	1925	1P	B	1	1	-	187	0.1827	22,700	3,769	300
Hawker Woodcock	1923	64	B	1	1	-	141	0.1427	20,550	2,979	280
N											
Nieuport Nighthawk	1919	70	B	1	1	-	151	0.1443	24,500	2,218	3 hrs

(Nighthawk intended as Sopwith Snipe replacement) ABC Dragonfly engine problems caused RAF to reject.
After Nieuport closed down, Gloster redesigned as 1921 Sparrowhawk, later re-winged as Grouse (prototype Grebe)..

Manufacturer & Aircraft	First Flight	No. Made	M.pln B.pln T.pln	No. Eng.	No. Crew	Max. bomb load (lb)	Max. mph	pwr/wt ratio (HP/lb)	service ceiling (ft.)	Max wt. (lb.)	Max. Range (miles)
P											
Parnall Pipit	1928	2P	B	1	1	-	173	0.1244	?	3,980	?
Parnall Plover	1922	13	B	1	1	-	142	0.1461	23,000	2,984	?
Parnall Puffin	1920	3	B	1	1	-	110	0.0900	?	5,000	?

Parnall Puffin was experimental amphibious seaplane

Manufacturer & Aircraft	First Flight	No. Made	M.pln B.pln T.pln	No. Eng.	No. Crew	Max. bomb load (lb)	Max. mph	pwr/wt ratio (HP/lb)	service ceiling (ft.)	Max wt. (lb.)	Max. Range (miles)
S											
Saunders A.10	1929	1P	B	1	1	-	200	0.1384	?	3,980	?
Supermarine Sea King (flying boat)	1920	2P	B	1	1	-	125	0.1053	?	2,850	2 hrs
V											
Vickers Type 123	1926	1P	B	1	1	-	149	0.1212	?	3,300	?
Vickers Type 143	1929	6	B	1	1	-	150	0.1442	20,000	3,120	?
Vickers Vireo	1928	1P	M	1	1	-	120	0.0901	14,750	2,553	?
Vickers Vixen (Fighter/Bomber)	1923	20	B	1	2	-	134	0.0984	20,000	5,080	664

Single example of all-metal version of Vixen produced as Vivid, first flight 1923

Manufacturer & Aircraft	First Flight	No. Made	M.pln B.pln T.pln	No. Eng.	No. Crew	Max. bomb load (lb)	Max. mph	pwr/wt ratio (HP/lb)	service ceiling (ft.)	Max wt. (lb.)	Max. Range (miles)
Vickers Wibault	1926	26	M	1	1	-	144	0.1532	23,000	2,970	300

Vickers Wibault was licence-built French Wibault company design

1920-29 Fighter aircraft continued on next page

APPENDIX 8, 1920-29

W, 1920-29 Fighter aircraft, continued

Manufacturer & Aircraft	First Flight	No. Made	M.pln B.pln T.pln	No. Eng.	No. Crew	Max. bomb load (lb)	Max. mph	pwr/wt ratio (HP/lb)	service ceiling (ft.)	Max wt. (lb.)	Max. Range (miles)
Westland Interceptor	1929	1P	M	1	1	-	192	0.1323	?	3,325	385
Westland Westbury	1926	2P	B	2	3	-	125	0.1143	?	7,787	?
Westland Wizard	1928	1P	M	1	1	-	188	0.1473	17,500	3,326	?

"Patrol aircraft 1920–1929"

Manufacturer & Aircraft	First Flight	No. Made	M.pln B.pln T.pln	No. Eng.	No. Crew	Max. bomb load (lb)	Max. mph	pwr/wt ratio (HP/lb)	service ceiling (ft.)	Max wt. (lb.)	Max. Range (miles)
Blackburn Iris	1926	5	B	3	5	-	118	0.0687	10,600	29,489	800
Iris was a flying boat (later developed as 1933 four-engined Perth)											
Blackburn Velos (float plane)	1925	22	B	1	3	-	107	0.0669	13,400	6,730	1300
R											
R38-class airship	1921	1	Project cancelled, structural failure and crash on fifth flight								
S											
Saunders Roe Cutty Sark (flying boat)	1929	12	M	2	2	-	90	0.0718	9,000	3900	315
A.17 Cutty Sark was first product of company after Alliott Verdon Roe and John Lord joined Sam Saunders											
Short Cromarty (flying boat)	1921	1P	B	2	4	-	95	0.0722	?	18,000	900
Supermarine Nanok (flying boat)	1927	1P	B	3	5	-	114	0.0791	10,920	16,311	640
V											
Vickers Valentia (flying boat)	1921	3	B	2	5	-	105	0.0563	?	21,300	?

1920-29 Reconnaissance aircraft on next page

APPENDIX 8, 1920-29

"Reconnaissance aircraft 1920–1929"

Manufacturer & Aircraft	First Flight	No. Made	M.pln B.pln T.pln	No. Eng.	No. Crew	Max. bomb load (lb)	Max. mph	pwr/wt ratio (HP/lb)	service ceiling (ft.)	Max wt. (lb.)	Max. Range (miles)
A											
Armstrong Whitworth Wolf	1923	6	B	1	2	-	110	0.0856	15,150	4,090	3¾hrs
Avro Bison	1921	3	B	1	4	-	108	0.0783	12,000	6,132	360
B											
Blackburn Airedale	1924	2P	M	1	3	-	120	0.0779	?	4,962	?
Blackburn Blackburn	1922	44	B	1	3	-	122	0.0755	12,950	5,962	4¼hrs
Boulton & Paul Bolton	1922	1P	B	2	3	-	?	0.0947	?	9,500	?
Bristol Bullfinch I	1922	2P	M	1	1	-	135	0.1326	22,000	3,205	4 hrs
Bristol Bullfinch II	1922	1P	B	1	2	-	120	0.1040	18,000	4,088	?
Bristol T. 84 Bloodhound	1923	4P	B	1	2	-	130	0.1003	22,000	4,236	3 hrs
E											
English Electric Ayr	1924	2P	B	1	2	?	127	0.0657	14,500	6,846	?
Ayr designed while Kingston built, both were flying boats: Ayr refused to take off. The day last Kingston finished, E.Electric closed aircraft design function until 1944											
English Electric Kingston (P.5 Cork + new hull and other changes)	1924	6P	B	2	6	-	105	0.0620	14,508	9,060	8/9hrs
English Electric bought Phoenix Dynamo (Leeds). Phoenix had designed and built the P.5 Cork flying boat to same requirement as 1916 Felixstowe F.5 and actually built 17 of the 163 F.5.											
F											
Fairey Fleetwing	1929	1P	B	1	2	-	169	0.1267	?	4,737	?
Fairey Fremantle (float plane)	1924	1P	B	1	5	-	108	0.0818	?	12,550	1,000
Fairey Fleetwing	1929	1P	B	1	2	-	169	0.1267	?	4,737	?
Fairey N.4 (flying boat)	1923	3	B	4	5	1,000	115	0.0822	14,100	31,612	9 hrs
H											
Hawker Duiker	1923	1P	M	1	1	-	125	0.0828	14,500	4,940	340
Hawker Hedgehog	1924	1P	B	1	3	-	121	0.0829	13,500	4,800	2½hrs

1920-29 Reconnaissance aircraft continued on next page

P, 1920-29 Reconnaissance aircraft, continued

Manufacturer & Aircraft	First Flight	No. Made	M.pln B.pln T.pln	No. Eng.	No. Crew	Max. bomb load (lb)	Max. mph	pwr/wt ratio (HP/lb)	service ceiling (ft)	Max wt. (lb.)	Max. Range (miles)
Parnall Pike (changeable, land plane to float plane)	1927	1P	B	1	2/3	-	127	0.0709	?	6,350	?
Parnall Peto (float plane)	1925	2	B	1	2	-	113	0.0692	11,300	1,950	2 hrs
A reconnaissance aircraft with backward-folding wings (carried in watertight hangar on submarine)											
Short Singapore I (S.5)	1924	1P	B	2	4	-	95	0.0539	?	18,000	900
Experimental aircraft: Metal hull version of 1921 Short Cromarty (flying boat) patrol aircraft											
Short S.6 Sturgeon	1927	2P	B	1	3	-	115	0.0837	?	6,213	?
Short S.3 Springbok (developed from 1920 Short Silver Streak)	1923	6P	b	1	3	-	105	0.0890	?	4,080	?
Short Springbok built in 3 versions (Springbok I & II, Chamois). Springbok 1 values											
Supermarine Scylla	1921	1P	Twin engined flying boat, never took off (taxy trials only)								
Supermarine Seagull	1921	34	B	1	3	1,000	80	0.0879	9,000	5,462	3½hrs
Supermarine Seagull was amphibian. See also 1948 Supermarine Seagull type 381											
Supermarine Seal	1928	2P	B	2	3	-	95	0.0821	10,950	5,800	?
Supermarine Seamew	1927	1P	Supermarine Seagull flying boat with revised hull								
Supermarine Sheldrake	1927	1	B	1	3	1,000	103	0.0738	?	6,100	250
Developed from Supermarine Seagull											
Supermarine Southampton	1925	83	B	2	5	1,000	95	0.0658	5,950	15,200	544
Supermarine Southampton flying boat developed from 1924 Supermarine Swan											
Supermarine Swan	1924	1	B	2	2	?	109	0.0490	10,200	13,710	300
Supermarine Swan originally built as amphibian. Loaned as flying boat to Imperial Airways											
V											
Vickers 131 Valiant	see Bomber aircraft										
Vickers Valparaiso (export)	1926	28	B	1	2	-	136	0.0922	19,500	4,720	478
Vickers Venture (export)	1924	6	B	1	2	-	129	0.0920	19,200	4,890	?
Valparaiso & Venture reconn./bomber: export versions of 1923 Vickers fighter/bomber											
Vickers Vespa	1925	15	B	1	2	?	139	0.1121	26,000	4,370	504

1920-29 Military Trainer aircraft on next page

APPENDIX 8, 1920-29

"Military Trainer Aircraft 1920-29"

Manufacturer & Aircraft	First Flight	No. Made	M.pln B.pln T.pln	No. Eng.	No. Crew	Max. bomb load (lb)	Max. mph	pwr/wt ratio (HP/lb)	service ceiling (ft.)	Max wt. (lb.)	Max. Range (miles)
A											
Avro Tutor	1929	606	B	1	2	-	120	0.0963	16,000	2,493	0.0963
B											
Blackburn Sprat	1926	1P	B	1	2	-	115	0.0854	17,500	3,220	?
Blackburn Sprat was a convertible land-seaplane to Air Ministry specification 5/24											
D (DH = De Havilland)											
DH. 53 Humming Bird	see Civil Utility aircraft										
H											
Hawker Tomtit	1928	35	B	1	2	-	124	0.0857	19,500	1,750	350
P											
Parnall Perch	1926	1P	B	1	2	-	115	0.0600	12,000	4,500	500
V											
Vickers Vendace	1926	5	B	1	2	-	119	0.0935	25,800	3,207	?
Vickers Vendace was a convertible land-seaplane to Air Ministry specification 5/24											
Vickers VIM	1920	35	B	1	2	-	100	0.0985	13,000	3,654	2¾ hrs
VIM = Vickers Instructional Machine, parts from Royal Aircraft Factory F.E.2 1915 military bomber but with dual controls and twice engine power. All sold to China.											

"Military Transport aircraft 1920-1929"

Manufacturer & Aircraft	First Flight	No. Made	M.pln B.pln T.pln	No. Eng.	No. Crew	Max. bomb load (lb)	Max. mph	pwr/wt ratio (HP/lb)	service ceiling (ft.)	Max wt. (lb.)	Max. Range (miles)
A											
Armstrong-Whitworth Awana	1923	2	B	2	2	25	97	0.0488	8,000	18,450	340
Avro Andover (1924)	1924	4	B	1	2	12	110	0.0573	13,500	11,500	460

1920-29 Military Transport aircraft continued on next page

APPENDIX 8, 1920-29

B, 1920-29 Military Transport aircraft, continued

Manufacturer & Aircraft	First Flight	No. Made	M.pln B.pln T.pln	No. Eng.	No. Crew	Max. bomb load (lb)	Max. mph	pwr/wt ratio (HP/lb)	service ceiling (ft)	Max wt. (lb.)	Max. Range (miles)
Beardmore Inflexible	1928	1P	M	3	2	?	109	0.0527	?	37,000	?
Used stressed skin principle of German Rohrbach aircraft. Wing span 157 ft. 6 in. (nearly 48 metres), which is greater than that of Boeing B-29 Stratofortress of Second World war (see max. weight)											
D (DH = De Havilland)											
DH.75 Hawk Moth	1928	8	M	1	1	3	127	0.0656	14,500	3,650	560
V											
Vickers Vellore (Vellore III twin-engined data)	1923	4	B	2	2	10	127	0.0808	?	13,000	300
4 aircraft built:- Velore I single-engined, carried 1,000 lbs. of cargo (mail), re-engined as Velore II. Velore III and IV and Vellox 10-passenger airliner had two engines											
Vickers Vernon	1921	55	B	2	3	11	100	0.0717	11,700	12,554	320
Vernon a conversion design of Vickers Vimy Commercial airliner of 1919, derived from 1918 Vimy bomber											
Vickers Victoria	1922	97	B	2	2	22	110	0.0642	16,200	17,760	770
Victoria a conversion design of Vickers Virginia bomber of 1922, a development of 1918 Vimy bomber 54 Vickers Victoria were converted to Vickers Valentia in the 1930s; see Appendix 9											
W											
Westland IV	1929	2P	M	3	2	6	?	0.0452	?	<6,300	420
Both Westland IV prototypes had 95 HP to 140 HP engine change, to become Wessex airliner; see 1930-39 airliner, Appendix 9											

"Military Utility aircraft 1920–1929"

Manufacturer & Aircraft	First Flight	No. Made	M.pln B.pln T.pln	No. Eng.	No. Crew	Max. bomb load (lb)	Max. mph	pwr/wt ratio (HP/lb)	service ceiling (ft)	Max wt. (lb.)	Max. Range (miles)
A											
Armstrong- Whitworth Ape	1926	3	B	1	2	-	90	0.0550	6,400	3,250	?
The Ape was an experimental aircraft, tail/rudder assembly adjustable in flight to investigate pitch trim											

1920-29 Military Utility aircraft continued on next page

APPENDIX 8, 1920-29

Manufacturer & Aircraft	First Flight	No. Made	M.pln B.pln T.pln	No. Eng.	No. Crew	Max. bomb load (lb)	Max. mph	pwr/wt ratio (HP/lb)	service ceiling (ft.)	Max wt. (lb.)	Max. Range (miles)
B, 1920-29 Military Utility aircraft, continued											
Bristol Boarhound	1925	4	B	1	2	-	135	0.0953	22,000	4,460	3 hrs
F											
Fairey Ferret	1925	3	B	1	2	-	135	0.0892	15,500	4,765	?
Fairey Long-range Monoplane (RAF aircraft)	1928	2	M	1	2	-	~130	0.0326	?	17,500	?
Fairey L.Range Monoplane: In 1929 the first aircraft crashed in a second attempt on the world distance record. In 1933 the second aircraft flew the record geographic distance of 5,410 miles, from Cranwell in England to Walvis Bay, South West Africa.											
W											
Westland Dreadnought	1924	1P	M	1	2	8	102	0.0652	?	6,900	?
Westland Dreadnought was all-metal experimental monoplane, "all-over aerofoil shape". Theoretical concept of Russian N. Woyevodsky. Crashed on first flight											

Civil Aircraft 1920-29 next page

APPENDIX 8, 1920-29

BRITISH CIVIL AIRCRAFT 1920-1929

pwr/wt ratio = power/weight ratio = [(total engine power) ÷ (max. weight)] = HP/lb

"Airliners 1920-1929"

Manufacturer & Aircraft	First Flight	No. Made	M.pln B.pln T.pln	No. Eng.	No. Crew	Max. passenger	Max. mph	pwr/wt ratio (HP/lb)	service ceiling (ft)	Max wt. (lb.)	Max. Range (miles)
A (ANEC = Air Navigation Engineering Company)											
ANEC III	1926	3	B	1	1	6	105	0.0680	14,508	5,591	450
Armstrong-Whitworth Argosy 124	1926	7	B	3	2	20	110	0.0656	?	19,200	405
Avro 547	1920	2	T	1	1	4	83	0.0533	?	3,000	230
B											
Boulton Paul Atlantic	1920	2P	B	2	1	7	149	0.1142	25,000	7,880	?
B.Paul Atlantic adaptation of B. Paul Bourges bomber (intended to replace DH.10)											
Bristol Grampus	None built										
Bristol Pullman	1920	1P	T	4	2	14	135	0.0901	15,000	17,750	~1000
Bristol Pullman developed from 1918 Bristol Braemar Bomber, which had 2 engines each wing driving paired in-line pusher/tractor propellers											
Bristol Seely	1920	1P	B	1	1	1	110	0.0800	18,000	3,000	?
Bristol Ten-seater (Brandon in RAF)	1921	3	B	1	2	8	110	0.0629	8,500	6,755	5½hrs
Type 65, Type 75 & Type 79 (Brandon) 3 different variants (Brandon high weight)											
Bristol Tramp	2 built in 1921: Two steam engines replaced 4 petrol engines in fuselage. Never flew										
D (DH = De Havilland)											
De Havilland DH.18	1920	6	B	1	1	8	125	0.0691	16,000	6,515	400
De Havilland DH.34	1922	12	B	1	2	10	128	0.0625	?	7,200	365
De Havilland DH.50	1923	38	B	1	1	4	112	0.0590	14,600	3,900	380
De Havilland DH.61 Giant Moth	1927	10	B	1	1	6-8	132	0.0714	18,000	7,000	450
De Havilland DH. 29 Doncaster	1921	2P	M	1	2	?	116	0.0600	?	7,500	?
DH.Doncaster was a monoplane cantilever-wing experimental version of DH.34. Eventually used as military/government transport											
DH.66 Hercules	1926	11	B	3	3	7	129	0.0808	13,100	15,600	525

1920-29 Airliners continued on next page

APPENDIX 8, 1920-29

Manufacturer & Aircraft	First Flight	No. Made	M.pln B.pln T.pln	No. Eng.	No. Crew	Max. passenger	Max. mph	pwr/wt ratio (HP/lb)	service ceiling (ft.)	Max wt. (lb.)	Max. Range (miles)
D, 1920-29 Airliners, continued											
DH.54 Highclere	1925	1	B	1	2	12-15	110	0.0578	?	11,250	400
DH.54 Highclere was extended version of DH.34 but was not adopted when Imperial Airways decided not to use single-engined aircraft (for safety reasons)											
H											
Handasyde H.2	1922	1P	M	1	1	6	115	0.0720	?	5,000	?
Handley Page Type W (W8f data)	1929	25	B	3	2	12	103	0.0646	13,000	13,000	>700
Handley Page Type W8 in 9 different variants (incl. W9 & W10), essentially conversions of O/400 bombers.											
First (twin-engined) W8 flew in 1921, 3-engined W8f flew in 1929											
R											
R36 (airship)	1921	1				During several trial flights, damaged/repaired/damaged/scrapped					
R80 (airship)	1920	1				Too small for intended use, eventually scrapped					
R100 (airship)	1929	1				After 1930 trans-Atlantic trial, eventually scrapped (see R.101)					
R101 (airship)	1929	1				After crash in France in 1930, all UK airship development curtailed					
S											
Saunders Kittiwake (flying boat)	1920	1P	B	2	2	7	110	0.0667	?	6,000	>340
Saunders Medina (flying boat)	1926	1P	B	2	2	10	115	0.0779	?	11,560	360
Short S.8 Calcutta	1928	7	B	3	3	15	118	0.0720	13,500	22,500	650
Short S.8 Calcutta: 3-engined adaptation of 1924 military Short Singapore I flying boat											
Sopwith Antelope	1920	1	B	1	1	2	110	0.0522	?	3,450	~450
Supermarine Commercial (Amphibian)	1920	1P	B	1	1	2	94	0.0614	?	5,700	312
Supermarine Commercial basis for Seal design (pre-prototype of Seagull reconnaissance aircraft)											
Supermarine Sea Eagle	1923	3	B	2	2	6	93	0.0595	?	6,050	230
W											
Vickers 170 Vanguard	1923	1	B	2	2	22	112	0.0703	16,400	18,500	?
Vickers Vulcan	1922	8	B	1	1	6-8	112	0.0667	16,400	6,750	430

1920-29 Sports, Racer, Tourer and Sailplane aircraft on next page

"1920-29 Sports, Racer, Tourer and Sailplane aircraft "
(includes 1923, 1924 and 1926 Lympne Light Aircraft Competition types)

Manufacturer & Aircraft	First Flight	No. Made	M.pln B.pln T.pln	No. Eng.	No. Crew	Max. passenger	Max. mph	pwr/wt ratio (HP/lb)	service ceiling (ft.)	Max wt. (lb.)	Max. Range (miles)
A											
Avro Avian	1926	405	B	1	2	-	105	0.0689	12,500	1,523	360
Avro Avis	1924	1	B	1	1	-	75	0.0352	?	995	?
B											
Beardmore Wee Bee	1924	1	M	1	2	-	87	0.0381	?	840	?
Blackburn Bluebird	1924	20	B	1	2	-	88	0.0577	?	1,385	?
B'burn Bluebird IV	1929	58	B	1	2	-	120	0.0571	?	1,750	320
Blackburn Pellet	1923	1	B	1	1	-	~160	0.1607	?	2,800	?
Boulton Paul Phoenix	1929	1	M	1	1	1	86	0.0367	?	1,089	?
Bristol Badminton	1926	1	B	1	1	-	160	0.2073	?	2,460	?
Bristol Brownie	1924	3	M	1	1	1	70	0.0368	?	870	100
Bristol Bullet	1920	1	B	1	1	-	155	0.2055	?	2,200	?
Bristol Racer	1922	1	M	1	1	-	~220	?	?	?	?

Bristol Racer had 480 HP Bristol Jupiter engine in circular streamlined fuselage.   Aerodynamic/control difficulties, never raced and was scrapped in 1924

Manufacturer & Aircraft	First Flight	No. Made	M.pln B.pln T.pln	No. Eng.	No. Crew	Max. passenger	Max. mph	pwr/wt ratio (HP/lb)	service ceiling (ft.)	Max wt. (lb.)	Max. Range (miles)
C (*RAF Cranwell designs)											
Civilian Coupé	1929	5	M	1	1	-	110	0.0667	?	1,500	?
Clarke Cheetah	1929	1	M/B	1	1	2	?	0.0516	?	678	?

Amateur built, could fly either as biplane or high-wing monoplane

*Cranwell CLA.2	1924	1	B	1	2	-	63	0.0357	?	897	?
*Cranwell CLA.3	1925	1	M	1	1	-	100	0.0604	?	530	175
*Cranwell CLA.4	1926	3	B	1	2	-	65	0.0410	?	874	?
D (DH = De Havilland)											
DH.60 Moth	1925	~1900	B	1	1	1	102	0.0606	14,500	1,650	320
DH.71 Tiger Moth*	1927	2	M	1	1	-	166	0.0939	?	905	?

* **not 1931 DH.82**: DH.71 first to be named "Tiger Moth".
High power engine (135 HP) replaced "usual" 85 HP engine for attempt on 100 km closed circuit record, achieving 193mph.

1920-29 Sports, Racer, Tourer and Sailplane aircraft continued on next page

APPENDIX 8, 1920-29

Manufacturer & Aircraft	First Flight	No. Made	M.pln B.pln T.pln	No. Eng.	No. Crew	Max. passenger	Max. mph	pwr/wt ratio (HP/lb)	service ceiling (ft.)	Max wt. (lb.)	Max. Range (miles)
D, 1920-29 Sports, Racer, Tourer and Sailplane aircraft, continued											
DH. 80 Puss Moth	1929	284	M	1	1	2	128	0.0585	17,500	2,050	300
G											
Gloster Gannet	1923	1	B	1	1	-	72	0.0152	?	460	140
Gloster II	1924	2	B	1	1	-	225	0.1887	?	3,100	?
Gloster III	1925	2	B	1	1	-	225	0.2605	?	2,687	?
Gloster IV	1927	3	B	1	1	-	295	0.2678	?	3,305	1.1 hr
Gloster VI	1929	2	M	1	1	-	351	0.3587	?	3,680	?
Gloster II, III, III & VI were designed to enter Schneider Trophy races (did not win). Gloster V not built											
Gnosspelius Gull	1923	2	M	1	1	-	70	0.0456	?	570	?
Gull: Designer Major O.T. Gnosspelius (Head of Research at Shorts) - Shorts built it											
H											
Halton Mayfly	1927	1	B	1	1	-	84	0.0348	?	920	?
designed by C.H. Latimer-Needham and built by Halton Aero Club (RAF Halton)											
Handasyde glider	1922	1	M	n/a	1	-	n/a	n/a	n/a	?	n/a
Handasyde Monoplane	1923	1	M	1	1	-	62	?	?	500	?
Handley Page 22/23	1922	3	M	1	1	-	?	?	?	430	?
L											
LPW Glider (semi-professional project)	1924	1	M	n/a	1	-	?	n/a	n/a	?	n/a
Designed and built by John Leeming, Tom Prince & Clement Wood (in 1922, founded Lancashire Aero Club)											
M											
Manuel Biplane Glider (enthusiast design)	1929	1	B	n/a	1	-	?	n/a	n/a	?	n/a
Bill Manuel design, mostly flown tethered to ground in propwash of Gloster Grebe											
Martinsyde Semiquaver	1920	1	B	1	1	-	161	?	?	?	?
P											
Parnall Elf	1929	3	B	1	2	-	116	0.0676	?	~1,500	?
Parnall Imp	1927	1	B	1	2	-	>110	0.0606	?	1,320	?
Parnall Pixie	1923	3	M	1	1	-	81	?	?	460	?

1920-29 Sports, Racer, Tourer and Sailplane aircraft continued on next page

APPENDIX 8, 1920-29

Manufacturer & Aircraft	First Flight	No. Made	M.pln B.pln T.pln	No. Eng.	No. Crew	Max. passenger	Max. mph	pwr/wt ratio (HP/lb)	service ceiling (ft.)	Max wt. (lb.)	Max. Range (miles)
R, 1920-29 Sports, Racer, Tourer and Sailplane aircraft, continued											
RAE (club) Zephyr	1923	1	B	1	1	-	53	0.268	?	635	?
RAE (club) Hurricane	1923	1	M	1	1	-	85	0.0582	?	550	?
S											
Salmon Tandem Monoplane	Monoplane produced for 1923 Lympne light aircraft trials but failed to fly										
Short Cockle	1924	1P	M	2	1		73	0.0531	?	1,205	?
Short Cockle was flying boat with novel duraluminium monocoque hull											
Short Mussel	1926	2	M	1	2	-	82	0.0412	?	1,576	260
Short Mussel was float plane with duraluminium floats											
Short Satellite	1924	1	M	1	1	-	72	0.0311	?	1,060	?
Simmonds Spartan	1928	48	B	1	1	1	100	0.0595	?	1,680	?
Supermarine Sparrow	1924	1	M	1	2	-	72	0.0407	11,000	860	?
1920s Schneider Trophy Entries #											
Short Crusader # (float plane)	1927	1	M	1	1	-	270	0.2987	?	2,712	?
Due to aileron control "cross" error on assembly for race, crashed and destroyed											
Supermarine S.4 # (float plane)	1925	listed "out of sequence in 1930-39 Appendix 9", alongside Supermarine S.6B									
Supermarine Sea Lion II #	1922	1	B	1	1	-	160	0.1579	?	2,850	?
Supermarine Sea Lion II flying boat winner of 1922 race											
Supermarine Sea Urchin #	Flying boat design intended as 1924 Schneider trophy contender, abandoned before construction										
Supermarine S.5 # (float plane)	1927	listed "out of sequence in 1930-39 Appendix 9", alongside Supermarine S.6B									
Supermarine S.6 # (float plane)	1929	listed "out of sequence in 1930-39 Appendix 9", alongside Supermarine S.6B									
V											
Vickers Vagabond	1924	1	B	1	1	1	77	0.0361	?	887	?
Vickers Viget	1923	1	B	1	1	-	58	0.0184	?	570	?
W											
Westland Widgeon (fixed wing, not the 1955 helicopter)	1924	26	M	1	2	-	104	0.0727	15,000	1,650	315

1920-29 Sports, Racer, Tourer and Sailplane aircraft, continued on next page

Manufacturer & Aircraft	First Flight	No. Made	M.pln B.pln T.pln	No. Eng.	No. Crew	Max. passenger	Max. mph	pwr/wt ratio (HP/lb)	service ceiling (ft.)	Max wt. (lb.)	Max. Range (miles)
W, 1920-29 Sports, Racer, Tourer and Sailplane aircraft, continued											
Westland-Hill Pterodactyl (series)	Pterodactyl Mk.I, Mk.IV & Mk.V built as tail-less"arrow-head" flying wings (inherently stable) experimental configuration but not converted to production. Derived from John Dunne 1910-1914 experiments.										

"Civil Trainer aircraft 1920-1929"

Manufacturer & Aircraft	First Flight	No. Made	M.pln B.pln T.pln	No. Eng.	No. Crew	Max. passenger	Max. mph	pwr/wt ratio (HP/lb)	service ceiling (ft.)	Max wt. (lb.)	Max. Range (miles)
B											
Bristol Jupiter F.2 Fighter (Trainer) (unusable as fighter)	1928	26	B	1	2	-	110	0.0985	22,150	3,250	340
Re-engined 1916 Bristol F.2B design. Observer gun unusable, 23 aircraft built as high-powered pilot trainer											
D											
DH.60 Moth	see 1920-29 Sports aircraft										
DH. 80 Puss Moth	see 1920-29 Sports aircraft										
Simmonds Spartan	see 1920-29 Sports aircraft										
Surrey Flying Services AL.1 (semi-professional)	1929	1	B	1	1	1	110	0.0792	?	1,200	200

"Civil Utility aircraft 1920-1929"

Manufacturer & Aircraft	First Flight	No. Made	M.pln B.pln T.pln	No. Eng.	No. Crew	Max. passenger	Max. mph	pwr/wt ratio (HP/lb)	service ceiling (ft.)	Max wt. (lb.)	Max. Range (miles)
A											
ABC Robin	1929	1	M	1	1	-	105	0.0588	17,000	680	340
Airship Development AD1	1929	1	Non-rigid airship used for advertising								
ANEC = Air Navigation engineering Company											
ANEC I (& ANEC II)	1923	3 + 1	M	1	1	-	74	0.0468	?	470	?
ANEC IV	1926	1	B	1	1	-	80	0.0304	?	1,150	?

1920-29 Civil Utility aircraft continued on next page

APPENDIX 8, 1920-29

Manufacturer & Aircraft	First Flight	No. Made	M.pln B.pln T.pln	No. Eng.	No. Crew	Max. passenger	Max. mph	pwr/wt ratio (HP/lb)	service ceiling (ft)	Max wt. (lb.)	Max. Range (miles)
A, 1920-29 Civil Utility aircraft, continued											
Austin Kestrel	1920	1P	B	1	2	-	110	0.0584	?	2,740	?
Avro 558	1923	2	B	1	1	-	?	0.0375	13,850	480	?
Avro 560	1923	1P	M	1	1	-	?	0.0425	?	471	?
B											
Bristol Primary Trainer	1923	28	B	1	2	-	96	0.0737	?	1,900	?
Originally built as 2-passenger Type 73 taxi/tourer aircraft, mostly Type 83 training aircraft (tandem cockpits)											
Bristol Type 92	1925	1	B	1	2	-	132	0.1324	26,000	3,400	?
Bristol 92 experimental type, to determine drag of different cowls on radial engines											
C											
Cierva Experimental autogyros											
Cierva/Avro C.8	1926	1P	n/a	1	1	-	100	?	?	?	?
Cierva/Avro C.9	1927	1P	n/a	1	1	purpose-built fuselage, no data					
Cierva/Avro C.12	1929	1P	n/a	1	1	1930: 2-man cockpit removed & floats added for first-ever rotary wing water-borne take-off					
Cierva/Avro C.17	1928	2P	n/a	1	1	-	90	0.0619	?	1,455	210
Cierva/Avro C.19	1929	>30	n/a	1	1	1	95	0.0750	?	1,400	300
D (DH = De Havilland)											
DH.37	1922	2	B	1	1	2	122	0.0829	21,000	3,318	?
DH.51	1924	3	B	1	1	2	108	0.0590	14,600	3,900	380
DH.53 Humming Bird	1923	15	M	1	1	-	73	0.0460	15,000	565	130
DH.53 originally built for light aircraft competition, later sold to RAF and export											
DH. 60 Moth	see 1920-29 Sports aircraft										
DH.80 Puss Moth	see 1920-29 Sports aircraft										
E											
English Electric Wren	1921	3	M	1	1	-	50	0.0179	?	420	?
English Electric Wren was essentially a motor glider											

1920-29 Civil Utility aircraft continued on next page

APPENDIX 8, 1920-29

Manufacturer & Aircraft	First Flight	No. Made	M.pln B.pln T.pln	No. Eng.	No. Crew	Max. passenger	Max. mph	pwr/wt ratio (HP/lb)	service ceiling (ft.)	Max wt. (lb.)	Max. Range (miles)
G, 1920-29 Civil Utility aircraft, continued											
Gloster A.S. 31 Survey	1929	2	B	2	3	-	131	0.1225	21,900	8,570	495
Specially ordered survey aircraft, needing good performance in hot climate											
H											
Handley Page HP.20	1921	After tests on DH.9A with added wing leading edge slots (the H.P 17), the HP.20 (DH.9A + new Handley Page monoplane wing + controllable leading edge slots) tested improvements in lift and increased stalling incidence.									
Handley Page HP.39 Gugnunc	1929	1P	B	1	2	-	112	0.0688	?	2,180	?
Handley Page Gugnunc was a one-off special low speed/high lift trials aircraft. It had wing leading edge slots and trailing edge flaps.											
Handley Page HP.32 Hamlet	1926	1P	M	2	1	6	114	0.0800	?	5,000	?
Hawker Cygnet	1924	2	B	1	2	-	82	0.0358	8,900	950	?
Henderson H.S.F.1	1921	1	M	1	1	5	105	0.0584	?	4,112	350
Henderson–Glenny Gadfly	1929	3	M	1	1	-	<80	0.0467	?	750	350
Henderson H.S.F.1, and Henderson–Glenny Gadfly were designs created for owner of Henderson School of Flying (built "in a shed")											
Hendy 302	1929	1	M	1	1	1	130	0.0684	?	1,900	?
Hendy Hobo	1929	1	M	1	1	-	130	0.1385	?	650	?
L											
Lowe Marlburian	1922	1	M	1	2	-	100	0.0667	?	~900	?
Self-design/build by T.H. Lowe, Newcastle-upon-Tyne (his 7th attempt at an aircraft). (The T.H. Lowe name is sometimes confused with a supposed brother F.H. Lowe)											
P											
Parnall Elf	1929	See Sports aircraft									

1920-29 Civil Utility aircraft continued on next page

APPENDIX 8, 1920-29

Manufacturer & Aircraft	First Flight	No. Made	M.pln B.pln T.pln	No. Eng.	No. Crew	Max. passenger	Max. mph	pwr/wt ratio (HP/lb)	service ceiling (ft.)	Max wt. (lb.)	Max. Range (miles)
S, 1920-29 Civil Utility aircraft, continued											
Saunders A.14 (flying boat)	1928	1P	B	2	5	-	97	0.0714	8,500	15,200	6½hrs
Saunders A.14 was a metal hull adaptation of 1925 Supermarine Southampton reconnaissance aircraft											
Saunders Helicogyre	Ministry specification for Isacco Helicogyre built by Saunders, transported by road to RAE, never flew										
Simmonds Spartan	see 1920-29 Sports aircraft										
Short Silver Streak	1920	1P	B	1	1/2	-	120	0.0836	?	2,870	450
Short Silver Streak first British all-metal aircraft (1918, German Dornier were first)											
Sopwith Grasshopper	1920	1	B	1	1	1	90	0.0599	?	1,670	?
W											
Westland Woodpigeon	1924	2	B	1	2	-	72	0.0411	?	779	?

Appendix 9

British Military and Civil Aircraft 1930–1939

Data in this Appendix is representative of aircraft type, usually early model. For exact data, refer to original sources.

BRITISH MILITARY AIRCRAFT 1930-39

APPENDIX 9, 1930-1939

P = Prototype(s) Only   (NF) = Night Fighter   (TB) = Torpedo Bomber   (F/B) = Fighter-Bomber

pwr/wt ratio = power/weight ratio = [(total engine power) ÷ (max. weight)]   = HP/lb

"Bomber aircraft 1930-1939"

Manufacturer & Aircraft	First Flight	No. Made	M.pln B.pln T.pln	No. Eng.	No. Crew	Max. bomb load (lb)	Max. mph	pwr/wt ratio (HP/lb)	service ceiling (ft.)	Max. wt. (lb.)	Max. Range (miles)
A											
Armstrong-Whitworth AW.19 (TB)	1934	1P	B	1	2/3	1,000	163	0.0926	21,000	8,750	?
Armstrong-Whitworth AW.23	1935	1P	M	2	4	2,000	162	0.0672	18,100	24,100	790
Armstrong-Whitworth AW.29	1936	1P	M	1	2	1,000	225	?	21,000	?	685
Armstrong-Whitworth AW.38 Whitley	1936	1,814	M	2	5	7,000	230	0.0684	26,000	33,500	1,650
Avro 679 Manchester	1939	203	M	2	7	10,350	265	0.0704	19,200	50,000	1,200
Avro Manchester developed into four-engined Lancaster (stretched wing), first flight 1941											
B											
Blackburn B-3 (TB)	1932	2P	B	1	2	2,204	142	0.0794	9,150	10,393	?
Blackburn B-7 (TB)	1934	1P	B	1	2/3	?	160	0.0996	20,000	7,027	540
Blackburn Baffin (TB)	1932	97	B	1	2	1,600	136	0.0742	15,000	7,610	490
Blackburn Botha (TB)	1938	580	M	2	4	2,000	249	0.1008	17,500	18,450	1,100
Blackburn Shark (TB)	1934	269	B	1	3	1,600	150	0.0937	15,600	8,111	625
Blackburn Skua	1937	192	M	1	2	500	225	0.1082	20,200	8,228	435
Boulton & Paul P.32	1931	1P	B	3	4/5	1,500	?	0.0760	?	22,700	?
Boulton & Paul BP.75 Overstrand	1933	28	B	2	3/4	1,500	148	0.0973	21,300	11,923	545
Boulton & Paul 75 Overstrand developed from 1926 Boulton and Paul 29 Sidestrand (4 by conversion)											
Bristol Beaufort	1938	1,821	M	2	4	2,000	272	0.1065	16,500	21,230	1,600
Bristol Blenheim	1935	4,422	M	2	3	1,000	266	0.1278	27,260	14,400	1,460
Bristol Bolingbroke	1939	626	M	2	3	1,000	288	0.1269	27,000	14,500	1,860
Bristol Bombay	1935	51	M	2	3/4	2,000	192	0.1001	24,500	20,180	2,230
AW.23, Bristol Bombay and HP.54 convertible between bomber and troop carrier											
D											
De Havilland DH.72	1931	1P	B	3	5	2,500	?	0.0832	?	21,462	?

1930-39 Bomber aircraft continued on next page

APPENDIX 9, 1930-1939

Manufacturer & Aircraft	First Flight	No. Made	M,pln B,pln T,pln	No. Eng.	No. Crew	Max. bomb load (lb)	Max. mph	pwr/wt ratio (HP/lb)	service ceiling (ft.)	Max wt. (lb.)	Max. Range (miles)
F, 1930-39 Bomber aircraft continued											
Fairey Albacore (TB)	1938	800	B	1	3	2,000	161	0.0897	20,700	12,600	930
Fairey Battle	1936	2,185	M	1	3	1,000	257	0.0954	25,000	10,792	1,000
Fairey Fox VI	1936	Fairey Fox first flew 1925, final (7th) version Fox VIR, flew 1934. See Appendix 8									
Fairey G.4/31 (TB)	1934	1P	B	1	2/3	680	157	0.0853	23,200	8,790	?
Fairey Gordon (based on 1917 Fairey III)	1934	1P	B	1	2/3	680	157	0.0853	23,200	8990	?
Fairey Hendon	1930	15	M	2	5	1,660	152	0.0600	21,400	20,000	1,360
Fairey P.4/34	1937	2P	M	1	2	500	283	0.1172	26,600	8,787	920
Fairey Swordfish (TB)	1934	2,391	B	1	2/3	1,500	143	0.0910	16,500	7,580	522
H											
Handley Page HP.46 (TB)	1932	1P	B	1	2	?	140	0.0778	?	10,600	?
Handley Page HP.47	1934	1P	M	1	2	1,000	161	0.0895	19,900	7,708	1,250
Handley Page HP.50 Heyford	1930	125	B	2	4	2,500	142	0.0621	21,000	16,900	920
Handley HP.52 Hampden	1936	1,430	M	2	4	4,000	247	0.0888	19,000	22,500	1,720
Handley HP.54 Harrow	1936	100	M	2	5	3,000	200	0.0804	22,800	23,000	1,096
Handley HP.57 Halifax (HP.61 Halifax Mk.III data)	1939	6,176	M	4	7	13,000	282	0.0994	24,000	65,000	1,860
Various versions of Halifax were built, sub-types HP.58, 59, 61, 63, 70 and 71. Most-produced HP.61 /HP.63 (Halifix Mk. III) used Bristol Hercules radial engines.											
Three variants of Hawker Hart: (Audax, Hardy & Osprey)	1931+	1950+	B	1	2	500	185	0.1110	22,800	4596	430
+1950 Hart variants: 761 Audax (1931), 47 Hardy (1934) and 142 Osprey (1931) for Royal Navy											
Hawker Hind (Hart variant)	1934	527	B	1	2	510	185	0.1208	26,400	5,298	430
Hawker P.V.4	1934	1P	B	1	2	570	183	0.1233	23,700	6,650	460
P											
Parnall G.4/31	1935	1P	B	1	2	1,500	165	0.0926	?	6,800	?
S											
Short S.29 Stirling	1939	2,371	M	4	7	14,000	282	0.0786	16,600	70,000	2,330
A half-scale Short Stirling prototypye (Short S.31) was also built, first flew 1938											

1930-39 Bomber aircraft continued on next page

Manufacturer & Aircraft	First Flight	No. Made	M.pln B.pln T.pln	No. Eng.	No. Crew	Max. bomb load (lb)	Max. mph	pwr/wt ratio (HP/lb)	service ceiling (ft.)	Max wt. (lb.)	Max. Range (miles)
S, 1930-39 Bomber aircraft, continued											
Supermarine 317	n/a	2P*	M	4	6	14,000	329	0.0902	32,000	59,007	3,679
*Winning submission to specification B.12/36. Two prototypes under construction destroyed in enemy bombing raid (Short Stirling, Handley Page Halifax and Avro Lancaster intended to perform to B.12/36)											
V											
Vickers 207 (TB)	1933	1P	B	1	2	2,000	159	0.0859	?	9,600	?
Vickers 253 (TB)	1934	1P	B	1	2	?	161	0.0760	?	8,350	?
Vickers Warwick	see 1930-39 Anti-submarine aircraft										
Vickers Wellesley	1935	177	M	1	2/3	2,000	228	0.0740	25,500	12,500	1,220
Vickers Wellington (Mk.1C data)	1936	11,461	M	2	6	4,500	235	0.0737	18,000	28,500	2,550
The Vickers Wellington was the most-produced multi-engined aircraft ever produced in Britain											
W											
Westland PV-3 (TB, but converted)	1933	1	B	1	2	?	163	0.1235	35,000	5,100	?
Westland PV-3 was a Wapiti converted for "flight over Mount Everest" – see below											
Westland PV-6	1933	This was the 1931 Westland Wallace prototype with adaptations (power, cockpit etc.)									
Westland PV-3 and PV-6 were private venture aircraft which flew the Houston-Mount Everest expedition – see also Appendix 14											
Westland PV.7 (T B)	1933	1P	M	1	2	1,100	173	0.1346	22,700	7,172	?
Destroyed in testing, pilot first in Britain surviving parachuting from enclosed cockpit											

"Anti-submarine aircraft 1930–1939"

Manufacturer & Aircraft	First Flight	No. Made	M.pln B.pln T.pln	No. Eng.	No. Crew	Max. bomb load (lb)	Max. mph	pwr/wt ratio (HP/lb)	service ceiling (ft.)	Max wt. (lb.)	Max. Range (miles)
V											
Vickers 207 (TB)	1934	see 1930-39 Bomber aircraft									
Vickers 253 (TB)	1934	see 1930-39 Bomber aircraft									

1930-39 Anti-submarine aircraft continued on next page

APPENDIX 9, 1930–1939

Manufacturer & Aircraft	First Flight	No. Made	M.pln B.pln T.pln	No. Eng.	No. Crew	Max. bomb load (lb)	Max. mph	pwr/wt ratio (HP/lb)	service ceiling (ft.)	Max wt. (lb.)	Max. Range (miles)
V. 1930-39 Anti-submarine aircraft, continued											
Vickers Warwick	1939	846	M	2	6	6,000	224	0.0822	21,500	45,000	2,300
Vickers Warwick designed as "big" twin-engined bomber (like Avro Manchester), sharing many Wellington components and similar features. Entered service already overtaken by the four-engined heavy bombers.											

"Fighter aircraft 1930–1939"

Manufacturer & Aircraft	First Flight	No. Made	M.pln B.pln T.pln	No. Eng.	No. Crew	Max. bomb load (lb)	Max. mph	pwr/wt ratio (HP/lb)	service ceiling (ft.)	Max wt. (lb.)	Max. Range (miles)
A											
Armstrong Whitworth A.W.16	1930	18	B	1	1	-	200	0.1491	26,100	3,520	235
Armstrong Whitworth A.W.35 Scimitar	1935	6	B	1	1	-	221	0.1793	?	4,100	?
A.W.35 developed for Norwegian Air force, 4 supplied											
B											
Blackburn F.3	Did not fly: damaged during taxy trials in 1931										
Blackburn Roc	1938	136	M	1	2	240	223	0.1119	18,000	7,950	810
Blackburn Skua	see 1930-39 Bomber aircraft										
Boulton Paul Defiant (N/F)	1937	1,064	M	1	2	-	304	0.1198	31,000	8,600	465
Bristol Beaufighter (NF/B)	1939	5,928	M	1	2	1,200	266	0.1260	19,000	25,400	1,750
Bristol Blenheim	see 1930-39 Bomber aircraft										
Bristol Type 123	1934	1P	B	1	1	-	235	0.1467	?	4,737	?
Bristol Type 133	1934	1P	M	1	1	-	260	0.1351	?	4,738	?
Bristol Type 146	1938	1P	M	1	1	-	287	0.1826	?	4,600	?
F											
Fairey Fantôme	1935	4	B	1	1	-	270	0.2245	?	4,120	?
Fairey Fantôme (Force) designed in Britain, 3 built in Belgium for Belgian Air force											

1930-39 Fighter aircraft continued on next page

APPENDIX 9, 1930-1939

Manufacturer & Aircraft	First Flight	No. Made	M.pln B.pln T.pln	No. Eng.	No. Crew	Max. bomb load (lb)	Max. mph	pwr/wt ratio (HP/lb)	service ceiling (ft.)	Max wt. (lb.)	Max. Range (miles)
G, 1930-39 Fighter aircraft, continued											
Gloster F.5/34	1937	1P	M	1	1	-	316	0.1556	32,500	5,400	?
Gloster F.9/37	1939	2P	M	2	1	?	360	0.1772	30,000	11,615	?
Gloster Gauntlet	1933	246	B	1	1	-	230	0.1625	33,500	3970	460
Gloster Gladiator	1934	747	B	1	1	-	253	0.1847	32,800	4,594	?
H											
Hawker Demon (Hart variant)	1935	305	B	1	2	-	182	0.1310	27,500	4,464	374
Hawker Hotspur (ex-Henley)	1938	1P	M	1	2	-	316	0.1346	28,000	7,650	?
Hawker Hurricane	1935	14,583	M	1	1	-	340	0.1631	36,000	7,850	460
(1941 Mk.IIC data)	The cannon-armed Mk.IIC was the first of the "Hurribomber" ground attack versions									(aux. tanks 960)	
Hawker Nimrod	1931	92	B	1	1	80	194	0.1230	28,000	4,050	?
Hawker P.V.3	1934	1P	B	1	1	-	224	0.1443	29,600	4,850	?
M											
Martin-Baker MB 2	1938	1P	M	1	1	-	305	0.1806	29,000	5,537	?
S											
Supermarine Spitfire	1936	20,351	M	1	1	-	370	0.2194	34,400	6,700	425 (Ferry)
(1941 Mk.VB data)	For "carrier-capable" variant of Supermarine Spitfire (1942 Seafire) see Appendix 10										
Supermarine Type 224	1934	1P	M	1	1	-	22B	0.1267	38,800	473	?
V											
Vickers Jockey (type 171 data)	1930	1P	M	1	1	-	218	0.1667	31,000	3161	?
	Vickers Jockey type 151 modified into Jockey II type 171, with more engine power										
Vickers Type 161 (C.O.W. Gun Fighter)	1931	1P	B	1	1	-	185	0.1582	?	3,350	?
	'Pusher' design fitted with Coventry Ordnance Works 37mm (1 ½ inch) automatic gun										
Vickers Venom	1936	1P	M	1	1	-	312	0.1504	32,000	4,156	?
	Derived as development of Vickers Jockey										
W											
Westland C.O.W. Gun Fighter	1930	1P	M	1	1	-	185	0.1248	27,900	3,885	?
Westland F.7/30	1935	1P	B	1	1	-	146	0.1156	?	5,207	?

1930-39 Fighter aircraft continued on next page

APPENDIX 9, 1930-1939

W, 1930-39 Fighter aircraft, continued

Manufacturer & Aircraft	First Flight	No. Made	M.pln B.pln T.pln	No. Eng.	No. Crew	Max. bomb load (lb)	Max. mph	pwr/wt ratio (HP/lb)	service ceiling (ft.)	Max wt. (lb.)	Max. Range (miles)
Westland Whirlwind (fixed wing aircraft)	1938	116	M	2	1	500	360	0.1546	30,300	11,445	800
Heavily armed (4 cannon) twin-engined aircraft and one of the fastest aircraft of the day. Engine problems delayed entry to RAF service, mostly used as ground attack.											

"Patrol aircraft 1930–1939"

Manufacturer & Aircraft	First Flight	No. Made	M.pln B.pln T.pln	No. Eng.	No. Crew	Max. bomb load (lb)	Max. mph	pwr/wt ratio (HP/lb)	service ceiling (ft.)	Max wt. (lb.)	Max. Range (miles)
B											
Blackburn Perth (flying boat)	1933	4	B	3	5	2,000	132	0.0651	11,500	38,000	1,130
Blackburn Sydney (flying boat)	1930	1P	M	3	5	1,102	123	0.0675	16,500	23,350	?
S											
Saunders-Roe A.33 (flying boat)	1938	1P	Written off during high speed taxi trials								
Short S.18 Knuckleduster	1933	1P	M	2	5	?	150	0.0838	15,500	18,500	1,040
Short S8/8 Rangoon	1930	6	B	3	5	1,000	115	0.0720	12,000	22,500	650
Short Singapore II (S.12)	1930	1P	B	4	5?	?	?	0.067?	?	27,500	?
Short Singapore III (S.19)	1934	37	B	4	6-7	1,100	136	0.0834	15,000	32,390	1,000
Short S.25 Sunderland	1937	749	M	4	9-11	misc.	210	0.0734	16,000	58,000	1,780
Knuckleduster, Rangoon, Singapore and Sunderland were flying boats											
V											
Vickers Warwick	see 1930-39 Bomber aircraft										

1930-39 Reconnaissance aircraft on next page

"Reconnaissance aircraft 1930–1939"

APPENDIX 9, 1930-1939

Manufacturer & Aircraft	First Flight	No. Made	M.pln B.pln T.pln	No. Eng.	No. Crew	Max. bomb load (lb)	Max. mph	pwr/wt ratio (HP/lb)	service ceiling (ft.)	Max wt. (lb.)	Max. Range (miles)
A											
Avro 652A Anson (incl. Anson XIX)	1935	11,020	M	2	3-4	360	188	0.0824	19,000	8,500	790
F											
Fairey S.9/30	1934	1P	B	1	2	?	136	0.1615	?	6,500	?
Fairey Seafox (Floatplane)	1936	66	B	1	2	?	124	0.0729	9,700	5,420	440
Fairey Seal	1930	91	B	1	3	500	138	0.0875	17,000	6,000	?
Seal based on 1927 Fairey IIIF... derived from 1917 Fairey III)											
H											
Hawker Hector (Hart variant)	1935	179	B	1	2	224	187	0.1640	24,000	4,910	300
S											
Saunders-Roe A.27 London	1934	31	B	2	6	2,000	135	0.0832	19,900	22,000	956
Saunders-Roe A.36 Lerwick	1938	21	M	2	6	2,000	214	0.0828	14,000	33,200	1,540
Short R/28 Sarafand	1932	1P	B	6	9	?	150	0.0707	44,753	13,000	1,450
Saunders-Roe London and Lerwick and Shorts Sarafand were flying boats											
Supermarine Scapa	1932	15	B	2	5	1,000	142	0.0653	15,500	16,080	1,000
Supermarine Sea Otter	1938	292	B	1	4	1,000	163	0.0965	17,000	10,000	690
Supermarine Stranraer	1934	57	B	2	6-7	?	165	0.0968	18,500	1,900	1,000
Supermarine Walrus	1933	740	B	2	3-4	600	135	0.0944	18,500	8,050	600
Supermarine Scapa, Sea Otter and Walrus were amphibious flying boats, Stranraer was not amphibious											

"Military Trainer aircraft 1930–1939"

Manufacturer & Aircraft	First Flight	No. Made	M.pln B.pln T.pln	No. Eng.	No. Crew	Max. bomb load (lb)	Max. mph	pwr/wt ratio (HP/lb)	service ceiling (ft.)	Max wt. (lb.)	Max. Range (miles)
A											
Airspeed AS.10 Oxford	1937	8,586	M	2	3	184	192	0.0933	23,500	7,500	~800
Avro 626 Prefect	1930	198	B	1	2	-	112	0.0764	14,800	2,750	240

1930-39 Military Trainer aircraft continued on next page

APPENDIX 9, 1930-1939

Manufacturer & Aircraft	First Flight	No. Made	M.pln B.pln T.pln	No. Eng.	No. Crew	Max. bomb load (lb)	Max. mph	pwr/wt ratio (HP/lb)	service ceiling (ft.)	Max wt. (lb.)	Max. Range (miles)
A, 1930-39 Military Trainer aircraft, continued											
Avro 636	1935	4	B	1	1-2	-	175	0.1406	18,000	3,271	?
Avro 652A Anson	see 1930-39 Reconnaissance aircraft										
D											
DH.82 Tiger Moth	1931	8,868	B	2	2	-	109	0.0712	13,600	1,825	302
F											
Fairey S.9/30	1934	1P	B	1	2	?	136	0.1615	?	6,500	?
Fairey Seafox (Floatplane)	1936	66	B	1	2	?	124	0.0729	9,700	5,420	440
G											
GAL.33 Cagnet	1939	1P	M	1	2	-	100	0.0302	?	2,976	?
GAL.42 Cygnet	see civil "Utility" aircraft, GAL.42										
H											
Heston T.1/37	1938	1P	M	1	2	-	159	0.0585	12,800	3,250	?
Hillson Helvellyn	1939	1P	M	1	2	-	110+	0.0600	?	1,500	?
M											
Miles Hawk Major	1934	64	M	1	2	-	205	0.1081	20,000	1,850	560
Miles Kestrel	1937	1P	M	1	2	-	296	0.1396	?	5,337	?
Miles M.2 Hawk Trainer	1935	27	M	1	2	-	150	0.0756	18,000	1,720	400
Miles M.15	1938	2P	M	1	2	-	?	0.0791	?	2,350	?
Miles Magister	1937	1,303	M	1	2	-	142	0.0705	18,000	1,845	380
Miles Master	1939	3,250	M	1	2	-	242	0.1561	25,100	5,537	393
Miles Mohawk	1936	1P	M	1	2	-	190	0.0741	?	2,450	?
Miles Mentor	1938	45	M	1	1	2	156	0.0738	13,800	2,710	?
Miles Nighthawk	1935	6	M	1	2	-	175	0.0833	23,000	2,400	?
P											
Parnall 382	1939	1P	M	1	2	-	155	0.0816	?	2,450	?
Percival Proctor	1939	1,143	M	1	2	-	160	0.0600	14,000	3,500	500
Proctor based on Percival Gull (tourer) design											

1930-39 Military Trainer aircraft continued on next page

APPENDIX 9, 1930-1939

R, 1930-39 Military Trainer aircraft, continued

Manufacturer & Aircraft	First Flight	No. Made	M.pln B.pln T.pln	No. Eng.	No. Crew	Max. bomb load (lb)	Max. mph	pwr/wt ratio (HP/lb)	service ceiling (ft.)	Max wt. (lb.)	Max. Range (miles)
Reid and Sigrist R.S.1	1939	1P	M	2	2-3	-	205	0.0418	24,000	4,900	900
Saunders Roe A29 Cloud (and A.19 Cloud Airliner)	1930	22	M	2	2	-	118	0.0716	14,000	9,500	380

A.19 Cloud was a 4 to 8 passenger airliner flying boat used by RAF as A.29 Cloud trainer (gunners and bomb aimers). Numbers are overall total, both versions.

"Military Transport aircraft 1930–1939"

Manufacturer & Aircraft	First Flight	No. Made	M.pln B.pln T.pln	No. Eng.	No. Crew	Max. bomb load (lb)	Max. mph	pwr/wt ratio (HP/lb)	service ceiling (ft.)	Max wt. (lb.)	Max. Range (miles)
B											
Bristol Bombay	1935	51	M	2	3-4	24	192	0.1001	24,850	20,180	2,230
D											
DH.95 Flamingo	1938	14	M	2	3	17	243	0.1033	20,900	18,000	1,345
G											
Gloster TC.33	1932	1P	B	2	4	30	142	0.0402	19,100	28,884	?
H											
Handley Page HP.43	1932	1P	B	3	3-4	30	118	0.0867	?	22,500	1,200
Handley Page HP.51	1935	1P	M	2	5	24	108	0.0767	?	18,000	950
Handley Page HP.51 was fore-runner to 1936 HP.54 Harrow bomber											
P											
Percival Petrel	1937	27	M	2	2	4-6	195	0.0745	21,000	5,500	750
V											
Vickers Type 264 Valentia	1934	28*	B	2	2	22	130	0.0667	16,250	19,500	696

* plus 54 conversions of 1922 Vickers Victoria (more powerful engines fitted)

Vickers Warwick see 1930-39 Bomber aircraft

1930-39 Military Utility aircraft on next page

"Military Utility aircraft 1930-39"

APPENDIX 9, 1930-1939

Manufacturer & Aircraft	First Flight	No. Made	M.pln B.pln T.pln	No. Eng.	No. Crew	Max. bomb load (lb)	Max. mph	pwr/wt ratio (HP/lb)	service ceiling (ft.)	Max wt. (lb.)	Max. Range (miles)
C											
Cierva C.30 (Autogyro)	1933	148	n/a	1	1	-	110	0.0875	?	1,600	285
Cierva C.40 (Autogyro)	1938	9	n/a	1	2	-	120	0.1041	?	1,950	200
D											
DH.93 Don	1937	30	M	1	1	2-3	189	0.0804	23,300	6,530	890
DH.84 Dragon	see 1930-39 Airliners										
DH.89 Dragon Rapide	see 1930-39 Airliners										
M											
Miles Mentor	see Military Trainer aircraft										
W											
Westland Lysander	1936	1,786	M	1	1	1	212	0.1374	21,500	6,330	600
Westland Wallace (revised Wapiti)	1931	104	B	1	2	-	158	0.1183	24,100	5,750	470

64 more Westland Wallace were made by conversion of 1927 Westland Wapiti

"Military (Uncategorised) aircraft 1930–1939"

Manufacturer & Aircraft	First Flight	No. Made	M.pln B.pln T.pln	No. Eng.	No. Crew	Max. bomb load (lb)	Max. mph	pwr/wt ratio (HP/lb)	service ceiling (ft.)	Max wt. (lb.)	Max. Range (miles)
Armstrong Whitworth A.W.19	1934	1P	B	1	2-3	-	163	0.0926	21,000	8,750	?
B											
Blackburn B-7	1934	1P	B	1	2-3	-	160	0.0996	20,000	7,027	540
Bristol Type 118	1931	2P	B	1	2	-	175	0.1250	25,600	5,200	?
Bristol 138	1936	2	M	1		-	123	0.0942	54.000	5,310	2¼ hrs
Bristol 138 was high altitude research aircraft. Two built, only one flew											
F											
Fairey G.4/31	1934	1P	B	1	2	-	157	0.1881	23,200	3,987	?

1930-39 Military (Uncategorised) aircraft continued on next page

APPENDIX 9, 1930-1939

Manufacturer & Aircraft	First Flight	No. Made	M.pln B.pln T.pln	No. Eng.	No. Crew	Max. bomb load (lb)	Max. mph	pwr/wt ratio (HP/lb)	service ceiling (ft.)	Max wt. (lb.)	Max. Range (miles)
G, 1930-39 Military (Uncategorised) aircraft, continued											
GAL.41	1939	1	M	2	2	2 passegers	110	0.0626	16,000	2,875	3½hrs
(part of overall proposal for GAL.40 pressurised airliner)			GAL.41 was adapted GAL.25 civil "Utility Aircraft" with a two-seat pressurised module in revised fuselage, used for research into cabin pressurisation								
H											
Handley Page H.P.46 (TB)	1932	1P	B	1	2	-	140	0.0778	?	10,600	?
Hawker Henley	1937	202	M	1	2	?	272*	0.1165	27,000	8,840	950
			Henley light bomber (some Hurricane parts) simplified into 2-seat target tug.... *Maximum speed quoted is when towing target								
S											
Saunders Severn	1932	1P	B	3	5	-	126	0.0655	8,930	22,000	6 hrs
(Saunders-Roe A7)			Saunders Severn last flying boat design by S.E. Saunders before A.V. Roe takeover								
W											
Westland PV.7	1933	1P	M	1	2	-	173	0.1146	22,700	7172	?

Civil Aircraft 1930-39 next page

BRITISH CIVIL AIRCRAFT 1930-39

APPENDIX 9, 1930-1939

pwr/wt ratio = power/weight ratio = [(total engine power) ÷ (max. weight)] = HP/lb

"Airliners 1930-1939"

Manufacturer & Aircraft	First Flight	No. Made	M.pln B.pln T.pln	No. Eng.	No. Crew	Max. passenger	Max. mph	pwr/wt ratio (HP/lb)	service ceiling (ft.)	Max wt. (lb.)	Max. Range (miles)
A											
Airspeed AS.4 Ferry	1932	4	B	3	1	10	112	0.0667	15,500	5,400	340
Armstrong Whitworth AW.15 Atalanta	1932	8	M	4	3	9-17	156	0.0648	14,200	21,000	640
Armstrong Whitworth AW.27 Ensign	1938	14	M	4	3+2	40	210	0.0667	24,000	66,000	1,370
Avro 618 Ten	1930	14	M	3	2	8	115	0.0679	16,000	10,600	348
(incl. Avro 619 Five (5 seats) and Avro 620 Six (6 seats) variants)	Avro 618 Ten was re-engined licensed copy of 3-engined Fokker VIIB/3m										
Avro 642 Eighteen	1934	2	M	2	2	12	160	0.0763	15,500	11,800	600
	Avro 642 Eighteen: 2-engined high wing Avro 618 Ten (+ one 4-engined special)										
Avro 652	1935	2	M	2	2	4	195	0.0773	21,500	7,500	787
	Avro 652 special order from Imperial Airways, use in India. Basis of 652A Anson										
Avro 652A Anson XIX (Avro nineteen)	see 1930-39 military reconnaissance aircraft (includes 56 Anson XIX airliner)										
B											
Blackburn H.S.T.10	1937	1P	M	2	2	12	204	0.0849	23,800	8,600	1,000
HST (High Speed Transport) project (also known as Blackburn B-9) had all-metal wing and fuselage skinning, abandoned in 1937....1,000 miles range with 6 passengers. Compare with 11-metal USA Douglas 210 mph DC-2, 14 passengers, 1,000 miles max range, 2nd in 1934 MacRobertson race England to Australia. (See also race winner 1934 DH.88 Comet Racer).											
D											
DH.91 Albatross	1937	7	M	2	3	22	225	0.0712	17,900	29,500	1,040
DH.84 Dragon	1932	202	B	2	1	10	128	0.0619	12,500	4,200	460
DH.89 Dragon Rapide	1934	727	B	2	1	8	157	0.0727	16,700	5,500	573
DH.86 Express	1934	62	B	4	2	12	166	0.0780	17,400	10,250	760
DH.95 Flamingo	1938	14	B	4	2	17	243	0.0533	20,000	18,000	1,345
F											
Fairey FC1 (as designed)	n/a	n/a	B	4	2	17	243	0.0533	20,000	18,000	1,345
1938 pressurised airliner 12-aircraft contract, cancelled October 1939 due to WW2 (see GAL.41 test aircraft, 1930-39 Military Uncategorised aircraft)											

1930-39 Airliners continued on next page

H, 1930-39 Airliners, continued

Manufacturer & Aircraft	First Flight	No. Made	M.pln B.pln T.pln	No. Eng.	No. Crew	Max. passenger	Max. mph	pwr/wt ratio (HP/lb)	service ceiling (ft.)	Max wt. (lb.)	Max. Range (miles)
Handley Page HP.42 (HP42 East)	1930	4	B	4	4	24	127	0.0786	?	28,000	500
Handley Page HP.45 (HP42 West)	?	4	B	4	4	38	127	0.0786	?	28,000	500
Heston Phoenix	1935	6	M	1	1	4	150	0.0621	20,000	3,300	500
M											
Miles Merlin	1935	4	M	1	1	4	155	0.0677	18,000	3,000	700
Miles Peregrine	1936	2	M	2	2	6	188	0.0788	?	5,200	?
S											
Saro A.19 Cloud	see 1930-39 Military Trainer aircraft										
Saro Windhover (amphibious flying boat)	1932	2	B	3	2	4/6	108	0.0632	9,680	5,700	400
Short Empire (S.23 data)	1936	42	M	4	5	17-24	200	0.0894	20,000	40,500	>760
Short Empire flying boats made in 3 sub-types: S.23 (31), S.30 (9) and S.33 (2).											
Short S.17 Kent (flying boat)	1931	3	B	4	4	16	137	0.0688	17,500	32,000	450
Shorts Mayo Composite -	When Composite, MTOWs were S.20: 20,800 lb, S.21: 27,700 lb										
{Short S.20 Mercury	1937	1	M	4	2	?	212	0.0942	?	15,500	3,900
{Short S.21 Maia	1937	1	M	4	3	18	200	0.0967	20,000	38,000	850
S.20 range value when operated as "composite" with (fuel) overload. Passenger numbers when operated "split"											
Short S.26 (not serial no.)	1938	3	M	4	3	24	209	0.0751	?	73,500	1,000
Short S.32 (not serial no.)	n/a	n/a	M	4	5+2	24	275	0.0704	?	71,000	3,420
Pressurised aircraft, started build but cancelled due to start of Second World War											
Short S.16 Scion (Scion II data)	1933	5/17	M	2	1	6	122	0.0563	11,500	3,200	370
Scion I (5), Scion II (17)... could be configured as landplane or floatplane											
Short S.22 Scion Senior	1935	6	M	4	2	12	140	0.0600	12,000	6,000	420
Short Scylla	1934	2	B	4	4	39	137	0.0663	?	33,500	?
Produced at eequest of Imperial Airways, as less expensive alternative to buying more Handley Page HP.42											
Short Valetta (float plane)	1930	1P	M	3	2	16	135	0.0703	16,000	22,400	520

1930-39 Airliners continued on next page

APPENDIX 9, 1930-1939

S, 1930-39 Airliners, continued

Manufacturer & Aircraft	First Flight	No. Made	M.pln B.pln T.pln	No. Eng.	No. Crew	Max. passenger	Max. mph	pwr/wt ratio (HP/lb)	service ceiling (ft.)	Max wt. (lb.)	Max. Range (miles)
Spartan Cruiser	1932	17	M	3	2	6	133	0.0629	15,000	6,200	310
Supermarine Type 179 (flying boat) (1931 estimated performance)	n/a	n/a	M	6	7	40	145	0.0699	11,000	75,090	12 hrs
W											
Abandoned before completion											
Westland Wessex (not 1958 helicopter)	1930	10	M	3	2	6	118	0.0667	14,900	6,300	420

"Mailplanes 1930-1939"

Manufacturer & Aircraft	First Flight	No. Made	M.pln B.pln T.pln	No. Eng.	No. Crew	Max. passenger	Max. mph	pwr/wt ratio (HP/lb)	service ceiling (ft.)	Max wt. (lb.)	Max. Range (miles)
A											
Avro 627 Mailplane	1931	1	B	1	1	-	170	0.1019	19,000	5,150	560
B											
Boulton & Paul P.64 Mailplane	1933	1P	B	2	3	-	185	0.0985	22,500	11,267	1,000
Boulton Paul P.71A	1935	2	B	2	2	-	195	0.1032	21,000	9,500	600

"Sports aircraft 1930-1939"
(includes Light aircraft, Racers, Tourers and Sailplanes)

Manufacturer & Aircraft	First Flight	No. Made	M.pln B.pln T.pln	No. Eng.	No. Crew	Max. passenger	Max. mph	pwr/wt ratio (HP/lb)	service ceiling (ft.)	Max wt. (lb.)	Max. Range (miles)
A											
Airspeed AS.8 Viceroy	1934	1	M	2	2	-	210	0.0921	?	6,300	1,400
Arrow Active	1931	1	B	1	1	-	144	0.0906	?	1,325	420
B											
British Aircraft Company Gliders	1930-35	~30	Series of 9 different models. (BAC VII version modified into motor-glider Planette in which owner crashed and was killed in 1933)								

1930-39 Sports, Racer, Tourer and Sailplane aircraft continued on next page

Manufacturer & Aircraft	First Flight	No. Made	M.pln B.pln T.pln	No. Eng.	No. Crew	Max. passenger	Max. mph	pwr/wt ratio (HP/lb)	service ceiling (ft.)	Max wt. (lb.)	Max. Range (miles)
1920-29 Sports, Racer, Tourer and Sailplane aircraft, continued											
British Aircraft Company Drone	1932	33	M	1	1	-	70	0.0500	12,500	460	300
Modified version (new engine) of Planette, by new company owner Robert Kronfeld											
C											
Chilton D.W.1	1937	4+3	M	1	1	-	112	0.0469	?	640	500
Comper Swift	1930	45	M	1	1	-	140	0.0761	22,000	985	380
D											
Dart Flittermouse	1936	1	M	1	1	-	64	0.0391	?	640	?
Dart Kitten	1937	4	M	1	1	-	95	0.0465	19,700	860	340
Dart Pup	1936	1	M	1	1	-	75	0.0383	?	705	?
DH.88 Comet Racer	1934	5	M	2	2	-	237	0.0829	19,000	5,550	2,925
DH.87 Hornet Moth	1934	164	B	1	1	1	124	0.0677	14,800	1,950	620
DH.81 Swallow Moth	1931	1P	M	1	1	-	117	0.0602	?	1,330	?
DH. T.K.2	1935	1	M	1	2	-	182	0.0919	?	1,600	?
DH. T.K.4	1937	1	M	1	1	-	230	0.0966	21,000	1,450	500
DH TK aircraft were De Havilland Technical School design and build											
G											
General Aircraft Cygnet	see 1930-39 Civil Utility aircraft										
Gordon Dove	1937	3	M	1	1	-	95	0.0212	?	1,323	400
Granger Archaeopteryx	see 1930-39 Civil Trainer aircraft										
H											
Heston Phoenix	1935	6	M	1	1	4	150	0.0621	20,000	3,300	500
K											
Kronfeld Monoplane	1937	1	M	1	1	-	73	0.0469	?	640	?
M											
Miles M.3 Falcon (-Six)	1934	36	M	1	1	2/3	145	0.0591	15,000	2,200	615
Miles M.2 Hawk	1933	47	M	1	1	1	115	0.0765	18,000	1,700	400
Miles M.2H Hawk Major	1934	64	M	1	1	1/2	150	0.1089	20,000	1,850	560

1930-39 Sports, Racer, Tourer and Sailplane aircraft continued on next page

APPENDIX 9, 1930-1939

Manufacturer & Aircraft	First Flight	No. Made	M.pln B.pln T.pln	No. Eng.	No. Crew	Max. passenger	Max. mph	pwr/wt ratio (HP/lb)	service ceiling (ft.)	Max wt. (lb.)	Max. Range (miles)
M, 1930-39 Sports, Racer, Tourer and Sailplane aircraft, continued											
Miles M.13 Hobby	1937	1P	M	1	1	-	~200	0.0950	?	1,527	?
Miles Monarch	1938	11	M	1	1	1	145	0.0591	17,400	2,200	600
Miles M.1 Satyr	1932	1	B	1	1	-	122	0-0833	?	900	?
Miles M.5 Sparrowhawk	1935	6	M	1	1	-	180	0.0840	12,470	1,750	415
Miles Whitney Straight	1936	50	M	1	1	1	145	0.0650	18,500	2,000	570
Collaborative design with Whitney Straight (Grand Prix driver, pilot & businessman)											
P											
Percival Gull	1932	48	M	1	1	2	145	0.0634	16,000	2,050	700
19 aircraft had the 200HP DH Gypsy Six engine, plus 4 more converted from Gull 4 model. Weight penalty of 195 lb but maximum speed increased to 178 mph. Vega Gull a further development											
Percival Mew Gull	1934	6	M	1	1	-	265	0.1130	?	1,460	550
Percival Vega Gull	1935	90	M	1	1	3	174	0.0631	17,000	3,250	660
R											
RAE (club) Scarab	1932	1	M	1	1	-	78	0.0492	?	650	200
Robinson Redwing	1930	12	B	1	1	-	95	0.0552	?	1,450	275
S											
Shackleton-Murray SM.1	1933	1	M	1	2	-	91	0.0552	?	1,450	250
Slingsby Gliders:-											
Slingsby T.1/T.2 Falcon 1	1931-37 (11)		M	n/a	1	-	n/a	n/a	n/a	506	n/a
Single seat sport glider, developed from Alexander Lippisch German Falke glider design of 1930.											
Slingsby T.3 Primary (Dagling)	1930	67	M	n/a	1	-	n/a	n/a	n/a	380	n/a
Developed from Alexander Lippisch German Falke glider design of 1926											
Slingsby T.4 Falcon 3	1935	9	M	n/a	2	-	n/a	n/a	n/a	899	n/a
Slingsby T.5 Grunau Baby	?	?	M	n/a	1	-	n/a	n/a	n/a	551	n/a
Licenced build of Edmund Schneider German Grunau glider design of 1926											
(After Second World War, Elliots of Newbury also licence-built this as Baby EoN)											
Slingsby T.6 Kirby Kite	1935	25	M	n/a	1	-	n/a	n/a	n/a	495	n/a

1930-39 Sports, Racer, Tourer and Sailplane aircraft continued on next page

1930-39 Sports, Racer, Tourer and Sailplane aircraft, continued

Manufacturer & Aircraft	First Flight	No. Made	M.pln B.pln T.pln	No. Eng.	No. Crew	Max. passenger	Max. mph	pwr/wt ratio (HP/lb)	service ceiling (ft.)	Max wt. (lb.)	Max. Range (miles)
Slingsby Gliders (continued):-											
Slingsby T.7 Kirby Cadet (RAF Cadet TX.1)	1935	513	M	n/a	1	-	n/a	n/a	n/a	376	n/a
Slingsby T.8 Kirby Tutor (RAF Cadet TX.2)	1937	106	M	n/a	1	-	n/a	n/a	n/a	570	n/a
Slingsby T.9 King Kite	1937	3	M	n/a	1	-	n/a	n/a	n/a	620	n/a
Slingsby T.12 Kirby Gull 1	1938	11	M	n/a	1	-	n/a	n/a	n/a	625	n/a
One Gull 2 (2-seat) variant and one Gull 3 also built											
Slingsby T.13 Petrel	1938	3	M	n/a	1	-	n/a	n/a	n/a	638	n/a
Development of Hans Jacobs German Schleicher Rhönadler design of 1932											
Schneider Trophy S-types (S.4, S.5 and S.6 listed in Appendix 8 but data shown here)											
Supermarine S.4: 1925	1925	1	M	1	1	-	239	0.2131	?	3,191	?
Crashed and destroyed in trials, ascribed to wing flutter											
Supermarine S.5: 1927 winner, 281.62 mph	1927	3	M	1	1	-	320	0.2776	?	3,242	?
Supermarine S.6: 1929 winner, 328.63 mph	1929	2	M	1	1	-	329	0.3292	?	5,771	?
SupermarineS6B: 1931 winner, 340.08 mph	1931	2	M	1	1	-	408	0.3861	?	6,086	?

"Civil Trainer aircraft 1930–1939"

Manufacturer & Aircraft	First Flight	No. Made	M.pln B.pln T.pln	No. Eng.	No. Crew	Max. passenger	Max. mph	pwr/wt ratio (HP/lb)	service ceiling (ft.)	Max wt. (lb.)	Max. Range (miles)
A											
Avro 631 Cadet	1931	35	B	1	2	-	112	0.0753	13,000	1,793	350
Avro Cadet series developed as smaller version of 1929 Avro 621 Tutor Military Trainer											

1930-39 Civil Trainer aircraft on next page

A, 1930-39 Civil Trainer aircraft, continued

Manufacturer & Aircraft	First Flight	No. Made	M.pln B.pln T.pln	No. Eng.	No. Crew	Max. passenger	Max. mph	pwr/wt ratio (HP/lb)	service ceiling (ft.)	Max wt. (lb.)	Max. Range (miles)
Avro 638,639,640, 643 Cadet	1933	36	B	1	2/3	1	112	0.0675	13,000	~2,000	~285
Cadet series originated in 1929 Avro 621 Military Tutor. Avro 638 Cadet had backward-folding wings, 639 had 3-seat cabin, 640 3-seat open, 643 as 631 with raised rear seat. 643 MkII had more powerful engine.											
Avro 643 Mk II Cadet	1935	61	B	1	2	-	118	0.0750	13,000	~2,000	~285
B											
Blackburn B-2	1932	42	B	1	2	-	112	0.0649	?	1,850	320
British Aircraft Manufacturing Swallow	1933	135	M	1	2	-	104	0.0567	17,000	1,500	420
British Aircraft Manufacturing Swallow was licenced and improved version of German Klemm L.25											
G											
Granger Archeopteryx	1930	1	M	1	1	-	95	0.0523	?	612	?
Granger brothers design as tractor-propeller version of swept-wing 1924 Westland-Hill Pterodacty aircraft, which themselves derived from John Dunne 1910-1914 experimental tail-less swept wing configurations.											
H											
Hillson Helvellyn	1939	1	M	1	2	-	~125	0.0600	?	1,500	?
M											
Marendaz Trainer	1939	1P	M	1	2	-	124	0.0699	?	1,500	35

"Civil Utility aircraft 1930–1939"

Manufacturer & Aircraft	First Flight	No. Made	M.pln B.pln T.pln	No. Eng.	No. Crew	Max. passenger	Max. mph	pwr/wt ratio (HP/lb)	service ceiling (ft.)	Max wt. (lb.)	Max. Range (miles)
A											
Aeronca 100/300	1935?	24	M	1	1	1	90	0.0058	14,000	2,006	190
Aeronca 100/300 was British licence-built production of Aeronaca C3, flown in USA in 1931 (Aeronautical corporation of America: the British venture was not successful)											

1930-39 Civil Utility aircraft continued on next page

APPENDIX 9, 1930-1939

Manufacturer & Aircraft	First Flight	No. Made	M.pln B.pln T.pln	No. Eng.	No. Crew	Max. passenger	Max. mph	pwr/wt ratio (HP/lb)	service ceiling (ft.)	Max wt. (lb.)	Max. Range (miles)
A, 1930-39 Civil Utility aircraft, continued											
Airspeed AS.5 Courier	1933	16	M	1	1	5	153	0.0615	13,500	3,900	635
Prototype Airspeed Courier originally built for Alan Cobham planning an attempt to fly to India non-stop, using air-to-air refuelling (never actually attempted).											
Airspeed AS.6 Envoy	1934	52	M	2	1	6	210	0.0548	22,500	6,300	650
Angus Aquila	1931	1	M	1	1	-	?	0.0571	?	700	?
Arpin A-1	1938	1	M	1	1	1	108	0.0539	?	1,261	5 hrs
Avro 641 Commodore	1934	6	B	1	1	4	130	0.0614	1,500	3,500	500
B											
Blackburn B-1 Segrave	1930	6	M	2	1	3	138	0.0727	14,000	3,300	450
Bristol Type 143	1936	1P	M	2	2	8	250	0.0455	?	11,000	1,250
British Aircraft Manufacturing Cupid	1935	1	M	1	1	1	149	0.0769	?	1,690	?
British Aircraft Manufacturing Eagle	1934	43	M	1	2	1	148	0.0542	16,000	2,400	650
G Handasyde design for British Klemm company, in 1935 renamed as British Aircraft Manufacturing company. (Klemm a German light aircraft company)											
British Aircraft. B.A. IV Double Eagle	1936	3?	M	2	1	4	165	0.0743	?	3,500	?
C											
Chrislea LC.1 Airguard	1938	1	M	1	1	1	118	0.0477	?	1,300	?
LC.1 was a R.C. Christophorides & B.V. Leak aircraft, built by their Chrislea Aviation Co.											
Cierva C.24 (Autogyro)	1931	1	n/a	1	2	-	115	0.0667	?	1,800	350
Cierva C.29 (Autogyro)	-	1	n/a	1	1	4	160est	0.120	?	5,000	?
Cierva C.30 (Autogyro)	see 1930-39 Military Utility aircraft										
Comper Mouse	1933	1	M	1	1	2	135	0.0587	?	2,215	600
Currie Wot	1937	2	B	1	1	-	95	0.0444	?	900	240
Wot designed by J.R. Currie as home-build: two built by Cinque Ports Aviation.											
D											
Dart Kitten	1937	4	M	1	1	-	95	0.0465	19,700	860	340
DH. 92 Dolphin	1936	1	B	2	2	6	~161	0.0618	?	6,600	?

1930-39 Civil Utility aircraft continued on next page

APPENDIX 9, 1930-1939

D, 1930-39 Civil Utility aircraft, continued

Manufacturer & Aircraft	First Flight	No. Made	M.pln B.pln T.pln	No. Eng.	No. Crew	Max. passenger	Max. mph	pwr/wt ratio (HP/lb)	service ceiling (ft)	Max wt. (lb.)	Max. Range (miles)
DH.90 Dragonfly	1935	67	B	2	1	4	144	0.0710	18,100	4,000	625
DH.83 Fox Moth	1932	154	B	1	1	3/4	106	0.0600	12,700	2,000	425
DH.87 Hornet Moth	1934	164	B	1	1	1	124	0.0667	14,800	1,950	620
DH.85 Leopard Moth	1933	133	M	1	1	2	137	0.0584	21,500	2,225	715
DH.94 Moth Minor	1937	c.140	M	1	2	-	118	0.0828	16,500	1,450	300
DH. T.K.1	1934	1	B	1	2	-	118	0.0828	?	1,450	?
Deekay Knight	1937	1P	M	1	2	-	125	0.0621	17,500	1,450	?

Short-lived company Deekay Knight designed an aircraft with a wing without ribs.

Manufacturer & Aircraft	First Flight	No. Made	M.pln B.pln T.pln	No. Eng.	No. Crew	Max. passenger	Max. mph	pwr/wt ratio (HP/lb)	service ceiling (ft)	Max wt. (lb.)	Max. Range (miles)
Desoutter Mk.I & II (first aircraft imported, 1929)	1930	6+41	M	1	1	2	125	0.0631	17,100	1,903	497

Desoutter Mk. I & II licence-build of F. Koolhoven F.K.41: 6 FK.41+41 as Desoutters

Manufacturer & Aircraft	First Flight	No. Made	M.pln B.pln T.pln	No. Eng.	No. Crew	Max. passenger	Max. mph	pwr/wt ratio (HP/lb)	service ceiling (ft)	Max wt. (lb.)	Max. Range (miles)
Dudley Watt D.W.2	1930	1	B	1	2	-	90	0.0547	?	1,224	?

F

Manufacturer & Aircraft	First Flight	No. Made	M.pln B.pln T.pln	No. Eng.	No. Crew	Max. passenger	Max. mph	pwr/wt ratio (HP/lb)	service ceiling (ft)	Max wt. (lb.)	Max. Range (miles)
Foster Wikner Wicko	1936	10	M	1	2	-	140	0.0650	20,000	2,000	480

Wicko impressed into WW2 RAF service as "Warferry"

G

Helmut J. Steiger designed and built ST-1as a wing-only structural test specimen by his Monospar company, re-named 1931 General Aircraft Company.

Manufacturer & Aircraft	First Flight	No. Made	M.pln B.pln T.pln	No. Eng.	No. Crew	Max. passenger	Max. mph	pwr/wt ratio (HP/lb)	service ceiling (ft)	Max wt. (lb.)	Max. Range (miles)
(Monospar) ST-2											
(Monospar) ST-3	1931	1P	M	2	1	2	110	0.0500	18,000	1800	?

ST-2 was wing only, ordered by govt. for experimental fit on 3-engined Fokker VIIb-3m (see Appendix 14)

ST-3 Built by Gloster for Helmut Steiger, as monospar-winged prototype aircraft

Manufacturer & Aircraft	First Flight	No. Made	M.pln B.pln T.pln	No. Eng.	No. Crew	Max. passenger	Max. mph	pwr/wt ratio (HP/lb)	service ceiling (ft)	Max wt. (lb.)	Max. Range (miles)
General Aircraft ST-4	1932	30	M	2	1	3	130	0.0667	15,000	2,550	540
General Aircraft ST-5											
General Aircraft ST-6	1933	2	M	2	1	3	138	0.0667	15,000?	~2,550	560
General Aircraft ST-7											
General Aircraft ST-8											
General Aircraft ST-9											
General Aircraft ST-10	1934	2	M	2	1	3	144	0.0706	16,000	2,550	594
General Aircraft ST-11	1934	2	M	2	1	3	160	0.0706	17,400	2,550	675

1932 ST-5 wing only, for Spartan monoplane

1934 ST-7 wing only, for Saunders Roe Cloud

1934 ST-8 wing only, test flown as change of wing on Italian Caproni Ca 97

1932 ST-5 wing only, for Italian Romeo Ra 39 sailplane, designed but not built

1930-39 Civil Utility aircraft continued on next page

Manufacturer & Aircraft	First Flight	No. Made	M.pln B.pln T.pln	No. Eng.	No. Crew	Max. passenger	Max. mph	pwr/wt ratio (HP/lb)	service ceiling (ft.)	Max wt. (lb.)	Max. Range (miles)
G, 1930-39 Civil Utility aircraft, continued											
General Aircraft ST-12	1935	10	M	2	1	3	158	0.0904	21,000	2,875	410
General Aircraft ST-18	1935	1	M	2	1	9	203	0.0793	19,500	11,350	900
General Aircraft ST-25	1935	30	M	2	1	3/4	142	0.0626	16,000	2,875	585
General Aircraft GAL.42 Cygnet	1937	10	M	e	1	1	135	0.0682	14,000	2,200	445
Prototype GAL.42 was C.R. Chronander & J.I. Waddington design & build, rights sold to General Aircraft											
H.J. Steiger left General Aircraft 1936, projects became "GAL" numbers from ST-25											
H											
Hafner AR III Gyroplane	1935	1P	n/a	1	1	-	120	0.1000	?	900	?
Helmy Aerogypt	1939	1P	M	2	1	3	160	0.0542	?	2,400	?
Helmy Aerogypt modified three times. Aerogypt IV data shown											
Hillson Pennine	1932	48	M	1	1	2	145	0.0634	16,000	2,050	700
Hinkler Ibis	1930	1	M	1	1	Found semi-derelict in Hinkler's garden in 1959					
Hordern-Richmond Autoplane	1936	1	M	2	2	-	98	0.0457	?	1,750	141
Edmund Horden design, built by Heston Aircraft											
Kay Gyroplane (autogyro)	1932	1	n/a	1	1	-	?	0.0815	?	920	?
David Kay built autogyro 32/1, damaged in 1933 crash, rebuilt to fly in 1935. Designed larger 33/1 (not built). 32/1 restored 1967 to static display standard											
L											
Luton LA.1 Buzzard	1936	1	M	1	1	-	95	0.0583	?	600	180
Luton LA.3 Minor	1939	1	M	1	1	-	105	0.0602	?	1,030	300
After LA.3 Minor flown successfully, redesigned as LA.4 minor for home build											
Luton LA.5 Major	1937	30	M	1	1	-	85	0.0735	?	750	180
M											
Martin-Baker MB 1	1938	1P	M	1	1	-	90	0.0457	?	700	200
Miles M.7 Nighthawk	1935	6	M	1	2	2	175	0.0833	23,000	2,400	?
Miles M.11 Whitney Straight	See 1936 Civil Sports aircraft										
Miles M.18	1938	3	M	1	1	1	142	0.0779	?	1,925	?

1930-39 Civil Utility aircraft continued on next page

APPENDIX 9, 1930-1939

Manufacturer & Aircraft	First Flight	No. Made	M.pln B.pln T.pln	No. Eng.	No. Crew	Max. passenger	Max. mph	pwr/wt ratio (HP/lb)	service ceiling (ft.)	Max wt. (lb.)	Max. Range (miles)
M, 1930-39 Civil Utility aircraft, continued											
Moss M.A.1	1932	1	M	1	2	-	130	0.0679	13,000	1,400	500
Moss M.A.2	1939	2	M	1	2	-	~130	0.0643	17,000	1,400	?
P											
Parnall Heck	1934	6	M	1	2	1	185	0.0741	16,700	2,700	605
Pobjoy Pirate	1935	1P	M	1	1	2	125	0.0563	?	1,600	?
S											
Shapley Kittiwake	1937	2P	M	1	1	-	~130	0.0563	?	1,600	?
Spartan Arrow	1930	15	B	1	1	-	106	0.0686	?	1,750	432
Spartan Clipper	1932	1	M	1	2	-	110	0.0577	?	1,300	?
Spartan Three Seater	1930	25	B	1	1	2	107	0.0714	?	1,680	260
Supermarine Air Yacht (flying boat)	1930	1	1	3	4	6	117	0.0675	6,500	23,348	?
	Supermarine Air Yacht was a special order for Hon. Arthur Ernest Guiness as "luxury touring" flying boat, with enclosed owner's cabin (bed and toilet included) and passenger cabin for 5 passengers. Despite replacing engines with higher power, rejected by Guiness as underpowered. He bought a Saro Cloud.										
V											
Vickers Viastra	1930	6	M	1/2/3	2	12	120	0.0850	?	12,350	535
8 variants of 6 airframes, with 1,2 or 3 engines (data for Viastra II)	Based on patents for all-metal aircraft designs of French aeronautical engineer Michel Marie Joseph Wibault										
W											
Watkinson Dingbat	1938	1	M	1	1	-	90	0.0457	?	700	200
	An ultra-light, restored to flying condition1959, crashed in 1975 and re-built, was still registered in 2010										
Willoughby Delta 8	1939	1P	M	2	2	-	183	0.1064	?	2,350	340
(also known as Delta-F)	Willoughby Delta 8 was pre-prototype concept demonstrator twin-engined flying wing configuration of larger 3 engined mailplane/airliner proposal. Crashed 1939 (mechanical failure), killing pilot and on-board sponsor.										

Appendix 10

British Military and Civil Aircraft 1940–1949

Data in this Appendix is representative of aircraft type, usually early model. For exact data, refer to original sources.

BRITISH MILITARY AIRCRAFT 1940-1949

APPENDIX 10, 1940-1949

P = Prototype(s) Only

pwr/wt ratio = power/weight ratio = [(total engine power) ÷ (max. weight)] = HP/lb

thrust/weight ratio = [(total engine jet thrust) ÷ (max. weight)] = lbf/lb

"Experimental aircraft" 1940–1949" (see also Appendix 14)

Manufacturer & Aircraft	First Flight	No. Made	M.pln B.pln T.pln	No. Eng.	No. Crew	Max. bomb load (lb)	Max. mph	thrust/weight ratio	service ceiling (ft.)	Max wt. (lb.)	Max. Range (miles)
A											
Armstrong Whitworth AW.52 (flying wing)	1947	2	M	2	2	-	500	0.2928	36,000	34,150	1,500
Proposed configuration as a possible bomber, the AW.52 was preceded by the half-scale AW.52G glider, first flown in 1945. In a test in 1949, the first full-scale AW.52 (with Rolls Royce Nene turbojet engines) entered an unstable oscillation and the pilot made the first life-saving ejection using a Martin Baker ejection seat. The second AW.52 had lower powered Rolls Royce Derwent engines, and was used in further research until 1953.											
Avro 707	1949	5	M	1	2	-	464	0.3400	?	10,000	?
(one third scale Vulcan delta research) Avro 707 built in 4 versions, 707, 707A (2), 707B, 707C (2-seater). Data for 707C											
D											
DH.108 Swallow (data for 3rd version)	1946	3	M	1	1	-	677	0.4200	35,425	~8,900	?
Tail-less research aircraft into high speed flight											
G											
Gloster E.38/39	1941	2	M	1	1	-	338	0.2295	32,000	3,748	410
Gloster E.38/39 was Britain's first turbojet aircraft											
H								pwr/wt ratio HP/lb			
HP.75 was research aircraft into tail-less flight											
Handley Page HP.75 Manx	1943	1	M	1	2	-	150	0.0700	15,000	4,000	?
M								thrust/weight ratio			
Miles M.52 intended as world first supersonic aircraft, cancelled 1946, build 80% complete (see also Miles Gillette Falcon (Appendix 14)											
Miles M.52	n/a	1	M	1	1	-	1,000	0.4878	50,000	8,200	?

1940-49 Experimental aircraft continued on next page

APPENDIX 10, 1940-1949

R, 1940-49 Experimental aircraft, continued

Manufacturer & Aircraft	First Flight	No. Made	M.pln B.pln T.pln	No. Eng.	No. Crew	Max. bomb load (lb)	Max. mph	thrust/weight ratio	service ceiling (ft.)	Max wt. (lb.)	Max. Range (miles)
North American P-51 Mustang ordered by UK for RAF, with single-stage supercharged Allison engine. Rolls Royce experimental change to two-speed supercharged Rolls Royce Merlin resulted in P-51B & P-51C (RAF Mk.III Mustangs). Much improved performance at 15,000 ft and higher altitude								**pwr/wt ratio HP/lb**			
Rolls-Royce Mustang Mk.X	1942	5	M	1	1	-	433	0.1562	40,600	10,913	?
S											
2nd Supermarine 510 modified to 517 before flight, later to 535 standard, as pre-prototype for 541 Swift (see Appendix 11)								**thrust/weight ratio**			
Supermarine 510	1948	2	M	1	1	-	635	0.3909	?	12,790	?
								pwr/wt ratio HP/lb			
Y											
R.T. Youngman developed double-slotted wing flaps added to modified Percival Proctor design by L.E. Baynes, aircraft built by Heston (see Appendix 14)											
Youngman-Baynes High Lift	1948	1	M	1	2	-	180	0.0714	?	3,500	?

"Bomber aircraft 1940-1949"

Manufacturer & Aircraft	First Flight	No. Made	M.pln B.pln T.pln	No. Eng.	No. Crew	Max. bomb load (lb)	Max. mph	pwr/wt ratio HP/lb	service ceiling (ft.)	Max wt. (lb.)	Max. Range (miles)
A											
Armstrong Whitworth AW.41 Albemarle	1940	602	M	2	4	4,000	265	0.0952	18,000	33,400	1,350
AW. 41 Albemarle initially conceived as a medium reconnaissance/bomber but no real improvement over 1936 Vickers Wellington. Became transport aircraft and glider tug.											
Avro 684	n/a	0	M	5	7	12,000	410	0.0952	50,300	68,000	2,300
Avro 684 intended as ultra-high altitude (beyond fighters) Lancaster, with 5th Merlin engine driving supercharger for all 4 "normal" engines. Not pursued											
Avro 683 Lancaster (Lancaster Mk.I data)	1941	7,377	M	4	7	14,000	282	0.0753	21,000	68,000	2,530
Lancaster was stretched-wing four-Merlin engines major variation of twin-engined 1939 Avro 679 Manchester.											

1940-49 Bomber aircraft continued on next page

APPENDIX 10, 1940-1949

Manufacturer & Aircraft	First Flight	No. Made	M.pln B.pln T.pln	No. Eng.	No. Crew	Max. bomb load (lb)	Max. mph	pwr/wt ratio (HP/lb)	service ceiling (ft.)	Max wt. (lb.)	Max. Range (miles)
A, 1940-49 Bomber aircraft, continued											
Avro 694 Lincoln	1944	604	M	4	7	14,000	319	0.0854	30,500	82,000	2,930
B											
Bristol 164 Brigand	1944	147	M	2	3	2,000	362	0.1267	26,000	39,000	2,800
Brigand (Buckingham derivative, conceived as Torpedo Bomber, 11 built as such but converted to bomber). Reliability problems when used in the tropics.											
Bristol 163 Buckingham											
Of 123 produced, only 54 built as bomber, intended to replace Blenheim. See 1940-49 Military Utility aircraft.											
Bristol Type 159	n/a	0	M	4	7	15,000	302	0.0845	25,300	71,000	2,500
Mock-up of this 4-engined heavy bomber produced but project curtailed, priority being given to fighters											
D											
De Havilland DH.98 Mosquito	1940	7,781	M	2	2	2,000	415	0.1368	37,000	25,000	1,500
DH Mosquito also used as night fighter and photo-reconnaissance aircraft.											
								thrust/ weight ratio			
E											
Canberra numbers include USA-built Martin B-57											
English Electric Canberra	1949	1,052	M	2	2	8,000	580	0.2691	48,000	55.000	3,380 (ferry)
								pwr/wt ratio (HP/lb)			
F											
Fairey Barracuda	1940	2,607	M	1	3	1,800	228	0.1163	16,600	14,100	686
Fairey Spearfish	1945	5(E)	M	1	3	2,000	292	0.1279	25,000	22,083	1,036
Fairey Spearfish cancelled as result of WW2 ending, eventually used as experimental aircraft											
S											
Supermarine 322	1943	2P	M	1	3	1,500	279	0.1083	?	12,000	825
Fairey Barracuda chosen over Supermarine 322											

1940-49 Bomber aircraft continued on next page

V, 1940-49 Bomber aircraft, continued

Manufacturer & Aircraft	First Flight	No. Made	M.pln B.pln T.pln	No. Eng.	No. Crew	Max. bomb load (lb)	Max. mph	pwr/wt ratio (HP/lb)	service ceiling (ft)	Max wt. (lb.)	Max. Range (miles)
Vickers Victory (1940 wind tunnel model tests)	n/a	n/a	M	6	?	22,000	352	0.0912	45,000	104,000	?
Vickers Windsor	1943	3P	M	4	6 or 7	15,000	317	0.1211	27,250	54,000	2,890

Intended as high speed Vickers Wellington replacement, eventually designed as four-engined high altitude bomber but overtaken by Avro Lancaster improvements

"Fighter aircraft 1940–1949"

Manufacturer & Aircraft	First Flight	No. Made	M.pln B.pln T.pln	No. Eng.	No. Crew	Max. bomb load (lb)	Max. mph	pwr/wt ratio (HP/lb) thrust/weight ratio	service ceiling (ft)	Max wt. (lb.)	Max. Range (miles)
B											
Blackburn B.44	B.44 concept intended as fighter operating from remote Pacific islands as a retractable hull flying boat fighter (see also Saro SR.A/1). No record of flying										
Blackburn Firebrand	Intended as naval strike/fighter, changed role:- see 1940-49 surface attack aircraft										
Blackburn Firecrest	1947	3P	M	1	1	500	380	0.1682	30,350	16,800	900
Boulton Paul P.92	Turret-armed fighter/ground attack aircraft, one half-scale version built & flown										
Bristol 164 Brigand	see 1940-49 Bomber aircraft										
De Havilland DH.103 Hornet	1944	388	M	1	1	1,000	475	0.2617	41,500	15,820	1,480
De Havilland DH.100 Vampire	1943	3,268	M	1	1	1,000	548	0.2704	42,800	12,390	1,220
	DH.100 prototype first flew as an experimental aircraft, became first prototype of DH Vampire										
De Havilland DH.112 Venom	1949	1,431	M	1	1	2,000	640	0.3149	39,400	15,400	1,080
	(incl. Sea Venom and French-built version Aquilon)										

1940-49 Fighter aircraft continued on next page

APPENDIX 10, 1940-1949

Manufacturer & Aircraft	First Flight	No. Made	M.pln B.pln T.pln	No. Eng.	No. Crew	Max. bomb load (lb)	Max. mph	pwr/wt ratio (HP/lb)	service ceiling (ft.)	Max wt. (lb.)	Max. Range (miles)
F, 1940–49 Fighter aircraft, continued											
Fairey Firefly	see 1940–49 Anti-submarine aircraft										
Fairey Fulmar	1940	600	M	1	2	200	272	0.1275	27,200	10,200	780
Fairey Fulmar developed from 1934 P4/34 prototype Bomber aircraft.											
								thrust/ weight ratio			
G											
Gloster E1/44	1948	3P	M	1	1	-	620	0.4359	44,000	11,470	410
Gloster Meteor (1948 F.8 data)	1943	3,947	M	2	1	2,000	600	0.4586	43,000	15,700	600
H											
Hawker Sea Hawk	1947	542	M	1	1	2,000	600	0.3220	44,500	1,650	480
Hawker Tempest	see 1940–49 Surface Attack aircraft										
Hawker Tornado	see 1940–49 Surface Attack aircraft							pwr/wt ratio (HP/lb)			
Hawker Typhoon	see 1940–49 Surface Attack aircraft										
Hawker Sea Fury	1945	864	M	1	1	2,000	460	0.1963	35,800	14,650	700
M											
Martin–Baker MB 3	1942	1P	M	1	1	-	415	0.1654	40,000	12,090	1,100
Martin–Baker MB 5	1944	1P	M	1	1	-	460	0.1683	40,000	12,090	1,100
Miles M.20	1940	2P	M	1	1	-	333	0.1575	32,800	8,000	920
S											
Supermarine Seafang	1946	18	M	1	1	2,000	475	0.2249	41,000	10,450	393
Supermarine Seafire	1942	2,646	M	1	1	-	359	0.2075	32,000	7,640	513
Supermarine Spiteful	1944	19	M	1	1	2,000	483	0.2387	42,000	9,950	564
Supermarine Attacker started from jet version of Spiteful								thrust/ weight ratio			
Supermarine Attacker	1946	185	M	1	1	-	590	0.4095	45,000	12,211	590

1940–49 Fighter aircraft continued on next page

APPENDIX 10, 1940-1949

Manufacturer & Aircraft	First Flight	No. Made	M.pln B.pln T.pln	No. Eng.	No. Crew	Max. bomb load (lb)	Max. mph	thrust/ weight ratio	service ceiling (ft.)	Max wt. (lb.)	Max. Range (miles)
S, 1940-49 Fighter aircraft, continued											
Saunders-Roe SR.A/1	1947	3P	M	2	1	2,000	512	0.4813	48,000	16,000	1¾hrs
Saunders Roe SR.A/1 was flying boat jet fighter, the only aircraft ever built with the Metropolitan Vickers F/2 axial compressor Beryl as power plant (ignoring Beryl follow-on Armstrong Siddeley Saphire development)											
								pwr/wt ratio (HP/lb)			
V											
Vickers Type 432	1942	1P	M	2	1	-	380	0.3322	38,000	9,150	1,500
Designed to same requirement as 1942 Westland Welkin											
W											
Westland Welkin	1942	77	M	2	1	-	385	0.2161	44,000	11,410	1,480
Westland Welkin was high altitude development of 1938 Whirlwind fighter. Never used operationally by RAF, suffered from reaching M_{CRIT} at altitude. 26 further engine-less airframes built.											

"Patrol aircraft 1940–1949"

Manufacturer & Aircraft	First Flight	No. Made	M.pln B.pln T.pln	No. Eng.	No. Crew	Max. bomb load (lb)	Max. mph	pwr/wt ratio (HP/lb)	service ceiling (ft.)	Max wt. (lb.)	Max. Range (miles)
A											
Airspeed AS.39 Fleet Shadower	1940	1P	M	4	3	-	126	0.0807	14,700	6,935	6 hrs
Avro 696 Shackleton	see 1940-49 Anti-Submarine aircraft										
G											
General Aircraft GAL.38 Fleet Shadower	1940	1P	M	4	3	-	115	0.0598	6,000	9,458	990
S											
Short S.45 Seaford (flying boat)	1944	10	M	4	8-11	4,960	242	0.0917	14,000	75,000	3,100
Developed from 1937 Short Sunderland											

1940-49 Patrol aircraft continued on next page

APPENDIX 10, 1940-1949

S, 1940-49 Patrol aircraft, continued

Manufacturer & Aircraft	First Flight	No. Made	M.pln B.pln T.pln	No. Eng.	No. Crew	Max. bomb load (lb)	Max. mph	pwr/wt ratio (HP/lb)	service ceiling (ft.)	Max wt. (lb.)	Max. Range (miles)
Short S.35 (Shetland I) and	1944	2P	M	4	11	4,000	263	0.0800	17,000	125,000	4,000
S.40 (Shetland II) flying boats											26 hrs
Designed as long-range Sunderland replacement, converted to transport but did not see service..											

"Surface Attack aircraft 1940–1949"

Manufacturer & Aircraft	First Flight	No. Made	M.pln B.pln T.pln	No. Eng.	No. Crew	Max. bomb load (lb)	Max. mph	pwr/wt ratio (HP/lb)	service ceiling (ft.)	Max wt. (lb.)	Max. Range (miles)
B											
Blackburn Firebrand	1942	223	M	1	1	4,000	342	0.1509	34,000	16,700	745
H											
Hawker Tempest	1944	1,702	M	1	1	2,000	432	0.1598	36,500	13,640	740
Hawker Tornado	1939	4	M	1	1	?	398	0.1650	34,900	10,668	?
Hawker Typhoon	1940	3,317	M	1	1	2,000	412	0.1930	35,200	13,250	510
W											
Westland Wyvern	1946	127	M	1	1	3,000	383	0.1450	28,000	24,550	910
Turboprop engine with additional 1,100lbf jet thrust											

"Anti-submarine aircraft 1940–1949"

Manufacturer & Aircraft	First Flight	No. Made	M.pln B.pln T.pln	No. Eng.	No. Crew	Max. bomb load (lb)	Max. mph	pwr/wt ratio (HP/lb)	service ceiling (ft.)	Max wt. (lb.)	Max. Range (miles)
Avro 696 Shackleton	1949	185	M	4	10	10,000	300	0.0912	20,200	86,000	1,950
											14½hrs
Built successively in three marks. In 1971 the first of twelve Mk.2 converted to AEW role flew											

1940-49 Anti-submarine aircraft continued on next page

APPENDIX 10, 1940-1949

B, 1940-49 Anti-submarine aircraft, continued

Manufacturer & Aircraft	First Flight	No. Made	M.pln B.pln T.pln	No. Eng.	No. Crew	Max. bomb load (lb)	Max. mph	pwr/wt ratio (HP/lb)	service ceiling (ft)	Max wt. (lb.)	Max. Range (miles)
Blackburn B-54 & B-88 (B-88 data)	1949	3P	M	2	3	?	320	0.2253	13,091	?	?
After cancellation of twin-coupled Napier turboprop engine, second aircraft became B-88 with Armstrong Siddeley Double Mamba engine. RN chose Fairey Gannet											
F											
Fairey Firefly	1941	1,702	M	1	2	2,000	316	0.1234	28,000	14,020	1,300
Fairey Gannet	1949	348	M	2	3	2,000	310	0.1399	25,000	22,487	944
44 of 348 Fairey Gannet aircraft built were later converted to AEW standard											5+ hrs
S											
Fairey Spearfish	1945	5	M	1	2	2,000	292	0.1279	25,000	22,083	1,036
Short Sturgeon	1946	28	M	2	3	-	366	0.1917	35,200	21,700	1,600
Sturgeon intended as carrier-borne strike aircraft, entered service as target tug											

"Reconnaissance aircraft 1940-1949"

Manufacturer & Aircraft	First Flight	No. Made	M.pln B.pln T.pln	No. Eng.	No. Crew	Max. bomb load (lb)	Max. mph	pwr/wt ratio (HP/lb)	service ceiling (ft)	Max wt. (lb.)	Max. Range (miles)
A											
Auster A.2/45	1948	2P	M	1	2	-	130	0.0743	15,500	3365	600
Auster AOP.6	1945	400	M	1	2	-	124	0.0671	14,000	2160	315
AOP.6 was post-Second Word War revised version of Taylorcraft Auster AOP											
E											
English Electric Canberra	see 1940-49 Bomber aircraft										
H											
Heston JC.6	1947	2P	M	1	2	-	125	0.0775	?	~3,095	~750
S											
Supermarine 381 Seagull (not 1921 aircraft)	1948	2P	M	1	3	-	260	0.1252	23,900	14,500	875
Supermarine Seagull type 381 amphibious flying boat could rescue 7 survivors											

1940-49 Reconnaissance aircraft continued on next page

APPENDIX 10, 1940-1949

1940-49 Reconnaissance aircraft, continued

Manufacturer & Aircraft	First Flight	No. Made	M.pln B.pln T.pln	No. Eng.	No. Crew	Max. bomb load (lb)	Max. mph	pwr/wt ratio (HP/lb)	service ceiling (ft.)	Max. wt. (lb.)	Max. Range (miles)
Taylorcraft Auster AOP	1942	1,630	M	1	3	-	130	0.0703	?	1,850	850
(UK licence-build, AOP versions)	Taylorcraft Auster AOP was UK adaptation of the USA 1930 C. Gilbert Taylor Cub ("forefather" of 1938 USA Piper Cub). USA Cub derivatives and sub-variants totalled 49,000 by end of production 1994. See also 1940-49 & 1950-59 "Civil Utility" Auster.										

"Military Trainer aircraft 1940–1949"

Manufacturer & Aircraft	First Flight	No. Made	M.pln B.pln T.pln	No. Eng.	No. Crew	Max. bomb load (lb)	Max. mph	pwr/wt ratio (HP/lb)	service ceiling (ft.)	Max. wt. (lb.)	Max. Range (miles)
A											
Airspeed Cambridge	1941	2P	M	1	2	-	237	?	24,800	?	~684
Avro Athena (tubo-prop)	1948	22	M	1	2	-	293	0.1574	29,000	8,130	550
B											
Boulton Paul Balliol	1947	229	M	1	2	-	288	0.1480	32,500	8,410	660
Boulton Paul P.112	P.112 cancelled before prototype complete										
Boulton Paul P.116	P.116 cancelled before prototype complete										
Bristol 166 Buckmaster	1944	112	M	2	3	-	352	0.0767	30,000	33,700	2,000
	Bristol 166 Buckmaster developed from Bristol 163 Buckingham bomber										
F											
Fairey Primer	1948	2	M	1	2	-	134	0.0740	19,500	1,960	383
	Oscar Tips of Avions Fairey designed Tipsy series, Tipsy M was last before 1940 invasion of Belgium. Parent UK company produced 2 post-war, as Fairey Primer										
G											
General Aircraft GAL.55 (glider)	1943	2P	M	n/a	2	-	225	n/a	n/a	2,350	n/a
General Aircraft GAL.45 Owlet	1940	1P	M	1	2	-	125	0.0652	?	2,300	?
H											
Handley Page Reading HPR1 Marathon	HPR1 was ex- bankrupt Miles M.60. Used by RAF as navigation trainer. see 1940-49 Civil Airliner aircraft										

1940-49 Military Trainer aircraft continued on next page

APPENDIX 10, 1940–1949

Manufacturer & Aircraft	First Flight	No. Made	M.pln B.pln T.pln	No. Eng.	No. Crew	Max. bomb load (lb)	Max. mph	pwr/wt ratio (HP/lb)	service ceiling (ft.)	Max wt. (lb.)	Max. Range (miles)
M, 1940-49 Military Trainer aircraft, continued											
Miles M.28 Mercury	1941	6	N	1	1	2-3	159	0.0600	?	2,500	355
Miles M.33 Monitor	1944	22	M	2	2	-	330	0.1613	29,000	21,075	2,750
Intended as target tug for RAF and RN, did not enter service											
P											
Percival Prentice	1946	>370	M	1	2-3	-	143	0.0598	18,000	4,200	396
Percival Prince	see 1940-49 Civil Airliner: Used by Royal Navy (FAA) as transport and navigation trainer										
R											
Reid and Sigrist R.S.3	1945	2	M	2	2	-	181	0.0901	24,000	3,550	4½hrs
In 1951, R.S.3 converted to R.S.4 Bobsleigh by RAE, for Prone Pilot research											
V											
Vickers Varsity	1949	163	M	2	4	-	288	0.1040	28,700	37,500	2648
Varsity developed from 1947 Valetta military transport: Longer fuselage and span, tricycle undercarriage. Multi-engined aircraft crew training. For bomber crew training, pannier underneath for prone bomb aimer											

"Military Transport aircraft 1940–1949"

Manufacturer & Aircraft	First Flight	No. Made	M.pln B.pln T.pln	No. Eng.	No. Crew	Max. passenger (troops)	Max. mph	pwr/wt ratio (HP/lb)	service ceiling (ft.)	Max wt. (lb.)	Max. Range (miles)
A											
Armstrong Whitworth AW.41 Albemarle	See 1940 Bomber aircraft										
H											
Handley Page HP.67 Hastings	1946	151	M	4	5	50	348	0.0813	26,500	80,000	1,690
Although a tailwheel design, shared lot of design elements with 1945 Handley Page Hermes airliner											
V											
Vickers Valetta	1947	262	M	2	4	34	258	0.1096	21,500	36,500	1,46

1940-49 Military Utility aircraft on next page

"Military Utility aircraft 1940–1949"

APPENDIX 10, 1940-1949

Manufacturer & Aircraft	First Flight	No. Made	M.pln B.pln T.pln	No. Eng.	No. Crew	Max. passenger	Max. mph	pwr/wt ratio (HP/lb)	service ceiling (ft.)	Max wt. (lb.)	Max. Range (miles)
A											
Auster Avis	1947	2P	M	1	1	3	115	0.0569	12,000	2,550	500
Auster Avis developed from J/1 Autocrat ("J family": see 1940-49 Civil Utility aircraft											
B											
Bristol Buckingham C.1	1943	123	M	2	3	4	336	0.1482	?	34,000	2,300
65 Buckingham C.1(conversion design from B.1, 54 + 4 prototypes built) used as fast communications aircraft											
Bristol 171 Sycamore (helicopter)	1947	180	H	1	2	3	132	0.0982	?	5,600	330
F											
Fane F.1/40	1941	1P	M	1	2	-	?	0.0533	?	1,500	?
G											
General Aircraft GAL.47	1940	1P	M	1	2	-	?	0.0557	?	1,615	?
M											
Miles M.32 Messenger	1942	93	M	1	1	3	135	0.0646	16,000	2,400	460
Developed from 1941 Miles Mercury military trainer											
S											
Saunders-Roe Skeeter (helicopter)	1948	~74	H	1	2	-	109	0.0977	12,800	2,200	260
Saro Skeeter first flew as Cierva (Weir) W.14											
Scottish Aviation Pioneer	1947	59	M	1	1	4	162	0.0897	23,000	5,800	420
W											
Westland WS-51Dragonfly (helicopter)	1948	133	H	1	1	3	95	0.0920	12,400	5,870	300
Licence-built version of USA Sikorsky S-51											

Civil Aircraft 1940-49 on next page

BRITISH CIVIL AIRCRAFT 1940-49
P = Prototype(s) Only

APPENDIX 10, 1940-1949

pwr/wt ratio = power/weight ratio = [(total engine power) ÷ (max. weight)] = HP/lb
thrust/weight ratio = [(total engine jet thrust) ÷ (max. weight)] = lbf/lb

"Airliners 1930–1939"

Manufacturer & Aircraft	First Flight	No. Made	M.pln B.pln T.pln	No. Eng.	No. Crew	Max. passenger	Max. mph	pwr/wt ratio (HP/lb)	service ceiling (ft.)	Max. wt. (lb.)	Max. Range (miles)
A											
Airspeed AS.57 Ambassador	1947	23	M	2	3	60	312	0.1000	25,000	52,500	550
Airspeed AS.65 Consul	1946	162	M	2	1	6	190	0.0958	19,000	8,250	900
Airspeed Consuls were refurbished ex-1937 AS.10 Oxfords (see Appendix 9)											
Armstrong Whitworth Apollo	1940	2P	M	2	3	31	330	0.0430	28,000	47,000	940
Avro Lancastrian	1943	91	M	4	5	9	310	0.0769	23,000	64,991	4,150
First nine Lancastrians were converted Lancasters, by Victory Aircraft in Canada											
Avro Tudor	1945	38	M	4	5	24	320	0.1073	30,100	76,080	3,630
Avro York	1942	258	M	4	5	56	298	0.0788	23,000	65,000	3,000
B											
Bristol 167 Brabazon	1949	1P	M	8	5-12	100	300	0.0731	25,000	290,000	550,0
Project cancelled in 1953, when second prototype incomplete. Second aircraft had change from 1st prototype piston engines to turboprop engines, never completed.											
Bristol 170 Freighter (and SuperFreighter)	see 1940-49 Cargo aircraft (Cargo: opening nose clamshell doors, Airliner: solid nose dome). SuperFreighter (SuperWayfarer as airliner) had 5ft fuselage stretch, room for 3 cars+20 passengers. One converted for 60 (no-cars) all-passenger.										
C											
Cierva W.15 Air Horse (helicopter)	1948	2P	H	1	3	24	140	0.0926	23,300	17,500	330
Cunliffe-Owen Concordia	1947	2P	M	2	3	12	223	0.1000	21,000	10,999	1,200

1940-49 Airliners continued on next page

APPENDIX 10, 1940-1949

Manufacturer & Aircraft	First Flight	No. Made	M.pln B.pln T.pln	No. Eng.	No. Crew	Max. passenger	Max. mph	thrust/ weight ratio	service ceiling (ft.)	Max wt. (lb.)	Max. Range (miles)
D, 1940-49 Airliners, continued											
D											
De Havilland 106 Comet 1	1949	21	M	4	4	48	490	0.1905	40,000	105,050	1,500
De Havilland type 106 Comet 1 was world's first jet airliner											
De Havilland 106 Comet 2											
15 built. Comet 2 fuselage strengthened, used by RAF, with altitude limit											
De Havilland 106 Comet 3	1954	1P	M	4	4	76	500	0.3333	40,000	120,000	2,700
De Havilland 106 Comet 4	1958	75	M	4	4	81	503	0.2593	42,000	162,000	3,225
								pwr/wt ratio (HP/lb)			
De Havilland DH.104 Dove	1945	542	M	2	2	8	230	0.0894	21,700	8,950	880
H											
Handley Page HP.81 Hermes	1945	29	M	4	5+2	82	350	0.0977	24,500	86,000	2,000
Developed as tricycle undercarriage partner of 1946 HP.67 Hastings Military Transport											
Handley Page Marathon (HPR.1 Marathon),	1946	43	M	4	2	20	233	0.0745	18,000	18,250	935
Handley Page (Reading) bought Miles Marathon project when Miles bankrupt											
M											
Miles M.26											
Miles M.26 proposals never proceeded beyond paper, except M.30 sub-scale test. M.26 covers 'X2 to X15' proposals for long-range (blended wing-body) transports											
Miles Merchantman											
see 1940-49 Cargo aircraft											
P											
Percival Prince	1948	75	M	2	2	3	223	0.0928	22,000	11,850	460
Planet Satellite	1949	1P	M	1	1	3	208	0.0757	22,000	2,905	1,000
Planet Satellite: two flights (hops), second flight magnesium alloy fuselage cracked on touchdown. Abandoned and finally scrapped 1958. Second fuselage used in 1952 Firth Atlantic helicopter.											

1940-49 Airliners continued on next page

APPENDIX 10, 1940-1949

S, 1940-49 Airliners, continued

Manufacturer & Aircraft	First Flight	No. Made	M.pln B.pln T.pln	No. Eng.	No. Crew	Max. passenger	Max. mph	pwr/wt ratio (HP/lb)	service ceiling (ft.)	Max wt. (lb.)	Max. Range (miles)
Short S.25 Sandringham	1943	(51)	M	4	5	24	206	0.0800	17,900	60,000	2,440
51 ex-RAF S.25 Sunderland flying boats converted to Sandringham (9 versions). Sandringhams included 23 "BOAC Hythe" and 1 "Ansett Islander".											
Short S.A.6 Sealand (amphibious flying boat)	1948	25	M	2	1 or 2	7	187	0.0747	20,600	9,100	660
Short S.45 Solent (flying boat)	1946	16	M	4	7	34	273	0.0866	17,000	78,000	1,800
Developed from 1944 Short Seaford patrol aircraft., plus 7 by conversion											
V											
Vickers VC.1 Viking	1945	163	M	2	2	36	263	0.0994	25,000	34,000	1,700
Viking was airliner fuselage on Wellington bomber wing, Bristol Hercules engines											
Vickers Viscount	1948	445	M	4	2	Viscount was world's first turboprop airliner					
(series 700 data)	First production (700) series, 1953					75	352	0.0948	25,000	65,000	1,507
(series 810 data)	Viscount 810 model, 1957					63	~350	0.1075	25,000	58,500	1,730

"Civil Cargo aircraft 1940–1949"

Manufacturer & Aircraft	First Flight	No. Made	M.pln B.pln T.pln	No. Eng.	No. Crew	Max. passenger	Max. mph	pwr/wt ratio (HP/lb)	service ceiling (ft.)	Max wt. (lb.)	Max. Range (miles)
B											
Bristol 170 Freighter	1945	194	M	2	2	44	225	0.0845	24,500	36,500	820
see also 1953 Superfreighter version (Appendix 11)											
M											
Miles M.57 Aerovan	1945	52	M	2	2	10	127	0.0517	13,250	5,800	400
Miles M.68	1947	1P	M	2	2	n/a	140	0.0474	?	?	290
Miles M.68: adapted Miles Aerovan with detachable "container box" for fuselage											
Miles M.71 Merchantman	1947	1P	M	4	1	20	163	0.0769	16,000	13,000	860
Miles Merchantman was scaled up M.57 Aerovan. Marathon wing similar											

1940-49 Civil Utility aircraft on next page

"Civil Utility aircraft 1940–1949"

APPENDIX 10, 1940-1949

Manufacturer & Aircraft	First Flight	No. Made	M.pln B.pln T.pln	No. Eng.	No. Crew	Max. passenger	Max. mph	pwr/wt ratio (HP/lb)	service ceiling (ft.)	Max wt. (lb.)	Max. Range (miles)
A											
Derived from WW2 (1942) army reconnaissance AOP Taylorcraft Auster Model J, Auster J/1 was basis of a family of light/trainer aircraft, J/1 Alpha was J/1 Autocrat conversion with more power (45 new-build Alpha included in Autocrat total). see also Appendix 11, 1950-59 Civil Utility.											
Auster J/1 Autocrat	1945	420	M	1	1	2	120	0.0541	14,000	1,850	320
Auster J/2 Arrow	1945	44	M	1	1	1	98	0.0517	10,000	1,450	320
Auster J3 Atom	1946	1	M	1	1	2	?	0.0406	?	1,601	?
Auster J/4 Arrow	1946	27	M	1	1	1	108	0.0563	12,500	1,600	317
Auster J/5 Adventurer	1947	59	M	1	1	2	125	0.0650	?	2,000	200
Auster J/5 Autocar	1949	202	M	1	1	3	116	0.0531	11,000	2,450	500

"Sports, Sailplanes and Motor Gliders 1940–1949"

Manufacturer & Aircraft	First Flight	No. Made	M.pln B.pln T.pln	No. Eng.	No. Crew	Max. passenger	Max. mph	pwr/wt ratio (HP/lb)	service ceiling (ft.)	Max wt. (lb.)	Max. Range (miles)
E											
Elliotts of Newbury (EoN)	1947	1P	M	1	1	3	~136	0.0426	?	2,350	?
(EoN A.P.4, Eon 1 data. Later change to higher power engine as Eon 2) The Newbury Eon was the only powered aircraft produced by Elliotts (designed for them by Aviation and Engineering Products, of Feltham). All other designs were gliders, responsibility taken by Slingsby in 1966 when Elliots abandoned glider work.											
EoN Type 5 Olympia (glider)	1947	150*	M		1	-	136	n/a	n/a	670	n/a
Series 1, 2 & 3... (Olympia 2 data)... total build includes 1950s versions... 1954 new type Series 4, 401, 402, 403, 415, 419... total all series 150*... see also Appendix 11.											
N											
Napier-Heston Racer	1940	1	M	1	1	-	~480	0.3403	?	7,200	18min.
Built to Napier concept, built by Heston Aircraft. Designed for world speed record attempt. Crashed on 1st flt											
S											
Short Nimbus (glider)	1947	1	M	n/a	2	-	?	n/a	?	1,200	n/a
A Shorts gliding club design, Nimbus was last aircraft to be designed, built and flown from Rochester works.											

1940-49 Sports, Sailplanes and Motor Glider aircraft continued on next page

APPENDIX 10, 1940-1949

Manufacturer & Aircraft	First Flight	No. Made	M.pln B.pln T.pln	No. Eng.	No. Crew	Max. passenger	Max. mph	pwr/wt ratio (HP/lb)	service ceiling (ft.)	Max wt. (lb.)	Max. Range (miles)
S, 1940-49 Sports, Sailplanes and Motor Glider aircraft, continued											
Slingsby T.21 (glider)	1944	226	M	-	2	-	104	n/a	n/a	1,049	n/a
Slingsby T.29A/B	1948	3	M	1	1	-	71	0.0458	11,400	807	n/a
Motor Tutor	Developed from 1937 Slingsby T.8 Tutor										
Slingsby T.30 Prefect (glider)	1948	~53	M	-	1	-	104	n/a	n/a	615	n/a
Slingsby T.31 Tandem Tutor (glider) (Cadet TX.3)	1949	~230	M	-	2	-	81	n/a	n/a	829	n/a

Appendix 11

British Military and Civil Aircraft 1950–1959

Data in this Appendix is representative of aircraft type, usually early model. For exact data, refer to original sources.

BRITISH MILITARY AIRCRAFT 1950-1959

APPENDIX 11, 1950-1959

P = Prototype(s) Only

wet thrust = with reheat

pwr/wt ratio = power/weight ratio = [(total engine power) ÷ (max. weight)] = HP/lb

thrust/weight ratio = [(total engine jet thrust) ÷ (max. weight)] = lbf/lb

"Experimental aircraft 1950-59" (see also Appendix 14)

Manufacturer & Aircraft	First Flight	No. Made	M.pln B.pln T.pln	No. Eng.	No. Crew	Max. bomb load (lb)	Max. mph	thrust/ weight ratio	service ceiling (ft.)	Max wt. (lb.)	Max. Range (miles)
A											
Avro 706 Ashton (renamed 689 Tudor 9)	1950	6	M	4	5	-	439	0.2439	40,500	82,000	1,725
Avro Ashton was Rolls Royce Nene jet-powered test aircraft adaptation of 1945 Avro Tudor. Used for research and jet turbine test bed (Rolls-Royce, Bristol and Armstrong Siddeley)											
B											
Boulton Paul P.111	1950	1	M	1	1	-	649	0.5036	35,000	10,127	?
Boulton Paul P.120	1952	1	M	1	1	-	~520	0.4054	?	12,580	?
P.120 was T-tailed version of P.111 (uncropped delta wing). Last BP design to fly											
E											
English Electric P.1A	1954	2	M	2	1	-	1,011	0.5540	60,000	27,007	?
English Electric P.1B	1957	3	M	2	1	-	1,390	0.5565	60,000	34,140	?
P.1A and P.1B were research aircraft leading to Mach 2 Lightning interceptor (see1950-59 fighter aircraft)											
F											
Fairey Delta 1	1951	1	M	1	1	-	628	0.5294	?	2,800	?
Fairey Delta 2	1954	2	M	1	1	-	1,300	0.7023	?	13,884	?
Folland Fo.139 Midge	1954	1	M	1	1	-	600	0.3684	40,000	4,500	?
Folland Midge was concept test aircraft and demonstrator for Folland Fo.141 Gnat											
H											
Handley Page HP.87 (glider)	1948?	1	M	n/a	1	-	n/a	n/a	n/a	?	n/a
One third scale crescent wing radio-controlled glider, low-speed handling trials of crescent wing planform shape of Handley Page Victor. HP.87 crashed on first flight, so HP.88 authorised by government											
Handley Page HP.88	1951	1	M	1	1	-	684	0.3258	?	14,640	?
Crescent wing test scale aircraft for Handley Page Victor crescent wing (modified Supermarine Attacker, Blackburn built). See Appendix 10 for Attacker data											

1950-59 Experimental aircraft continued on next page

S, 1950-59 Experimental aircraft, continued

Manufacturer & Aircraft	First Flight	No. Made	M.pln B.pln T.pln	No. Eng.	No. Crew	Max. bomb load (lb)	Max. mph	thrust/ weight ratio	service ceiling (ft.)	Max wt. (lb.)	Max. Range (miles)
Saunders-Roe SR.53	1957	2P	M	2	1	-	1,400	0.5548	60,000	17,575	?
Research aircraft prior to Saunders Roe SR.177 design to specification F.155T for turbojet/rocket interceptor											
Supermarine 508 (research towards Scimitar)	1951	1	M	2	1	-	~600	?	?	?	?
Three Supermarine "research aircraft" built, first two with thin, unswept wings and butterfly tail and tailwheel undercarriage. Second modified before flight with hinged rear fuselage to give all-flying tail, becoming type 529. type 529: 2nd "508", rear fuselage reconfigured, and additional aerodynamic features (see below) type 525: 3rd aircraft, swept wings and cruciform tail (see below).											
Supermarine 510 (pre-prototype of Swift)	1950	2	Both 510 modified, 1st into 517 before flight, 2nd into 528								
Supermarine 517	1950	(1)	Modified first 510, rear fuselage adjustable (in flight), for pitch trim								
Supermarine 525	1954	1	M	2	1	-	647	0.4615	28,169	42,600	?
Supermarine 528	1950	(1)	Modified second 510, larger more swept wing, engine reheat available								
Supermarine 529	1952	1	Revised version of type 508 with representative armament & additional equipment								
Supermarine 535	1950	(1)	Further modified 528, longer nose and nosewheel, engine reheat								

"Bomber aircraft 1950–1959"

Manufacturer & Aircraft	First Flight	No. Made	M.pln B.pln T.pln	No. Eng.	No. Crew	Max. bomb load (lb)	Max. mph	thrust/ weight ratio	service ceiling (ft.)	Max wt. (lb.)	Max. Range (miles)
Avro 698 Vulcan (B.Mk.1 data)	1952	136	M	4	5	21,000	645	0.2378	55,000	175,000	~4,600
6 Mk.2 aircraft converted to air-to-air refuelling tankers											
Avro 730	n/a	0	M	2	1	~2,000*	1,320	0.5548	60,000	17,575	?
Avro 730 ordered 1955, to OR.330 (reconnaissance). OR.336 (tactical nuclear strike – *Red Beard) added later. Project cancelled as a result of 1957 Defence Review											

1950-59 Bomber aircraft continued on next page

Manufacturer & Aircraft	First Flight	No. Made	M.pln B.pln T.pln	No. Eng.	No. Crew	Max. bomb load (lb)	Max. mph	thrust/ weight ratio	service ceiling (ft.)	Max wt. (lb.)	Max. Range (miles)
H, 1950-59 Bomber aircraft, continued											
H											
H. Page HP.80 Victor (B.Mk.1 data)	1952	86	M	4	5	35,000	627	0.2156	56,000	205,000	6,000
Bomb load over 21,000lb resulted in significant range penalty. Blue Danube and later Strategic nuclear weapon Some aircraft (Mk.1 and, later, Mk.2) converted to tanker air-to-air refuelling tankers											
S											
Short SA.4 Sperrin	1951	2P	M	4	5	20,000	564	0.2261	45,000	115,000	3,860
V											
Vickers Valiant	1951	107	M	4	5	21,000	567	0.2857	54,000	140,000	4,500
Blue Danube and later Strategic nuclear weapon. Some aircraft converted to air-to-air refuelling tankers											

"Fighter aircraft 1950–1959"

Manufacturer & Aircraft	First Flight	No. Made	M.pln B.pln T.pln	No. Eng.	No. Crew	Max. bomb load (lb)	Max. mph	thrust/ weight ratio	service ceiling (ft.)	Max wt. (lb.)	Max. Range (miles)
A											
Avro 720	n/a	0	M	2	1	-	1,320	0.5548	60,000	17,575	?
Avro 720 was 1953 rocket/turbojet interceptor, to meet specification F.155T. Cancelled engine ended project											
D											
De Havilland DH.112 Sea Venom	1951	see DH.112 Venom (Appendix 10)									
De Havilland DH.110 Sea Vixen	1951	145	M	2	2	~2,000*	690	0.4706	48,000	41,575	790
DH Sea Vixen had option of tactical nuclear strike capability (*Red Beard weapon)											
E											
English Electric Lightning (F.6 data)	1957	332	M	2	1	-	1,300	0.6995 (wet)	70,000	45,750	850
for the 5 experimental prototypes pre-Lightning, see P1A & P1B (on previous page)											
F											
Folland Fo.141/144 Gnat	see 1950-59 Military Trainer aircraft										

1950-59 Fighter aircraft continued on next page

APPENDIX 11, 1950-1959

G, 1950-59 Fighter aircraft, continued

Manufacturer & Aircraft	First Flight	No. Made	M.pln B.pln T.pln	No. Eng.	No. Crew	Max. bomb load (lb)	Max. mph	thrust/ weight ratio	service ceiling (ft.)	Max wt. (lb.)	Max. Range (miles)
Gloster Javelin	1951	436	M	2	2	-	710	0.5699	52,800	43,165	954
H											
Hawker Hunter	1951	1,972	M	1	1	-	715	0.4124	50,000	24,600	1,900 (Ferry)
Hunter first flight date is prototype. First production (F.1) flight 1953											
Hawker P.1121											
Mach 2.5 PV proposal, abandoned after 1957 Defence Review (see section 5.15)											
S											
Saunders-Roe SR.177	n/a	0	M	2	1	-	1,500*	0.8518	67,000	28,174	?
SR.177 and research aircraft SR.53 cancelled as a result of 1957 Defence Review											
*SR.177 theoretical performance, to specification F.155T											
Supermarine 544 Scimitar	see 1950-59 Surface Attack aircraft										
Supermarine 541 Swift	1951	197	M	1	1	-	713	0.3311	45,800	21,673	630
Swift first flight date is prototype. First production (F.1) flight 1952											
V											
Vickers Type 559	n/a	0	M	4	2	-	1,700	0.8040	60,000	62,190	32min
Vickers 559 was rejected proposal to same F.155T spec. as Avro 730 and SR.177											

"Surface Attack aircraft 1950–1959"

Manufacturer & Aircraft	First Flight	No. Made	M.pln B.pln T.pln	No. Eng.	No. Crew	Max. bomb load (lb)	Max. mph	thrust/ weight ratio	service ceiling (ft.)	Max wt. (lb.)	Max. Range (miles)
B											
Blackburn Buccaneer (1963 S2 version data)	1958	211	M	2	2	4,000	667	0.3581	40,000	62,000	2,300 (Ferry)
Buccaneer had Red Beard or WE.177A tactical nuclear weapon capability											
S											
Supermarine 544 Scimitar	1956	76	M	2	1	4,000	736	0.6579	46,000	34,200	1,422
Scimitar had option of tactical nuclear strike capability (Red Beard or WE.177A weapon)											

1950-59 Patrol aircraft on next page

"Patrol aircraft 1950-59"

Manufacturer & Aircraft	First Flight	No. Made	M.pln B.pln T.pln	No. Eng.	No. Crew	Max. bomb load (lb)	Max. mph	pwr/wt ratio (HP/lb)	service ceiling (ft.)	Max wt. (lb.)	Max. Range (miles)
S											
Short Seamew	1953	26	M	1	2	1,844	236	0.1060	?	15,000	750
Described by some as "a camel amongst racehorses", Seamew never reached service											
Westland Whirlwind (helicopter)	1953	>360	H	1	2	?	109	0.0962	13,000	7,800	334
Whirlwind was "Anglicised" licence build of USA Sikorsky H-19											
Westland Wessex (helicopter, HC.2 data)	1958	382	H	2	2	troops	132	0.1148	12,000	13,500	310
Wessex was "Anglicised" licence build of Sikorsky H-34 but re-engined with turboshaft. First batches: one Napier turboshaft engine. Later models two de Havilland Gnome turboshaft engines.											

"Reconnaissance aircraft 1950–1959"

Manufacturer & Aircraft	First Flight	No. Made	M.pln B.pln T.pln	No. Eng.	No. Crew	Max. bomb load (lb)	Max. mph	pwr/wt ratio (HP/lb)	service ceiling (ft.)	Max wt. (lb.)	Max. Range (miles)
A											
Auster AOP.9	1954	182	M	1	2/3	-	127	0.0742	18,500	2,330	242
Avro 730	see 1950-59 Bomber aircraft										

"Military Trainer aircraft 1950–1959"

Manufacturer & Aircraft	First Flight	No. Made	M.pln B.pln T.pln	No. Eng.	No. Crew	Max. bomb load (lb)	Max. mph	thrust/ weight ratio	service ceiling (ft.)	Max wt. (lb.)	Max. Range (miles)
B											
BAC Jet Provost	1954	734	M	1	2	2,160	440	0.2717	36,750	9,200	900
F											
Folland Gnat (single seat Gnat F.1 for Finland data)	1955	422	M	1	1	-	695	0.5205	48,000	9,040	500
Folland Gnat total includes Fo.140 (1), Fo.141 (237), Fo.144 (105) and 89 built as Ajeet (India), 10 of which were Gnat conversions. (Fo.144 built after HSA take over)											

1950-59 Military Trainer aircraft continued on next page

APPENDIX 11, 1950-1959

H, 1950-59 Military Trainer aircraft, continued

Manufacturer & Aircraft	First Flight	No. Made	M.pln B.pln T.pln	No. Eng.	No. Crew	Max. bomb load (lb)	Max. mph	pwr/wt ratio (HP/lb)	service ceiling (ft.)	Max wt. (lb.)	Max. Range (miles)
Handley Page HPR2 Basic Trainer	1950	2P	N	1	2	-	173	0.0950	20,500	4,421	485
								thrust/ weight ratio			
M											
Miles Student	1957	1P	M	1	2	-	298	0.2256	?	3,900	620
								pwr/wt ratio (HP/lb)			
P											
Percival Provost	1950	461	M	1	2	500	200	0.1250	25,000	4,399	560
S											
Slingsby T.38 Grasshopper (glider)	1952	115	M	n/a	1	-	80	n/a	n/a	550	n/a

"Military Transport aircraft 1950–1959"

Manufacturer & Aircraft	First Flight	No. Made	M.pln B.pln T.pln	No. Eng.	No. Crew	Max. passenger	Max. mph	pwr/wt ratio (HP/lb)	service ceiling (ft.)	Max wt. (lb.)	Max. Range (miles)
A											
Armsronng Whitworth Argosy (AW.650 & AW.660 data)	1959	74	M	4	4	69	~315	0.0941	23,000	105,000	3,450
B											
Bristol 192 Belvedere (helicopter)	1958	31	H	2	3	19	138	0.1562	12,000	19,000	460
Type 192 total includes 5 Bristol 173 as development prototypes (1st flight 1952)											
Blackburn B-101 Beverley	1950	49	M	4	6	80	238	0.0844	16,000	135,000	1,300
Bristol 175 Britannia	see 1950-59 Civil Airliners										
P											
Percival Pembroke	1952	128	M	2	2	8	186	0.0801	22,000	13,489	1,166

1950-59 Military Utility aircraft on next page

"Military Utility aircraft 1950–1959"

APPENDIX 11, 1950-1959

Manufacturer & Aircraft	First Flight	No. Made	M.pln B.pln T.pln	No. Eng.	No. Crew	Max. passenger	Max. mph	pwr/wt ratio (HP/lb)	service ceiling (ft.)	Max wt. (lb.)	Max. Range (miles)
F											
Fairey Ultra-light Helicopter	1955	6P	H	1	2	-	~100	0.2500	4,800	1,800	180
Saunders-Roe P.531 (helicopter)	1958	6P	H	1	2	1	121	0.0855	3,800	3,800	242
Saro P.531 later developed by Westland into Scout (1960) & Wasp (1962) helicopters											
Scottish Aviation Twin Pioneer	1956	87	M	2	2	13	165	0.0877	20,000	14,600	695
W											
Westland Whirlwind (helicopter)	see 1950-59 Patrol aircraft										

Civil Aircraft 1950-59 next page

BRITISH CIVIL AIRCRAFT 1950-59

APPENDIX 11, 1950-1959

P = Prototype(s) Only

pwr/wt ratio = power/weight ratio = [(total engine power) ÷ (max. weight)] = HP/lb

thrust/weight ratio = [(total engine jet thrust) ÷ (max. weight)] = lbf/lb

"Airliners 1950–1959"

Manufacturer & Aircraft	First Flight	No. Made	M.pln B.pln T.pln	No. Eng.	No. Crew	Max. passenger	Max. mph	pwr/wt ratio (HP/lb)	service ceiling (ft.)	Max wt. (lb.)	Max. Range (miles)
A											
Aviation Traders ATL-90 Accountant	1957	1P	M	2	2	28	295	0.1081	?	32,000	2,070
Aviation Traders only in-house complete design, intended as DC-3 replacement											
B											
Bristol 175 Britannia (1958 Series 310 data)	1952	85	M	4	4/7	139	397	0.0962	24,000	185,000	4,430
Bristol Britannia Long-range (series 310) version, first flight 1957											
Bristol 170 SuperFreighter (passenger version SuperWayfarer)	1953	20*	M	2	2	56	225	0.0900	24,500	44,000	1,270
*Type 170 Superfreighter stretched fuselage version of 1945 original Freighter, up-rated engines. 20 built, two more converted basic 170 Freighter (Appendix 10)											
D											
De Havilland DH.114 Heron	1950	150	M	4	2	17	~215	0.0711	18,500	13,500	805
F											
Fairey Rotodyne (compound Gyroplane)	1957	1P	G	6	2	40	191	0.1697	13,000	33,000	450
H											
Handley Page HPR-3 (piston) Herald	1955	4P	M	4	2	47	~300	0.1024	27,900	34,000	1,640
Handley Page HPR-7 (Dart) Herald	1958	50	M	2	2	56	~310	0.0979	29,700	43,700	1,635
HPR-7 total includes two HPR-3 converted to HPR-7											
S											
Saunders-Roe Princess (Flying boat)	1952	3P	M	10	6	105	380	0.1304	39,000	345,025	5,720
V											
Vickers Vanguard	1959	44	M	4	2/3	139	425	0.1333	30,000	141,000	1,830

1950-59 Airliners continued on next page

1950-59 Airliners, continued

Manufacturer & Aircraft	First Flight	No. Made	M.pln B.pln T.pln	No. Eng.	No. Crew	Max. passenger	Max. mph	thrust/ weight ratio	service ceiling (ft.)	Max wt. (lb.)	Max. Range (miles)
Vickers V-1000 (Airliner version VC-7)	n/a	n/a	M	4	?	100	~600	0.2957	?	231,000	4,143
V-1000 RAF transport (to be VC-7 with same wing in Airliner guise) cancelled 1955, shortly before roll-out											

"Civil Cargo aircraft 1950–1959"

Manufacturer & Aircraft	First Flight	No. Made	M.pln B.pln T.pln	No. Eng.	No. Crew	Max. passenger	Max. mph	pwr/wt ratio (HP/lb)	service ceiling (ft.)	Max wt. (lb.)	Max. Range (miles)
A											
Armstrong Whitworth AW.650 Argosy	see 1950-59 Military Transport aircraft										
Auster B.4	1951	1P	M	1	1	3	~120	0.0692	?	2,600	300
Auster B.4 was unsuccessful light cargo adaptation of Auster J-series aircraft											
B											
Bristol 170 Superfreighter	see 1950-59 Airliners										
W											
Westland Westminster (helicopter)	1958	2P	H	2	2	40	155	0.1770	?	33,000	120

"Sports aircraft 1950–1959"

Manufacturer & Aircraft	First Flight	No. Made	M.pln B.pln T.pln	No. Eng.	No. Crew	Max. passenger	Max. mph	pwr/wt ratio (HP/lb)	service ceiling (ft.)	Max wt. (lb.)	Max. Range (miles)
B											
Britten-Norman BN-1	1951	1P	M	1	1	-	84	0.0873	?	630	?
BN-1 Finibee pre-dates formation of B-N company. Intended as club ultra-light											

1950-59 Sports aircraft continued on next page

APPENDIX 11, 1950-1959

Manufacturer & Aircraft	First Flight	No. Made	M.pln B.pln T.pln	No. Eng.	No. Crew	Max. passenger	Max. mph	thrust/weight ratio	service ceiling (ft.)	Max wt. (lb.)	Max. Range (miles)
M, 1950-59 Sports aircraft continued											
Miles M.77 Sparrowjet	1955	1	M	1	2	-	228	0.2750	?	2,400	271
B											
Twin-jet racing aircraft, converted from 1935 prototype of piston-engined Miles Sparrowhawk											
Somers-Kendall SK-1	1955	1	M	1	2	-	323	0.2200	?	1,500	400
SK-1 racing monoplane was designed by Hugh Kendall (ex-Miles aircraft Chief Test Pilot) for J 'Nat' Somers, owner of the land of Southampton Airport. Kendall also designed M.76 glider.											

"Sailplanes 1950-59"

Manufacturer & Aircraft	First Flight	No. Made	M.pln B.pln T.pln	No. Eng.	No. Crew	Max. passenger	Max. mph	pwr/wt ratio (HP/lb)	service ceiling (ft.)	Max wt. (lb.)	Max. Range (miles)
E											
Eon Type 5 Olympia series (series 4 onwards)	1954										
EoN Type 5 Olympia 1 first flight 1947, see Appendix 10. The Type 5 Olympia series was modified several times, Olympia 1, 2 & 3 changing type in 1954 into Olympia 4, 401, 402, 403, 415 & 419, total number all Olympia *150. See Appendix 10 Sailplanes for Olympia 2 data											
EoN Type 9 K-1	1954	1P	M	-	2	-	126	n/a	n/a	1,000	n/a
– Kendall K.1 (glider) Also known as Miles M.76											
Experimental lightweight sailplane (contracted by British Gliding association). Miles M.76 design, with plastic wing from Miles and wooden fuselage from Elliotts. Wing failed in load tests. Elliott back-up wooden wing used to complete.											
S											
Slingsby T.38 Grasshopper	see 1950-59 Military trainer aircraft										
Slingsby T.34 Sky	1950	16	M	n/a	1	n/a	113	n/a	-	800	n/a
Slingsby T.37 Skylark	1953	2	M	n/a	1	n/a	130	n/a	-	666	n/a
Slingsby T.41Skylark 2	1953	63	M	n/a	1	n/a	134	n/a	-	679	n/a
Slingsby T.42 Eagle	1954	17	M	n/a	2	n/a	147	n/a	-	1,239	n/a
Slingsby T.43 Skylark 3	1957	70	M	n/a	1	n/a	134	n/a	-	789	n/a
Slingsby T.45 Swallow	1957	117	M	n/a	1	n/a	141	n/a	-	701	n/a

1950-59 Civil Utility aircraft on next page

"1950-59 Civil Utility aircraft"

APPENDIX 11, 1950-1959

Manufacturer & Aircraft	First Flight	No. Made	M.pln B.pln T.pln	No. Eng.	No. Crew	Max. passenger	Max. mph	pwr/wt ratio (HP/lb)	service ceiling (ft.)	Max wt. (lb.)	Max. Range (miles)
A											
Auster J/1B Aiglet	1950	86	M	1	1	2	126	0.0650	18,000	2,000	220
Auster J/5 Aiglet Trainer	1951	77	M	1	2	1	127	0.0591	12,500	2,200	275
Auster J/5 Alpine	195?	10	M	1	2	1	128	0.0578	22,000	2,250	460
Auster Atlantic	1957	1P	M	1	1	3	~150	0.0685	?	2,700	?
Auster J family developed from Taylorcraft Auster, Model J (originally 1942 Taylorcraft Auster AOP)...	1940s standard, see Appendix 10: 753 aircraft: J/1 Autocrat & Alpha 420, J/1 Avis 2, J/2 Arrow 44, J/3 Atom 1, J/4 Arrow 27, J/5 Autocar 180, J/5 Adventurer 59. Two prototypes J/1 Avis built (replaced by J/5 Auotcar)...										
(First to fly J/1 Autocrat, 1945, data in Appendix10)	1950s standard: 174 aircraft: J/1B Aiglet 86, J/5 Aiglet Trainer 77, J/5 Alpine 10, J/5 Atlantic 1 J1/U Workmaster listed in 1950-59 Agricultural aircraft										
E											
Edgar Percival E.P.9	see 1950-57 Agricultural aircraft										
F											
Firth Atlantic (helicopter)	n/a	1P	Atlantic construction abandoned 1955 before flight								
	Firth Atlantic (helicopter, twin outrigger rotors) used Planet Satellite aircraft fuselage (which "hopped", 1949).										
Hants and Sussex Aviation Herald	1953	1P	M	1	1	-	92	0.0444	?	900	?
	H&S Herald the only design attempted by Hants and Sussex Aviation										
S											
Scottish Aviation Twin Pioneer	1955	87	M	2	2	13	165	0.0877	20,000	14,600	791
T											
Taylor J.T.1 Monoplane	1959	~115	M	1	1	-	105	0.0623	?	610	230
	The J.T.1 was a home-build design of John Taylor (some 100 built worldwide)										
Thruxton Jackaroo	1957	(19)	B	1	2	2	102	0.0596	?	2,180	20
	Thruxton Jackaroo was based on converted DH.82 Tiger Moths, modified with a four-seat cabin in a widened fuselage. Built by Jackaroo Aircraft, formed 1957 (later acquired by Rollason Aircraft and Engines)										

1950-59 Agricultural aircraft on next page

"1950-59 Agricultural aircraft"

APPENDIX 11, 1950-1959

Manufacturer & Aircraft	First Flight	No. Made	M.pln B.pln T.pln	No. Eng.	No. Crew	Max. passenger	Max. mph	pwr/wt ratio (HP/lb)	service ceiling (ft.)	Max wt. (lb.)	Max. Range (miles)
A											
Auster B8 Agricola	1955	9	M	1	1	2	127	0.0625	20,000	3,840	220
Auster J1/U Workmaster	1958	10	M	1	1	2	104	0.0679	13,700	2,650	225
E											
Edgar Percival E.P.9	1955	27	M	1	1	5	146	0.0683	17,500	4,320	580

Appendix 12

British Military and Civil Aircraft 1960–1969

Data in this Appendix is representative of aircraft type, usually early model. For exact data, refer to original sources

BRITISH MILITARY AIRCRAFT 1960-1969

APPENDIX 12, 1960-69

P = Prototype(s) Only

pwr/wt ratio = power/weight ratio = [(total engine power) ÷ (max. weight)] = HP/lb

wet thrust = with reheat   thrust/weight ratio = [(total engine jet thrust) ÷ (max. weight)] = lbf/lb

"Bomber aircraft 1960-69"

Manufacturer & Aircraft	First Flight	No. Made	M.pln B.pln T.pln	No. Eng.	No. Crew	Max. bomb load (lb)	Max. mph	thrust/ weight ratio	service ceiling (ft.)	Max wt. (lb.)	Max. Range (miles)
B											
BAC TSR-2	1964	3P	M	2	2	10,000	1,500	0.5915	40,000	103,500	2,877
	(only 1 flew)		Cancelled 1965: see Section 6.3					(wet)			(Ferry)

"Fighter aircraft 1960–1969"

Manufacturer & Aircraft	First Flight	No. Made	M.pln B.pln T.pln	No. Eng.	No. Crew	Max. bomb load (lb)	Max. mph	thrust/ weight ratio	service ceiling (ft.)	Max wt. (lb.)	Max. Range (miles)
H											(Ferry)
HS.Harrier (incl. AV-8A)	1967	344	M	1	1	5,000	730	0.8530	51,200	25,200	2,129
HS.P.1127/Kestrel	1960	15P	M	1	1	-	710	0.8824	?	17,000	?
(Vectored thrust VTOL aircraft)	For VTOL, thrust/weight ratio > 1. Maximum weight take off is rolling take-off, where weight > max thrust										

"Patrol aircraft 1960–1969"

Manufacturer & Aircraft	First Flight	No. Made	M.pln B.pln T.pln	No. Eng.	No. Crew	Max. bomb load (lb)	Max. mph	thrust/ weight ratio	service ceiling (ft.)	Max wt. (lb.)	Max. Range (miles)
H											
HS.801 Nimrod	see 1960-69 Anti-submarine aircraft										

1960-69 Surface Attack aircraft on next page

"Surface Attack aircraft 1960–1969"

Manufacturer & Aircraft	First Flight	No. Made	M.pln B.pln T.pln	No. Eng.	No. Crew	Max. bomb load (lb)	Max. mph	thrust/ weight ratio	service ceiling (ft.)	Max wt. (lb.)	Max. Range (miles)
B											
BAC Strikemaster	1967	146	M	1	2	3,000	481	0.2730	40,000	11,500	1,382
S											
SEPECAT Jaguar ('A' data) (joint BAC-Breguet project, 50%-50%)	1968	543	M	2	1	10,000	1,056	0.2956	45,900	34,612	2,190

"Anti-submarine aircraft 1960–1969"

Manufacturer & Aircraft	First Flight	No. Made	M.pln B.pln T.pln	No. Eng.	No. Crew	Max. bomb load (lb)	Max. mph	thrust/ weight ratio	service ceiling (ft.)	Max wt. (lb.)	Max. Range (miles)
H											
HSA HS.801 Nimrod	1967	51	M	4	13	20,000	575	0.2533	44,000	192,000	5,755
Numbers made include 3 Nimrod 'R' Elint aircraft											
								pwr/wt ratio (HP/lb)			
W											
Westland Sea King (helicopter)	1969	344	H	2	2-4	various	129	0.1551	?	21,400	764

"Military Trainer aircraft 1960–1969"

Manufacturer & Aircraft	First Flight	No. Made	M.pln B.pln T.pln	No. Eng.	No. Crew	Max. bomb load (lb)	Max. mph	thrust/ weight ratio	service ceiling (ft.)	Max wt. (lb.)	Max. Range (miles)
B											
British Aerospace 125	see 1960-69 Civil Business aircraft category: 125 used as Dominie navigator trainer by RAF										

1960-69 Military Transport aircraft on next page

"Military Transport aircraft 1960–1969"

APPENDIX 12, 1960-69

Manufacturer & Aircraft	First Flight	No. Made	M.pln B.pln T.pln	No. Eng.	No. Crew	Max. passenger	Max. mph	thrust/ weight ratio	service ceiling (ft.)	Max wt. (lb.)	Max. Range (miles)
A											
Armstrong Whitworth AW.681	n/a	nil	M	4	?	?	~490	0.3044	25,000	181,000	4,801
AW.681 STOL logistics support aircraft cancelled 1965, before build											
								pwr/wt ratio (HP/lb)			
B											
Beagle B.206	1965	79	M	2	1	6	258	0.0907	27,100	7,499	1,620
H											
HSA HS. 780 Andover	1963	31	M	2	2/3	52	320	0.1273	24,000	51,000	1,425
S											
Short SC5/1 Belfast	1964	10	M	4	5	250	352	0.0997	30,000	230,000	5,300

"Military Utility aircraft 1960–1969"

Manufacturer & Aircraft	First Flight	No. Made	M.pln B.pln T.pln	No. Eng.	No. Crew	Max. passenger	Max. mph	pwr/wt ratio (HP/lb)	service ceiling (ft.)	Max wt. (lb.)	Max. Range (miles)
B											
Bell H-13 Sioux (helicopter, Westland licence build)	1965	265	H	1	1	3	105	0.0881	16,100	2,952	273
USA Bell H-13 (1945 1st flight) rights sold to Augusta (Italy). UK manufacture under licence from Augusta by Westland, as Sioux AH.1 (250, RAF) and Sioux HT.2 (15, RN)											
W											
Westland Scout	1960	~150	H	1	1/2	4/5	131	0.1292	17,700	5,300	315
Westland Wasp	1962	133	H	2	2	4	120	0.1909	12,200	5,500	303
Scout and Wasp helicopters developed from 1958 Saunders Roe P.531, after Westland takeover											

Civil Aircraft 1960-69 next page

BRITISH CIVIL AIRCRAFT 1960-69
P = Prototype(s) Only

APPENDIX 12, 1960-1969

pwr/wt ratio = power/weight ratio = [(total engine power) ÷ (max. weight)] = HP/lb
thrust/weight ratio = [(total engine jet thrust) ÷ (max. weight)] = lbf/lb

"Airliners 1960–1969"

Manufacturer & Aircraft	First Flight	No. Made	M.pln B.pln T.pln	No. Eng.	No. Crew	Max. passenger	Max. mph	pwr/wt ratio (HP/lb)	service ceiling (ft.)	Max wt. (lb.)	Max. Range (miles)
A											
Aviation Traders Carvair	1961	21	M	4	2	85	250	0.0786	18,700	73,800	2,300
Aviation Traders Carvair was unpressurised cargo conversion of Douglas DC-4, with side-hinging fuselage nose door (flight deck moved to hump on top, akin to later Boeing 747). Developed as bigger replacement of 1953 Bristol SuperFreighter, 5 cars+22 passengers. Carvair also used as passenger-only											
								thrust/ weight ratio			
B											
BAC One-Eleven (1-11 series 500 data)	1963	244	M	2	2	119	~541	0.2402	35,000	104,500	1,705
BAC Two &Three-Eleven	1968 BAC 2-11 narrow-body and 1971 BAC 3-11 wide-body were proposals, shelved										
BAC-Sud Aviation Concorde (joint project, 50%-50%)	1969	20	M	4	3	120	1,354	0.3107	60,000	412,000	4,488
The 20 Concorde built include 2 pre-prototype & 4 prototypes. Engine dry thrust value.											
								pwr/wt ratio (HP/lb)			
Britten-Norman BN-2 Islander	1965	>1,280	M	2	1/2	9	170	0.0909	13,200	6,600	874
BN-2 Islander remains in production (2020)											
H											
Handley Page Jetstream	1967	30+	M	2	2	16	282	0.1025	25,000	12,566	1,380
After 30 production aircraft completed, Handley Page insolvent 1970. Jetstream build continued by Scottish Aviation: see Appendix 13											
Hawker Siddeley HS.748 (First flight as Avro 748)	1960	380	M	2	2	58	~310	0.0981	25,000	46,500	1,066

1960-69 Airliners continued on next page

APPENDIX 12, 1960-1969

Manufacturer & Aircraft	First Flight	No. Made	M.pln B.pln T.pln	No. Eng.	No. Crew	Max. passenger	Max. mph	thrust/ weight ratio	service ceiling (ft.)	Max wt. (lb.)	Max. Range (miles)
H, 1960-69 Airliners, continued											
Hawker Siddeley HS.121 Trident 1	1962	39	M	3	3	101	580	0.2672	35,000	128,000	1,350
Hawker Siddeley HS.121 Trident 2	1967	50	M	3	3	115	580	0.2527	35,000	142,000	2,700
Hawker Siddeley HS.121 Trident 3	1969	28	M	4	3	180	570	0.2742	35,000	150,000	2,235
S											
Short SC.7 Skyvan	see 1960-69 Cargo aircraft										
V											
Vickers VC10	1962	54	M	4	4	151	580	0.2686	43,000	334,878	5,850
VC.10 data. Number made includes larger Super VC.10											

"Business aircraft 1960-1969"

Manufacturer & Aircraft	First Flight	No. Made	M.pln B.pln T.pln	No. Eng.	No. Crew	Max. passenger	Max. mph	thrust/ weight ratio	service ceiling (ft.)	Max wt. (lb.)	Max. Range (miles)
B											
British Aerospace 125 (series 600 data)	1962	1,720	M	2	2	14	522	0.3000	41,000	25,000	1,796

"Civil Cargo aircraft 1960-1969"

Manufacturer & Aircraft	First Flight	No. Made	M.pln B.pln T.pln	No. Eng.	No. Crew	Max. passenger	Max. mph	pwr/wt ratio (HP/lb)	service ceiling (ft.)	Max wt. (lb.)	Max. Range (miles)
S											
Short SC.7 Skyvan	1963	149	M	2	1/2	19	202	0.1144	22,500	12,500	694
1960-69 Sailplane and Replica aircraft on next page											

APPENDIX 12, 1960-1969

"Sailplane and Replica aircraft 1960–1969"

Manufacturer & Aircraft	First Flight	No. Made	M.pln B.pln T.pln	No. Eng.	No. Crew	Max. passenger	Max. mph	pwr/wt ratio (HP/lb)	service ceiling (ft.)	Max wt. (lb.)	Max. Range (miles)
E											
EoN Type 10, 460 series	1960	55	M	n/a	1	-	136	n/a	n/a	630	n/a
After four 460 prototypes, 463 and 465 standard production											
S											
Slingsby T.49 Capstan	1961	34	M	n/a	2	-	135	n/a	n/a	1,250	n/a
Slingsby T.50 Skylark 4	1961	65	M	n/a	1	-	142	n/a	n/a	829	n/a
Slingsby T.51 Dart	1963	82	M	n/a	1	-	?	n/a	n/a	750	n/a
Slingsby T.53	1967	21	M	n/a	2		142	n/a	n/a	1,279	n/a
Replica aircraft – with engines											
Royal Aircraft Factory SE.5A replica built by Miles	1965	2	B	1	1	-	?	?	?	?	?
Initially constructed for film "The Blue Max"											
Slingsby T.56 (as 1916 S.E.5A)	1970	6	B	1	1	?	?	?	?	?	?
based on reduced scale of 1937 Currie Wot bi-plane design. Used in film "Darling Lili"											
Slingsby T.57 (as 1916 Sopwith Camel)	1969	1	B	1	1	?	?	?	?	?	?
Slingsby T.58 (as 1917 Rumpler C.IV)	?	2	B	1	2	?	?	?	?	?	?

"Civil Utility aircraft 1960–1969"

Manufacturer & Aircraft	First Flight	No. Made	M.pln B.pln T.pln	No. Eng.	No. Crew	Max. passenger	Max. mph	pwr/wt ratio (HP/lb)	service ceiling (ft.)	Max wt. (lb.)	Max. Range (miles)
A											
Auster D.4	1960	15	M	1	1	2	110	0.0568	13,200	1,900	500
Auster D.4 was development of Auster Arrow (see Appendix 10)											
Auster D.6	1960	4	M	2	1	3	121	0.0659	14,000	2,200	?
4-seater version of 1949 Autocar (see Appendix 10)											
Auster Tugmaster	1960	(34)	M	1	2	-					
Auster Tugmasters were glider tug conversions of surplus Taylorcraft Auster 1942 AOP (see Appendix 10)											
Beagle Airedale	1961	43	M	1	1	3	140	0.0655	?	2,750	940
Beagle Airedale was development of 1960 Auster D.6 (see above)											

1960-69 Civil Utility aircraft continued on next page

APPENDIX 12, 1960-1969

Manufacturer & Aircraft	First Flight	No. Made	M.pln B.pln T.pln	No. Eng.	No. Crew	Max. passenger	Max. mph	pwr/wt ratio (HP/lb)	service ceiling (ft.)	Max wt. (lb.)	Max. Range (miles)
B, 1960-69 Civil Utility aircraft, continued											
Beagle B.206	1962	79	M	2	1	6	258	0.0907	27,100	7,499	1,620
Beagle B.218	1962	1P	M	1	1	3	185	0.0453	21,700	3,200	1,000
Beagle Husky	1960	179	M	1	1	2	125	0.0653	12,800	2,450	460
Beagle Husky was revised Auster Alpha (see 1945 J/1 Autocrat) more powerful engine (started as Auster D.5)											
Beagle B.121 Pup	1967	176	M	1	1	3	127	0.0625	?	1,600	?
Beagle Terrier	1961	(64)	M	1	1	1	104	0.0604	?	2,400	320
Beagle Terriers were rebuilt Taylorcraft Auster 1942 AOP.6 (see Appendix 10)											
Britten-Norman BN-2 Islander	see 1960-69 Airliners										
C											
Cierva-Rotorcraft CR Twin (h'copter, Grasshopper III)	1969	3	H	2	1	4	130	0.0857	20,000	3,150	500
NAC Freelance	1969	2	M	1	1	3	117	0.0597	11,200	1,925	600
Desmond Norman took the NAC Freelance design with him when he left Britten-Norman (Britten-Norman had been taken over by Fairey)											
S											
Scottish Aviation Bulldog	1969	328	M	12	1	-	150	0.0851	16,000	2,350	621
Original prototype was Beagle 121 Pup development as Beagle 125 Bulldog, before Beagle wound up											
T											
Tipsy Nipper	1957	110	M	1	1	-	101	?	?	?	200
Designed by E.O. Tips (Avions Fairey, Belgium). Produced in Belgium & UK (Slingsby, in UK until closed by 1968 fire, Nipper Aircraft 1968-71). Now "Home build"											
W											
Wallis WA-116 Agile (Autogyro)	1961	10+	A	1	1	-	100	0.1039	10,000	550	130
One was "Little Nellie", appearing in 1967 James Bond film "You Only Live Twice"											

Appendix 13

British Military and Civil Aircraft 1970–2019

Data in this Appendix is representative of aircraft type, usually early model. For exact data, refer to original sources.

BRITISH MILITARY AND CIVIL AIRCRAFT 1970-2019

APPENDIX 13, 1970-2019

P = Prototype(s) Only   pwr/wt ratio = power/weight ratio = [(total engine power) ÷ (max. weight)] = **HP/lb**

wet thrust = with reheat   thrust/weight ratio = [(total engine jet thrust) ÷ (max. weight)] = **lbf/lb**

"Fighter aircraft 1970-2019"

Manufacturer & Aircraft	First Flight	No. Made	M.pln B.pln T.pln	No. Eng.	No. Crew	Max. bomb load (lb.)	Max. mph	thrust/ weight ratio	service ceiling (ft.)	Max wt. (lb.)	Max. Range (miles)
L											
Lockheed Lightning II (JSF)	2006	491+	M	1	1	18,000	1,200	0.6100 wet 0.4000 dry	>50,000	70,000	>1,200

Lift fan augments vertical thrust of deflected jet exhaust to permit Short Take-off/Vertical Landing operations. Originally indigenous USA-only Joint Strike Fighter programme (joint USAF/USN/USMC) but international co-operation encouraged. On behalf of UK, BAE Systems the only non-USA Tier One (15%) design and manufacture contributor to airframe. In production (491 as of Dec. 2019), total expected 3,184 by 2035.

Manufacturer & Aircraft	First Flight	No. Made	M.pln B.pln T.pln	No. Eng.	No. Crew	Max. bomb load (lb.)	Max. mph	thrust/ weight ratio	service ceiling (ft.)	Max wt. (lb.)	Max. Range (miles)
E											
Eurofighter Typhoon	1994	see Multi-purpose aircraft									
P											
Panavia Tornado ADV (joint international, BAe share 45%)	1979	218	M	2	2	-	1,490	0.5355 (wet)	50,000	61,700	2,650 (Ferry)

see also 1974 Tornado IDS/ECR Surface Attack version

"Surface Attack aircraft 1970-2019"

Manufacturer & Aircraft	First Flight	No. Made	M.pln B.pln T.pln	No. Eng.	No. Crew	Max. weapons + passenger	Max. mph	pwr/wt ratio (HP/lb)	service ceiling (ft.)	Max wt. (lb.)	Max. Range (miles)
A											
AgustaWestland AW.159 Wildcat (helicopter)	2009	62*	H	2	2	missiles & 6 troops	193	0.2058	?	13,228	483
B											
BAe Hawk 200	1986	62	M	1	1	multi	644	0.2811	50,000	20,064	554
BAe Harrier II	1985	143	M	1	1	8,000lb	662	0.7016	50,000	31,000	2,417 (Ferry)

1970-2019 Surface Attack aircraft continued on next page

P, Surface Attack aircraft, continued

Manufacturer & Aircraft	First Flight	No. Made	M.pln B.pln T.pln	No. Eng.	No. Crew	Max. bomb load (lb)	Max. mph	thrust/ weight ratio	service ceiling (ft.)	Max wt. (lb.)	Max. Range (miles)
Panavia Tornado IDS/ECR (joint, BAe share 45%)	1974	774	M	2	2	19,840	1,490	0.5355 (wet)	50,000	61,700	2,417 (Ferry)

"Patrol and Reconnaissance Aircraft 1970–2019"

Manufacturer & Aircraft	First Flight	No. Made	M.pln B.pln T.pln	No. Eng.	No. Crew	Max. bomb load (lb)	Max. mph	thrust/ weight ratio	service ceiling (ft.)	Max wt. (lb.)	Max. Range (miles)
B											
BAe Nimrod AEW Mk.3 (conversion of MR.Mk.1)	1980	3P+8	M	4	12	-	580	0.2586	43,999	187,800	~5,750
Cancelled 1986 with 11 aircraft completed (none delivered) out of 11 ordered											
BAE Systems Nimrod MRA4 (MR.Mk.2 fuselage and empennage)	2004	2P+3	M	4	10	22,000	571	0.2669	36,000	232,315	6,910
Cancelled 2010 after 5 aircraft completed (out of final order for 9, reduced from 21 originally ordered)											

"Military Trainer aircraft 1970–2019"

Manufacturer & Aircraft	First Flight	No. Made	M.pln B.pln T.pln	No. Eng.	No. Crew	Max. bomb load (lb)	Max. mph	thrust/ weight ratio	service ceiling (ft.)	Max wt. (lb.)	Max. Range (miles)
BAE Systems Hawk	1974	>717	M	1	2	6,800	638	0.3250	44,500	20,000	1,565
See also separate entries for Surface Attack BAe Hawk 200 and USMC Trainer T-45 Goshawk											
BAe/McDonnell-Douglas T-45 Goshawk (50%-50%)	1988	221	M	1	2	Training only	645	0.3925	44,500	14,081	805

1970-2019 Military Trainer aircraft continued on next page

F, 1970-2019 Military Trainer aircraft, continued

Manufacturer & Aircraft	First Flight	No. Made	M.pln B.pln T.pln	No. Eng.	No. Crew	Max. bomb load (lb)	Max. mph	pwr/wt ratio (HP/lb)	service ceiling (ft.)	Max wt. (lb.)	Max. Range (miles)
F, 1970-2019 Military Trainer aircraft, continued											
FLS Sprint (originally Trago Mills SAH-1)	1983	3	M	1	2	-	175	0.0780	10,000	2,050	575
FLS Sprint: Originally intended as replacement for BAe Bulldog RAF trainer. FLS taken over more than once, eventually by Edgley in 2007 (now intended as home-build)											
S											
Short Tucano	1986	160	M	1	1/2	-	315	0.1524	34,500	7,220	1,035
Brazilian Embraer EMB-312 Tucano, with Shorts heavily modified design for 130 aircraft manufactured under licence by Shorts for RAF, 30 more exported											
Slingsby T.67 Firefly	1974	>250	M	1	2	-	224	0.1020	19,000	2,550	468
Originally French Fournier RF-6,all-wood design, sold to Slingsby. T-67 changed design to composite construction, changed the engine and other improvements.											

"Military Multi-purpose aircraft 1970–2019"

Manufacturer & Aircraft	First Flight	No. Made	M.pln B.pln T.pln	No. Eng.	No. Crew	Max. bomb load (lb)	Max. mph	pwr/wt ratio (HP/lb) [thrust/weight ratio]	service ceiling (ft.)	Max wt. (lb.)	Max. Range (miles)
A											
AugustaWestland AW.101 (joint venture, 50% each)	1987	145*	H	3	3-4	multi.	192	0.1957	15,000	32,188	517
*still in production, 2019, AW fully absorbed into Leonardo group (ex-Finmeccanica)											
E											
Eurofighter Typhoon (BAE Systems share 37.42%)	1994	565*	M	2	1	multi.	1,550	0.7846 (wet)	65,000	51,800	1,800
*still in production. For EAP pre-prototype experimental aircraft, see Appendix 14											

1970-2019 Multi-purpose aircraft continued on next page

APPENDIX 13, 1970-2019

Manufacturer & Aircraft	First Flight	No. Made	M.pln B.pln T.pln	No. Eng.	No. Crew	Max. bomb load (lb)	Max. mph	pwr/wt ratio (HP/lb)	service ceiling (ft.)	Max wt. (lb.)	Max. Range (miles)
W, 1970-2019 Multi-purpose aircraft, continued											
Westland Lynx (helicopter)	1971	450	H	2	2/3	multi.	201	0.1906	?	11,750	328
For civil version of Lynx, see 1979 W.30 Airliners											

Civil Aircraft 1970-2019 next page

BRITISH CIVIL AIRCRAFT 1970-2019

APPENDIX 13, 1970-2019

P = Prototype(s) Only

pwr/wt ratio = power/weight ratio = [(total engine power) ÷ (max. weight)] = HP/lb

thrust/weight ratio = [(total engine jet thrust) ÷ (max. weight)] = lbf/lb

"Airliners 1970-2019"

Manufacturer & Aircraft	First Flight	No. Made	M.pln B.pln T.pln	No. Eng.	No. Crew	Max. bomb load (lb)	Max. mph	thrust/weight ratio	service ceiling (ft.)	Max wt. (lb.)	Max. Range (miles)
B											
BAe 146/RJ(-200/RJ85 data)	1981	387	M	4	2	100	491	0.3006	35,000	93,000	2,269
								pwr/wt ratio (HP/lb)			
British Aerospace ATP	1986	64	M	2	2	64	325	0.1050	25,000	50,550	1,134
BAe Jetstream 31	1980	386	M	2	2	19	303	0.1226	25,000	15,332	783
BAe Jetstream 41	1991	100	M	2	2	29	340	0.1375	26,000	24,000	891
Britten Norman Trislander	1970	72	M	3	1/2	16	180	0.0780	13,160	10,000	1,000
S											
Scottish Aviation Jetstream	1974	36	M	2	2	16	282	0.1466	25,000	12,566	1,380
Scottish Aviation took over Jetstream production after 30 aircraft completed, when Handley Page bankrupt in 1970: see Appendix 12											
Short SD.330	1971	141	M	2	2	30	281	0.1046	26,000	22,900	1,053
Short SD.360	1981	165	M	2	2	36	251	0.1051	20,000	27,100	992
Westland W.30 (helicopter)	1979	41	H	2	2	19	150	0.1914	?	12,800	299
Westland W.30 is civil variant of 1971 Lynx military (Multi-purpose) helicopter											

"Business aircraft 1970-2019"

Manufacturer & Aircraft	First Flight	No. Made	M.pln B.pln T.pln	No. Eng.	No. Crew	Max. bomb load (lb)	Max. mph	thrust/weight ratio	service ceiling (ft.)	Max wt. (lb.)	Max. Range (miles)
CMC Leopard	1988	2P	M	2	1	3	540	0.2745	55,000?	2,550	2,204
Data for second prototype (had more powerful engines)											

1960-69 aircraft continued on next page

"Sport aircraft 1970–2019"

Manufacturer & Aircraft	First Flight	No. Made	M.pln B.pln T.pln	No. Eng.	No. Crew	Max. passenger	Max. mph	pwr/wt ratio (HP/lb)	service ceiling (ft.)	Max wt. (lb.)	Max. Range (miles)
A											
AMF Chevron 2-32	1983	41	M	1	2	-	75	0.0380	10,010	842	230
AMF Microflight built Chevron 2-32											

"Sailplanes and Motor-Gliders 1970–2019"

Manufacturer & Aircraft	First Flight	No. Made	M.pln B.pln T.pln	No. Eng.	No. Crew	Max. passenger	Max. mph	pwr/wt ratio (HP/lb)	service ceiling (ft.)	Max wt. (lb.)	Max. Range (miles)
S											
Slingsby T.59 Kestrel	1970	105	M	n/a	1	-	155	n/a	n/a	1,041	n/a
Initially licence-built German Glasflügel 401, several T.59 Slingsby variants produced											
Slingsby T.61 Falke (RAF Venture T.1/T.2)	1971	76	M	1	2	-	118	0.0385	>15,000	1,170	435
Motor glider (licenced-built German Scheibe SF 25B) used by RAF Air Training Corps											
Slingsby T.65 Vega	1977	34+	M	n/a	1	-	160	n/a	n/a	1,120	n/a
Constructed after Slingsby acquired by Vickers											

"Civil Utility and Agricultural aircraft 1970–2019"

Manufacturer & Aircraft	First Flight	No. Made	M.pln B.pln T.pln	No. Eng.	No. Crew	Max. passenger	Max. mph	pwr/wt ratio (HP/lb)	service ceiling (ft.)	Max wt. (lb.)	Max. Range (miles)
1970–2019 Civil Utility aircraft											
ARV Super2	1985	~40	M	1	2	-	118	0.0700	?	1,100	311
1970–2019 Agricultural aircraft											
NAC Fieldmaster	1981	10	M	1	1	1	165	0.0750	18,200	10,000	1,150

Appendix 14

British Experimental Aircraft 1919–2019

This appendix lists miscellaneous aircraft produced in Britain for experimental purposes after the end of the First World War. Government-authorised 'X' registered experimental aircraft 1917–19 are separately listed in section 2.3 and the earliest "finding out how to fly" experimental aircraft of the early years (up to 1919) are included in Appendix 7. Experimental aircraft used to research the behaviour of features which might or might not become part of the design of an eventually-produced machine are included (such as the P1A and P1B high speed research aircraft preceding the English Electric Lightning). Other experimental aircraft were used to investigate and develop aeronautical technology, or other research such as exploring the upper atmosphere.

Prototypes of aircraft which were created with the intention of development to enter series production, such as the many pre-Second World War competitive but unsuccessful submissions for military aircraft, are included in Appendices 7 to 13, listed as prototype elements (P). Production aircraft adapted for an experiment which were more than purely scientific (such as a test bed for a new engine for another project (e.g. the Lancaster tail-mounted Metropolitan Vickers F2/1 axial flow jet engine, the Rolls-Royce "Dart" turboprop flight test using the Wellington bomber, or the Gloster Meteor Rolls-Royce "RB.50 Trent" turboprop test aircraft) are not listed here. Home-built aircraft are excluded, as are unmanned and remotely-piloted air vehicles (UAVs and RPAVs).

Where an experimental aircraft listed in this Appendix is also mentioned in the main text, this is cross-referenced, as is any duplication in the lists of aircraft in Appendices 7 to 13.

Manufacturer and Aircraft	First Flight	No. Made	Purpose	Noted in Chapter (or in Appendix)
A				
Armstrong Whitworth Ape	1926	3	"Fully adjusting": investigating configuration	(A.8)
Armstrong Whitworth AW.52	1947	2	"Flying wing" research, originally intended for application to a possible bomber or airliner.	(A.10)
Avro 707	1949	5	Low and high speed delta wing aerodynamics (for Vulcan research)	5.12, (A.10)
Avro Ashton 706	1950	6	Jet powered aircraft trials, with associated systems such as cabin pressurisation. New engines in fuselage-mounted pods were trialed (Rolls-Royce Avon and Conway, Bristol Olympus and Orpheus).	(A.11)
B				
BAC 221	1964	1	Fairey Delta 2 conversion: To investigate supersonic "Ogival" wing (for Concorde)	7.1
BAe EAP	1986	1	Concept-proving for Eurofighter Typhoon	8.7
BAe 146 FAAM	2004	1	BAe 146 conversion to Facility for Airborne Atmospheric Measurements (climate research)	9.2

B Experimental aircraft continued next page

APPENDIX 14: EXPERIMENTAL AIRCRAFT (continued)

Manufacturer and Aircraft	First Flight	No. Made	Purpose	Noted in Chapter (or in Appendix)
B, continued				
Baynes Bat	1943	1	Tail-less glider (as possibility to carry tanks)	2.8
Beardmore Inflexible (Rohrbach IV)	1928	1	Largest aircraft in the world in 1928, all metal stressed skin, licensed from Rhorbach	(A.8)
Blackburn B-20	1940	1	Retractable flying boat hull (drag reduction)	-
Blackburn C.A.15C	1932	2	Two identical aircraft except one a biplane, one a monoplane, for comparison at RAE	-
Boulton Paul P.6	1918	1	Biplane, 5ft gap between wings to air test different aerofoil sections (change top wing)	2.2, (A.7)
Boulton Paul P.111	1950	1	Tailless Delta wing transonic tests	(A.11)
Boulton Paul P.120	1952	1	T-tail delta wing development of P.111 (crashed & destroyed, due to tail flutter1952	(A.11)
Brennan Helicopter	1924	1	First helicopter flight in the world (poor control). Crashed due to malfunction 1925	2.9
Bristol 92	1928	1	Engine cowling aerodynamic drag research	(A.8)
Bristol MR.1	1917	2	To develop all-metal construction techniques	-
Bristol 138 Monoplane	1936	1	High altitude research (world record, 30 June 1937, 53,937ft)	-
Bristol T.188	1962	3	Supersonic aerodynamic research	2.10, 7.1
Bristol Tramp	2 Built 1921 Never flew		Air Ministry/RAE idea: Central engine with transmission to wing propellers ... see also Boulton & Paul Bodmin and Parnall Possum	B&P Bodmin and Parnall Possum in (A.8)
C				
Cierva/Weir Autogyros	1926 -on	1	35 Experimental types C.6 to C.40, plus successful C.30 of 1933 (148 built)	5.9, (A8, A.9)
D				
de Bruyne Snark (Aero Research Ltd.)	1934	1	4-seat cabin monoplane with bakelite bonded stressed ply-balsa-ply thin wooden monocoque fuselage and wings, for test and demonstrating very light bonded stressed skin construction. At first refused a Certificate of Airworthiness until complete fuselage static testing proved the strength.	2.8
de Bruyne -Mass Ladybird (Cambridge Aeroplane Construction Co.)	1938	1	A single-seat cabin monoplane of lightweight plywood construction completed by Johan Nicolaas Mass.	2.8
de Havilland DH.29 Doncaster	1921	2	Ministry monoplane long-range experiments	(A.8)
de Havilland DH.108	1946	3	Tail-less transonic aerodynamic research	5.1, (A.10)
de Havilland Spider Crab	1943	1	First flying as experimental aircraft, became prototype of DH.100 Vampire (see A.10)	(A.10)
de Havilland T.K.5	1939	1	DH tech. school canard research. Did not fly	-

E Experimental aircraft on next page

APPENDIX 14: EXPERIMENTAL AIRCRAFT (continued)

Manufacturer and Aircraft	First Flight	No. Made	Purpose	Noted in Chapter (or in Appendix)
E				
English Electric P.1A .....and P.1B	1954 1957	2 3	Pre-prototypes for English Electric Lightning	5.10, 5.15, 6.3, (A.11)
F				
Fairey Delta 1	1956	1	Transonic delta-wing aerodynamics	(A.11)
Fairey Delta 2	1954	2	Supersonic aerodynamic research (one converted to BAC.221 for Concorde)	5.10, 7.1, (A.11)
Fairey Jet Gyrodyne	1951	1	Compound autogyro (test for Rotodyne)	5.9
Fairey Long-range Monoplane	1928	2	In 1933 the second aircraft flew the record geographic distance of 5,410 miles.	(A.8)
Folland Fo.108	1940	12	Dedicated testbed for different engines	-
Folland Fo. 139 Midge	1955	1	Lightweight jet fighter concept demonstrator	5.14
G				
General A/craft GAL.41	1939	1	Conversion of GAL.25 for research into cabin pressurisation	2.7, (A.9)
General A/craft GAL.56 (4 versions) & GAL.61	1944	5	Tail-less swept wing research gliders. After fatal GAL.56/01 fatal crash, GAL.61 never flown.	-
Gloster E.28/39	1941	2	First UK jet engine powered aircraft trials	4.2, (A.10)
Gloster Meteor "Prone Pilot"	1954	1	Tests for controllability (high 'g' environment alleviation for pilot)	(A.10)
Gloster E.1/44	1948	2	Single-engine jet fighter (contingency that new jet engine supply problems would delay twin-engined Gloster Meteor). Engine supply resolved, E.1/44 specification changed, two aircraft scrapped part-built and revised aircraft produced. Continued into post-war era as research aircraft	3.1, (A.10)
H				
Hafner A.R.III Gyroplane	1935	1	Experiments leading to standard "swash plate" helicopter rotor control	5.9, (A.9)
Hafner Rotachute	1940	7	Man-carrying skeletal autogyro glider for dropping assault troops onto battlefield	5.9
Hafner Rotaplane	1943	1	Jeep-carrying enlarged version of Rotachute	5.9
Handley Page H.P.17	1920	1	DH.9 fitted with slotted wing	(A.8)
Handley Page H.P.20	1921	1	First aircraft with controllable wing slots	(A.8)
Handley Page Gugnuc	1929	1	Low speed/high lift trials aircraft	(A.8)
Handley Page H.P.75 Manx	1943	1	Tail-less wing experiments	(A.10)
Handley Page HP.88	1951	1	Supermarine Attacker, with early wing shape of Handley Page HP.80 Victor bomber	5.12, (A.11)
Handley Page HP.115	1961	1	Low speed slender delta control experiment (for Concorde)	7.1
Hawker P.1052	1948	1	Swept wing jet aircraft experiments	5.12
Hawker P.1072	1950	1	Rocket motor test aircraft (in tail of 3rd Sea Hawk prototype)	-

H Experimental aircraft continued next page

APPENDIX 14: EXPERIMENTAL AIRCRAFT (continued)

Manufacturer and Aircraft	First Flight	No. Made	Purpose	Noted in Chapter (or in Appendix)
H, continued				
Hawker 1081	1950	1	Nene-powered after-burning P.1052 (potential for RAAF Meteor replacement)	5.13
Hawker P.1127/Kestrel	1960	15	Vectored jet VTOL flight testing (pre-prototype Harrier, with Pegasus engine)	6.3, (A.12)
Hillson Bi-mono	1941	1	Biplane with jettison-able upper wing	-
Hillson FH.40	1943	1	Hurricane converted to Bi-mono (never used)	-
Hunting H.126	1963	1	Blown flap aerodynamic research	-
M				
Miles M.3E Gillette Falcon	1944	1	Low speed tests for supersonic M.52 with "razor thin" wing and all-moving tail	for M.52, 5.10, (A.10)
Miles M.6 Hawcon	1935	1	Thick wing aerodynamic research	-
Miles M.30	1942	1	Blended wing-body experimental sub-scale aircraft (see 1940s M.26 design study series)	(A.10)
Miles M.35 Libellula	1942	1	Tandem wing concept-proving man-carrying, scaled concept	-
Miles M.39B Libellula	1943	1	5/8 scale of larger version of M.35	-
Miles M.52	n/a	0	Designed 1942-46. Never completed supersonic design	5.10, (A.10)
Miles Peregrine BLS	1939	1	Modified (2nd prototype) with Boundary Layer Suction (BLS) on wing top surface	(A.9)
Monospar-winged Fokker F.VII (ST-3)	1931	1	Steiger monospar wing replacing original Fokker F.VII wing, saving 560lb weight	(A.9)
P				
Parnall Parasol	1930	2	Aerofoil lift/drag measurement in flight, alternative wings, adjustable in flight	-
Parnall Peto	1925	2	"Confined space" float plane... in hangar on deck of submarine. One crashed, one lost (submarine sank after hangar flooded)	(A.8)
Parnall Prawn	?	1	1930-built single-engined flying boat with nose-mounted engine tilting to avoid propeller touching water – not known ever to have flown.	-
R				
Reid and Sigrist R.S.4 Bobsleigh	1951	1	RAE-Converted R.S.3 for prone pilot tests	2.8, (A.10)
Rolls Royce Mustang Mk.X	1942	1	Rolls Royce experimental USA North American Mustang aircraft change of engine, to two-speed supercharged Rolls Royce Merlin.	2.7 (note 5) (A.10)
Rolls-Royce Thrust Measuring Rig	1954	2	Man-carrying jet-lift VTOL experimental hovering rig (no wings)	6.3
Saunders-Roe A.37 Shrimp	1939	1	Half-size version of early proposal for Sunderland replacement	-
Saunders-Roe SR.53	1957	2	Initial pre-prototype jet/rocket interceptor	5.15
Short Cockle	1924	?	First all-metal flying boat in the world	(A.8)

S Experimental aircraft continued on next page

APPENDIX 14: EXPERIMENTAL AIRCRAFT (continued)

Manufacturer and Aircraft	First Flight	No. Made	Purpose	Noted in Chapter (or in Appendix)
S, continued				
Short S.21 Maia/S.30 Mercury Composite	1937	1 set	Piggy-back Mercury launch from Maia, to extend Mercury range	2.7, (A.9)
Short S.6 Sturgeon	1927	2	Duraluminium aircraft durability testing	(A.8)
Short S.7 Mussel	1926	2	Duraluminium float durability testing. Eustace Short died of heart attack in second example, just after landing on River Medway	(A.8)
Short S.31	1938	1	Half-scale pre-prototype of Short S.29 Stirling	-
Short SB.1	1951	1	One third scale glider to test aero-isoclinic wing concept	-
Short SB.4 Sherpa	1953	1	Powered aircraft, aero-isoclinic wing	-
Short SB.5	1952	1	Changeable wing high sweep control tests and tailplane position (for English Electric Lightning	6.3
Short SC.1	1957	2	Lift-fan VTOL concept testing	6.3
Short Silver Streak	1920	1	First UK all-metal aircraft (used as starting point for Short Springbok design)	(A.8)
Supermarine 508	1951	3	Swept-wing/V-tail twin-engined transonic flight research	5.13, (A.11)
Supermarine 510	1948	2	Single-engined transonic flight research	5.13, (A.11)
Supermarine 517	1953	(1)	1st Supermarine 510 modified with adjustable rear fuselage (to increase pitch trim range)	5.13, (A.11)
Supermarine 525	1954	(1)	Revised 3rd 508 with swept wings	5.13, (A.11)
Supermarine 528	1951	(1)	After short trials, modified into 535 with tricycle undercarriage	5.13, (A.11)
Supermarine 529	1952	(1)	Revised 2nd 508, with modified fuselage	5.13, (A.11)
W				
Westland-Hill Pterodactyl (3 versions of Mk1, plus Mks.IV & V)	1924 to 1934	7 in 5 Mks.	Pterodactyl Mk.I, Mk.IV & MK.V built as tail-less"arrow-head" (inherently stable) flying wing experiments, which flew but not converted to production	2.8, (A.8)
Westland Dreadnought	1924	1	Air Ministry-sponsored experimental eight-passenger flying wing, instability caused fatal crash on first flight	(A.8)
Westland PV-3..... and Westland PV-6	1933	1 ea.	Adapted Westland Wapiti as Houston-Westland PV-3 and Wallace as Houston-Westland PV-6 for Lady Houston-financed expeditionary joint flight over Mount Everest (25 January 1933, world record 35,000ft altitude).	(A.9)
Willoughby Delta 8 (sometimes known as Delta -F)	1923	1	Flying wing scale version of 36-passenger proposed airliner (twin boom) (crashed 1939, project terminated)	2.8, (A.9)
Y				
Youngman-Baynes High Lift	1948	1	High lift test bed for system of slotted flaps (used Percival Proctor fuselage)	2.8, (A.10)